Sport, Culture and Society

It is impossible to fully understand contemporary society and culture without acknowledging the place of sport. Sport is part of our social and cultural fabric, possessing a social and commercial power that makes it a potent force in the world, for good and for bad. Sport has helped to start wars and promote international reconciliation. Governments commit public resources to sport because of its real and perceived benefits. From the bleachers to the boardroom to the senate or cabinet, sport matters.

Why should governments invest in sport and what difference does it make to people's daily lives?

Now available in a fully revised, researched and updated new edition, this exciting, comprehensive and accessible textbook introduces the study of sport, culture and society. International in scope, the book explores the key perspectives that shape our understanding of sport's power and popularity while critically examining many of the assumptions that underpin that understanding.

Placing sport at the very heart of the analysis, and including real and relevant sporting examples throughout, the book introduces the student to every core topic and emerging area in the study of sport and society, including:

- the history and politics of sport
- the economics and financing of sport
- sport and globalisation
- sport and the media
- sport and education
- sport, violence and crime
- sport, the body and health
- sport and the environment
- sport, religion and spirituality
- alternative sports and lifestyles
- sporting mega-events and the Olympics
- sport, poverty and international development
- sport and social change

Each chapter includes a wealth of useful features to assist the reader, including chapter summaries, highlighted definitions of key terms, practical projects, revision questions, boxed case studies and biographies, and guides to further reading, with additional teaching and learning resources available on a companion website.

Sport, Culture and Society is the most comprehensive and thoughtful introduction to the socio-cultural analysis of sport currently available, and sets a new agenda for the area. It is essential reading for all students with an interest in sport.

Grant Jarvie is Professor and Deputy Principal at the University of Stirling, and is also working with the University of Toronto. He was born in Scotland and went to school in Edinburgh. He advises governments on a wide range of areas, including sport, education, health, research and the funding of universities. He has held ministerial appointments to the board of national sports agencies and comes from an international sporting family. He was awarded an honorary doctorate in 2009 in recognition of his work to promote international cooperation between countries. He has led three departments and two research centres across four universities. He has served as acting principal/provost and has been invited to talk all over the world.

James Thornton is an international management graduate from Heriot-Watt University. Upon completion of his degree, he moved to Wellington to work in sports marketing and volunteer with Street Football Aotearoa, the Homeless World Cup's partner organisation in New Zealand. James is now based in London and works as a marketing executive for an events company.

Having read this book, if you think it can be improved in content, please contact or send Sport in Focus case studies to: grantjarvie1@gmail.com.

Sport, Culture and Society

An Introduction

Second edition

Grant Jarvie
with James Thornton

Routledge
Taylor & Francis Group

LONDON AND NEW YORK

First published 2006
by Routledge

This second edition published 2012
by Routledge
2 Park Square, Milton Park, Abingdon, Oxon OX14 4RN

Simultaneously published in the USA and Canada
by Routledge
711 Third Avenue, New York, NY 10017

Routledge is an imprint of the Taylor & Francis Group, an informa business

© 2006, 2012 Grant Jarvie

British Library Cataloguing in Publication Data
A catalogue record for this book is available from the British Library

Library of Congress Cataloging in Publication Data
Jarvie, Grant, 1955–
    Sport, culture and society: an introduction/by Grant Jarvie. – 2nd ed.
    p. cm.
    1. Sports – Social aspects. I. Title.
    GV706.5.J383 2012
    306.4′83 – dc23   2011036858

ISBN: 978–0–415–47855–7 (hbk)
ISBN: 978–0–415–48393–3 (pbk)
ISBN: 978–0–203–88380–8 (ebk)

Typeset in Perpetua and Bell Gothic
by Florence Production Ltd, Stoodleigh, Devon

MIX
Paper from
responsible sources
FSC   FSC® C004839
www.fsc.org

Printed and bound in Great Britain by
CPI Antony Rowe, Chippenham, Wiltshire

For Mairi,
Kate, David, Colin and Margaret

Governments Change, Policies Change,
But the Need Remains the Same

Contents

CONTENTS

Sport in Focus

Acknowledgements

This book has been researched during periods of sabbatical research leave granted by the University of Stirling, for which I am extremely grateful. I am lucky to work in such a beautiful and supportive research environment. Different groups of students, colleagues, conference audiences, local sports groups and Ministers of Sport have been invaluable in helping to both refine and challenge the thinking on much if not all of the content of this book.

Colin Jarvie, who has acted throughout as photographic consultant, was asked to do the impossible in terms of photograph production, but I learned a lot from his interventions and the book is all the better for them.

Simon, Josh and Aimee have all been patient, supportive and great to work with.

Abbreviations

AEN	Asia-Specific People and Environmental Network
AFC	Asian Football Confederation
AIOWF	Association of International Olympic Winter Sports Federations
ANC	African National Congress
ANOC	Association of National Olympic Committees
ANTENNA	Asian Tourism Network
ASEAN	Association of South-East Asian Nations
ASOIF	Association of Summer Olympic International Sports Federations
BBC	British Broadcasting Corporation
BSA	British Sociological Association
BSkyB	British Sky Broadcasting Group
BSSH	British Society for Sports History
BWSF	British Workers Sports Federation
CAF	Confederation of African Football
CAS	Court of Arbitration for Sport
CONCACAF	Confederation of North and Central American and Caribbean Football
CONMEBOL	Confederation of South American Football
EEC	European Economic Community
EFTA	European Free Trade Association
ENGSO	European Non-Governmental Sports Organisation
FA	English Football Association
FIFA	Fédération Internationale de Football Association
FS	Fabian Society
GAA	Gaelic Athletic Association
GANEFO	Games of the Newly Emerging Forces
GNAGA	Global Network for Anti-Golf Course Action
IAAF	International Association of Athletics Federations (formerly International Amateur Athletics Federation)
ICAS	International Council of Arbitration for Sport
ICC	International Cricket Council
ICCPR	International Covenant on Civil and Political Rights
IESCR	International Covenant on Economic, Social and Cultural Rights
ILO	International Labour Organization

IMF	International Monetary Fund
INSP	International Network of Street Papers
IOC	International Olympic Committee
ISA	International Sumo Association
JSA	Japanese Sumo Association
KS	Kladt-Sobri Group
MLB	Major League Baseball
MYSA	Mathare Youth Sports Association
NASS	North American Society for the Sociology of Sport
NASSH	North American Society for Sports History
NBA	National Basketball Association
NCAVA	National Coalition Against Violence
NGO	non-governmental organisation
NHL	National Hockey League
OFC	Oceania Football Confederation
OHCHR	Office of the United Nations High Commissioner for Human Rights
OPHR	Olympic Project for Human Rights
PASO	Pan American Sports Organization
ROK	Republic of Korea
RSI	Red Sports International
SNP	Scottish Nationalist Party
SWSI	Socialist Workers Sports International
TNC	Transnational Corporation
UAE	United Arab Emirates
UEFA	Union of European Football Associations
UN	United Nations
UNEP	United Nations Environment Programme
UNICEF	UN Children's Fund
USSR	Union of Soviet Socialist Republics
WHO	World Health Organization
WTO	World Trade Organization

Introduction

In the 1920s and 1930s, the Social Credit Movement made a number of progressive suggestions with regard to the use of sport in society. Barack Obama was elected President of the United States of America on a wave of progressive optimism and plea for change. The importance of sport was acknowledged during the presidential campaign but how should we think progressively about sport today?

OBJECTIVES

This chapter will:

- introduce the study of sport, culture and society;
- explain the structure and rationale for this new edition;
- comment upon the role of the student, academic and researcher interested in sport;
- introduce different levels of analysis in the study of sport, culture and society;
- explain the main features of the book and how to use them;
- outline the content of the four different parts to *Sport, Culture and Society*.

KEY TERMS DEFINED

Sport: A human activity, usually associated with a degree of physical exertion, in which skill is accomplished in performance or contest, and for which there is either a competitive outcome (winner, loser or position), a measurable achievement (logged by the rowing machine or the timer's stop watch) or some further perceived benefit (health, fitness, pleasure/fun).

or An individual or group activity pursued for exercise or pleasure, often involving the testing of physical capabilities and taking the form of a competitive game.

Culture: The total of the inherited ideas, beliefs, values and knowledge that constitute the shared bases of social action.

Society: The totality of social relationships among organised groups of human beings or animals.

INTRODUCTION

It is impossible to fully understand contemporary society and culture without acknowledging the place of sport. We inhabit a world in which sport is an international phenomenon. It is important for politicians and world leaders to be associated with sports personalities; it contributes to the economy; some of the most visible international spectacles are associated with sporting events; it is part of the social and cultural fabric of different localities, regions and nations; its transformative potential remains evident in some of the poorest areas of the world; it is important to the television and film industry, and the tourist industry; and it is regularly associated with social problems and issues such as crime, health, violence, social inequality, labour migration, economic and social regeneration, and poverty.

The research that informs *Sport, Culture and Society* has moved on from the first edition (2006), as have some of the arguments and frameworks for explaining sport. The Sport in Focus sections help to illustrate the power of sport today. So much has happened since 2006 – the importance of sport was such that it was acknowledged by both Barack Obama and

John McCain during the 2008 presidential campaign in the US. On the eve of the election of the new president of the United States, both Barack Obama and John McCain were interviewed on the half-time show of *Monday Night Football*. Asked the same questions, they differed significantly on only one: if you could change one thing about American sports what would it be? McCain offered something worthy about sorting out the steroid problem, while Obama wanted a college football play-off. Obama is not only the first black president of the United States, but the first president to identify himself primarily as a basketball fan. Reagan played football at college, the Bushes senior and junior are both baseball men, Clinton did play basketball at Oxford, but Obama's basketball credentials are good. It has been widely reported that he shook off Election Day nerves by playing basketball. In *Dreams from My Father*, Obama writes 'I was trying to raise myself to being a black man in America and, beyond the given of my appearance, no one around me seemed to know what that meant'. One thing it means is, in basketball, the dominance of African Americans on the basketball court is so well established and documented that it is hardly commented upon. In 2009, the Washington Wizards, Obama's new local team, had 15 players on the roster, 13 of them African Americans. Basketball is allegedly the only native sport the US has managed to sell to the world. Baseball and American football have an international following, but only basketball rivals soccer as potentially 'the global game', if such as thing exists. Obama's presidency coincided with an aggressive expansion by the National Basketball Association (NBA). One of the problems it faced was the NBA draft laws, which are the American method of dividing up young talent, and might just be too socialist for European employment law (Markovits, 2003: 28).

In 2010, the FIFA World Cup was held not just for the first time in South Africa, but for the first time in Africa. The event was acknowledged by UNESCO as a powerful means of accelerating development and supporting African integration – the 2010 FIFA World Cup was marketed around the world as Africa's Hour. In 2011, former US President Bill Clinton, supporting the unsuccessful US bid to host the 2022 FIFA World Cup, suggested that few things in the world had done more to help poverty and the poorer nations of the world than football. The winners in the competition to host the 2018 and 2022 FIFA World Cups were Russia and Qatar, but the announcement was surrounded by a controversy of corruption in world football during the same year that betting scandals had affected cricket, snooker and motor racing, to name but three sports.

Society and the world in which we live have changed since 2006. We can identify at least four developments that impinge upon contemporary sport in society. These are, first, an emerging shift of the economic centre of the world from the North Atlantic to South and East Asia has meant that the relationship between sport and capitalism itself could be shifting. Second, the 2008 worldwide financial crisis has impacted upon global flows of finance in and out of sport in different parts of the world. Third, the emergence of a new bloc of developing countries has meant that the make-up of international sporting competitions has accommodated new countries and, in some cases, old entities no longer exist. Finally, the systematic weakening of the authority of states, of national states within their territiories and in large parts of the world, has meant that new tensions between sporting nations have emerged and, in some cases, this has meant bigger is better (e.g. Europe playing together in golf) and, in other cases, this has meant traditional sources of funding and support based upon traditional ties is diminishing (e.g. across Eastern Europe). Some treat such events as nothing more than a temporary phase in human history and, as such, we do not need to fundamentally rethink how we might understand sport, culture and society, while others see it as the latest manifestation of capitalism and development that represents a fundamental transformation of world politics.

Sport continues to be a potential resource of hope for some. In September 2008, Pamela Jelimo returned to the Rift Valley village in Kenya that she had left four months earlier to compete in the Beijing Olympic Games. She returned by helicopter with her 800m Olympic gold medal around her neck and £650,000 in her bank account. For a nation that has been producing Olympic running champions for more than 40 years, Kenya's first woman Olympic gold medal winner transformed the schoolgirl into one of Kenya's running celebrities. The financial winnings for 2008 for the daughter from a one-parent family of nine shoeless children, who lived in two temporary huts in a rural village where the average wage is less than £12 per month, amounted to at least US$1.3 million. Much of the money from her athletics was used to help with local investment in Eldoret, both for her own family but also supporting the broader local community. This example is about the personal story of one girl's escape from poverty through her athletics, but it is also a broader, very public example of the transformative capacity of sport.

We live in a world in which both rich and poor identify with sport. This can be said despite the fact that an immense gap exists between the rich and poor parts of the world, and without accepting uncritically the myth of global sport. Sport's social and commercial power makes it a potentially potent force both for good and for bad. Historically, it has been a tool of dictatorship, a symbol of democratic change; it has helped to start wars, but also facilitate international reconciliation and development. Almost every government around the world commits public resources to sporting infrastructure because of sport's perceived benefits to improving health and education, creating jobs, and preventing crime. Sport matters to people. The competing notions of identity, internationalisation, national tradition and global solidarity that are contested within sport all matter far beyond the reach of sport. Cities around the world vie for sporting prominence, but not all cities have the capacity or capability to do so. Sport in Focus 0.1 considers the criteria and winners of the ultimate sport city awards and some key questions that may arise from the evidence provided.

Why are so few cities from Africa represented? How does Europe compare with Asia or America? Vancouver, New York and Chicago are listed as having a significant presence and, by and large, cities are chosen not from the periphery of certain economies, but from the centre. Do the major American, European or Asian cities see themselves as being the homes of a sporting or wealthy class, and does public provision in these cities mean that all categories of people experience sport and what they have to offer?

Generation after generation of students, researchers and teachers have raised social, economic, political and historical questions in relation to sport's organisation, its distribution and the part it has played in the allocation and exercise of power. Many of these people are employed by universities and colleges that also have a role to play in both supporting and challenging the societies they are part of. The scope and content of sport, culture and society can be wide-ranging, while various specialised sub-areas continue to give rise to degree courses, specialist texts, and particular forms of policy intervention and specialist research

SPORT IN FOCUS 0.1: ULTIMATE SPORT CITIES

Category	Winner
Hosting experience – events	London
Hosting experience – federations	Lausanne
Facilities	Melbourne
Transportation	Berlin
Accommodation	Shanghai
Government support	Melbourne/Singapore
Legacy	Manchester
Quality of life	Vancouver
Public sports interest/participation	New York
Security	Monte Carlo
Marketing	Glasgow

Rank	City	Points	Population	2008 Rank	2006 Rank
1	Melbourne	486	Large	1	1
2	Singapore	431	Large	N/A	N/A
3	London	423	XL	4	5
4	Berlin	411	Large	2	4
5	Sydney	407	Large	3	=2
6	Vancouver	391	Medium	5	11
7	Manchester	374	Small	N/A	N/A
8	Dubai	326	Medium	N/A	N/A
9	Paris	315	Medium	6	=2
10	New York	302	XL	N/A	7
11	Glasgow	291	Small	N/A	N/A
12	Doha	274	Small	12	N/A
13	Madrid	267	Medium	9	6
14	Moscow	264	XL	14	19
15	Budapest	263	Medium	13	N/A
16	Rio de Janeiro	226	Large	N/A	16
17	Shanghai	216	XL	21	N/A
18	Beijing	203	XL	18	8
18	Chicago	203	Medium	N/A	14
20	Johannesburg	197	Large	N/A	N/A
21	Monte Carlo	194	Small	N/A	N/A
22	Rome	180	Medium	N/A	13
23	Lausanne	175	Small	N/A	N/A
24	Valencia	161	Small	22	N/A
25	Istanbul	160	XL	16	12

Source: Adapted from information provided in Sport Business International

groupings. The potential eclectic coverage of ideas, together with a sound grasp of sport itself, provide for a stimulating avenue not only to developing sport, but also to analysing it, demystifying it, and ultimately attempting to contribute to social change and intervention in the world in which we live.

DEFINITIONS, STRUCTURE AND RATIONALE OF THE BOOK

The book is written for those researchers, students, teachers and others who are thinking about sport as a social phenomenon, and the extent to which sport contributes to the very social fabric of communities. It examines critically many of the assumptions relating to sport and questions the extent to which the substantive basis for such claims made by sport exist. The objective of the book is not only to encourage students and others to reflect upon sport, drawing upon concepts, ideas and themes, but also to produce a body of original substantive research from different sports, societies and communities. The position taken throughout this book is that, while it is important to explain and understand sport in society, the more important intellectual and practical questions emanate from questions relating to social change. The book aims, in a small way, to continue to influence research agendas and policies involving sport.

In addition to the broader definitions provided in 'Key terms defined' above, sport has also been described as:

- a ritual sacrifice of human energy;
- providing a common cultural currency between peoples;
- a means of compensating for deficiencies in life;
- a mechanism for the affirmation of identity and difference;
- business rather than sport;
- a social product;
- a contested arena shaped by struggles, both on and off the field of play;
- a euphemism for Western or capitalist sport; and
- a form of humanitarian aid and international development.

A genuine social understanding of sport remains crucial to our understanding of the world in which we live. Sport needs to be contextualised critically and evaluated in order to explain why sport is the way it is today. The approach that continues to differentiate this text from other recent but equally important explanations of sport in society is that it does not just attempt to understand the relationship of sport in society, but also continues to reassert the question of social change and intervention.

What is the transformative value of sport? Can sport truly make a difference to people's lives? Political scientists and policy experts have been asking *where is the evidence to substantiate the claims made by sport today?* These questions are as important today as they were in the past. The late Palestinian activist and American intellectual Edward Saïd (2001: 5) was explicit about the public role of the intellectual as being 'to uncover and contest, to challenge and defeat both an imposed silence and the normalised quiet of unseen power wherever and whenever possible'. The former Olympic and Commonwealth athlete Kip Keino, talking about the power of sport to act as a resource of hope for both individuals and communities, is more explicit when he points out that 'I believe in this world that sport is one of the tools that can unite youth – sport is something different from fighting in war and it can make a difference' (interview with the author, February 2007). Is this what we mean when we say that sport can be part of a progressive resource of hope in keeping alive different visions of the world that we both live in and could live in? The role of the public intellectual in the field of sport is desperately needed as a partial safeguard against a one-dimensional world of sport in which what is not said tells you perhaps more than what is actually said. The informed student of sport who can develop the skills of presenting complex issues in a communicative way, participate in public debates about sport and even promote debates about sport is very much needed. The role of the public intellectual working with sport and through sport to bring about change has recently been championed by Dominic (2011), Bairner (2009) and Jarvie (2007), but also on a day-to-day basis in many countries of the world as the impact of recessions, financial challenges and standards of living impact upon life.

We hope that the content of this book will help many on that journey and help readers to reflect upon and inform public debates about, for example, sport and the environment; sport and the limits of capitalism; sports finance; sport and poverty; sport, internationalism and nation building; and sport, social inequality and the law. Raising awareness about social issues within sport and answering social problems that arise out of and between different sporting worlds may occur at different levels or entry points.

LEVELS OF ANALYSIS IN SPORT, CULTURE AND SOCIETY

It has already been suggested that the study of sport, culture and society involves a number of complex factors, all of which impinge upon the nature of sport at different levels. Students and researchers need organising frameworks, or at least points of entry and exit into and out of debates about sport. The notion of levels of analysis or entry points offers a useful organising framework for locating any analysis of sport. The levels below are not exhaustive, but illustrative of different ways of organising and prioritising knowledge about sport, culture and society.

Level 1: Epistemology and new frameworks

Just as different politicians reflect divergent party agendas and philosophies, so too does the body of knowledge that is sport, culture and society champion numerous problematics or approaches to the study of sport. Researchers reflect divergent viewpoints and bodies of knowledge that influence the practice of research and the questions that they want to ask about sport. The different paradigms or perspectives or eclectic approaches to the study of sport are many, and although conventional theories are not as popular as they were, many different frameworks thinking about sporting issues and practices remain. Four emergent strands of thought that help to answer the question 'what is a good society?' include left communitarianism, left republicanism, centre republicanism and right communitarianism. All of these approaches raise particular questions and suppress others – a point that is illustrated and developed further in Chapter 1. Students and researchers of sport, culture and society will need to decide and reflect upon where they are coming from in an epistemological sense or, at the very least, from what standpoint they wish to constructively engage with other bodies of knowledge about sport per se. (Epistemology is not equated solely with theory or frameworks, but see Chapter 1 for further comment on the relationship between epistemology, sports theory and the problem of values.)

Level 2: Sport and culture

This traditionally refers to the values, ceremonies and way of life characteristic of a given group and the place of sport within that way of life. Like the concept of society, the notion of culture is widely used in the sociological, anthropological and historical study of sport. It has traditionally encouraged the researcher and student to consider the meanings, symbols, rituals and power relations at play within any particular cultural setting. The notion of culture may be operationalised at a national, local or comparative level. Consequently, examples may include the place of sport within Irish or Kenyan culture; the meaning of the Tour de France to the French or sumo wrestling to the Japanese; the extent to which basketball reflects the new audacity of American society; the extent to which sport in South Africa during the apartheid era actively challenged the dominant definition of sport through politicising and empowering the idea that one cannot have normal sport in an abnormal society; the part played by the stance of some Zimbabwean cricketers not to play cricket for Zimbabwe as long as President Mugabe remained in power; or whether the tragedy and symbolism attached to the 2009 African World Cup being held in Angola offered real optimism that life itself was progressing in Angola. By examining the extent to which certain representations of culture within the media or readings of cultural texts by audiences reinforce certain cultural messages or meanings about sport, we are able to question the world in which we live in today.

Level 3: The nation

The role of sport in the making of nations is one of the most discussed areas in sport, culture and society. The precise nature of nations and nation states varies, as do the forms of nationalism that are often associated with different sports. The extent to which we understand the complex ways in which sport contributes to national identity, civic and ethnic nationalism and internationalism remains an open question. In order to understand sport fully, students and others need to comprehend processes and patterns of national and international change in sport, as well as the distinct content of national sports policies or the criteria for selection to national teams. At its most celebrated, the relationship between sport and nations is illustrated through events such as the Tour de France in France, the All-Ireland Hurling Final in Ireland, and cricket in India or England. At another level, it is illustrated by world leaders such as Kofi Annan, Mao Zedong or Nelson Mandela, who have commented upon sport's role in the building of society, reconciliation and hope. (See Chapter 6 for an examination of the part sport has played in nation building and national identity.)

Level 4: Global sport

The notion of global sport implies the processes by which sport reflects the growing interdependence of nations, regions and localities within a global or world political economy. In studying global sport, it is important to identify processes that transcend or cross national boundaries. Research into global sport has highlighted certain processes, ideoscapes, ethno-scapes, mediascapes, financescapes and technoscapes. International sporting organisations, such as the Fédération Internationale de Football Association (FIFA), often convey the message of marketing, administering and controlling global football. The notion of global sport has tended to be criticised from a number of viewpoints, including those of nationalists and internationalists. The development of global sport should not be considered in isolation from social welfare reform, anti-globalisation or anti-capitalism. Protests have targeted global sporting companies and highlighted the role of cheap labour, often children's labour, in the production of international sporting goods. The global economic recession and collapse of financial markets have certainly raised the question of trust and ownership of global financial companies and banks. Sport has not been immune from these events. (See Chapter 4 for a further discussion of sport, commercialisation and finance, and Chapters 5 and 20 for a further discussion of global sport, globalisation and anti-globalisation protests.)

Level 5: Neighbourhood and community sport

Geographically, the neighbourhood has been the area around one's home and usually displays some degree of homogeneity in terms of housing type, ethnicity or socio-cultural values. The term 'neighbourhood' is closely associated with a particular, although not the sole, definition of community. Neighbourhoods usually display strong allegiances to local sports teams, provide a focus for intergenerational discussions about 'golden sporting eras' and provide a basis for the development of community solidarity, but also rivalry, with other neighbour-hoods or communities. Accounts of sport's social role in communities and the part played by sport in the regeneration of deprived urban areas bring into question the effectiveness of sport. Metcalfe's (2006) study of the mining communities in the north-east of England identifies factors that have impinged upon neighbourhood or community sport, such as population stability and the physical layout of the community, town or village. The term 'community' has tended to denote a social group that is usually identified in terms of a common habitat, common interest and a degree of social cooperation, but it can also, in an applied sense, refer to a community of sportspeople, artists and students, as well as the international or national community. As a term, it has been historically associated with the German *Gemeinschaft*. More recently, it has been suggested that, within left-wing discourses, it has become more popular in the twenty-first century than the term 'social class', which used to be the 'holy grail' of various labour movements. The challenge over the use of such concepts as community and neighbourhood is whether they can be resurrected in new ways, in new shapes or in new incarnations to help make sense of the world and sport today.

Level 6: Policy intervention

The term 'policy' is derived from the Greek *politeia*, meaning government. The general principles of sports policy, like all policy, guide the making of laws and the administrative and executive governance of sport, as well as acts of governance per se in international and domestic affairs. Policy intervention in sport takes many forms, such as anti-drug policies or anti-discrimination policies, or policies restricting the movement of players from one club to another or one country to another, which may be viewed as anti-competitive. Sports policies may reflect particular political ideologies, but policies in general are not the same as doctrines, which may be viewed as the system of values and beliefs that may help to generate policies and that purport to describe the ends to which policy is the means. Nor are policies the same as philosophies, which tend to be the underlying justification for doctrines and policies together. Sports policy is one of the major practical means of intervention in sport. The different perspectives on sports policy put it somewhere in the middle ground between sports doctrine and sports philosophy. Houlihan (2008) provided a commentary on politics, power policy and sport, and infers the term 'policy intervention' as applying to something bigger than specific decisions but smaller than general social movements. Political outlooks differ radically over whether sports policy is or should be a reflection of some underlying philosophy, but most agree that policy should be consistent, reasonable and acceptable to those with power to oppose it. One last point is to suggest that there is no choice between the engaged and neutral ways of policy intervention. Seeking a morally neutral stance among the many forms of sports policy and decision making that impact upon the world of sport would be a vain effort. (See Part 4 of this book for a more in-depth coverage of some of the ways in which policy has been used to bring about social change in sport.)

Level 7: The sport or sporting event

A particular sport may provide the focus or framework for arranging the research material or essay. Many historical, sociological, political and other frameworks for analysing sport have been organised around case studies of particular sports or clubs. Some of the most superficial questions about a particular sport can lead to further investigations and enquiries about gender relations; social inequality; nationhood; the distribution of economic, cultural and social resources; social change; human rights; the environment; the role of the state; poverty; the urban and the rural; the global and the local; freedom and dependence; insiders and outsiders; and many other areas of investigation that fall within the remit and duty of the socially committed student, academic or politician to explore. Any number of sports or illustrative examples could be provided, and I have limited myself here to briefly mentioning the following that have been drawn from both past and more recent contributions to the field of sport, culture and society. Alabarces' (2000) investigation of football in Latin America raises issues about globalisation, colonialism, tradition and identity; Ray's (2001) study of the Highland Games explores issues of ethnicity, racism, Scottish–American heritage, social networks and power; Guha's (2002) study of cricket in India raises and answers questions about colonisation, the indigenous cricket experience, nation, caste and religion; Maguire's (2005) study has furthered our understanding of the relationship between sport, power and globalisation; Pitsiladis *et al.*'s (2007) inter-disciplinary examination of running in East Africa attempts to explain the phenomenal success of Kenyan and Ethiopian runners; Jarvie *et al.*'s (2008) study of the political economy of the 2008 Beijing Olympic Games informs us about the importance of Olympic sport and special events within the 'New China' of the twenty-first century; while Kingsley's (2012) study of American surfing questions whether surfing actually provides a radical alternative lifestyle. These studies and others help us to understand why some nations may want to host sporting events, why it is beyond the reach and capability of some, and why others would prefer to do it in partnership with other nations.

Level 8: The historical period or theme

The historical study of sport has been one of the most active and interventionist in helping to interpret past and present sport. It has also brought to the study of sport, culture and society the discipline of sustained micro-level archival research methods that have helped to qualify unsubstantiated grand narratives of sport. Chronologically, the study of sport, culture and society may be approached century by century or time period by time period, as for example in Vamplew's (1988) study of professional sport and commercialisation between 1875 and 1914; Metcalfe's (1991) study of power in Canadian amateur sport between 1918 and 1936; Pfister's (1990) study of female physical culture in nineteenth- and early twentieth-century Germany; Parratt's (1989) study of working-class women and leisure in late Victorian England; Kidd's (1996) account of the struggle to control Canadian sport; Burnett's (2000) study of sport in Lowland Scotland before 1860; Huggins's (2008) overview of sport in the lives of the British upper classes between 1500 and 2000; Stead and Williams's (2008) significant reminder that, in a country where the rugby union team is a source of national pride, boxing has also had a special place in the psyche of the Welsh nation; or Hedenborg's (2009) account of the challenges to the ten existing special orders of sport on post-war Sweden. The study of what and why in the history of sport has also been influenced by other ways of presenting the history of sport, whether it be thematically or in terms of ancient, modern or post-modern perspectives about sport, culture and society. The history of sport may be presented with different emphases: quantitatively, economically, theoretically, semiotically, heroically, conservatively, reverently and/or chronologically. There are many historical levels of analysis from which to approach the study of sport, culture and society. (See Chapter 2 for further coverage of the historical contribution to the study of sport, culture and society.)

Level 9: Social divisions and inequality

It is impossible to think about sport, culture and society without realising that sport means different things to different groups of people, or that different policies or forms of social mobilisation are aimed at empowering different groups of people. The meanings that often divide sport are those of class, ethnicity, gender, age, nationality, black or white, European or non-European, and disabled or physically impaired. Many of these social divisions have become separatist, and fail to acknowledge the connection between and within different forms of social inequality in sport. Various accounts of sport, culture and society have accorded priority to different forms of social division and social inequality; for example, the relationship between rich and poor parts of the world informs Arbena's (1999) study of sport in Latin America; issues of race, racism and multiculturalism inform Back *et al.*'s (2001) study of the changing face of English professional football; issues of social class and social stratification are central to Scheerder *et al.*'s (2002) account of sport in Belgium and other parts of Europe; gender, feminism and different experiences of women are central to Fan Hong's (1997) study of women in sport in China; while notions of imperialism and post-colonialism are crucial to Hwang's (2001) accounts of sport in Taiwan. Sorek's (2007) analysis of Arab soccer in a Jewish state provides a very specific insight into the contemporary role of sport in legitimising and challenging contemporary inequality between Arabs and Jews in Israel. Theberge (2009) draws our attention to the blurred professional boundaries and divisions that have been involved in the social construction of the field of sports medicine. However, important questions remain: are equalities fair and just? How do these social divisions intersect? Should priority be given to any form of social division? And should we not at least recognise that the gap between rich and poor in sport remains? The study of sport and social inequality should not simply examine a random selection of different sections of society, but rather the issues of hierarchy, social division, fairness and social injustices that impact upon all people's lives per se. (See Part 4 for a more detailed account of these social divisions in terms of sport.)

Level 10: International development and sports aid

New dimensions to the understanding of sport, culture and society are being added or further developed as a result of an increasing emphasis on the part played by sport in terms of international development and/or sport as a facet of humanitarian aid. Sport, in a number of ways, has been seen to be part of a programme of social intervention and welfare aimed at supporting people who have been traumatised by conflict, in the promotion of programmes of conflict resolution, and by helping in situations of military conflict where sport is used to draw people out of routines of violence. The work of Levermore and Beacom (2009) suggests that sport can contribute to the development process, particularly where traditional approaches to development have found it difficult to engage with communities. In part, the benefits from using sports as a development tool or for peace building involve not just sport, but education through sport. Such programmes have long since been viewed as agents of social change for individuals, with the rationale being that they can provide opportunities for lifelong learning and sustain not just education, but an involvement in sport and physical activity; increase knowledge and skills, and, in a broader sense, contribute to the knowledge economy; foster social capital through building relationships, networking and making connections; and support development programmes across the world that use sport as a tool or incentive for participation.

It is the ability to combine sport with other social forces such as education through sport that has facilitated an increased profile for sport by agencies such as UNICEF, UNAIDS and

SPORT IN FOCUS 0.2: SPORT AND RELIGION IN AMERICAN SPORT – KURT WARNER AND FAITH

Many athletes, such as former NFL quarterback Kurt Warner, attribute their sporting success to their faith in religion. Warner's career was one of great highs and lows. He was released in 1994 by the Green Bay Packers and ended up stacking shelves on the night shift at his local supermarket. Nevertheless, his faith and determination led him back to the NFL, where he had a successful career that included three Super Bowl appearances, winning one with the St Louis Rams in 2001.

Warner became a devout Christian after seeing his wife cope well with extreme personal tragedy, thanks to her faith in God. Warner was open about his faith throughout his career, and often spoke of how it helped him to achieve the level of success he did. In 2000, before his winning Super Bowl appearance, he stated:

> Who am I? I am a devout Christian man; I am not a football player. That is what I do. When I throw a touchdown pass, my thoughts are on how I can use this success on the field as a platform to glorify and praise my Lord Jesus Christ.

In the aftermath of winning Super Bowl XXXIV, he was asked to describe his winning pass, but instead replied that he had Jesus to thank for the victory. Similarly, in the build up to the 2009 Super Bowl, Warner again stated how important his faith was:

> Everybody's going to be tired of hearing this, but I never get tired of saying it. There's one reason that I'm standing up on this stage today. That's because of my Lord up above. I've got to say thanks to Jesus, you knew I was going to do it, but I've got to do it.

Whether one is religious or not, it is evident that many athletes, like Kurt Warner, gain confidence from their faith, which inspires them to incredible achievements in sport. This is examined further in Chapter 14.

the World Health Organization. Studies at this level can look at the role of international development as a form of sports aid country by country, or case study by case study, or evaluation of initiatives one by one.

Many other levels of analysis could be added in order to ask a number of key questions about sport, culture and society today. It would be remiss if those working in universities did not want future generations of students to say that their university experience prepared them for life in an increasingly interdependent world, or those studying or living sport did not recognise the wider world of sport, culture and society. Is the relationship between sport and religion today any greater in contemporary America than it was in the early twentieth century? Many examples may be provided, but each of the chapters in this book try to provide some evidence, and illustrate key examples in the Sport in Focus sections.

ORGANISATION OF THE BOOK

The book is organised into four main parts, with each part providing an introduction for the reader. Part 1 explores the broader context, including the epistemological and ontological context or framework in which contemporary sport may be understood; it introduces a number of common concepts and theories that have been utilised in the explanation of sport; it acknowledges the lessons of history and what these bring to the study of sport; and it asserts that one of the tasks and promises of sociological theory has always been to help us draw bigger diagnostic pictures of sport, culture and society. How these particular tools, theories and evidence are used, and for what purpose, should be the exclusive prerogative of social actors themselves in specific social contexts, and used on behalf of their values and interests. It also introduces the relationship between finance, economics and commerce, and its broader influence upon sport. With these pictures, the student of sport can begin to understand and comprehend the socially and politically situated nature of their work and being.

Part 2 examines some of the international, national, post-colonial and local contexts in which sport operates. One of the enduring problems with core introductory texts that have addressed these issues is that the analysis of sport, culture and society has tended to be dominated by, or at least sensitive to, an American perspective, without critically questioning this or alternative points of view (Coakley and Pike, 2009; Coakley, 2003; Nixon and Frey, 1996). The interaction between such processes as imperialism, post-colonialism and internationalism may have a much louder voice in any comprehensive analysis of sport in today's world. New circumstances call for strengthened international frameworks capable of constraining the use of political violence. Equally, there should be a call for self-examination by the West of its attitudes towards other worlds of sport and the international role of sport in contributing to humanitarian causes. One of the advances in the analysis of sport, culture and society over the past decade has been the impact made by social, cultural and urban geographers who have researched and mapped out crucial bodies of work in relation to sport and the city, sport and space, sport and the body, sport and post-colonialism, and urban sporting cultures. Part 2 of this book critically examines the relationship between global sport and different communities while identifying some of the core international players, organisations and institutions that have impacted upon or brought about social change in sport in many different parts of the world. It considers some key social institutions that influence world sport, such as the media, the law and education.

Part 3 focuses upon issues of identity and lifestyle, and other key social issues. Sport is not immune from key social and political concerns about the environment, religion, violence and the search for a better society or lifestyle. Identity politics through sport seem to have been premised upon the acceptance that all social groups have essential identities. The rise of identity politics in sport forms a convergence of cultural and political style, a mode of logic, a badge of belonging, a claim to insurgency, a recovery from exclusion and/or a demand for representation. The long overdue opening of political initiatives to minorities, women and a multitude of voiceless people in sport has developed into a method of its own. Identity politics on its own is not enough. At the same time, the pressures for alternative forms of sport and physical activity mean that the social and physical profile of sport itself is changing. Early research indicates that a crop of activities that might be loosely termed 'extreme sports' are firmly embedded within counter-cultures, but a more contemporary analysis indicates that a broad range of groups are looking for a better society. These and other issues form the basis of Part 3.

In Part 4, our attention turns to matters of social change, social movement, development and social intervention. While Parts 1, 2 and 3 are about analysing and substantiating the world of sport, Part 4 thinks about sport as a resource of hope. It is based upon the premise that, while it is crucial for students and researchers of sport, culture and society to analyse and empirically test the social world of sport, it is also important to identify areas in which sport has campaigned, or ought to campaign, for change. Much of the existing research carried out by social researchers and students interested in sport has sought to destroy many taken-for-granted myths about sport, critically appraise and evaluate the actions of the powerful in sport and their impact upon the less powerful, and inform and champion the promise of sport in terms of social policy and community welfare. It is only relatively recently that sport's contribution to human rights campaigns has been recognised. It has been said that sociology is the power of the powerless, and yet there is no guarantee that, having acquired a sociological understanding of sport, one can dissolve or disempower the resistance put up by the tough realities of everyday life. The power of understanding is no match for the pressures of coercion allied with resigned and submissive common sense. If it were not for this understanding of sport in society, the chance of further freedoms being won through and in sport would be slimmer still.

Finally, some of the main influences that have informed the thinking behind this book are pulled together. The whole project is mindful that sport can make a difference to communities and societies, and that, while policies and governments may change in different parts of the world, the need for many people remains the same.

HOW TO USE THE NEW BOOK

The book provides a comprehensive introduction to the study of sport, culture and society. There is a sustained attempt to critically analyse, describe and explain sport today as a social, cultural and political phenomenon. The position taken throughout this book is that, while it is important to explain and understand sport in society, the more important intellectual and practical questions emanate from questions relating to social change.

The core questions at the heart of this text are:

- What empirical evidence can we draw upon to substantiate aspects of sport, culture and society? (What is happening in sport?)
- What theories, ideas and concepts can we draw upon to explain and analyse this substantive evidence? (How can we make sense of what is happening in sport?)
- What capacity does sport have to transform or intervene to produce social change? (What can be done to produce change?)
- What is the contemporary role of the student, intellectual, researcher and universities in the public arena? (What are you going to do about it?)

15

One of the objectives of the book is to encourage students to reflect upon sport, drawing upon concepts, theories and themes, but also on a body of substantive research from different sports, societies and communities. It is the constant interplay between theory, explanation, evidence and intervention that is one of the hallmarks of the approach adopted. Put more simply, the student of sport, culture and society will continually be faced with three interrelated challenges. Although the production of knowledge and policy rarely comes in such a neat package or process, these can be summarised as: (i) What evidence do you have? (ii) How are you going to make sense of it? and (iii) What recommendations are you going to make as a result these first two exercises?

The book is supported by a wealth of additional sources of information, provided in a number of forms. These include:

- chapter previews and objectives that outline the main areas covered in each chapter;
- photographs that provide visual illustrations from sport, culture and society settings;
- Sport in Focus boxes that provide empirical information that complements, where appropriate, the area being covered in each chapter;
- key concepts and definitions that act as a guide to the core ideas and concepts covered;
- study questions designed to test knowledge and promote critical reflection upon the subject matter of each chapter;
- sample projects that may be used as a databank of exercises to sharpen and refine not only transferable research skills, but also a sensitivity to the social world of sport;
- a list of at least five websites that will assist and support the body of knowledge in each chapter (these websites provide access to a range of information and are not all sports-specific – be prepared to explore each website thoroughly in relation to the topic in which you are interested); and
- additional support through access to supplementary PowerPoint documents and test banks of questions.

SUMMARY

This introductory discussion of sport, culture and society has outlined the structure and rationale that has informed the content of this book. It has highlighted the need not only to draw upon substantive evidence and explain that evidence, but also the necessity to link this exercise to policies and attempts to produce social change. It has championed the cause of the researcher, teacher, intellectual and student of sport who really wants to understand more than just the popularity, importance and relevance of sport in today's world. It has provided an introduction to some of the tools of the trade that help to equip and enlighten the enquiring student who is fascinated and caught up in the power, potential and passion of sport and related areas. It is one thing to identify the key areas of concern of our time, but it is also vital to identify silences, since what is not being said often tells us as much about sport as that which is being said. Nonetheless, sport, Nelson Mandela once said, is a force that mobilises the sentiments of a people in a way that nothing else can. Can it, or will it, remain a vehicle for social capital, community solidarity, critical scholarship, and a resource of hope and fun for a long time to come? Bill Clinton, the former US president suggested that football does more for poverty in poor nations than almost any other intervention. Barack Obama (US), Desmond Tutu (South Africa), Lula de Silva (Brazil), Wen Jiabao (China) and many others have all commented in various ways on the relationship between sport, culture and society.

GUIDE TO FURTHER READING

Boykoff, J. (2011). 'The Anti-Olympics'. *New Left Review*, 67 (January/February): 41–61.

Cashmore, E. (2010). *Making Sense of Sports*. London: Routledge.

Coakley, J. and Pike, E. (2009). *Sports In Society: Issues and Controversies*. Boston, MA: McGraw Hill Companies.

Donnelly, P. and Coakley, J. (2011). *Sport: A Short Introduction*. London: Routledge.

Houlihan, B. (2008). *Sport and Society: A Student Introduction*. London: Sage.

Levermore, R. and Beacom, A. (2009). *Sport and International Development*. New York: Palgrave Macmillan.

Obama, B. (2008). *The Audacity of Hope*. New York: Three Rivers Press.

Sherry, E., Karg, A. and O'May, F. (2011). 'Social Capital and Sport Events: Spectator Attitudinal Change and the Homeless World Cup'. *Sport in Society*, 14 (1): 111–125.

QUESTIONS

1 Outline and develop five different levels of analysis by which you might begin to reflect upon sport, culture and society.

2 Critically discuss in detail the importance of sport in today's world.

3 List four ways in which society has changed since 2006.

4 What is the public role of the intellectual and/or student involved in the study of sport, culture and society?

5 Define and reflect upon use of the following terms: 'sport', 'culture' and 'society'.

6 How else might sport be described?

7 What are the core questions at the heart of this book, and how do they relate to one another?

8 Give at least five different groups of people who might be affected by the divisive nature of sport.

9 Much is made of the term 'good society'. At least four strands of contemporary thinking on this term exist – what are they?

10 What are some of the key social issues and problems facing the student of sport, culture and society?

PRACTICAL PROJECTS

1   Interview five people who are 10, 20, 30 or 40 years older than yourself and ask them to talk about what sport was like when they were your age. Compile a short report on how sport has changed over time, based upon your interviews.

2   Read the sports coverage of two national newspapers or websites over a period of three months, and list the social issues and problems that appear. Based upon your results, write a short report on the ways in which sport reflects broader social issues and problems in society.

3   Access the website www.google.co.uk and type 'sport + society' in the search space. Read the articles listed and then carry out five other searches of your own choice in relation to sports topics, such as 'sport + poverty' or 'sport + environment' or 'sport + politics'.

4   Read the manifesto of any political party and see if it refers to sport. Suggest five sports policy recommendations that reflect the core values of the political party you have chosen.

5   Draw a flow chart of networks from key people in your life or someone else's life whom you or they have met through sport. Consider and reflect upon the potential for sport to introduce and sustain networks of people.

KEY CONCEPTS

Community ■ Culture ■ Development ■ International ■ Epistemology ■ Global Sport ■ Nation ■ Neighbourhood ■ Sport ■ Society ■ Social Change ■ Social Inequality

WEBSITES

FIFA worldwide programmes of support
www.fifa.com/aboutfifa/worldwideprograms/index.html
A dedicated website that provides information about FIFA's role in terms of social responsibility and sport.

A factbook of information on different countries
https://www.cia.gov/library/publications/the-world-factbook/
The CIA World Factbook is one of the most authoritative international factbooks about different countries. Use it as a resource to find out necessary background information on different parts of the world.

Sport in Europe

www.sport-in-europe.eu

Sport in Europe focuses upon the relationship between the EU and sport.

The Foreign Policy Centre

www.fpc.org.uk

A progressive foreign affairs think tank. Use the search facility to find information on sport and foreign policy.

The International Olympic Movement

www.olympic.org

The official website of the Olympic Movement. Explore this resource with a view to finding out about Olympism in action or the changing nature of countries involved, and where major events are held.

ONLINE RESOURCE CENTRE

Visit the online resource centre that accompanies this book to access more resources. www.routledge.com/cw/jarvie

Part 1

The broader context

INTRODUCTION

The four chapters that form the first part of this book examine broader contexts that have informed our knowledge about sport, culture and society.

Sport theory and the problem of values

Theory provides us with different frameworks for thinking about sport in society. Is it still as relevant to the study of sport today and, if so, what are the new ways of thinking about or framing sporting problems and issues? The constant interplay between theory and evidence helps to examine taken-for-granted sporting assumptions. Sporting myths need to be constantly challenged and re-evaluated. How these particular tools, theories and evidence are used, and for what purpose, should not be the exclusive prerogative of researchers and students themselves, but used in specific social contexts and on behalf of the individual's or group's values and interests. The accuracy, rigour and relevance of theory and evidence provide a basis not only for critically examining popular and unpopular sports issues, but also providing students with solutions and explanations to particular sporting problems. It is vital to make decisions, but to make the right decisions, and frameworks and evidence help you to evaluate and come to decision-making moments.

Sport, history and social change

How does the history of sport help us to understand the development of sport today? The socio-historical development of sport tells students of sport where and when particular sporting practices emerged. It owes as much to cross-comparative contexts as it does contemporary historiography. It acknowledges the influence of the past on the present, but also the dangers of thinking solely contemporaneously. By enabling us to know about other centuries and other cultures, an understanding of the socio-historical development of sport provides students with one of the best antidotes to any temporal sporting parochialism, which assumes that the only time is now, and geographical parochialism, which assumes that the only place is here. The emphasis on social change, sporting trends and past solutions to problems forms the core to understanding how sporting worlds are the way they are. Histories also provide a vast resource of solutions in relation to what has been done in the past when similair situations or contexts or problems have arisen.

Sport, global finance and economics

Economics is about choice and is at the heart of the decision making about sport. Economics and finance are not the same, but it is difficult to fully understand notions of global sport without an introduction to how sporting finances flow in and out of different forms of sport. What is the economic impact of certain sports in certain places? Sport, like other commodities, is affected by decisions that are made about resources. How has sport been affected by the financial recession? Where is the economic power in sport, who holds it and how does the potential redistribution of sporting finance impact upon different places, teams, communities and individuals? Is sport a form of global trade? These and other themes are at the heart of Chapter 3.

Sport, politics and culture

What are the politics of sport and culture? Chapter 4 identifies the ways in which sport has figured within the political field. Politics has been variously described as being centrally concerned with sport when sport is involved with: (i) civil government, the state and public affairs; (ii) human conflict and its resolution; or (iii) the sources and exercise of power. A contemporary view might be that politics only applies to human beings, or at least to those beings that can communicate symbolically and thus make statements, invoke principles, argue and disagree. The politics of sport occurs in practice when people disagree about the distribution of resources and have at least some procedures for the resolution of such disagreements over sport. This is particularly pertinent to the analysis of sport, culture and society, where competing definitions of this relationship struggle for dominance within and outside the sporting world.

Chapter 1

Sport, theory and the problem of values

How has sport helped society think about differences, and have university employees opposed inequality wherever it exists?

Sporting celebrities, such as Lionel Messi, often champion social causes. How can sporting ambassadors help to sustain or enable campaigns that help people today?

PREVIEW

Key terms defined ■ Introduction ■ Cricket in Pakistan ■ Thinking about sport, culture and society (1) ■ Thinking about sport, culture and society (2) ■ The research process ■ West and Anti-West ■ Contemporary themes in sport ■ Globalisation ■ Identity ■ Social Inequality ■ Culture and power ■ Development and freedom ■ New ideas and fresh thinking ■ Left and right communitarianism ■ Left and right republicanism ■ In search of common ground and social change ■ Summary

This chapter will:

- discuss the role of theory in analysing sport;
- outline the relationship between sports theory and values;
- consider different theoretical approaches to analysing sport;
- consider the common ground between different traditions of social thought and sport; and
- reject the notion of neutral or value-free sport.

KEY TERMS DEFINED

Globalisation: A historical process involving a fundamental shift or transformation in the spatial scale of human social organisation that links distant communities and expands the reach of power relations across regions and continents. It is also something of a catch-all phrase often used to describe a single world economy after the collapse of communism, though sometimes employed to define the growing integration of the international capitalist system growing in the post-war period.

Epistemology: The study of how we can claim to know something. It is about our theories of knowledge.

Identity: The understanding of the self in relationship to an 'other'. Identities are social and thus are always formed in relationship to others. Constructivists generally hold that identities shape interests; we cannot know what we want unless we know who we are. But because identities are social and are produced through interactions, identities can change.

Power: In the most general sense, the ability of a political actor to achieve its goals.

Ontology: The study of what is. It is about the nature of being.

INTRODUCTION

In approaching the study of sport for the first time, it is useful to think about contemporary approaches to the study of sport, culture and society. One of the peculiarities of most *general* books in this area is that many, but not all, are still discussed largely in isolation from a broader or dated context and, to a lesser extent, the societies of which they are part. Many sporting texts are not written from the standpoint of the critical thinker, economist or political scientist, all of whom have used concepts, ideas and theories as a basis for explaining and understanding sport as part of social life. Studies of sport have helped to provide insights into different ways of understanding the world of sport. Yet, all have made domain assumptions, adopted starting points, prioritised certain questions and marginalised others.

In other words, they are not neutral or value-free. It is necessary to understand where different questions about sport come from and why they are being asked. Those interested in the political element will ask questions about wealth as in Sport in Focus 1.1.

SPORT IN FOCUS 1.1: WHERE AND WHO EARNS THE MOST FROM SPORT?

The table below lists the top 12 salary earners in one recent year, but the interesting questions are not so much who earns the most, but where is the concentration in wealth – which sports, which countries or even continents – and how do you distribute wealth in a more equitable way?

Rank	Team	League	Avg Annual (£)	Avg Week Pay (£)
1	Barcelona	La Liga	4,944,211	95,081
2	Real Madrid	La Liga	4,597,895	88,421
3	New York Yankees	MLB	4,222,688	81,206
4	LA Lakers	NBA	4,087,961	78,614
5	Orlando Magic	NBA	3,979,446	76,528
6	Chelsea	Premier League	3,762,923	72,365
7	Inter Milan	Serie A	3,749,777	72,111
8	Boston Red Sox	MLB	3,744,502	72,010
9	Denver Nuggets	NBA	3,743,859	71,997
10	Manchester City	Premier League	3,664,741	70,476
11	Utah Jazz	NBA	3,643,527	70,068
12	Bayern Munich	Bundesliga	3,612,724	69,475
163	Celtic	SPL	971,220	18,677
181	Rangers	SPL	768,845	14,778

At the same time, many people are asking questions such as what now for social theory? Who are the key thinkers of our time and how are these impacting upon our understanding of sport, culture and society? One thing is clear, and that is that those working with theory today have much more freedom to think from a broader international range of social theory and are not constrained by any one theory born out of one nation or even continent. Students, teachers and researchers of sport, culture and society must look to think internationally, draw upon international examples and continually think and act against the grain of academic orthodoxy.

At the time of writing this chapter, the world's newspapers were struggling to frame an explanation surrounding the fact that three or four members of the Pakistan cricketing team had been allegedly found to be taking bets that may or may not have influenced the outcome of certain cricket matches. Different countries, newspapers and sports agencies were all competing to try to frame, contain or expose further the story of the day. There is no value-free way of engaging with this incident. At first glance, this might have been about whether cricket is above or below the law and whether the cricket authorities or the legal authorities should resolve the incident. It may also be about the way in which money is associated differentially with different sports or whether gambling – as it is in horse racing – is an accepted part of the culture of certain sports and not others. Alternatively, different cultures might approach the issue of betting or gambling in sport differently. The issue is really no different from that facing the researcher who has to frame or think about sporting problems and issues in a particular way and continually reflect upon the interplay between theory and evidence.

One of the basic problems facing anyone who tries to understand contemporary sport, culture and society is that there is so much material to look at that it is sometimes difficult to distinguish that which matters most. Theories are not simply some grand formulaic model that helps to explain sport, but rather theory can be a sort of simplifying device that assists you with deciding what matters most. The first edition of this book outlined particular approaches to thinking about sport, culture and society. Some of these form the basis of Sport in Focus 1.2 and 1.3, which outline several sets of questions. The approach that is taken within Sport in Focus 1.2 and 1.3 is an attempt to relate some of these frameworks to some contemporary social issues. How would you use such questions to help you think about sporting icons such as Tiger Woods that have slipped from being ideal role models, or the extent to which democratic or post-colonial tensions between countries help us explain why certain countries are awarded the FIFA World Cup? The examples used here cannnot be exhaustive, but they illustrate the practical aspects of this knowledge by relating the questions to sport in American, Canadian and other societies. Other examples from a broad range of countries will be used throughout this book. New ideas and new ways of thinking have undoubtedly influenced the analysis of sport, culture and society, and these are also developed throughout this chapter.

THE VALUE OF THEORY TO FRAMING THE ANALYSIS OF SPORT, CULTURE AND SOCIETY

When asked what the value of theory is to framing the analysis of sport, culture and society, the following are some of the most common answers given:

- Asking theoretical questions is crucial to allowing us to explain or generalise about sport, culture and society.
- Theory or hypothesis testing is a necessary part of approaching or organising research.
- Theory is equally capable of illuminating circumstances or destroying certain cherished myths that are often taken for granted without being tested.
- A good theory stimulates new ideas and is fruitful in terms of generating further areas of research or study.
- It helps frame and illuminate the process of decision making and why some decisions take the format that they do and others are rejected.

Sport, culture and society, like other bodies of knowledge, has its own perspectives, ways of seeing things and of analysing human actions, as well as its own set of principles for

SPORT IN FOCUS 1.2: FRAMING DIFFERENT FORMS OF THINKING ABOUT SPORT

You can apply these frameworks to ask questions about your sport or your country, or both.

Functionalism

- Socio-emotional function, wherein sport contributes to the maintenance of socio-psychological stability.
- Socialisation function, wherein sport contributes to the inculcation of cultural beliefs and mores.
- Integrative function, wherein sport contributes to the harmonious integration of disparate individuals and diverse groups.
- Political function, wherein sport is used for ideological purposes.
- Social mobility function, wherein sport serves as a source of upward mobility.

Symbolic interactionism

- What does sport mean to oneself, or what place has sport played in the individual's biography?
- How has one's personal identity been affected by sport over time?
- To what extent have feelings about sport been influenced by a process of interaction with others?
- How do sports form a pattern of association and interaction?
- How do athletes in certain situations reciprocate with and against one another?

Interpretative sociology

- To what extent are sportspeople conscious of their actions?
- How have sportspeople's careers in reality been experienced?
- What socialisation experiences are involved in the process of becoming an athlete?
- How have media audiences internalised or interpreted the representations of sport in the media, particularly television?
- To what extent is status helpful in explaining sport and social order?

Process sociology

- What are the principal processes that have been involved with the development of sport?
- Has sport become more or less violent over time?
- What have been the core figurations that have influenced the shifting balances of power in sport?
- How might the globalisation of sport be explained?
- Do we have a reality-congruent body of knowledge about sport?

SPORT IN FOCUS 1.2—*continued*

Political economy

- Who profits from sport and how is it organised under global capitalism?
- How is wealth produced through sport and who benefits from this wealth?
- Are different groups that are involved in sport exploited?
- How might a materialist understanding of history be produced?
- How might global capitalism impact upon the trade of sports people to different countries?

interpretation. It has become increasingly inter-disciplinary and more relaxed, even since the arrival of the first edition of this book. It is, first and foremost, a distinct body of knowledge, but it also has fluid boundaries in that it draws upon other bodies of knowledge; for example, in the search for solving classical sociological problems or the social issues of the day. Fundamentally, both practical and scholastic social questions are not about interpreting the world of sport, but about how to change it. As a tentative summation of what is entailed in thinking sociologically about sport, it is important to develop the habit of viewing human actions as elements of wider figurations or social networks. Sport does not exist in a value-free, neutral social, economic, cultural or political context, but is influenced by all of these contexts. It is people that make decisions. The value of sociology to the study of sport, culture and society is primarily that it provides a multitude of different ways of thinking about the human world. The way one chooses to think about sport will ultimately depend upon the values and political standpoint from which one views the human world. Thinking sociologically about sport is more than just adopting a common-sense approach to sport, in that the art of thinking sociologically may help the student of sport to be more sensitive to the human conditions that constitute the different worlds of sport. Thinking sociologically about sport may help us to understand that an individual's personal experience of sport is ultimately connected to broader social and public issues.

It has been said that sociology is the power of the powerless and yet, as one exponent has pointed out, there is no guarantee that, having acquired sociological understanding, one can dissolve or disempower the resistance put up by the tough realities of everyday life. The power of understanding is no match for the pressures of coercion allied with resigned and submissive common sense (Bauman, 1990: 18). Despite being written more than twenty years ago, as with other references the reader needs to think about whether such a statement helps you understand the world today a little bit better. If it were not for this understanding, the chance of further freedoms being won through and in sport would be slimmer still. Sociological thinking helps the cause of freedom. The service that sociology is well equipped to provide is to render to the human condition the promotion of a mutual understanding and tolerance as a potential condition of shared freedom. Sociology provides a basis for better understanding of not just societies and cultures, but also of ourselves. In reality, politics, philosophy and economics also help with this and therefore should not be ruled out as providing part of an answer to a problem simply because of disciplinary boundaries. As readers of this book will find out, the philosopher and Nobel Prize-winning economist Amaryta Sen has as much of an impact as sociologists or other people working within the field of sport.

A significant number of recent theories have involved the term 'post' as a basis for demarking a change in emphasis or time period. This is not new given that such a list of 'posts' might include post-Fordism, post-colonial, post-communist, post-feminism, post-humanism, post-industrial, post-modernism and post-structuralism, to name but a few, all of which have different epistemological or ontological premises for embarking upon any understanding of sport, culture and society. Some of the key questions that are associated with some of these approaches are illustrated in Sport in Focus 1.3.

Perhaps the real value of post-modernist, post-colonial, post-democratic and post-structuralist thinking about sport is that it challenged previous authoritative bodies of knowledge about sport. Thinking about sport, culture and society is never static, and the way in which the framing of sport, culture and society might be approached has changed even between the publication of the first and second editions of this book. The core issues that face sport today not only require new ideas, but also a fundamental shift in human consciousness. The idea that people can change, need to change and through changing can contribute to a better world is just as important today. In the same way, questions about the capacity and capability of sport to contribute to change, to help with international development, to affect different rates of violence and be part of a progressive solution to twenty-first-century society and imagining is just as relevant today. According to Elliott (2009: 347), one of the new tasks of social theory consists of examining the political conditions under which the planet is shared, and highlighting problems of violence, disease, malnutrition and rising levels of poverty. There is an emerging idea that today's social coordinates are being rewritten around the politics of survival, sharing, community and inequalities of capacity, as well as capability and the resources of hope that sport can potentially bring or mobilise to help with such contemporary problems.

As such, it is as much about ontology or a way of being as it is about epistemology or ways of knowing. The two terms 'epistemology' and 'ontology' are worth elaborating upon at this point. Epistemology, from the Greek word *episteme*, meaning knowledge, is concerned with theories or a theory of knowledge that seeks to inform how we can know the world we inhabit. Important divisions within the philosophy of knowledge have been between rationalism or idealism and empiricism. In a sociological sense, epistemology tends to emphasise the way in which forms of knowledge have been influenced by social structure. Ontological arguments are also an explicit feature of sociological theory in that they attempt to establish the nature of fundamental things that might exist in the world, or of ways of being in the world. Ontology may refer simply to the study of being, yet at times it is worth distinguishing the ontology of a belief or practice from the theory that explains it. Thus, at a lived or micro-level, the solutions to the problem of sporting violence in its different forms in different countries, for example, might be different from the theories that explain it.

Among the ontological sociological issues that researchers of sport, culture and society may have to consider are where they stand in relation to the nature of social facts, whether sociology is a contemporary or historically based subject, the relationship between material-ism and idealism, structure and agency, or what is the essence of social class or social division

29

SPORT IN FOCUS 1.3: FRAMING DIFFERENT FORMS OF THINKING ABOUT POST-SPORT

The following are indicative questions that have been associated with different forms of thinking about sport in society involving the term 'post'. The term 'post' usually refers to a shift in time period, a change in method or a change in approach.

Post-modernism

Questions that might arise out of an approach to sport informed by post-modernism:

■ What are the characteristics of post-modern sport that suggest that the boundaries of sport have moved beyond modernity?

■ To what extent do children of the bourgeoisie dominate the discussion of post-modern sport?

■ If modern sport has failed, what promise does a post-sport world hold?

■ Is the athletic body, the sporting body or the healthy body a source of discipline and pleasure?

■ To what extent has sport become a pure event devoid of any reference to nature, and susceptible to imagined or synthetic images?

Post-democracy

Questions that might arise out of an approach to sport informed by a post-democratic approach:

■ How should sport be organised in a post-democratic world?

■ To what extent has the rise in corruption within sport reflected a post-democratic world?

■ What is the significance of global sports firms in influencing sport today?

■ Is the nature of sport different between democratic and post-democratic worlds, and, if so, how?

■ What should be done to promote trust in a post-democratic sports world?

Post-colonialism

Questions that might arise out of an approach to sport informed by post-colonialsim:

■ To what extent has the process of external imperialism and/or colonialism influenced the development of sport?

■ To what extent has the history of sport been challenged and changed by non-Western perspectives?

■ How has Western sport controlled non-Western sport?

■ Is the nature of sport different in Western and non-Western worlds, and, if so, how?

■ How do other ways of seeing things help us inform a more progressive sporting world?

SPORT IN FOCUS 1.3—*continued*

Historical–sociological

Questions that might arise out of an approach to sport informed by historical––sociological forms of thinking:

- How has sport been affected by the historical period in which it is located?
- To what extent have contemporary sporting problems and issues been adequately covered, or do sports journalists, politicians and writers tend to retreat into the present?

in the twenty-first century. Thus, a theorist attempting to explain the world of sport in society or even what is a social fact will utilise different paradigms of thought or bodies of knowledge to explain the way things are or could be. Some of the most prominent approaches have been symbolic interactionism, structuralism, Marxism, feminism, post-modernism, post-structuralism, post-nationalism and figurational sociology, all of which try to construct knowledge or ways of seeing the world and the place of sport within it.

In order to establish that theory is necessary, it might be useful to consider two things: (i) the role and importance of theoretical thinking and (ii) the relationship between theory and research. A point that needs to be made here is that theoretical thinking is not a process divorced from sport or everyday life. Theoretical thinking is not the obscure and esoteric exercise that it is so often characterised as, but rather the rigorous and continual systematic attempt to make use of particular tools in order to interpret the world around us or solve a problem or provide for a programme of change, action or critical thinking. What sociological theory may provide is a mode of critique, a language of opposition and a promise that the potential for radical transformation actually exists. The role of the sociological researcher and student interested in sport is not simply to destroy myths about sport, but also to ensure that the choices that are made about sport and the worlds in which it operates are genuinely free, regardless of whether these choices are libertarian, on the one hand, or staunchly communitarian, on the other.

In the same way that the relationship between sport and capitalism was a common theme within much of the critical Marxist or socialist literature on sport produced towards the end of the twentieth century, the notion of global sport and the accompanying language of globalisation have increasingly and uncritically dominated social, cultural and political debates about the nature of sport in the first decade or more of the twenty-first century. It is as if, at some point, a resolution between the inherent tensions brought about by globalisation and capitalism has been achieved, and that sport and its relationship to capitalism has lost its meaningfulness as a way of thinking about sport in the world today. If we reduce the various theoretical forms of appeal to sport – globalisation, capitalism, a shift in the economic centre of the world or the importance of frameworks aimed at thinking about religion – as a basis for simple abstraction about the social world, then we need to jettison such an approach. If we view theory as useful shorthand for a set of collectively practised prompts to reflection

31

– in other words, if we raise sport through all its activities and forms as a basis for reflexivity about the very nature of sport and the world itself – then we are subjecting sport and the world we live in to a qualitative assessment. Theory can help to lay the foundations for this assessment, which, in turn, may extend to the notion of a critique of sport that is often ignored by mainstream, orthodox and traditional sports practitioners. This is but one of the core healthy progressive functions of theory or frameworks – the function of criticism.

One of the fundamental functions of theory and sociology is that it contributes to a form of critique of existing forms of culture and society. A sociology dominated by Western thinking is itself problematic; as such, there is just as much credibility in the enduring claim that the practice of sociology demands invoking what C. Wright Mills (1970) referred to as the 'sociological imagination' as there is in Amaryta Sen's (2006) reminder that the Western mind has many stereotypes and that, in a world of unprecedented opulence, millions of people living in rich and poor countries are still unfree. This is a threefold exercise that involves a historical, anthropological and critical sensitivity. The first effort of the sociological imagination involves recovering our own immediate past and understanding the basis of how historical transformation has influenced the social and cultural dimensions of life. The second effort entails the cultivation of an anthropological insight. This is particularly helpful in that it lends itself to an appreciation of the diversity of different modes of human existence and cultures throughout the world, and not just those associated with the materiality of life in the West or advancing modern capitalist societies. Through a better understanding of the variety of human cultures and societies, it is asserted that we can learn or facilitate a better understanding of ourselves. The third aspect of the imagination is a combination of the first two in that the exercise of the sociological imagination avoids a critical analysis based upon the here and now, and involves the potential of grasping an understanding of social relations between societies throughout the world.

Theory is also a necessary part of the research process and there are a number of possible explanations for this. First, it can inform the type of research that is undertaken in that the particular theoretical approach adopted will influence both the types of questions examined and the particular types of research methods adopted. This is because of the close relationship between certain theories and certain methods or, put more simply, certain theoretical approaches have a disposition to certain methods. Second, theory informs how the data collected may be interpreted, not simply because certain conclusions may be derived as a result of the approach adopted, but also as a result of the type of theoretical scrutiny that is applied to data and empirical evidence. Finally, theory may act as a stimulus to pursue particular research topics and questions. In all of these approaches the accumulation of knowledge is continually evolving, although that which was taken for granted in the past might be superseded by contemporary ways of thinking. Earlier findings and previous ways of knowing may be returned too, in the light of changing world conditions or new ways of thinking about data or the fact that the same continuing themes prevail; for example, the relationship between rich and poor, or that the genuine transformative capacity of sport has never been realised.

Since at least the 1960s, the scope and significance of the study of sport, culture and society has expanded rapidly. The breadth of perspectives, frameworks and ideas that have been brought to bear upon sport has led some to be critical, a rivalry which has been viewed as a source of potential weakness, while others have welcomed the breadth of perspectives as a basis for strengthening sociology's position as an integrative force for research into all social and developmental aspects of sport. While the importance of particular approaches and ways of knowing about sport will ultimately become less eclectic as one develops, in the first instance students and researchers of sport, culture and society need to be familiar with some of the main contemporary approaches to thinking about sport, culture and society in the world in which we live. For a more complete history of the body of sociological knowledge that has influenced ideas about sport, culture and society, this second edition of the book should be read alongside the first edition. This next section deliberately limits itself to several contemporary themes. The key themes are:

- globalisation;
- identity;
- social inequality;
- culture and power; and
- development and freedom.

CONTEMPORARY THEMES: SPORT IN SOCIAL THOUGHT

One of the tasks and promises of sociological theory has always been to help us draw bigger diagnostic pictures of sport, culture and society. With these pictures, students and researchers can begin to understand and comprehend the socially and politically situated nature of their work and being. Associated with this is the fact that critical analysts of sport, culture and society must also consider or decide upon their preferred entry point into any social or political analysis of sport. In other words, where do you, as an individual, club or group, stand upon particular issues in sport such as inequality and social division, the way in which money is controlled and distributed in sport, the processes involved in the long-term development of sport, the way in which research findings are used to create policy decisions that impact upon communities and cultures, or the extent to which sport should be used as a way of changing or drawing attention to people's lives in different parts of the world? In a sociological sense, does sport help to produce or reproduce social, cultural and/or economic capital?

It might be useful to elaborate upon the term 'problematic' at this point. Each of the approaches outlined above and all other forms of analysis are 'problematic', not in the sense that they are wrong or unethical, but that, at various levels of sophistication, they have provided the basis for the organisation of a field of knowledge or research about sport. In this sense, this book speaks of a problematic as a definite structuring of knowledge about sport that organises a particular research enquiry into making certain kinds of questions about sport possible or permissible, and making other questions suppressed or marginalised. In other words, the problematic in which one chooses to operate as a student or researcher will, in part, determine the sorts of questions that are asked about sport. At the same time, it will also highlight what questions are not being asked and why.

What, then, are *some* of the main contemporary epistemological or theoretical developments that have influenced our understanding of sport, culture and society? It is impossible to adequately cover and evaluate all of the above and there is no one theoretical position that dominates the area. The coverage of various theoretical developments should not simply limit itself to sociology, since other trends and influences from the social sciences and humanities from different places might also be involved just as much as discussions of freedom, truth, subjectivity, validity, culture and politics.

Globalisation

There remains much debate over the consequences of globalisation on everyday life, and it is the focus of an extended discussion in Chapter 5. At least three approaches exist – global sceptics, global radicals and global transformationalists. The question that is often asked is whether it is possible in the foreseeable future to have a democratic global state and what key forums provide the basis for discussing global problems. The United Nations has often been mentioned as one such forum that at least attempts to provide a platform for different global voices. In supporting the 2005 Year of Sport, the United Nations under Kofi Annan also recognised the role of sport in assisting with peace and international development. Attempts to hold an increasing number of international sporting events in China, South Africa, India and Brazil acknowledge the fact that sport cannot be deemed global unless it holds major events in key population areas of the world. Global democracy through sport is not just about the question of governance in sport, but also about holding public discussions about sport all over the world. The tradition of the public discussion through a multitude of different forums is a very practical antidote to the fears of parochialism or the practice of global sport that is not connected to notions of global poverty and global fairness through sport.

Proponents of globalisation typically argue that we live in an age in which a new kind of international world has emerged, one that is characteristic of global competition for markets, consumers and culture. A facet of the free-market form of globalisation has been that markets have decided whether we will have pensions in our old age; whether people suffering from ill health in Africa will be treated; and what forms of games and sports will be supported, or even whether certain regions will have football clubs or not. Critics of globalisation insist that the process and development of global sport has neither been created completely nor produced a world that may be defined by rampant free markets or passive nation states. The movement for global change is often referred to as an anti-globalisation or anti-capitalist movement.

Questions that might arise out of an approach to sport informed by globalisation theory may include:

- Do we have global justice or injustice in sport?
- To what extent are peripheral sporting nations in the world dependent upon, or devalued by virtue of, their relationship to core sporting nations?
- Have national and local forms of sport been marginalised as a result of globalisation?
- To what extent is global sport a euphemism for Western or American forms of sport?
- Are sporting organisations such as FIFA and the IOC global sporting organisations?

Identity

The concept of identity has had a long history in relation to sport. Formulaic constructions of identity in sport have become a symptomatic feature of much of the present body of knowledge that informs our thinking about sport in society. Yet, it is perhaps time to move on or at least think differently about a concept that has grown out of all proportion, is vaguely misrepresented and, at times, appears to be a signature phrase or rationale in itself for talking or writing about a wide range of topics such as sport and nationalism, sport and religion, and sport and ethnicity to name but three areas where the word is loosely used. The term 'identity', while tending to assert a common essence to which special meanings are attached, is in itself weaker than terms such as 'recognition'. Is it not recognition in and through sport that collective identities are seeking to establish, challenge and consolidate, rather than just identity in itself?

It is precisely this notion of the relationship between recognition, redistribution and justice that needs to be placed at the heart of the normative debate about social identity. That is to say, the emphasis to date, certainly for much of the sports research in this area, has been placed too heavily on the notion of identity and not the social. Therefore, the idea that research and teachings into identity and sport that reifies sporting identity/identities does relatively nothing to determine or redress the cultural harm that is caused by reified models of identity in sport. It is crucial that such representations that are promulgated as authentic or true accounts of identity in sport are questioned, their authority and coherence closely examined, and alternative, more social-orientated models of intervention provided (Parker and Harris, 2009).

It is not whether any identity can be chosen, but whether sporting identities offer choices, alternative identities or combinations of identities, or indeed freedoms from any one identity. Identifying with others can be very important for living in a society or community, but at least two distinct issues exist in relation to sport and other public spheres. First, that identities are nearly always plural and the importance of one form of identity does not necessarily mean that other identities are not important. Second, that choices have often to be made and therefore divergent sporting loyalties and priorities are all competing for precedence over one another. These issues surrounding the question of sport, recognition and identity are explored further in Chapters 6 and 16.

Social inequality

Two key themes running throughout sport, culture and society are those of socio-economic inequalities and geopolitical inequalities. These two planes or platforms of injustice are not in opposition to one another, but are in fact at the heart of both understanding and changing the nature of the contemporary relationship between sport and capitalism. Certainly, the global financial crisis and the decidedly post-neo-liberal response to it may mark the end of neo-liberalism's end as an economic regime. We may be seeing the beginning of new waves of mobilisation aimed at articulating a more open future. A neo-liberalism in crises will not bring an end to social inequality or uneven development, but sport has its part to play in narrowing the gap between rich and poor, both within and between countries and places.

Sport is as much about inequalities of capability as it is about inequalities of income and, if the promise of sport is realised, then it can act as an important resource of hope for some. There remains a compelling need in the contemporary world to ask questions not only about the politics and economics of globalisation, but also about the vision for the future and the conception of the global world that people want to live in. Future patterns and experiences of sport and social inequality very much depend upon the extent to which opposition to global sport and/or sport and capitalism can, in fact, develop its own alternative version or the vision as a basis for providing alternatives to how sport could or should be. Other chapters in this book will reflect upon the relationship between sport and the environment, but ecological differences between countries also point to the fact that ecological inequalities are also a concern that impacts upon sporting provision.

Questions that might arise out of an approach to sport informed by placing issues of social inequality at the core may include:

- How do you narrow the gap between provision for rich and poor in and through sport?
- To what extent are inequalities in life chances improved by projects that use sport as basis for building improved capabilities?
- What actual lasting impact does the hosting of major sporting events have on the local people and communities in which these events take place – do they make a difference?
- Are social divisions in sport changing or increasing or decreasing, and to what extent are we still separate and unequal?
- To what extent can the twinning of the politics of social inequality with ecological sustainability offer an alternative starting point for sport today?

Culture and power

The Canadian writer Richard Gruneau (1999: 125) argued more than a decade ago that, where there is no truth, only power, and where power is said to circulate everywhere, politics can only be understood as an ongoing localised tactical project. In this sense, one form of domination or subordination is as relevant as any other, so political struggles through sport could easily be seen as little more than an arena of choice closely associated with one's self-identity. Without any normative standards for evaluating the politics of sport, or when some forms of power are more prevalent than others at any point in time, or for evaluating the conditions by which different political agendas come into conflict with one another, social criticism loses its potential. When a hazy perception of culture and power divorced from politics threatens to exist, thinkers about sport, culture and society run the risk of being enslaved by an imaginary illusory force. Culture and power can be just as much a force for freedom as it can be a force for captivity (Sen, 2006: 13). The question about sport is not about whether culture matters, but how does it matter and how do different cultures of sport operate today.

All-consuming evolutionary approaches to culture tend to marginalise issues of power and social differentiation between and within groups. If everything within a particular way of life is seen as culture, it is difficult to distinguish between different aspects of culture or the relationship between subcultures. The notions of power or social inequality or social differentiation need not be silent within all-embracing anthropological notions of culture. Thinking critically about sport necessitates researchers continually questioning why they think the way they do and never taking for granted that the way they think is the correct way. This provides a starting point for any self-conscious reflection.

Cultural or social anthropological approaches to sport have reflected upon:

- What is the symbolism attached to sporting rituals, customs and traditions?
- What can cultural materialism tell us about sport and games in traditional, tribal, folk or non-Western cultures?
- What are the limits and possibilities of viewing sport as an institution and, therefore, a component of culture?
- How have sporting ceremonies and festivals evolved?
- What does the anthropological study of play tell us about sport?

The advantage of a broader cultural approach to the study of sport, culture and society is that it allows the student to move beyond the conventional analysis of politics at the level of the state or the ways in which, for example, governments use sport as an instrument of nation building or as a facet of health policy. This does not mean that the study of the way in which the state uses sport is irrelevant, but that the cultural politics in civil societies, between civil society and the state, and within the practices and institutions considered to be of the state must also be taken into account when analysing the politics of sport. Cultural politics is understood to be potentially everywhere and, therefore, it has a broad social context. The broader cultural approach to sport has involved the work of Bourdieu, Habermas, Baudrillard and Gramsci, but also Anderson, Morretti, Klein, Mertes, Bull and a whole host of writers from a broad range of countries and platforms that have helped to provide a more vibrant understanding of cultural practice itself.

- What are the cultural politics of sport?
- How does a particular definition of sport become dominant at any given point in time?
- What is the relationship between sport, power and culture now?
- How is a particular definition of sport challenged, struggled over and transformed?
- What is the meaning and symbolism of sport within the context of a changing global political order?

It is to its credit that much of the research into sport, culture and society has acknowledged the changing socio-economic and geopolitical shifts in a changing world order. The section on social inequality above touched on this, while the section on development and freedom below touches upon uneven development and geopolitical inequalities.

Development and freedom

Capitalism still continues to produce a sense of outrage, despite the fact that the classical Marxist triangle has been broken and is most unlikely to be restored. Yet, the impact of new thinking on inequalities of capability, as well as inequalities of wealth, can be seen to have impacted upon both individual countries and organisations such as the United Nation and the World Bank. Geographers and urban historians such as Harvey (2010) have boldly addressed the geo-economics and politics of uneven development. Uneven development at the global scale has been matched by social and geographical unevenness within national formations or nation states. New world orders are emerging and yet the trade of athletes between countries seems to flow mainly in one direction, despite some notable exceptions.

Levermore and Beacom's (2009: 9) review of sports projects that were aimed at sport and development tended to initially group such projects around certain themes. These were those that were aimed at helping with (i) conflict resolution and international understanding; (ii) building physical, social, sport and community infrastructure; (iii) raising awareness, particularly through education; (iv) empowerment; (v) direct impact upon physical and psychological health, as well as general welfare; and (vi) economic development/poverty alleviation.

The redistribution of resources and income have nearly always been central to the critique of neo-liberal approaches to sport, but writers such as Sen (2009) in *The Idea of Justice* have moved this view to accommodate the idea that, while resources matter, so too does what people are able to do with those resources – in other words, their capabilities. You can, at times, increase people's income without necessarily people's ability to choose for themselves the kinds of lives they aspire to lead. By the same rationale, the sports development project that is time-limited and dependent upon short-term funding may help with raising awareness of sport and development issues without necessarily producing an increased capability set to help create more equal and sustainable choices for people through sport. What much of the sport and development literature has failed to capitalise upon is not so much the notion of sport, development *and* freedom, but sport and development *as* freedom.

NEW TIMES, NEW IDEAS AND FRESH THINKING

New times, political shifts and changing balances of power all demand fresh thinking and new ideas. There is no agreed understanding of many of the concepts and ideas introduced in either this book or the first edition but what is evident is that the world in which we live in has changed as a result of the economic recession that occurred between the first and second editions of this book. Notions of justice, globalisation, equality, authority, poverty, the big society, the networked society, the age of austerity and/or audacity are all contested ideas about different parts of the world or different issues facing the world today. At the same time, contests over different solutions, policies and approaches to sport continue to occur between different sports administrators, participants, researchers politicians or teachers, as they may also occur between any two people who subscribe to different political ideologies. The claim that any position can be dismissed on the grounds of ideology does, in fact, remove the possibility of having any healthy debate over any particular sports issue. If having a particular ideological position negates what a person has to say, then the same is true of the person making that criticism. In other words, the criticism deprives itself of the context and structure needed for effective criticism. This is not so much an argument against ideology, but a warning against simply accepting uncritically all ideologies as a form of universalism.

SPORT IN FOCUS 1.4: FRAMING DIFFERENT BUT NEW FORMS OF THINKING ABOUT SPORT IN A GOOD SOCIETY

Left communitarianism

Neo-liberalism rests upon the premise of the individual as an isolated competitive profit maximiser. But human beings are social creatures and they need to both recognise and make a virtue of their interdependency. Left communitarian sport within this vision of a good society would stress a social vision of sport based upon solidarity and mutuality. The market would be kept firmly in its place, a strong emphasis would be placed upon the role of sport in civil society, and collective action and economic equality would be key concerns.

Left republicanism

The task of progressive politics would be to radically disperse power and opportunity, and rebuild sport within a stronger public sphere. The state would be restructured so that individuals would participate more in the decision making process. Sport would be required to figure strongly within the wider context of grassroots social movements and the ownership of sport would have to provide opportunities for individual asset ownership.

Centre republicanism

The task of progressive politics would echo that of left republicanism in that the dispersal of power and opportunity would be seen to be important. The relationship between sport and the state would be in a decentralised direction. A strong emphasis would be placed upon sport and civil liberties, sport freedom and lifestyles, with a potential taxation burden being placed upon taxing sport's unearned wealth and any damage to the environment.

Right communitarianism

Right communitarianism emphasises the need to fill a moral vacuum created by a combination of neo-liberalism in the economy and lifestyle liberalism in society. This requires the rebuilding of a strongly moralistic civil society to meet social needs that neither the free market nor conventional welfare state can meet. The role of sport and social entrepreneurship would be important as dependency on the welfare state was reduced. State policy would limit sport's market freedom. A nihilist liberal politics of arbitrary freedom through sport would be replaced by an emphasis on sport to help with a collective morality in society.

Ideological positions are often imprecise and fluid but it is clear that, in many countries – the UK, the US, Brazil and France being but a few – changing ideological landscapes are emerging. Obviously, the way in which different parts of the world are handling the economic turmoil of the economic recession vary, but at least four

SPORT IN FOCUS 1.4—*continued*

progressive perspectives have dominated current new thinking – the restructuring of the state, re-moralising of societies, expanding the role of civil society and the spreading of asset ownership. All of these may impact in different ways upon sport, culture and society in different parts of the world.

One of the fundamental roles of the student or public intellectual interested in sport is to question critically and understand the very nature of why sport is the way it is and what it could or should be. The promise of fully understanding and grasping the complexity of sport, culture and society necessitates a broader understanding of sport and theory. This can be a very practical understanding of how different frameworks help to inform not only the sociological imagination, but also the policy advisor, political activist, public speaker or student of sport who wants to think and reflect socially about sport, culture and society. In a discussion of social theory today and towards 2025, Elliott (2009) is correct to raise the question about the future of social theory and whether recent developments in society, culture or politics give us any indication of where social theory might be heading, and whether it will promote a good or better society. Will social theory continue to energise sizeable publics in 2025 or continue to drive key ways of thinking about sport, culture and society?

Sport in Focus 1.4 emphasises some of the new strands of thinking that are informing notions of a good society.

SUMMARY: IN SEARCH OF COMMON GROUND AND SOCIAL CHANGE

Each of the major approaches mentioned, and many others, can claim to illuminate some part of the complexity that is sport, culture and society. Writing better histories and more inclusive progressive theory means the pursuit of complexity rather than totality. Whatever position or story that the student of sport, culture and society wants to tell about the changing nature of sport in different cultures or societies, they can always be more complex and always partial. The student of sport needs to provide reality-congruent bodies of knowledge by continually evaluating the continual interplay between theory, evidence and the broader context. Reality, just as sociology, needs history (and geography), and so does theory need evidence. Purely theoretical accounts of sport, culture and society are just as unsatisfactory as those empirical accounts of sport that exude findings without any theoretical grounding or explanation. The constant interaction between theory and evidence remains one of the best defences against the imposition of grand theory or dogma or empiricism without explanation. The student of sport, culture and society should never be value free, or far less value neutral. It is impossible to develop theoretical or problematic frameworks by which one can understand sport, culture and society in contemporary life by adopting a value-free position.

Students, like researchers, carry with them domain assumptions that inform their ontological existence and not just the approach to sport, culture and society. It might be suggested in the first instance that the student of sport, culture and society has at least three strategies. The first strategy might be to reproduce or replicate the conventional scientific enterprise laid down by certain domain assumptions or epistemological rationales. The second strategy might be to produce scientific status in one's work without necessarily replicating existing practices or studies of sport, culture and society, but adding meaning to the object of enquiry. However thoroughly explored the world of sport described by science might be, it remains meaningless if the student or researcher of sport, culture and society does not attempt to recover the meaning of reality. This might be simply deemed as a more reflective position. Finally, it might be that the strategy option is neither replication nor reflection, but one of effect. The aim here is to demonstrate how the knowledge one has accumulated and the values one believes in can be demonstrably effective in pursuing practical ends in the analysis of sport, culture and society. To put this very simply, all the above approaches to sport, culture and society might be thought of in terms of epistemology, ontology and intervention. All the above approaches help equip the student to cope with the future role of the intellectual as public servant and destroyer of myths. All of the above approaches are also relevant to thinking about the role of universities in society today and those employed by them.

The object of the exercise does not rest solely with explanation, but with a sustained effort to produce social change, and challenge inequalities and myths. Understanding lies in the linkage between personal values, the interpretation of evidence, and the epistemological vantage point from which to arrive at the conclusions or recommendations made by any particular piece of work, essay or research project. Simply stated, it lies in the reflexivity and critical consciousness inherent within a much more inclusive form of social and economic imagination. Ultimately, the student of sport, culture and society needs to decide upon an entry point into the battleground over the particular issue, debate or social phenomenon being studied. In all of this, critical social and historical analysts should acknowledge the socially and economically situated nature of their work. The process of producing social change necessitates the need for multi-layered, committed perspectives that move beyond just an explanation of what is going on in sport, culture and society.

GUIDE TO FURTHER READING

Anderson, E. (2010). *Sport, Theory and Social Problems*. London: Routledge.

Carrington, B. (2010). *Race, Sport and Politics: The Sporting Black Diaspora*. London: Sage.

Elliott, A. (2009). *Contemporary Social Theory: An Introduction*. London: Routledge.

Giulianotti, R. (2011). 'Sport, Transnational Peacemaking and Global Civil Society: Exploring the Reflective Discourses of Sport, Development and Peace Project Officials'. *Journal of Sport and Social Issues*, 35 (1): 50–71.

Hwang, D. and Chiu, W. (2010). 'Sport and National Identity in Taiwan: Some Preliminary Observations'. *East Asian Sport Thoughts: The International Journal of the Sociology of Sport*, 1 (1): 39–71.

41

Sen, A. (2006). *Identity and Violence: The Illusion of Destiny*. London: Allen Lane.

Therborn, G. (2007). 'Mapping Social Theory'. *New Left Review*, 43 (January/February): 63–116.

White, S. (2009). 'Thinking the Future-Ideological Map'. *New Statesman,* 7 September: 19–28.

QUESTIONS

1 Explain the role of theory in the investigation of sport, culture and society.

2 Compare and contrast any three approaches to social thought that have framed our understanding of sport.

3 Explain how you might establish how a particular theory is necessary.

4 Explain ways in which a commitment to any particular problematic or epistemology might bring about social change.

5 List at least six ways in which sports research has informed what we know about sport and development.

6 What new ideas have impacted upon the notion of a good society, and what part does sport have to play in this, if any?

7 List four common ways in which countries have dealt with the recent economic recession.

8 In searching for common ground, what strategies are open to the student of sport, culture and society?

9 Define the following terms: 'sport', 'power', 'problematic', 'society' and 'post-colonialism'.

10 To what extent do values influence the study of sport, culture and society?

PRACTICAL PROJECTS

1 Through discussing sport with your friends, link five personal sporting troubles they may identify to broader public issues about sport.

2 Write down five policy directives that would be at the heart of any policy aimed at tackling social inequality.

3 Chose any five sports clubs and ask members of the club what badges, flags and songs are associated with supporters or club members. Use the evidence to write a short report on what the club stands for and what values or symbols are associated with the club.

4 Design and implement a small survey aimed at gathering empirical information about the voting patterns of (a) fans, (b) sports club members or (c) any other specific sport or exercise population. What does the information gathered tell you about sport and political values?

5   Investigate the committee or executive membership of any sports club or organisation over a five-year period and explain the process of election or appointment to the committee or executive.

KEY CONCEPTS

Culture ■ Development ■ Epistemology ■ Freedom ■ Globalisation ■Historical sociology ■ Identity ■ Ontology ■ Political economy ■ Power ■ Problematic ■ Social inequality ■ Sport ■ Theory ■ Values

WEBSITES

British Sociological Association
www.bsa.co.uk
The home of the British Sociological Association and information about its work, including the BSA Sport and Leisure Study Group.

Fabian Global Forum
www.fabianglobalforum.net
A forum for information about global issues.

Foreign Policy in Focus
www.fpif.org
An international foreign policy think tank that keeps you in touch with world events as they happen. Use the search facility to track down particular pieces on sport.

Social Theory
www.socqrl.niu.edu/FYI/theory.htm
www.sussex.ac.uk/spt/cst
http://sportpolitics.blogspot.com/
Some websites that provide information about different social theorists and theories.

Sport and Citizenship – Sport Serving Society
www.sportetcitoyennete.org
A dedicated international forum that publishes up-to-date briefings on key social issues involving sport. The publications are very useful summaries of key current policy concerns.

Chapter 2

Sport, history and social change

What important changes have taken place in sport over the past 50 years and how would you evaluate progress? Women's football is not a new phenomenon. The picture above, showing Leith Ladies, is evidence of organised women's football being played in Scotland as early as 1938. Source: *Trustees of National Museum of Scotland.*

PREVIEW

Key terms defined ■ Introduction ■ The scope of a history of sport ■ Why sports history matters ■ Dangers of contemporary history ■ Milestones in the history of women in sport and society ■ Change and continuity in sport ■ Race and sport milestones ■ comparative physical cultures ■ Sporting plausibility and complexity ■ Change and the meaning of sport ■ Sporting past, heritage and mythology ■ The Naismith Memorial Basketball Hall of Fame ■ Making sporting heritage and golden sporting moments ■Golden sporting moment ■ The invention of tradition and sports popular memory ■ Historical and sporting forces ■ sport and post-feminism ■ sport and post-modernism ■ sport and post-colonialism ■ Where stands the history of sport today? ■ Summary

OBJECTIVES

This chapter will:

- answer the question why sports history matters;
- evaluate the historical contribution to sport, culture and society;
- consider the value of historical sociology, popular memory, heritage and tradition to the study of sports history;
- critically discuss some of the major forces that have influenced modern sports historiography; and
- explain why the historical contribution to the study of sport and social change cannot be left to questions about identity history.

KEY TERMS DEFINED

Historiography: The art of, or employment of, writing history.

Heritage: Something inherited at birth, such as personal characteristics, status and possessions.

Imperialism: Domination or control by one country or group of people over others, in ways assumed to be at the expense of the latter.

Social History: Any study of the past that emphasises predominantly 'social' concerns. Social history often refers to the history of ordinary people.

Tradition: A set of social practices that seeks to celebrate and inculcate certain behavioural norms and values, implying continuity with a real or imagined past, and associated with widely accepted rituals or forms of symbolic behaviour.

INTRODUCTION

Social historians ask questions about the nature and place of sports in given times among given peoples, and about how and why people constructed particular forms of sport, where these sports have travelled to around the world and what they mean to different groups of people. The socio-historical development of sport tells us where and when particular sporting practices emerged. It owes as much to acknowledging cross-comparative contexts as it does to contemporary social history. The stories of people's sporting experiences located and understood within the context of their time and place are a valuable part of the story of sport, but they also help to shed light on many, if not all, of the core themes in this book and more. This chapter introduces some of the core historical forces and rationales that are used to explain why, when and how sport has changed.

The process of producing social change itself entails the need for multi-layered committed perspectives that move beyond explanation of what is going on in sport, culture and society. History is an important part of this committed perspective. To paraphrase Polley (2008: 70), while it may be easy to view history as a storehouse of valuable factual information, sports historiography is about 'our interest in roots and origins and our desire to know what happened and why'. The plurality of possibilities that is provided by sports history has been enriched by other histories of social divisions and a much richer international set of histories of sport that have helped to illuminate the history of sport in other communities. The history of sport is no longer a monolithic history of sport in the West. The dangers of unqualified identity histories of sport remain evident. The reviews of the field by Booth (2010) and Osborne and Skillen (2010) have made further inroads into debates about emancipation, realism, truth and objectivity, while ancient sporting histories remind us of the illusion that

SPORT IN FOCUS 2.1: AN INSIGHT INTO THE VALUE OF A HISTORY OF SPORT

Personal attributes:

✔ self-awareness
✔ insight into your own life and personal identity
✔ a way of seeing and understanding the world past and present
✔ tolerance and empathy
✔ open-minded
✔ understanding different perspectives
✔ healthy scepticism
✔ questioning and making connections

Skills:

✔ synthesising and analysing information rigourously and sensitively
✔ critical thinking
✔ how to write about ideas
✔ how to talk about ideas
✔ independent reasoning
✔ self-discipline and professionalism

Purpose:

✔ social responsibility
✔ good citizenship
✔ potential desire to change the world

Passion:

✔ for history

sacred sporting tales and myths have little or no significance to humanity today. Pope and Nauright (2010) provide an overview of sports history. Sport in Focus 2.1 gives an insight into a history of sport and its value to students.

By enabling us to know about other centuries and other cultures, an understanding of the social-historical development of sport provides one of the best antidotes against both a temporal sporting parochialism, which assumes that the only time is now, and a geographical parochialism, which assumes that the only place is here. There is not only here and now, there is also there and then. In sport, one of the best defences against retreating into the present is sports historiography, in part because it helps us understand how other sporting worlds have developed. The impact of historical interventions and ideas upon the study of sport has been one of the richest and most enduring. As with other areas, it has had to answer post-modern debates about facts, objectivity and truth, and post-colonial debates about the non-Western worlds, colonialism and other histories and representations of sport, while at the same time adding plausibility and complexity to what we know about sport in the past and present.

WHY SPORTS HISTORY MATTERS

While the following list is not exhaustive, it is perhaps illustrative of the areas in which the historiography of sport has helped to illuminate what we know about sport, culture and society. The following are not in any order; rather, they form the bulk of what have been key areas of investigation or topics or questions over the past 10 or 15 years. The historiography of sport is still being constructed and the areas listed below will not necessarily be the agendas of the future. On the other hand, any attempt to construct a synthesis of what we know about the contribution of sport to past and present cultures and society would have to acknowledge some or all of the following general bodies of sporting history or themes:

- the roots of sport in ancient societies;
- sport in the Middle Ages;
- sport in colonial and post-colonial societies;
- women's sporting experiences from at least the nineteenth century;
- nineteenth- and twentieth-century working-class sport;
- rich internal sporting histories of clubs or events;
- sport in the lives of different racial, ethnic and indigenous groups;
- the social formation and transformation of sport within the historiography of various nations;
- sporting tradition and the making of heritage and mythology;
- post-sporting histories, such as post-modernism, post-colonialism and post-feminism;
- comparative and cross-cultural histories of sport and physical cultures; and
- oral histories and biographies of sporting heroes and heroines.

The history of sport teaches students and researchers many things, not least of which is that it instils a sense of caution with regard to dogmatic generalisation and theorising. Many of the above themes have provided rich, detailed micro-histories of sport that have stressed the continual interplay between change and continuity. It makes little sense to argue that women have more power in sport today without acknowledging the power and influence of women in sport in the past. To argue that sport has become increasingly global implies that sport today is being compared with sport in a previous period. The *process* of globalisation or urbanisation or commercialisation or professionalisation implies that some sort of change has taken place over time and, therefore, to talk of commercialisation in sport is to suggest that the levels of commerce associated with sport have increased or decreased. When governments insist that participation rates in sport have improved, it is necessary to compare rates of participation in sport over a period of time. History teaches students that social surveys, upon which much policy information on sport depends, only really provide a snapshot or moment in time, and cannot really be understood without acknowledging or exploring further what went on before.

You cannot begin to understand the significance of rugby union in Wales without knowing about the social, cultural and economic history of Wales. Similarly, the symbolic relationship between the Grey Cup (ice hockey) and Canada, or the Super Bowl (American football) and the US, or the All-Ireland Gaelic Football Final and Ireland, or Wimbledon (tennis) and the UK, cannot be fully explained without substantiating and acknowledging that such sporting occasions are also social institutions that have increasing or decreasing levels of importance to various nations because of the historical association between these events and the cultural and national historiography of the respective nations. It is crucial to acknowledge that sport has been played differently at different times in different nations and places.

Dangers of contemporary sport

Perhaps the historiography of sport's unique contribution lies in its potential to unshackle minds from the constraints of the present. An important role for the history of sport is to liberate students from the chronological aridity and constraint of the present, or what others have termed a retreat into the present (Elias, 1983). Contemporary sport, at times, may seem more accessible to the sporting enthusiast or student of sport, but contemporary 'tunnel vision' fails to acknowledge the fact that the history of sport can tell us a great deal about contemporary sport.

It is often assumed that the popular involvement of women in sport is relatively modern, and yet the historiography of women's sport has done much to alter our views about sport in society. Much of this body of work has moved beyond identifying particular women as sporting heroines or victims of patriarchy. Adams (2010) demonstrates that gendered segregation has not always been fundamental to the organisation of competitive sports. Hargreaves's (2000) oral histories of Muslim, aboriginal and black women have crucially intervened to provide a far less Euro-centric picture of world sport (this body of work is one of the few that is sensitive to the way in which the story of women's experiences of sport over time has been overlaid by class and race); Vertinsky (1994) has explored the changing nature of women's control over their own bodies at given points in time; Crosset's (1995) oral testimonies from US women professional golfers illuminate and describe an evolving process within a world of sport where what is required to achieve success as a golfer is clearly at odds with wider expectations of what it takes to make it as a woman; while Vicky Paraschak

(1990, 1995) has documented and explored the strategies adopted by native Inuit peoples, including women, who have historically struggled to maintain the values, often utilitarian, of traditional sports and pastimes threatened by the march of modern sport. More recently, Kay (2010) has speculated about a window of lost opportunity in women's sport in post-war Britain.

Sport in Focus 2.2 is an *illustrative* history of the development of women's sport but much of the historical research into sport that has emerged over the last few decades has moved the history of sport far beyond simple chronology – important as it is.

Accounts of women and sport in the nineteenth century emphasise participation in terms of patrons, spectators and players (Tranter, 1998; George, 2010). In Scotland, wealthy women presented sporting prizes, such as the miniature silver curling stone that Mrs Houison-Crawford of Craufurdland gave for competition between the curlers of Fenwick and Kilmarnock. The number of women who had access to sport at the start of the nineteenth century was small, but not as small as the number of women who boxed, as two did on Glasgow Green in 1828. The first ladies' golf club was established at St Andrews in 1867, shortly followed by ladies golf clubs at Musselburgh (1872), Carnoustie (1873), Panmure (1874) and Perth (1879). Almost two-thirds of the 42 founding members of the Avon Lawn Tennis Club at Linlithgow in 1880 were female; in some cases, the number of females equalled and exceeded the number of males in the Tennis Club Championships, as happened in the Braid Club in Edinburgh in 1895. The point that is being illustrated here is that sports historiography can help to qualify, complement and add to present-centred approaches to the study of sport, culture and society.

The danger of thinking solely in contemporaneous terms is that of remaining blinkered to the past and the extent to which contemporary oral histories and testimonies, past newspaper accounts of sport, government archives, photographs, club histories, minutes and other forms of historical knowledge are all sources of evidence that potentially stop researchers from retreating into the present. They are important in evaluating trends and rates of development and critically evaluating whether change has taken place or not. They also serve as a reminder of the necessary evidence-based nature of sports historiography. The history of sport helps to define and answer sporting problems, provide evidence and illuminate the context in which sport has developed or could develop.

Change and continuity in sport

In his history of sport and society since 1945, Polley (1998) demonstrates ways in which sport has figured in the post-war British historical experience. The argument is that sport has literally given physical form to debates about gender, class, ethnicity, the nation, the state and commerce in Britain since 1945. This succinct conclusion is worth commenting upon in some detail, since it serves as an illustration and reminder of one of the crucial facets of historical work, namely evaluating and mapping out the extent to which change and continuity have or have not occurred. Polley (1998: 161) notes that, while continuity and change may be relative concepts and that problems may exist with various interest groups contesting whether change has been good or bad for sport, nonetheless it is one of the challenges and duties of the historian to analyse and chart such developments.

49

SPORT IN FOCUS 2.2: A SELECTED HISTORY OF MILESTONES FOR WOMEN IN SPORT

1500 BC   Female bull jumpers in Crete defy death.

1000 BC   Atalanta out-wrestles Peleus; the women-only Herean Games take place in Greece.

440 BC   Kallipateira sneaks into the Olympic Games and men devise the first sex test to keep women out.

396 BC   Princess Kyniska of Sparta is the first female Olympic champion, winning the chariot race.

1424   Madame Margot outplays Parisian men at *jeu de paume*, an early version of tennis.

1900   Women are included on the programme of the modern Olympic Games competing in golf and tennis; tennis player Charlotte Cooper of Great Britain becomes the first woman Olympic champion.

1922   Suzanne Lenglen makes her Wimbledon debut.

1924   The Fédération sportive féminine internationale organises the first Women's Olympic Games in Paris; in one day alone, 20,000 spectators watch 18 world records broken in track and field.

1926   Alexandrine Gibb spearheads the formation of the Women's Amateur Athletic Federation of Canada (WAAF) to initiate international competition for Canadian women; the second Women's Games are held in Gothenburg, Sweden, with entries from 10 nations.

1928   Staging the only feminist boycott in Olympic history, the British women stay away from the Games to protest the lack of women's Olympic events.

1930   The third Women's Games are held in Prague.

1934   The fourth and last Women's Games are held in London, England.

1936   The Women's Games are cancelled in exchange for a nine-event Olympic programme for women.

1948   Fanny Blankers-Koen of the Netherlands is the first mother to be an Olympic gold medallist.

1956   Skier Guiliana Chenal-Minuzzo of Italy is the first woman to take the Olympic oath at the opening ceremony.

1966   Sex tests (gender verification) for women are adopted in international sport.

1968   Enriqueta Basilio becomes the first woman to light the Olympic flame.

1975   The United Nations declares International Women's Year; women tennis players win pay parity at the US Open.

1986   Debi Thomas becomes the first female black American athlete to compete at the Winter Olympics and wins bronze in the singles figure skating.

SPORT IN FOCUS 2.2 — *continued*

1996	3,626 women compete at the Olympic Games in Atlanta – 32 per cent more than in Barcelona – in part, due to the recognition of women's soccer, softball and triple jump as Olympic events.
2002	Vonetta Flowers becomes the first black American athlete to win gold at the Winter Olympic Games.
2007	The Wimbledon Tennis Championships offer equal prizes to male and female competitors for the first time, bringing it in line with the other Grand Slam events.
2007	Pamela Jelimo becomes the first Kenyan woman to win an Olympic gold medal.
2010	The LPGA votes to allow transgender women golfers a chance to play on the tour by eliminating the 'female at birth' clause from the LPGA's constitution.
2011	Japan become the first Asian team to win the Women's Football World Cup.
2012	Women's boxing appears in the Olympic Games for the first time.

In his summation of the development of British sport, Polley (1998, 2008) mentions some of the changes that have taken place since 1945 as being that: the state has a more structured relationship with sport; sport has become less insular through embracing international developments; a transition from amateur to professional management structures emerged; rates of commercialisation associated with sport have changed; women have more access to sport than in 1945; social mobility has altered the class appearance of British sport; sport has become more ethnically diverse; there has been a certain degree of hybridisation in sport itself with combined rules sports emerging in certain contexts (i.e. combined rules for shinty/hurling international matches between Scotland and Ireland); and there is a greater diversity of sport available for people to participate in.

On the other hand, there has been a great deal of continuity since 1945 and many of the changes, asserts Polley (1998: 162), may have been quantitative rather than qualitative differences. The structure of British sport, with the emergence of governing bodies of sport, enforcement of standardised rules and regulations and the development of regular competition remains intact; voluntarism and amateurism continue to inform, in part, the way in which mass sport is administered and played; the maintenance of club colours, names and cultures reinforces notions of continuity; and sport continues to be part of the debate about inequality and opportunity. That is, as Holt and Mason (2000: ix) put it, 'Post-war sport had its own agenda which has to be understood in its own terms'.

Sport in Focus 2.3 provides some milestones in the emergence of changing race relations in British sport, and yet the experience of racism in 1881 would be different from the

SPORT IN FOCUS 2.3: RACE AND SPORT MILESTONES

1881	Guyanese-born Andrew Watson captains Scotland, becoming the first black international footballer.
1936	Jesse Owens wins four gold medals for the US at the Olympics in Berlin.
1947	Jackie Robinson becomes the first black Major League Baseball player of the modern era, debuting for the Brooklyn Dodgers.
1971	Evonne Goolagong wins the French Open and Wimbeldon, becoming the first Aborigine to win a tennis Grand Slam.
1977	Commonwealth leaders agree to discourage sporting links with apartheid South Africa.
1977	Laurie Cunningham becomes the first black footballer to play for England.
1982	During World Cup finals, the National Front actively recruits at England matches.
1999	Foundation of Football Against Racism in Europe.
2006	England bowler Monty Panesar becomes the first Sikh to represent any nation except India in tests.
2011	Former caddy to golfer Tiger Woods talks of the golfer in racist terms.
2011	Manchester United defender Patrice Evra alleges that he was subjected to racist abuse from Liverpool striker Luis Suarez during a match between the two sides in October. At the time of writing, the English Football Association are investigating the incident.

experience of racism in sport in 2012, precisely because the context and the period were different. Sporting milestones such as that below allow researchers to comment upon both continuity and change in relation to racism in British sport.

Comparative physical cultures

The uses of historiography in exploring comparative physical cultures, as Holt (2000) reminds us, can help with defining comparative sporting problems and, more importantly, understanding the context because, for Holt (2000: 54), 'sport history has been overwhelmingly concerned with establishing the context under which sports could develop'. Comparative work on sport has illuminated links between the making of identity and nationalism. Students and researchers of sport, culture and society may want to take up some of Holt's challenges: to develop comparative analysis of the way sporting heroes and heroines in different cultures are produced and projected; to compare sport and physical culture in any two great cities or capitals of the world – Edinburgh and Paris, Madrid and Moscow,

Beijing and Kolkata, London and Washington, Nairobi and Glasgow, or Tokyo and Seoul, to name but a few; to examine how sporting excellence has been produced in two different regions; or to compare the values associated with body cultures in nineteenth-century Germany and Britain, Denmark and Pakistan, or Italy and Kenya. While, historically, processes such as urbanisation, industrialisation and colonialisation have profoundly influenced the development of sport and physical culture, it is doubtful whether such experiences have been the same for any two nations, regions or continents. Thus, some of the best comparative cross-cultural work needs history to properly understand the totality of the underlying forces that have impacted upon the development of sport and physical culture in different places.

The fundamental purpose of comparative cross-cultural work applies to both historiography and other areas of investigation, notably anthropology and sociology, but as a component of critical reflection upon sport, culture and society the comparative lessons include understanding more about 'others', both in terms of sports geography (place and space) and sports historiography, understanding the subtleties and nuances of sport in terms of time and place, and both are different. The work of the archaeologist informs both cultural and historical knowledge about sport and physical culture. Cave dwellers placed pictographs of sporting and physical pursuits on cave walls. Perhaps the social and political value of comparative cross-cultural work is that it enhances interpretation and helps to undermine the formation of stereotypical or Euro-centric or insular, parochial, inward-looking thinking about sport. It is invaluable, for example, in thinking about how a particular sport or place stands in relation to general claims about global sport or globalisation. It enhances the complexity of knowledge and understanding about sport and helps to challenge orthodox or complacent claims about core or mainstream sport by arming the student with alternative and residual forms of sport from many places and times.

Furthermore, resistance to Westernisation has a strong presence in the world today. It can take many forms, from being critical of ideas that are seen as Western but are not actually Western in origin to more overt forms of anti-Western sentiment such as championing Asian values to insisting that Islamic ideals must, in essence, be deeply hostile to everything the West stands for. Part of the fixation and reaction against the West lies in the history of colonialism but, more fundamentally, in the more complex histories of exploitation and humiliation. As shall be explained later, it is vital to recognise the richness and diversity of Western and non-Western sporting cultures and places, and different traditions as being just that – different, but not better or worse – so that a stratification of sporting tastes and forms is ranked as if it is some sort of world order. More than anything else, comparative physical cultures must be explored, compared and valued so that, ultimately, the complexity and multidimensionality of sport, culture and society can be seen as being international, humane and more complete than it hitherto has been.

Sporting plausibility and complexity

Despite the intervention made by various forms of post-history of sport, one of the historical lessons remains embedded within the plausibility and supremacy of the historical evidence collected. Without entering a theoretical debate on issues of dogma, dogmatism and ideology in the history of sport, for some historians the supremacy and plausibility of the research evidence provides the foundation for separating the history of sport from sport as fiction and myth. Like the physiologist or economist, the historian of sport aims to increase the sum of our knowledge about sport. Like other areas of investigation that inform our knowledge about sport, culture and society, common issues about the relationship between theory and evidence, description and explanation, and universality and reliability all exist. A large part of the conviction of the story that the historian wants to tell us about sport lies in the accumulative, exhaustive and plausible range of sources that are brought to bear upon any historical problem.

To insist upon the supremacy of the evidence and the centrality of the distinction between verifiable historical fact and fiction is not the holy grail of the professional historian. Within historians of sport, however, there is, one suspects, a consensus on *matters of substance*, despite the varied and complex histories of sport that are told. Polley (2003: 51) reminds us that generations of historians have been trained to find evidence, interpret it and then come to a plausible conclusion. One of the crucial facets of the making of plausible histories of sport is that the student or researcher of sport, culture and society must, at some point, answer the question of whether or not the historical evidence is sufficiently complete to provide a solution to the sporting problem or historical question of sport. Good histories of sport, culture and society acquire cumulative plausibility without claiming to be right or wrong (Holt, 2000: 50). Methodology is not a replacement for thinking and interpretation. This can be done without being descriptive or exaggerating any *truth* claims, nor adopting a grand narrative stance.

Sociologists, too, have recognised the need for complex sporting histories, but the meaning of the word 'complex' varies. The nature and plausibility of the range of sources of evidence is of primary concern to the historian. This is somewhat different from the challenge laid down by Gruneau (1999: 127), who suggested that the post-modern assault on studies of sport and social development means that writing better history and more inclusive theory involves the pursuit of complexity rather than totality. The challenge is to write theoretically informed histories of sport that are sensitive to multiple and uneven paths of change. The difference between those who write sociological and historical accounts of sport, culture and society is perhaps a matter of emphasis on the nature of the approach that is adopted, rather than not recognising the value of sport from a historical sociological point of view. Such an approach has become increasingly the norm as boundaries between disciplines have waxed and waned.

Change and the meaning of sport

Whether you see the history of sport primarily as an art, as a way of structuring the world through the narrative or stories that you want or have to tell about sport, or whether you conceive of the history of sport as a science, getting as close as possible to the actuality of the past by the rigours of methodologies or accumulation of evidence brought to bear upon it, what cannot be done is to prevent the history of sport from focusing upon social change as part of its *raison d'être*. The history of sport would make little sense in a society that did not change, and equally in a society that did not see change as a fundamental category of existence. Trends, transformations, developments, continuities and changes are perhaps much of the essence and function of the history of sport. How sport has been influenced by the historical epoch in which it moves or is located remains one of the core questions that needs to be addressed by any student or researcher of sport, culture and society.

If answering the above question is one of the reasons why the history of sport matters, then a further core reason is to explore the *meaning* of sport. The degree to which the meaning of sport has paralleled social change is an issue that encompasses some of the most basic questions that might be asked about the changing relationship of sport to processes of globalisation, urbanisation, modernisation, democratisation, bureaucratisation, American-isation and rationalisation, as well as such issues as social inequality, social division and poverty. The importance of understanding the changing meaning of sport is at the heart of Hill's study of sport, leisure and culture in twentieth-century Britain (Hill, 2002). The sentiments expressed in the conclusions of this study are worth emphasising. Two crucial points are prioritised: first, 'if our study of sport and leisure does not attempt to tease out the *meaning* of what we do in our free time and to place it in some context of contestation and negotiation, it seems to me not to be a very significant aspect of our lives' and, second, that, 'if the study of sport and leisure is not political in the broadest sense of the word, then it isn't worth a damn' (Hill, 2002: 187). This sentiment echoes Hobsbawm (1997: 140), who insisted that political partisanship, together with scholarship and plausibility, can often serve to counteract the increasing tendency to look inwards to the academy. It might be that much political partisan scholarship in the history of sport remains trivial, engaged in proving a predetermined truth, doctrine or narrative. But if plausibility coupled with partisanship helps to produce new ideas, then the history of sport needs to continue to connect with broader historical and social forces that have brought about social change. This helps in terms of not just thinking about how sport is or has been, but also, and perhaps more importantly, what it can or should be. Thus, the history of sport, for example, has a direct relevance to the contemporary governance of sport, because it adds plausible and yet partisan directives for the governance of sport.

SPORTING PAST, HERITAGE AND MYTHOLOGY

The sporting past has been central to issues of tradition and heritage. The heritage industry spends millions on constructing national and local heritages. Sports halls of fame are as important to sporting culture as the laboratory is to the sports scientist. The Manchester United Football Museum, as Vamplew (1998: 269) reminds us, attracts in excess of 150,000 paying customers per year. National sporting histories are displayed in museums in Prague, Helsinki, Melbourne and Edinburgh, while specialist sports halls of fame in the US are to be found for most popular sports. Sports museums and halls of fame are often celebrated as the public face of sports historiography. The celebration of the sporting past, sporting heroes and heroines and inter-generational exchanges over the golden era of a particular sport have all involved issues of selection, nostalgia, myth and romanticism.

Sports museums and halls of fame are useful sites to explore questions about local and national identity, while at the same time catering for the commercial and heritage-driven

SPORT IN FOCUS 2.4: NAISMITH MEMORIAL BASKETBALL HALL OF FAME

1959	Chuck Hyatt	1980	Jerry Lucas	1995	Kareem Abdul-Jabbar
1959	Hank Luisetti	1980	Oscar Robertson	1995	Anne Donovan
1959	George Mikan	1980	Jerry West	1995	Vern Mikkelsen
1959	John Schommer	1981	Tom Barlow	1995	Cheryl Miller
1960	Vic Hanson	1982	Hal Greer	1996	Kresimir Cosic
1960	Ed Macauley	1982	Slater Martin	1996	George Gervin
1960	Branch McCracken	1982	Frank Ramsey	1996	Gail Goodrich
1960	Charles Murphy	1982	Willis Reed	1996	Nancy Lieberman
1960	John Wooden	1983	Bill Bradley	1996	David Thompson
1961	Bennie Borgmann	1983	Dave DeBusschere	1996	George Yardley
1961	Forrest DeBernardi	1983	Jack Twyman	1997	Joan Crawford
1961	Bob Kurland	1984	John Havlicek	1997	Denise M. Curry
1961	Andy Phillip	1984	Sam Jones	1997	Alex English
1961	John Roosma	1985	Al Cervi	1997	Bailey Howell
1961	Chris Steinmetz	1985	Nate Thurmond	1998	Larry Bird
1961	Ed Wachter	1986	Billy Cunningham	1998	Marques Haynes
1962	Jack McCracken	1986	Tommy Heinsohn	1998	Arnie Risen
1962	Harlan "Pat" Page	1987	Rick Barry	1999	Kevin McHale
1962	Barney Sedran	1987	Walt Frazier	2000	Robert McAdoo
1962	John Thompson	1987	Bob Houbregs	2000	Isiah Thomas
1963	Robert Gruenig	1987	Pete Maravich	2001	Moses Malone
1964	Bud Foster	1987	Bobby Wanzer	2002	Magic Johnson
1964	Nat Holman	1988	Clyde Lovellette	2002	Drazen Petrovic
1964	John Russell	1988	Bobby McDermott	2003	Dino Meneghin
1966	Joe Lapchick	1988	Wes Unseld	2003	Robert Parish
1969	Dutch Dehnert	1989	William Gates	2003	James Worthy
1970	Bob Davies	1989	K.C. Jones	2004	Drazen Dalipagic
1971	Bob Cousy	1989	Lenny Wilkens	2004	Clyde Drexler
1971	Bob Pettit	1990	Dave Bing	2004	Maurice Stokes
1972	Paul Endacott	1990	Elvin Hayes	2004	Lynette Woodard
1972	Marty Friedman	1990	Neil Johnston	2005	Hortencia Marcari
1973	John Beckman	1990	Earl Monroe	2006	Charles Barkley
1973	Dolph Schayes	1991	Nate Archibald	2006	Joe Dumars
1974	Ernest Schmidt	1991	Dave Cowens	2006	Dominique Wilkins
1975	Joe Brennan	1991	Harry Gallatin	2008	Adrian Dantley
1975	Bill Russell	1992	Sergei Belov	2008	Patrick Ewing
1975	Robert Vandivier	1992	Lusia Harris-Stewart	2008	Hakeem Olajuwon
1976	Tom Gola	1992	Connie Hawkins	2009	Michael Jordan
1976	Ed Krause	1992	Bob Lanier	2009	David Robinson
1976	Bill Sharman	1992	Nera White	2009	John Stockton
1977	Elgin Baylor	1993	Walt Bellamy	2010	Cynthia Cooper-Dyke
1977	Charles Cooper	1993	Julius Erving	2010	Dennis Johnson
1977	Lauren "Laddie" Gale	1993	Dan Issel	2010	Gus Johnson
		1993	Dick McGuire	2010	Karl Malone
1977	William Johnson	1993	Ann Meyers	2010	Ubiratan Pareira
1978	Paul Arizin	1993	Calvin Murphy	2010	Scottie Pippen
1978	Joe Fulks	1993	Uljana Semjonova	2011	Dennis Rodman
1978	Cliff Hagan	1993	Bill Walton	2011	Chris Mullin
1978	Jim Pollard	1994	Carol Blazejowski	2011	Arydas Sabonis
1979	Wilt Chamberlain	1994	Buddy Jeannette	2011	Artis Gilmore

culture of tourism. Sport in Focus 2.4 illustrates the role of honour in one major sport in one country: the Naismith Memorial Basketball Hall of Fame recognises outstanding contributions to the sport. In the box they are ordered by the year they were inducted. Players must be fully retired for five years to be eligible for induction.

There are several specific reasons why sports historians might question the contribution of the sports museum to sports history. For instance:

- sports museums cater for the nostalgia market and an institutionalised version of the golden age;
- errors of fact, myth and interpretation are both perpetuated and problematic;
- the sporting artefacts are often displayed without sufficient explanation or context;
- the financial imperative often gets in the way of historical objectivity;
- halls of fame and, to a lesser extent, sports museums can be shrines to sporting heroes and heroines – they tend to glamorise sporting events and achievements and, therefore, display an uncritical approach to the material; and, following on from this,
- the controversial or unsavoury sporting past is often marginalised.

It is possible to be critical of sporting heritage, not just because of its association with conservation and a conservative ideology that can be imperialistic, nostalgic, exclusive and part of a nationalistic response to the need to conserve national history and identity, but also because heritage can construct a national fable and glorify and sanitise the past by developing sporting myths. The making of sporting heritage has glorified golden sporting moments and often been part of a reaction or a need to re-assert particular values that are often anti-democratic.

MAKING SPORTING HERITAGE AND GOLDEN SPORTING MOMENTS

Heritage is something of a rhapsody on history. The real value of heritage lies in its perennial flexibility and the strength of the emotions it evokes. Celebratory and commemorative reflections on past sporting experiences tend to merge historical sporting incidents, folk memories, selected traditions and often sheer fantasy in order to interpret the sporting past in a way that is meaningful to a contemporary group. The danger is that the bits of the past that seem most significant continually change relative to the present. Heritage representations are often regarded by sports historians as inherently artificial or inauthentic – a sort of staged authenticity involving mythical history to meet commercial and/or tourist demands. The markets, and market values, are viewed as subsuming everything and nothing is valued in itself, only as heritage currency.

Contrasts between idealised pasts and problems of the present are often implicit in celebrations of sporting heritage or golden moments in sports history. The golden era vintage of sports historiography is often underpinned by the notion that sport in the past was better, not just in terms of performance, but more regarding conduct and style, than sport in the

57

SPORT IN FOCUS 2.5: GOLDEN SPORTING MOMENT

Evonne Goolagong won Wimbledon in 1971 having defeated fellow Australian Margaret Court in the final. She then took nine years, 4 July 1980, to win the title again, by which time she became the first mother to win Wimbledon since Dorethea Lambert Chambers in 1914. In autumn of 1979, she became the fifth player to pass $1 million in career earnings. Evonne Goolagong Cawley became the first, and to date the only, Aborigine to win a Grand Slam event (two Wimbledon titles, one French and four Australian Open Championships).

present and that person *w* in year *x* would have run, jumped or fought better than person *y* in year *z*. At the turn of this century, Muhammed Ali was rightly or wrongly declared to be the athlete of the twentieth century not just because of his athletic ability, but because of the various political stances he took on certain issues and because of his enduring popularity and celebrity status with the public. In other words, he is drawn upon as an inspiration to today's sport and society. Many golden and historically important sporting moments exist. Sport in Focus 2.5 points out that, in 1971, Evonne Goolagong became the first Aborigine woman to win a Grand Slam tennis title.

Polley (2008) reminds us of two ways in which views of the past are mobilised in relation to the present. The first is to invoke nostalgia and a belief in a golden age. This often takes the form that sport in the past was purer and that contemporary sport has become corrupt: politics, drugs, commercialisation, violence and professionalism are raised as the usual suspects to denounce contemporary sport as not being like it was in the 'good old days' when football crowds regularly exceeded 100,000 in the stadium. Changes in tradition often give rise to puritan conservative defences of the past, as demonstrated by critical responses to the broadening of sports in the Olympic programme to include sports such as beach volleyball. The second way is when the past is mobilised to add weight and authenticity to celebration of the present. Scotland's campaign at the turn of the twentieth century to host golf's Ryder Cup between Europe and the US was premised upon the ideology of Scotland being 'the home of golf'. A similar 'coming home' theme was raised through the notion of 'football coming home' that accompanied England's 1996 European Championship campaign. Both these types of image, Polley (1998: 3) asserts, share some common ground in the sense that nostalgia is used in the first instance in a sentimental, reactionary and backward-looking comparison between past and present sport, while the second attempts to champion the present by drawing upon links to the past.

The mythology of golden-age sports historiography is nowhere better encapsulated than in Ramachandra Guha's (2002) *A Corner of a Foreign Field: The Indian History of a British Sport*. Guha (2002: xv) observes that the commercialisation of modern cricket and the corruptions that have come in its wake have led some commentators to speak of a time when this was a 'gentleman's game'. In truth, it is added:

there was no golden age, no uncontaminated past in which the playground was free of social pressure and social influence – cricket has always been a microcosm of the fissures and tensions within Indian society: fissures that it has both reflected and played upon, mitigated as well as intensified.

(Guha, 2002: xv)

The colonial history of cricket is replaced by an indigenous account of cricket in which the overarching themes of Indian history, race, caste, religion and nation are to the fore. The history of cricket is located within the context of Indian historiography itself and might be viewed within the notion of the post-colonial because it provides an alternative history to that of the Imperial game variety, in which cricket in India is seen to develop as part of an explicitly colonial environment. It is also *subaltern* in that it develops from some of Guha's earlier work in which the notion of subaltern, originating in Gramsci's notion of the subaltern classes, is used as a perspective to combat the persistence of the colonial perspective (Guha, 2002). It is perhaps worthwhile reading Guha's (2002) account of cricket alongside Bose's (2006) more recent social history of the place of cricket in Indian society.

Perhaps the most important conclusion to be drawn from the above illustrations is the way in which the past is continually renegotiated through sporting history, culture, identity and meaning, and nowhere is this more self-evident than in the way in which the celebration of sport in different parts of the world draws upon the selection or invention of tradition to commemorate a lost past or a sense of injustice, or to assert a particular set of identities.

THE INVENTION OF TRADITION AND SPORT'S POPULAR MEMORY

Sporting traditions, like traditions in general, may be seen as a set of social practices that seek to celebrate and inculcate certain behavioural norms and values, implying continuity with a real or imagined past and usually associated with widely accepted rituals or other forms of symbolic behaviour. Signs, symbols and artefacts play a central role in the development of sporting culture, traditions and myths. Here, there is a potential overlap with anthropological or ethnological contributions to the study of sport, culture and society. Some of the most common sporting traditions would involve sporting festivals, the display of flags, the way in which ceremonies associated with sporting occasions are conducted, and the singing of songs or ritual chanting at sporting events, all of which evolve over time. The following elements seem to be contained within the idea of a sporting tradition:

- traditions are essentially shared, in that there are solitary sporting habits but no solitary sporting traditions, and are understood as such;
- they denote a class or form of intentional actions along with the thoughts, beliefs, perceptions and associations that motivate them;
- they are often associated with certain forms of conservatism in order to assert the validity of respect for the past;

- they create a background of shared expectations against which deviance and originality may be evaluated – hence the phrase 'deviating from the norm', implying deviating from tradition or the way things are usually done; and
- they are often associated with theories of the state and its institutions, since they themselves are offshoots of tradition, invented or otherwise – the term traditionalism may be used in reference to any policy or practice founded in the defence of tradition.

Many traditions may be fabrications, and those that are perceived to be relatively long-standing may, in fact, be relatively recent inventions or selections of tradition. The standard example of an identity culture that anchors itself in the past by means of invented tradition or myths dressed up as history is nationalism. The past is continually recreated to explain and give meaning to the present. Imagined sporting communities select from history and from tradition that which provides a feeling of connectedness with both those who went before, those present and those separated by time and space. The selection of tradition is an act of identification by which we distil our many statuses and roles into those that we find most meaningful. Selected traditions effectively accomplish what traditions are meant to provide: a coherent sense of self, community and other. The fabrication of sporting tradition often consists of anachronism, omission, decontextualisation and, in extreme cases, lies. The following is but an example of invented tradition or myth that has helped to mobilise support for a particular point of view or identity history.

The difference between sporting myth and reality is central to Collins's (1996: 33) account of the 1895 split between rugby union and rugby league. Collins argues that a comprehensive mythology has been developed around William Wollen's painting of the 1893 rugby 'Roses Match' between Yorkshire and Lancashire. The original painting hangs at Twickenham, the home of England's national rugby union side, while a reproduction of it hangs in the clubhouse of Otley Rugby Union Football Club in Yorkshire. The rivalry between the two codes of rugby union and rugby league was such, contends Collins (1996: 33), that those players that went on to play rugby league and turned professional have been painted over, or at least removed by the artist. Such a story is a myth, but one that Collins (1996: 34) contends has been valuable to rugby union and rugby league for a number of reasons: it signified the alleged power of rugby union over rugby league; it downplayed the importance of the 1895 split that, in reality, devastated rugby union; and the painting also served rugby league in that it fitted into the popular pattern of belief that rugby union discriminated against rugby league.

Just as the myths surrounding the Wollen painting have become accepted as facts, Collins (1996: 40) goes on, so too has mythology affected the explanation for the split between rugby union and rugby league in 1895. The painting, he argues (Collins 1996: 38), reproduces the myth of amateurism, the north/south divide and the role of the northern businessman as core factors in promoting the split between the two codes of rugby. Alternatively, it is suggested that the real cause of the 1895 split between rugby union and rugby league was the coming of the working-class player to rugby in the 1870s and 1880s, and the reluctance of the rugby union hierarchy to allow this participation to develop on an equal footing. It is realistic, therefore, to suggest that the bifurcation of rugby in England into two codes was primarily a symptom of class tension and struggle in Victorian sport and society.

The role of memory in determining social and historical accounts of sport, culture and society is relatively recent, in the sense that only a few (but gradually increasing) studies have drawn heavily upon oral history. Memory is structured, in part, by group identities: one remembers one's childhood, one's neighbourhood as part of a local or national community or one's working or non-working life as part of a broader working or non-working group of people. One's memories are shared with others, told in stories, and are thus social memories that tell a particular story about the past or how it was. Such memories help to shape people's lives and their association, romantic or otherwise, with places, times and activities. Memories are important in creating an awareness of sports places and sporting pasts. Memory is an important facet of oral sporting history and it helps to facilitate intergenerational interaction about sporting occasions or places or infamous or famous moments.

A sense of shared history and experience is an important part of geographical memory. Hague and Mercer's (1998) study of the role of memory in shaping the relationship between a community and a sports team is evident in their account of the relationship between Raith Rovers Football Club and the Scottish town of Kirkcaldy. Founded in 1883, Raith Rovers first played as a full member of the Scottish Football League in 1902. Arguably the most memorable moment in the club's history was winning the Scottish First Division in the 1994–95 season, obtaining promotion to the Scottish Premier Division and gaining entry to the European UEFA Cup during the 1995–96 season by winning the Scottish Coca-Cola League Cup the year before. Playing the famous German club Bayern Munich and, for a short spell, leading the German champions by 1–0 have become an important part of the club's folklore. An equally important cup tie was allegedly played between Raith Rovers and a defunct existing local league club, St Bernard's, during the 1923–24 season. The infamous St Bernard's cup tie is recalled in Hague and Mercer's study as an example of memory passing on historical knowledge from, in this case, a father to his son:

> As far as I can remember, Rovers lost a silly goal and, despite battering the opposing goal nearly all the match, were unable to draw level or indeed take the lead. However, as my Dad used to say, that's what happens in football. I already told you that my father was responsible for introducing me to the Rovers and Stark's Park when I was six.
>
> (Hague and Mercer, 1998: 111)

Sporting memory is, therefore, a further link to the past and tradition, but tradition, like heritage and oral history, always has to balance historical plausibility with idealised inventions or selections of tradition or the past. Because visions of heritage and tradition most commonly alter and even distort history in appealing ways, what we perceive as heritage and tradition often replaces history and becomes memory (Ray, 2001: xii). When a selected past is remembered, it may be a celebration of national unity, such as in Hill and Varsasi's (1997) story of the creation of Wembley Stadium, the twin towers and the English FA Cup Final, but in doing so we also emphasise what divides us from all those with 'other' memories, or perhaps a different memory of the same selected past. In Nova Scotia, the symbolism and practice of Scottish–American Highland Games and a romanticised and cleansed Scottish heritage can feed racial tensions. In Northern Ireland, in 2002, the attitude of nationalist football fans to the Northern Irish Catholic Celtic football player Neil Lennon playing for his country in front of a predominantly loyalist crowd is a reminder of ways in which extremists can use heritage in a sporting context as a justification for violence. Thus, it is worth remembering that sporting traditions and sporting heritage can include and exclude, empower and victimise.

HISTORICAL AND SPORTING FORCES

The challenges to more than just the conventional wisdom about how we should think about sport per se have been influenced by a number of historical and sporting forces. Substantial bodies of new research have indicated that sports historiography has become more open to different ways of thinking about sport, change and continuity. Sports historiography is not limited to the impact of industrialisation or modernisation or the impact of any particular period upon sport. Any rigid distinction between different forms of sport in the nineteenth or twentieth centuries would fail to acknowledge the possibility of traditional forms of sport surviving and existing today, despite the onslaught of history and time.

The idea of various 'post' periods and philosophies of sport is thrown around rather readily within discussions of social change. In one sense, the 'post' prefix with reference to historical change can be rather simple. Abstractly, it is as if time period 1 is pre-x, and will have certain characteristics associated with lack of x. Time period 2 is the high tide of x, when many things are touched by it and changed from their state in time 1. Time period 3 is post-x. This implies that something new has come into existence to reduce the importance of x by going beyond it in some sense; some things will, therefore, look different from both time 1 and time 2. However, x will still have left its mark, there will be strong traces of it still around. More interestingly, the decline of x will mean that some things start to look rather like they did in period 1 again. 'Post periods' are therefore seen as being rather complex, but they need not be.

The following are three 'post labels': post-feminism, post-modernism and post-colonialism. But what are they? Do they help us understand sport? And what is wrong with the post-history debate?

Sport and post-feminism

Post-feminism has at least two meanings: a popular sentiment that women can have power without losing their femininity and a more academic sentiment that, as a result of the development of new ideas and knowledge, a label which distances itself from feminist theory as it has been previously understood is required. Post-feminism incorporates a critique of previous assumptions that have been made about the self, the social, the political, the historical, the textual and the West. It is here, for example, that the work of Jennifer Hargreaves (2000) on sport and Muslim women, Vicky Paraschak (2007) on sport in the lives of Inuit women and Fan Hong's (1997) historical account of Chinese women and sport are all valuable in the sense that they collectively and individually have challenged the parochial vision of sport and physical culture as it has been described and championed by Western feminism.

■ **62**

Women's under-representation in sport is a long history in itself. However, one of the major recent points of change in some parts of the world has been the relative political mobilisation of women in sport. Many countries have tried to address women's under-representation in sport by adopting gender equity policies, yet in a review of 24 European countries, Fasting (1989) concluded that a considerable gap still existed between intent and achievement. If we are deemed to have entered a post-feminist world, then it would seem logical to assume that the demands of the post-feminist world of sport have superseded the demands of the feminist world of sport. At the beginning of the twenty-first century, women still occupy a marginal position in sport in nearly every country of the world (Kay, 2003: 102). It is also worth noting that, in *Leisure and Feminist Theory*, not post-feminist theory, Wearing (1998) alludes to the idea of women in a post-modern world as having a certain vibrancy and vitality because it allows for the celebration of diversity, difference and self-confidence without the imposition of any all-embracing imposed theory from above. To paraphrase Wearing (1998: 145), it may be possible for sports historiography to acknowledge ideas from 'post' theories so that sport is re-signified as an appropriate space for the diversity of women from all parts of the world. The crucial intervention here is to invoke the notion that sport can provide possibilities for women of colour, as well as working-class and middle-class women to 'rewrite or resignify women's subjectivities so that they are no longer inferiorized' (Wearing 1998: 145).

A good deal of post-feminism's attraction comes perhaps from the substantive manifestations of 'girl power' and the self-assured displays of confident young sportswomen, and the challenge that this poses to old-fashioned, essentialist feminism with its conventional images of feminism as being dowdy, embittered and self-pitying. The differences between women are confidently accentuated within post-feminism and, as such, issues of sporting diversity are perhaps more open in post-feminist sport than they were within feminist sport. It remains to be seen whether a more powerful, younger, energetic post-feminism can obliterate the problems of nature and inequality that older forms of feminism contested. As such, it would be important to note both the continuities and changes in sport that have been brought about as a result of post-feminism.

Sport and post-modernism

Adding to the introductory comment upon post-modernism provided in Chapter 1, a number of specific attempts have been made to provide a post-modernist introduction to sports historiography (Hill, 1996, 2002). The term 'post-modernism' is a multi-layered concept that directs our attention to a variety of social and cultural changes that took place towards the end of the twentieth century. The philosophy of the Enlightenment in the eighteenth century heralded the notion of modernity within a historical period when industrial production, rationality, positivist science, objectivity, and belief in absolute truths, order and stability prevailed. Post-modernity refers to the period following modernity in which all of these certainties were challenged. This critique of modernity has provoked two responses: a conservative one that tries to conserve some or all of the aspects of modernity, and a more radical one that attempts to harness the plurality and freedom of thinking and method that have been released by the post-modern critique and changing historical circumstances.

63

Championing the cause for a post-modern future in British sports historiography, Hill (1996, 2002) has suggested that issues of identity and meaning may provide historians with fruitful future lines of investigation. Hill (1996: 19) skillfully steers a path between the conventional and the radical when he argues that it might be rewarding for sports historians to turn their attention to matters of sport as ideology, symbol and text, while he also argues that the conventional features of the historian's craft provide the equipment to undertake such a task. The importance of uncovering and interrogating the sporting experiences of ordinary people from below, Hill (1996: 19) goes on, means that oral history, in particular, has an important role to play in uncovering accounts of sport that hitherto have been hidden from history. It seems that Hill, in one sense, is encouraging students and researchers to at least grasp the opportunity provided by post-modern epistemology to tell different stories or narratives about sports historiography, while at the same time remembering the craft of the historian in terms of plausibility, reality, evidence and perhaps even the ghost of labour history. The scepticism of modernity's grand theory is coupled with an empirical enthusiasm for uncovering the experiences of sport and of what sport has meant to people hitherto hidden from sports history. In this sense, sports historiography provides an important empirical addition to the continuing search for a historiography from below, rather than a history of leaders, personalities and famous sporting institutions.

There is good reason to listen to much of what post-modern sports historiography has to offer, and yet much remains to be done if sport is to witness a change as a result of a transition from modernity to post-modernity. At a philosophical level, it is doubtful if the assault on truth or the anti-realism inherent within post-modernism will do much to uphold the task of socially committed students or sports historians who are not afraid of clarity, but see their role as explaining complex ideas and problems clearly.

Sport and post-colonialism

As a term, 'post-colonialism' may refer to both the effects of colonisation and the efforts being made by various communities to develop anti-colonial strategies. In Chapter 1, the notion of post-colonialism was referred to in three senses: (i) as a historical term or stage of development in which post-colonialism has replaced colonial legacies; (ii) as a geographical term that connects those places in the world that have been affected by the imperial process; and (iii) as a particular method or epistemology that focuses upon the forces of oppression and coercive domination that operate within the contemporary world, and consequently examines the part played by sport within the politics of anti-colonialism and neo-colonialism. In this sense, post-colonial theory's intellectual commitment involves engaging in new forms of theoretical work that is closely linked to activism and social change within the world today, and specifically those parts of the world that have been affected by colonialism and imperialism.

In Chapter 7, three important questions are raised. These are simply referred to here as the what, when and how of the relationship between sport and post-colonialism. Post-colonial sport could be said to have arrived when the first 'Third World' sports workers arrived in 'First World' sport. The disadvantages of the term 'Third World' have been generally denounced, since it has a negative connotation, suggesting that, in a hierarchical sense, it comes after the first and second worlds. Alternatively, the term 'tricontinental', or three continents, is often used to refer to the land masses of Latin America, Africa and Asia. It presupposes that the history of European expansion and the occupation of most of the available global land mass occurred between 1492 and 1945. Any consideration of the relationship between sport and post-colonialism would necessitate looking at the way in which sport has developed and diffused from these places. As a form of critique of global sport, the politics of post-colonial sport necessitates an examination and exposure of Euro-centric or Western forms of dominance in world sport. For instance, does global sport reflect a dominance of the North over the South? One of the general assumptions of post-colonial studies is that many of the wrongs, if not crimes against humanity, are a product of the dominance of the North over the South. If nothing else, the study of post-colonial sport provides the opportunity to examine Western ontological assumptions about 'other' sports. Post-colonial sport provides an important point of engagement with Western sport that should warn students and others against accepting any uncritical account of Western sport.

As with all attempts at periodisation, objections have been raised about what should be included and excluded from post-colonialism as a historical period. A substantive concern is the inclusion of any countries that did not have a colonial past in the sense that Africa, India and the Caribbean did. All of this simply serves as a reminder that the specifics of the what, when and how of post-colonialism and the study of post-colonial sport are not the same, for example, for Latin America, Australia, Canada, South Korea, Taiwan, Turkey and Iran. Some have argued that the debate about post-colonialism has been superseded by the power of globalisation or a network society, and yet the post-colonial era still involves different kinds of anti-colonial struggles that have given rise to changing geographies and have grown out of not theory, but activism in the world today.

The selection of the above 'posts' is a fraction of those influences on the history of sport, culture and society that could have been considered. In 1989, Francis Fukuyama's (1989, 1992) essays on the end of history seemed to symbolise, or at least announce, that we were living in the aftermath of the historical age in which the big concepts of the nineteenth and twentieth centuries had been or were about to be retired. The end of the history of sport in these terms would have meant that liberal capitalist sport had triumphed universally. It had triumphed over all the concerns and values associated with Marxist, feminist, colonial and modernist accounts of sport that had hitherto been retired as causal historical or social forces that impacted upon sport, culture and society. Beyond the end of history was only boredom, with no values to struggle over other than what Fukuyama would have viewed as parochial sporting issues, such as religion or nationalism.

There are a number of shortcomings associated with such developments, and it should be no surprise to students of sport, culture and society that many of the facets of sport that were consigned to retirement are alive and well. The post-worlds are all worlds without centres. They are worlds without any fixed authority or absolute centre or ideology around which policy or intervention can be organised, not even post-colonialism. National governments or national sports organisations may continue to act as if they have authority, but global capitalism or global sport evades control and can be both *everywhere* and *nowhere*.

65

The predicament for the study of sport, culture and society is what to do with the vast number of 'posts' – post-industrialism, post-modernity, post-tradition and even post-history – and what they tell us about sport and the world we live in. Post-isms have proliferated everywhere at a speed that has led to much confusion. They agree only in the view that things are not what they used to be, that we are living in a different world and that the prefix 'post' points us to beyond. But to what remains unclear – new worlds, new sport, new attitudes and new values? Radically varying lists of 'posts' have impacted upon not just sport, culture and society, but upon sports historiography. The post world is a world in which relativity and discourse rule. There are no absolutes because language, style, image and so on are part of a discourse, and there is no way of proving or disproving a discourse. The post world of sport, culture and society is a world in which it is impossible to distinguish reality because everything is allegedly the appearance of reality. We can look at the 'post worlds' of sport as either a joyous liberation into a free play of 'post' discourses or narratives in which nothing counts and everything is relative, or as a tragedy in which meaning is everything and of no significance, and the latter is probably the hangover resulting from too much of the former. There are no values and the negative thrust of the post world is not counterbalanced by the positive thrust of progress or social change or a more humanitarian account of world sport.

So where stands the history of sport today?

Perhaps one of the most important points to know about any subject or area is what its purpose is, or what it gives us. The discussion about sport, history and social change presented in this chapter has gone some way to answer that question. We need a history of sport that provides access to the past, but one that also explains the inter-connected nature of the contemporary world of sport. We need a history of sport that explains how sporting relationships have emerged and how different social, cultural and political traditions of sport have formed but also interacted. The history of sport continues to offer genuine new discoveries but also fosters tools, methods and insights that can help to provide a better understanding of the world in which we live in and how it has emerged. The history of sport continues to embrace important debates, challenges and uncertainties but it has a substantive core of research that tells us about different worlds of sport. If social history is taken to mean an analysis of the lives of ordinary people, then clearly gaps exist in what we know about sport in the lives of ordinary people in different parts of the world. We do not, for instance, have as yet a global or world history of sport, but we have a number of local, regional, national and international histories of sport. Historians of sport are increasingly aware that questions of the past are not separate from the challenges of the present or from having a part to play in the provision of alternative or possible forms of sport that need to be confronted and explored as part of a more complete history of sport today. The notion of any global sport from a historical perspective would necessitate taking a view of sport from different parts or angles on contemporary sport. A view of any global history of sport would have a different view, depending on whether the view of history was a view from the south, north, east or west. The history of sport today needs to continue to expand its geographical offer, while at the same time addressing all of the major issues presented in this chapter. It continues to be work in progress.

SUMMARY

What is generally being suggested here is that no informed debate on sport, culture and society can take place without reference to the historical dimensions or processes involved in the making of sport. All aspects of social and cultural life are based upon socio-political and economic events of the past. The past is therefore a permanent dimension of the human consciousness, an inevitable component of the institutions, values, traditions, customs and patterns of human society. The sporting past is much more than just chronology and, as such, the historiography of sport must not be reduced to a simple chronology of events. Rather, sport must be properly located within the social, cultural and historical context in which it moves or is located.

The production and dissemination of sport historiography has many audiences, genres and functions. The main audiences are not mutually exclusive and, indeed, sports historiography may benefit from a greater rate of exchange between the academic study of sports history that is produced for journals and monographs; popular sports history as part of sporting post-war development that has helped to confirm and mythologise a sense of tradition through sport; the production of sports history through museums and heritage sites; the production of sports history for television and film; and socially committed sports history that seeks out the excluded and fills in gaps to produce a more complete body of knowledge about sport, culture and society. The deconstruction of political or social sporting myths that pass as sports history remains one of the main responsibilities of the sociologist and the sports historian. They and others are responsible both for destruction of myth, despite the onslaught of post-modern sports history, and the production of more reality congruent bodies of knowledge about the historiography of sport.

The history of sport matters for a number of reasons: (i) it helps to avoid a parochial or insular understanding of sport; (ii) it stops research retreating into the present; (iii) it provides the tools by which to evaluate change, whether it be social or otherwise, continuity and meaning; (iv) it helps, like sociology, to destroy sporting myths; (v) it warns against uncritical acceptance of sporting heritage, traditions and identities; and (vi) it helps to illuminate past themes, events and changes in their own terms as mattered at the time, and therefore sport in the past is explained on its own terms without necessarily having to call upon whatever vogue theory exists to re-interpret the past.

All human beings, institutions and collectivities need a past, and sport is no different. All histories of sport are part of a larger and more complex world and, therefore, a historiography of sport designed for only a particular section or part of that world cannot on its own be good history. In other words, although identity sports historiography may be comforting to particular groups, left on its own it can be dangerous if it leads or contributes to forms of fundamentalism. The history of sport and what it has to offer sport in terms of solutions to current problems is a vast resource of tried and tested policies, interventions and case studies, but also a methodology that helps, through comparative and historical data, keep things in perspective. The question of how violent sport and society is today can only be answered, in part, by thinking and evidencing how violent sport and society has been in the past before coming to a more rounded judgement about any particular case or country.

GUIDE TO FURTHER READING

Bale, J. and Cronin, M. (2003). *Sport and Post-colonialism.* Oxford: Berg Publishers.

Guha, R. (2002). *A Corner of a Foreign Field: The Indian History of a British Sport.* London: Picador.

Hill, J. (2002). *Sport, Leisure and Culture in Twentieth Century Britain.* Basingstoke: Palgrave.

James, C. L. R. (1963). *Beyond a Boundary.* London: Stanley Paul.

Osborne, C. and Skillen, F. (2010). 'Introduction. The State of Play: Women in British Sports History'. *Sport in History,* 30 (2): 189–196.

Park, R. (2011). 'Physicians, Scientists, Exercise and Athletics in Britain and America from the 1867 Boat Race to the Four-Minute Mile'. *Sport in History,* 31 (1): 1–31.

Polley, M. (2008). 'History and Sport'. In Houlihan, B. (ed.) *Sport and Society.* London: Sage, 56–75.

Schultz, J. (2011). 'Contesting the Master Narrative: The Arthur Ashe Statue and Monument Avenue in Richmond, Virginia'. *International Journal of the History of Sport,* 28 (8/9) May: 1235–1251.

Vamplew, W. (1998). 'Facts and Artefacts: Sports Historians and Sports Museums'. *Journal of Sports History*, 25 (2): 268–283.

QUESTIONS

1   Explain the dangers of thinking contemporaneously about sport.

2   What does the study of history add to an understanding of sport, culture and society?

3   Outline some of the concerns that historians might have with sporting heritage.

4   Outline a history of (i) racism in British sport or (ii) possible milestones in the development of women's sport.

5   Describe a number of invented sporting traditions and explain the ways in which myth, memory and tradition all help to mobilise the past in the present.

6   Discuss Guha's analysis of cricket within the context of Western and/or anti-Western resistance.

7   What is (i) post-modern sports history and (ii) post-colonial sports history?

8   Critically evaluate the debate about sport's 'post' histories.

9   Discuss the value of developing comparative histories of sport.

10   How does history help to provide an understanding of the broader context of sport, culture and society?

PRACTICAL PROJECTS

1   Visit a sports museum and assess whether it sets its artefacts in context.

2   Interview a parent or older relative about a famous sports incident and produce a short press report.

3   Carry out an Internet search for information in relation to the history of:

   (i)   a particular sport;

   (ii) a sports organisation; and

   (iii) a national sport.

   Explain how the historical content of each of these is presented.

4   Explore further any one of the many sporting myths that exist. Draw upon a range of primary sources in order to write 1,000 words on the sporting myth.

5   Compare the coverage of sport in one local and one national newspaper of 10 and 5 years ago. Write a 1,000-word report on how sport has changed over the past 10 years.

KEY CONCEPTS

Biography ■ Comparative ■ Continuity and change ■ Feminist sport history ■ Heritage ■ Historiography ■ Identity ■ Myth ■ Oral history ■ Social change ■ Social history ■ Tradition ■ Transformation

WEBSITES

International Society for the History of Physical Education and Sport
www.umist.ac.jk/sport/ishpes.htm
The International Society for the History of Physical Education and Sport provides for both an international and comparative perspective on physical education and sport. Its membership list and contacts provide for an international network of researchers interested in the history of physical education and sport in the broadest sense of the terms. It is a membership-based society.

International Society of Olympic Historians
www.olykamp.org/isoh
A specialist society dedicated to exploring and recording Olympic history, whether it be fact, mythology, specific country focus or thematic. An international network of researchers interested in exploring facets of Olympic history.

69

The British Society for Sports History

www.umist.ac.uk/sport/index2/htm

The British Society for Sports History is a membership-based society that also runs the *Sports Historian* journal. It is one of the oldest history of sport societies and, although its focus is mainly the British Isles, this is not at the expense of a broader international perspective. It holds an annual conference.

The North American Society for Sports History (NASSH)

www.nassh.org

One of the largest international societies with an interest in sports history. It hosts both an international journal and annual conference. Memebership is drawn from many different countries but mainly the US and Canada.

Canadian Sports History Review

http://journals.humankinetics.com/shr-back-issues

A journal that prioritises an interest in Canadian or Canadian-related aspects of sports history.

Chapter 3

Sport, economics and global finance

Does the hosting of major sporting events in different parts of the world help to redistribute wealth throughout the sport?

The 2022 FIFA World Cup, at the time of writing, is scheduled to take place in Qatar. Who benefits from this?

PREVIEW

Key terms defined ■ Introduction ■ Club ownership ■ The economics of sport ■ 2009 Tennis budgets and Wimbledon prize money ■ Economic impact studies ■ Cost–benefit analysis of sport ■ European models of sport and American professional models of sport ■ Economic histories ■ Global trade and finance ■ The uneven global trade in muscle ■ Top sponsorship deals for 2009 ■ World's most valuable sports teams ■ Financing of the Beijing Olympic Games ■ Cultures of capitalism, business and sport ■ Summary

OBJECTIVES

This chapter will:

■ explore and introduce some of the economic and financial aspects of global sport;

■ explain the research that informs the economics of sport;

■ consider the impact of global trade and finance on selected sports;

■ describe the relationship between sport and varieties of capitalism; and

■ provide some necessary background to a further analysis of global sport in Chapter 5.

KEY TERMS DEFINED

Dependence: The state of being connected to and subordinate to someone or something.

Economics: The social science concerned with the production and consumption of goods and services, and the analysis of the commercial activities of a society.

Capitalism: A system of production in which human labour and its products are commodities that are bought and sold in the marketplace.

Development: A multidimensional process that normally notes a change from a less to a more desirable state.

Political Economy: The branch of politics concerned with the nature of the wealth of nations, and the political aspects of economic policy making.

Neo-liberalism: Developed in the 1970s, it advocates measures to promote economic development, and is used to guide the transition from planned to market economies in former communist countries.

INTRODUCTION

While it is correct to question whether the era of globalisation has come to an end, it is undeniable that commerce and capital continue to spread around the globe. One consequence of the era of globalisation was that financially powerful individuals and companies continued to invest in sport. Rupert Murdoch started as an Australian newspaper heir; entered the world of satellite and terrestrial television; started the Australian Rugby League to meet the demands of his company, Fox Network; holds contracts for Major League Baseball coverage; up until 2004 he owned the Los Angeles Dodgers; and continues to be the controlling investor in different companies in different countries, all of which value the rights to broadcast sport. Football clubs have come to depend upon the media income to help pay the wages commanded by their players. Lord Sugar once dubbed this the 'prune juice economics' of the game because all of the money the clubs earned went straight out again in the form of salaries. On average, income from broadcasters accounts for about 40 per cent of the turnover of Premier League sides, but the actual figures vary wildly depending upon the size and success of the club.

Another such individual is Malcolm Glazer, owner of the American National Football League team Tampa Bay Buccaneers (but also holding the controlling interest in Manchester United of the English Premier League), who, in 2003, entered into a joint marketing venture with the New York Yankees. The Glazer family bought Manchester United in a £790 million leveraged buyout deal. They paid £272 million in cash and borrowed the remainder in bank loans. Although the family restructured the debt in 2006, it cannot be paid off easily. From the Glazers' perspective, the financial logic is simple – it assumes that United's players will be good enough, year in and year out, to generate from ticket sales, television rights and commercial deals the money needed to service the debts. Together, these income streams provided turnover of £145 million in the last six months of 2009. Media income accounted for 36 per cent of the club's £278 million sales in 2009. Yet, financial power can very quickly lead to issues of ownership and governance in sport and society. The social consequence of this financial power extends to the localities and communities in which these clubs are located. Studies of changing patterns of sports finance have warned about the impact this can have on local sports clubs (Morrow, 2003; Szymanski and Zimbalist, 2005). Many Manchester United fans have already protested against the Glazers' ownership of the club by shunning the club's official red colours in favour of the green and gold of the railway workers who funded the club in the nineteenth century.

It would be a mistake to assume that the flow of global sporting finances is between Western nations, and this chapter attempts to at least acknowledge the question that many economists are asking, namely – when will China's economy leapfrog America's to become the world's biggest economy? When Goldman Sachs made its first forecasts for the BRIC economy (Brazil, Russia, India and China) in 2003, it predicted that China would overtake America in 2041. This date has now been revised to 2027 (*The Economist*, 18 December 2010: 133). If real GDP in China and America continue to grow at the same annual average pace as over the past 10 years and nothing else changed, China's GDP would overtake America's in 2022. The flow of sportsmen and sportswomen into European professional sport from Asia is a part-acknowledgement of the need to attract players who are recognised as national icons within China, South Korea and Japan. Glasgow Celtic Football Club signed Chinese international defender Du Wei in 2005, followed by Zheng Zhi in 2009; Japanese midfielder Shunsuke Nakamura in 2008; and South Korean Ki-Sung in 2009. The classic example lies with Manchester United, who have tapped into market to the tune of perhaps tens of millions of pounds by the acquisition of South Korean national team captain Park Ji-Sung. In the sponsorship market, there are a clutch of big hitters in South Korea. In the summer of 2009, Chelsea Football Club and Samsung Electronics, part of the world's biggest conglomerate, renewed their shirt sponsorship deal for a further three years, an agreement that was previously worth £11 million a year.

Having introduced the importance of economics and finance to providing a more complete analysis of sport today, this chapter explores various aspects of global finance and economics and, by doing so, contributes to a much more complete analysis of sport, culture and society

73

than that provided in the first edition. This chapter is divided into four parts: (i) an overview of the economics of sport; (ii) an account of how sport figures unevenly within global trade and finance arrangements; (iii) an implicit need to consider the relationship between various cultures of capitalism, and not simply capitalism and sport; and (iv) an overview of the international political economy and sport.

THE ECONOMICS OF SPORT

As Sport in Focus 3.1 shows, the economics of some sports, such as tennis, can be fairly detailed but the economics of individual sports, interesting as they are at times, do not tell us much about economics. The analysis of tennis could provide an insight into different wage–labour relations and expenditure in one Grand Slam tennis event but the conclusion that men and women are paid almost equally in terms of prize money per hour spent on court is perhaps not typical of other sports.

In 1956, Rottenberg's analysis of the baseball labour market in the *Journal of Political Economy* partly signified the acceptance of the economics of sport as a sub-discipline of economics (Rottenberg, 1956). According to Rottenberg's invariance proposition, free agency would yield the same talent distribution as the reserves system in American baseball. Many economists attracted to the economics of sport continue to be labour economists and, consequently, much of the research is dominated by issues of salary discrimination, distribution of earnings, profit maximisation, attendance revenues, restrictions of players' mobility, revenue-sharing schemes and salary caps, the impact of the franchise in professional sport, and different models of transatlantic sport represented by American and European professional sport models. It is perhaps helpful to suggest that the economics of sport is not much different from economics in that economics, in part, is about choice and is at the heart of the decision making about sport, but it is also about asking how can sport help answer certain economic questions and propositions.

Sloane's (2004) overview of the economics of sport acknowledged that, in his view, while individual sports such as tennis, athletics, boxing, golf and horse racing were features of interest to the economist, they did not face the same scale of problem of allocation of resources through competition as that of professional team sports. The account proceeds to summarise the challenges of professional football clubs, the impact of television revenue as a basis for transforming rugby union, the implications of the athletes' freedom of contract in North America, team performance and managerial change in the English Football League, and the regulation of the broadcasting of sporting events. The first volume of the *International Journal of Sports Finance*, published in 2006, investigated the value of Major League Baseball ownership, the efficiency of the UK fixed-odds betting market for Euro 2004, the auctioning of TV sports rights, and the development of a profitability model for professional sports leagues based upon a case study of the National Hockey League. Some three years later, the *Scottish Journal of Political Economy* (2007) covered a range of research papers on the Champions League and Coase Theorem, the rational expectations of the pro sports leagues, and an analysis of whether the centralisation of media rights does improve competitive balance or improve weaker teams.

SPORT IN FOCUS 3.1: LAWN TENNIS ASSOCIATION'S 2009 BUDGET

The Lawn Tennis Association (LTA) is the national governing body of tennis in the UK. Like other sports associations, it has a wide range of commitments. To fulfil these obligations, it is important that associations budget correctly. Below is a breakdown of the LTA's 2009 budget.

Activity	% Budget allocation (£ million)
Competition	17.9
Business Operations	11.7
Coaches	9.1
Commercial	8.4
Player Programmes	8.2
Resources	4.3
Total	59.7

The chart shows that the LTA sets aside the largest proportion of its budget for competition. Wimbledon is the association's premier event and it is held for two weeks during the summer each year. It is one of the four tennis Grand Slams and is the only one to be played on grass. Wimbledon is by far the greatest source of income for the association.

However, there is a cost to hosting such a high-profile event, and that is why the LTA earmark so much funding for competitions. The graphs below show how much prize money is paid out to the men's and lady's finalists. In 2009, the prize money for the four finalists totaled £2.6 million, or 4.35 per cent of the total LTA budget. Therefore, it is important that sports associations strike a balance between developing new talent and rewarding the elite players.

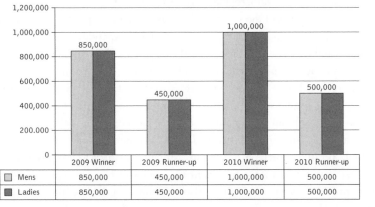

Wimbledon Prize Money (£)

	2009 Winner	2009 Runner-up	2010 Winner	2010 Runner-up
Mens	850,000	450,000	1,000,000	500,000
Ladies	850,000	450,000	1,000,000	500,000

The economics of sport according to Sandy *et al.* (2004: xiii) provides an excellent framework for covering standard economic topics such as, for example, marginal revenue, profit and utility maximisation, cartel behaviour, worker productivity, monopoly behaviour and practice, cost–benefit analysis, stock market flotation, anti-trust laws, supply and demand of athletes in the labour market, discrimination, economic development, uneven development, economies of scale, economies of scope, incentives, and competitive balance. However, it is also crucial to note that theories informed by economic thinking about sport have helped to inform explanations about cores and peripheries, imperialism and colonialism, uneven development, and well-being and happiness.

Economic impact studies

Research on the economic impact of sport has attempted to measure the direct and indirect effects of sport and major sporting events on economic variables such as employment, output or gross domestic product (GDP), and the impact of sport on urban and regional regeneration. The value of sport to community *x* or country *y* through event *z* has been the focus of many economic impact studies. Economists often use economic impact statements to analyse the potential effects of a development on a variety of activities. Economic impact studies are similar to cost–benefit analyses but do not need the full overall approach that is contained within cost–benefit studies. A cost–benefit analysis compares the perceived benefits of an activity with the actual costs of undertaking the activity or event. Private investors tend to be concerned with the economic rate of return on any investment, whereas public investment invariably considers the broader social return produced by the investment. Many economists remain wary of the claims made by such studies on the grounds that analysts tend to overstate the benefits, understate costs, misapply multipliers and fail to take account of the economic activity that does not take place as a result of a sporting event. Few long-term economic impact studies have been funded but, nonetheless, economic impact studies have found a place in the evaluation of the impact of sport in different situations.

Studies of the economic impact of sport may be classified according to type: regular sports competitions, such as major sports championships in football, rugby, cricket, etc.; one-off annual events, such as the FA Cup; mega-events, such as the FIFA World Cup or the Olympics; and smaller, one-off irregular major events, such as athletics meetings. Kasimati's (2003) review of 13 studies of the summer Olympics concluded positive impacts on a number of economic variables, including GDP, employment and expenditure. Blake's (2005) studies carried out for candidate countries for the 2012 Olympics again found evidence of a positive impact on income and employment. Most of the studies for the impact of regular sports competitions, such as league sports, have been carried out in the US. The context in the US is specific, as major league sports teams can move around from city to city and are able to use the threat to move to leverage public subsidies. Hence, much of the research has focused on whether the public subsidies are justified. Many economic impact studies take no account of the possible positive effect on inward investment that may follow a successful sporting event if a host city is able to use the event to rebrand itself and improve its international rating as a 'premier league' city. It is also difficult to calculate the monetary value of regeneration – both in terms of environmental impact and in terms of any change in the well-being of local residents. Few economic studies attempt to measure the 'feel-good' factor or 'psychic income' (Crompton, 2001) associated with major sporting events. 'Psychic income' takes many forms. It includes a sense of community and common purpose. However, a US study by Rushen (1999) of the impact of the Pirates team on Pittsburgh, which did consider the opportunity costs, in terms of taxation, expenditure and employment effects, found that the Pittsburgh was better off with the team than without it.

Comparison of national pastimes

It could be alleged that baseball and football transcend national borders more than any other sports but it is the comparative analysis of these two sporting passions that provide a focus of Szymanski and Zimbalist (2005). A broader comparative economics of North American and European sports can be found in the earlier overview by Barros *et al.* (2002) and provides one of the most succinct accounts of European and North American models of sport, but it is the former study that this discussion draws upon. Written by economists, this study explores the way in which the two sporting traditions of baseball and football have generated different possibilities for the commercial organisation and exploitation of the respective sports. The research questions are not simple to answer but, at a general level, the authors suggest that their approach to the problems of baseball and football provide for a better comparative perspective on national sporting pastimes in both America and Europe. One consequence of the era of globalisation has been the spread of commerce and capital around the world. Many of the same individuals and/or companies who have invested in one sport may also view the other sport as lucrative.

Sports leagues in the US are organised in an entirely different way from football leagues in the UK. Team owners control the franchises and their locations. Teams tend to be provided with the opportunity of monopoly over certain territories, when leagues expand existing owners charge a substantial fee to the new owners and leagues benefit from a variety of antitrust laws. In the UK, leagues are open, a hierarchy of leagues exist, poorly performing teams are relegated while the strongest are promoted. Teams are not provided with territorial monopolies and rarely – exceptions do exist – extract large public subsidies from local government. The openness of football enables a city or region to host a major football league team. Relocations between cities, although not within cities, are rare. The three main regulatory issues that impact upon American sport are free agency for players, breakaway leagues and franchise relocation. The economists conclude that the organisation of football and baseball will never be the same, nor should they be, but that they reflect the societies where they were created. However, cross-cultural comparisons help to create alternative solutions to problems, create a greater degree of open-mindedness about how arrangements could be and, in this sense, the provision of alternative models can be, at times, a force for change.

The final part of the study comparing the national pastimes of baseball and football sets out a number of lessons that can be drawn from crossing cultures. They include:

- The origins of the two sports evolved out of different social groups with the evolution of the American model being more commercial.

- A number of specific themes have given rise to a soccer crisis, and these include a hierarchy of governance in football, a hierarchy of league competition, the operation of clubs as not-for-profit associations, and the over-reliance on regional and national political support for investment and financial rescues.
- Baseball's dilemmas are of a different order, and include:
  - a fixation on short-term results at the expense of long-term vision;
  - falling participation rates among African Americans; and
  - the establishment of an effective anti-doping policy and securing improve labour relations.
- Yet, both sports have a cultural centrality within their respective societies that, despite management issues and problems, helps to ensure that they could continue to evolve as national pastimes.

Economic histories

While economics can be embedded in historical change to various degrees, they cannot be divorced from it without any substantial loss of realism. It is perhaps fair to say that economic historians as economists or economists as historians may, at times, live in an uneasy coexistence. Economists might agree on the value of history for their discipline but not all historians would necessarily agree on the value of economics. It is safe to say that economies and thinking about economics is both historically and culturally specific. Why, for example, did industrial capitalism not develop in China rather than Europe? Economic choices might also be significantly limited, be historically constrained or enabled by periods of growth. Important questions about uneven development should not be constrained by historical or economic models of explanation. At the same time, an understanding of the world economy, not to mention any particular part of it, necessitates a sensitivity to complex economic histories rather than, for example, an all-consuming model of modernisation or the fact that, for decades, the Russian Revolution was seen to provide an alternative to capitalism as opposed to being a potential variety of capitalism.

Economic histories of sport have themselves declined in popularity. Significant examples such as Tranter's study of sport, economy and society in Britain between 1750 and 1914, or Vamplew's classic study of the turf, which depicted one of the first social and economic histories of horse racing, or Williams's (1991) classic essay on rugby in Wales, which provided an account from grand slam to grand slump and located a history of rugby football in Wales during periods of not economic growth, but recession, stand to remind students and researchers of sport, culture and society of the value of economic histories of sport. Very few economic histories of women's sport exist and, to that extent, much work needs to be done in this regard.

GLOBAL TRADE AND FINANCE

Transnational corporations use sports as vehicles for introducing their products around the world. Transborder production arises when a single process is spread across widely dispersed locations, both within and between countries. This might be compared with territorial-based production. With the growth of global production, a large proportion of international transfers of sports goods and services may entail intra-firm trade within transborder companies. A considerable proportion of international trade of sports goods often involves transworld brand names and companies. Through transborder production and transworld products, the global trade of sports goods and services has become an important facet of trade for some world-based firms.

At least four key points might be made here:

- While territorial borders can constrain trade through different forms of protectionism, the proliferation of sports goods and services around the world has not generally been hindered by territorial distance.
- A number of states have created special economic zones in order to attract global or international factories.
- Contemporary sports commerce involves transborder marketing of global brand-name products.
- Invariably, the amount of trade between different parts of the world, even continents, is uneven and, in some cases, unjust.

Finance and, in particular, global finance has experienced considerable degrees of growth, recession and creeping stability since the 1980s. The extent to which the financial recession of 2008 impacted upon sport in parts of the world will be touched upon shortly but, in the first instance, a number of key points and qualifications need to be made. First is to recognise the unevenness with which the globalisation of trade and finance has both spread and the extent to which any economic recession affects trade in some countries more than others. Second, the continuing importance of territoriality in the current global economy. Third, that on both economic and social grounds, the relaunch of economic development supported by some huge financial mechanism that functions with different standards to those recently upheld by globalised US finance.

The uneven global trade in muscle and sponsorship

The international flow of athletes from Kenya has recently been referred to as a global trade in muscle in which Kenyan athletes have switched allegiance from the country of their birth to the oil-rich states of Qatar and Bahrain (Simms and Rendell, 2004). This scramble for African talent, write Simms and Rendell (2004), may be equated with the exploitation of Africa's mineral wealth during different periods of colonial rule; the assertion being that those living in poverty provide the muscle while the rich countries of the world capture the benefits. The new scramble for Africa started as early as the 1960s, with athletes being lured to American colleges, but now the oil-rich countries of the world simply buy athletic talent that is then lost to Africa. Gyulai (2003) recognises that the freedom of movement of athletes may give rise to conflicting interest between different member federations of the International Association of Athletics Federations (IAAF), but believes that there should be no exception to the increased mobility of individuals within the rules of free-market trade and global sporting capitalism. The IAAF notes that the rules with regard to the movement of athletes should not be to the detriment of the member federations (Gyulai, 2003). Kenya has recently moved to try to stem the flow of athletes out of Kenya by tightening up on the circumstances and conditions under which athletes may be granted visas to leave the country.

In the same way that the all-too-easily accepted truths about globalisation have ignored the uneven and differentiated forms of capitalism emerging in the twenty-first century, so too is it crucial not to ignore the injustices and uneven patterns of sports labour migration. It is essential that any contemporary understanding of global sport must actively listen and engage with other sporting communities, places and voices. Perhaps it is impossible for humanity or global sport to arrive at an understanding of the values that unite it, but if the leading capitalist nations ceased to impose their own ideas on the rest of the sporting world and started to take cognisance of 'other' sporting cultures, then the aspiration of global sport may become more just and less charitable. It is not charity that Africa or African runners want, but the tools by which Africans can determine their own well-being and life chances in a more equable sporting world (Jarvie, 2005; McAlpine, 2005). If large parts of Africa are kept poor as a result of unfair trade arrangements that facilitate cheap European and American imports that keep parts of Africa poor and dependent, then why should the resources afforded by running not be viewed as a viable route out of poverty for those that can make it?

Globalisation has not been experienced everywhere and by everyone to the same extent. In general, transborder trade and finance has developed furthest (i) in East Asia, North America and Western Europe; (ii) in urban areas relative to rural districts; and (iii) in wealthier and professional circles. Supraterritorial trade and finance have developed disproportionately in the north and, most specifically, in the cities. Foreign direct investment, credit card transactions, stock market capitalisation and transborder loans tend to flow within the north rather than between north, south, east and west. Transborder markets and investments can be shown to have contributed significantly to a growing wealth gap between countries. Sport in Focus 3.2 and 3.3 both address this unevenness of distribution of wealth. The former highlights the fact that the flow of money associated with the top sporting sponsorship deals in 2009 benefited only a few countries.

Manchester United is the most valuable sports team in the world. This is based on the club's global appeal and their ability to exploit these markets, particularly in Asia. The team claim to have 330 million followers and 139 million core fans. Sport in Focus 3.3 shows that (i) during 2009–10, the top 25 wealthiest sports teams in the world resided within 4 countries; (ii) 2 sports dominate the league of wealthiest sports teams; and (iii) the South, in particular Africa, does not appear in this league table.

The list is almost completely dominated by American football from the NFL. Only 5 teams from other sports have made the top 25. However, it is important to note that the NFL teams have much lower revenue than the other sports teams on the list. For example, FC Barcelona is bottom of the table, yet their revenue is far greater than any of the NFL teams. The value of American football teams stems from the value of an NFL franchise and all the commercial ties that come with it.

SPORT IN FOCUS 3.2: TOP SPONSORSHIP DEALS OF 2009

Sponsor/ Industry/ Country	Event or activity	Reported value (US$ m)	Years	Deal type
1 Rostelecom Telecommunications Russia	Sochi 2014 Winter Olympic Games	260	5	New deal
2 MegaFon Telecommunications Russia	Sochi 2014 Winter Olympic Games	260	5	New deal
3 Aeroflot Airlines Russia	Sochi 2014 Winter Olympic Games	180	5	New deal
4 Rosneft Oil/Petrol Russia	Sochi 2014 Winter Olympic Games	180	5	New deal
5 Omega Watches/Timing International	IOC 2010–2020	80	8	Renewal
6 Gillette Personal care USA	MLB corporate sponsorship	72	3	Renewal
7 Adidas Clothing – Sports France	Olympique Lyonnais	70	10	New deal
8 Anta Clothing – Sports China	Chinese Olympic Committee	70	4	New deal
9 Bwin Gambling/Lottery Spain	Real Madrid	65.85	3	Renewal
10 Carlsberg Drinks – Beer UK	FA	60	4	Renewal

Financing of the Beijing Olympic Games

If the above provides an insight into the way in which sports labour migration and other aspects of global sports trade and finance impacts upon one or two countries through one or two sports, namely athletics in one part of Africa, then what follows is a more detailed insight into the financing of one Olympic Games in one country. In 2008, Beijing held the very first Olympic Games in China. As other chapters in this book illustrate, the hosting of major sporting events is complicated – not all cities, or even countries, can afford to stage

SPORT IN FOCUS 3.3: WORLD'S MOST VALUABLE SPORTS TEAMS, 2009–2010

	Team	Sport	Value (US$ bn)	Revenue (US$ m)
1	Manchester United	Soccer	1.83	459
2	Dallas Cowboys	American Football	1.65	280
3	New York Yankees	Baseball	1.60	441
4	Washington Redskins	American Football	1.55	345
5	New England Patriots	American Football	1.36	302
6	Real Madrid	Soccer	1.32	563
7	New York Giants	American Football	1.18	230
8	Arsenal	Soccer	1.18	369
9	New York Jets	American Football	1.17	227
10	Houston Texans	American Football	1.15	256
11	Philadelphia Eagles	American Football	1.12	250
12	Tampa Bay Buccaneers	American Football	1.09	241
13	Chicago Bears	American Football	1.08	241
14	Denver Broncos	American Football	1.08	240
15	Baltimore Ravens	American Football	1.08	240
16	Ferrari	Motorsport	1.05	308
17	Carolina Panthers	American Football	1.05	238
18	Cleveland Browns	American Football	1.03	235
19	Kansas City Chiefs	American Football	1.03	228
20	Indianapolis Colts	American Football	1.03	233
21	Pittsburgh Steelers	American Football	1.02	235
22	Green Bay Packers	American Football	1.02	232
23	Miami Dolphins	American Football	1.02	242
24	Tennessee Titans	American Football	1.00	232
25	FC Barcelona	Soccer	1.00	513

Note: Values are equity plus net debt.
Source: Forbes.

the Olympic Games. What follows is a fairly detailed discussion of the financing of the Beijing Olympic Games.

Beijing's economy has been growing at a fast pace over the last two decades, reaching an average annual increase of 17.5 per cent in its revenue. There was allegedly a sufficient guarantee for the supply of capital and other resources from the public and private sectors to meet the needs of the Beijing Olympic Games. The investment in infrastructure to support the Games was compatible with the long-term economic and social development plan of Beijing. The Beijing Olympic Committee Organising Group (BOCOG) budget, with its associated guarantees, was aimed at ensuring the success of the Games and provided the basis of the opportunities the Games would bring. A financial guarantee of support for Beijing to host the 2008 Olympic Games was given by the Chinese Central and Beijing Municipal Governments. A copy of this guarantee was jointly signed by the Minister of Finance of China, the Chairman of the State Development and Planning Commission of China, the Director of the Beijing Finance Bureau and the Chairman of the Beijing Development and Planning Commission. The financial guarantee included:

- funding of any BOCOG revenue shortfalls, should they occur;
- pre-financing of all BOCOG expenditures prior to receipt of Games revenue;
- the construction of the infrastructure within Beijing to support the Games; and
- the construction of the venues and facilities required to host the Games.

The Central and Beijing Municipal Governments pledged that consumer prices and hotel rates in and around Beijing would be effectively managed to ensure that prices were fair and reasonable during the Games period. A guarantee to achieve this level of price control had been jointly signed by the Chairman of the State. For the services provided directly by BOCOG via rate card (such as transportation, radio and telecommunications, and rentals of technical equipment and offices), a final price list would be submitted to the IOC for their approval prior to the hosting of the Games. BOCOG assets at the conclusion of the Games would include the furniture, equipment and temporary fixtures purchased by BOCOG for the conduct of the Games. Assets in this category would include items of a practical nature (for example, sports equipment and computers) and items of a memorabilia nature (for example, the look of the Games and ceremony assets). It was anticipated that a significant portion of the items would be disposed of via public tender and/or auction. The funds received from the sale of any assets were to be included as revenue for BOCOG. The sports venues, the Olympic Village, the Media Village and other facilities used to host the Games are owned by the relevant government authorities or private organisations. These government authorities and private organisations are responsible for the ongoing operation and maintenance of the facilities as part of the Beijing legacy.

The current Chinese industrial and commercial tax regime (excluding tariffs and agricultural tax) comprises 17 specific taxes. Of these, the following taxes applied for the hosting of the Olympic Games in Beijing: business tax; value-added tax (VAT); consumer tax; corporate income tax; individual income tax; vehicle and road tax; and stamp duty. BOCOG was legally responsible for civil obligations and liabilities. Under Chinese Taxation Law, BOCOG would be a taxpayer. In support for the Olympic Movement, the Chinese Government promised that BOCOG would be exempt from taxes. This exemption included revenues from the sale of broadcasting rights for the Games, from the Olympic marketing programme, and from sponsorship activities, whether the party that made payments to BOCOG was resident in China or elsewhere. In support for the Olympic Movement, the Chinese Government promised, upon approval by the Legislature, to exempt the IOC and other Olympic participants from taxes otherwise required under Chinese Taxation Law. These would include: business tax and withholding tax on income from the Beijing Olympic Games (for example, income from the sale of television rights); individual income tax due in China for participating athletes in conjunction with various monetary prizes; VAT levied on the proceeds from the sale by BOCOG of sponsored commodities and post-Olympic sale of assets; and reimbursement to BOCOG of the VAT levied on commodities received as donations or sponsorships or purchases for its own use. While the Chinese Government could grant tax exemptions within China, residents in foreign countries were required to pay withholding or similar taxes in their respective countries for payments to BOCOG for media rights, the Olympic marketing programme and other sponsorships. In addition, BOCOG would negotiate with the governments of the countries concerned regarding exemptions for these taxes, if necessary.

The forecast budget for the Beijing 2008 Olympic Games was prepared on the basis of a conservative forecast of receipts and expenditure. The process of preparing the budget included: consultation with the Governments of China, the Beijing Municipality and other relevant local areas; consultation with experts both nationally and internationally for each budget item; detailed review and analysis of the budgets of previous games, particularly Sydney; consultation with the IOC and the Chinese (National) Olympic Committee (COC); and a comprehensive review of the budget process by Arthur Andersen and Bovis Lend Lease, who had specialist knowledge relating to the Sydney Games. The planning and budgeting for the Games resulted in an outcome with little or no risk to the IOC and with significant opportunities for the IOC, Beijing, China and the world. In particular, the projected budget resulted in a surplus and contained responsible contingencies built into each budget item. The Chinese and Beijing Municipal Governments were committed, and had the financial strength to support BOCOG and all other aspects of the preparation for and hosting of the 2008 Games. The Chinese Central Government, Beijing and other city Governments concerned guaranteed that the facilities and venues for the Games would be constructed as scheduled, while the Chinese people would offer full support for the Games. The Games generated significant business opportunities within Beijing and China.

What follows is a summary of the forecast receipts, payments and surplus for the 2008 Games. The projected revenues from the Olympic lottery, the Olympic coin programme and government subsidies have been endorsed by the competent authorities. Written confirmation has been obtained from the IOC on the split of revenues from TV rights and from the TOP sponsorship programme. The revenue from television rights of the 2008 Olympic Games allocated to BOCOG was estimated at US$833 million at 2008 prices, which would be US$709 million when converted to 2000 prices. TOP sponsorship BOCOG was to be allocated a share of approximately US$200 million of the revenue from the TOP programmes, which would be US$130 million. Beijing Organizing Committee for the Olympic Games (BOBICO) approached a number of multinational and large Chinese corporations on the prospect of sponsorships. It was expected to receive US$130 million in sponsorships and services from 10–15 multinationals, large corporations and manufacturers of special equipment. The total licensing revenue for the Beijing 2008 Games was estimated to be about US$50 million. To meet the needs of the Games for various equipment, supplies and related services, BOCOG budgeted US$20 million worth of supplies and services from official suppliers at home and abroad. BOCOG, in consultation and cooperation with the People's Bank of China, which is China's central bank, asked the governing institution to issue 1.5 million gold and silver Olympic coins. This was expected to generate, for BOCOG, revenue of US$8 million. BOCOG, in consultation and cooperation with the State Post Bureau, asked the governing institution to issue Olympic stamps. BOCOG and the Ministry of Finance operated an Olympic Games Lottery between 2001 and 2008. The lottery was expected to generate US$180 million in revenue. BOCOG estimated sales of 7 million tickets at home and abroad, which was expected to generate further revenue of US$140 million. Donations from business enterprises, social organisations and individuals were estimated to be US$20 million. The disposal of assets revenues arising from the disposal of assets owned by BOCOG were estimated to be worth US$80 million. The Central and Beijing Municipal Governments provided BOCOG with US$100 million in subsidies. Revenues from the licensing and leasing of commercial premises in the Olympic complexes, from the leasing of space, equipment and facilities of the Municipal Programme Council (MPC) and the International Beijing Council (IBC), and from the rentals of accommodation in the Olympic Village before and after the Games was estimated to be worth a further US$46 million.

Cultures of capitalism, commerce and sport

The term 'global capitalism' has become commonplace, and there is much to suggest that capitalism is organised on a global basis. Huge sums of money are transmitted across the world on a global basis. Companies do not produce money in one country for export to another country but run manufacturing or other operations in many different countries in different parts of the world. Markets for goods, services, capital and labour are the realities of global capitalism but they also impact unevenly upon people's lives in different ways. The notion of global sport and global capitalism is explored further in Chapter 5 but, for the time being, two points need to be made: (i) that sport is not immune from such realities mentioned above and (ii) that different varieties or cultures of capitalism exist.

There are initially two ways of reflecting about sport and capitalism. The first is to think of capitalism in terms of what it represents as a set of contemporary relationships between people and countries. The truth about sport as a universal creed is that it is also an engine of injustice between nations and peoples. The second is to think of the relationship between sport and capitalism in historical terms. Sport potentially provides a resource of hope for many people and places but it also runs the danger of aligning itself with historical calls proclaiming the principles of equality, justice and the eradication of poverty. Past interventions through sport have not sufficed to make a reality of any of these aforementioned possibilities.

The trends and pressures of contemporary capitalism can seem relentless but it is important to explore alternatives rather than simply assume that any universal model of neo-liberal thinking is the only worthwhile model. At least two major economies are central to any discussion of intensifying international financial competition. Both India and China have developed their position within the global economy through highly unorthodox and interventionist economic policies. In China, privatisation is occurring before democratisation, with China moving towards a closer relationship with globalisation on its own terms – in other words, what has been referred to as creeping towards capitalism with Chinese characteristics. Social, economic and cultural changes have been afoot in China following the

85

perceived failure of Mao's egalitarian socialism in which an understanding of China's own approach to consumerism, Confucianism and communism is only part of the guidebook to making sense of China today. There has been a close East Asian alliance between China and Japan that may eventually wish to challenge any perceived US-led world order. There is dialogue with Tibet, Hong Kong has been handed over and Beijing hosted the 2008 Olympic Games. The awarding of the Olympic Games in many ways encapsulates the challenge that is China, in that the promise and possibilities are framed not in terms of the strengths and weaknesses of communism and capitalism, but the tantalising notion of reconciliation, internationality and wealth limited by divergent views and solutions to issues such as democracy, corruption and rural poverty – problems that, in themselves, are widespread internationally and involve places and spaces that are far beyond the boundaries or borders of China.

The flow and distribution of resources between Europe and Asia resulting from television broadcasting has been subject to criticism by many Asian broadcasters. The way forward, according to Total Sports Asia, is firstly to recognise the unique characteristics of the Asian broadcasting market and facilitate local operators controlling the international sports opportunities that arise out of different parts of Asia. The example of Asian broadcasting is utilised here to illustrate and emphasise the dynamics of sporting capital and the potential of the local in the South to challenge and produce change within broader international sporting opportunities that have traditionally been controlled outwith the South.

Some, such as Nair (2010: 9), go as far as to argue that it is time for Asia to rewrite the rules of capitalism. The triumph of consumption-based capitalism has created the crisis of the twenty-first century: climate change, environmental damage and the depletion of natural resources have all been contributory factors. A Western economic model that defines sporting success and success in general as consumption-driven could be challenged by alternative values coming out of Asia, suggests Nair (2010). Policy makers, she goes on, need to challenge the vested interests of consumption-driven capitalism, not least of which is on the basis that expectations need to be aligned with current constraints under which all societies must operate. The relationship between sport and capitalism needs to demonstrate that issues of capability and inequality are as important as any economic gap. Narrowing that gap requires the gap in capability, as well as the economy to be reduced further.

Most orthodox accounts of the commercialisation of sport illustrate that sport has moved from being a pastime to a business, that sponsorship, branding and commodification are all important in sustaining professional sport on a mixed-economy basis. When sport becomes increasingly commercialised, when it becomes a spectacle, then it is necessary to ask in whose interests it has developed in this way (the sponsor, the spectator or the consumer?) and the extent to which different trends in the quest for excitement can be produced. Corporate executives recognise that sports can satisfy and produce links with athletes, events, teams and places. Commercial sites are often spaces and places where powerful people with financial resources can package certain values and ideals in such a way that sport in a particular form is taken for granted. Commercialisation, as Coakley and Pike (2009: 423) point out, not only leads to changes in the internal structures and goals of certain sports, but also the orientations of those involved in sports. Those who control, sponsor and promote sport generally seek new ways to expand markets and maximise profits. Issues of economic justice, global income inequality and transparency are not always at the forefront for those who are driving the globalisation of commercial sports.

Wheaton's (2005) early accounts of the commercialisation of lifestyle sports is an example of this phenomenon where the author acknowledges that alternative sports (similar to, but not to be confused with, extreme sports) have the capacity to adapt, change, resist and conform in places to the pressures of American capitalism in the form of consumerism and individualism. The global commercial images and alleged interests of alternative sports are invariably controlled by multinational and transnational corporations and media organisations. Even sports such as surfing, which had the potential to create a powerful liberation ethic of individual self-expression, anti-establishment sentiment, emotional attunement to nature and the world and the personal pursuit of pleasure, could not escape from becoming a variant or form of capital accumulation. Yet, as we shall consider later, the commercial model is not the only model of sport to provide for exciting or even pleasurable moments.

The reality of any new relationship between sport and capitalism today would need to acknowledge not only that different varieties of capitalism exist in different parts of the world, but also that sport may be able to contribute, in some very small way, to a better world that aims to realise some form of sporting social justice and a better quality of life for many. If a new progressive global sport, culture and society is to mean anything in the twenty-first century, then it needs to assist with a redistribution of hope for both the hopeful and the hopeless. The acceleration of positive thinking through sport in the new emerging worlds is to be welcomed – not least of which it challenges the consumption-driven dominant Western models of sport.

SUMMARY

The vast sums of money generated by sport in different parts of the world means that the laws of economic competition and sporting competition have an important part to play not just in the organisation and regulation of a specific industry, but also the dynamics of sport within and across cultures and societies. It is perhaps inevitable that, wherever sums of money through sport change hands, questions about economic competition, cost and benefit, impact and value for money will be raised. The political economy of sport is international by nature and is, in part, ruled by the flow of global capital – a breakaway transnational football league might still be a future testing ground for globalised sport.

The globalisation of world sport involves, among other things, issues surrounding the flow of global finance, trade and economics. While avoiding the pitfall of economic determinism, no account of sport, culture and society would be complete without an exploration of the economic dimension of sport. Global trade and finance have spread unevenly between different regions and circles or networks of people. The trade of athletes and patterns of labour migration are not uniform. The flow of finance attached to ownership of football clubs often happens as if national barriers to transborder commerce can be breached at will. This, in fact, is not the case, since states still exercise a significant influence over global trade and finance. In their different ways, all of these insights note that global finance and trends towards economic globalisation represent a key facet of the contemporary world. This may, at times, be exaggerated but the geography of global sport today needs to illustrate that the proliferation of economic transactions may be constrained or limited by many things, but less and less is territorial distance between parts of the world a factor.

Yet, fundamentally, the economics of sport, like economics in general, is about choice and evidence. It is at the heart of decision making; whether it be governments, sports or individuals, they are all faced with making decisions about resources. In this sense, economics is not a subject but a way of thinking, a potential framework, for looking at a variety of issues. It has both a socio-economic and geopolitical relevance to the analysis of sport, culture and society that is very practical in that economic and financial decision making has major consequences, and is therefore an indispensable body of evidence.

GUIDE TO FURTHER READING

Ahlfeldt, G. and Maening, W. (2010). 'Stadium Architecture and Urban Development from the Perspective of Urban Economics'. *International Journal of Urban and Regional Research,* 34 (3): 629–646.

Bridgland, F. (2010). 'Big Men, Big Money: No Holds Barred for the Wrestlers More Famous than Footballers'. *The Sunday Herald,* 18 April: 32.

Campbell, R. (2011). 'Staging Globalization for National Projects: Global Sports Markets and Elite Athletic Transnational Labour in Qatar'. *International Review for the Sociology of Sport,* 46 (1): 45–60.

Morrow, S. (2003). *The People's Game? Football, Finance and Society.* Basingstoke: Palgrave Macmillan.

Pine, N. (2010). 'The Role of Athletics in the Academy: An Alternative Approach to Financial Investment'. *Journal of Sport and Social Issues,* 34 (3): 475–480.

Pope, D. and Schweitzer, M. (2011). 'Is Tiger Woods Loss Averse? Persistant Bias in the Face of Experience, Competition and High Stakes'. *American Economic Review,* 101 (1): 129–157.

Runciman, D. (2006). 'They Can Play but They Can Never Win' *New Statesman,* 29 May: 14–18.

Scottish Journal of Political Economy (2007). Special Edition on the Economics of Sport.

The Sunday Times (2011). 'The Sunday Times: Sport Rich List'. 15 May: 1–15.

Szymanski, S. and Zimbalist, A. (2006). *Handbook on the Economics of Sport.* London: Routledge.

QUESTIONS

1 What key themes have dominated the economics of sport as presented by labour economists?

2 How can sport help us to explain key economic problems and issues?

3 Discuss at least three terms central to understanding the financial and economic development of global sport.

4 What can the data presented in Sport in Focus 3.1 tell us about the economics of tennis in one year?

5   Compare baseball and football as national sporting pastimes. What lessons can be learned from this cross-cultural exercise?

6   The hosting of the FIFA World Cup in South Africa in 2010 was seen by many as a great success not just for South Africa, but for Africa. It has been argued by some that it is unlikely that an African team will win the World Cup in the near future – why?

7   Explain how the 2008 Beijing Olympic Games was financed.

8   Argue against the notion that only two forms of relationship exist between sport and capitalism.

9   Use the information provided in Sport in Focus 3.2 to critically analyse the flow of sponsorship money to some, but not all, parts of the world during 2009.

10 Consider the ways in which global trade and finance affects the provision of sport.

PRACTICAL PROJECTS

1   Select any sport or any club and source the end-of-year financial accounts of the club. Write a short performance analysis of the club's finances using terms such as income, costs, surplus/deficit. What percentage of the costs are attached to (a) staff costs and (b) non-staff costs?

2   Look at the fact sheets that are published by the International Olympic Committee following any major Summer or Winter Olympic Games. Argue for or against the financial success or failure of any one Summer or Winter Olympic Games. Identify at least five key financial facts associated with any games.

3   Select a period of one year and look at the International Athletics Federation Handbook as a basis of analysing the migration of athletes from one country to another. On the basis of what you find, write a 2,000-word account on the key trends and explain some of the factors that give rise to the migration of athletes.

4   Source the annual Global Sports Salaries published by Sporting Intelligence and discuss the top earners, where they play and in which sports.

5   Examine the *Sunday Times* Rich List over a two- or three-year period and comment upon changing trends in wealth distribution (i) between the Sports Rich List and the Rich List; (ii) between sports on the Sports Rich List; and (iii) between athletes on the Sports Rich List.

KEY CONCEPTS

Capitalism ■ Consumption ■ Dependency ■ Development ■ Economics ■ Franchise ■ Globalisation ■ Investment ■ Micro-economics ■ Neo-liberalism ■ Political economy ■ Profit ■ Surplus

WEBSITES

Deloites Football Finance Reports
www.deloitte.com/assets/Dcom-Ecuador/Local%20Assets/Documents/Estudios%20generales/Football%20Money%20League.pdf
A series of annual reports on the finances of world football and some other sports.

Stefan Szymanski Reports on Sports Finance and Economics
http://bunhill.city.ac.uk/research/cassexperts.nsf/RecentPublications?ReadForm&parent unid=2CC5FB92963E1C04802573DA00500532&form=RecentPublications
A source of papers on sports finances and economics provided by one of the world's leading commentators on sport and the economy.

The economy and sports
www.sportanddev.org
A resource that provides information on sport's role in international development.

The International Labour Organization and Sport
www.ilo.org/global/lang—en/index.htm#a2
Use this website to specifically research work on sport sponsored by the International Labour Organization. Place the word sport in the search facility and discover.

A factbook of information on different countries
https://www.cia.gov/library/publications/the-world-factbook/
The CIA world factbook is one of the most authoritative international factbooks about different countries. Use it as a resource to find out necessary background information on different parts of the world.

Chapter 4

Sport, politics and culture

How important has sport been to bringing about change in South Africa?

It is crucial that current and future students and researchers of sport, culture and society recognise the socially situated nature of their work and engage with the future politics of sport.

Sport sometimes creates a space for different countries to talk to one another when other avenues have failed.

PREVIEW

OBJECTIVES

This chapter will:

■ evaluate the relationship between sport, politics and culture;

■ question certain arguments about sport and culture;

■ consider some of the political successes and failures in world sport;

■ illustrate the connection between personal sporting troubles and public issues; and

■ provide examples of some of the future areas of political involvement with sport.

KEY TERMS DEFINED

Community: A social network or group of interacting individuals usually, but not always, concentrated in a defined territory; a human association in which members share common symbols and wish to cooperate to realise common objectives.

Politics: The practice of the art or science of directing and administering states or other political units, or the pursuit of achieving one's goals or outcomes.

State: A distinct set of political institutions whose specific concern is with the organisation of domination, in the name of the common interest, within a delimited territory.

Power: In the most general sense, the ability of a political actor to achieve its goals – see Chapter 15.

Government/Governance: The resolution of conflicts of interest. It can occur at every level in society; it is inherent in social relationships, and needs to be contrasted with the state.

INTRODUCTION

Power refers to the capacity of an individual or group to command or influence the behaviour of others. Power is vested in people who are selected or appointed by a socially approved procedure, is regarded as legitimate and is often referred to as authority. Power may also be exercised through social pressure or persuasion, or by use of economic or even physical force. Sport has not generally been central to the issue of determining the outcome of international power struggles, of who gets what, when and how, but it has made a contribution to a number of successes and failures in international politics.

The social character of political struggles over the past 40 years or more has tended to revolve around issues of class, gender and ethnicity. In other words, the conventional social patterning of the politics of sport has been heavily dependent upon categorical notions of class structure, gender and ethnicity as the main drivers of politics of sport in the West. As Chapter 17 eschews forms of social division and social inequality are both complex and in a state of flux. The twenty-first century involves new tribes and new forms of social inequality that are just as complex as those social patterns that moulded sport in the past.

The politics of sport was given a succinct overview by Houlihan (2002: 212), who suggested that the literature could be divided into two broad schools of thought: (i) politics in sport that direct our attention to the use made by governments of sport and the process by which public policy is made and implemented; and (ii) politics in sport that lead to a consideration of issues concerned with the way in which sports organisations use power to pursue their own sectional interests at the expense of other social groups. Contained within the former group would be themes relating to the role of the state, including issues of sport and national identity, sport and economic development, sport and foreign policy, and the promotion of individual state interests. By contrast, the latter would include an examination of the power of sports organisations in determining the nature of sporting opportunity, an examination of sport both as a source of profit and as a vehicle for the transmission of capitalist values, and issues of equality of access to sport. Both Houlihan (2008) and Coakley and Pike (2009) describe government involvement in sport as having some or all of the following purposes: safeguarding public order; maintaining health and fitness among citizens; promoting prestige and power at different levels; promoting a sense of identity; producing values consistent with dominant ideology in a community or society; support for political leaders and government; promotion of economic development; and serving as a tool of foreign policy. Sport in Focus 4.1 considers some foreign policy themes in relation to the game of baseball.

Very rarely does a relatively recent serving politician or diplomat provide an insider's view into the politics of sport, but Cha's (2009) *Beyond the Final Score: The Politics of Sport in Asia* is such an account, and its greatest single strength is the opportunity that it affords to understand the cultural diplomacy that surrounded not just the spectacle of the 2008 Beijing Olympic Games, but also the broader cultural diplomacy surrounding sport in Asia and between Asia and other parts of the world. At least four arguments are raised in the beginning of the study:

- that sport matters in the world of politics because it can provide opportunities for diplomatic interventions at times when other forms of international relations and mediation are not working;
- that sport provides a popular prism through which nation states can and do present an image or identity to both the rest of the world and their own people;
- that sport can be a facilitator of change within a country; and
- that each of these arguments is extremely relevant as background to understanding the importance of the Beijing Olympic Games to the Beijing authorities.

The analysis of Olympic Games prior to 2008 provides examples of the politics of sport in terms of truces, terrorism, boycotts and bans, both cultural politics with a small p and superpower Politics with a large P. However, Cha's work also looks forward to the London Summer Olympic Games of 2012 and the Sochi Winter Olympic Games of 2014.

93

SPORT IN FOCUS 4.1: BASEBALL IN US FOREIGN POLICY

Governments have used sports deliberately in the service of war and conquest. In the US, for instance, baseball prepped the nation for World War I with its close-order drills at ballparks. Ball players used their throwing skills to train soldiers in tossing hand grenades. Baseball accompanied the endless US military and corporate interventions in the Caribbean and Latin America, including Nicaragua, Mexico, Panama, Colombia and the Dominican Republic – even Brazil, Chile and Argentina. Baseball became a powerful symbol of American involvement in World War II, which took the game to Africa, the Middle East, and South and East Asia.

In its war abroad, Major League Baseball (MLB) International Incorporated became a significant operator in the then emerging era of globalisation, cutting costs by exporting its cheap labour havens abroad. In 2011, MLB offered $1 million in earthquake relief, yet organised baseball and its allied industries made hundreds of millions of dollars on the backs of Haitian workers making balls, apparel, merchandise and other equipment.

According to Albert Spalding, whose sporting goods company was an early supporter of American expansionism: 'The United States has no lands or tribes to conquer but it is only to be expected that baseball will invade our new possessions and [demonstrate] that possession's American-ness'.

Whatever definition of the politics/sport axis is used, it is likely to be highly contested because there has been disagreement as to which aspects of social life are political. The content of, and approach to, the coverage of sport, politics and culture in this chapter emanates from a particular sense of the term 'politics' that eschews and rejects the notion of sport as being separate from the very social forces that influence it. At a bare minimum, sport is not unaffected by social, economic and political activity. The politics of sport is no longer just about whether sport reflects a particular political system, but whether sport should be viewed as a set of values, or as a social movement or political practice.

CRICKET, POLITICS AND CULTURE

At one level, the significance of cricket in social and political terms is no different from any other sport in that it has been shaped and reconfigured by the socio-economic and geopolitical forces that have been operating in different places at different times. The discussion of cricket that follows serves to introduce the significance of the politics of cricket with both a large P and a small p.

Almost 50 years after it was first published, *Beyond a Boundary* (James, 1963) remains a classic example of a study of the politics of cricket and culture. The book is about cricket, but also the West Indies, poverty, being black and colonialism. Cricket is presented as a sport and a metaphor, the property of the colonisers and the colonised. Its originality as a study of the game of cricket was neither as a cricket book nor an autobiography, since it symbolised and expanded a conception of humanity as the West Indies burst on to the stage of world history. The core of the book was the chapter on 'What is Art?' – in which James explores the aesthetic experience of cricket. His idea was to explore the cricketer in action but as an expression of public art in which, in this case, man is placed in his social environment. The cricketer in the West Indies was depicted at the time as a modern expression of the individual personality pushing against the limits imposed upon his or her full development by society. James recognised that an almost fanatical obsession with organised games was not merely an innocent social activity, but also a potential signifier of oppression and liberation. It provided a statement about an expanded conception of humanity, as well as the necessity to break from the colonial legacy that had affected the development of the West Indies at a particular point in time. Non-white cricketers came first to challenge, then to overthrow, the domination of West Indian cricket by members of the white plantocracy. By the 1980s the transformation of West Indian cricket had come full circle – from being a symbol of cultural imperialism to being a symbol of Creole nationalism. Sport in Focus 4.2 provides an overview of the key themes relating to cricket, politics and culture that are depicted in *Beyond a Boundary*.

The politics of cricket have been evident everywhere the game has been played and developed, and the following four examples illustrate that the politics of cricket, in both socio-economic terms and geopolitical terms, has been almost entirely context-specific.

Cricket and Germany

Adolf Hitler played cricket, raised his own team to play British prisoners during World War I, and then declared the game unmanly and tried to rewrite its rules. Macintyre (2010), drawing upon an account by Locker-Lampson, describes how, in 1923, shortly after the Munich putsch, Locker-Lampson met some British officers who had been prisoners of war in southern Germany during World War I. (John Locker-Lampson MP was the founder of the Sentinels of Europe, a blue-shirted group of right-wing activists dedicated to fighting Bolshevism. He was not the only upper-class English Member of Parliament who supported Nazism.) Hitler, then a lance corporal in the German army, was recovering in hospital from his wounds. He asked the British officers whether he could watch a game of cricket and then assemble his own team with a view to a friendly match against the British. Hitler declared the game insufficiently violent for German fascists, and had an ulterior motive for wanting to play the game and alter the rules, which he wanted to be 'Nazified'. Allegedly, he suggested the removal of cricket pads since these artificial bolsters were dismissed as unmanly and un-German. Sport in fascist thinking of the time was merely a tool through which to forge a Nazi mentality. German sport has only one task, declared Joseph Goebbels – 'to strengthen the character of the German people, imbuing it with the fighting spirit and steadfast camaraderie necessary in the struggle for its existence' (Macintyre, 2010: 23) – an approach that would find its full expression in the Nazi Olympic Games of 1936.

95

SPORT IN FOCUS 4.2: THE POLITICS OF CRICKET IN *BEYOND A BOUNDARY*

James's triumph in this 1960s classic was to reinvigorate the values of cricket with a new political energy, not only by beating the masters at their own game, not by changing the game, but by destroying its values and reinterpreting those very values as a vehicle for political change. In summary, it might be suggested that:

■ The originality of *Beyond a Boundary* was more than just a critical study of cricket in the Caribbean in that it symbolised a new and expanded conception of humanity as black West Indian and formerly colonial peoples burst on to the stage of world history.

■ It viewed the contours of Victorian cricket as essentially being the contours of imperial cricket.

■ Victorian cricket reversed the process of transporting aristocratic values and allowed the Indians to assess their colonial rulers by Western values and to find the rulers somewhat wanting. It became important to beat the colonisers at their own game.

■ Cricket is viewed in the West Indies as more than just cricket, but as a form of art, politics and moral philosophy.

■ Cricket is viewed as a privileged site of colonial rule and asks of the colonisers the classic question, 'what do they know of cricket who only cricket know?'.

■ The cricketer was, at the time, a modern expression of the individual personality pushing against the limits imposed on his full development by the mentality of an imperial or colonised society.

■ Cricket and English literature were complementary in that they were viewed as cultural and ideological expressions of the same social order, a bourgeois order grounded in capitalism.

■ The struggle over cricket was a classical struggle over the values associated with the game in a particular context at a particular point in time.

Cricket and Zimbabwe

Beyond a Boundary was the heading of a leading newspaper article on sport and politics that hit the headlines when the English cricket team refused to play a match in Zimbabwe as part of the 2003 Cricket World Cup. Zimbabwe is a former colony to which Britain had clear and stated obligations. In Harare and Bulawayo, where the cricket matches involving England were scheduled to be played, the shortage of fuel had in December 2002 almost paralysed the transport system. Famine threatened the lives of seven million people as a result of

President Robert Mugabe's policies, which included land seizures and repatriation of land from white farmers to black supporters of Mugabe's political party. The International Cricket Board wanted England to play in Zimbabwe for fear of loss of revenue from not playing the game. The country that the England cricketers would have been protected from was the Zimbabwe that saw people sprint from their shacks at the noise of an approaching truck carrying maize meal, the staple diet of the impoverished nation. At the time of the tour, a chronic fuel shortage existed, but a special reserve supply of fuel was to be used to shuttle the cricketers about Zimbabwe. The patron of the Zimbabwe Cricket Board, President Mugabe, would have been given the opportunity to stage-manage the six international cricket matches scheduled to be played. The politics of cricket in Zimbabwe, then, was not just about specific issues of lost cricket revenue, but also land seizures, relations between coloniser and colonised, black and white, human rights and poverty. In the end, the players refused to play, forfeited the points from the abandoned matches and eventually failed to progress to the later stages of the tournament. Furthermore, the almost obscene deafening silences in the academic world over certain aspects of the politics of cricket in Zimbabwe occurred, and still occur in a way that would almost have been unthinkable during the last quarter of the twentieth century or even the era of apartheid sport in South Africa.

Cricket, India and Pakistan

In April 2002, George W. Bush told the Palestinian people that everyone must choose whether they were with the civilised world or with the terrorists. Many people around the world may have recalled Ghandi's famous reply when asked what he thought of Western civilisation – he replied that it would be a good idea. Almost three years later, another Indian leader, Dr Singh, invited the Pakistani President to join him at the New Delhi cricket ground to watch India play Pakistan. In April 2005, speaking after signing a joint peace agreement in the Indian capital Delhi, the two leaders, Manmohan Singh and Pervez Musharraf, agreed that peace between the two nuclear rivals was irreversible. On the same day, the two leaders watched the start of the final day of the one-day international cricket match between India and Pakistan. A match eventually won by Pakistan, a match in which the result had been secondary to the process of attempted reconciliation and internationalism between two nuclear rivals who had fought three wars since partition in 1947.

Yet, the social politics of cricket and other sports in the relationship between the two countries is perhaps more evident in a later event involving the proposed marriage of an Indian tennis player and a Pakistani cricket player. During November 2010, the Indian tennis star, Sania Mirza, and the Pakistani cricket hero, Shoalib Malik, announced that they were getting married. Mirza, once a national heroine after becoming the first Indian woman to break into the WTA top 40 had her sponsorship contract with Cadbury Bournvita cancelled one week after the news of the wedding broke because of the adverse publicity. There were demonstrations in India, where Mirza's picture was burnt by right-wing Hindu nationalists, and yet on the other side of the border there were celebrations in Malik's home town and the marriage was publicly supported by the head of the Pakistani Cricket Board and Miss Pakistan. The former Pakistan prime minister, Nawaz Sharif, suggested that the political differences between the two countries could be resolved through a similar positive approach

97

to relations between the two countries. In India, cross-border marriages, because of the relations between the two countries, are a cultural shock. The decision of the couple to stay in Dubai instead of Pakistan also provides insights into the social and political ties between New Delhi and Islamabad.

SPORT AND THE POLITICS OF CULTURE

The aforementioned discussion of cricket, politics and culture allows for a number of points to be made about sport, politics and culture. The term 'culture' has been associated with sport in a number of different ways, ranging from ideas about culture that tended to exclude sport and other forms of popular culture to more inclusive definitions of culture that have recognised sport as an important purveyor of cultural meanings, values and identities. The relationship between sport and the politics of culture has rested upon some or all of the following arguments: the notion of culture as being defined by a particular definition of the arts that excludes sport; sport as a site of popular struggle between different social groups; sport as contributing to a particular way of life of different subcultures; sporting involvement and consumption as being viewed as a badge of distinction involving the production and reproduction of cultural capital; sport as contributing to forms of cultural policy; sport as contributing to forms of cultural identity; sport as one form of the broader notion of body culture; and, finally, the evolution of sporting traditions, rituals and meanings being best understood from an anthropological approach to culture.

Sport contributes to the politics of culture in a number of ways, and all of these have vested interests and support from different social and political groups.

Sport, cultural policy and the arts

It is significant that nearly all the hostility towards the term is associated with elitist definitions of the word 'culture' that historically have been associated with high/low cultural debates, notably in the arts. High art, in this sense being associated with the word 'culture', has been separated in some way from popular art or other forms of popular culture. The hostility to the artistic notion of culture stems from its exclusivity and association with some sort of intellectual superiority for those who are seen as cultured. At least four points need to be made here:

- An elitist definition of culture often associated with high culture of the arts is one of many notions of culture that exist, but at times it has been a powerful definition of culture that has done sport no favours, despite the fact that sport has contributed to literature, arts and film.
- The word 'culture' here is closely associated with a context in which intellectual growth is fostered within a certain narrow range of classical activities.
- Historically, culture, according to this view, would have little or nothing to do with sport, and the only sports that would be allowed into the academy would be the sports of the elite or the leisured classes.

98

- This is an approach to culture that devalues other forms of culture – particularly those that are not included in this particular definition of culture: working-class culture and some traditional forms of culture.

Within the context of this book, it fails to acknowledge the role of sport in terms of social, economic, human or cultural forms of capital. In this sense, the word 'culture' is used in an artistic, sometimes elitist, intellectual sense and is, for example, completely different from the anthropological notion of culture. The usage of the term 'culture', as described above, is neither neutral nor value-free.

The scope of cultural policy in different parts of the world varies; some policies include sport and some do not. The scope of specific policies also reflects divergent political ideologies. Clear statements of principles tend to govern most cultural policies and these might include the following: for citizens to achieve individual creativity; equality of access to cultural life; to safeguard freedom of expression; to promote cultural pluralism and diversity; to promote a flourishing of cultural life; to support cultural renewal and quality; to preserve and use cultural heritage; and to promote international cultural exchange. Sport as a facet of cultural policy is influenced by values, political perspectives, nationality, attitudes towards the arts, the very definition of culture itself, the issues of access, and the place of sports culture in all of the aforementioned.

Sport power and popular struggle

It became common throughout the latter part of the twentieth century to talk of the transformative or reproductive capacity of sport to bring about change. It was not uncommon for students of sport in society to consider in detail the role of sport as a site of popular struggle. The Gramscian influence upon sports research fired an intellectual and very practical form of intervention that highlighted both the political symbolism and the practical social struggle over sport as a form of popular culture. Popular culture is one of the sites where the struggle for and against a culture of the powerful is engaged: it is also the stake to be won or lost in that struggle.

The impact of this intervention into the politics of sport was that work on sport, power and culture was undertaken for some or all of the following reasons: (i) to consider the relationship between sport, power and culture; (ii) to demonstrate how a particular form of sport had been consolidated, contested, maintained or reproduced; and (iii) to highlight the role of sport as a site of popular struggle and resistance. Struggles over the legitimate use of the sporting body, over times to take part in sport and spaces to play in, all contributed to ongoing debates about the social and political meanings articulated through sport. The major contribution made by this body of work was the due recognition of, and priority given to, the sport, power and culture problematic, and that the politics of sport could not be simply limited to analysis of government and policy intervention into sport.

The notion of culture does not stand still; it is not homogeneous, and other things matter in relation to determing people's lives. The extent to which notions of cultural liberty and freedom figured greatly in 1980s discussions of sport, power culture is relative to the time but they are important in the twenty-first century. Cultural freedom may include the liberty to question past traditions and authority in sport and young people may view it as an important facet of changing their way of life. Cultural liberty is also struggled over when a society does not allow a particular community to pursue a particular sporting tradition or lifestyle and in this sense culture creates or contributes to a sense of captivity rather than freedom or liberty.

Sport, anthropology and identity

Ethnography is at the heart of both a social and cultural anthropology of sport that has moved beyond the traditional cross-cultural study of play, games and sport in non-modern or tribal societies. Anthropological work, in particular, has tended to unpick the complexity of play, games, athleticism, exercise, and sports and the body in different settings. Traditionally, analysis of culture derived from anthropology has tended to refer to culture as a whole way of life, an all-consuming notion of culture in which anthropologists spoke of the cultures of various peoples, the cultural materialism or etymology associated with people or settings, or the evolution of culture in different comparative contexts. Dyck (2000) identifies four specific anthropological themes in his recent overview of the anthropological study of sport.
    These are:

1   how the game is played, in which sociologists *are reminded* that the very terms 'games', 'sports' and 'athletic competitions' are readily distinguishable by their composition, purpose and complexity;
2   sport provides a major venue for displaying the body in public, recognising and exploring the bodily dynamics and attractions of wrestling in India, bodybuilding in America or training the body in China or Japan all illustrate the opportunity for cross-cultural fieldwork into different games and sports;
3   the celebratory and communicative powers of sport are prominent in many ritual or theatrical sporting displays that invoke themes such as nostalgia, memory and the notion of celebrity, which are all constructed differently in different cultural settings; and
4   fieldwork on the issue of boundaries and the way in which sports reinforce, redefine, invent and transgress boundaries and identities.

This has helped to substantiate the way in which sporting differences and similarities are involved in the making of a multitude of social identities and imagined communities. The way in which sport contributes to a form of social and cultural identity has helped individuals address questions about the idea that sport can contribute to different forms of cultural identity has developed alongside the rise of identity politics. In an increasingly impersonal world, sport may help different groups of people answer questions such as: who am I? Who is like me? Whom can I trust? The argument that tends to underlie accounts of sport and cultural identity is that sport, in a positive way, helps with recognition and representation. In my view, such accounts fail to recognise that identity politics on its own is not enough. This can be said without rejecting the idea that sport can provide some genuine insights into understanding aspects of sexism, racism, colonisation and cultural imperialism. It is both

100

theoretically and politically problematic because such accounts of sport and cultural identity tend to reify the notion of identity, and stop short of recognising issues of status and the redistribution of wealth. The way in which sport helps different groups with problems of prestige, status and identity cannot be uncoupled from issues of injustice and the redistribution of wealth in sport.

Sport, distinction and the body

The notion that sport may contribute to the process of distinction and the acquisition of cultural capital has most closely associated with the work of the late French sociologist Pierre Bourdieu. The theory of cultural capital sees culture as a system of symbols and meanings, and derives its analytical framework from notions of social practice and the social reproduction of symbols and meanings. Bourdieu suggests that habitus results from a calculation between opportunities and constraints, and between what is desirable (subjective) and what is probable (objective).The distribution of sporting practices among and between social classes is determined by three factors: economic capital, spare time and cultural capital. Those sports that required a higher or lower degree of economic capital are separated, in part – into those that require property and purpose-built, often private facilities – as opposed to those that are low cost and played in public places. The crucial point here is that some sports may have a certain social currency and become a badge or symbol of social division. For some, participation in sport and physical activity was deemed an important part of their body habitus, whereas, for others, it was viewed as a waste of time.

The relationship between sport, culture and the body has figured in a burgeoning corpus of literature. Some reasons might be given:

- the importance of the body as both a personal project and a cultural project, which has given rise to political economies of the body that ask questions about who owns the body and what cultural tastes and patterns of consumption give rise to the body as being marketed in certain ways;
- feminism and women's control over their own bodies;
- the ageing body and what this means, and how this is presented in different parts of world;
- the leisured body, as opposed to the worked body, and how issues of work hard and play hard have impacted upon the body, both mentally and physically – the notion of why people 'flog themselves to death' in the gym after a stressful day at work might be given as an illustrative example here; and
- the post-colonial body and how the body has been framed and thought about in terms of imperialism, colonialism and post-colonialism, and cosmopolitanism.

There has been a well-documented discussion of culture in both social and political discussions about sport (Jarvie, 2006: 67–72). This has broadly taken two forms of thinking, which may be referred to as epistemological and historical bodies of work about sport, culture and society. The first point refers to the fact that there is/has been a theoretical epistemologically driven debate about sport, politics and culture; the second point refers to the fact that sport continues to play an unprecedented role in contemporary cultural politics. International politics and culture may, at times, seem to be a long way away from the world of sport but, as illustrated above and below, all aspects of social life are considered to be potentially political, and sport is no different from other areas where political power is active. The relationship between sport and the state perhaps should not be the sole or even the central focus of any sport, politics and culture, since such an approach could fail to illuminate new forms of politics that traditional models of politics have tended to, at best, marginalise and, at worst, ignore.

POLITICAL SUCCESS AND FAILURES IN WORLD SPORT

The social and political forces that have forged post-twentieth-century sport wax and wane within the international arena. This international space itself is relatively weak in the sense that only social actors and actions can influence what can be done in sport. The international political space that is available to sport comprises two broad areas. First, there is the geo-political plane that provides the broad parameters by which governments influence the politics of sport within and between national boundaries, and, second, there is the socio-cultural/economic plane that influences the relationship between sport, power and culture. It is necessary to view these two areas or social spaces as being mutually interactive.

Political successes in sport

It is impossible to list all the major or minor political successes and failures in world sport. Sporting activity has been associated historically with political protests that have championed human rights, progressive socialism and social equality. Sport has also been associated with violence, fascism, individualism and strong nation states. The following might be viewed as some of the most significant successes and failures in which the politics of sport has figured over the past 50 years or more. The discrediting of racism in sport and the recognition that sport has been inextricably associated with colonialism have progressed significantly since the late 1960s when the 1968 Mexico Olympic Games witnessed Black Power protests against the condition of black people, primarily (although not solely) in America. The protest drew attention to the denial of black American human and civil rights, but also to the subtle politics of black athletic involvement in world sport. To this might be added the part that sport played in the overthrow of apartheid in South Africa; the role of cricket in the decolonising of the West Indies; and the part played by baseball in drawing attention to imperialism in Cuba.

The post-war argument that sport could benefit within the then advanced capitalist countries through increased expenditure on the welfare state meant that a social welfare approach to sport was adopted in social reformist countries, such as the former West Germany, Sweden, Denmark, Norway, Finland and Holland, to name but a few. The Nordic countries have had a long history of democratic popular sports movements, with their independence being protected in legislation. The organisation of sport in Sweden, for example, has often been heralded as being based upon a model of social welfare and as being more democratic in terms of its organisation. For almost five decades, Sweden has been

SPORT IN FOCUS 4.3: THE SOCIALIST FOOTBALL CLUB

Sports teams are rarely perceived to have political ties, which is why the German football team FC St. Pauli is an unusual case. Based in Hamburg's red-light district, the club is often described as the most left-wing sports team in the world. It is known for making a stand against issues such as racism, homophobia and the commercialisation of football. The club's unofficial emblem is the skull and crossbones, which embodies the fans' punk attitude and has turned it into a 'kult' club not just in Germany, but also throughout the world.

For much of its history, St. Pauli was a club like many others, originating in a working-class dockland area and with an unspectacular record on the field. However, in the political unrest of the early 1980s, the club went through a transition. The surrounding neighbourhood became an area of left-wing politics and counter-culture. Many of the new locals began to support St. Pauli and, in time, the club's culture changed to reflect the political movement in the district.

In a move to oppose the right-wing, neo-fascist hooligan culture spreading through European football during the 1980s, St. Pauli officially banned right-wing nationalist activities and displays at their stadium. They also launched anti-racism and anti-homophobia initiatives. Over the years, the club has continued to champion good causes. In 2006, while the rest of Germany hosted the FIFA World Cup, St. Pauli hosted the Wild Cup. This was a tournament of unrecognised nations, giving non-FIFA nations such as Tibet and Gibraltar the chance to play international football.

St. Pauli also stands against the commercialisation of football and attempts to operate under socialist principles. While rivals Hamburg earn millions from stadium naming rights, St. Pauli have pledged never to change the name of the Millerntor Stadion.

Some argue that St. Pauli's refusal to accept the commercialisation of German football has left it at a disadvantage. According to former club president Corny Littmann, the club has almost €30 million less to spend in the 2010/2011 season than its league rivals. Furthermore, manager Holger Stanislawski recently stated, 'St. Pauli can't afford to be a social utopia anymore'.

However, despite this, the club is not quite the downtrodden underdog it is perceived to be. St. Pauli was promoted back into the top division for the 2010/2011 season. Moreover, some critics claim that the club has sold out on their socialist policies. The club has a large sponsorship deal in place with German car maker Dacia, and, according to sports marketing agency UFA Sports, it sells $8.6 million worth of merchandise each year to its 11 million worldwide fans.

Undoubtedly, St. Pauli will carry on supporting good causes, and the skull and crossbones flags will continue to fly in the stands. However, it remains to be seen if St Pauli can maintain a hard-line political stance on finances in the cut-throat and commercialised world of twenty-first-century European football.

known for its social welfare model that has been a hypothetical compromise between communism and capitalism. In practice, it has meant far-reaching government involvement in the private sphere fuelled by a strong conviction that social engineering can achieve the kind of justice that the ruling political party holds to be the ultimate truth. One of the main characteristics is the assumed duty of politicians not only to alleviate poverty, but also to redistribute wealth, including the wealth generated from sport, across Swedish society. The feminist movement questioned and partially transformed male leadership of movements for liberation and equality in which traditional gender roles remained unchanged. One of the areas of conflict and struggle is funding for women's involvement in sport, exercise and physical activity. Sports policy in Canada during the 1990s, in many ways, gave a contradictory message to women in that, while supporting the development of a set of structures aimed at addressing and rectifying gender inequality in sport, the federal state also legitimated the ideology of masculine superiority by continuing to provide more funds and sporting opportunities for males than for females. The feminist movement might be viewed as one of the left's successes both in sport and international social relations. However, its impact in sport has been uneven across countries and more work needs to be done in several parts of the world, notably Africa, China or the Islamic world.

The use of sport as a sanction to publicise human rights violations has led to attempts to isolate or draw attention to human rights records, such as those in Iraq, Nigeria and Chile. In the mid-1990s, several members of Iraq's national football squad alleged that Uday Hussein, the son of the then Iraqi leader Saddam Hussein, ordered them to be tortured after they lost a World Cup qualifying match 1–0. The players claimed they were locked in cells beneath the headquarters of the Iraqi Olympic Committee and beaten on the soles of their feet. FIFA investigated the allegations, but concluded that Iraq could remain in FIFA. In 1995, Nigeria was subject to sanctions because of its violation of human rights. Between 1974 and 1976, Israel was excluded from the Asian Football Confederation. The politics of Israeli sports remain under-researched. Kidd and Donnelly (2000), Giulianotti and McArdle (2004) and, more recently, Jarvie et al. (2008) explored the contribution that sport has made to the struggle for human rights. The aspirations for democracy and liberation evoked under the banner of human rights cannot be achieved without human rights in sport. The Sports Act in Finland came into force in 1998 and stated that the purpose of the Act was: (i) to promote equality and tolerance and to support cultural diversity and sustainable development of the environment through sport, (ii) to support recreational, competitive and top-level sports and associated civic activity, (iii) to promote the population's welfare and health; and (iv) to support the growth and development of children and young people through sport (Kidd and Donnelly, 2000: 145).

The struggle between nations as a war without weapons and within certain nations over blood sports and the broader relationship between humans and animals has witnessed some successes through, for example, the ban on hunting with dogs in some countries. However, blood sports have had a long history and it is open to question as to whether this has formed political success or political failure given the resurgence in interest among the right. The history of blood sport has a very wide meaning. In the Mayan game of *pitz* (Feffer, 2010b), one of the first team sports in human history, two sets of players squared off in a ball court that could stretch as long as a football field. The object of the game was to use hips and elbows to keep the ball in the air and, if possible, get it through a hoop set high on a stone wall. The ball was roughly the size and heft of a human head. Indeed, given the sheer number of decapitations in the *Popol Vuh*, the sacred Mayan text that prominently features the game, scholars have not ruled out the possibility that the teams sometimes played with the heads of sacrificial victims. It is also probable that, at the conclusion of the game, one team or the other fell *en masse* beneath the priests' daggers. *Pitz* was intimately connected to the religious rituals of the Mayans. But it was also a re-enactment of war. Team sports faithfully reproduce the conditions of a battlefield: two irreconcilable foes, displays of courage and endurance, team loyalty as a form of tribalism or nationalism, the veneration of winners and the castigation of losers. Were the Mayans especially bloodthirsty in their combination of play and sacrifice? No more so than Romans egging on the gladiators at the Coliseum. It was not that long ago that we dispensed with ritual re-enactments and treated war as a spectator sport. In July 1861, Washingtonians took their picnic baskets out to Bull Run stream in Manassas to take in the show and root for one side or the other. (Today, partisans cheer the home team from the safety of the living room, and TV networks are generally careful not to show too much carnage to ruin the evening meal.) Sports and war have long had an intimate connection. The marathon was born during the Greek victory over the Persians at Marathon in 490 BC, when a Greek messenger allegedly ran 25 miles to Athens to announce the victory. The biathlon – skiing and shooting – began as training for Norwegian soldiers. Boxing, fencing and martial arts all bring hand-to-hand combat into the sporting world. Like *pitz*, the Olympics are a ritual re-enactment of battle, where nations compete for gold and glory, and it invariably involves the spilling of blood.

Sports have been bloodied by their association with politics. But politics, too, has become a blood sport. Like *pitz*, what goes on inside the sacred ring known as the beltway is a fight to the death between two opposing teams. A Republican siding with the Democrats has become as unheard of as a Yankees pitcher striding over to the Red Sox dugout and offering to throw a few for the other side. Team loyalty is absolute. If you don't vote the party line, the party will sacrifice you in the next elections.

To return to a more contemporary context of blood sports, in one part of the UK – England – the pro-hunting lobby has often appealed to the civil liberties argument on the basis that the freedom to choose one's recreation may be seen as one of the modern jewels of democracy. Liberty, it is agreed, is a vital principle, but this does not mean carte blanche to do as one pleases, for it should always be tempered by respect for others, or even the wishes of the majority. Contemporary debates relating to the relationship between animals and humans have raised the issue of the feelings and thoughts of all living beings, not just humans. For example, in the classical English fox hunt, does the fox's opinion matter? If so, it would surely choose to be somewhere else than at the heart of an ancient recreational pursuit that involves the killing of foxes. Does the fox have a right to a civil liberty as a living being, or is this simply the preserve of the human world? While the left has been quick to condemn certain blood sports on the grounds of animal rights, it has, in part, failed to justify policies on angling and other popular sports.

Political failures in sport

If the aforementioned are illustrative of some of the contemporary political successes or partial successes involving sport, then equally a number of failures need to be mentioned. The capacity for violence has been fatally underestimated by the left, and the association between right-wing groups and violence in sport imploded throughout the 1980s as rampaging football hooligans left their mark on the football landscape. Russell (1997) has suggested that football may well have played an important part in popular Tory Britain of the late twentieth century in fashioning middle-class perceptions about working-class Britain. Attempts by clubs to deal with football hooliganism of the 1980s and 1990s were reported with heavy political rhetoric of the right about law and order, social class and the 'English disease' – football hooliganism. Football, according to the *Sunday Times*, was 'a slum sport played in slum stadiums and increasingly watched by slum people who deter decent folk from turning up' (Taylor, 1987: 171–191). By the same token, the violence associated with anti-hunt marches aimed at pressurising British political administrations to ban blood sports failed to halt the violence associated with fox hunting, at least in England, since the Watson Bill (www.scotland.gov.uk/library2/doc16/bhwd-02.asp) that banned hunting with dogs in Scotland. This was one of the first pieces of legislation passed by the Scottish Parliament that came into being in 1999. The violence associated with animals is much more than just the issue of fox hunting, since it may also be associated with many other areas, such as horse racing on the flat and over jumps, or eventing, showjumping and polo, or greyhounds in coursing, or fishing, to name but a few sports in which animals are viewed as either performers or prey. A succession of left- and right-wing coalition and majority governments in Britain has struggled to contain violence in sport.

The rise of a powerful individualism, which had little or no respect for mutual ownership or cooperation in sport, has led to an extreme individualistic sports culture, but also to the decline in social capital and civic society, which Putnam (1995) called 'bowling alone'. Putnam used the notion of social capital to comment critically upon the process of what he called civic disengagement from American life. By this, he referred to the decline in participation, not just in formal political activity, but also in all kinds of social activities, including sport and physical activity. The decline of social capital allegedly included decreasing membership in voluntary organisations, decreased participation in organised activities, and a decrease in time spent on informal socialising and visiting. Americans were viewed as becoming less trusting of one another, with a close correlation existing between social trust and membership of civic associations. The late twentieth- and early twenty-first-century legacy of the New Right's *Kulturkampf* (cultural battle) has changed the values of the public domain and contributed to the formation of a culture of distrust that has tended at times to corrode the promise of citizenship, equity and accountability in sport. For every volunteer or sports worker delivering a service, there seem to be numerous administrators, agencies or otherwise looking over their shoulder to check their work. The implosion of communism in the 1990s may be viewed as a negative turn on an epochal scale for both non-communist as well as communist sport. The planned sports systems collapsed, sporting nations were reconfigured and absorbed into primarily Western, global or American sports configurations. Different forms of corruption mediated sporting practice and, as such, agents' control of athletes, the development of international sports manufacturing on the back of child labour and the sexual exploitation of young high-performance athletes have all continued to be part of an international sporting world that is in need of social, if not ethical, direction and leadership.

It might be suggested that while, traditionally, sport has always been viewed as an avenue of social mobility for some of the world's most talented athletes, the gap between rich and poor throughout the world remains a chasm between the wealthy and the not so wealthy. For example, Hari (2002: 24) reminds us that poverty is plainly a factor in the formation of what have become labelled 'feral children', the right-wing press's term referring to some of the most disadvantaged kids in Britain who have been raised without family support or without homes in urban inner-city housing estates. Kids Company is a responsive network set up in many of Britain's inner cities that aims at helping these children. Talking of these kids, Hari (2002: 25) reports, 'It's not like these kids want much, they only ever have one pair of trainers, not five, but it is not unreasonable for them to want one pair'.

For poor British kids, many areas are desolate, shrinking amounts of public space with no leisure centres; children who might once have played in parks, fields or even streets now have nowhere to go. While middle-class parents may deal with the absence of public space for their children through the consumption of expensive hobbies or clubs or buying houses with gardens, these are not options available to other children. The relative success of projects designed to help children in inner cities such as Birmingham lies not in any one social solution, but in a range of social networking by disenfranchised agents working outside the mainstream provision that solely identify with the needs of these children. Sport has effectively failed the poor and, as yet, the transformative potential of sport in many of the poorest parts of the world has not been fully realised.

Each of these sketches of some of the political successes and failures in world sport is far from exhaustive, but they serve to illustrate that the politics of sport is not just present in and between states, but also in markets and, most importantly, in social patterns or groups. It is within a triangle of states, markets and social patterns that political ideas about sport gain ascendancy and political action occurs (Sport in Focus 4.4). The following example illustrates the interaction of the state, markets and social patterns in Kenya, notably gender. Lornah Kiplagat and Lina Cheruyiot, two of Kenya's women athletes, have spoken openly about the personal troubles of exploited and mistreated young women athletes in Kenya who have to struggle against not only *market exploitation* by commercial shoe companies, or *state control* over the issue of passports, which make it difficult for a young girl athlete to travel to international competitions, but also the 'macho' culture or the *social patterning* of Kenyan society.

C. Wright Mills (1970) identified the sociological imagination as the comprehension of history and personal biography, and the relations within the two in any given society. By this standard, when one seeks to examine a particular aspect of social life such as sport, it is necessary to make a sustained effort constantly to relate personal biographical concerns in sport to broader public issues in culture and society. The above example from Kenyan athletics illustrates that one of the enduring hallmarks of the politics of sport has been the acknowledgement that many personal sporting concerns may transcend the level of personal sporting biography to become more of a public issue. Maria Isabel Urrutia is another

107

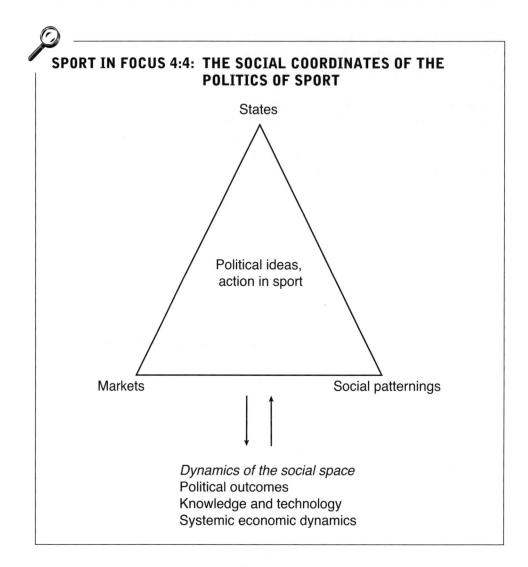

States

Political ideas,
action in sport

Markets   Social patternings

Dynamics of the social space
Political outcomes
Knowledge and technology
Systemic economic dynamics

international female athlete, who won a gold medal in weightlifting at the Sydney 2002 Olympic Games. She was not only the first ever South American woman to win an Olympic gold in 100 years, but also the winner of Colombia's first ever gold medal. Urrutia was born into a family where 9 of the 14 children died before she began her athletic career. The town in which she was born was chosen by chance, since it was then the only public hospital in the country that could deliver babies free of charge. Commenting on her Olympic victory, the athlete hoped that her success would reach out to others exactly like her: poor, black and female. She went on:

> as a poor person I hope others see that you can make a living, see the world and get an education through sport and that girls who are now 13 realise that they do not have to become teenage mothers.

The challenge to students of sport is to be able to recognise their own moral commitment to the normative component of the political perspective and then, through disciplined enquiry, test the evidence against the political or social assumptions to reform or confirm our beliefs as best we can.

TWENTY-FIRST-CENTURY POLITICS OF SPORT

Any speculative forecast about post-twentieth-century politics of sport must acknowledge the enduring dynamics of the capitalist system, and accept that it is crucial to move beyond the polarised debate of left and right in sport, since any modern radical politics of sport can no longer be viewed in simple terms, such as socialism versus capitalism or identity politics. It should be noted that newly emerging forms of politics might coexist with traditional ones rather than replacing them. The old political issues of sport's contribution to issues of employment, inequality, poverty and identity have not disappeared; they have to compete for social and political space with life politics, environmental politics, and fundamental non-Western cultural expressions through sport.

The social space occupied by the politics of sport historically has tended to be associated with distinct social categories or social patterns, such as class, gender or ethnicity, or the interaction between some or all of these factors. The dynamics involved in the politics of sport, particularly those associated with social categories or patterns, might be better thought of in the following continua: irreverence – deference and collectivism – individualism (Sport in Focus 4.5).

Irreverence and deference refer to existing inequalities of power, wealth and status in sport, while collectivism and individualism refer to high or low degrees of collective identification and organisation. The twenty-first century is much more irreverent as a result of the declining power of deferential class politics associated with amateur and imperial sport. Traditionally, the sporting left in the West has tended to be driven by the irreverent collectivism of the socialist working-class or anti-imperialist movements, while other radical progressive currents for women's rights or human rights have been, by comparison, more individualist in character. The traditional sporting right tended to be institutionally collectivist, while liberalism (both old and new) leaned towards deferential individualism – deferring to those of allegedly superior status. In other words, a culture of deference and colonialism was reproduced both within and between sports. One of the major characteristics of any post-twentieth-century politics of sport in the West has been the relative erosion of previously strong forms of traditional deference, religious as well as socio-political.

Deference has eroded in some societies and cultures, while in others it has become more fundamental. The decline of erstwhile authority has given rise to other forms of fundamentalism that are not irrelevant to post-twentieth-century sport, politics and culture. In February 2003, a football team from Baghdad, Al-Nafid, made a trip to opposition-controlled Northern Iraq, where they were to take on Irbil, the top Kurdish team in Iraq's national league. To reach Irbil, the Baghdad players had to travel across a reinforced Iraqi frontline, past freshly dug army trenches and up into the mountains of Kurdistan. Prior to the game, they expressed their complete support for Saddam Hussein in the war against

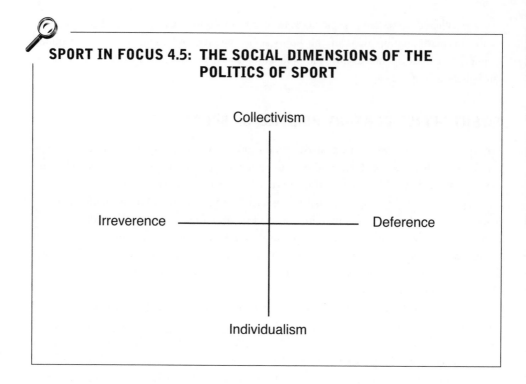

SPORT IN FOCUS 4.5: THE SOCIAL DIMENSIONS OF THE POLITICS OF SPORT

American and British imperialism and the then-impending invasion of Iraq. Baghdad's 20-year-old goalkeeper, Saif Aldin Zaman, explained that 'we love President Hussein', while Mista Qalan, a defender, said 'we will fight to the death' (L. Harding, 2003: 1). Before running out on to the pitch Al-Nafid players broke into several chants of 'we don't want a war' and 'we give our blood, our blood for our Saddam' (L. Harding, 2003: 1). The Kurdish home crowd appeared at kick off to have forgotten the traditional enemy, Saddam Hussein, since they broke into long a series of anti-Turkish songs in protest against an American-backed plan that would involve thousands of Turkish troops pouring into Kurdish Iraq. Most ordinary Kurds now regard the Turks as more of a threat than the Iraqi army. On the other hand, having lost the game 1–0, Zaman was sanguine in defeat: 'we have good relations with the Kurds . . . we are not fighting them anymore' (L. Harding, 2003: 2).

The grip of patriarchy too has been significantly loosened as women's rights and questions of gender equality have come onto the sporting agenda virtually everywhere in the world. What might be termed the social modernisation of sport, resulting from economic change, education and players having more control over their labour, has meant that many different kinds of deference have been eroded, affecting not only women and young people, but also other significant social groups. One element of this erosion of deference has been the struggle over new forms of rebellious collectivism. Indigenous peoples have organised in defence of their rights, including the protection of cultural rights, such as traditional sports and pastimes.

In some senses the challenge to contemporary sport comes not from the West, but from many of the post-colonial re-evaluations of sport. Perhaps the political field of the future will contain more elements of life politics in sport around issues of health, exercise, extreme sports, ageing, or environmental issues, the impact of sporting tourism in different parts of the world or, alternatively, the impact of technology. The latter and, in particular, the power of the media have raised questions about public order controls and public service communications, as well as control over sporting outcomes.

The study of sport, politics and culture is not an exact science and it must be remembered that the twenty-first-century politics of sport is slightly more than a decade old. That being said, in the immediate future, say the next 5 to 15 years, the following concerns are likely to impact upon any sporting politics:

- sport and poverty;
- human rights and aid in sport;
- sporting irreverence and identity;
- post-colonial sport;
- sport and the environment;
- lifestyle politics;
- sport and corruption; and
- hosting of major sporting events.

One final point that needs to be addressed in both this and the next chapter is the way in which the politics of sport is influenced by the idea of global politics. Chapters 5 and 7, in particular, elaborate further on global sport, global governance and global politics. In drawing this chapter to an end, it is beneficial to provide an endnote on sport and global politics. One of the arguments supporting the idea of globalisation is that an emerging global polity is evolving that involves transnational, social and political movements, and the beginnings of a transfer of allegiance from the state to sub-state, transnational and international bodies. The Ryder Cup golf tournament between Europe and America is but one example of the way in which sport supports a transnational European Sports development that helps with promoting allegiance and recognition to Europe. The migration of sportspeople across continents means shifting patterns of sports personnel and trends that have implications for centres and peripheries.

Any contemporary idea of global politics involving sport should acknowledge that, if technology can provide a physical infrastructure for global sport, then politics – ideas, interests and power struggles – can provide a normative infrastructure for global sport. The global politics of sport necessitates an attention to the fragile way in which international or transnational political processes provide some sort of order to sport or fail to be governed at all. At best, global politics of sport helps to distort the relationship between forces of statism, cosmopolitanism and/or internationalism. Sport is not immune to questions about the changing nature of political communities in today's world. It is recognised as having an important part to play in international interventions in areas of need. Many of the poorest countries in the world continue to defy repeated attempts by international communities to provide sustainable help. Sport has historically been used as a key facet of humanitarian aid and a proven avenue of social mobility for many athletes from developing countries. The real development and global political challenge remains one of closing the gap between a rich world and a poor world in which some of the world's poorest people – the bottom billion

111

– face a tragedy that is growing inexorably worse. Projects such as Peace and Sport are targeted at parts of the world such as Haiti, which have experienced some of the issues alluded to above (www.peaceandsport.org). Helping the bottom billion remains a key challenge facing the world and the question is whether sport and global politics have a part to play. It is a question that is addressed in Parts 2, 3 and 4 of this book.

SUMMARY

Sport in certain parts of the world might not be defined as a social democratic system, but the promise of sport might be that it can be an inspiration, a way of being, a manner of acting based upon both democratic and social values. The politics of sport, then, is all that bears on the attempt to order sporting relations, and is not simply limited to the conventional approach that encompasses the everyday processes of involvement in sport by politicians, parties and parliaments – important as this may be. The value of such an approach is that it helps individuals understand that the social and political dimensions of sporting activity can reveal how personal troubles within sport are, in fact, related to broader public issues. The basic idea is that sporting involvement and practice is not value-free, but involves complex interactions, not least of which are the dynamic relations of power between states, markets and social patterns. Sport has always been an arena in which various social actors and groups can actively rework their relationships and respond to changing conditions as a whole. The resources to do this have invariably been uneven, both between and within different groups and sports. There is no single agent, group or movement that can carry the hopes of humanity but there are many points of entry or engagement into a debate about sport that offer good causes for optimism that things can get better. It is crucial that current and future students and researchers of sport, culture and society recognise the socially situated nature of their work and engage with the future politics of sport.

GUIDE TO FURTHER READING

Cha, V. (2009). *Beyond the Final Score: The Politics of Sport in Asia*. New York: Columbia University Press.

Featherstone, S. (2011). 'Late Cuts: C.L.R James, Cricket, and Postcolonial England'. *Sport in History,* 31 (1): 49–62.

Feffer, J. (2010). 'Blood Sports'. *Foreign Policy in Focus,* 5 (14) April: 1–8.

Gilchrist, P. and Holden, R. (2011). 'Introduction: The Politics of Sport, Community, Mobility and Identity'. *Sport in Society,* 14 (2): 151–159.

Jarvie, G. (2008). 'Sport as a Resource of Hope'. *Foreign Policy in Focus,* 18 August: 1–8.

Kietlinski, R. (2011). 'One World One Dream? Twenty-first Century Japanese Perspectives on Hosting the Olympic Games'. *Sport in Society,* 14 (4): 454–465.

Levermore, R and Beacom, A. (2009). *Sport and International Development*. New York: Palgrave Macmillan.

New Statesman (2009). 'Alex Ferguson on Football Politics and Much Else'. *New Statesman,* 22 March: 20–24.

Shor, E. and Yonay, Y. (2011). 'Play and Shut Up: The Silencing of Palestinian Athletes in Israeli Media'. *Ethnic and Racial Studies,* 34 (2): 229–247.

Therborn, G. (2001). 'Into the 21st Century'. *New Left Review,* 10 (May): 87–111.

QUESTIONS

1 Why is the notion of power important to the politics of sport?

2 What does the term 'global politics' imply? Is it relevant to sport today?

3 The politics of sport in Asia outlines four ways in which sport and politics are related – what are they?

4 Explain the role of baseball in US foreign policy.

5 What have been some of the key political successes and failures in sport?

6 Explain the politics of cricket in two different settings.

7 What social dimensions make aspects of sport political? Answer using two illustrative case studies.

8 Are personal troubles linked to public issues and, if so, to what extent might these relationships influence any future politics of sport?

9 What areas are likely to be the focus of any politics of sport in the near future?

10 Comment upon the ways in which sport in politics today might be viewed as global.

PRACTICAL PROJECTS

1 Carry out a content analysis of the political party manifestos in your country of residence. Explain the importance of sport to the political parties and, where possible, compare the different political approaches to sport.

2 Design a strategy or 10-point policy aimed at increasing the involvement of one of the following in sport:

    (i) women;
    (ii) a specific minority group of your choice;
    (iii) the poor; or
    (iv) the elderly.

3 Find out how much money is spent on sport in your country and the rationale for spending that money on certain sports and activities.

4 Examine the process by which any four presidents of any four national sporting bodies get appointed or elected and write a 1,000-word report on sport and democracy based upon the evidence.

5   Listen to the content of the opening addresses of any major world sporting event and compare this with the coverage of main reasons for hosting the event in the national newspapers. Write a 1,000-word report on the politics of the event.

KEY CONCEPTS

Community ■ Colonialism ■ Cosmopolitanism ■ Cultural policy and identity ■ Development ■ Global politics ■ Power ■ Popular struggles ■ Public issues ■ Racism ■ Social patterning ■ Statism ■ Welfare state

WEBSITES

European Football Players Union
www.fifpronet.com/
FIFPro is the worldwide representative organisation for all professional footballers.

The Centre for Sports Policy Studies
www.physical.utoronto.ca/Centre_for_Sport_Policy_Studies.aspx
Access to campaigns, projects and publications involving the University of Toronto Centre for Sport Policy development and advocacy.

The International Olympic Committee
www.olympic.org/ioc
The official website of the Olympic Movement contains a number of valuable sources of information about Olympism in sport.

Political Studies Association Sports Group
www.sportpolitics.net/
The dedicated Political Studies Association runs a specialist politics of sport sub-group. You can access the annual conference presentations and overviews through this website.

When politics enters sports
http://blogs.reuters.com/sport/2010/05/05/when-politics-enters-sports/
A debate about politics and sport that draws upon US basketball as the focus for discussion.

ONLINE RESOURCE CENTRE

Visit the online resource centre that accompanies this book to access more resources.

Part 2

Sport, globalisation and other communities

INTRODUCTION

The six chapters that form the second part of this book examine the notion of global sport and, in particular, the national, international or global and post-colonial contexts and debates about sport, culture and society. The first theme at the heart of this section is whether we should think of the world as one place or many and, consequently, one global sports product or process, or many sports products or processes, including the national, international, local and global. The second important theme within this section is the issue of power and governance and who is or should be involved in influencing the world of sport today. Globalisation and reactions to it illustrate the uneven distribution of power in today's world of sport. Part 2 explores some of the broader implications and reflects upon some key normative issues that may be posed for sport, culture and society. The power of sport itself may be limited but the combination of what sport and education can deliver should not be dismissed.

Global sport and globalisation

The study of global sport has been examined from the point of view of the processes involved in the move towards something called global sport. The characteristics of global sport have included the changing rates of migration of sports personnel; the transfer of sports finance on a global scale; the delivery of sport through the media on an international scale; the exchange of ideas about sport throughout the world; the emergence of transnational sports organisations; and the extent to which sporting tastes and cultures have moved across national boundaries to be consumed in different corners of the Earth. An understanding of globalisation is central to an understanding of the changing nature of contemporary sport, culture and society. While global sport has been documented and discussed at length, less has been said about anti-globalisation or globalisation in the future. To what extent is sport part of the challenge to global sport? To what extent is global sport myth or reality? The coverage of global sport in Chapter 5, therefore, is inclusive of these questions but also how we should make sense of global sport today.

An important dilemma is the extent to which sport is viewed primarily in global terms or international terms, and this provides the focus of attention in Chapter 6.

Internationalism, reconciliation and sport in the making of nations

Has the emergence of global sport weakened national and international sport? Does sport have a role to play in developing national identity or is it a substitute for political nationalism? It has often been assumed that the latter has, in fact, been the case, and that the increasing influence of global sport has meant that national sport has been affected. The increasing international or cosmopolitan nature of sport brought about by, for example, the migration of athletes across national boundaries has resulted from the realisation that the contemporary sports world is a smaller place, but also from the focus of sport having, in part, shifted from the national to the international and global arena. Perhaps it is more appropriate to talk of international sport and not global sport? Chapter 6 critically assesses the notion of nationalism and international sport and rejects the idea that sport should simply be thought of in global or local terms. On the issue of identity through sport, it is suggested that it is not identity that countries and individuals are seeking through sport, but recognition and, in some cases, reconciliation. This provides an ideal link to Chapter 7, which extends further a discussion of sport in other communities.

Sport, community and others

The extent to which Western sport, power and influence have been challenged and, indeed, viewed as part of the problem within many non-Western nations has raised a substantial post-colonial critique of sport, culture and society. Non-Western sporting concerns are raised throughout this book, but are the particular focus of Chapter 8. If colonial sports history was the history of sports involvement within the imperial appropriation of the world, then post-colonial sports history must be concerned with certain peoples of the world appropriating sport for themselves. This chapter initially focuses upon the relationship between sport and post-colonialism by considering three questions; what, when and how is post-colonialism associated with sport? It is generally acknowledged within this chapter that historians and geographers have carried out much substantive work that has uncovered and re-interpreted the colonial influence upon sport. Post-colonial sport is not Third World sport. The disadvantages of the term 'Third World' have been well documented in terms of its hierarchical relation to other worlds. The International Amateur Athletics Federation has stated that its aim is to remove cultural and traditional barriers to participation in athletics, which may imply that indigenous practices and culture may be viewed as something that has to be removed in order that Western forms of athletics and sport might take their place. The post-colonial critique draws upon a broad range of areas as a basis of effective political intervention. If the role of the student or scholar is to uncover the contest, to challenge and defeat an imposed silence and the normalised quiet of unseen power, then post-colonial sport and the role of sport in humanitarian terms must have a much louder voice in the world today. At the very least, the orthodoxy of global sport must be more progressive and humanitarian in terms of its governance and mode of arbitration.

Sport, law and governance

Is there a crisis of confidence in global sport? What possibilities are there for adopting a more inclusive approach to corporate sporting governance? How can and should sport be regulated? Is sport above the law, and to what extent should sporting governance being influenced by sport's own court of arbitration? In relation to the debate about global sport, the challenge facing the world of sport is whether such a notion can be sustained, given (i) the influence of corruption that has influenced the development of international sport; (ii) that sporting governance occurs at so many different levels that it is rarely coordinated or seen to be committed to international justice or social reform; and (iii) the power of European and American models of professional sport and the issue of whether non-Western forms of sport can modernise and become powerful players in the international arena while at the same time holding on to values, beliefs and traditions that are perhaps not governed by Western values. To what extent can the law help to embrace those other communities discussed in Chapter 7?

Sport, media and television

One of the major power players in sport today remains the media and, in particular, television and the changing rates of commercialisation associated with mediated sport. Sporting spectacles dominate television in many parts of the world. The timing of major world sports events is influenced by peak viewing times for different countries around the world. Terms such as 'old media' and 'new media' are now readily used in relation to their specific influence upon sports, culture and society. But what do the terms mean and what exactly is the scope of their influence? The media, in many ways, have colonised sport and, as a result, sport at various levels has become dependent upon media rules, but without completely losing its separate identity. The emergence of private media has provided sport with wider exposure. Tools for developing financial solidarity have emerged in Europe, as witnessed by the UEFA Champions League system. European institutions have taken measures to ensure that, inter alia, free broadcasting of major sporting events is limited. Perhaps one of the greatest challenges facing sport today is the extent to which sport participates, obtains a stake within the media and is not simply the passive recipient of media politics and policy. Indeed, society needs to exercise oversight and control over the media system and its mode of communication, for the dangers of one-dimensional politics, society, football or any other sport are all too evident. At the same time, the media that profit from sports need to take more responsibility for promoting grassroots sports and its important social and educational role. This, in part, links to a much broader discussion of the relationship between sport, education and social capital in Chapter 10.

Sport, social capital and education

Education is often viewed as a key element in not only transforming societies, but also a right for all. Education is often deemed a key to social mobility and social capital. Education for all was adopted by 160 countries as a Millennium Development Goal.

Education and sport, and education through sport, are often hidden but indispensible tools in reaching marginalised groups of people. We often hear of the contribution that sport can make in terms of producing economic capital but what social capital can be built or sustained through education and sport combined? It is argued that it is unrealistic to expect sport to sustain a notion of social capital or civic engagement without addressing certain issues such as education for all. Is it about ensuring that all people are equipped to discharge the duties and exercise the right of citizenship and democracy? The importance of education through sport was recognised by Europe when it dedicated 2004 as the European Year of Education through Sport, but what about other parts of the world? Does sport have a role to play in transforming the prospects of those whom education currently fails or cannot reach? It is the power of sport and education combined that is deemed as an important resource of hope – a theme that is taken further in Part 4. Sport, social capital and education is the final chapter in Part 2.

Chapter 5

Global sport and globalisation

Is sport truly a global phenomenon and what values are associated with global sport?

Has the axis of world sporting power shifted within Asia?

OBJECTIVES

This chapter will:

- explore the notion of global sport;
- critically evaluate the myth and reality of globalisation;
- consider the emergence and characteristics of global sport;
- ask whether the global era has ended;
- consider some alternatives to the notion of global sport; and
- question the notion of globalisation as being an appropriate term to describe the development of international sport.

KEY TERMS DEFINED

Cosmopolitan: Composed of people or elements from all parts of the world or from many different spheres.

Development: A multidimensional process that normally notes a change from a less to a more desirable state.

Globalisation: A historical process involving a fundamental shift or transformation in the spatial scale of human social organisation that links distant communities and expands the reach of power relations across regions and continents. Often used to describe a single world economy, although sometimes employed to define the growing integration of the international capitalist system.

Internationalisation: The term is used to denote high levels of international interaction and interdependence. The term is often used to distinguish the position from globalisation. The processes of internationalisation are often shaped by inter-state and transnational agreements.

Neo-liberalism: Represents the re-assertion of the classical liberal concern to promote the maximum possible liberty and/or economic efficiency. Developed in the 1970s, it advocates measures to promote economic development, and is used to guide the transition from planned to market economies in former communist countries.

INTRODUCTION

The term 'global sport' and the associated processes of globalisation are not uncommon within discussions of contemporary sport, culture and society. This has tended to take place at two levels: the extent to which the globalisation of sport itself has occurred, and the extent to which sport makes a contribution to other globalisation processes. The existence of world satellite information systems, global patterns of sports consumption and consumerism, and the emergence of global sports competitions such as international tennis matches, the Olympic Games or other international sports tournaments have all contributed to the idea that the world of sport is more of a single entity. Such a notion tends to overlook the complexity of international sport that is, in itself, both historically variable and multidimensional. It is one thing to say that sport x is the most popular sport in the world and has increased its international presence, and another to say that sport x is global. Can you think of a truly global sport or product that exists in every country of the world?

One of the obvious objections to both notions of global sport and globalisation is that it is but a buzz word to denote the latest phase of capitalism. It is important to point out that discussions of global sport, while accepting that there are powerful reasons for viewing globalisation as a new phase of development, also need to recognise that globalising forces are not all necessarily either good forces or progressive forces. Not everybody has a voice in global sport and although many valuable studies of sport have tended to revolve around a comparison between the local and the global, few, if any, studies of global sport have considered the parochial versus the global or the parochial versus the international. The debate over global sport covers many relevant aspects and issues that illuminate aspects of contemporary sport but the criticisms of global sport today also need to be seriously addressed. The radically uneven distribution of power and voice in sport today often makes for a distorted politics of global sport in which the interests of the few more often than not take precedence over the interests of the majority.

It is difficult to deny or challenge the fact that the world has become a smaller place or that the sports clothes people wear or the relentless coverage of sport on television has helped to evoke the idea of global sporting products or experiences. However, it is meaningless to equate the sporting experiences of young women in Cuba or Afghanistan with those of a teenage American or German. The experiences are as similar as they are different. In other words, in order to understand the sporting world of these young people, it is necessary to resist the temptation to treat sporting experiences as if they were even or universal or equal. There is little evidence to suggest that even American sporting forms have become global. On the other hand, one of the world's most popular international sports, football, while increasing in popularity within the US, is still of secondary importance to other sports inside America. The notion of global sport, therefore, is difficult to define as a product since it is not homogeneous or universal, and consequently those who have attempted to explain the emergence of global sport have tended to refer to the process or development of global sport. It is hard to miss the powerfully inclusive ideas of belonging and quest for recognition that moves so many people to challenge what they see as unfairness or corruption in contemporary global sport. On a broader level, the anti-globalisation critique is perhaps one of the most globalised moral movements or social network operations in the world today. It is necessary, therefore, to consider some of the current criticisms of global sport and globalisation while, at the same time, recognising the promise and possibilities of sport.

The term 'globalisation' has been poorly defined, often meaning different things to different people. In particular, it is often unclear whether people are dealing with globalisation in all its forms or whether they are referring to economic or political or cultural, or all three aspects of it. Globalisation is the process by which interaction between humans, and the effect of that interaction, occurs across global distances with increasing regularity, intensity and speed. Much of the debate about globalisation gives the impression that the process is relatively new, and yet most analysts tend to agree that globalisation has, in fact, been under-way for centuries. Some go as far as to say the era of globalisation has ended, while some argue that global forms of inequality are increasing.

Possibly the central argument has been whether globalisation actually promotes or produces economic well-being throughout the world. Its critics argue that its emergence is one of the key causes of increases in poverty and inequality. The volume of research on global sport produced by Maguire (1999, 2005) and Jung Woo and Maguire (2009) helps to provide an overview of some of the key questions that face researchers attempting to explain global sport. They may include those already outlined in Chapter 1, but also the following:

- Are globalisation processes one-dimensional or multidimensional?
- What is the main dynamic behind globalisation in terms of monocausal or multicausal factors?
- Does globalisation lead to unity, a perception of unity or fragmentation?
- Are globalisation processes intended or unintended?
- To what extent does global sport actually exist?
- Does globalisation make world sport more or less democratic?
- Is global sport merely Western imperialism in a new form?
- Is sport a globalising or anti-globalising force in itself?

One of the most popular arguments supporting the notion of global sport has been the increasing global media coverage of international sports events, such as the Olympic Games. But a closer examination of the content of television coverage of events may suggest that the commentary is based upon not so much internationality as nationality and forms of subtle cultural nationalism. Television companies such as the American networks traditionally have attracted viewers to their Olympic coverage by stressing political controversies, along with asserting national interests and symbols. The globalisation of sport has often been closely associated with economic interests, and the differences between national interests and identities, and corporate interests and identities, are often blurred and contradictory.

It would be misleading to suggest that the notion of globalisation remains unchallenged. For those on the left, the sharing and cross-fertilisation of different sporting cultures is something to be celebrated. Sporting culture is richer, more diverse and caters for different lifestyles and tastes. Those on the right tend to argue that globalisation poses a threat to traditional, in particular national, sporting heritage, and it has weakened the position of national or even local sporting traditions that have been marginalised, at best, and eradicated, at worst. There has also been opposition from other parts of the world; they argue that the notion of global sport in terms of the governance of world sport tends to conceal traditional Western, or even colonial, power bases that need to be replaced by representatives of a post-colonial world of sport.

SPORT IN FOCUS 5.1: THE GLOBAL NATURE OF FORMULA ONE

The table below shows the circuits used in each round of the 2012 Formula One season. The races are split across five separate continents. While there is a concentration of circuits in Europe, with the exception of Africa the circuits are well spread across the globe. This displays the global appeal of the sport.

Round	Circuit	Grand Prix	Continent
1	Bahrain International Circuit, Sakhir	Bahrain GP	Asia
2	Albert Park Grand Prix Circuit, Melbourne	Australian GP	Oceania
3	Sepang International Circuit, Kuala Lumpur	Malaysian GP	Asia
4	Shanghai International Circuit, Shanghai	Chinese GP	Asia
5	Korean International Circuit, Yeongam	Korean GP	Asia
6	Istanbul Park, Istanbul	Turkish GP	Europe
7	Circuit de Catalunya, Barcelona	Spanish GP	Europe
8	Circuit de Monaco, Monte Carlo	Monaco GP	Europe
9	Circuit Gilles Villeneuve, Montreal	Canadian GP	North America
10	Circuit of the Americas, Austin	United States GP	North America
11	Valencia Street Circuit, Valencia	European GP	Europe
12	Silverstone Circuit, Silverstone	British GP	Europe
13	Hockenheimring, Hockenheim	German GP	Europe
14	Hungaroring, Budapest	Hungarian GP	Europe
15	Circuit de Spa-Francorchamps, Spa	Belgian GP	Europe
16	Autodromo Nazionale Monza, Monza	Italian GP	Europe
17	Marina Bay Street Circuit	Singapore GP	Asia
18	Suzuka Circuit, Suzuka	Japanese GP	Asia
19	Buddh International Circuit, Greater Noida	Indian GP	Asia
20	Yas Marina Circuit, Yas Island	Abu Dhabi GP	Asia
21	Autódromo José Carlos Pace, São Paulo	Brazilian GP	South America

WHEN DID GLOBAL SPORT START?

Sport in Focus 5.1 considers some contemporary evidence from one sport and asks whether this sport is global.

Globalisation is not a new phenomenon. The process of globalisation has been ongoing throughout human history but the rate of progress and effects of certain actions have accelerated and decreased the process at various periods in its development. Critics of globalisation insist that the process and development of global sport has neither been created completely, nor has it produced a world that may be defined by rampant free markets or passive nation states. Some have suggested that, although the global era may not have been completely created, it has come to an end as the more local, fundamental and international forces such as the United Nations or religious fundamentalist groups increasingly assert their influence today. Maguire's (1999: 75–94) classic study and discussion of the complex process of development of global sport identifies five stages in what is more specifically referred to as phases of global sportisation, none of which are historically concealed periods of time. They rather refer to phases of development, some of which may overlap at the edges of the beginning and ending of certain phases. This simply asserts that processes of development do not suddenly stop at one period and begin at a certain date, but are more fluid in the transition from one phase to the next. It remains the most comprehensive study of global sport.

Phase one refers to an initial sportisation phase from about the 1550s to the 1750s, during which many of the antecedent folk origins of modern sport emerged alongside the incipient growth of national communities. The initial sportisation process involved the emergence of sport as a form of physical combat, primarily in England, not Great Britain or Alba or Ancient Caledonia, or other ancient societies. Phase two refers to the period from about the 1750s to the 1870s when the processual nature of sportisation involved the formation of voluntary associations or sports clubs. The patronage bestowed upon sports such as cricket, boxing, folk football, fox hunting, association football and rugby led to a calming down of violence compared to the previous period, as well as a spurt in the shift towards modern male achievement sport. Folk games became less widely practised. Phase three refers to the period from about the 1870s to the 1920s, when the diffusion of English sports and pastimes to continental Europe also involved the export of the amateur ethos and notions of fair play. These commingled with other European forms of achievement sport. The last quarter of the nineteenth century witnessed the international spread of sport, the growth of competitions between national teams, the establishment of international sports organisations and the international acceptance of rules. Phase three, in essence, entailed the differential diffusion of sport and the emergence of inter-state competition between nations. Phase four, from 1920 to 1960, is when, according to Maguire et al. (2002: 365), sport can be seen to have become a global idiom. English-speaking peoples dominated international sporting governing bodies. Non-Western peoples not only resisted and re-invented forms of Western sport, but increasingly challenged the Western domination of global and/or male sport. The further phase Maguire refers to as a period from about 1960 to 1990 is a time when Cold War Olympic politics between capitalist sport and communist sport diminished with the collapse of the Berlin Wall and the fragmentation of the former Union of Soviet Socialist Republics (USSR); women secured further changes and recognition in world sport; former colonial nations defeated the former colonial masters at their own game, as evidenced by the West Indian dominance of world cricket in the 1960s and 1970s; Anglo/Euro and American control of global sport was challenged, with African and Asian countries securing more power in FIFA and the IOC; and a resurgence of European traditional sports and games served as a reminder that residual forms of sport in different parts of Europe have a strong traditional base – in Catalonia, France, Germany, Belgium, Switzerland, Ireland, Spain and Switzerland, to name but a few places where there is a strong regional/national affinity for indigenous forms of sport. All this can be alluded to without forgetting the global power of the media and the mass consumption of international and local sporting tastes and preferences.

GLOBALISATION: WHAT IS IT?

Globalisation has been described, at one level, as the widening, deepening and speeding up of world interconnectedness. Sceptics of global sport would not regard global inter-connectedness as evidence of globalisation and, therefore, the key issue remains the extent to which the term is understood and/or accepted. Realists, liberals, Marxists and construc-tivists all testify to having different theories of globalisation. For realists, while an increasing interconnectedness between economies and societies might be a trend, it does not, for realists, alter the most significant feature of contemporary global organisation, namely the territorial division of the world into nation states. For liberals, globalisation undermines realism since it undermines the role of the nation state. The increased interconnectedness between societies is both economic and technological, and has advanced to such an extent that it is impossible to view nation states as concealed units, but rather to see them as part of a cobweb of social relations. Marxists argue that globalisation may be the latest stage in the development of international capitalism in which global forms of inequality are increasing rather than decreasing. Finally, for constructivists, the act of intervening or moulding globalisation provides a great chance to create cross-national social movements aided by modern technology and social networking. They argue that other theories underestimate the possibilities that exist to shape globalisation.

The term has been used to reflect the compression of the world and the intensification of the world's consciousness as a whole. The term has become ubiquitous because there is no agreed definition of its meaning. This, in part, explains the extent to which it has figured within many international public debates, including debates about the nature and ethics of international sporting organisations and the power of international sporting finance to determine sporting practices, such as the timing of Olympic competitions or World Cup finals, or where major sporting events are placed. There is little point in seeking to deny the fact that global capitalism has affected the way sport is administered, packaged and watched, but this has not been an even process. For some, globalisation and global sport is nothing more than neo-liberalism and equates to market forces controlling sport, minimising the role of the state in terms of sports provision and inequality within sport being non-problematic. Critics of this agenda denounce global sport and globalisation as being a vehicle of global exploitation that has produced sports goods on the back of cheap labour, helped to maintain global poverty levels and maintained different levels of inequality in sport, particularly in terms of access of women and ethnic minority groups to positions of power in global sport.

There are primarily two competing approaches to globalisation. One encompasses a community of human citizens and is worked for, for instance, by environmentalists who talk in terms of thinking global and acting local. The other is of an unregulated free market where capital is king or queen and international corporations leave the poor to struggle with the consequences of deregulation, privatisation and international plundering. Proponents of globalisation typically argue that we live in an age in which a new kind of international world has emerged, one that is characteristic of global competition for markets, consumers and culture. A facet of the free-market driven form of globalisation has been that markets have decided whether we will have pensions in our old age, whether people suffering from ill health in Africa will be treated, and what forms of games and sports will be supported or even whether certain regions will have football clubs or not.

It is worth asserting at this point that globalisation is a highly uneven set of processes whose impact varies over space, time and between groups. Global forces and many international sports bypass many people and places. In many localised parts of the world, the development of sport is for local or national consumption and not for global or international consumption. Even within many international sporting cities or places where sporting mega-events are held, certain neighbourhoods within these cities or places where poverty or disadvantage prevail will, at one level, remain peripheral to the event itself and, at another level, to the working of the international sporting economy. It should be recognised that the current situation of social and economic disadvantage in many parts of the world has been triggered on a macro scale by the actions of transnational corporations based in a city or place often on the other side of the world. The uneven penetration of global sporting markets and sports is not simply a question of which sporting institutions, industries, people and places are affected, but how they are affected. The unevenness of globalisation and global sport is, therefore, apparent at all levels of society and culture. Sport in Focus 5.2 attempts to outline some of the key characteristics of globalisation and sport.

LEVELS OF CONTEMPORARY GLOBALISATION

Functional descriptions of global sport have a tendency to isolate particular elements of globalisation processes without relating them to one another. In what follows, the relationship between sport and globalisation is articulated at a number of different levels, but very rarely do these levels operate in isolation from one another. Ultimately, any strategy that is aimed at producing change needs to be unitary and totalising in nature rather than being fragmentary and locked into a form of dualism that views globalisation as simply good or bad, monocausal, deterministic, or in terms of the relationship between core and peripheral nations within the global economy. At a minimal illustrative level, globalisation can be articulated at the level of politics, culture, economics, technology and society.

Political globalisation

Political globalisation might refer to the increasing number and power of international sporting organisations that influence or govern international sport. Prime among these bodies would be the International Olympic Committee (IOC) or the Fédération Internationale de

SPORT IN FOCUS 5.2: SOME CHARACTERISTICS OF GLOBALISATION AND SPORT

- Globalisation and sport is not a new phenomenon. The processes of sports globalisation have been ongoing throughout human history, but the rate of progress and effects have accelerated since at least the 'early modern' period of the late sixteenth century.

- Globalisation involves both an intensification of *worldwide* sporting relations through time–space compression of the globe, and local sporting transformations involving enhancement of local sporting identities, as well as of *local* consciousness of the world of sport.

- In the global–local sporting nexus, global forces are generally held to be most powerful and their control more spatially extensive.

- Global sporting forces are mediated by locally and historically contingent forces as they penetrate downwards, coming to ground in particular places.

- A number of 'trigger forces', such as technology and social networks, underlie sporting globalisation but the dominant force is generally regarded to be economic.

- Globalisation reduces the influence of national governing bodies of sport.

- Globalisation through sport operates unevenly, bypassing certain institutions, people and places. This is evident at the global scale in the disparities between booming cities of sport and declining sporting regions.

- The differing interests of actors means that global sporting forces are sometimes embraced, resisted or exploited at lower levels.

- The mobility of capital diminishes the significance of particular sports places, although it may also strengthen local sports identity by occasionally engendering a defensive response by local actors.

Football Association (FIFA). Alongside these increasingly genuine world sporting organisations might be the establishment of a number of national or continental sports organisations, such as the European Traditional Sports and Games Association or the American Baseball Association. The very spread of international sports organisations can also be seen as a response to the process of political globalisation whereby the types of problems confronting national sports organisations can no longer be addressed locally or nationally. Political globalisation is seen in arrangements for the concentration and application of power in sport.

In discussions of globalisation at the political level, one question that has tended to predominate has been that of the nation state. What kind of national autonomy do nations and national sporting organisations or cultures lose under any contemporary or new world order? Is it really not merely a new kind of domination or colonisation? In particular, when the term globalisation is used contemporaneously, are we not really referring to the spreading political and economic power of the US or China? Are we not really discussing the subordination of nation states indirectly or directly to American or Asian power? Discussions of global sport rarely acknowledge the existence or impact of any international order or hierarchy of states that make up the globalised interdependent world in which we live in. Not all cities can be Olympic cities, not all regions want to or have the capability to compete or host international sporting mega-events and, even if they did, power in world sport is still exercised by the few. More generally, in the place-bound daily lives of ordinary sportspeople, particularly those outside the mainstream of global sport or advanced capitalism, global sport may promote a search for local identity in a mobilised international world. This element of sport in an internationalised society is considered further in Chapter 6 and one of the key issues is the extent to which the principles of international order reflect the contemporary reality of globalised states.

Economic globalisation

Economic globalisation refers to the increasing occurrence, speed and intensity or production of trading and financial exchange across national boundaries. This includes the trading of sports personnel and, for example, increasing rates of labour migration within and across national boundaries. Indeed, economic globalisation might be taken to refer to a series of linked phenomena that have emerged over the last 30 years or more. The increasing flow of sporting finances would include the international flow of finance brought about as a result of trading of players, prize money and sporting endorsements. Economic globalisation is seen in arrangements for the production, exchange, distribution and consumption of sport. The underlying assumption that supports the reality of globalisation is that the pace of economic transformation and, in some cases, recession has been so great it has created a new world order in which states cannot control their economies and the world economy is more interdependent than ever. While some have tried to define globalisation as simply time–space compression, others prefer to refer to it as the integration of the world economy.

Globalisation as a force is, in varying degrees, evident in all the principal sectors of social activity, including sport. In the economic sphere, patterns of worldwide trade, finance, production, governance and labour migration are all supporting at least an international, if not global, capitalist economy. The operation and control of sporting finances and the informal and formal sporting economy contributes to which countries are sporting winners and which countries are sporting losers. Such a principle has led to such questions as when an African nation will win the FIFA World Cup. Economics and technology remain key engines of global sport.

Cultural globalisation

Cultural globalisation refers to the growth and exchange of cultural practices between nations and peoples. Many researchers point to the way in which new technologies, such as commercial television, the Internet and other forms of mass communications, have created a world that increasingly consumes identical products. The Internet is central to democratic international cultural exchange in that shared sporting interests and enquiries can be accessed internationally between people involved in sport. Thus, there are now specific sports websites and email networks that individuals from different cultural backgrounds share, which represent facts, meanings, beliefs, preferences, tastes and values. Sport itself has been viewed as a cultural product that lies at the heart of the telecommunications attempt to attract international audiences. Cultural globalisation is also seen in arrangements for the production, exchange and expression of sporting symbols. Patterns of cultural globalisation are complex, given the international diffusion of culture, global media networks and social networks. Few cultures, if any, are hermetically sealed off from cultural interaction.

Social globalisation

Shifting patterns of migration from North to South, East to West to East, from peripheries to centres have turned patterns of migration, immigration and social welfare into a major global issue. Movements of sporting personnel and patterns of labour sports migration from place to place are not immune. Patterns of global income inequality also impact upon sporting choices and options for some people. There are several main concepts of global sporting inequality, all of which have social consequences. Furthermore, sport has been identified as a powerful and cost-effective tool to help achieve international development goals, including the Millennium Development Goals that aim to eradicate or reduce poverty, hunger, child mortality and disease, and to promote education, maternal health, gender equality, environmental sustainability and global partnerships by 2015. SportAccord, the umbrella organisation for all Olympic and non-Olympic international sports federations, recently established a sports social responsibility agency. It would seem that an increasingly recognised obligation of some international sports agencies is to care for society.

Sport in Focus 5.3 is illustrative of five different cultural, social and/or economic flows that may help to characterise the development of contemporary globalisation processes: ethnoscapes, technoscapes, financescapes, mediascapes and ideoscapes. All these processes develop at different speeds and have impacted upon global sport at different rates.

CHALLENGES TO GLOBALISATION

While global sport, as illustrated in this chapter, may have developed as a result of different stages of development, it has also been suggested by Gray (2001: 25) that the era of globalisation has come to an end. The dozen years between the collapse of the Berlin Wall and the al-Qaeda attack on the twin towers of the World Trade Center in New York on 11 September 2001 might have marked the end of an era. The West greeted the collapse of communism – though it was itself a Western utopian ideology – as a triumph of Western values. The end of a way of life was welcomed as an opportunity to further develop a global free market. This part of the world was to be made over in an image of Western modernity – an image deformed by a market ideology that was as far removed from any human reality as Marxism had been. Following the attacks on New York and Washington, the conventional view of globalisation as an irresistible historical trend seems to have changed. It may be that

SPORT IN FOCUS 5.3: GLOBAL SPORT – FLOWS AND PROCESSES

- Sporting ethnoscapes might involve the migration of professional or non-professional sports personnel through player, manager or coach transfers.
- Sporting technoscapes would include sports goods, equipment, landscape-building for golf courses and transporting of sports technology, which is now a multi-million pound business.
- Sporting financescapes refer to the global flow of finance brought about through the international trade of players, prize money, endorsements and sporting goods.
- Sporting mediascapes refer to the sports–media complex that transports sport across the globe at different times in different countries, and delays events and recordings to suit viewing times of international and national audiences.
- Sporting ideoscapes are bound up with the ideologies or philosophies expressed by, in and through sport: professionalism, amateurism, sport for all, liberal notions of integration, and critical notions of exploitation. All these different ideologies compete in the battle for how world sport is, should be or could be.

we are back on the classical terrain of history, where international conflict is waged not over ideologies, but over religion, ethnicity, territory and the control of natural resources. The attempt to force life everywhere into a single mould was bound to fuel conflict and insecurity. Perhaps if sport is to develop a greater degree of social currency, then the notion of international sport should be considered in place of global sport, not least because the values associated with global sport and globalisation seem to have melted down as sporting markets, as well as financial markets going into free fall during the economic recession that occurred during 2008.

Certainly, a number of alternatives to the notion of global sport have emerged more recently. These are outlined in more depth in subsequent chapters within Part 2, but also Parts 3 and 4. These alternatives are not exhaustive but several are worth briefly introducing at this stage.

Global or international sport

Some have argued that it is necessary to distinguish between international and global sport. Are the Scottish Highland Games and gatherings that take place in different parts of the world examples of global sport or international sport, or something else altogether? There is the international and/or North American image that is presented through magazines such as *Celtic World*, which continues to report and carry stories of the Scottish Highland Games to all corners of the Celtic world and beyond. It is, in many senses, an image that contributes to an international or Celtic image of the Scottish Highland Games. If you visit the Scottish

Highland Games 2010 website, you will be promptly transported to Scottish Highland Games in Waipu, New Zealand (1871); the Auckland Highland Games and Gathering (1980); Turakina Highland Games (1856); Highland Games Sychrov – near Prague (2001); the Tri-Annual Highland Gathering at Leeuwarden (1998); the Hengelo Scottish Games – Netherlands (2002); and the Highland Games Association of Western Australia. The language and appeal of these activities now extends around the world. The web pages of the Highland Games Association of Western Australia receive daily hits from many corners of the globe in a way that would have been unthinkable 10, 20 or 30 years ago. All of these developments are testament to the place of traditional and non-traditional Highland Games as perhaps being international, although not a global form of culture.

Is FIFA a global organisation? FIFA is undoubtedly one of the most powerful sporting organisations in the world. It controls world football and is comparable with the IOC as one of the most influential world sporting organisations. The growth of the game is such that it is estimated that, globally, the football industry is worth US$250 billion annually, which means that it has a higher financial turnover than companies such as Mitsubishi or General Motors. If you look at the FIFA website, the organisation talks of FIFA as being the governing body of the world's most popular sport, a game played by some 200 million people throughout the world. It has more than 200 member organisations, more than any other sports organisation, including the International Olympic Committee. It talks of football moving millions on all continents; its emblem is two stylised footballs in the shape of the globe – the symbolic quotation 'of a global fraternity united in sport'. FIFA is supported by a worldwide spread of confederations that include the AFC in Asia, CONCAF in North and Central America and the Caribbean, CONMEBOL in South America, UEFA in Europe and OFC in Oceania. Contracts for the rights to televise the 2002, 2006 and 2010 World Cups are such that television viewing in poorer regions such as parts of Africa and Asia is distributed free of charge, whereas special fees are charged to the wealthier nations of the world.

What is being suggested here is that much of the debate about global sport has tended to accept the idea of globalisation as, at least, an inexorable free-market process, which is best characterised through use of the term 'globalisation'. It might be suggested that the term 'internationalisation' is equally appropriate, if not more so, given that patterns of labour migration in sport have become increasingly international without specific trends developing along regional rather than global lines. As such, the terms 'global sport' and 'globalisation' need to be employed very carefully because of their analytical value in helping to portray a more reality-congruent picture of sport today.

The core issue is whether globalisation, and therefore global sport, can be regarded as having any defining contemporary order and legitimacy. There is reason for scepticism about globalisation as the exclusive hallmark of any contemporary world order. Rather than refer to one global order, it may be more reality-congruent to refer to global sport as being made up of an international order of globalised states. If it can be convincingly proven that global sport is not some entity that overrides the activities of states, and that globalisation is but an element of state transformation, then the notion of a globalised state can take precedence over globalisation. By extension, the notion of a more or less globalised state does not make redundant the notion of an international sporting order, or indeed an international order. Consequently, we arrive at the notion of an international sporting order consisting of globalised states that may provide a better normative framework for thinking about sport today. What might be distinctive about sport today is a merging of old and new international sporting orders in which the constituent actors are more or less globalised states.

Global or anti-global sport

There is considerable evidence of resistance to globalisation. We should acknowledge that the values associated with globalisation and global sport have been subject to pressures for change. The movement for global change is most commonly referred to as an anti-globalisation or anti-capitalist movement. Other terms that are sometimes associated with oppositional threads to globalisation are 'anti-free trade' and 'anti-imperialist'. Some have argued that this movement emerged in Seattle in the mid-1990s as a result of protests against the World Trade Organization and the International Monetary Fund. Others maintain that it began more than 500 years ago when colonists first told indigenous peoples that they were going to have to do things differently if they were to develop or be eligible for trade. Whatever the point of origin, the privatisation of every aspect of life and, in particular, the transformation of every activity and value into a commodity has resulted in a number of oppositional threads that have taken the form of many different campaigns and movements.

There are two competing concepts of anti-globalisation, one termed 'radical' and one termed 'moderate'. The radical wing views globalisation as a process largely designed to ensure that wealthy elites become wealthier at the expense of poorer countries. It would argue, for instance, that globalisation undermines the working conditions and pay of sports personnel in wealthy countries, while at the same time exploiting cheap sports labour in other parts of the world. The radical wing sees transnational corporations as the main cause of the problem, in that they have so much power that international sporting organisations undermine the power and decision making of national governing bodies of sport. Furthermore, it is suggested that indigenous sporting cultures have been threatened as a result of global sport or capitalist sport, which has tended to market uniform sports products across the globe. Whereas, 20 years ago, children in local communities might have worn the sports gear of local sports teams, children today tend to wear more uniform sports brands such as Nike. The view expressed here is that globalisation, as a process, is fundamentally flawed and immoral.

The moderate wing, although more difficult to define, tends to share the view that globalisation has the potential to be good or bad. It has the potential to provide for a sharing of cultures paid for out of the economic growth provided by free trade, but because the institutions and rules that govern the world are currently controlled by wealthy elites, then inequality, instability and injustice are inevitable. In a sporting context, a corollary of this might be to argue that traditional cultural rights and sporting traditions need to be at least equally recognised as socially and culturally, if not economically, as important as market-supported forms of commercialised sport. For the moderate wing, the solution to many of the above problems lies with reforming the institutions that govern world sport. Many non-Western countries are sceptical about anti-global or social movements that are rooted in the West.

SUMMARY

There is no single theory of globalisation or global sport. The idea of globalisation and global sport has become the source of intense political dispute. Perhaps the central argument in terms of globalisation has been the extent to which it promotes economic well-being throughout the world. For its proponents, the spread of free trade encourages enterprise, economic growth, jobs and wealth creation. For its critics, globalisation is seen as a key cause of rises in poverty and inequality. Global sport, like globalisation, operates unevenly, bypassing certain institutions, people and places. The impact of globalisation processes upon sport is one of the core areas of investigation and reflection in sport, culture and society. The way in which global sport seems to be changing has been the subject of heated debate. For its proponents, the sharing and cross-fertilisation of different sporting cultures and tastes is something to be celebrated. For its critics, global sport is seen to undermine traditional sporting heritages of nations that are key to people's sense of their belonging, and these have been undermined by the commingling of diverse sporting tastes and forms. Indigenous sporting cultures have been replaced by market-driven sport that can be sold in the marketplace or prove to be popular to television viewers.

The term 'anti-globalisation' has been associated with a movement for global change that is an extremely loose network of individuals and campaigning organisations seeking to transform the way in which globalisation is proceeding. Moved by the thesis that global relations are primarily anatagonistic and adversarial rather than mutually supportive, anti-global protesters often see globalisation as imposing a number of penalties, such as the failure of global force to provide a moral voice. If a summary were possible of the basic differences between radical and moderate approaches to global sport, it might be along the following lines: while the radical wing sees fundamental flaws in the whole process of global sport, the moderate wing is more open to the potential good that may be derived from all forms of globalisation. The true potential of global sport for moderates is undermined by globalisation's domination by a neo-liberal agenda and undemocratic sporting structures.

Finally, it is worth re-asserting that the world is both spectacularly rich and distressingly impoverished. There is often an unprecedented richness of sporting choice in the contemporary world and yet it is also a world of impoverished choice. Depending upon where you are born, children can have the means, facilities and capability to have a sporting way of life or face the likelihood of desperately deprived lives, and even here sport has been seen to develop capability in some of the most impoverished parts of the planet. This is explored further in Part 4.

Some have suggested that the term 'international sport' might be a more reality-congruent term than 'global sport' given the debate on whether the global era has ended or not. The ideas associated with internationalism, cosmopolitanism and sport's dynamic role in the making of nations are examined further in the next chapter.

GUIDE TO FURTHER READING

Allison, L. (2005). *The Global Politics of Sport.* London: Routledge.

Campbell, R. (2011). 'Staging Globalization for National Projects: Global Sport Markets and Elite Athletic Transnational Labour in Qatar'. *International Review for the Sociology of Sport,* 46 (1): 3–22.

Harvey, J., Horne, J. and Safai, P. (2009). 'Alterglobalisation, Global Social Movements and the Possibility of Political Transformation Through Sport'. *Sociology of Sport,* 26 (3).

Hayes, G. and Karamichas, J. (eds) (2011). *Olympic Games, Mega-Events and Civil Societies: Globalisation, Environment and Resistance.* Basingstoke: Palgrave.

Jung, W. and Maguire, J. (2009). 'Global Festivals through a National Prism. The Global National Nexus in South Korean Media Challenge of the 2004 Athens Olympic Games'. *International Review for the Sociology of Sport,* 44 (1): 5–25.

Maguire, J. (2005). *Power and Global Sport: Zones of Prestige, Emulation and Resistance.* London: Routledge.

Mertes, T. (2002). 'Grass-Roots Globalism'. *New Left Review,* 17 (October): 101–112.

Poli, R. (2010). 'Understanding Globalization Through Football: The New International Division of Labour, Migratory Channels and Transnational Trade Circuits'. *International Review for the Sociology of Sport,* 45 (4): 491–506.

Sen, A. (2006). *Identity and Violence: The Illusion of Identity.* London: Allen Lane.

Sobel, A. (2009). *Challenges of Globalization: Immigration, Social Welfare and Global Governance.* London: Routledge.

QUESTIONS

1 What are the implications of globalisation for local, national and international sport?

2 What do the terms 'liberalism', 'capitalism' and 'globalism' mean?

3 Describe and evaluate any four themes that have contributed to the debate about global sport.

4 When did global sport come into being and how has it progressed to date?

5 What criticisms have been made of the values associated with global sport?

6 What is the cosmopolitan and local critique of global sport?

7 The debate about global sport has been dominated, in the late twentieth century, by figurational or process sociology. Does this approach offer an adequate framework for analysing global sport?

8 What does the evidence provided in Sport in Focus 5.2 actually tell us about one global sport?

9 What are the anti-global critiques of global sport?

10 What are some of the factors that affect the migration of athletes across the globe?

PRACTICAL PROJECTS

1   Empirically calculate the migration of players from different countries into any sport of your choice over the period of one season. Describe and interpret the pattern of sports labour migration.

2   Map out the names of the different countries that have participated in the Olympic Games since 1948. Use this data to argue for or against the Olympic Games becoming truly global or simply international.

3   Using the Google search engine, develop five detailed case studies of sport that might be used to substantiate sport as a facet of anti-globalisation.

4   Consult the website of any major international sports organisation to obtain information on the nature and scale of its presence in different parts of the world. Use the data as a basis for finding out more about the organisation, its objectives, its investments in different countries and its policies towards all, or some parts, of the world.

5   Write a report of about 1,500 words on a web-based investigation into child labour in sport.

KEY CONCEPTS

Anti-globalisation ■ Capitalism ■ Constructivism ■ Cosmopolitanism ■ Globalisation ■ Internationalism ■ Liberalism ■ Marxist ■ Nationalism ■ Neo-liberalism ■ Realism ■ Transnational corporations

WEBSITES

Focus on the Global South
www.focusweb.org/
A dedicated resource that draws attention to campaigns and issues affecting the Southern Hemisphere.

Global Social Forum 2011
http://fsm2011.org/en/frontpage
The programme and debates from the 2011 Global Social Forum, including a concept note on the caravan of sport.

One World
www.oneworld.net
A dedicated resource promoting the concept of One World and the issues that affect it. Look at the issues affecting your country.

Globalization 101

www.globalization101.org/

A students' guide to globalisation.

The Global Site

www.theglobalsite.ac.uk

A gateway to world politics, society and culture.

Football Against Child Labour

www.un.org/pubs/chronicle/2002/p19

The UN Chronicle provides an archived list of articles. Use the search facility to identify all the articles relating to sport.

Chapter 6

Internationalism, reconciliation and sport in the making of nations

Nelson Mandela once said that we can reach more people through sport than we can through political or educational programmes. Can sport really help bring about reconciliation?

PREVIEW

Key terms defined ■ Introduction ■ European Sports Policy ■ Sport and nationalism ■ Sport's role in the making of nations ■ Sport, recognition and identity ■ Sport and identity ■ Sport, nationality and globalisation ■ Sport, nationalism and their futures ■ Nationality and the Old Firm ■ Nationality, New Zealand and the Rugby World Cup ■ International sport and internationalism ■ Past and present sport and internationalism ■ International sports labour migration ■ Dispersal of power in sport ■ Sporting governance and states of denial in world sport ■ Sport as reconciliation ■ Olympic truces, diplomacy and international relations ■ Global or local sport: A false choice ■ Summary

OBJECTIVES

This chapter will:

- evaluate some of the ways in which sport has contributed to nation building;
- suggest that sport and its relationship to nationalism and internationalism can provide a particular qualification of the global–local thinking about sport;
- illustrate the part played by sport in processes of reconciliation within nations;
- look at the emergence of new nationalisms in relation to sport; and
- introduce the notions of internationalism and cosmopolitanism as part of the global–local continuum of sport.

KEY TERMS DEFINED

Diplomacy: A communications process between international actors that seeks, through negotiation, to resolve conflict short of war.

Internationalism: Increase of interactions between nation states.

Nationalism: The idea that the world is divided into nations that provide the overriding focus of political identity and loyalty, which in turn demands national self-determination.

Old Firm: Used to describe Glasgow Celtic vs Glasgow Rangers Football matches.

Power: In the most general sense, the ability of a political actor to achieve its goals.

Transnational: Extending beyond the boundaries and interests of a single nation.

INTRODUCTION

It has often been suggested that nationalism is becoming obsolete as a result of globalisation and that the relationship between sport and nationalism is weakening. Nation states may no longer be viewed as absolute governing powers able to impose outcomes on all dimensions of policy, including sporting policy. They nonetheless remain an influential locus of power because of their relationship to both territory and populations. Populations remain territorial and subject to the citizenship of a national state not in the sense that they are all-powerful, but because they still have a central role to police the borders of a territory and, to the extent that they are potentially legitimately democratic, they remain representative of the citizens within fluid border territories. The corollary is that national governing bodies of sport and national sports agencies continue to be vital to the governance of sport within certain countries. At the same time, international decisions and forces also influence the governance of national sport.

The nationalism that is connected to sport may be constructed by many different forces; be manifested within and between different types of nationalism; be real and imagined;

be a creative or reflective force; and be both positive and negative, transient and temporary, multifaceted and multi-layered and/or evolutionary in its format. Cronin (1999, 2005) asks a number of pertinent questions concerning the ways in which sport is inextricably linked to the forces of nationalism. Are countries in the search for a new national identity appropriating sport? How has the relationship between sport and nationalism developed? Why is it so important in contemporary society, and what should we do with it or about it? While it is increasingly difficult to sustain the argument that a single sport represents any one nation, nonetheless, certain 'nation-specific' games, such as Gaelic games, American football, shinty, Australian rules football, or pelota, still thrive despite the advances of global sport, and continue to play a central part within various national cultures.

Initially, the points that need to be made here relate to the changing geography of the world. It is crucial to recognise that the content of the relationship between sport, nationalism and national identities is fluid in terms of time and place. The potential weakness in thinking of the nation as only a place, or linking a particular sport to a particular nation, is that these cases run the danger of becoming fixed in content, time and space. This is a view that fails to acknowledge the nation or territory as a process that is neither fixed nor immutable. Territorial expansion or contraction is one of many ways in which the nation as a place changes over time. But the idea of what the nation is or which sports represent the nation also changes in relation to the social, cultural and political contexts.

The content, timing and symbolism of sport, nationalisms and identities in South Africa today are completely different from the content, timing and symbolism of sport, nationalisms and identities that existed during the apartheid era. Both sets of experiences are part of the process of South African sport and South Africa. In this sense, it might be suggested that there is no single essential nation, only a South Africa that embraces different territorial spaces and times. South African sportsmen and sportswomen, such as Nelson Mandela, Zola Budd, Hassan Howa, Sam Ramsamy, Jasmat Dhiraj, Basil d'Olivera, Justin Fortune and Sydney Maree, all express the idea of belonging to a South African nation or solid community moving up or down history.

Aborigines were vastly under-represented in most Australian sports and virtually non-participants in many others. In only three sports were Aboriginal men proportionately successful, namely Australian rules football, boxing and rugby league. Hargreaves' (2000: 85) groundbreaking discussion of Aboriginal sportswomen noted that these sporting heroines are part of two worlds of sport and two forms of nation building, namely the imperial culture of Australia's mainstream sport and the indigenous sporting culture of the indigenous nations within the nation state that is Australia. Aboriginal women have forged sporting opportunities in both mainstream sport and Aboriginal sport, and yet Australian sport cannot be properly understood outside the contexts of discussions about racism, colonisation, post-colonialism and how Aboriginal sportspeople such as Evonne Cawley and Cathy Freeman have, or have not, been portrayed, represented and empowered within Australia.

In an earlier discussion of the role of sport in the making of nations, it was concluded that the word 'nation' might be used to describe a human community that has acquired national consciousness, since it is clear that national consciousness is different from other forms of collective consciousness (Jarvie, 2006; Harris and Parker, 2009). If one accepts the notion that nation states are no longer viewed as absolute governing powers, but are simply one class of powers, then sport must reflect the changing system of world power that operates from global to local or to international levels. What was missing from this earlier discussion on sport in the making of nations was any recognition of the notion of internationalism or sport in an international society. This is where an international society may be taken to mean an association of distinct political communities that accept some common values, rules and institutions. International society is potentially an important sphere of human freedom. The contribution of sport to national identity is perhaps obvious but not so the case of sport in relation to international society. Perhaps the contribution that competitions such as the Ryder Cup golf tournament between Europe and the US afford the opportunity to make the argument that sport can be an appropriate vehicle for the promotion of a European identity and citizenship. The European Court has certainly helped to assert that sport is the most organised of European activities, with 2007 being a landmark year for sport at a European level. In 2007, the European Commission adopted a White Paper on Sport that provided a framework for sport at a European level. Sport in Focus 6.1 outlines some of the thinking on a broader notion of European identity and citizenship.

Historically, the social benefits of internationalism as a reality-congruent form of globalisation are strong. The challenge for sport is for it to cross the boundaries of prejudice and parochialism and recognise that sporting loyalties to local, regional and national sporting forms also need to coexist alongside internationalism. In this sense, sport and globalisation emerge as the natural enemy of bigotry and inward-looking varieties of sporting patriotism and nationalism. Thinking globally and acting locally was one of the many slogans of the 1960s. The debate about global sport has tended to dismiss the debate about international sport and internationalism as socialist utopias of the nineteenth and twentieth centuries. Internationalism is associated, almost uncritically, with the creation of a specific international working-class culture, beginning with songs and the celebration of May Day, and reaching its most advanced forms within the socialist and communist internationals of the inter-war period. There were certainly international worker organisations for sport, theatre, youth, students, film, photo, nature lovers and tourism. The vitality of the international women's movement, environmental and ecological groups, and peace and human rights protests tell us that any understanding of globalisation and global sport needs to account for internationalism and international sport in new ways. While globalisation poses serious problems for any sovereignty-based international society, it is open to question as to whether it incorporates forms of internationalism or cosmopolitanism.

The discussion that follows is developed around the following themes. What is the relationship between sport and nationalism? Are countries and individuals searching for recognition through sport? What is the future of sport and nationalism? What is the relationship between sport and internationalism? To what extent might the notions of internationalism and cosmopolitanism add to our understanding of the complexity of global sports processes? As an extension of the arguments developed in the previous chapter, this chapter suggests that sport has not been at the forefront of global or international change. Nor has it been dormant or unaffected by changing boundaries. The advance of globalisation does not make the state redundant; many would argue that it makes the state more necessary as a guarantor of civil and human rights. Internationalism has made, and continues to make, a small contribution to these and other sporting developments.

SPORT IN FOCUS 6.1: WHAT IS THE ROLE FOR SPORT IN THE PROCESS OF BUILDING EUROPEAN IDENTITY AND CITIZENSHIP?

Some evidence

As of March 2010, the Eurobarometer survey of sport and physical activity indicated that:

✔ 40 per cent of EU citizens do sport at least once a week;

✔ 700,000 sports clubs are involved; and

✔ 10 million volunteers are involved.

Some arguments for

✔ Europeans have little interest in European institutions and identity.

✔ Sport can help break down barriers and help people get to know each other.

✔ The European Ryder Cup golf tournament promotes a European identity.

✔ Sport can be a common denominator and a vehicle for education and citizenship.

✔ Sport provides a gateway through which a common European identity can be constructed.

✔ Sport is at the heart of multiple European Issues – social inclusion, EU law, citizenship, diversity, volunteering, tackling racism.

Some advocacy

Sport has a strong potential to contribute to smart, sustainable and inclusive growth and new jobs through its positive effects on social inclusion, education, training and public health.

European Commission, 2011: Developing
the European Dimension in sport

Sport, like nothing else, empowers people. It has the potential to inspire and motivate, since it shines a light on what people can do . . . sport connects people and communities. It knows no distinctions or race, language or culture.

Androulla Vassiliou, European Commissioner for Education,
Culture, Multilingualism and Youth, 2010

SPORT AND NATIONALISM

General discussions of nationalism and sport are often problematic because of the 'slipperi-ness' of the term. Nationalism is perhaps more complex than the conceptual tools we have at our disposal. The value of Cronin's (1999) early typology of nationalisms is that it highlights a much broader set of ideas than simply that of civic or ethnic nationalism. Four approaches to the historical origins of nationalism are presented. First, there is the *primordialist* view on nationalism, which asserts that nationalism is rooted in the land. Primordialists champion the dangerous notion that nationalism is a product of ethnicity that can be rooted in history. Second, there is the *modernist* view that nationalism is a product of the modern age. Thus, the origins of the formation of nationalism are specifically tied to a particular historical epoch. Third, there is the *statist* view, which suggests that nationalism itself, more than anything else, is associated with the idea of the state. Statists argue that the state uses sport to manage forms of state identity and allegiance. Finally, there are the *political mythologists* who locate the ideology of nationalism within the imagined or mythical symbols of national repre-sentation. The objective of this form of nationalism is to suggest that nations share a sense of community.

There are many different concepts associated with nationalism, and any cursory discussion is illustrative of the fact that different types of national communities and identities exist in different parts of the world. There are many different notions of the nation or nationalism or identity, and to reduce the terms to some form of rational universalism simplifies the concepts and the reality of sport in the making of nations. Whatever the nation in question, the quest for identity inevitably involves questions of representation, nostalgia, mythology and tradition. Many nations are fabrications or constructions, many states are not nations and indeed many nations are not states. Modern states and stateless nations have often required an explicit sense of loyalty and identification that has, at times, been mobilised through identification with certain symbols, icons, hymns and prayers, all of which are continually changing over time.

The implications of specific comparisons, contrasts and distinctions used to define nationalism are, like different viewpoints on its origins, rarely value-free. Nationalism can, at times, be seen to be positive in relation to narrow local attachments or feudal loyalties while, at the same time, being viewed as a negative social force in relation to ideologies of civic community. It can seem positive in the context of combating forms of imperialism and yet negative in relation to other supra-national phenomena, such as humanity or international class or gender solidarity. The issue of the values associated with nationalism or nationhood depends on what one is comparing it against and, as such, the specifics of any situation will often prove to have a greater explanatory potential than broad generalisations.

Much of the debate has centred upon distinctions between civic forms of nationalism and ethnic forms of nationalism. The former is often closely associated with citizenship and territory, while the latter is often associated with ties of blood. A significant problem with notions such as ethnic and civic nationalism is that they are used to describe certain types of abstract social relationships. Yet, what is crucial is not the level of abstraction or meaning, but the underlying relationship to the reality within which the experience is lived out. Ethnic forms of nationalism cannot be freely chosen. They imply, for example, that you are a Hutu, a Croat, a Catalan, a Basque, a Scot, a Welsh or English person, or you are not. You cannot opt out because, within this framework, ethnicity is conveyed at birth. Within the ever-changing twenty-first century, multiplicities of identity are the norm.

This distinction between absolutist civic and ethnic nationalism can be criticised on a number of grounds, not least the forms of racism embedded within either absolute definition of nationalism. In absolute cases, it is impossible to keep blood and soil apart and, despite modern attempts at ethnic cleansing in territories such as Croatia and Serbia or between ethnic groups such as Hutus and Tamils in Tanzania and Ethiopia, in practice such forms of nationalism can never be absolute. Multiculturalism and hybridity are embedded in nearly every place, and any claim that the state or stateless nation has to a single culture, a single identity or single form of nationalism becomes almost impossible to sustain. When the English Conservative politician Norman Tebbit sought to apply his racist cricket test rule – if you live in England, you should support the national English cricket team, even if it is playing against your country of origin – he failed to acknowledge this very point. People have many complex allegiances and it might be suggested that both ethnic–nationalist absolutism and civic-state absolutism are untenable in a post-nationalist world. Both diminish active personal choice, one more so than the other, and hence are fundamentally illiberal.

Politicians from various political parties, including nationalist political parties, have used the emotions associated with different sports to rally support for the nation. In the 1960s, the then Labour Prime Minister, Harold Wilson, made great political mileage out of England's football victory in the 1966 World Cup. Throughout the 1970s, Julius Nyerere of Tanzania often remarked that, in developing nations, sport helped bridge the gap between national and global recognition. Immanuel Wallerstein suggested that African citizens could feel affection for the victorious athlete and the nation (Jarvie, 1993). He said that this affection might not have existed in the first instance, given the social and ethnic divisions within African nation states. The process necessary to develop this affection depended on athletes accepting the politics of the nation and working with the party structures. Jim Sillars, the then Deputy Leader of the Scottish National Party (SNP), following his defeat in the 1992 General Election, chastised the Scottish electorate for not voting for the nationalist cause, maligning them for being '90-minute patriots' and saving their nationalist fervour for major sporting occasions (*The Herald*, 24 April 1992: 1). In other words, sport as a form of cultural nationalism served as a substitute for voting for the political nationalism of the Scottish National Party, in that patriots could show an affinity for the nation on various sporting occasions without necessarily voting for nationalist parties.

During the 1980s, a key element of African National Congress (ANC) policy in South Africa was 'One can not play normal sport in an abnormal society'. By the 1990s, President Mandela argued that sport had become part of the new glue that held the nation together. This was exemplified by South Africa's victory in the 1995 Rugby World Cup, a victory viewed as being symbolic of a new post-apartheid era. In 1995, it was rugby, not football, that symbolised for many the establishment of a new rainbow nation and the hope that the future would get better. Yet, it was football that was important for the ANC prisoners held on Robben Island during the apartheid years and it was the 2010 Football World Cup in South Africa that carried the hopes of not just the African National Congress, but also

143

South African society and the majority of the African continent itself. It is hard to establish the extent of the progress between 1995 and 2010, the period between the two sporting World Cups held in South Africa, but Archbishop Desmond Tutu was in no doubt about what the progress, the challenge and the hosting of the World Cup could do for South Africa:

> The restoration of pride and dignity as we host the world's sporting event is priceless. Despite the strides that have been made since Nelson Mandela was elected President in 1994, many of us are still haunted by the traumas of our past. Our self-esteem was profoundly damaged, our ability to dream compromised. We have built millions of houses and hundreds of schools, clinics, libraries and sports centres. We have held four successful elections and transformed most of our institutions. We have a black Chief Justice, a women governor of our reserve bank and we have served on the Security Council of the United Nations. We have won the Rugby World Cup twice, the African Cup of Nations and even contributed significant resources towards England's winning of cricket's World Twenty. But hosting the 2010 football World Cup is the big one. Because football is a sport that unifies like no other.
>
> (Tutu, D. 2010)

The symbolism of sport has also helped to promote national identity and sentiment at major sporting events. Sport has helped provide a sense of cultural autonomy to such places as Catalonia in Spain, Brittany in France, or Taiwan. Specific sporting success has helped to foster a close symbolic link between specific sports and specific places, such as athletics and Kenya; football and Brazil; ice hockey and Canada or Sweden; golf and Scotland; sumo wrestling and Japan; cycling and France; baseball and Cuba; and hurling and Ireland. The idea that sport and sporting achievements contribute to a nation's greatness and national identity, and at times help to transcend internal strife and social deference, is but one argument that has been dressed up in a number of guises and commented upon extensively over the last decade or more (Hwang and Chiu, 2010).

Sport, at times, has also been implemented in the politics of imperialism and national reconciliation. In the build-up to the 2002 football World Cup, jointly hosted by Japan and the Republic of Korea (ROK), Emperor Akihito of Japan acknowledged that Japan's imperial family was descended from the Kingdom of Paeckche, an ancient Korean civilisation. Following Japan's annexation of Korea in 1910, and the subsequent 35 years of colonial rule, Emperor Akihito used the then imminent sporting event to break the ice between the two nations. The co-hosting of the World Cup was the first time since World War II that Japan and Korea had cooperated over an event. The two countries made attempts to normalise relations in the run-up to the event. Japan dropped its visa requirements for ROK short-stay visitors, while Seoul removed a ban on broadcasting Japanese music. In reality, any reconciliation over the colonial past, remarked one of Japan's first Korean residents, would not come about through football but through ordinary Korean and Japanese people being brave enough to acknowledge the past and move on (*The Financial Times Weekend*, 25 May 2002: 10). At times, football travels beyond the confines of national identity, reconciliation and national politics. In the first match of the 2002 football World Cup in Japan and

ROK, Senegal defeated its former colonial rulers, and the then world champions, France. The country's president praised the success of the team in terms of defending the honour of Africa (*The Times Higher*, 14 June 2002: 19).

The relationship between sport and nationalism, and the role that sport has played in the making of nations have tended to rely upon some or all of the arguments listed in Sport in Focus 6.2.

A particular facet of the way in which sport has contributed to the making of nations has been to suggest that sport has contributed to national identity. The debate about sport and national identity has often been confused with a country's search for recognition and, in some cases, national identity can be viewed as resistant to a more powerful super-power form of national identity, a point that is made by Hwang and Chiu (2010) in their essay on sport and national identity in Taiwan. Because international sporting competitions, they argue, continue to be nation-centred and individual athletes tend to be attached to a country's sporting organisation, the athlete's identity is necessarily tied to the nation and, conversely, the nation's identity is linked to the athlete. This poses problems when the national identity is steered by a dominant system, such as when Japan controlled the majority of Taiwan's sporting organisations. It is necessary, therefore, to consider the relationship between sport, national identity and recognition as a further strand of the discussion about sport in the making of nations.

SPORT IN FOCUS 6.2: ARGUMENTS RELATING TO SPORT IN THE MAKING OF NATIONS

- Sport acts as a form of cultural nationalism.
- Sport acts as a substitute for political nationalism.
- Sport can contribute to both ethnic and civic forms of nationality, many of which may be mythical, invented or selected.
- Sport helps with the process of national reconciliation.
- Sport provides a safety valve or outlet of emotional energy for frustrated peoples or nations.
- Sport helps to build national identity and patriotism.
- Nations denied national sports representation have, at times, vested great national sentiment in specific clubs or sports, such as 'Barça' (Barcelona, capital of Catalan Spain).
- Nationalist support for sport has been a natural reaction against the pressures arising out of the development of global or international sport.
- Sport contributes to the building of national consciousness.
- Sport has contributed to the politics of cultural imperialism and colonialism.
- Sport can contribute to forms of resistant national identity.

Sport, recognition and identity

It is often argued that it is not identity that nations want, but recognition and a re-distribution of resources. The usual contemporary approach to identity politics in sport tends to start from the idea that identity is constructed dialogically. The proposition is that identity is forged by virtue of the fact that one becomes an individual subject only by virtue of recognising and being recognised by another subject or group. Recognition is seen as being essential to developing a sense of self, and being misrecognised involves suffering a sense of distortion of one's relation to one's self and consequently feeling an injured sense of identity. This logic is transferred on to the cultural and political terrain. As a result of repeated encounters with the stigmatising gaze and the resultant internalising of negative self- or group-images, the development of a healthy cultural identity is affected. Within this perspective, the politics of recognition through sport is mobilised as a potential strategy in the repair of self- or group-dislocation by affirmative action that challenges derogatory or demeaning pictures of the group. The argument is that members of misrecognised groups or national groups suffering from a lack of identity can jettison such images in favour of self-representations of their own making and collectively produce a self-affirming culture of recognition. Add to this public assertion, the gaining of respect and esteem from society at large, and a culture of distorted misrecognition changes to being one of positive recognition.

This model of how identity politics in sport may operate contains some genuine insights into the effects and practices of racism, sexism, colonisation, nationalism, imperialism and other forms of identity politics that operate through sport, and yet the model is both theoretically and politically problematic in that such an approach leads to both the reification of group identity and the displacement of resource distribution. The problems of displacement and the reification of social and political identities in sport are serious insofar as the politics of recognition displaces the politics of redistribution and may actually promote inequality. To promote identity politics in sport as opposed to the politics of recognition runs the danger of encouraging separatism, intolerance, chauvinism, authoritarianism and forms of funda-mentalism. This, then, is the problem of reification and identity politics in sport. What is being argued here is the need to develop accounts of recognition in sport that can accommodate the full complexity of social identities instead of promoting reification and separatism. This means developing accounts of recognition in sport that allow for issues of redistribution, rather than displacing or undermining such concerns in relation to sport, culture and society.

By means of summary, it might be suggested that some or all of the following arguments listed in Sport in Focus 6.3 have been utilised in an examination of identity politics in sport. It has been suggested here that students, teachers and researchers exploring identity politics in sport need to avoid decoupling the politics of identity in sport from social issues relating to the redistribution of wealth and power in sport. National identity in sport should not be viewed as an end in itself and, by the same token, it is not being suggested that recognition in sport can be remedied by redistribution of resources. Properly conceived struggles for recognition in sport can assist in the redistribution of power and wealth, and should be aimed not at a promotion of essential national fundamentalism, but interaction and cooperation across gulfs of difference in sport.

SPORT IN FOCUS 6.3: THE RELATIONSHIP BETWEEN SPORT AND IDENTITY

- Essentialist arguments view identity in sport as fixed and unchanging.

- Sporting identity is linked to essential claims about nature, self and/or culture.

- Sporting identity is relational and differences are established by symbolic marking in and around sport. Sport contributes to both the social and symbolic processes involved with the forging of identities.

- Sport simply reflects the changes that have accompanied the age of identity and, in this sense, identity in sport refers to a period or phase in history.

- Identity politics in sport is reproduced and maintained through changing social and material conditions.

- Identity in sport involves classifying people into different permutations of 'us' and 'them'.

- Identity in sport involves both the promotion and obscuring of certain differences.

- Identities in sport are not unified, and contradictions within them involve negotiation.

- Identity politics in sport, when reified, leads to forms of fundamentalism.

- The quest for identity through sport involves the quest for recognition.

A status model of recognition

There is no neat theoretical model that can be used to neatly resolve the dilemma of national identity and recognition in sport. However, the dilemma can be softened in various ways by acknowledging, in part, that the status model at least continues to recognise that social justice and a redistribution of wealth provides a social framework for thinking about sport, culture and society. The status model recognises that not all distributive injustices in sport can be overcome by recognition alone, but it at least leaves the door open for a politics of redistribution. Unlike the identity model in sport, the status model continues to strive to understand recognition in sport alongside distribution. The status model of national identity politics in sport works against tendencies to displace struggles for redistribution. It recognises that status subordination is often linked to distributive injustice and, therefore, any notions of identity in sport would be closely aligned with notions of injustice and social change in sport. The status model also avoids the problem of reification of group identities because the status of individuals and sub-groups within groups is part of the total pattern of recognition and social interaction. Thus, identity in sport can invoke notions of social and political solidarity without masking forms of authority and power within such a collective form of identity. For example, the initial phase of policy development in post-apartheid sport in South Africa practically illustrates that recognition in sport in the new South Africa was a collective effort but also it was argued that that the international community should compensate South Africa for past injustices in some way.

Today's struggles for recognition in sport often assume the disguise of identity politics in sport. This is usually aimed at countering demeaning cultural representations of social, cultural, national or local groups in sport. The result of misrecognition in sport is that the struggle for identity by emphasising differences has enforced forms of separatism, conformism and intolerance but, more importantly, has displaced struggles for economic justice with the formation of reified identities. What is required is not the rejection of the politics of recognition in sport, but rather an alternative politics of recognition that can remedy misrecognition without fostering displacement and separatism or reification. The forgotten notion of status can provide a possible basis for examining recognition and struggles for redistribution in sport and with the help of sport. The status model of sport tends to reject the view that misrecognition is free-standing and it accepts that status subordination is often linked to distributive justice. Identity in sport cannot be understood in isolation, nor can recognition be abstracted from distribution.

The concept of identity and national identity in particular has had a long history in relation to sport. It has been suggested in this chapter that the concept is not sufficient or weighty enough to encompass all the differences or representations presented through sport. Consequently, there is an urgent need to rethink recognition in sport. Contemporary struggles for recognition in and through sport often take on the guise of identity politics. This is often aimed at championing the cause for a particular social difference or form of representation from disenfranchised or less powerful sections of sport. It has been suggested in this chapter that such approaches are mis-conceived on at least three accounts: (i) the failure to foster authentic collective identities across differences has tended to enforce separatism, conformism and intolerance; (ii) the struggle for identity politics in and through sport has tended to replace struggles for economic justice and wealth redistribution, which condemns different sporting groups to suffer grave injustices; and (iii) the failure to realise that, while levels of social and national inequality between and within certain groups may be decreasing, levels of poverty remain on the increase. Identity politics in sport is not enough and alternative forms of thinking about recognition in sport that make a real difference need to be urgently addressed. Only by looking at alternative conceptions of redistribution and recognition can we meet the requirements of justice for all, and sport has a part to play.

Sport, nationality and globalisation

Before considering the future relationship between sport and nationalism, we will examine the assertion that the relationship between sport and nationality has diminished in importance as sport has become more global. As mentioned earlier, it has been suggested that nationalism is becoming obsolete as a result of globalisation. This seems doubtful and, on those occasions when the perceived global imagined community comes into view – the millennium, concerts to raise money for world hunger or AIDS victims, the Olympic Games, the football World Cup, the World Athletic Championships, or Princess Diana's funeral – these are but occasional and *rarely total* global events. That said, there has been an increased rate or occurrence of globalisation or internationalisation of sport over the past 20 years is entirely different from saying that sport is global or that the end point of the global era has arrived.

In a review of national responses to globalisation in sport, Allison (2002: 353) maintains that the degree of globalisation impacting upon different cultural, political and economic areas is not only complex but also different from sector to sector. Thus, while the global governance of sport may be advanced, this is only relative to other less advanced areas, such as the global or international governance of environmental regulation or human rights. It is argued that, in sport, the alleged global governance results from a combination of factors, many of which are international by nature. Three examples are provided: (i) international organisations involved in the governance of sport whose leaders and authority are often virtually unaccountable; (ii) transnational corporations, particularly in the media, that sponsor sport; and (iii) the growth of an effective system of international law that has influenced elements of sport, such as the 1995 Bosman ruling, which outlawed certain aspects of the football transfer system to bring it, at the time, more in line with European legislation on the freedom of workers to travel within Europe. Moreover, the Monopolies and Mergers Commission of the UK government intervened to stop the media mogul Robert Murdoch – through his ownership of British Sky Broadcasting – from taking over Manchester United Football Club.

A subtle version of these arguments has been to suggest that, as a result of globalisation and the diminishing power of nationalism, sport and society have become increasingly homogeneous. Bairner (2001) is unequivocal that any analysis of the above should stop short of arguing that global forces have resulted in greater homogenisation or Americanisation. To speak of Americanisation in such terms is to distort reality and, in agreement with Maguire, Bairner (2001) concedes that any assessment of global sport should accommodate the idea that globalisation has resulted in increasing varieties and diminishing contrasts. In other words, while various societies have become increasingly similar to one another, each country also has afforded its inhabitants a far greater choice of sports to play and watch.

The term *glocalisation* is coined to refer to the extent to which sport and nationality have resisted globalisation. Yet, global capitalism through the sponsoring of international sporting competition has ensured that national sporting identities remain to the fore, indeed are 'flagships of the global sporting economy' (Bairner, 2001: 176). It is for this reason, the author goes on to say, that we can talk of nationalism having successfully resisted the encroachment of globalisation's homogenising tendencies. Sport and globalisation have become accomplices in the process whereby the importance of national identity has been unsure (Bairner, 2001: 176). Thus, it is concluded that sport will continue to play a part in allowing nations to resist global homogenisation.

All of the above serves to illustrate that, in terms of world sport today, the issues are perhaps not so much about the question of national democracy versus global governance of sport, but more about the complex interaction between local, national, international, post-colonial and global forces, all of which are potential points of entry into any analysis of the changing nature of contemporary sport.

SPORT, NATIONALISMS AND THEIR FUTURES

It is perhaps misguided to forget the power of nationalism and its relationship to sport. The idea that sport and sporting achievements contribute to a nation's greatness and transcend internal strife and social deference remains as potent in the twenty-first century as it has been in the past. Following the war in Afghanistan, the former Tottenham Hotspur football captain Gary Mabbutt was involved in the organising of football matches between peacekeeping forces in the area and Afghan citizens in Kabul during February 2003. A spokesperson for the Ministry of Defence suggested that football was a global language and that more matches in the future would be played between peacekeeping forces and local people. During the American and British invasion of Iraq in the early part of 2003, it was suggested that, when the fighting was over, the Football Association and, in particular, the then England football captain David Beckham, should play a role in restoring normality and peace to Iraq. Indeed, during the early part of the war, British forces played a football match against local people in Umm Khayyal and more than 1,000 spectators turned out to watch the home side win (*Sunday Express*, 5 April 2003: 11). The 2011 Asian Football Cup was hosted in Qatar and involved 15 Asian countries plus Australia. While the event may not have been viewed as a symbol of political reconciliation, it was less than a decade earlier that some of the countries playing in the 2011 Asian Football Cup were labelled as being part of the 'axis of evil' by UK and American administrations. Yet, here was a new axis of relations through football. The fixture lists included teams from North Korea, Iraq and Iran. Journalists were given the chance to write; Iraq took on Iran and lost 1-0, but there were no casualties on or off the field. Furthermore, Australia refused to let geography or politics stand in the way of a football tournament and joined the 15 Asian football nations in Qatar to play against the likes of Bahrain and Bhutan. Identity, including national identity, at times is dependent upon recognition by others and the desire for recognition. Legitimation means that the international sporting domain can sometimes serve as a force for reconciliation between nations in a way that other social or political spheres cannot.

The nation state remains a unit of political currency and it is perhaps helpful to outline several ways in which the relationship between sport and nationalism may have a future. The changing configuration of nation states is such that it would be a brave person who would predict the future make-up of international sports competitions, such as the football, rugby or cricket World Cups or the Olympic Games or the Asian or Pan American Games or any other international sporting event. The effect of proliferation of nationalisms and nation states over recent decades only serves to confirm this point. The complex relationship between sport and nationalisms, rather than waning, seems to be waxing and certainly shows no signs of dying.

For example, sport continues to play an important role in the construction of national consciousness in modern China. The complexity of sport in post-Maoist China is evident in the fact that Chinese leaders in the build-up, and subsequent gaining of the right, to host the 2008 Olympic Games in Beijing used sport and, in particular, Western sports in what Hwang and Chui (2010) describes as an attempt to break out of Asia and advance further into the international arena. At the same time, specific attempts to modernise traditional forms of sport and exercise are resisted for fear of enhancing Western ideas of democracy. Following the bombing of the Chinese Embassy in Belgrade on 8 May 1999, the immediate response of the Chinese government was to ban the broadcasting of American National Basketball Association (NBA) games on national television. NBA teams were popular among 79 per cent of Chinese teenage television viewers at the time. On the other hand, the traditional form of exercise known as *quigong* featured in a public protest staged by more than 10,000 members of the Falun Gong in Beijing on 25 April 1999. The government responded by saying that 'this kind of gathering affected public order and it was completely wrong to damage social stability under the pretext of practising martial arts and traditional sports' (*Central Daily News*, 29 June 1999: 7).

National or international case studies?

The social composition of contemporary sports teams also needs to be contextualised within the changing social history of any one particular club. Celtic Football Club was the first UK and Scottish football club to win the European Football Championship back in 1967. A club with a strong Irish history, the international and cosmopolitan make up of the football team in 2011 is far from national, in that it contains multiple nationalities. It at least raises the question as to whether the football team with a proud Irish history playing in the Scottish Premier League is best described as national or international or global. Sport in Focus 6.4 and 6.5 outline the nationalities of different players in the one team and the contribution of one nation's athletes to other teams.

There are at least four immediate arguments that may initially be put forward to assert that the relationship between sport and nationalism is likely to have a future. First, in a sovereign sense the nature of the nation state may change, but the existence of sports teams representing territorially defined nations or regions aspiring to be nations is likely to continue. Second, nationalist-orientated governments or organisations such as the African National Congress or the Palestinian Liberation Movement, or forms of national sovereignty such as Great Britain (however fragile the union may be) are likely to promote distinctive sporting policies. Third, distinctive nationalist sporting organisations such as the Gaelic Athletic Association will continue to provide a national focus for traditional national sports. Finally, whether these are sporting or otherwise, an international society as an association of states cannot totally rely upon supra-national bodies to make and enforce laws, since these require states to accept legal and constitutional limitations above and below. In this sense, the nation state, or new forms of sovereignty involving national factions, remain central to any proposed international economy, society or culture. Sport as an entity is managed both nationally and internationally – it is not a question of either/or.

Nationalisms have continued to rise in regions and territories that have expressed a wish to break away from existing states. In some senses, it is correct to point out that the contemporary relationship between nationalism and the nation state is, at best, contradictory, if not illusory. Just as nationalism is growing in importance, nation states appear to be losing their powers as they are, in part, challenged by global or international powers such as those exercised by the International Monetary Fund, the Court of Arbitration for Sport, the World Bank, the European Union and the International Olympic Committee. All these forces would seem to have eroded the power of the independent state or national sports organisation. So

151

SPORT IN FOCUS 6.4: NATIONALITIES OF OLD FIRM PLAYERS 2010/2011

	Squad size	Nationalities	Scottish players	Percentage Scottish (%)	Percentage foreign (%)
Celtic	29	17	6	21	79
Rangers	25	9	14	56	44

Celtic players	Position	Nationality	Rangers players	Position	Nationality
Lukasz Zaluska	GK	Poland	Alan McGregor	GK	Scotland
Fraser Forster	GK	England	Neil Alexander	GK	Scotland
Emilio Izaguirre	DF	Honduras	David Weir	DF	Scotland
Daniel Majstorovic	DF	Sweden	Kirk Broadfoot	DF	Scotland
Jos Hooiveld	DF	Netherlands	Sa_a Papac	DF	Bosnia
Du-Ri Cha	DF	South Korea	Richard Foster	DF	Scotland
Mark Wilson	DF	Scotland	Steven Whittaker	DF	Scotland
Charlie Mulgrew	DF	Scotland	Madjid Bougherra	DF	Algeria
Glenn Loovens	DF	Netherlands	Gregg Wylde	DF	Scotland
Andreas Hinkel	DF	Germany	Kyle Bartley	DF	England
Thomas Rogne	DF	Norway	Lee McCulloch	MF	Scotland
Richie Towell	DF	Rep of Ireland	Maurice Edu	MF	USA
Efraín Juárez	MF	Mexico	Steven Davis	MF	N Ireland
Scott Brown	MF	Scotland	John Fleck	MF	Scotland
Shaun Maloney	MF	Scotland	Vladimír Weiss	MF	Slovakia
Niall McGinn	MF	N Ireland	Jamie Ness	MF	Scotland
Joe Ledley	MF	Wales	Kyle Hutton	MF	Scotland
Marc Crosas	MF	Spain	Kenny Miller	ST	Scotland
Sung-Yueng Ki	MF	South Korea	Kyle Lafferty	ST	N Ireland
Paddy McCourt	MF	N Ireland	Steven Naismith	ST	Scotland
Biram Kayal	MF	Israel	Nikica Jelavic	ST	Croatia
Freddie Ljungberg	MF	Sweden	James Beattie	ST	England
James Forrest	MF	Scotland	Rory Loy	ST	Scotland
Kris Commons	MF	Scotland	David Healy	ST	N Ireland
Oliver Kapo	ST	France	El Hadji Diouf	ST	Senegal
Georgios Samaras	ST	Greece			
Anthony Stokes	ST	Rep of Ireland			
Daryl Murphy	ST	Rep of Ireland			
Gary Hooper	ST	England			

SPORT IN FOCUS 6.5: NEW ZEALAND-BORN PLAYERS AT THE 2007 RUGBY WORLD CUP

The table below shows the flexibility of national representation in rugby. There were more players at the 2007 World Cup from New Zealand than from any other country. The 47 New Zealand-born players, along with their national team, are listed below. Interestingly, the New Zealand squad included eight foreign-born players in its 30-man squad.

	Name	National team		Name	National team
1	Boss, Issac	Ireland	25	Mexted, Hayden	USA
2	Carter, Dan	New Zealand	26	O'Reilly, Philip	Japan
3	Ellis, Andrew	New Zealand	27	Oliver, Anton	New Zealand
4	Evans, Nick	New Zealand	28	Pala'amo, Fosi	Samoa
5	Fa'atau, Lome	Samoa	29	Parker, Sonny	Wales
6	Freshwater, Perry	England	30	Polu, Junior	Samoa
7	Griffen, Paul	Italy	31	Robertson, Kaine	Italy
8	Hayman, Carl	New Zealand	32	Robins, Bryce	Japan
9	Hore, Andrew	New Zealand	33	Robinson, Keith	New Zealand
10	Howlett, Doug	New Zealand	34	Seveali'I, Elvis	Samoa
11	Jack, Chris	New Zealand	35	Smith, Conrad	New Zealand
12	Johnston, Cencus	Samoa	36	Sole, Josh	Italy
13	Kelleher, Byron	New Zealand	37	Somerville, Greg	New Zealand
14	Lafaiali'I, Leo	Samoa	38	Tagicakibau, Sailosi	Samoa
15	Lealamanua, Kas	Samoa	39	Taukafa, Ephraim	Tonga
16	Leo, Daniel	Samoa	40	Thompson, Kane	Samoa
17	Leonard, Brendon	New Zealand	41	Thompson, Luke	Japan
18	Little, Nicky	Fiji	42	Thorne, Reuben	New Zealand
19	MacDonald, Leon	New Zealand	43	Tialata, Neemia	New Zealand
20	Makiri, Hare	Japan	44	Va'a, Justin	Samoa
21	Mauger, Aaron	New Zealand	45	Williams, Ali	New Zealand
22	McAlister, Luke	New Zealand	46	Williams, Gavins	Samoa
23	McCaw, Richie	New Zealand	47	Woodcock, Tony	New Zealand
24	Mealamu, Kevin	New Zealand			

why has there been an increase in national movements wanting a state of their own? One answer is that a homogeneous view of the viable nation state is over, if it ever existed, and national vision must be redefined. Sport could be viewed as a good indicator of modern nationality and internationality in the sense that international sports teams are less dependent upon players being born in the country which they play for. Indeed, many international athletes have played for different countries and they are national, by definition, if they play for the national side.

In a rapidly global or internationalising world, many of the traditional things that helped us with a sense of belonging – nation states with relatively homogeneous populations, sports teams of home-grown nationals, well-established local communities, allegiance to local teams or to history and tradition – are all being challenged. To know thyself is a fundamental human need. Having some idea of who we are helps us to define how we ought to live and conduct our daily affairs. In other words, who or what we are either as an individual or nation or international community helps determine how we may conduct or live out our lives. Sport, through allegiance to all of the above, can help different configurations or groups to know themselves.

SPORT AND INTERNATIONALISM

While past and present commentaries upon sport, culture and society have mapped out the complex relationships between sport and nationalism, and sport and globalisation, less has been said about notions such as internationalism and, to a lesser extent, cosmopolitanism. It is not as if such notions have not been relevant to the history of sport, but discussions of global sport and sport in the making of nations have tended to marginalise the very vivid role that sport has had in terms of internationalism.

Undoubtedly, the world is changing rapidly and much of what has been advocated about sport diminishing contrasts and increasing varieties of nationalism and globalisation remains crucial to our understanding of sport, culture and society today. As the examples in Sport in Focus 6.6 illustrate, this is not at the expense of the role that sport has played in terms of internationalism, or at least particular versions of it. It is important, therefore, to remember the complexity of the global–local axis, and for students of sport, culture and society to appreciate that notions such as internationalism and cosmopolitanism, as well as orientalism, are pertinent to understanding the dynamic processes that are impacting upon the post-millennium world of sport. Few political notions are at once so normative and so equivocal as internationalism. Whatever sense is given to the term 'internationalism', logically it depends upon some prior conception of nationalism. At the turn of the millennium, while nationalisms as a force have proved to be alive and well, it has been within certain limits. Paradoxically, internationalism and internationality may be viewed as having positive values *both* as a defence against, for example, American unilateralism, and as a form of American hegemony. Sport in Focus 6.6 considers evidence in relation to sport and internationalism.

On the one hand, American unilateralism itself may be viewed as a creeping notion of internationalism that needs a series of checks and balances to be put in place. On the other hand, the international community also needs to assert itself, not least over the issue of human rights for all people and not just those conforming to American internationalism.

SPORT IN FOCUS 6.6: PAST AND PRESENT EXAMPLES OF SPORT AND INTERNATIONALISM

1928	The entry of women into Olympic athletics after being excluded for 32 years.
1931	The worker Olympics held in Vienna, involving 8,000 worker athletes from 23 countries held under the banner of internationalism and peace.
1936	Jesse Owens winning four gold Medals at the 'Nazi' Olympic Games held in Berlin.
1964	The expulsion of South Africa from the Olympic Games, thus heralding the official international anti-racist campaign against apartheid.
1984	The Algerian athlete Hassiba Bourghiba winning an Olympic gold medal and screaming as she crossed the line on behalf of all oppressed women.
1988	The Seoul Olympic Games, which were the first Olympic Games for years not to be affected by more than a token boycott.
1995	Nelson Mandela wearing a baseball cap and Springbok shirt following South Africa's victory in the Rugby World Cup held in South Africa, so demonstrating the need for the new 'rainbow' nation to work together and respect one another.
1998	France's victory in the football World Cup held in France with an international team that proclaimed its representation of the new ethnically integrated France.
2003	Liverpool and Celtic football fans during the quarter final of the UEFA Cup competition singing the same songs together and wearing scarves with Liverpool and Celtic printed on the same scarf.
2010	The first Youth Olympic Games held in Singapore involving 3,600 athletes between 14 and 18, and 205 delegations.
2011	Novak Djokovic, on winning the Australian Open Tennis Championship, announcing in his victory speech that those suffering and homeless as a result of Australian floods should know that they are not alone.

Internationally, Islamic fundamentalism and orthodox Catholicism muster as residual places for an alternative form of life that is equally international, but also less captive to the world of consumption. The dangers of Americanism and Britishness as forms of Western internationalism under the banner of human rights are problematic. They provide, in the name of the international community, the forces to blockade, bomb or invade peoples or states that displease them (Cuba, Yugoslavia, Afghanistan, Iraq, Egypt), while at the same time nourishing, financing and arming states that appeal to them (Turkey, Israel, Saudi Arabia, Pakistan). As for the Chechens, Palestinians, Tutsi, Sahrawi, Nuer and other peoples, some without a state, they are left to a world of charity that cannot, after all, be ubiquitous.

Some of the key arguments

Sport is not exempt from the uneven gaze of human rights, as the last part of this book illustrates. Some, or all, of the following arguments may be associated with sport and internationalisms:

- The international governance of sport is relatively advanced in the twenty-first century, and the relationship between sport and specific national territories cannot be fully understood without recognising the part played by transnational organisations and international forces of development.
- Sport in specific times, and at specific places, has contributed to specific forms of internationalism. Sport, at times, may be a catalyst in reviving or sustaining international sentiment and, in this sense, sport has reflected, rather than led, political sentiment.
- Sport can help with the process of reconciliation.
- The hybridity associated with post-modern international sport has meant that sport operates in both a post-nationalist and post-colonial phase of development and yet, at the same time, it is important to recognise that post-colonial sport has impacted upon sport's historical role as an agent of both imperialism and colonialism.
- The nation state and forms of internationalism provide potential sites of hope for the 'other' worlds of sport outside the gaze of the transnational sports corporation.

There are a number of ways in which sport might be thought of being actively international rather than national. All of these in turn serve as a qualification and warning vis-à-vis accepting too uncritically the notion of global sport. First, historically, international contacts through sport have provided opportunities for European workers to understand those factors that divided nations with a view to attempting to overcome them. The available evidence from the stories of worker sports movements throughout Europe and beyond suggests, above all, that worker sportsmen and sportswomen were internationalists and supported causes such as anti-fascism, which tended to circumvent national boundaries (Jones, 1988; Kruger and Riordan, 1996).

By 1930, worker sport united well over four million people, making it by far the most popular working-class cultural movement. Certainly, one of the most interesting aspects of worker sport in Britain was the way in which sport was used to forge links with the continental worker sports movement in Germany, France, Austria, Italy, Finland, Israel, Canada, Czechoslovakia and the former Soviet Union. The principle of internationalism flowed over into the sports arena with sport festivals, and Workers' Olympiads became popular forums for continental socialists. If international peace was to be advanced by bringing together workers, then sports events had to be organised effectively and in such a way as to develop political awareness, as well as sporting progress. The provision for worker sports events spread throughout Europe to the extent that, between 1926 and 1934, as many as 966 national and international sporting events had been organised under the auspices of the Socialist Worker Sports International (SWSI), which had 1.3 million members by 1927 from eighteen different countries (Jones, 1988: 170). If nothing else, the worker sports movement strengthened a rather weak internationalistic ethic among continental workers during the first half of the twentieth century. Despite political difficulties, worker sport helped to stimulate some form of common European ethos or internationalism through sporting contact.

Second, at an empirical level, contemporary studies have concluded that certain aspects of sport today may be more international, regional and local rather than global. Therefore, a second way in which international sport might be thought of as a critique of globalism is empirically. A particular critique of globalisation is borne out in McGovern's (2000) study of the migration patterns of foreign football players into the English Football League between 1946 and 1995. McGovern writes that the idea of globalisation producing a global football market is naive. The author presents a case study of the football labour market where globalisation might reasonably have been expected. The empirical evidence provided lends support to the idea that international labour migration might reasonably have been expected to be one of the defining features of globalisation as far as football is concerned. Within the football industry the employers – the clubs – tend to be permanently fixed to specific geographical locations, while the employees – footballers – can move within certain limits between cities, continents and countries. Towards the end of the twentieth century, the increased mobility of footballers led to the popular view that the football industry was undergoing a process of globalisation, mostly because of the increasing numbers of European clubs importing players from a wide range of countries. Because of the social embeddedness and historical patterns of recruitment involved in football migration, McGovern concluded that labour market migration in football was characterised by a process of internationalisation and that the recruitment of players was influenced by a range of social, economic and political factors that were national and international in origin, if not British. Thus, it is important to distinguish between the terms 'globalisation' and 'internationalisation', where internationalisation refers to the extension of activities across national boundaries, whereas globalisation refers to the geographical extension of economic activity across national boundaries, as well as the functional integration of such internationally dispersed activities. There was no evidence in the study to suggest that international sources of recruitment had been functionally integrated into the labour market practices of English football clubs between 1946 and 1995. While the market for professional football players was clearly becoming more international in nature, this trend (McGovern, 2000: 38) was developing along regional rather than global lines.

Third, at a relational level, sport may influence new generational attitudes towards past conflicts across national boundaries. Following the 2002 FIFA World Cup, co-hosted by Japan and the ROK, a new Japanese internationalism may have been encouraged through football. In an editorial entitled, 'A Key Role for the World Cup Generation', *Chosun Iibo*, a leading ROK newspaper, stated that the World Cup had awakened young people's pride in the ROK and that the performance of its football team, which reached the semi-finals of the tournament, seemed to have left young Japanese with the impression that South Korea was 'cool' (www.fpcj.jp/e/shiryo/jb/0223.html). Japan's relations with the ROK, as indicated previously, have been tense, the two nations having been close but hostile neighbours, and yet some feel that the co-hosting of the World Cup, together with the performance of the ROK team, laid the groundwork for future internationalism between Japan and the ROK. A leading Japanese paper, *Asahi*, referred to this as a new

157

easy-going nationalism that transcended borders; it suggested that the relations between Japan and the ROK were entering a new international era.

Fourth, sport today might be thought of as being cosmopolitan and providing a popular basis for internationalism. The terms 'cosmopolitan' and 'internationalism' are neither historically dead, nor irrelevant to the debate on sport. The changing composition of sports teams, even national teams, is more cosmopolitan than it has been in previous decades, and supporters are being asked to associate with a range of identities rather than with any one national team defined in only territorial terms. This factor may merely add to its complexity. Historically, cosmopolitanism has combined two distinct ways of thinking about sport. On the one hand, it designates an enthusiasm for different sporting customs and rituals. The combined rules of shinty/hurling matches, which take place every year between Ireland and Scotland, allow for a merging of their two sets of rules, enabling a completely different form of game to take place. The term 'cosmopolitan' allows for the blending or merging of customary differences that may emerge from multiple local sporting customs.

On the other hand, cosmopolitan sport projects a theory of world sporting governance and corresponding citizenship. In other words, the structure of the hypothetical underlying unity of the cultural meaning of the term 'cosmopolitan' is also carried over to the political meaning of the term – cosmopolitan sporting structures or events would also imply more cosmopolitan sporting citizens. The cosmopolitan ideal (and it is an ideal) envisages a federation or coalition of sporting bodies and states rather than an all-encompassing representative sporting structure in which members can deliberate about sport on a global scale. That is to say that cosmopolitan sport is neither local nor global and is closer to the term 'international'. The transformation of local sport into 'glocal' sport may, at some point, require recognition of cosmopolitanism. This may include: (i) elements of sporting mobility in which people have the means, opportunity and right to travel to and experience other places through sport; (ii) an openness to other peoples and cultures and a recognition of 'other' sporting traditions and customs as being of value; and (iii) a commitment to voluntary sports activity involving communities outside one's own locality. It might be that sporting coverage through international television coverage has contributed to an awareness of a shrinking sporting world and a more cosmopolitan awareness of the world of sport.

By contrast, internationalism seeks to establish global relations of respect and cooperation based upon acceptances of differences in polity as well as culture. Internationalism is not necessarily at odds with national sporting sovereignty. Internationalism allows for multinational sporting forums, for there are few other ways to secure the support of weaker peoples, societies or sporting groups. However, this is not globalisation, nor is it cosmopolitan sport. Forms of cosmopolitan sport may spring from the comfortable culture of middle-class sporting tastes and choices. Internationalism may be said to be more inclusive of an ideology of the domestically restricted, recently relocated, the provisionally exiled and the temporarily weak. Cosmopolitan sport is not a new modern form of internationalism but rather the two are incompatible. They both serve to warn the student of sport, culture and society that the choice between local or global sport is not that simple and, in many ways, is a false choice. The following are four arguments that should be kept in mind when reflecting upon the debate about global/local sport.

The dispersal of power in international sport

The dispersal of power in world sport means that the control, management and organisation of sport do not simply occur at local or global levels. In pre-devolution times, UK sport remained a centrally controlled function of government, directed by the Westminster government through the respective national offices and agencies. After 1999, within a devolved Great Britain, power in sport has been dispersed to the respective parliaments in Scotland and Wales, although a UK sports cabinet and Sports Council still exists. An examination of the calculus of power in sport today, by comparison with, say, the 1950s, would partially conclude that power in world and national sport has been increasingly dispersed as sport has become more irreverent. The control of sport through deference to the old establishment world order or amateur class ideals of due deference and respect has been eroded. In 1904, membership of FIFA was limited to seven countries: France, Belgium, Denmark, the Netherlands, Spain, Sweden and Switzerland. By 2003, membership of this same organisation had been extended to 204 members spreading across all continents and, in 2011, membership of FIFA numbered 208 countries. The staging of international tournaments, such as the African Nations Cup, affects European football clubs, such as Chelsea, Rangers, Celtic, Manchester United, Barcelona, A.C. Milan, etc., in a way that was unthinkable 20 years ago. Power in world sport is increasingly international, although national sports organisations are not powerless.

Sporting governance and states of denial in world sport

The dispersal of power in world sport might have diminished the power of national governing bodies in certain sports, but it has also meant the development of a crisis of confidence in global sport. Many major sports have been shaken by issues ranging from bribery and corruption, match fixing, and player trafficking, to strike action among the players, international bureaucracy out of control and a lack of trust in sporting governance. The headline controversies may feed into wider debates about whether sporting bodies have the capacity to deal with contemporary challenges, change and the world of agents, player power, the growing role of the courts, the needs of sponsors, new media rights and technological advances, both fair and foul. Added to this is the fact that the old structures of loyalty and identity have been losing their authority as sport has become more irreverent; a healthy distrust of authority has encouraged a more egalitarian commitment. So the need for transparency, accountability and movement to a state of trust rather than official denial in sport is needed today.

It is about putting in place structures that can give those who play and follow sport more confidence that those in charge are doing the right thing. The global era has presented fundamental challenges for sporting governance, but it has also created the opportunity for sport to be a force for internationalism. At the very least, it should create a reflex suspicion of official denials. Good governance refers to the democratic values that sports organisations must implement, and this is sometimes confused with systematic governance.

Sport as reconciliation

The role of sport in terms of reconciliation is perhaps one of the most important humanitarian ways in which sport can contribute to the world today. The twentieth century was one in which the world witnessed more great wars than in the previous century. The beginning of the twenty-first century has shown no early signs of national conflict decreasing between or within nations. In Northern Ireland, different community groups have generally recognised the cultural importance of sport in reconciling civil, national and religious tensions in a divided Ireland as set out under the Good Friday Agreement between the British and Irish Governments. In South Africa, shortly after the collapse of the apartheid government, the Head of the Department of Sport and Recreation within the Governments of National Unity's Ministry of Sport stated, in 1997, that mutual recognition would be given to the critical role that sport was destined to play as a catalyst for change and reconciliation within the new South Africa. Sorek's (2007) study of Arab soccer examined how football can potentially be utilised as both a field of social protest and as a channel for social and political integration between Arabs and Jews, and Palestine and Israel.

Olympic truce, diplomacy and international relations

International sporting organisations, such as the IOC, are in many senses contradictory when it comes to internationalism and humanitarian causes. The IOC, in support of the 2000 Sydney Olympic Games, spent US$230 million on a series of advertisements around the theme 'Celebrate Humanity'. This exercise was designed to encourage viewers and those attending the Olympic Games to see the event as a celebration of the best that humanity had to offer in terms of health, internationalism and sport. At the same time, the Sydney Olympic Games Committee assembled a security apparatus to prevent protesters using the Olympic Games as a vehicle for highlighting Australia's record on human rights. Thirty thousand private security guards, four thousand state military personnel and thousands of state police were charged with ensuring that the Sydney Olympic Games was a peaceful Olympic Games.

Acknowledging the contradictory messages given by international sporting organisations does not necessarily negate the way in which international sporting organisations and sport are implicated within international relations. Following the break-up of the Federal Republic of Yugoslavia in 1992, the IOC revived the notion of 'Olympic Truce'. The original stated objective of the IOC was to defend the interests of athletes, protect the Olympic Games and consolidate unity within the Olympic Movement. However, UN Security Council Resolution 757 of 1992 listed sport as a recognised element within any sanctions policy, so a compromise was reached permitting the athletes of Yugoslavia to participate in the Barcelona 1992 Olympic Games as individuals. The support for the concept of an Olympic Truce is note-worthy in terms of recognising the role of international non-governmental organisations (NGOs) in influencing and brokering international relations (Beacom, 2000). A further Olympic Truce was launched on 24 January 1994 to cover the period of the Lillehammer Winter Games given the continuing conflict in Yugoslavia. This Olympic Truce involved representations from the World Health Organization (WHO), UNICEF, the Red Cross, the

UN High Commissioner for Refugees and the Norwegian Government, who had to resolve the issue of evacuating National Olympic Committee (NOC) leaders and athletes from Sarajevo so that they could compete in the Winter Olympic Games. Thereafter, any potential Olympic Truces arising out of any global, local, national or international situations has become an item permanently on the agenda of the UN General Assembly in the year prior to an Olympic Games. The UN flag also flies at all Olympic Games competition sites. The examples above do not reflect internationalism per se, but they do help to illustrate that a straightforward choice between global and local sport is too simplistic, if not false.

Local or global sport: a false choice

The assertion is often made that global sport has eroded local sport. The corollary is that globalisation has reduced the power of national sporting agencies to be self-sufficient. Those who support local and national sporting traditions and forms often romanticise a lost world of traditional, local and national sporting forms. The argument is that global sport, and in particular global market capitalism and the multinationals, including sports firms such as Nike and Adidas, and international sporting organisations, should be restricted or regulated, or even reduced. If that is done, they say, a return to the golden age of local sporting self-sufficiency will be assured. This characterisation may be somewhat unfair, but it represents a view about sport, culture and society advocating the protection of the local, regional and national against the global. A further contemporary facet of this argument is that, within an increasingly global sporting community in which diversity of choice is dictated by the marketplace, there is a need to protect and value the diversity of our sporting communities and traditional sporting cultures.

A question that faces students of sport, culture and society is to what extent can global sporting events assist in influencing cosmopolitanism, internationalism and global solidarity? It may be suggested that the development and discussion of global sport is not simply a question of thinking globally and acting locally, but of recognising that the actual transformation of local sport and the role of sport in the making of nations involve issues of recognition, internationalism and cosmopolitanism.

SUMMARY

Sport in the future will continue to play an important part in response to the questions 'who are we?' and 'who do we wish to become?'. The foundations of identities in different parts of the world are crumbling and many segmented sporting communities are changing from traditional local forms of sporting identity to those of a more international nature. The idea that identity history and identity politics are not enough has been one of the common themes throughout this book. Sporting identities, such as allegiances to national sports teams, often invoke a desire to be patriotic, nationalist and different. Sport can also evince a desire to be similar.

While sport, at times, reproduces the politics of contested national and other identities, it should not be at the expense of an acceptance of the possibility of internationality or focus upon common humanity. Living sporting identities are in constant flux, producing an ever-changing international balance of similarities and differences that may contribute to what it is that makes life worth living, and what connects us with the rest of the changing world. If we are to come to terms with the contemporary crisis of sporting identities, then we need to transcend the nationalist or global–local simplicities and celebrate difference without demonising it. Increasing similarity of sporting tastes, choices and aspirations can exist without implying homogeneity. As such, the notion of international sport and new forms of internationality must remain part of the vocabulary of global and regional sporting debates not just because it is a more reality-congruent way of explaining the governance of sport today, but because it tempers the all-consuming notion of globalisation and provides grounds for explaining the 'other' worlds of sport outside the transnational corporation. The notion of other sporting worlds is developed further in Chapter 7.

GUIDE TO FURTHER READING

Baylis, J., Smith, S. and Owens, P. (2008). *The Globalisation of World Politics*. Oxford: Oxford University Press.

Cardoza, A. (2010). 'Making Italians? Cycling and National Identity in Italy: 1900–1950'. *Journal of Modern Italian Studies*, 15 (3): 354–377.

Holden, R. (2011). 'Never Forget You're Welsh: The Role of Sport as a Political Device in Post-Devolution Wales'. *Sport in Society*, 14 (2): 272–288.

Hwang, D. and Chiu, W. (2010). 'Sport and National Identity In Taiwan' East Asian Sport Thoughts'. *The International Journal for the Sociology of Sport*, 1: 39–73.

Fraser, N. (2000). 'Re-thinking Recognition?'. *New Left Review*, 3 (May/June): 107–120.

Giulianotti, R. and Armstrong, G. (2011). 'Sport, the Military and Peacekeeping: History and Possibilities'. *Third World Quarterly*, 32 (3): 379–394.

Jarvie, G. (2003). 'Internationalism and Sport in the Making of Nations'. *Identities: Studies in Global Culture and Power*, 10 (4): 537–551.

Olsen, K. (2008). *Adding Insult to Injury: Nancy Fraser Debates Her Critics*. London: Verso.

Piggin, J., Jackson, S. and Lewis, M. (2009). 'Knowledge, Power and Politics: Contesting Evidence Based National Sports Policy'. *International Review for the Sociology of Sport*, 44 (1): 87–102.

Tiessen, R. (2011). 'Global Subjects or Objects of Globalisation? The Promotion of Global Citizenship in Organisations Offering Sport for Development and/or Peace Programmes'. *Third World Quarterly*, 32 (3): 571–587.

QUESTIONS

1 Explain how sport is associated with nationalism.

2 Discuss and critically evaluate Cronin's typology of nationalisms.

3 Consider whether sport is governed by global or international factors.

4 Outline the ways in which sport can help with internationalism.

5 Critically evaluate the notion that sport is either global or local.

6 Explain the significance of recognition as a critique of national sporting identity.

7 Outline the ways in which sport contributes to identity.

8 What does the empirical evidence presented in Sport in Focus 6.5 and 6.6 allow us to say about sport and national identities?

9 Outline the ways in which sport can help with reconciliation.

10 What does the evidence presented in Sport in Focus 6.8 allow us to say about sport?

PRACTICAL PROJECTS

1 Observe the national opening ceremonies of the last four Olympic Games and explain how the sporting world has changed over this 16-year period.

2 Examine the nationalist policies of four national parties of your choice that have used sport as a vehicle for promoting nationalism and nationhood. Write a critical report describing and contrasting the four case studies you have chosen.

3 Use the Internet to collect information about the way in which sport has assisted with reconciliation and international diplomacy. Write a short report based upon four case studies that you have developed as a result of your search for information.

4 Interview ten people at any international sporting setting and collect their views on the importance of the role of sport to the cultural and/or political identity of the country.

5 Examine the FIFA website and explain the ways in which this international sporting organisation attempts to contribute to solidarity, internationalism and peace.

KEY CONCEPTS

Cosmopolitanism ■ Denial ■ Displacement ■ Fundamentalism ■ Globalisation ■ Internationalism ■ Misrecognition ■ Nationalism ■ National identity ■ Recognition ■ Reconciliation ■ Reification ■ Resources ■ Symbolism

WEBSITES

Council of Europe on Education, Youth and Sport
www.coe.int/lportal/web/coe-portal/what-we-do/education-and-sports/sport-for-al
An explanation of why the Council of Europe sees sport and education as making an important contribution to the lives of young Europeans.

United Nations and Sport
www.un.org/sport
The key website and resource for answers to why the United Nations is interested in sport. Look at the resources and fact sheets for detailed information on sport, peace and development, and other social areas.

Scholarly sports sites
www.ucalgary.ca/library/ssportsite
One of the most complete scholarly web-based sports sites, which should be interrogated with specific topics in mind.

World Football Governing Body
www.fifa.com
A resource for up-to-date information on world football.

Football Observatory
www.eurofootplayers.org/
The CIES Football Observatory – one of the cornerstones of the vast CIES Observatory project, dedicated to the statistical analysis of sport in all its diversity.

Chapter 7

Sport, community and others

Does sport help to build a level of trust between communities, including 'other' communities?

PREVIEW

Key terms defined ■ Introduction ■ Sport and community ■ What is communitarianism? ■ Critique of communitarianism ■ Sport, civil society and engagement ■ Ownership of sports clubs ■ Community stakeholder model ■ Other sporting communities ■ Senagalese wrestling ■ Trobriand Island cricket ■ Wushu ■ Globalisation and 'other' state forms ■ Post-colonialism – what is it? ■ Sumo wrestling ■ Post-colonialism and sport ■ How, what and when was post-colonial sport? ■ Sport in Australia ■ Sport in India ■ Football in Africa ■ Not yet global or post-colonial sport ■ Sport, power and the South ■ All-African Games ■ The Asian Games ■ The Pan American Games ■ Social dimensions of global sport ■ Summary

OBJECTIVES

This chapter will:

■ examine the argument that sport is good for the community;

■ consider different theoretical approaches to the term 'communitarianism';

■ explain what is meant by 'other' sporting communities;

■ explore the notion of post-colonialism and post-colonial sport;

■ consider the utility of post-colonialism in relation to sport; and

■ discuss other ways of highlighting sport in other parts of the world.

KEY TERMS DEFINED

Communitarianism: Advocacy of a social order in which individuals are bound together by common values that foster close communal bonds.

Democracy: Usually describes a form of political rule that is justified and exercised by the people for the benefit of the people.

Post-colonial: A field of inquiry and collection of concepts aimed at illuminating, as well as criticising, the cultural, intellectual, literary and epistemological dominance of the modern West over countries previously colonised by Western imperial power.

Volunteer: An individual who provides support or services at no financial cost to an organisation or association, such as a charity, a political association or a sports club.

INTRODUCTION

The contribution that sport can make to community has been a common theme within historical, sociological and political thinking about sport (Jarvie, 2003; Okayasu *et al.*, 2010; Wilkinson, 2010). As a term, the word 'community' is often invoked to imply democratic legitimacy, citizenship, part of civil society or a feel-good factor. For some, the term has simply been used as a synonym for the people or society or the state and an antonym for the private sector and competition. Sport in different parts of the world is often associated with community building, social welfare, social capital and stereotypical notions of making a contribution to working-class communities (Bauman, 2001). The latter often refers to a lost network of trade unions, craft associations, friendly societies, cooperatives, women's organisations, religious organisations, sport and social clubs, causes and campaigns and unitary organisations. Community, in this sense of the word, may be characterised by close-knit bonds or social relationships but more often than not the term refers loosely to a collection of people in a given location – a particular town, city or nation. Community as place is often viewed as warm and friendly.

People rarely have bad words to say about the community or sports policies or initiatives that are premised upon rationales of contributing to the community (Nicholson and Hoye, 2008). The associational nature of sport in Denmark may be viewed as a particular example of sport in the community that involves a high degree of local democracy but is more than just the local community (Eichberg, 2004). Sport in Denmark belongs to the non-governmental sector and is dependent upon an active degree of voluntarism. Despite substantial public support, the freedom and independence of sports organisations, federations, associations and clubs, are respected by the public authorities. The voluntary contribution is regarded as a valued aspect of democracy within Danish civil society. Sport remains at arm's length from government. Sports associations, like all cultural associations in Denmark, are approached from an ideal perspective characterised by notions of solidarity, reciprocity, community and personal initiative. Solidarity in a sports association can be manifested as responsibility for the whole, which each individual is a part of. The whole that the association is part of will often be a local community, and association and solidarity through sport necessitates a broader sense of awareness of the needs of the broader local community. Sport occupies a central position in the consciousness of young Danish people and, therefore, it is deemed as having the opportunity to inspire the form of solidarity and responsibility inherent within Danish democracy.

A wide range of thinkers, socialists, conservatives, nationalists and, more emphatically, fascists have, at different times, styled themselves as anti-individualists. In most cases, anti-individualism is based upon a commitment to community and the belief that self-help and individual responsibility are a threat to social solidarity. In social and political thought, the term 'community' usually has deeper implications, suggesting a social group or neighbourhood, town, region, group of workers or other group, within which there are strong ties and a collective identity. A genuine community is, therefore, often distinguished by the bonds of comradeship, loyalty and duty. Some of these terms are often readily used to describe the notion of particular sporting communities, be they local fans, places, national supporters or groups of people who wear a badge of allegiance to a particular sport such as marathon running or wushu in China or baseball in Cuba, Japan or America. The notion of identity is often a surrogate term for community, where community refers to the social roots of individual identity. Both the notions of identity and community, although hotly desired, often remain imagined rather than real (Palm, 2003).

Sport has the potential for good in all parts of the world, but not if the forms of sport are pre-ordained and governed solely by the fundamentalism of the free market or Western sport. Global sport on its current commercially driven path risks the recolonisation of the world by Western commercial sporting values and dogma that fail to recognise other rich sporting cultures, societies and peoples. Protecting and empowering social and cultural diversity through sport must, therefore, be seen as a crucial part of any progressive approach towards sport in the world. The poorest countries in the world must be given improved access to world sport in a way that respects the values of the 'other'. Development is itself a matter of justice, and global sport, if it is to be truly global, has to respond to the fundamental aspirations of sport in all parts of the world, to be recognised on mutual terms

167

and not simply through the dogma or values of the major power brokers in world sport who tend to be located in the northern hemisphere (Sen, 2009).

To view global and Western sport as a corpus of dogma allows us to question the values in the idea of an aspirant global sport rather differently. All major dogmatic systems, whether or not they are dogmatic about the free market or religion or world sport, need to avoid the twin pitfalls of absolutist and relativist attitudes towards sport, both of which are forms of fundamentalism. Absolutist standpoints run the risk of regarding Western sport as a sacred set of commandments brought to the developing South by the developed North. Those who lag behind are pressurised or compelled to convert to the faith of Western sport, thus raising barriers to encouraging a greater participation in international sporting festivals staged in or by the West from, for example, Islamic women or Trobriand Island cricket or sumo wrestlers or wushu.

The relativist view, on the other hand, considers that Northern or Western sport is designed to suit only the Northern or Western sporting hemispheres and need have no meaning for 'other' places or communities. To assume that there can be no communication between major sporting doctrines from different parts of the world is, in itself, a form of fundamentalism that treats indigenous or local belief systems as closed and inflexible. Both variants of Western sporting dogma present countries of the South with a simple alternative: either to transform their sporting practices by denying who they are, or remain who they are, but give up any idea of transforming sport and them. Perhaps it is impossible for humanity to arrive at an understanding of the values that unite it, but if the countries of the North cease automatically to impose their own ideas on the rest of the sporting world and start to take due cognisance of other sporting cultures in a common exercise of critical self-examination, the aspirations of global sport may become more just and less charitable. On the other hand, the balance of power in the world is changing and sport itself is not immune from changing balances of social and economic power in which an increasing number of sporting voices are non-Western.

WHAT IS COMMUNITARIANISM?

The notion of community means different things to different groups and, by means of summary, Sport in Focus 7.1 illustrates some of the most common characteristics of the term 'community' as it is used today. Approaches that place an importance upon the notion of community are usually referred to as forms of communitarianism. Communitarianism is a very good example of a phenomenon that reveals common ground in the relationship between political and social theory and practical politics. Different traditions of social and political thought have all emphasised the ideal of community. Communitarians have tended to view community not simply as an object of analysis, but as the true source of values, particularly of self-reliance and self-help. Recurring themes are those of social justice, mutuality, a rejection of individualism, social networks, power devolved to local communities, and an emphasis on family, neighbourhood and kin. Furthermore, it is suggested that community, rather than the individual or the state, should be the main focus of analysis.

Communitarianism might be thought of as being divided into at least three categories: the social, the political and the vernacular (Frazer, 2000: 180; Olsen, 2008). Social communitarianism consists of a core group of texts or abstract canons that have developed a sustained attack on the philosophy of liberal individualism. The arguments are very much centred upon a number of abstract notions that question our knowledge of social processes and values (epistemology); the nature of the individual and the social world (ontology and metaphysics); and the nature or issue of what we do value and what we should value (ethics). Political communitarianism relates to a core set of policy ideals or positions and arguments adopted by politicians who have attempted to propel the notion of communitarianism on to the twenty-first-century political agenda. The alleged strength of such a policy is that it lies beyond left and right politics. Vernacular communitarianism is more concerned with the ideas, ideals and values of a range of social actors and movements who think of their central *raison d'être* as being that of community activists and that community building is the most important political project.

Liberal individualism is a natural target for forms of communitarianism that seek to establish solidarity and mutuality. From the communitarian point of view, the central defect of liberalism is its view of the individual as an asocial, atomised self. The critique of liberal individualism arises out of its (rightly or wrongly) assumed dominant position not simply

---

SPORT IN FOCUS 7.1: SOME OF THE MOST COMMON CHARACTERISTICS ASCRIBED TO THE NOTION OF COMMUNITY

- There is no such thing as 'the community' as a homogeneous entity. There are many and overlapping communities, with new forms developing all the time. Some are chosen by their members, some are the product of ascribed characteristics.

- Communities exist beyond geography; they encompass a wide range of social ties and common interests that go beyond proximity or common residence.

- Communities benefit and enhance the lives of individuals, through fellowship, development and learning, and engendering a strong sense of mutual rights and responsibilities.

- Communities can give the individual a sense of identity and culture.

- Communities must be democratic, giving people a collective say over their destinies.

- Communities must be tolerant towards and respect other communities, and, where disputes arise, there must be mediation by law.

- Communities, in their diverse forms, create a civic society where the forces of decency can act to countervail antisocial behavior.

- Community is usually expressed through association with others in voluntary institutions.

within academic thought, but also key political institutions such as the free market, individualism and the rule of law. The individual, according to liberal thought, must be protected from the state. Communitarian engagement with liberal individualism tends to include some or all of the following arguments. First, that liberal theories of rights are overtly individualistic and fail to recognise that bonds of obligation are not necessarily freely chosen, and that mutuality, reciprocity and cooperation are pre-conditions of human life. Second, while an individual rights culture is historically admirable, it has gone too far, in that it produces a society that has encouraged people to think of themselves as disconnected from others. This, it is argued, leads to a distortion or misunderstanding of the real meaning of rights per se. Finally, communitarians point to a wholly undesirable and unintended upshot of a society that emphasises too many rights and too little duty or mutuality. It is, therefore, within the gap between the state or governmental provision and free market ideals, and the perception of their twin failure, that communitarianism as social theory and political practice has become popular.

The emphasis on community rather than the individual or the state has raised questions about the lack of definition over the term 'community'. Are we talking about community as place or community as a set of interests? Some feminists, while supporting the notion of communitarianism, have implied that terms such as 'community' are hierarchical and that communitarian arguments are non-egalitarian (Fraser, 2009). The claims of individual liberty and rights versus the claims of community raise difficult issues of the common good, public interest, and notions of justice and exclusion. The communitarian stance has particular implications for any understanding of justice. Liberal theories of justice tend to be based upon assumptions about personal choice and individual behaviour that, communitarians argue, make sense because they apply to the individual without society, community or others. Thus, for communitarians, universalist theories of justice must give way to ones that are strictly local.

Are sporting communities more likely to be formed through friendship or friendship-like relations arising through work and associational ties? If so, then one might expect notions of community to be closely tied to issues of social capital and civil society. Borrowing Anderson (1991)'s concept of imagined communities, writers such as Bricknell (2000) suggest that the very ideal of local imagined communities remains highly emotive and a potent political and social symbol to those it includes and those it excludes. Others, such as Krieger (2000), tend simply to refer to two categories of community – actual and imagined. For others, such as Doherty and Misener (2008), community sport is specifically about social networks of individuals, volunteers and potential social capital, while others, such as Sen (2006, 2009), refer to community as a form of captivity, developed through the colonised mind and lacking in real diversity of thinking.

Communitarians maintain that cosmopolitans underestimate the role that separate communities play in the moral lives of human beings. Its proponents often contend that individuals acquire their most fundamental human rights and responsibilities as members of particular communities and not as members of the human race. Communitarians do not deny that societies have obligations to one another, but they insist that it is appropriate that most human beings are moved more by attachments to their community than by appeals to common humanity. Thus, in some versions of sport and communitarian thinking, it is presumed, explicitly or by implication, that one's identity with one's community sports club or team must be part of the principal or dominant identity a person has. This approach has the effect of possibly rejecting normative judgements about sport, identity and community that allow for cross-cultural exchange and mutual understanding of other communities, cultures, and the healthy possibility of choice. Community sporting choice and identity does not require jumping out of nowhere into somewhere but it opens up the possibility of moving from one place to another and lessens the chance of the parochial.

It must be acknowledged that all concepts are continually contested on an ongoing basis. The notion that there is a proven link between communitarianism and social capital or that friendship is a prerequisite for continual development are all valid critiques that might be questioned by robust empiricists or non-athletes. In response to many of these criticisms, communitarians stress the importance of community, social capital and a strong civil society, and the practical goal of an inclusive community with layered loyalties. The notions of communitarianism and community are likely to remain active but often illusory or slippery principles and/or notions of not just contemporary social thought and political practice, but also the normative or real potential of sport to form bonds or bridges between groups of people.

SPORT IN FOCUS 7.2: ARGUMENTS IN SUPPORT OF THE IDEA THAT SPORT HELPS IN THE MAKING OF COMMUNITIES

- The associational nature of sport helps in the production and reproduction of social capital.

- Sport contributes to a sense of civic pride and civic boosterism.

- Sport has a vital role to play in the regeneration of deprived urban communities.

- Sports facilities can provide an important contribution to the physical infra-structure of communities, provide a social focus for community and, consequently, influence people's perceptions of neighbourhood.

- The power of sport has been diminished, along with the decline of civil society and social capital.

- A strong sense of collective identification with some teams rather than being communitarian has been divisive.

- Sport alone cannot sustain vibrant living communities.

- Global sporting markets and patterns of consumption have marginalised and replaced local sporting identity and taste.

- The mutual ownership of sports clubs can contribute to social capital within the community.

The assertion that local sports clubs provide communities with a sense of place and identity is one of the popular contributions that sport can make to communitarian thinking. Other arguments are outlined in Sport in Focus 7.2.

It is worthwhile exploring some of these themes in more detail.

Sport, civil society and engagement

The view that it is good to have sources of power in society that are independent of the state was both popular and controversial as early as the eighteenth century (Keene, 1988). By the twenty-first century, civil society has come to be defined in not just social, but political and economic terms. Thus, civil societies today have been described as a constellation of forces that provide a series of checks and balances upon the power of the nation state or the local state. At a micro-level, civil society is also the terrain of civil and community associations that are potential forces of civic engagement and mutuality. These forces might include the market in all its forms or professional associations or mutual societies or voluntary public bodies or sports associations, to name but a few of the bodies that actively hold the middle ground between the government, the state and the individual.

The idea that sport and other forms of cultural activity may be viewed as sites of civic engagement has often led to the suggestion that such activities might be viewed as important arenas of community revitalisation. Community fun runs and sponsored marathons are often used as a means of subsidising sporting provision in areas where state provision for sport is inadequate. Such perspectives reflect a change of emphasis from viewing urban regeneration or community development in purely economic terms to one that places a greater emphasis on people and the development of social capital. The role of professionals in the development of civil society or the development of social capital may be paradoxical. As Harris's (1998: 144) insightful contribution suggests, the horizontal, equitable nature of civil society makes professional efforts to strengthen civil society somewhat problematic because professionals usually have more power than the people they often serve, and the conventional top-down approach to the development of community and civil society is not likely to bring about the desired outcomes. Such an observation is as true today as it was when Harris made the remark.

Sporting activity, historically, has been associated with political protests that have championed human rights, progressive socialism and social inequality. Sport and physical activity, as Harris (1998: 145) has asserted, has played its part in 'fostering self-esteem, human agency and social equity . . . an important step toward strengthening and expanding civil society'. Daniel Tarschys, then Secretary General to the Council of Europe, suggested in 1995 (although it remains true today):

> that the hidden face of sport is also the tens of thousands of enthusiasts who find, in their football, rowing, athletics and rock climbing clubs, a place for meeting and exchange, but above all, the training ground for community life.

Harris goes on to assert that, within this microcosm, people learn to take responsibility, to follow rules, to accept one another, to look for consensus and to take on democracy 'seen

172

in this light sport is par excellence, the ideal school for democracy'. If this is the case, then community itself must mean more than just a common bond between individuals or a sense of belonging and obligation to others. The term 'community' must therefore mean, in part, democratic community in which members of the community or the club have a real say over decisions affecting them.

The issue of ownership of community-based sports clubs needs more careful consideration. The importance of the sports club to the city or the community has been widely recognised and yet, in the increasingly commercial global sport marketplace, there remains the danger of certain sports clubs becoming increasingly divorced from the local or grassroots fan base. Increasingly, demutualised societies and communities have failed, in most cases, to give sports fans any form of stakeholding in the community sports club. The conventional wisdom in relationship to the ownership of sports clubs remains that of the profit-maximising, investor-owned plc, with the public sector remaining the natural and unchallengeable giants of the modern economy (Morrow, 2000a). In the twenty-first-century global economy, a number of third sector, non-profit-making organisations continue to flourish. When it comes to building sustainable forms of social capital, generated by a sense of local self-responsibility, neither the private sector nor the public sector seem to offer the ideal solution. The private sector has a history of crowding out the third sector from capital markets and the public sector of bludgeoning mutual or cooperative ventures out of existence. There will continue to be many areas of economic activity where investor-owned, profit-maximising companies will remain dominant but there are many other instances where there remains a need for stronger state/civil regulation or a different form of ownership, or possibly a combination of both. When consumers or employees become owners, their sense of self-esteem, responsibility and participation can be transformed.

It is not unnecessary to dismiss a debate about mutuality as irrelevant to sport. Sport, in many ways, is ideally suited to mutuality because of the way in which groups attach themselves to a sporting ideal or common objective. The idea of football trusts that developed in England is simple: if supporters want an increased say in the way that football clubs are run, they can achieve it only by ownership. Supporters Direct, as a unit of the Football Trust in England, supplies legal and financial advice in addition to model constitutions, while the Co-op Bank helps with funding. The first Scottish attempt to form a mutual trust, operating upon co-operative principles, was made by a small group of shareholders in Celtic Football Club back in January 2000 (*Scotland on Sunday*, 23 January: 6).

The community stakeholder model provides but one model of possible conduct for sports clubs who, first, aim to demonstrate that they are a vital part of the community and, second, aim to promote and sustain social and economic capital through facilitating the community role in the decision-making structures of the sports club (Morrow, 2003). The organisational thinking behind increasing community ownership of sports clubs owes much to the principles of mutuality. The cooperative is but one organisational form that is based upon the notion of mutuality. The above case is but an illustrative example that questions the inaccurate assumption that the profit-maximising investor plc is the natural form of sports organisation for the professional sports club. Cooperative, mutual philosophies work best when there is a clear opportunity and incentive for people to work closely together for practical mutual interest in increasingly demutualised societies. In truth, few democratic governments have

173

got to grips with the important issue of community ownership of sports clubs and organisations. Its natural pragmatism whispers that which works is right, but there is a danger that in rejecting the sterility of the polarised argument about state versus private ownership, the case for diversity in forms of ownership goes unexamined. Ownership matters. The socially excluded need a sense of ownership. One of the most intransigent aspects of twenty-first-century welfare reforms in Britain is that the poorest 15 per cent cannot afford to put cash aside to save for retirement – because they lack capital either in terms of savings or real estate (Hargreaves, 1999). In all the meanings of that word, the issue of ownership and community lies at the very heart of a larger debate concerning sport's contribution to civil society.

OTHER SPORTING COMMUNITIES

The term 'other' sporting communities, as it is used in this chapter, is drawn from the post-colonial critique of the colonial or imperial worlds and, consequently, the way in which sport developed in many countries. The term, at one level, refers to something separate from oneself but, as it is used in this chapter, it primarily refers to the articulation of differences between and within imperial, colonial and often European stereotypes and actions associated with people, sports and places. Bhabha (1983) has talked about the 'other' in terms of the regimes of truth that are produced by colonialism or imperialism. Such truths invariably view indigenous, non-European or non-Western forms of sport as inferior.

The term 'other' can refer to colonised 'others' who are marginalised by imperial thinking, values and actions. Those 'others' are identifiable by their difference from the centre, the colonial; the mainstream has perhaps become the subject and focus of anticipated mastery and domination by the imperial ego. Post-colonial and subaltern studies of sport seek to uncover 'other' material accounts of sport in colonised countries such as Africa, India, China and Australia. The 'other' is often the marginalised or the forgotten, or viewed as less important within the overall notion of global sport.

Different bodies of research into sport, culture and society have attempted to ensure that 'other' sporting worlds are forever present. Anthropologists have brought to our attention the significance of the Mayan ball game pok-ta-pok, karuta in Japan, Bachama wrestling, sports of the Samoans, dart matches in Tikopia, cockfighting in Bali, ritual rural games in Libya, Aboriginal sport, the structure of Trobriand Island cricket, Indian running, Kalenjin runners in Kenya, Tarahumara runners in Mexico, sumo in Japan, the role of sports among the Maori, the training of the body in China, the alleged use of *juju* in football in Tanzania, the role of football for Palestinians in Jordan, or football among the Baga of Guinea. Sport in Focus 7.3 provides a glimpse into change in sport in one non-Western state.

Geographers have contributed to the opening up of sport in 'other' places, locations and landscapes, while at the same time calling for imaginative geographies of sport (Bale, 1994, 2002a, 2003, 2007). The spatial dynamics of sports has contributed to a greater understanding of the geographical diffusion of sport, talent migration, the relocation of sports clubs and the changing content of the sporting landscape. This work has included analysis of running in Kenya, sports stadiums in Scandinavia, the way in which African footballers are reported in the Western press, images of Rwandan high jumpers, memory and identity in one local

SPORT IN FOCUS 7.3: SENEGALESE WRESTLING

In the West African state of Senegal, wrestlers can receive up to £130,000, with prize money totalling millions of dollars. Wrestlers can earn more than famous footballers in Senegal. Young wrestlers know that a successful wrestling career can help them move on from crippling poverty. The top fighters wrestle in front of 80,000 fans in Dakar's main stadiums. One observer noted that changes in wrestling represent changes in African society. In the past, the wrestlers represented the village and the community and, while elements of this still exist, it is now all about the individual and the city (Bridgland, 2010).

Scottish football community, women athletes and Islam, a geography of baseball, and athletic representation in the colonial world. Perhaps it is useful, at this point, to consider two examples in more detail.

Trobriand Island cricket and wushu are illustrative of 'other' sports. European missionaries introduced cricket to the Trobriand Islands in the 1920s and 1930s as part of an overall colonising mission that included the usual requisite changes in dress, tradition, social practices and values. Very quickly, the Trobriand Islanders refashioned the game to meet local needs. The number of players in the team was not restricted, as long as they were even. Bowling actions were replaced by spear-throwing actions that, in turn, because of their accuracy, led to shortening the stumps. The ball was made from local materials and the fall of each wicket was accompanied by dance celebrations, while teams practised elaborate celebratory rituals. Games were invariably accompanied by feasting and became part of the inter-village political activities. The 'other' cricket in the case of the Trobriand Islanders was not inferior or marginal, but an essential part of Trobriand culture with deep ritual significance.

Wushu, the collective phrase for Chinese martial arts, is one of the most widespread traditional sports in China. Many other Asian martial arts have originated from its wide variety of fighting techniques. Within China, wushu has displayed a number of local variations, and collectively the All-China Federation of Trade Unions has estimated that almost three million Chinese people practise wushu on a daily basis for both physical and spiritual needs (Jarvie *et al.*, 2008). At one and the same time, wushu represents a traditional Chinese sport and a modern form of Chinese culture, looking to acquire Olympic status and recognition. It nonetheless runs the risk of being influenced or re-invented by American–Chinese culture, given the significant place that martial arts have found in the American imagination. The American and potential Olympic fascination with the 'other' therefore gazes at wushu through Western eyes, while looking to re-invent or colonise the tradition within the American imagination, thus potentially reducing its oppositional potential to Western culture. Since the 1980s, both the Chinese Wushu Association and the International Wushu Federation have lobbied for wushu to be included as an official Olympic sport. In post-colonial terms, the inculcation into 'modern sport' of traditional Chinese wushu by Olympic, American and

Western forces would most likely lead to hybridity, which commonly refers to the creation of new transcultural sports forms by contact between the colony and the 'other'.

While the above is illustrative of some of the 'other' worlds of sport, what follows is illustrative of the changing dynamics of state development in different parts of the world. One of the most serious flaws of conventional discussions about globalisation is its blindness to strongly differentiated state forms that have developed over the past 40 years. These serve as a reminder of the increasingly diverse and deferential world in which we live. Social modernisation resulting from economic change, education, mass communication, calls for formal democratic rights, and transnational migration has impacted upon different parts of the world in a very uneven way. Successful state forms have included the welfare statism that has been deployed and consolidated in much of Western Europe. The more outward developmental model adopted by East Asia, characterised by state planning, control of banks and credit, and aggressive world market export-orientated structures, has also been successful. The Asian development states have been more concerned with political and cultural protection against unwanted foreign influences, with Japan and South Korea both being tenacious about incoming foreign investment. If the East Asian models of state development have been relatively successful, there have been less successful state models that have been more inward looking. With the exception of North Korea and China in Asia, the former communist state models have disintegrated. China, Vietnam, Cambodia and Laos have all staked out new courses of development. China, the largest country on the planet, has become history's most successful development state, with a 20-year growth rate per capita of almost 10 per cent per year. Tourism has helped Cuba to survive, while in the post-colonial African states, government-encouraged socialist ambitions have struggled to overcome administrative chaos, ethnic tensions and rising poverty (Huish, 2011).

In the same way as globalisation has been blind to the uneven and differentiated models of state formation emerging in the twenty-first century, the same might be said about our current knowledge of global sport (Amir, 2011; Bloomfield, 2010). It is impossible at this stage to draw up a balance sheet of the combined effects of globalisation and other social forces with their many contradictions, exceptions and unevenness. By the same token, it is also impossible to map out the changing patterns of global sport. But it is essential that any contemporary understanding of sport, culture and society must actively listen to and engage with other sporting communities, places and voices. If nothing else, the dynamic body of work that contributes to what we know about sport and post-colonialism is helping with this sensitivity. The post-colonial critique of colonial sport serves as a reminder that 'other' sporting communities contribute to and influence global sport. Its overall value lies in it being a safeguard against inward-looking parochialism and the conscience of cosmopolitan sport, lest it forgets 'other' traditions of sport, the poor or the use of cheap labour in sporting production, or the humanitarian power of sport in 'other' parts of the world.

POST-COLONIALISM – WHAT IS IT?

If colonialism exists in support of Western powers, it is debatable whether colonialism has declined at all. Post-colonialism may signify changes in the official power structure after a period of de-colonisation, as well as colonialism's enduring effects, particularly as they are manifested interpretatively. 'Post-colonial theory' is an umbrella term that covers different critical approaches, and is particularly critical of European thought in areas as wide-ranging as philosophy, history, literary studies, anthropology, sociology, political science and sport, and culture and society. Within this perspective, the term 'post-colonial' refers not to a simple periodisation, but rather a radical methodological revisionism and wholesale critique of Western structures of knowledge and power.

As mentioned in Chapter 1, at a general level, post-colonialism presents a challenge to previously accepted values and criteria for ways of looking at and thinking about the world. The need to rewrite sport, culture and society arises, in part, from forms of intervention, such as post-colonialism, which assert that our past knowledge of sport has been disproportionately influenced by specific ideologies of the dominating powers, usually European and invariably colonial, and that 'other' sporting communities are not sufficiently represented in that which currently accounts for the literature on global sport. The history of global sport has been disproportionately influenced by the ideas or ideals of nineteenth- and twentieth-century imperialism. These include an assumed superiority of Western, often white, sporting cultures that have promoted historically questionable ideologies of sport relating to fair play, amateurism, athleticism, the role of sport in the civilising process, the marginalisation of indigenous sporting forms as inferior to Western, often European, sporting forms, and sport's particular links with forms of religion that gave rise to phrases such as 'muscular Christianity'. In the latter, a fundamental clash of cultures is exposed in the very words that prioritise particular sports and a particular religion.

'Other' sports have, in some cases, aligned themselves with aspects of religion and athleticism, but have had to develop a certain level of hybridity. Sumo is a traditional Japanese wrestling sport that has always included a strong element of religion and ritual. A fundamental clash of cultures and values is evident in Guttmann and Thompson's (2001: 139) account of sumo wrestling in Japan in which they write that, from the 1890s onwards, many Japanese intellectuals have struggled with the problem of understanding Japanese society and the place of sumo as a modern and a traditional sport. Some of sumo's traditions pre-date the nineteenth century but, as Guttmann (1996: 380) concludes, the elders who traditionalised twentieth-century sumo were quite successful in that sumo flourishes today as baseball's most serious rival among spectator sports in Japan. Together, the two sports symbolise Japan's desire to be simultaneously a traditional and a modern society (Okayasu et al., 2010).

Sumo also encapsulates the clash between a sport that has at least a 2,000-year-old history and the struggle to survive against the inroads being made by sports such as soccer, following the success of the national soccer team in the 2002 FIFA World Cup. Traditionally the number one sport in Japan, sumo wrestling has been hit by reduced sponsorship, and falling attendances and television viewing figures. At the same time, soccer is fast capturing the minds of a new generation. Corporate sponsors have fallen away as Japanese companies such as Mitsubishi, Nissan, Posco and SK Corporation have looked to support more international sports, such as golf and soccer. Ticket sales to tournaments fell by 15 per cent between 2000 and 2002, while television ratings were, at the end of 2002, 50 per cent down on the 1998 figures. There is also the alleged problem that match fixing has become common in the sport. Japanese gangs, known as the yakuza, are said to control betting on fights.

177

The Japanese Sumo Association (JSA) has responded by cutting seat prices, selling tickets at convenience stores, claiming to have solved the problem of match fixing and attempting to add internationality by luring foreign wrestlers to fight Japanese sumo wrestlers. In 1998, the IOC provisionally recognised the Tokyo-based International Sumo Federation (ISF), thus boosting the sport's chances of making it into the Olympic Games. In 2001, sumo's amateur world championship featured women for the first time. At the 2005 World Games, men's and women's sumo will make their debut for the first time at this high-profile event for non-Olympic sports. The view of the ISF is that the rise of women's sumo should only strengthen the case for the sport to be represented at the Olympic Games. The official Japanese argument on this issue is that judo is an Olympic sport, but that sumo is older and better (www.amateursumo.com). In 2002, however, IOC President Jacques Rogge had condemned the sport's gargantuan competitors as presenting the wrong image, claiming that it was ugly and bad for one's health (*Sunday Herald*, 15 June 2003: 18).

This can be said while still recognising that sumo shares some of the problems of contemporary sport. For the first time since 1946, the JSA, in February 2011, cancelled the grand national tournament over allegations of match fixing. The police were called in to investigate 13 senior wrestlers and the Japanese Prime Minister Naoto Kan called the match fixing a betrayal of the people. In the 2011 allegations, the JSA Chairman commented that text messages found on mobile phones suggested that 13 senior wrestlers were involved. One reportedly went into the detail of how he would attack and the other would fall, in exchange for hundreds of thousands of yen. This follows on from another scandal over illegal betting in 2010, which saw live television coverage of the sport dropped by the national broadcaster NHK.

These problems may be approached in two ways. One is to stress the difference between Japan and the West, since the West invariably characterises or invents Japan as it wants to see it in terms of being rational, progressive, scientific, individualistic, meritocratic, lacking material wealth but having spiritual qualities. The other possible way is to differentiate Japan and 'Japaneseness' from the West, while at the same time maintaining and constructing Japan's own definition of 'Japaneseness'. Both of these approaches can be seen in Japanese assessments of the relative merits of imported Western sports and indigenous traditional martial arts and sumo. If the West, in this case, is viewed as the 'other', it is the interaction between Japan and the 'other' that makes it possible for Japan to differentiate itself from other nations. In other words, 'Japaneseness' has to be imagined by the 'other', as well as by its own members. Japan constructs its images of Western sports just as the West constructs its images of Japanese sport and 'Japaneseness'. Western sport can be viewed as individualistic, secular, involving modern forms, players' rights and labour unionism, whereas something as traditional as sumo can still be viewed as spiritual, hierarchical, ritualistic, and yet struggling equally with twenty-first-century professional sporting problems.

POST-COLONIALISM AND SPORT

Normally, three meanings are given to the term 'post-colonial'. First, it is the end of a period of time in the sense that the old colonial control has diminished. Second, post-colonial refers to a stage of development in which post-colonialism has replaced colonialism. This may be

SPORT IN FOCUS 7.4: QUESTIONS ON A POST-COLONIAL APPROACH TO SPORT

- To what extent has the process of external imperialism and/or colonialism influenced the development of sport?

- How has Western sport controlled the development of sport in non-Western parts of the world?

- To what extent has the history of sport been written or challenged by non-Western perspectives?

- Is the nature of sport different in Western and non-Western parts of the world and, if so, how?

- Do the notions of hybridity or orientalism help us to explain sport?

viewed as a goal or aspiration that necessitates a critical examination of today's sporting content and representation. In this sense, post-colonialism might refer not so much to a state of being after colonialism, but the process by which we might reach that particular aspiration or state of being. Finally, the term 'post-colonial' might be viewed as a method that adopts a post-colonial approach to sport. Sport in Focus 7.4 highlights some questions that might arise out of a post-colonial approach to sport.

In one of the most comprehensive introductions to sport and post-colonialism, Bale and Cronin (2003) raise three crucial questions, which we need to elaborate upon before considering whether the term is reality-congruent, for example, in places where the US has moved offensively in both sport and society in general (Ali, 2003). Two of the questions raised by Bale and Cronin refer to the 'how' and the 'what' of post-colonial sports, in which the 'how' refers to methodology and the 'what' refers to some illustrative forms of post-colonial enquiries into sport. As mentioned in the introduction to this book, one of the potential roles of a student, researcher or intellectual working in the field of sport, culture and society is to uncover, contest, challenge and ultimately defeat both imposed silences and the normalised quiet of unseen power. In terms of doing post-colonial sport, this refers to the general goal of opening up the injustices or the silences within global sport in relation to 'other' sporting communities. It means a challenge to the values of Western sport, so that what might first appear as odd and out of 'place' no longer becomes out of 'place'.

More specifically, Bale and Cronin (2003: 9) see in the context of sports and body cultures post-colonial method, involving emphasising aspects of sport in the relations between coloniser and colonised; re-interpreting and providing alternative understandings of sport; displaying an awareness of the way in which sport and body culture have resisted colonisation; and the removal of post-colonial sport from universal or general metropolitan ideas or policies about sport. In a very practical sense, if it is generally accepted that sporting festivals and world championships are too big, then in any downsizing we must ask which sports will

179

SPORT IN FOCUS 7.5: POST-COLONIAL SPORTS

- Forms of body culture that have survived colonialism, such as Rwandan high jumping.

- Indigenous local forms of body culture that have been transformed into modern sports, such as lacrosse, ice hockey and shinty.

- Body cultures that were re-invented by a former colonising power, such as baseball and basketball in the US.

- Colonial sports that have been modified by former colonies into national sports, such as Gaelic and Australian football.

- Sports that have travelled with the colonising powers and have adopted 'other' styles, such as Brazilian football and Kenyan running.

- Sports that have developed a degree of hybridity, such as Trobriand Island cricket or combined-rules shinty/hurling matches.

go, which countries will go and in whose interest it is that such a downsizing policy is accepted? As Bale, more than anybody else, has done over the past decade, this means challenging, for example, the European construction of athleticism of various groups of 'other' people in the colonised world. It means giving a voice to 'other' sporting communities in terms of their own values. What, then, are post-colonial sports? Several illustrative types of post-colonial sports are provided in Sport in Focus 7.5.

One final question: 'when' was post-colonial sport, and is it worth discussing this in more detail?

When are sports post-colonial?

Although the term 'post-colonial' has a clear chronological meaning, designating the period after which independence had been secured from colonial governance, from the late 1970s the term has been used in a variety of different ways, not least of which has been a denouncing of the literary impact of colonialism. Originally used by historians to refer to periods after World War II, in which post-colonial states emerged, it is clear that there is no one fixed starting date for post-colonialism or post-colonial sport, but a number of post-colonial sports. 'Post-colonial sport' is not a term that can be precisely pinned down. Rather, it can be articulated in different ways in different places at different times, while still maintaining the common core problematic thrust of attempting to develop a healthy degree of suspicion and self-consciousness about what has passed as colonial, imperial and even neo-colonial sports. The hyphenated term 'post-colonial sports' denotes a particular historical period or epoch, after colonialism. But the plurality of the term 'sports' also indicates not just the number of sports, but also a number of epochs or historical periods in which sport in different places may have taken on different post-colonial politics. Post-colonial sports are not contained by tidy common categories of historical periods or dates, although they remain firmly bound up with historical experiences, particularly after independence from colonial governance.

In attempting to answer the 'when' of post-colonialism and sport, Bale and Cronin (2003) offer the following suggestions: (i) when the first 'Third World sports workers' arrived in the 'First World'; (ii) the period following independence from nineteenth-century imperialism when sport played such an important part in transmitting values; and/or (iii) the present and future attempts to challenge international sports organisations that continue to promote a colonising policy towards sport in an attempt to achieve global expansion for any particular sport. Many of the specific studies of sport and the body contained within *Sport and Post-colonialism* also struggle with the 'when' issue of post-colonial sports. In Hay's (2003) analysis of Australia as a post-colonial sporting society, he specifically refers to the evolution of Australian sport within a post-imperial context. This draws upon Australia's ambivalent relationship to the sporting metropolis or centre, by which Hay means British and American sport, and also Australia's own attitude and actions towards ethnic minority and Aboriginal Australian sport. For Mills and Dimeo (2003), the body is a central and unique way to inform the relationship between sporting activities in both colonial and post-colonial South Asia. The 'when' of this research refers to post-colonial India and, in particular, the way in which football has acted for the colonisers as an 'idiom and as a technology for imagining and transforming the Indian body' (Mills and Dimeo, 2003: 157). Given that India and Pakistan gained independence in 1947, the framework for this particular contribution to sport and post-colonialism revolves around pre- and post-1947 reflections upon sport and the Indian body.

Finally, the post-colonial refers to post-colonial states in particular parts of Africa and thus the issue of 'when' relates to the period following the ending of colonial rule in Africa, not the lingering effects of colonialism; this refers to the lingering lived experiences of Africans inhabiting this post-colonial Africa. Specifically drawing upon this second meaning, Vidacs's (2003) account of Cameroon football is set against the context of the 1998 Football World Cup in France in which the ideal world of football and justice outside of Cameroon was deemed to be lacking. Cameroonians, like other Africans (Vidacs, 2003: 237), create outside models of great nations to make sense of their own lives. The football ideal of the level playing field was smashed in 1998, and this gave rise to bitterness and despair among many Cameroonians. Following the defeat of the Cameroon football team, the problems of football in a post-colonial Africa were hidden or explained by an anti-FIFA, anti-white and anti-European account for the failure of the Cameroon football team to live up to the ideal of post-colonial football.

Attending to the cultural, historical, social, political and geographical differences of post-colonial sports is crucial. But, as the above examples illustrate, the specific 'when' of post-colonial sports cannot be answered in the singular. The specifics of 'when' in regard to post-colonial sport would need to take cognisance of the fact that India and Pakistan gained independence in 1947, Ceylon (now Sri Lanka) in 1948, Ghana, the first majority rule independent African country, in 1957, followed by Nigeria in 1960. Jamaica and Trinidad

181

and Tobago followed suit in the Caribbean in 1962 and, more recently, Hong Kong passed from Britain to China in July 1997.

The post-colonial sporting world would also need to take cognisance of the way in which sport has contributed, or could contribute, to anti-colonial struggles in those countries recently occupied. Should China's human rights record in Tibet, for example, have influenced the awarding of the 2008 Olympic Games to Beijing? Or should the awarding of the 2002 World Cup to Japan and South Korea have recognised those Koreans who cannot return to their own country at this time? Perhaps at this point in development of research into post-colonial sports, it is wise to suggest that detailed historical work on aspects of local post-colonial sports should serve as a defence against simplistic historical or geographical generalisations. 'Post-colonial sport' should not be a generalising term, but students and researchers of sport, culture and society may inevitably link differences and think comparatively across differences, as well as between 'other' sporting communities.

Not yet global or post-colonial sport

The power of sport to make money has been one of the key drivers behind the expansion of sport. Three of the main drivers behind the aspiration of global sport have been money, technology and the quest for cultural recognition on the international playing field. The impact of new technology has meant that the world itself has seemingly become a smaller place. Television and new media have contributed to new home-centred forms of entertainment. Telecommunications, in general, have also brought a richer diversity of world sports into people's homes. At the same time, developments in communications technology have made it more difficult to shield a state population from impressions of the outside world.

While the breakdown of selected economic frontiers may have allowed sport to become more international, part of the problem facing Northern-dominated professional sports organisations has been their assumptions concerning the rest of the world. These assumptions have, in part, been born out of a colonial or Western mentality. There are at least two modes of contemporary thinking about contemporary sport that display such a mentality. First, there is the notion that the professional sports market is dominated by professional sports that have been propagated in the West, and that professional sports enterprises around the world have followed this model. Part of this assumption has been to suggest that international trends emerging in sport have been examples of Americanisation rather than of globalisation. The argument is supported as a result of the outcome, power and explosion of sports on television, particularly on pay and cable platforms, such as Fox in the US, Star TV in Asia, BSkyB in Britain and Foxtel in Australia. Television will continue to expand its markets throughout Asia and Africa, and yet such vast warehouses of sports entertainment are also accompanied by the not-so-subtle reinforcement of the consumption experiences that have become commonplace in the US, but not perhaps in 'other' parts of the world.

The core problem, however, remains one of cultural compatibility and recognition that the professional Western sports model is not the only way to deliver sport. The Western model seems to want to continue to re-invent sport in the rest of the world in its own image, a universal approach that does not recognise or value the fundamentally different value systems that operate in different parts of the world. It is incomprehensible to imagine such a model of professional sport prospering in parts of the Middle East, simply because the values of professional sport are incompatible with the wider cultures. Sport, in the above form, will struggle to make significant inroads into the Middle East and other Islamic nations until sport managers abandon the need to inculcate Western values. It is doubtful if, in the early part of the twenty-first century, the promise or aspiration of global sport is worth dilution of the distinctive national ethnic and religious cultures. Attempts to represent sport both in and from 'other' sporting worlds have involved issues of hybridity, mimicry, orientalism, myth and invented sporting traditions. Sport might have become increasingly international, but not yet global or post-colonial.

SPORT, POWER AND THE SOUTH

In terms of terminology, there are several problems associated with notions such as First World sport or Third World sport, not just in terms of the very language reproducing a hierarchical stereotype, but the terms themselves have changed over time. The term 'Third World' was first used in 1952 to designate those countries that were aligned with neither the US nor the former Soviet Union during the Cold War period. Third World sports, by definition, followed the same geographical demarcation as those sports associated with the local indigenous Third World. The term 'First World' was widely used to refer to the dominant economic and political powers of the West, while the term 'Second World' was used to refer to the Soviet Union and its allies. The term 'tricontinental' has often replaced the term 'Third World' as a geographical and cultural description of the three continents of Latin America, Africa and Asia, while the North and South divide refers to countries in the Northern Hemisphere or the Southern Hemisphere (Huish, 2011).

Yet, there needs to be a word of caution here in accepting too readily a definition or process of globalisation that acts purely against the interests of the southern hemisphere. It has been relatively easy for Islamic countries and those countries of the South to denounce imperialism, globalisation and global sport as unjust. It is necessary, however, to guard against seeing global sport and globalisation as simply imperialism or yet another form of unequal exchange between the North and the South. To dismiss globalisation and global sport purely in terms of imperialism obscures the extent to which some Arab countries have different stakes in globalisation in that they provide oil and, by continuing to feed the West, such countries actively feed globalisation. It also fails to acknowledge the power of the Asian economy or the way in which sport in Japan may synthesise Western and traditional cultures. Alternatively, a significant body of research into baseball in the Dominican Republic suggested that the development of Latin baseball was conditioned, in part, by a dependency upon the power of the American baseball leagues to attract the best players and undermine baseball at 'home'. However, in the early part of the twenty-first century, such argument would fail to acknowledge the extent to which Latino baseball players might play in Japanese or American leagues, and therefore reduce the power of the American hold on baseball by playing the interests of Japanese baseball off against the power of US baseball.

As examples of the development, background and symbolism of sports in 'other' communities, the All-African Games, the African Nations Cup, the Asian Games and the Pan American Games are a particularly fertile soil for thinking more internationally about sport, culture and society in places other than Europe.

All-African Games

Attempts had been made to hold African Games in Algiers as early as 1925 and in Alexandria in 1928, but they failed owing to, among other reasons, colonial politics and economic difficulties. The impact of colonialism was such that, in the early 1960s, the Friendship Games were held among French-speaking countries in Africa. At the conference of African Ministers for Youth and Sport held in Paris in 1962, it was decided that the Games would thereafter be called the Pan-African Games, as they would include countries other than those colonised by the French. The All-African Games eventually emerged in 1965 as a force for African solidarity and as a means of uniting the continent against South Africa's apartheid regime. That same year, the Games were granted official recognition by the IOC. Some 2,500 athletes from 30 independent African states attended the 1965 All-African Games held in Brazzaville, Congo. The sixth All-African Games were held in 1995, with the inclusion of (post-apartheid) South Africa for the first time (Levinson and Christensen, 1996: 4). The 2003 eighth All-African Games were hosted in Abuja, Nigeria, with the specific mission to act 'as a wake-up call for an African continent threatened by war, disease, hunger and poverty, to respond positively to the challenge by using sports as a strong weapon' in this struggle (www.8allafricagames.org). As the world has viewed the images and cries for help highlighted by the international singer and songwriter Bob Geldof in parts of Africa such as Ethiopia, it is often forgotten that humanitarian political leaders, such as Nelson Mandela, the former South African President, have repeatedly stated that football is a force that mobilises the sentiments of a people in a way that nothing else can (*Observer*, 13 July 2003: 14). More recently, former US President Bill Clinton suggested that football has done more for poor countries in the world than almost anything else. Sport in Focus 7.6 provides an insight into how sport can help.

The Asian Games

The Asian Games are held for the purpose of developing inter-cultural knowledge and friendship within Asia. The Games are intended as a forum for cultural exchange, with the official programme including both sport and the arts. The roots of the current Games date back to 1913 when the Far East Championships were held, involving China, Japan and the Philippines. The modern Asian Games, the invention of tradition, were re-established at India's suggestion following World War II and were first held in New Delhi in 1951. Eleven nations and some 489 athletes competed in the first Games. Israel attended, but Syria did not; Pakistan, only recently separated from India, refused to attend, while communist China and Vietnam boycotted because India refused to recognise either government. The fourth Asian Games, held in Jakarta, Indonesia, in 1962, witnessed a move to establish a separate structure, termed the Games of the Newly Emerging Forces (GANEFO). Such a move was

SPORT IN FOCUS 7.6: FOOTBALL, RWANDA AND CAMEROON

The promise that football holds in Africa may be illustrated by two recent examples of the complexity, difference and possibilities that are part of African football. The first example is drawn from the 2003 African Nations Cup match between Rwanda and Uganda. The match was characterised by scenes of violence between players, and between the players and police (Carlin, 2003: 14). A couple of early saves by the Rwandan keeper Mohammed Mossi incited the 60,000 crowd to claim that the Rwandan goalkeeper was using supernatural powers. Abubaker Tabula of Uganda started digging behind the Rwandan goal to find the offending *juju* – a witchcraft doll placed by the Rwandans behind their goal. Mayhem followed, with the referee ordering the players to leave the pitch. Half an hour later, the game resumed and Rwanda went on to win 1–0. Celebrations across a united Rwanda followed in a country that, less than 10 years earlier in 1994, had endured the government-incited massacre of 800,000 Tutsis and as many people murdered on any one day for 100 days as died in the September 11 attack on the World Trade Center in New York. Following the match, Hutus and Tutsis, genocide killers and genocide survivors, danced in the streets of Rwanda together, while the then Tutsi President Paul Kagame was joined at the airport by almost half the country's eight million people to meet the Hutu captain and the victorious football team (*Observer*, 13 July 2003: 14). The president announced there and then that new presidential elections would be held the following month, the first since his coming to power. It was generally acknowledged that only football could have had such a huge impact upon the task of national reconciliation in one of the world's most ethnically divided and damaged countries.

In June of 2003, the Cameroon footballer Marc Vivien Foé died during a semi-final of the Confederations Cup match in which Cameroon was aiming to become the first African nation to qualify for the final of a major World Cup football tournament. The death of the football star was front-page news across Europe and Africa, with the *Cameroon Tribune* summing up the loss to the nation in the phrase 'a giant is killed in combat' (*The Herald*, 28 June 2003: 4). One of the poorest nations in the world, Cameroon has a life expectancy of well below 50, an average annual wage of £350 and, at the time, was on the brink of war with Nigeria over contested oil territories. It is home to around 130 different ethnic groups and several languages. There are few things with the potential to unite and reconcile Cameroon, but since 1990 the footballing 'Lions' of the national team have succeeded in bringing people together in a way that few other aspects of life can. It is viewed as an opportunity for Cameroon to compete and succeed on an equal footing with the rest of the world. The final against France went ahead despite the death of the player. This led to criticism of the President of FIFA, Sepp Blatter, from the French captain, Patrick Vieira.

185

in clear opposition to the Western powers. Both China and the then Soviet Union supplied money and sent athletes. GANEFO survived long enough to show the West that the Asian nations could organise alternative games.

The Olympic Council of Asia was formed in 1982, with 43 countries and regions affiliating by 2003. The traditional Asian game of kabbadi was featured at the Beijing Games of 1990, but most of the events remained modern and Western. In 1994, the Asian Games were hosted by Hiroshima, Japan, and symbolised the regeneration of the city; Kazakhstan became the first ex-Soviet Asian Republic to attend the Games, and was another illustration of the dynamic changing geography of world sport (Levinson and Christensen, 1996: 22). The emblem for the 1994 Asian Games depicted a dove, the symbol of peace and the 'H' of Hiroshima, reflecting Hiroshima's desire for peace. The slogan accompanying the emblem expressed the wish that the Games would foster mutual respect among the Asian peoples as they worked to build an attractive, dynamic Asia for the twenty-first century.

The 2002 Games were hosted by Busan in South Korea. North Korea participated for the first time in games held in South Korea; North Korea's national anthem was played for the first time in South Korea, the law banning the display of North Korean flags being set aside for the Games, although it was still illegal for individual South Koreans to fly North Korean flags. Internal Chinese colonialism meant that Taiwan was represented as Chinese Taipei and athletes from Taiwan were forced to march behind the Chinese banner. Afghanistan participated in the 2002 Asian Games, the first since the Taliban came to power, despite the lack of facilities or sporting infrastructure in Afghanistan.

The 2006 Games were hosted in Doha, Qatar. Qatar is a state of only 600,000 inhabitants and one of the issues to be resolved is the demand made by some Muslim states with regard to sportswear worn by some Muslim women athletes. As a result, Western-dominated sportswear manufacturing companies have been accused by some Islamic nations of exploiting women athletes and not developing suitable sportswear for women in Islamic countries. There is also the issue of various interpretations of the Koran, which raises issues of modest dress worn by women, but is in fact interpreted by some Islamic sections as the obligatory covering up of limbs and even the face, and raises questions as to whether the issue is one of faith and religion or a mixture of faith and patriarchy. Qatar sent a team of women athletes to Busan in 2002 in preparation for 2006. At the time women of Qatar were expected to compete in a number of events , with the official website at the time reading that Qatar 'intends to train women volunteers, referees, technicians, officials and athletes so that they can attain international standards while still respecting Islamic values'. While Islamic fundamentalism might be viewed in the West as problematic, it is no more so than one of the other forceful ideologies of the twenty-first century, namely global and domestic free markets extending as widely and as rapidly as possible.

The Pan American Games

At the 1932 Los Angeles Olympic Games, representatives from Latin American countries proposed a regional games for all the Americas. A Pan American Sports Congress was proposed for 1942, but it was not until 1948 in London that such an event took place. The founding Pan American Games took place in Buenos Aires in 1951, in what was termed a

SPORT IN FOCUS 7.7: THE RIO DE JANEIRO PAN AMERICAN GAMES

In 2007, Brazil showed the rest of the Americas how successful the Pan American Games can be. Hosted in city of Rio de Janeiro, it set a new precedent for the Pan American Games by producing an event at a near Olympic Games level.

The Pan American Sports Organization (PASO) declared the event the most successful in the history of the Games, due to the incredible support from government at all levels. Furthermore, the Games saw exceptional audience interest, with the highest public attendance and largest television audience in Pan American history.

A total of 5,633 athletes from 42 National Olympic Committees (NOCs) took part in 332 events in 34 sports and in 47 disciplines. During the Games, 95 new Pan American records were set; 2,196 medals were awarded; 1,262 doping control tests were performed and around 15,000 volunteers participated in the organisation of the event.

Rio de Janeiro was the most expensive Pan American Games ever, with a budget of $2 billion. This money was used to greatly improve the sporting infrastructure of the city, including constructing the Estádio Olímpico João Havelange and renovating the Estádio do Maracanã.

Brazil's triumphant and smooth hosting of the Games demonstrated to the international community that the country had the ability to successfully host the largest of sporting events. Consequently, Brazil won the bid to host the 2014 FIFA World Cup, while Rio de Janeiro will hold the Olympic Games in 2016.

However, what will become of the Pan American Games in the future? Whether the event can maintain the level of interest developed at the Rio de Janeiro games remains to be seen. Ultimately, this lies in the hands of the organising committees for Guadalajara 2011 and Toronto 2015.

festival of sport and international friendship. Twenty-two countries and 2,500 athletes competed in 19 events. The organisation governing the Games was renamed in 1955 as the Pan American Sports Organization (PASO). In 1979, Puerto Rico spent US$60 million on new facilities for the Games. Cuba hosted the 1991 games and set new records in the numbers of athletes and countries participating. The US's economic embargo on Cuba meant that only $1.2 million of the original agreed figure of $9 million from television rights reached Cuba. The Games returned to Argentina in 1995, with more than 5,000 athletes from 42 countries competing in 37 sports. The Games' slogan 'América: Espírito, Sport, Fraternité' uses the principal languages of the hemisphere, but is also in itself a symbol of various forms of colonialism (Levinson and Christensen, 1996: 288). The phrase, loosely translated, means 'the American spirit of friendship through sports'. PASO, currently made up of the 42 nations of North, Central and South America and the Caribbean, continues to govern the Games.

The three examples given above illustrate the cultural politics of sport in other worlds. The dialogue about Southern sport, and in particular Latin American sport, often starts from the position that the power structures of global sport have not materially shifted since the end of the imperial era. Such an argument runs the risk of passing over the differences within and between sports in other communities in the southern hemisphere. The cultural politics of sport presents neither a homogeneous picture of the West, nor sport on the three continents. A substantive body of work relating to the relationship between sport in Africa, Asia and the Americas, particularly those countries south of the US, might be further enhanced by linking the politics of sport in anti-colonial or post-colonial struggles with the politics of sport and anti-globalisation. The geography of the current anti-globalisation protests signals a new world political landscape, and the seeds of what have been sown in Chiapas or Porto Alegre or Seattle or Genoa or Barcelona point towards an entirely new ideological, political and geographical shift.

It is not necessary to see this as irrelevant to sport, culture and society, and indeed such issues are explored further in Parts 3 and 4 of this book, but the potential emergence of a global three-way split in the values associated with contemporary sport and other sporting communities is as serious as the ideological differences that divided sport in the twentieth century. The following are but three contemporary developments that mark the return of ideology into world sport:

■ aggressive American expansionism with American sports and television companies seeking a greater share of global sport – American-dominated transnational sports companies are able to come and go as they please in many of the poorer countries of the world;

■ sport and progressive globalisation or internationalisation, in which the pursuit of a genuine multilateral effort in sport is leading to greater economic, political and social equality in and through sport; and

■ sport and physical culture within Islamic fundamentalism either allowing for the opening up of or mutual respect for the place and presence of Islamic sport and body culture or conflict, in which the values associated with sport and physical culture are positioned as an alternative to American neo-liberal expansionism or progressive globalisation.

Only one of these three ideologies has the potential for contributing to the reality of global sport.

Finally, it might be suggested that the social dimension of global sport is destined to remain an empty slogan as long as there exists a relative imbalance between the means for the peoples of the South to propose to the North their own interpretation of global sport and the common ground between the different worlds of sport, values and societies. There is much more to this than the production of a post-colonial understanding of sport in other communities, or the proliferation of hybrid sporting alternatives, or a redistribution of some of the wealth brought about through international sport. Yet, if nothing else, the value of a post-colonial understanding of sport is that it serves as a constant reminder that attending to the cultural, historical, social, political, economic and geographical differences of other sports is paramount to an understanding of sport, culture and society. Comparative modes of thought about sport remain a valuable means of critique, and need not lead to generality and universalism, but are also a safeguard against fundamentalism or identity sporting politics. The role of sport in international development is complex (Darnell and Black, 2011).

SUMMARY

The themes of community and the place of sport in the community have been commented upon for more than half a century. There remains a substantive moral and political dis-agreement between those who value community in itself and those who value it instru-mentally. This chapter has argued that it is unrealistic to expect sport to be totally responsible for sustaining a sense of community or citizenship, or even for reinforcing notions of social capital. However, sports projects and the place of sport within both imagined and active senses of communities can make a valuable contribution. More importantly, it is the potential contribution that sport makes to civil society, the space between the state and the individual, that provides sport with the opportunity to promote a communitarian philosophy based upon mutuality and obligations rather than individualism and some ideological notion of sport for all.

In answer to the question 'is sport good for the community?', it might be useful to qualify any notion of universality by suggesting that:

- sport can play a positive role in a number of wide-ranging community initiatives that can help to sustain a sense of community;
- sport on its own is not the solution to community social and economic problems but it can be part of the solution;
- policy advisers and social theorists need to test empirically a number of statements concerning the role of sport and its associated outcomes in specific settings before concluding on the issue of sports relationship to communities; and
- communities themselves change over time, and whether one is talking about a com-munity of Internet sport enthusiasts or the place and space associated with sport in the geography of communities recognition must be given to the fact that the relationship between sport and the community is never static but always changing.

The term 'community' is often missing in the worlds we inhabit and yet it is potentially a crucial quality to a happier life. The worlds of sport and beyond would be safer, more secure and less vulnerable if community was more of a reality. Given the insecurity and concerns about safety in a rapidly globalising interdependent world, we need to gain control over the conditions under which we struggle with the challenges of life and, for most people, such control can only be gained by working collectively. If there is to be any notion of active community in a world of many individuals, it needs to be a community woven together from sharing and mutual care. If sport can help to provide moments of safety, security and hope for vulnerable groups of people, then it has a part to play in creating a community of concern and responsibility for the equal right to be human and the equal ability to act on that right. At present, those excluded from sport in many parts of the world do not have access to that right.

A body of work on sport has focused on an evaluation of colonial and post-colonial sport. Post-colonialism is not the only idea that has drawn attention to sport in *other communities*. This chapter has considered the strengths and weaknesses of post-colonialism as an idea that draws attention to the dynamics of sport in other communities. There are many under-studied regions, places and peoples of the world that are not included within the umbrella terms of 'post-colonialism' or, indeed, 'global sport'. There is a greater danger in global sport or free-market sport being adopted as a euphemism for Western sport. Nonetheless, the social and political dynamics of contemporary sport necessitate not only an understanding of 'other' sporting communities; the value of sensitivity to other sporting communities is one of the best defences against inward looking parochialism, nationalism and a sole concentration upon identity sporting politics.

A final related issue might be the right of all people to have access to sport, to participate in sport and to be represented through sport. A sensitivity to the expanding world of sporting communities has, at least at the time of writing this book, begun to present itself through a number of significant and sustained bodies of sporting work that have opened up particular avenues into 'other' sporting communities. Yet, as alluded to earlier in this chapter, perhaps the overall value lies in its method as a safeguard against inward-looking parochialism and as the conscience of cosmopolitan sport, in case it forgets 'other' traditions of sport, the poor or the use of cheap labour in sporting production, or the power of sport in 'other' parts of the world.

GUIDE TO FURTHER READING

Amir, G. (2011). *Global History: A View from the South.* Oxford: Pambazuka Press.

Bauman, Z. (2001). *Community: Seeking Safety in an Insecure World.* Cambridge: Polity Press.

Bale, J. and Cronin, M. (2003). *Sport and Post-colonialism.* Oxford: Berg.

Bloomfield, S. (2010). *Africa United.* Edinburgh: Cannongate.

Darnell, S. and Black, D. (2011). 'Mainstreaming Sport into International Development Studies'. *Third World Quarterly,* 32 (3): 367–378.

Huish, R. (2011). 'Punching Above It's Weight: Cuba's Use of Sport for South–South Co-operation'. *Third World Quarterly,* 32 (3) April: 417–433.

Jiwani, N. and Rail, G. (2010). 'Islam, Hijab and Young Shia Muslim Canadian Women's Dioscusrsive Constructions of Physical Activity'. *Sociology of Sport,* 27 (3): 251–267.

Nicholson, M. and Hoye, R. (2008). *Sport and Social Capital.* London: Elsevier.

Okayasu, I., Kawahara, Y. and Nogowa, H. (2010). 'The Relationship Between Community Sports Clubs and Social Capital in Japan: A Comparative Study Between the Comprehensive Community Sports Clubs and Traditional Community Sports Clubs'. *International Review for the Sociology of Sport,* 45 (2): 163–186.

Wilkinson, J. (2010). 'Personal Communities'. *Sociology,* 44 (3): 453–471.

QUESTIONS

1 Compare and contrast at least four different ways in which sport is said to contribute to the notion of community.

2 What do the terms 'communitarianism', 'community stakeholder' and 'social capital' mean?

3 What are some of the characteristics often ascribed to the notion of community?

4 Describe the associational nature of sport in Denmark.

5 Explain what is meant by 'other' sporting communities.

6 How might the notion of post-colonial sport provide a critique of global sport?

7 Provide a short but detailed history of the Asian Games, The Pan American Games or the All-African Games.

8 Why might the terms 'First World' and 'Third World' be seen as problematic?

9 Define any two of the following terms: 'other', 'post-colonial', 'imperialism' or 'volunteering'.

10 Provide a brief history of the either the All-African Games or the Pan American Games.

PRACTICAL PROJECTS

1 Identify one socially excluded group of your choice. Develop a policy document designed to promote social inclusion in sport.

2 Look at the constitution of three different sports clubs, and compare and contrast the different ways in which the constitution promotes or discourages communitarianism or mutual obligations to the community in which the clubs are located.

3 Interview ten different local people, taking into account different generations of people, and ask them how sport has helped to develop or fragment social cohesion within the neighbourhood. Based upon your findings, write a report on sport and community within your neighbourhood.

4 Alongside the huge disparities in wealth between rich countries and poor countries is also the idea that sport in the world is unequal and unfair. Examine the sports that are represented at the Olympic Games and make a list of those traditional sports in non-Western countries that are not represented.

5 Explore further one of the websites provided in this chapter with a view to finding out about either the All-African Games or the Asian Games, and provide a short history of this event.

KEY CONCEPTS

Civil society ■ Civic engagement ■ Colonialism ■ Communitatrianism ■ Democracy ■ Hybridity ■ Imperialism ■ Mutuality ■ North/South divide ■ Orientalism ■ Other ■ Periphery ■ Power ■ Third World ■ Voluntarism

WEBSITES

All-African Games
www.allafricagamesmaputo.com/
The official website of the 2011 All-African Games.

2014 Asian Games
www.ocasia.org/Game/GameParticular.aspx?GPCode=32
The official website of the 2014 Asian Games in Incheon.

The 2011 Pan American Games
www.guadalajara2011.org.mx/ENG/01_inicio/
The official website of the 2011 Pan American Games.

UNESCO on traditional games and sports
www.unesco.org/new/en/social-and-human-sciences/themes/sport/physical-education-and-sport/traditional-sports-and-games/
UNESCO's approach to traditional games and sport as the basis of community spirit and a celebration of cultural roots.

Scottish Highland Games
www.shga.co.uk/
The official website of the Scottish Highland Games Association.

Chapter 8

Sport, law and governance

Is sport just, fair, transparent and accountable?

Should violence, corruption and/or the taking of drugs in sport be dealt with within the international sporting community or outside the jurisdiction of sport itself?

PREVIEW

Key terms defined ■ Introduction ■ FIFA World Cup Bids 2010 ■ Foul play in cricket ■ Sport and corruption ■ The Kakuta affair ■ Sport and the law ■ How should sport be regulated? European and US models ■ Sports regulation and the market ■ Is sport above or below the law? ■ Bosman Ruling ■ Webster Ruling ■ International Court of Arbitration in Sport ■ Sporting governance ■ Sporting institutions ■ A debate about sporting institutions ■ The deep challenge of global sport democracy ■ Zimbabwe and the 2003 Cricket World Cup ■ Pakistan, Corruption and cricket 2010 ■ Challenges for global sport ■ Summary

OBJECTIVES

This chapter will:

- look at the relationship between sport and the law;
- examine the role of sport's independent Court of Arbitration;
- evaluate the allegation that corruption is an identifiable feature of sport;
- answer the question 'what is democracy in relation to sport?'; and
- consider broader questions of sporting governance and the need for regulation.

KEY TERMS DEFINED

Cartel: Where two or more businesses reach a formal or informal agreement to limit competition among themselves; (for example, by fixing similar prices).

Constructivist: An approach that concerns itself with the centrality of ideas and human consciousness, and stresses a holistic and idealist view of structures.

Global governance: The evolving system of political coordination among public authorities and private agencies seeking to realise common purposes or resolve collective problems through the making and implementing of global or transnational norms, rules, programmes and policies.

Realist: An approach that sees power as the prime motivation or driving force of all political life. Adopts a limited view of power that focuses on the group and not the individual.

INTRODUCTION

This chapter provides a critical comment upon law and governance within international sport. The issues of sports governance and sports law have been freely used in contemporary discussions about the sporting world (Glendinning, 2009). The theme of governance has a prominent place in discussions about global sport and whether or not it is possible, or even desirable, to develop a more progressive approach towards the reform of sporting structures, regulations, practices and laws. We know that the duality of sport means that it unites and divides, is fair and foul, healthy and destructive, expressive and controlled, myth and reality, and both public and private in terms of team ownership. Living with an increasingly international entity that is sport today involves a mutual responsibility for all that comes with twenty-first-century sport. Arguably, the enduring moral problem of global sport is the vast gap between and within different sporting worlds. One thing that, so far, has escaped global sport has been the collective ability to act globally.

Taken in isolation, the 2010–11 allegations about FIFA World Cup bid corruption, match fixing by Pakistani cricketers and gambling by Ted Forstmaan would be worrying, but the fact that that they have all happened in one year not only raises questions about the relationship between commercialisation and sport, but also the power of governance that is or is not being exercised by governing bodies of sport. FIFA, the international custodian of football, is publicly embroiled in allegations of corruption in the process that led to the awarding of FIFA World Cups to Russia and Qatar. The enormous contract value of hosting a World Cup places FIFA members in a commercially privileged position. The point about Ted Forstmaan's gambling is not just about potential corruption, but about responsibilities of governance. Whether or not Forstmaan was exerting influence or using inside knowledge is irrelevant since he contravened the regulations of the International Tennis Federation by gambling, as a tournament owner, on the outcome of a tennis tournament. Many international federations struggle to balance a primary and principle objective of promoting sport with increasing private sector involvement where the primary and principle objective is commercialisation. The goal of commercialisation can, at times, obscure or subsume the responsibility to create a fair competition and a legitimate winner. As Sport in Focus 8.1 illustrates, it is not as if the relationship between sport and corruption is new and, therefore, governing bodies have a lot of case study material to learn from.

There has been a resurgence of interest in issues relating to sports governance; so too there has been a specialist development in sport and the law. The implicit notion that sport is above the law or has separate mechanisms for dealing with sporting problems and issues has produced not only a burgeoning body of case study material, but also a body of literature that has begun to add to our knowledge about sport, law and society; the governance of sport; commercial regulation of sport; regulation of the sports workplace; and comparative directives such as European Community law. At the heart of this chapter, then, are some straightforward questions. If global sport exists, should a system of global sporting governance exist? Is sport above or subject to the law and, if so, what law, national, international and/or a specific sports judiciary?

The contemporary sporting landscape is characterised by a highly dense network of organisations. It remains open to question as to whether it is possible to refer to a system of global sporting governance. Are current international sporting regimes dependent upon certain underlying power structures of Western dominance and Western preferences, and how sustainable is this given the changing power balances and levels of cultural diversity within sport today? The analysis of the relationship between North and South introduced in Part 1 is not irrelevant to matters of governance and regulation, since issues of governance and regulation may be viewed as both a problem and a solution for those analysing the different experiences of the industrialised North and the marginalised South. Arguably, global sport is primarily shaped by relations between three groupings (North America, Western Europe and East Asia) but it is a moot point as to whether global sporting governance is attempting to regulate and manage inequalities between these groupings.

Good governance is often associated with sets of guiding principles such as transparency, democracy, effective management, responsibility, coooperation, representativeness and ethics. The term 'governance', as it has been used in sport, has tended to be closely related to organisational theory, management and the governance of sport per se (Hoye et al., 2010).

195

SPORT IN FOCUS 8.1: A RECENT HISTORY OF FOUL PLAY IN CRICKET

1994   England's Michael Atherton was fined £2000 for illegeally rubbing sand on the ball in a Lord's Test against South Africa.

2000   South Africa captain Hansie Cronje was banned for life for taking £68,000 from bookmakers to throw games against India.

2000   Pakistan captain Saleem Malik was banned after match-fixing claims over tours of South Africa and Zimbabwe.

2001   India's Sachin Tendulkar was banned for one game for scuffing the seam of the ball during a match against South Africa.

2006   Pakistan captain Inzaman ul-Haq brought the game into disrepute after accusations of ball tampering at the Oval.

2010   Stand-in Pakistan captain Shahid Afridi received a two-game ban after biting a ball's seam to gain an illegal advantage against Australia.

2011   After accusations of accepting cash to bowl no-balls during a Test match against England in 2010, Pakistani cricketers Salman Butt, Mohammad Asif and Mohammad Amir were given bans of 10 years, 7 years and 5 years respectively by the International Cricket Council. On 30 November, the three players were convicted of on-field corruption in a UK court.

The concept of governance is intrinsically bound up with that of globalisation. It remains imprecise as a term but might loosely be referred to as consisting of self-organising inter-organisational networks. It is essential to stipulate that governance is much more than government. This chapter begins at another level: that any progressive notion of global sport necessitates paying attention to a system of governance at both national and international levels. It is tempting to suggest that a system of global sporting governance is already evolving, based on various relationships between the sporting organisations of nation states; supranational federations, such as UEFA; international sporting institutions, such as the International Athletics Association or the International Olympic Association or FIFA; multinational corporations, such as those which finance major sporting events; non-governmental sporting organisations; quasi-autonomous government quangos; and others. The most difficult, perhaps impossible, task is to ground these institutions in forms of democratic accountability.

Good governance means recognising the specificity and values of sport but it also means recognising its failings and its continual struggle to combat issues of corruption, gambling, drug taking and player trafficking, violence, and child protection, to name by a few issues. Sport in Focus 8.2 provides a short case study of one such incident. The Kakuta affair, named after a young French footballer illegally recruited by Chelsea, brings to the forefront the issues of safeguarding young players, international training systems and the international

SPORT IN FOCUS 8.2: THE KAKUTA AFFAIR AND ITS IMPLICATIONS

The Kakuta Affair was a case surrounding the controversial transfer of the young French forward Gaël Kakuta from RC Lens to Chelsea FC. The case involved issues around the rights of smaller football clubs in Europe to hold on to young players they had invested in and developed. It was expected to be a benchmark case that would influence future transfers of youth players in Europe.

Kakuta began his football career in 1999 as an eight-year-old in RC Lens's youth system. However, in 2007, he controversially moved to Chelsea to join their youth team. RC Lens were dismayed by the loss of one of their top prospects, and sought legal action against Chelsea.

In August 2009, the FIFA Dispute Ruling Chamber concluded that Kakuta was in breach of contract and was banned for four months from competitive action and fined €780,000, for which Chelsea were deemed jointly and severally liable for also. Chelsea were punished further with a transfer ban until January 2011, and ordered to pay RC Lens training compensation of €130,000.

transfer of underage players. Regulating the international transfer of athletes is an important governance issue that crosses nation state, regional and, in some cases, multinational regulatory frameworks.

However, instead of this ruling setting a precedent for future cases of youth player 'stealing', the whole case descended into farce. Chelsea took the case to the Court of Arbitration for Sport (CAS) to appeal the decision. The original decision by the FIFA Dispute Ruling Chamber was cancelled when RC Lens could not produce any evidence of a contract between the club and Gaël Kakuta. Chelsea and Kakuta had their respective bans rescinded and were liable to pay nothing, although in an act of good faith Chelsea paid RC Lens the original €130,000 training compensation fee.

As of March 2011, there is still no legal framework in Europe for the 'stealing' of youth players by the top clubs. Furthermore, this is a global issue, with teams in South America particularly susceptible to the loss of youth players to more illustrious clubs in Europe. Ultimately, the Kakuta affair has done little to tackle this issue.

Many sports organisations at an ideological level think of themselves as being democratic despite operating exclusive sport for *some* policies. In this sense, democracy remains one of the key ideologies for sport, governance and society. It could be suggested that contemporary liberal democracy, as practised throughout Western sport, is lacking in a number of fundamental ways. Notably, it is lacking in its inability to control the way in which global sports companies exploit world labour markets, or the way in which certain sports fail to recognise individual differences of, for example, age, ethnicity, gender and even class. Sport in the West tends to be undemocratic in at least one sense, in that large sections of the population remain disenfranchised when it comes to voting for positions of power and

197

influence within sporting clubs and organisations. The football authorities in Great Britain and even governments view sceptically the setting up of supporter-owned football trusts or an increased community stake in the sports plc model of governance. There have been few opportunities in Britain or the US to develop the sort of ownership pattern practised within Barcelona Football Club or to develop a system of free associations that characterise the very essence of democratic sport in certain Scandinavian countries, such as Sweden or Denmark.

The issue of democracy has been one that has been readily debated within sport, culture and society. There are various national sports organisations that claim to be more democratic by the fact that they operate at arm's length from government, and yet the notion and future of democracy is rarely in itself questioned. Today, the connotations of the word are so favourable that organisations and forms of state control that have no claim to being referred to as being 'democratic' still use the term. As a descriptive term, democracy is closely associated with majority rule and yet there is no real consensus as to what majority rule really means. For example, do issues relating to majority rule or the democratic nature of sport include:

- Who are to count as the people and what is a 'majority of them'?
- Why, if at all, should majorities rule minorities?
- Which system of democracy should be preferred – a direct or representative one?
- What are the dangers of majority rule for minority rights?

Sport has long been viewed as a graphic symbol of meritocracy despite the fact that sociologists and others have been questioning the substantive basis for such a claim for more than half a century. The question remains, however, as to whether the popular image of sport as an unquestioned democracy of ability and practice is somewhat exaggerated, if not mythical. Generally speaking, the term 'democratisation' tends to imply a widening degree of opportunity or a diminishing degree of separatism in varying forms of sports involvement. The term has also been used to describe the process whereby employees or clients have more control over sporting decisions and sporting bodies. The expansion of opportunities in sport might be used, at one level, to argue that sport, at least in the West, has become more open. Moffat (2000: 33) suggests that the reality, in Britain at least, is that the extremes of privilege and poverty remain sharply drawn.

Should golf clubs that are in receipt of public monies be allowed to operate exclusive policies? Just as progressive globalisation needs a system of democratic governance at both a national and international level, so too does sport. Sport, law and governance are therefore linked to other notions, such as democracy, ownership and power. The danger is that, in a world of global sporting interdependencies, with no corresponding global or international sporting polity and few tools of global sporting justice, the rich of the sporting world are free to pursue their own interests, while paying little attention to the rest.

SPORT AND LAW

The contemporary relationship between sport and the law can be partially gleaned from the topics covered by the magazine *Sportsbusiness* listed in Sport in Focus 8.3. The last few years have witnessed growth in litigation involving sports matters. The threat of players' strikes in Britain and America has illustrated the growing influence of players' unions in disputes over earnings and players' rights. The part played by sport and Internet gambling has raised questions over whether specific laws concerning data protection stop at the state or national border or are, in fact, subject to international laws. The celebrity status of sportsmen and sportswomen enables them to cash in on their fame through endorsements and merchandising, yet many sport stars have instigated legal action in order to own their own name for the purposes of using it as a domain name on the Internet. The employment contracts of football managers and players have often appeared to be 'unique' in character when compared to those of executives in other sectors of employment. The difference between a violent tackle in some sports and that which amounts to an act of violence is sometimes hard to define, and varies within and between sporting codes – for example, ice hockey, water polo, wrestling, boxing, rugby union and rugby league.

Terrorist attacks in different parts of the world have meant that contracts to host sporting mega-events now have to cover the possibility of event cancellation, and so insurance companies consider the extent to which insurance coverage operates in such circumstances. The attack on teams travelling through countries to participate in the 2010 African Nations Cup raised concerns about the safety of players. The matches of the 34th Ryder Cup golf tournament between Europe and the US were postponed following the events of 11 September 2001 in New York. It has been suggested by many that, in terms of regulating the use of drugs in sport, there cannot be one system of doping regulation that applies equally to all sports because the nature of sporting activity varies. As the genetic code is unravelled, the issue for sport will be the extent to which genetic manipulation is used to enhance prowess and performance. It seems clear from this very superficial glance at some legal issues that sport is likely to provide plenty of employment for lawyers in the present and the future.

It might be fruitful at this point to answer the question 'what is the law?'. For practical purposes, the law in Scotland is, according to Stewart (2000: 1), what the Queen in parliament says it is, although it must be acknowledged that customary law is the body of decisions of the courts of law. The basic form of law making or legislation is the Act of Parliament that may produce specific sports legislation. It is interesting to note that certain Nordic countries, such as Finland, have the equivalent of a Sports Act that ensures a statutory minimal level of provision for sport in Finland. The law for many sports administrators remains the rulebooks of their governing bodies, and such internal laws often rightly or wrongly provide a mini legal system for those subscribing to it.

At another level, European law is viewed as superior to both Scots law and the laws of the UK parliament. European Community law is the body of law created by the founding Treaties of the European Community, the Treaty of Paris (1951) and the Treaties of Rome (1957). The European Commission has applied European Community law to the sports sector and has probably had the biggest impact, since, as Middleton (2000: 86) asserts, 18 out of the 23 Directorates in the European Commission have impacted directly or indirectly upon European sport. A number of legal cases have been brought before the European Commission, covering such issues as broadcasting rights, the freedom of movement of players across Europe, the employment of foreign players, nationality clauses and quotas, and community competition rules covering concerns such as the regulation and monitoring of

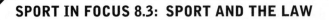

SPORT IN FOCUS 8.3: SPORT AND THE LAW

The following topics form the basis of the main themes covered in sport and the law articles in *Sportsbusiness* between 2000 and 2012:

- the impact of anti-trust law upon US professional sport;
- the ways in which sport is affected by the Human Rights Act of 1998;
- the regulatory framework surrounding the selling of television sports rights and online sports broadcasting piracy;
- the impact of insolvency upon sports rights transactions;
- the harmonisation of sports doping rules and regulations;
- the movement of professional players internationally;
- the licensing laws relating to online sports gambling;
- the separation of image rights from playing contracts;
- the impact of collective bargaining as a mechanism to resolve player disputes;
- the effects of competition law upon the setting up of sports leagues; and
- concerns about money laundering in sport.

ticket sales by agencies. The European Convention on Human Rights has recently been incorporated into UK law by virtue of the Human Rights Act of 1998, which means that sport is now subject to this legislation.

The emergence of new countries, new borders and over-arching memorandums of understanding provides Europe with a volatile mix of constraints and opportunities. The governance of sport in and between countries is varied, complex and ever changing. The challenges for sport are immense and have led some commentators to argue that sport is in a state of crisis, and that international sporting agencies and transnational corporations are more famous for corruption and corporatism rather than social responsibility. A series of guidelines for modernising sporting governance, emphasising stakeholder participation, greater transparency and cooperation between governments, the European Union and the governing bodies of sport all remains work in progress rather than working within a progressive framework for sporting governance. The implementation of the Treaty of Lisbon, in which Article 165 deals with sport, allows the European Union the competence to support, coordinate or supplement actions in this domain. While sporting organisations and European member states have the prime responsibility for conducting sporting affairs, Europe has recognised the need for a sports framework that goes beyond the national framework.

How can and should sport be regulated?

In an examination of the regulation of professional team sports it was concluded that considerable confusion exists over exactly what stance should be taken towards professional team sports and competition law (Sloane, 2002: 64). Should professional sports team leagues be treated as natural monopolies, cartels or joint ventures? What is the appropriate definition

200

of the market? How should sports law cater for global sport in which at least two completely different models of professional sport operate – namely, the US model and the European model? The special features of professional team sports mean that treating them like other industries would seem an unlikely way to maximise consumer welfare, while a carte blanche exemption from competition law would leave open the route to monopoly abuse of power. If a US-style player draft system were to operate in Europe, it would probably fall foul of the freedom of mobility of labour legislation guaranteed by the Treaty of Rome. Salary cap provision would, at present, be difficult to implement within the context of European sport, although it has been operationalised within both rugby league and rugby union. In terms of promoting a redistribution of wealth in professional sport, a more equal revenue sharing policy would add to both the uncertainty of outcome of matches, but would also help to control labour costs. Yet, it is likely that such a scheme would be resisted by the G14 group of European football clubs because it would reduce their ability to compete in the cash-rich European club competitions.

It is necessary to comment briefly upon US and European models of professional sport before turning to the question of regulation (Barros *et al.*, 2002). The dominant model of sport in America is a professional sport model that celebrates profit maximisation and commercial objectives. Teams are organised into leagues that operate as sealed cartels. Player contracts are organised on a collective bargaining basis between players' unions and team owners. Teams enter into collective agreements that restrict the scope of economic competition. The three central general internal laws of the US model are: (i) a sporting contest is uninteresting unless its outcome is uncertain; (ii) in team sports, a contest is made more uncertain by establishing an equal distribution of economic resources among the teams; and (iii) an equal distribution of economic resources is best achieved either by limiting the role of economic power in hiring players or equalising economic power through income redistribution.

Generally, the European model of professional sport is dominated by football and, by and large, European soccer or football leagues engage in far fewer restrictive practices, while revenue sharing is almost unknown, as is joint merchandising. No attempts have been made to equalise the redistribution of player talent that exists in the sense that there is no draft system, no team roster limits, other than those determined by income, and no salary caps. Players trading for cash is the norm within the European model. Larger differences in income exist between the top and bottom clubs than in the North American model, while a system of relegation and promotion is a distinctive feature of European professional football. It has been suggested that European team owners and managers are motivated by goals other than profit maximisation, although the trend of placing more and more football teams on the stock exchange would seem to contradict such a hypothesis. The major difference is that the leagues in Europe are not effectively sealed and, therefore, European competition exists. Finally, sporting competition within the European model is more complex and is generally inconsistent with balance-enhancing measures. Thus, the ability of players to move to the highest bidder is greater than in the US, where collective bargaining and strong anti-trust laws exist as the norm. Player unions are fragmented across Europe, while a limit of one per country means that employers have almost been able to bypass the unions. Even if a single European union for players became established, there is still no equivalent of anti-trust exemption from the collective bargaining agreements that dominate the US professional sport model. In Europe, the European competition authorities give teams almost no incentives to write long-term contracts and the market for players is much more individualistic and liberal.

The issue of regulation cannot be seen in isolation from different market models of sport and, as Foster (2005) acknowledges, at least five different market models for sport might be suggested in relation to the legal regulation of sport. These might be summarised as shown in Sport in Focus 8.5. The *pure market model* tends to view sport purely in terms of business. Money comes before sporting success and unregulated economic competition is a means to this end (Foster, 2000). The dominant ideology is that competition is the best regulator. Within this model, governing bodies of sport have broad functions, but they mainly provide a loose regulatory framework in which profit maximisation occurs. The public interest is generally ignored and sports fans have limited powers in terms of resisting exploitation. There is a network of contracts between economic units with individualistic ideologies. Within this model, the normal form of regulation is the market, with the normal means being the contract as the legally binding authority. In stark contrast to this view, the *defective market model* exposes the limitations of the pure market model, the main one being that, within the free market model, the weakest economic units are usually eliminated. Sporting competition tends to need equal economic strength, and monopolies of success are bad for sporting business. Unpredictable values are a key facet or value of this model. Governing bodies of sport and the competitions that they license are often the monopoly controllers of sport. They can use this power to restore sporting balance by re-allocating resources. The main legal method of regulation in a defective market is competition policy. Thus, if the market fails, competition law can be used to counterbalance monopolies or abuse of power.

The *consumer welfare model* provides a critique of the pure market model. Different interests may be linked through contracts, but there can be very unequal economic power between respective contracting parties. The fan or consumer has weak market power against the sports club. Players have historically had weak or limited economic power against their employers. Players and clubs, at times, need protection against federations that can take decisions over them with major economic consequences. The legal form of regulation is protective legislation to protect the weaker party, or to allow a greater protection of the wider public interest. The fourth model alluded to is the *natural monopoly model*. One of the arguments to support statutory-backed regulation is that the regulated industry is a natural monopoly and, therefore, market competition is absent. A natural monopoly is characterised by a single seller, a unique product and barriers to ease entry to the market. Sport, it is claimed, has these characteristics and, therefore, needs a regulatory structure that assumes it is a private monopoly likely to ignore the interests of the public. Competition law is an inappropriate mechanism of regulation because the market cannot be freed if there is a natural monopoly; an alternative regulatory strategy is therefore needed.

During the summer of 2003, the European, if not the world, financial football market was shaken as a result of the Russian businessman Roman Abramovich securing a majority stake in the ownership of London-based Chelsea Football Club (*The Herald*, 15 July 2003: 30). Overnight, the club became the wealthiest in the world as a result of the £140 million

SPORT IN FOCUS 8.4: SPORT REGULATION AND THE MARKET

Model	Values	Form of regulation	Governing bodies
Pure market	Profit/private interest (shareholders)	Contract/intellectual property	Maximise commercial opportunities
Defective market	Equal sporting competition (teams and players)	Competition law	Reallocate
Consumer welfare	Fans and viewers	Protective legislation	Widen democracy and accountability
Natural monopoly	Public interest	Independent regulator	Overcome rival organisations
Socio-cultural (traditional)	Private club	Immunity/ voluntarism	Preserve sporting values
Socio-cultural (modern)	Fairness, internal constitutionism and rule of law	Supervised self-government	Preserve sporting values with due process

Note: There has been increasing concern about the ineffectiveness of sports administrators in the modern world of international sport. It has been suggested that a solution may lie in increased regulation. The alternative view is that legal intervention disrupts good administration of sport.

Source: This table has been adapted from Foster's (2005) insightful research into sports regulation.

initial investment. The alleged link between sport, governance and corruption has a further case study as a result of this development. The source of Abramovich's wealth has been linked to a number of oil companies within the former Soviet Union. The oil magnate's wealth flourished under the patronage of the former Russian president, Boris Yeltsin. Abramovich assumed control of the Sibnyeft oil company, among others, and was appointed governor of the Chukotka region of northern Russia, which he declared bankrupt, leaving many public sector workers unpaid. It is this money that has allegedly become the new money behind Chelsea Football Club. From virtually sliding into liquidation in the late 1990s, Chelsea had assumed the mantle of the richest club in the world, seemingly prepared to outbid anyone for many of the world's available football stars. Within two weeks of assuming control, £13 million had been released for two players, £100 million was reported to have been made available to sign the French internationals Patrick Vieira and Thierry Henry from Arsenal Football Club, while a bidding war was started with Manchester United through a further £20 million being put aside for the services of the Brazilian Ronaldinho. At a time when this self-regulating football business had been hit by deflation, the notion of such wealth being made available to one club may yet have alarming consequences for other clubs struggling to stay afloat within the financial footballing climate since 2003. A handful of clubs in each country has contested the major honours each year, but if the alleged people's game still harbours any slim ambition of being a responsible meritocracy rather than a plutocracy, then the impact of such a development may be problematic, and it is unlikely to be benign. As mentioned above, the football market is unlikely to be freed if a natural un-regulated monopoly of domestic or European football emerges.

Finally, there is the *socio-cultural model* that promotes the notion that sporting values are dominant and profit is ancillary. The autonomy of sport is valued, with the historical governance of sport taking a number of forms, such as the private club with voluntary administrators, or supervised self-government through, for example, undemocratically elected British sports quangos. This allows governing bodies to be autonomous and regulate the sport without too much external intervention. This requires internal constitutionalism, due process and good governance. In short, the socio-cultural model argues for autonomous self-government with constitutional safeguards to protect sporting values. The problem with such a model is that it is often difficult to define exactly what values are being protected and promoted, since global sport has been increasingly linked with corruption, vested interests and a distinct lack of democracy, if not at the level of participation, certainly at the levels of power, governance and privilege.

Is sport above or below the law?

Given the above, it is tempting to suggest that Western sport, in terms of both the US and European models of professional sport, enjoy a certain degree of autonomy and internal policing. Perhaps the most vivid international example of this is the Court of Arbitration for Sport (CAS), originally created by the International Olympic Committee in 1983. In 1994, a Paris Agreement meant the creation of the International Council of Arbitration for Sport (ICAS) and a new structure of the CAS. This was signed by the highest authorities representing the sports world, viz. the presidents of the IOC, the Association of Summer Olympic International Federations (ASOIF), the Association of International Olympic Winter Sports Federations (AIOWF) and the Association of National Olympic Committees (ANOC). The funding of CAS is shared between the different groups that constitute ICAS. These are the IOC, ANOC, ASOIF and AIOWF.

The business of CAS in the early days tended to be dominated by Western sports problems, with few, if any, cases coming from Asia or Africa. CAS has two divisions: the ordinary division (which deals with commercial disputes) and the appeals division (which deals with the facts and the law in relation to sporting matters, such as doping, voting mechanisms and cruelty to horses). At the 1996 Olympic Games in Atlanta, CAS developed an ad hoc division (AHD) that facilitated a 24-hour resolution to a dispute (Morris and Spink, 2000: 67). Generally speaking, a dispute may be submitted to the Court of Arbitration for Sport only if there is an arbitration agreement between the parties that specifies recourse to the CAS. Article R27 of the Code of practice governing the procedures and rules of governance stipulates that the CAS has jurisdiction solely to rule on disputes connected with sport. Since its creation, the CAS has never declared itself to lack jurisdiction on the grounds of a dispute not being related to sport. In principle, two types of dispute may be submitted to the CAS: those of a commercial nature, and those of a disciplinary nature. Since the World Conference on Doping in Sport, held in March 2003, the Olympic Movement and numerous governments

SPORT IN FOCUS 8.5: CAS RULINGS – THE BOSMAN RULING

The judgement passed in the Bosman case

The Bosman case – the first one of its kind in the legal history of football – made it necessary to reconsider the transfer of players and the restrictions foreign athletes face in EU countries. The Bosman judgement refers to transfer fees, on the one hand, and to nationality clauses in sport, on the other. The principles in the decision apply to all sports federations and not just to football. As far as transfer fees are concerned, the decision refers to the professional and semi-professional athletes of a sports federation, athletes who are being sponsored and athletes who generate an income from advertising. The limitations of the decision are that it refers solely to situations after a contract has run out.

The facts of the case

Mr Jean-Marc Bosman agreed to switch to the French club US Dunkerque shortly after his contract with the Belgian club RC Liege had run out, but was unable to do so because the two clubs failed to reach agreement on the transfer fee. The Belgian Football Federation refused to grant the required transfer approval to the French club. Because of the delay, US Dunkerque withdrew the contract with Bosman. He brought an action for compensation before the Belgian courts for loss of income, requesting that the case be referred to the European Court of Justice.

Summary of the outcome

The judgement passed by the European Court of Justice addressed two totally different problems, although the legal basis is the same in both cases: Article 48 of the Treaty Establishing the European Community. No transfer fees are paid if a player moves from one member state to another after their contracts have expired (special regulations apply to nationals of third countries and to countries that have concluded an association agreement). As far as the nationality clause is concerned, it is generally invalid to restrict the number of EU nationals in a club/team.

The consequences of the judgment passed in the Bosman case

The consequences of the Bosman judgment for sport are far-reaching. The example of the professional footballers in England shows that the quota of foreigners in the English football leagues has risen sharply. The sums paid by English clubs for international transfers has also risen since the Bosman case, as more and more football clubs are looking further afield to foreign countries in their efforts to find new players. This revival in the transfer market has led, among other things, to the football clubs attempting to tie their players to their clubs by having them to sign long-term contracts.

have promulgated the World Anti-Doping Code, Article 13 of which states that the CAS is the appeals body for all international doping-related disputes.

There are at least four issues or challenges in relation to the power of CAS:

- the enduring perception that CAS is owned or influenced by the federations that fund it and that it is second best but cheaper than the law courts;
- major sporting organisations such as FIFA and IAAF have still to subscribe or submit to the jurisdiction of the tribunal;
- with regard to the institutional structures that make up CAS, the interests of the athletes are not necessarily given a fair hearing in terms of athlete representation on the boards; and
- significant room exists for closer collaboration between CAS and other sporting arbitration schemes within different national and international frameworks, sporting or otherwise.

It may be that such a development would curtail or at least limit the number of cases reaching CAS to those of a particularly contentious or novel dispute.

The development of CAS and ICAS is but one contemporary example of the juridification of sport that simply adds to the paradox about sporting autonomy. Sport would appear to have a diminishing degree of freedom as it becomes more commercialised and, in a simple sense, as sport becomes more commercial, the need for law and forms of regulation increase. The myth of sporting autonomy has historically been used as an argument against legal intervention in sport. It has appeared in various forms and disguises:

- Sport and the law are separate realms and the relationships within the world of sport operate differently from the legal norms of fixed rules, rights and duties.
- A degree of relative autonomy from the law should exist because sport may also be viewed as a leisure pursuit, and sport is, therefore, for pleasure, not profit.
- In this area of activity, sport is a private activity, pre-eminently within civil society and outside the confines of the state.
- Sport should create its own internal law that negates the need for external regulation and intervention.

The establishment of CAS may be viewed as an attempt by sport to forestall further intervention from the external law, and yet nationally and internationally the trend would appear to be one of increasing rates of juridification in sport. CAS merely helps to facilitate this process in terms of sport itself.

There seems to be a further paradox at the centre of the debate about sport, law and governance that merely adds to the question as to whether global sport is myth or reality. Global sport is not a panacea for a world of sport that is borderless, prosperous, even democratic and accountable. Globalisation cannot be understood as a single driving force. We do not have a simple form of global sporting governance that one might expect if the notion of global sport was a possibility or reality. The regulation of sport usually portrays or reflects the triumph of market-led values. Even the most cursory examination of sport and the law would suggest that, while sport is regulated both internally and externally, perhaps the more

SPORT IN FOCUS 8.6: CAS RULINGS – THE WEBSTER RULING

The judgment passed in the Webster case

The Webster ruling established case law for Article 17 in FIFA's 'Regulations on the Status and Transfer of Players'. Article 17 was created by FIFA and the European Union to give professional footballers the same rights as other EU workers. Under the rule, a footballer between the ages of 23 and 28 may sever ties with his or her club, so long as he or she has served three years of a four- or five-year contract. Furthermore, a player over 28 can terminate his or her contract if he or she has completed two years of its duration. The ruling has serious implications for the entire football market.

The facts of the case

In 2006, Scotland's Andy Webster became the first footballer to invoke Article 17. This allowed him to move from Scottish club Heart of Midlothian to Wigan Athletic in the English Premier League by buying out the final year of his contract. After a contractual disagreement with Hearts owner Vladimir Romanov, Webster was excluded from the first team for the remainder of the 2005/2006 season. Unhappy with his circumstances, Webster invoked Article 17 and released himself from his contract at the end of the season.

Summary of the outcome

FIFA ruled that Webster had to pay £625,000 to Hearts based on future wages, earning potential and legal costs. Both parties were unhappy at this decision – Hearts valued the Scotland defender at around £4 million, and Webster argued the compensation payment due was excessive. The case was taken to the CAS, where it was decided that the amount Webster should pay to Hearts was £150,000. The figure was based on the remaining value of Webster's contract with Hearts.

The consequences of the judgment passed in the Webster case

In the aftermath of the Webster case, there was great speculation on how great an impact this would have on football transfers. FIFA President Sepp Blatter was disappointed with the decision, commenting, 'The decision which CAS took is very damaging for football and is a pyrrhic victory for those players and their agents, who toy with the idea of rescinding contracts before they have been fulfilled'.

Many in the media predicted that the Webster ruling would be Bosman-like in its implications, and would have a profound influence on the football transfer market. Speculation mounted that stars such as Cristano Ronaldo, Frank Lampard and Cesc Fàbregas could use the new ruling to switch to clubs in other countries. In reality, there have been very few transfers using Article 17, with Jonás Gutiérrez's move to Newcastle from RCD Mallorca being the most high-profile. Curiously, Andy Webster returned to Heart of Midlothian in February 2011, signing a two-and-a-half-year contract.

important challenge facing world sport is whether the notion of global sport can be sustained given that:

- there have been clear indications that it is in crisis in terms of various forms of corruption;
- sporting governance occurs at a multitude of different levels and is rarely coordinated or committed to international justice or social reform; and
- while transatlantic forms of sport in both Europe and America may continue to modernise, it is hard for non-Western forms of sport to modernise and become powerful players in the international sports forums while, at the same time, holding on to values that are perhaps not governed by Western laws, beliefs, values or traditions.

If non-Western countries continue to follow their own road towards economic and social modernisation through sport, then it is only to be expected that future disputes between, for example, Western and Asian values over issues such as human rights, gender and religion in sport will persist. It is only reasonable to expect resistance and expressions of disappointment from the countries of the Southern Hemisphere that perceive international or global sport to be following a Northern sporting agenda.

Somehow, the translation of the moral impulse into universal globally binding standards of honesty, fairness, justice and responsibility has gone astray in global sport. What the hidden artificial hands of the morally sensitive controllers of international sport do bears little resemblance to any sustained social commitment to the power of sport when tough choices have to be made between profit and more socially committed forms of international governance in sport. Arguably, the true function of our incipient global sporting institutions is the perpetuation and reinforcement of a polarising trend that merely reproduces and extends the gap between rich and poor sporting nations. In a world of global dependencies with no corresponding global polity and few tools of global justice, the rich of the sporting world are free to pursue their own interests while paying little attention to the rest.

SPORTING GOVERNANCE IN QUESTION

The accelerated spread of global sporting relations has had a number of important implications for patterns of governance in world sport. Any notion of progressive globalisation through sport requires a system of democratic governance at both national and international levels, and yet the increasing level of corporate sporting involvement has brought into question the relevance of corporate governance to sport today. The challenges for sport are immense and have led some commentators to argue that global sport is in a state of crisis and that international sporting agencies and transnational corporations are more famous for corruption and corporatism, rather than for a positive social role. Katwala (2000a) insists that the global era presents fundamental challenges for sporting governance, but also the opportunity for sport to become more of a force for internationalism. The path of transformation from the traditional amateur association to a socially responsible global sports industry is far from complete. Katwala (2000a) goes on to suggest a series of guidelines for modernising sporting governance, emphasising stakeholder participation, greater transparency, and cooperation between governments, the European Union and the governing bodies of sport.

The problems of world sports organisations are similar to other organisations with visions that are primarily concerned with money, material wealth and unregulated profit. In free-market sport, accountability often means the boardroom's responsibility to shareholders and the company's responsibility to the customer. Yet, until relatively recently, shareholders had rarely challenged or effected principled changes in corporate policies, and sporting consumers had often been captives of an oligopoly. Mechanisms for access and participation in market-based governance of sport are often determined by wealth and income. One needs capital to become a shareholder. One needs power to influence and participate in FIFA or UEFA decisions. Very few people receive invitations to attend meetings of bodies such as Nike or other major sponsors of international sport, and almost all of the participants come from a narrow and highly privileged circle. Shareholder-owned companies or organisations are, arguably, far more accountable than bodies such as the IOC, FIFA and UEFA.

Some of the most important sociological questions concerning global sport relate to issues of accountability. How can sporting organisations, such as the IOC, that seek to speak for the whole world, and especially the youth of the world, and represent peace and harmony between nations, justify the ways in which they conduct their business? Lenskyj's (2000) study of the internal workings of the Olympic industry examines the rationale, the processes and outcomes of the Olympic bidding process, the efforts made by cities and countries to win IOC votes, and the responses of communities and citizens who are left with the aftermath of an Olympic Games when the show has left town and country. The study portrays a culture of corruption and collusion in a body consistently purporting to speak for universal human values. It is often forgotten that anti-Olympic protest groups in cities such as Nagano, Toronto, Sydney, Berlin and Atlanta have often portrayed a different interpretation of the work of the IOC.

The role of international sporting organisations within world sport may be viewed from at least three different positions. Sport in Focus 8.7 outlines three divergent views about international sporting institutions and the extent to which they can or cannot affect change. Institutionalists regard the world as an arena of inter-state cooperation. They argue that international sporting organisations will play an increasingly important and positive role in the governance of global sport, and will ensure that the benefits of global sport are spread widely throughout the world. However, several pre-conditions are necessary for this to occur. These conditions include: the existence of mutual interests that make joint gains from cooperation between sporting nations; rational choices and a long-term relationship between a relatively small number of sporting organisations, such as FIFA and UEFA; and reciprocity according to agreed standards of behaviour. Under these conditions, institutionalists argue that national sporting organisations will agree to be bound by the rules, norms and decisions of the international sporting organisation or institution. Institutionalists are optimistic about the possibility of progressive steps towards increased rates of international governance within world sport based upon cooperation, mutuality and negotiation.

Realists disagree with institutionalists and reject the notion that international sporting organisations are the primary solution to universal sporting problems and issues. They argue that the institutionalist model does not account for the unwillingness of powerful sporting organisations to sacrifice power relative to other sporting organisations. The position adopted

209

SPORT IN FOCUS 8.7: A DEBATE ABOUT SPORTING INSTITUTIONS

Institutionalist (or 'neo-liberal institutionalist')	Realist (or 'neo-realist')	Constructivist
Under what conditions will states create international sporting institutions?		
For mutual gains (rationally calculated by states).	Only where relative position *vis-à-vis* other states is not adversely affected.	Sporting institutions arise as a reflection of the identities and interests of states and groups which are themselves forged through interaction.
What impact do sporting institutions have on international relations?		
Expands the possible gains to be made from cooperation between sporting organisations.	Facilitate the coordination of policies and actions but only insofar as this does not alter the balance of power among states.	Reinforce particular patterns of interaction, and reflect new ones.
The implications for globalisation and aspects of global sport.		
Sporting institutions can manage globalisation to ensure a transition to a more 'liberal' sporting world.	Institutions will 'manage' globalisation in the interests of dominant and powerful states.	Changing patterns of interaction and discourse will reflect in sports' responses to global sport.

is that the governance of international sporting bodies will always reflect the interests of the dominant governing bodies of sport. When these powerful sporting bodies wish to coordinate international sports policy with others, they will create appropriate institutions, which will be effective only for as long as they do not diminish the power of the dominant sporting nations vis-à-vis other states. For realists, cooperation and institutions are heavily constrained by underlying calculations about power and vested interests. From a realist perspective, it follows that anti-global sports campaigners are right to argue that international sporting organisations do not work for the interests of poor sporting nations.

Finally, constructivists pay more attention to how institutions, states and other forces construct their preferences, thus emphasising the part that identities, dominant beliefs and contested values have to play in the process of negotiation. They argue that the interests, normative ideas and beliefs of, for example, the organisation, sporting body or national association influence the identities of sporting institutions. They reject the realist position on the grounds that it is wrong to assume that sporting bodies can only be mere reflections of power politics, whether it is the government of the day or institutions at a more micro-level.

In other words, sporting identities and interests are more fluid and turbulent than the realists realise. A constructivist approach to global sporting institutions would highlight the actors and processes involved in globalisation that are neglected within realist or institutionalist approaches. For example, the protesters who are active within anti-global sporting campaigns would be part of the construction of an ongoing dialogue about sporting institutions that affects state, national and international facets of sport in several ways. The globalisation of sport is thus viewed not just as a process affecting and managed by states, but rather the governance of global sport and indeed globalisation are shaped by a mixture of interests, beliefs and values about what sport is and what sport should be and can be. The existing sporting institutions doubtless reflect many of the interests of powerful states; however, these interests are the products of how sporting organisations and companies and people interact, and are therefore always subject to re-interpretation and change.

One of the many practical strategies in the move towards a more equitable approach to international sporting governance is the need to closely regulate transnational corporations (TNCs). There are at least two factors that explain how transnational sporting corporations have managed to escape genuine regulation of their behaviour. These are: (i) *legal limitations* in terms of regulating corporate accountability and, in particular, the fact that international law is still largely focused upon state-to-state legal frameworks; and (ii) *power imbalances between powerful TNCs and comparatively weaker states* that result from governments globally courting the economic wealth of TNCs, and collectively the TNCs lobbying governments for preferential terms and conditions with regard to bidding for mega events or contracts to build capital-intensive sports facilities. Yet, on an international scale, this leads to a potential imbalance of investment in certain countries that does little to help sustain a sporting infrastructure in the poorer parts of the world. Transnational corporations have invaluable resources that, if harnessed correctly, could bring many sporting benefits to all of the countries in which they operate.

THE DEEP CHALLENGE OF GLOBAL SPORTING DEMOCRACY

Perhaps the emergence of a more socially committed approach to global sport has to start from actively acknowledging the huge differences of opportunities, wealth, democracy, sporting tastes and models of professional sport that divide the world. The deep challenge facing global sport is to outline the mechanisms by which sport can be seen to contribute to social and economic welfare on an international scale. At the international level, the more powerful sporting nations would seem to have the power to enforce many of the rules and decisions affecting world sport and yet there are perhaps unprecedented opportunities at the beginning of the twenty-first century in that sport is free from the cold war politics of the twentieth century. Perhaps the most obvious and disturbing concern is the extent to which the core institutions of sport are trusted and sensitive to ways of addressing the interests of the majority in the non-Western world. The chief causes of inequality in global sport remain twofold: the transformation of global sport by financial capital and the displacement of democratic political power in sport by unaccountable market power.

Sport, historically, has always been viewed as a pathway to social mobility or an avenue out of poverty for talented sportspeople. The marketability of sportswear has contributed to

211

the situation where children as young as 13 are now effectively sold to the highest bidder. In May 2003, Freddy Adu, a 13-year-old American schoolboy, signed a $1 million deal with Nike. Why should Nike spend that amount of money on a schoolboy who plays soccer in a country in which soccer is a minority sport? The answer lies in Nike's desire to gain an even bigger share of the £10 billion global market in sports shoes. Freddy Adu had only been playing soccer for five years when he arrived from Ghana with his mother Emilia, who had won a Green Card lottery to live in the US. He is tipped to become a future world soccer star and, to that end, in Nike's view, they cannot afford not to sign him up, or let rival companies such as Reebok or Adidas secure Adu's signature, in case he turns out to be a superstar. In an increasingly youth-obsessed sports world, Freddy Adu is not particularly well paid in comparison to other child sport stars. Only days before Freddy signed his contract, Nike signed a contract for $90 million with 18-year-old Lebron James, a high school basketball player who had never appeared in a professional match. The merest hint that a young sportsperson may become a star is enough to spark a bidding war between multinational companies (*Observer*, 1 June 2003: 21).

The example is insightful for a number of reasons, not least of which is that it is one of many millions of examples of sporting talent moving from relatively poor countries to rich countries with little, if any, compensation or redistribution of monies from the rich part of the world to the poorer parts. The example of Freddy Adu is merely illustrative, but in this one example there are issues of child labour, the power of unregulated financial capital, the seduction of living the American dream and the migration of football talent to the football cities of the sporting world without any recognition, in financial terms, of the part played by the periphery or the Ghanaian Football Association. The consequences of such a view of sporting progress for global sport are simply that the rich sporting nations stay rich and the poor but talented sporting nations are mined for sporting excellence without any recourse to the redistribution of wealth. The production of wealth derived from global sport could be geared towards human aims. Western liberalism needs to strive for honesty about the implications of lifestyle preferences not just for its own societies, but also for other members of the global or international community.

Zimbabwe and the 2003 Cricket World Cup

Examples at this point might be drawn from situations arising out of the involvement of Zimbabwe in both the 2003 Cricket World Cup and the subsequent cricket tour of England in May 2003. England's progress to the last four of the 2003 Cricket World Cup was ultimately ended when the International Cricket Council ruled that England should forfeit points for not playing their first match in Harare against Zimbabwe. The English captain, Nasser Hussain, pleaded with both the UK Labour government, the international cricket authorities and the English Cricket Board (ECB) to rule on the issue of whether England should play Zimbabwe, given that Zimbabwe was ruled by an illegitimate regime whose head of state, Robert Mugabe, was patron of the Zimbabwe Cricket Union. More than half of the country's 13 million people were suffering from starvation, and yet the players would have been put up in the best hotels, the cricket team would have been shuttled around in special cars using petrol from a special reserve supply (given that the average motorist at the time had to queue for two days for petrol). The Libyan government had stopped oil deliveries to Zimbabwe because the government had not made its payments. Human rights groups, such as the Amani Trust, which used to monitor and publicise human rights violations in Zimbabwe, folded because of state-sanctioned harassment and intimidation. Both the US and UK governments at the time refused to use any sanctions or enforce international human rights laws. In the end, the English cricketers themselves made a decision not to play, and their progress in the Cricket World Cup was ultimately affected by this decision, a decision that the sporting authorities and British government felt they could not make.

The Cricket World Cup in South Africa was followed by a test series against Zimbabwe that took place in May 2003 (Tatchell, 2003: 16). Only players and officials uncritical of President Robert Mugabe were eligible for selection. Earlier in the year, two team members, Andy Flower and Henry Olonga, wore black armbands to mourn the death of democracy in Zimbabwe. They failed to make the team to travel to England and were subjected to death threats. Other critics of Zimbabwe had also been removed, including the coach Kevin Curran, the trainer Malcolm Jarvis, the former captain Alistair Campbell and the all-rounder Guy Whittal. Gagging orders were written into the contracts of the players who made the trip. Most of the officials who make up the Zimbabwe Cricket Union are also members of Robert Mugabe's political party Zanu-PF. The president's authority was required before the tour could go ahead. The ECB not only agreed to play two test matches against Zimbabwe in 2003, but also signed a commercial contract with the Zimbabwe Cricket Union to play a return series in Harare in 2004, with the promise of financial compensation made for England's withdrawal from its World Cup fixture in 2003.

The challenge to sporting democracy in Zimbabwe is, to paraphrase C. L. R. James, beyond a boundary. The paradox of the 2003 Cricket World Cup involving Zimbabwe in a tournament hosted by South Africa was that, during the apartheid era, the African National Congress urged the international community to exert economic and cultural pressure on the governments of P. W. Botha and F. W. De Klerk. The demise of the apartheid regime was aided by international sporting sanctions invoked against South Africa under the slogan 'You cannot have normal sport in an abnormal society'. Perhaps President Thabo Mbeki's South African government should have supported the struggle for democracy in Zimbabwe by exercising authority upon the cricket authorities and others to impose similar sanctions against Zimbabwe during the 2003 Cricket World Cup. Furthermore, if the English cricket authorities were interested in supporting not only sporting democracy, but also a more social sporting agenda, it would have to answer at least two questions: why is England playing cricket against a Zimbabwe squad whose members have had to pass a political loyalty test? Are there times when the values associated with sport should not be purely economic ones? The example above has been used simply as a short case study in relation to the challenge facing global sporting democracy. Zimbabwe versus England cricket relations would have benefited from a degree of international support that, rather than upholding the amateur adage of 'Keep politics out of sport', might have been better served by acknowledging that, here, sport was all about politics. That was certainly how President Mugabe saw it, and the opposition who failed to turn up.

Pakistan, corruption and cricket 2010–2011

The relationship between cricket, Pakistan and India has been complex. In April 2002, many people around the world might at the time have recalled Ghandi's famous reply when asked what he thought of Western civilisation – he replied that it would be a good idea. In April 2005, speaking after signing a joint peace agreement in the Indian capital Delhi, the two leaders Manmohan Singh and Pervez Musharraf agreed that peace between the two nuclear rivals was irreversible. On the same day, the two leaders watched the start of the final day of the one-day international cricket match between India and Pakistan. A match eventually won by Pakistan, a match in which the result had been secondary to the process of reconciliation and internationalism between two nuclear rivals.

As alluded to in Chapter 4, in 2010, three Pakistan cricketers, Mohammed Aamer, Salman Butt and Mohammad Asif, found themselves at the centre of allegations of cricket match fixing during September 2010. Mazhar Majeed, the 35-year-old businessman at the centre of the allegations allegedly told the Pakistan players to deliberately bowl no-balls in return for £150,000. The immediate onus rested upon the International Cricket Council's anti-corruption and security unit. The Pakistan cricket board initially resisted pressures to drop the players from the touring Pakistan team until police investigations had been completed. The Indian Premier League has been a money spinner for many of the world's top cricketers. An estimated £227 million was gambled on India's Premier League in 2009, despite the fact that betting is illegal. Yet, the deterioration in relations between India and Pakistan during 2008 meant that many Pakistan cricketers missed out. A Pakistan cricketer can earn about £25,000 a year but this is dwarfed by the flow of finance associated with the Indian Premier League. This has led some observers to suggest that this is part of the reason why Pakistan cricketers may have been open to inducements. Former Pakistan captain Ramiz Raja commented that an entire generation had been left rudderless and hopeless by the acts of its favourite players, while Pakistan's prime minister at the time, Yousuf Raza Gilani, noted that the match fixing allegations 'have bowed our heads in shame' (*Observer*, 5 September 2010: 8). On 3 November 2011, the three Pakistani cricketers became the first sportsmen convicted of on-field corruption in a UK court since 1960.

Challenges for global sport

At first glance, the notion of global sport would seem to provide possibilities and opportunities for regulating sporting governance and finance to ensure a more equitable redistribution of sporting wealth.

Any clear template for how sport in the world should be governed has not accompanied the transition towards a more global notion of sport. The governance of global sport is multi-layered, complex, national, local and international, but in all of these, states, sporting agencies, the sports market, civil societies and governing bodies of sport have all suffered from shortfalls with respect to popular participation and access, consultation and debate, inclusion and representation, transparency and accountability. Forms of global sporting governance through market-driven channels would seem to imply deep inequalities and the rule of efficiency overriding democracy. Suprastate sports organisations would appear to

SPORT IN FOCUS 8.8: CHALLENGES FOR GLOBAL SPORT

- Global sport must advocate a distinctive social agenda for sport.

- Social democracy must become a distinctive feature of global sporting reform.

- Global sporting institutions must be active in publicising human rights violations in sport and, linked to this, the places and cities chosen to host sporting mega-events must undergo a human rights audit as part of the selection process.

- Global sport should institutionalise a global framework for sporting mobility and migration.

- Sport needs to monitor child labour violations in sport and in the production of sport merchandising.

- Sport may be seen as a popular vehicle for debating and promoting global politics.

- Models of sporting governance need further to embrace local communities as stakeholders in the mutual governance of sport.

- Given popular support for sport, international sporting and/or other sanctions are options that may be used to help further sporting democracy.

suffer from severe democratic deficiencies. At the moment, it is unclear whether and how democracy can be adequately realised in a more global sporting world. Above all, Western sport embedded within national and increasingly European sporting governance, as well as the continuing dominance of American sporting capital, seems incapable of showing the historical imagination needed to grasp the radical challenges facing world sport. If global sport means recognising common situations, sharing a single world of sport, then the gaps between West and non-West, rich and poor, democratic and democratising, or even England and Zimbabwe, will need a different kind of consciousness.

Global sport cannot make a significant difference to globalisation, but it can make a contribution, as Part 4 of this book attempts to explain. However, in the meantime, it is sufficient to suggest here that the enduring deep challenge for forms of global sporting democracy might involve some or all of the ideas outlined in Sport in Focus 8.8.

SUMMARY

Just as globalisation is very uneven in its effects, so too is global sport. The notion of a level playing field is, of course, a sporting metaphor, but even the most superficial glimpse at sport in the twenty-first century would suggest that international finances, global markets and forms of governance are far from progressive in terms of their impact upon sport itself. The concentrations of wealth and power in world sport have the capacity to sustain and develop new inequalities within sports, between sports and among sporting nations. According to the rich list compiled by Deloitte-Touche, all of the top 20 wealthy clubs are based in Europe. During 1999, global expenditure on sport sponsorship trebled but its distribution was unbalanced, with 37.8 per cent of the sum being spent in North America; 36.4 per cent being spent in Europe; and 20.8 per cent in Europe, with South America way behind and Africa virtually out of the reckoning (Callaghan and Mullin, 2000: 43). As mentioned at the beginning of this chapter, the enduring moral problem of global sport remains that of the vast gap between different sporting worlds, organisations and peoples. It is tempting to suggest that, while international sporting politics during the cold war era was the political divide between East and West, the crucial divide in the twenty-first century is that of the North versus South divide. A sporting paradox exists in the sense that world sport, while striving to be more inclusive, is so expensive that only certain parts of the world can afford to compete for hosting mega events such as the various sporting World Cups or the Olympics.

This chapter has reviewed different potential forms of regulation and governance that may or may not impact upon sport. It is perhaps inevitable that, as sport becomes more and more enmeshed with the world of finance, then the law and lawyers in different parts of the world are sure to benefit first and foremost. Yet, if the management of global or international sport is going to progress, then it needs to adopt certain forms of structural reform and common rules that have the potential to lead not so much to recognition of sporting power and wealth, but to the redistribution and regulation of sporting power and wealth. At the very least, sporting organisations have to be increasingly accountable and transparent, and be aggressive about representing key community or local stakeholders in the governance of sports organisations. This chapter has suggested some of the ways in which this might progress, while the next chapter illustrates how unjust and different the nature of sport is in other communities. It is crucial that students and researchers read these two chapters together, and not in isolation from one another.

GUIDE TO FURTHER READING

Blitz, R. (2011). 'FIFA Set to Launch Probe into Bribery Allegations'. *Financial Times*, 11 May: 1–3.

Brown, K. and Connolly, C. (2010). 'The Role of Law in Promoting Women in Elite Athletics: An Examination of Four Nations'. *International Review for the Sociology of Sport*, 45 (1): 3–21.

Chaker, A. N. (2004). *Good Governance in Sport*. Strasbourg: Council of Europe.

Foster, K. (2005). 'Alternative Models for the Regulation of Global Sport'. In Allison, L. (ed.). *The Global Politics of Sport*. London: Routledge, 63–86.

Glendinning, M. (2009). 'Crimes and Misdemeanours: The Latest Hot-Spots in Sports Law'. *Sportsbusiness International*, 151 (November): 48–52.

Hoye, R., Nicholson, M. and Houlihan, B. (2010). *Sport and Policy: Issues and Analysis*. Oxford: Butterworth-Heinemann.

Marquand, D. (2004). *Decline of the Public Realm*. Cambridge: Polity Press.

Morrow, S. (2003). *The People's Game? Football, Finance and Society*. Basingstoke: Palgrave.

Sport et Citoyenneté (2010). *Special Edition on The Governance of Sport in Europe*, 10 (December).

Tatchell, P. (2003). 'Ambassadors of Tyranny: Zimbabwe Cricket Tour'. *New Statesman*, 19 May: 16.

QUESTIONS

1 Describe and compare at least four different models of sports regulation.

2 Argue for and against the idea that sport is above the law.

3 Describe the work of the International Council for Arbitration in sport.

4 Critically evaluate the debate about different approaches to thinking about international sporting institutions.

5 What are the key challenges facing global sport in terms of democracy, governance and the law?

6 Describe the case material presented by Bosman, Kakuta and Webster.

7 Explain the differences between institutionalist, realist and constructivist approaches to sporting institutions.

8 Explain the differences between American and European approaches to governance in sport.

9 Describe how the terms 'cartel' and 'monopoly' help to describe the governance of modern sport.

10 Contrast the issues surrounding Zimbabwean and Pakistani cricket.

PRACTICAL PROJECTS

1 Investigate the websites of any two sports arbitration agencies and list the cases that have been brought before the court/agency in the last three years.

2 Prepare a portfolio including at least ten legal case studies involving sport.

3 Review the constitution of ten local sports clubs in your area and determine whether each club is governed in a democratic way. You may want to consider asking how elections to the committees are made or how decisions by the committee are operationalised.

4 Examine the constitution of one professional sports club in your area and identify what the club pledges to do for the players, shareholders and the community. Design a community stakeholder model of governance for the club.

5 Identify legal companies who specialise in sports law and see if you can arrange an interview with a lawyer to discuss how the law is influencing sport today.

KEY CONCEPTS

Accountability ■ Arbitration ■ Cartel ■ Constructivist ■ Democracy ■ Governance ■ Institutionalist ■ Juridification ■ Justice ■ Monopoly ■ North/South divide ■ Power ■ Realist ■ Regulation ■ Transparency

WEBSITES

Sports Court of Arbitration
www.tas-cas.org/news
A dedicated forum for up-to-date information on sport and the law cases.

Sport and the Law Research
www.sportslawjournals.com/
An international platform for sport and the law journals.

Governance in Sport
www.governance-in-sport.com/Koss.pdf
A dedicated resource on sport and governance issues.

Sport and Citizenship
www.sportetcitoyennete.org/version3/page_anglais.php
A European think tank based on promoting citizenship through sport.

World Anti-Doping Agency
www.wada-ama.org/
The work of the World Anti-Doping Agency can be found at this site.

Chapter 9

Sport, media and television

It is fast, accessible and connected but what role does social media have in the battle to be a star or secure a sporting event?

OBJECTIVES

This chapter will:

- illustrate the importance of sport to both the old and new media;
- consider ways in which the media mediates sport;
- explain the ways in which sport has developed a relationship with the Internet;
- introduce and critically discuss the notion of an information age; and
- provide illustrative examples and sources for further information.

KEY TERMS DEFINED

Democracy: A political or social unit governed ultimately by all of its members.

Fourth World: Used to represent the people in regions that are bypassed by most forms of technology but it can also be synonymous with stateless, poor, and marginal nations.

Monopoly: Exclusive control of the market supply of a product or service.

Network: Any structure of communication for individuals and/or organisations to exchange information, share experiences, or discuss political goals and tactics.

Social media: The various online technology tools that enable people to communicate easily via the internet to share information and resources. Social media can include text, audio, video, images, podcasts and other multimedia communications.

INTRODUCTION

Old and new forms of media play a fundamental role in the consumption, ownership and delivery of sport. The specificity of sport and its relative autonomy in decisions concerning sport have been fundamental to the development of sport, and yet the lucrative power of the media has threatened this relationship in certain sports. Sports will argue that they need a space in which the social and commercial world attach value to sport and, therefore, a dependency on the forms of media to achieve this goal are seen as important. At the same time, the digital age is distinguished by a rapid transformation in the kinds of technological mediation through which forms of sport and people communicate. The traditional face-to-face sports reporter using his or her landline telephone calls and postal mail to report on sport has been joined by email, mobile telephone calls, text messaging, instant chat messaging, web boards, social networks, photo sharing, video sharing, multiplayer online gaming and much more. While sport is still challenged by the positives and negatives of the power of television sponsorship and endorsements, new forms of media also present new issues. Yet, the fundamental purpose of communication technologies still remains in that it allows people to exchange messages without being physically co-present.

Not everybody has access to this new media sports world. The story of online sports media history is also a story of changing users and influencers. The digital sports divide is simplistically framed between those who have access to the Internet and those who do not. Location certainly matters. The website Internet World Stats estimate that, as of 2009, 73.9 per cent of North Americans use the Internet, 60.1 per cent of people in Oceania/Australia, 50.1 per cent of Europeans, 30 per cent in Latin America/Caribbean countries, 23.7 per cent of Middle Easterners, 18.5 per cent of Asians, and 6.7 per cent of Africans. On average, just under a quarter of the world's population use the Internet. In many areas where Internet use is low, mobile phone use is far more pervasive, in that 61.1 per cent of the world's population use mobile phones, with the higher uptake, in comparison with internet usage, driven by use of mobile phones in Brazil, Russia, India and China. Who is excluded from digitally mediated forms of interaction is neither random nor inconsequential. The market forces driving the development of online gambling have both economic and social consequences. The attempts by sports clubs to develop their own media capacity operates in a very uneven world but elite clubs will continue to chip away at retaining their core media rights while exploiting the reach of new media technologies. The battle to control sport in the digital age is not new.

At the same time, the speed of social networking and information flows means that people have power. While the 2010 Vancouver Winter Olympics proved to be a success not just for Vancouver, but Canada as a whole, activists, artists and anti-Olympic protesters were not slow to use old and new media forms in protest against the Winter Olympics (Boykoff, 2011). Social media such as Twitter, Facebook and Flickr provided activists with an alternative set of information streams although the received wisdom from Vancouver 2010 was that, while such media enable people to create content and generate numbers at protest events, these are primarily most effective as short-term event-driven services since they are also policed. Protesters using YouTube during the Games found that a number of videos were swiftly removed and that activist groups did not have the resources or time to fight the censorship. Well aware of such problems, the anti-Olympic activists in Vancouver also placed numerous adverts in the *Vancouver Sun* to help inform local people about why they were protesting.

SOCIAL MEDIA, DEMOCRACY AND CHANGE

The bid to host the 2018 FIFA World Cup was won by Russia, and yet the analysis of the way in which different nations used the social media to support the respective bids highlights the new role that the social media has in the battle to secure major sporting events. Although England lost the bid, it probably won the social media battle. According to the three main social media channels, Facebook, Twitter and YouTube, the England bid had more than 25 times the number of Twitter followers of Russia, Holland/Belgium and Spain/Portugal. Campaign managers want people around the globe to find out easily about the strengths of the respective bids and, therefore, England targeted football fans across 145 countries. The idea was to build a global presence to build both interest and excitement for a respective country outside of that country. A continual flow of press releases, website text,

SPORT IN FOCUS 9.1: SOCIAL MEDIA AND EUROPEAN WORLD CUP BIDS

	England	Holland/ Belgium	Russia	Spain/ Portugal
Facebook likes	306,280	9,338	515	2,784
Twitter followers	6,295	614	–	2,032
YouTube subscribers	321	95	21	21

video and conversations were continually released through the England 2018 Facebook page and Twitter feed. Sport in Focus 9.1 highlights the social media standings of three European World Cup bids as of 9 November 2010.

Most forms of media, old or new, do not depend upon sports coverage but television and newspapers rely on sports coverage as a basis for commercial success. Television coverage is serious business in the US. Sports network companies such as ESPN invest heavily in new technologies, including HD and 3D, in order to remain competitive in the sports coverage market. The sports network became a money earner for its owners, Walt Disney, by becoming dominant in the American home market. The reach of ESPN sport in January 2011 was such that it involved 46 channels in 200 countries with 300 million subscribers. One 10-year deal to cover Monday night NFL games cost nearly £1.3 billion per year. ESPN's biggest UK audience was for a Manchester United versus Tottenham Hotspur match in October 2010, which was watched by an estimated 1.2 million subscribers.

We know a lot more about the consumption of sport on television. The number of television viewing hours of Davis Cup tennis matches between different tennis nations stood at 839 hours in 1989, 1,219 hours in 1993, 1,460 hours in 1998 and 1,660 hours in 2000. The 2000 UEFA Champions League football final was viewed in more than 200 countries, and involved more than 300 hours of coverage worldwide, using 80 broadcasters and more than 100 television channels. Media coverage is central to the hosting of the Olympic Games. In March 2004, the IOC began the bidding process for the European TV rights to cover the 2008 and 2012 Olympic Games. The US bidding process had already been completed, with NBC securing the rights as a result of a $2.2 billion package. The Internet is allowing unprecedented levels of interconnectedness and interactivity. The number of worldwide Internet users has grown rapidly and the range of activities that can be completed online continues to expand. Visitors to the Wimbledon tennis championship official website rose from 100,000 in 1995 to 9.04 million in 2000; while Internet hits stood at 2 million in 1995, they had risen to 2,340 million by 2000. While the Internet provides new possibilities for sport, some worry that Internet usage in general may undermine human relationships and communities by contributing to rising levels of social isolation and anonymity.

The media industry has become increasingly globalised over the past three decades, with the following being some of the key trends:

- The ownership of the sports media is increasingly concentrated in the hands of the larger media conglomerates; private ownership of the media is threatening if not eclipsing public service provision and ownership.
- Media companies purveying sports coverage operate across national borders.
- The sports media industry is dominated by a small number of multinational corporations.

The illusion of inhabiting one world of sports coverage is, in part, a result of the international scope of sports media and communications. An international world of sports information and an international system of sports production, distribution and consumption has come into being.

Given the positioning of the major European and American media companies in the world sports–media complex, many believe that the developing countries have been subject to a new form of media imperialism. Is international television sport a form of Western cultural imperialism? On a bigger scale, critics worry that the concentration of media power in the hands of a few companies or powerful individuals, such as Rupert Murdoch or Italy's President Silvio Berlusconi, is undermining the workings of democracy.

Resolutions, meetings and manifestos calling for a new world order in international information structures and policies have been a feature of the international media scene since at least the 1970s. The original impulse came from the non-aligned nations, many of whom gained independence in the post-war years. These same years witnessed the rapid development of what was then the new communications media and the era was constantly characterised as the Information Age – one in which information would be the key to power and affluence. To many developing countries, it was clear that multinational companies that were based in the most powerful nations dominated the flow of information, including sports information. As Sport in Focus 9.2 indicates, in 2004, all of the top 17 sports media-related companies were based in either Europe or America, with 11 of these 17 companies registered in either New York or London. Political independence had not been matched by independence in the economic and socio-cultural spheres. A number of non-aligned countries saw themselves as victims of cultural colonialism, and sport was viewed as a contributor to this process. In 2000, sport contributed to 7 per cent of the broadcasting genres around the world, with the others being news and special events at 18 per cent, entertainment at 30 per cent, fiction at 44 per cent and others at 1 per cent (Jarvie, 2006: 133).

Yet, Asian pay broadcaster ESPN Star Sports recently claimed that it was on the verge of a golden era given that Indian pay television had witnessed significant expansion in 2010 and 2011. Live India international cricket coverage was still the key subscription driver in the country but golf, football, motor sports and tennis all experienced growth. ESS reported that, in 2010, it reached approximately 90 per cent of total cable and satellite households. At the same time, the value of sports advertising around the Indian sports genre was expected to rise to 14 billion rand, with the value of sports subscription expected to rise to 7.7 billion rand. Growing penetration of digital TV technology and fragmentation in the satellite segment have been the main trends in India's TV industry during 2010 (Gupta, 2011).

The strong symbiotic relationship between sport and the media often suggests that they are one and the same thing but it is crucial to point out that sport and the media is not sport per se the same thing, but rather that it is sport that has been mediated for the sports–media complex. Many, if not all, aspects of media sports are social, economic and political constructions that carry messages, are controlled by human beings, and provide selected representations of reality. Sports through the media carry messages about gender, race, class, nationhood, violence and what is good and what is bad sport. Much of the research into media sport has concentrated upon an examination of the meanings, messages and representations provided through the process of producing media-sport. Critics of multi-national capitalism's control of the sports media frequently complain of the tendency towards a cultural convergence and homogenisation of, for example, sports television coverage across the globe. This is also a major criticism of the discourse on cultural imperialism that takes sport and capitalism as its target. Is the Fourth World excluded from the new sports information age of the twenty-first century? Is it astonishing that we see so little of sport in Asia or sport in Africa or sport in Latin America on European TV and yet key American sporting dates such as the Super Bowl final or the final of the US Open tennis championships or US PGA golf championships regularly appear as major productions in the annual sports television coverage of major world sporting events?

The social and cultural implications of the reconfiguring of the new sports media landscape relate to issues of democracy and access and the creation, or not, of new public spheres of media sport. Developments such as pay-per-view television sport and subscription are seen to introduce an increased element of consumer responsiveness into programming, while the more developed forms of sports interactivity associated with video, digitalisation and the Internet allow the sports fan and other consumers to organise their own way through particular sports media experiences. Theoretically, the Internet can provide each of us with the ability to create our own spectator sport realities and experiences. The Internet is also seen to offer positive possibilities for groups previously marginalised. Alternatively, critics have pointed to the increasing gap between the information rich and the information poor in a new or evolving media sport universe. Novick (2004: 24) points out that, to 'free marketeers and sports fans alike the new world of television sport is a joy' but the same author goes on to point out that not only do many not have access, but that the 'free market was not set up for the benefit of the poor'.

SPORT AND THE MEDIA

Live sport and the sports media are, in one sense, two different entities in that the experience of live sport for the sports fan in the stadium is a different experience from sitting in front of the computer or standing at the sports bar; even the last two forms of media sport are different. By its very definition, the sports media is sport mediated by the media and, as a result, students, teachers and researchers need to question the influence of such processes, the stories told, the impact of technology on what we think about sport, and the extent to which worldwide exposure to Internet sport exists in reality and the price of its development – not just in economic terms, but also in social terms. The coverage of sport and the media

SPORT IN FOCUS 9.2: 2004 SPORTS-RELATED MEDIA COMPANIES

Company	Exchange	Symbol	MC (millions)	1yr % change	3 mnth % change
AOL Time Warner	NYSE	AOL	$81,834.04	61	23
British Sky Broadcasting Plc	LSE	BSY	£14,670.58	28	18
Cablevision Systems Corp	NYSE	CVC	$7,568.98	−4	7
Carlton Communications Plc	LSE	CCM	£1,824.35	143	26
Clear Channel Communications Inc.	Nasdaq	CCU	$27,799.65	13	11
Comcast Corp	Nasdaq	CMCSK	$332.54	32	4
Eckoh Technologies Plc	LSE	ECK	£49.33	N/A	−20
Fox Entertainment Group Inc.	NYSE	FOX	$27,781.04	12	11
Granada Plc	LSE	GAA	£3,744.02	111	15
Interpublic Group of Companies Inc.	NYSE	IPG	$6,541.39	30	12
News Corporation Ltd	ASX	NCP	A$64,751.63	9	−2
Seven Network Ltd	ASX	SEV	A$1,483.23	31	−1
SportsLine.com Inc.	Nasdaq	SPLN	$68,295.82	60	37
Television Corp Plc	LSE	TCP	£26.45	−42	9
Vivendi Universal	Paris	EAUG	€23,177.04	39	20
Walt Disney Co.	NYSE	DIS	$48,641.33	38	7
Wireless Group	LSE	TWG	£102.76	73	38

Source: *Sports Business*, 89, March 2004: 40.

in this section is divided into two discussions, the first providing a brief history of the relationship between sport and media, while the second is more thematic and gives a topical and theoretical synopsis of sport and the media.

The development of a match made in heaven?

The influence of the mass media and sport has contributed to a significant body of research in the area of sport, culture and society not just in terms of television, but all forms of media communication that have provided sports information and entertainment (Cashmore, 2010). The study of media sport in the conventional sense might be approached by analysing the part played by the different forms of media that have contributed to sports information and sports entertainment. The domination of the sports–media relationship by television and new media styles should obscure the fact that sport has sustained a relationship with the press and radio, in some cases, for more than a century. Sport was marginal to the news agenda of the respectable press of the nineteenth century. Sport could not compete for space in the restricted copy-space environment and yet, as early as 1751, a specific sporting press existed in the form of *The Racing Calendar*, which helped the Jockey Club publicise the rules of racing. The growth of popular gambling was a second and more economic rationale for the growth of an early sporting press.

Modern sport and the modern press, argues Mason (1993: 3), grew up together. The newspapers provided free publicity, described the main events, published the results and, in the early years of the nineteenth century, provided prizes, management, commitment and even judges and referees. Newspapers and the sporting press, Mason (1993: 4) goes on, helped in the formation of specific sporting subcultures that grew up around particular sports and particular events. The early coverage of sport in the British press might broadly be divided into three categories: the evening and the Saturday sports specials; the national daily papers; and the Sundays and the specialist sporting press. In 1890, Britain could boast of the existence of *Sporting Life*, *The Sporting Chronicle* and *Bell's Life in London*. Racing coverage was the staple diet for all three but they also covered sports such as quoits, football, pedestrianism and golf. By 1900, the Sunday papers were selling up to 2 million copies; the *News of the World* gave 14 per cent of its space to sport, especially racing, cricket, football and athletics. By 1905, 15.75 per cent of an enlarged paper was reserved for sporting coverage. By the 1930s, the *People* devoted 10 per cent to sport, a figure that rose to 20 per cent in the 1950s (Mason, 1993: 8).

A simple content analysis of the national British daily papers in 2004 illustrated that the national dailies devoted over 200,000 words to football. Horse racing was the next most popular sport after football in terms of coverage in column inches. More recently raw data from the coverage of some of the major national and international newspapers for 24 January 2011 is presented in Sport in Focus 9.3. It illustrates the amount of space devoted to sport as a percentage of the total number of pages.

Some of the contemporary issues about the relationship between sport, the press and radio are not new. How close should sport be to the press? Is the media's role to celebrate the present or sit in critical judgement? How far should the press be prepared to criticise the role of sport in society or to what extent does the price of investment in sport mean an increased stake in the decision-making process about how sport is organised, presented, when it is played, who is displayed and what sort of commentary or interpretation should be placed around the story or the visual pictures of sport? The close relationship between sports editors and boxing promoters in America during the inter-war years meant that sports journalists expected big pay-offs in return for favourable publicity. To what extent have things changed today? The press rarely question the politics of sport, and only when corruption or scandal arise does the notion of questioning the values associated with sport or the press ever shake the conventional framework or the parameters for thinking about the symbiotic relationship between sport and the media – a relationship that, in the contemporary era, is dominated by sport, television and new media forms.

Sport first appeared on British screens in June 1937 when the British Broadcasting Corporation (BBC) transmitted pictures of the Wimbledon tennis championships to about 2,000 households. Ten years earlier, having secured its charter in 1927, the BBC used its service to carry commentaries and reports on a wide range of sports, with the FA Cup Final, the Cambridge and Oxford University boat race and the Derby horse race all recording popularity with listeners during the 1920s and 1930s. Radio was something of a forerunner to television but, until the middle of the 1950s, the BBC had a broadcasting monopoly of both radio and television. It should be remembered that audiences for television sport before World War II were insignificant by today's standards, with viewing figures for both the 1938 and 1939 FA Cup Finals being approximately 12,000 each.

During the 1940s and 1950s, particular individual sporting bodies and rights owners offered resistance to the televising of events. The British Boxing Board of Control was particularly vociferous about its resistance to television, noting at the time that, in the US, television had a detrimental effect on boxing audiences, with reductions of as much as 80 per cent in some cases. Yet, as a major purveyor of national culture, the BBC in the 1950s viewed the coverage of sport as one of its statutory obligations. Whannel (1992: 21) points out that the corporation believed it had a function analogous to the press, possessing an obligation to report and broadcast on all relevant areas of social activity such as football, which showed record attendance figures of 41 million during the 1948/1949 season. By 1964, the BBC had extended its coverage by providing its first football highlights programme, *Match of the Day*, and, during the last 40 years of the twentieth century, various television companies have been in competition for the right to broadcast sport.

Initially, the BBC and ITV in Britain acted as a cartel, thus limiting how much would be paid for the right to broadcast live sport. However, during the 1980s and 1990s, the advent of Rupert Murdoch and his company British Sky Broadcasting (BSkyB) meant that an initial price war for the battle to show live sport emerged with the advent of satellite television. In 1991, Murdoch reportedly paid £191.5 million for the rights to show 60 English Premier League football matches per season between 1992 and 1997. BSkyB's monopoly of Premier League football coverage was challenged in 2003 when the European Commission raised two key objections: (i) to the monopoly coverage of broadcasting rights that limited consumer access to live football coverage and (ii) to the way in which the football league was acting as a cartel in the selling of football coverage. The lack of exclusivity has meant the fall in rights fees and, consequently, the drop in money available to football clubs who, in turn, are looking to the new media as possible outlets for football content as a way of balancing the loss of revenue from television fees. In 1998, Manchester United became the first club to brand its own channel, with MUTV broadcasting on a national and international basis.

Themes and issues: a brief overview

The study of the media in relation to sport, culture and society has tended to be dominated by television rather than the print media. Within this form of communication, research has distinguished between at least three aspects, production, content and audience. The production of media messages through sport involves the study of the structures and finances

SPORT IN FOCUS 9.3: INTERNATIONAL COMPARISON OF SPORT COVERAGE IN THE NEWSPAPERS

The table below compares the coverage of sports in the newspapers of the US and the UK. The research looked at three newspapers in each country on Monday 24 January 2011. It shows that sports news in both countries is dominated by one sport in particular: American football in the US, and soccer in the UK. It also illustrates that newspaper reporting in both countries follow different sports in general. Tennis is the only sport to feature in both lists.

Newspaper	No. of pages	Pages of sport	% of total devoted to sport	Most covered sport*	Second most covered sport	Third most covered sport
USA Today	32	10	31	American football (50%)	Basketball (15%)	Golf (7.5%)
New York Times	48	7	15	American football (71%)	Tennis (11%)	Surfing (5%)
LA Times	56	8	14	American football (41%)	Basketball (19%)	Golf (12.5%)
The Times	108	34	31	Soccer (59%)	Cricket (13%)	Tennis (6%)
The Telegraph	68	28	41	Soccer (54%)	Rugby (18%)	Tennis (7%)
The Herald	46	20	43	Soccer (48%)	Athletics (11%)	Rugby (10%)

*Percentage of the total devoted to specific sport

of the institutions that frame the production of the sports media. Media organisations exist within legal frameworks that, in part, determine their activity. In Britain, for example, the BBC, for the time being, remains a public corporation while media super companies regularly try to influence large sections of the media market and create the situation where a few large companies cover global sports media production. The increasing control of sports production by US firms has had an inevitable impact upon sports coverage in terms of which sports are covered, when TV viewing times of major sporting events are scheduled and the impact of advertising during the coverage of the sports event. The vision of sport through the Internet, for example, in the hands of a few media conglomerates stands in stark contrast to the idea of a free and unrestricted electronic realm in which individual sports choice is relatively free from corporate messages.

The production of the media message invariably involves hierarchisation, personalisation, narrativising and framing of events for a particular audience. The production of sport for television involves all four of these processes. As such, it is crucial that students, teachers and researchers continually consider how television and other forms of media sport production are represented and organised for public consumption. What production practices and professional and political ideologies inform the representation of sport on television and what is the cultural, social and economic relationship between a sports event and a mediated sports event? How will a producer frame and edit coverage of a particular sports event? What narratives will be attached to sports stars and celebrities? Will the coverage of sport in the twenty-first century be dominated by sports performance or a more critical coverage of the sporting world?

The second part of the communication process involves a consideration of content. In attempting to maintain and maximise television viewing figures for sport, what strategies should be used in terms of determining balance between commentary and visual effect? Does the excitement generated in the commentary serve to camouflage the lack of excitement in a sports event or do particular visual shots and styles help to create, rather than report, a particular sporting event? In the 1980s, Clarke and Critcher (1985) argued that the transformation of sport to televised sport was a form of ideological production in which competitive individualism, local, regional and national identities and male superiority were all presented as natural, rather than the specific selection of content. Feminist scholarship has also been concerned with the documentation and presentation of gender differences through sport in the media. The reproduction of the sports media gaze, it may be suggested, continues to associate women with appearance rather than performance and, consequently, feminist scholars have pointed out that the content of sports media production, at times, places women athletes as the object of this sports gaze rather than the subject (Kennedy and Hills, 2009).

A third part of the communication process concerns the audience and, in particular, audience reception. The consumption of mediated sport by the sports fan often requires locating and understanding sports fandom within its broader social context. Is sports fandom a male ritual? How does the media cater for the female or ethnic sports audiences? To what extent should public service television viewing have a strict regulatory policy on sports violence or should, as in some Scandinavian countries, sports violence be banned from peak viewing hours? Boyle and Haynes (2004) point out that even mediated football consumption is experienced differently by sports fans that have their own sense of tradition, community and place. To some extent, the challenge for the new sports media is how to capture that sense of belonging to class and community, and in some cases gender, that is important to the sports fan. The pleasures involved in sports viewing are complex, while the experience of viewing is often ritualised and communal as opposed to the more individual or solitary experience of viewing television. Whannel (2002: 295) is right to assert that it is the distinctiveness of sport and its uncertainty that make it an elusive product to package for an audience. The notion of the global sports fan or audience is, in many ways, a myth because the level of intensity with which different audiences in different countries interact with different sports is far from homogeneous.

229

Despite the advent of the new media and the suggestion that we live in a new information age, the media still have an extremely limited range of topics or themes, with sport being but one form of production. The media have only a limited capacity to transmit a full and complete picture of sport and, therefore, they have to continue to pick and choose what will feature and how to present it. Thus, at least two main filters operate in translating sport into a sports media product. The first filter of selection is that of general news or audience value, and the higher the value the more likelihood that the media will cover it. The second filter consists of the rules of presentation that are picked up from the codes of theatre performance and the discourses of popular culture such as storytelling, personification, conflicts between mythical heroes and heroines, drama, archetypal narratives, verbal duels, actions with symbolic overtones and reporting rituals, all of which transform the logic of sport into the logic of the media. The media stage, as pre-structured by these twin filters, has a capacity to handle sport in a number of different ways. It can create a celebratory sporting spectacle or it can destroy sporting careers. It can transform the aesthetics of sport beyond that which is real sport.

The logic of the media is closely interwoven with its economic structure. In the case of the privately owned media, the products are first and foremost commodities, since sales figures, sports ratings in the case of the sports media, are a primary justification for activity. Heightened private sector competition has led to an intensification of the rules that are inherent in the production of the sports media and, as with other areas of production, the pressure for ratings that afflicts commercial sports coverage is also being felt within public broadcasting systems. There is a sharp tension between media logic and sports logic and between the uncompromising filters inherent in media production time and the time required to cover sport.

As the sphere of sport falls under the influence of the media logic, it changes to the extent that sport becomes dependent upon media rules but without completely losing the reality of real sport. The term 'colonisation' is justified in the sense that the almost unconditional surrender of sport, at least in all its visible publicly accessible aspects, involves the colonisation of sport by the media systems. At least three forms of entertainment are provided by the sports media event, pseudo sports events, image projection events and pseudo sports actions. All of these modes of media sport are used with increasing professionalism and frequency. The mass media sports stage, particularly that of television, is subject to a complex and highly selective set of conditions for producing or covering sports material, which limits access and cannot be easily circumvented. The logic of selection and presentation of sports coverage affects who and what gets on centre stage, and for how long. At a very simple level, the commentary and the visual presentation of sport is not neutral in that texts and images are organised to tell a particular story.

At least five conventions for analysing the visual content might be mentioned:

1 the transformation of the sports event into a television, film, podcast or media event;
2 the balance between the impulse to produce realism and/or entertainment is different but the two distinct approaches are tensions that are ever present;
3 the ideal pursuit of providing maximum action in a minimum amount of time;

4   while visual framing through the camera lens produces a presence for some action and people, it also produces absences, with the tendency, for example, to focus on winners rather than losers, men rather than women, the sport of the Western world as opposed to other worlds, and popular rather than minor cultural sports; and

5   time itself is manipulated as a result of the editing process.

Five types of visual effects that are available to television sports audiences that are not available to the live audience might include: changing the size of the image, manipulating time to dramatise action through slow motion or instant replays, collapsing the actual time of an event through edited highlights, a specific focus on isolated action within the event, and the provision of comparative statistical information.

Given that significant parts of the world of sport have bought into the logic of the sports–media complex, it is perhaps difficult to consider what an alternative sports–media complex might entail. However, it is also relevant to remember that the relationship between sport and the media is not only economic, but also social and cultural, and while it might not be of equal parts, it is one of inter-dependency. The politics of an alternative sports media needs to remember that any audience is not passive but active, and as potential consumers of both real sport and mediated sport, strategies for change might include those of sports media criticism, internal reform within the sports media industry, the development of a sports media reform league, audience resistance, with all of the aforementioned strategies not being mutually exclusive but, to some extent, mutually supportive. The object is for viewers, sports fans, sports readers and others to publicly resist the ready-made incorporation into the sports audience commodity. The object of viewers is to point out the silences or absences within world sports coverage. Perhaps fundamental change will only occur when sports audiences change their orientation towards sports coverage to one of seeking real information about sport and its progressive potential rather than simply seeking to be entertained through the production of a spectacle.

It is not only the major sports that have the attention of the public but also those outside of the limelight. Potential sponsors may consider the notion that, for example, in the US, coverage of skating is one of the best vehicles for reaching women aged 25–54 as a target audience. Bowling, as a participatory sport, has 50 million Americans a year playing the game, mainly for social reasons (Wilner, 2004: 14). The challenge, even in the new media age, is to strike a balance between real sport and entertainment, between commerce and culture, between economic and social motives, and between coverage of the local and the global. An ongoing struggle continues in terms of directing the sports media gaze and resources to the silent parts of the world that receive little coverage or attention and yet have indigenous vibrant sporting heritages. The larger project of truly democratising the media will also demand a transformation of audience expectations and uses of the media. The task of democratising the rules of sports media selection and presentation may be one of the single biggest challenges that a more progressively orientated form of sports coverage will face in the future, despite the advent of sport on the Internet and the advent of broadband. Yet, the real threat to democracy for the UK lies in the erosion of competition within the British media and the consequences that this has for choice of entertainment and values.

Perhaps the time has come for politicians in different countries to state where they stand on the issue of democratic pluralism in the media.

SPORT, ONLINE AND THE INTERNET

Many see the Internet as exemplifying an image of the new global order. Users of the Internet live in cyberspace, meaning the space of interaction formed by a global network of computers that compose the Internet. It has been suggested that, in cyberspace, we are no longer people but messages on one another's screens (Baym, 2010). At least two broad categories of opinion exist. On the one hand are those observers who view the online world as fostering new forms of electronic relationships, often anonymous, but supplementing existing face-to-face interaction. Distance and separation allegedly become more tolerable. Others critically view the time interacting through the Internet as a threat to interaction in the physical world, which leads to social exclusion, isolation, less quality time for families, with the lines between work and home life becoming blurred as many employees seek to work from home. An analogy would be that people spend more time watching sport than going to sport and participating in sport, and therefore some of the fabric of social life for some groups is weakened.

The Internet is but one new form of communication that is associated with a new media age, others being digital television and mobile telephony. The impact of the new media has brought into question the extent to which television may continue to be the main platform for viewing sport in the twenty-first century. The promise of the Internet as a platform for communication lies in the possibility of a global, boundary-less audience for sport, coupled with a direct threat to future coverage of sport through national broadcasting corporations or indeed the old media. With specific reference to the football industry, Boyle and Haynes (2004: 166) remind us that the new media age has seen two related media systems develop a new relationship of coexistence – namely the global Internet and the nation-centred television service. They go on to suggest that the digital age is increasingly one driven by commercial values and the wider economic climate, in which the market remains the central driver of the digital economy. The new media have become increasingly concentrated and commercialised and they continue to encroach upon the functioning of what Habermas (1989) refers to as the public sphere – the places or arenas where the public congregate to debate or discuss issues of general concern and where opinions are formed, places where individuals, in principle, could come together as equals in a forum for public debate and sociability. The question remains: to what extent is real sport as a facet of the public sphere influenced or eroded by the development of new media forms?

Sport in Focus 9.4 is illustrative of how sports clubs are now using social media and just how popular it is.

The Internet has proved to be an effective medium for expanding an online sports gambling industry. A report from investment bank Merrill Lynch predicts that the online gambling industry will turn over £123 billion ($177 billion) by 2015, with online sports betting worth £100 billion ($144 billion). By 2001, the growth of the market had reached such a stage that more than 1,800 online sports betting and casino operations operated worldwide, all looking for part of the estimated $4.6 billion revenue generated through the e-gambling industry.

SPORT IN FOCUS 9.4: SPORTS CLUBS AND SOCIAL MEDIA

Social media have become one of the most powerful tools of communication in the modern world, and sports teams are becoming more aware that a social media presence is a key way to engage with supporters. Websites such as Facebook and Twitter have become important parts of a team's media output.

Clubs can communicate directly with fans on team news, ticket sales, promotions, and behind-the-scenes information to make fans feel more connected. It also gives the supporters a chance to air their views on the team, good or bad. In return, clubs can hope for more loyal supporters, a larger fan base, and increased revenues from these improvements.

Below is a list of the top 10 most popular sports teams on Facebook. While, unsurprisingly, the list is dominated by the huge names of world sport, such as FC Barcelona, Manchester United and the LA Lakers, the list does throw up two big surprises. Turkish football clubs Galatasary and Fenerbahçe sit proudly above sporting giants such as the Dallas Cowboys, AC Milan and the New York Yankees that place just outside the top ten. The table also shows how fast social media is growing for sports teams. In less than six months, most of the clubs on the list had doubled their number of Facebook fans.

Top 10 Most Popular Sports Teams on Facebook, 16 September 2010		Top 10 Most Popular Sports Teams on Facebook, 3 March 2011	
Club	Fans	Club	Fans
1 Galatasary	4,492,556	1 FC Barcelona	10,211,973
2 FC Barcelona	4,464,641	2 Man Utd	9,920,797
3 Real Madrid	3,580,163	3 Real Madrid	9,415,194
4 Fenerbahçe	3,010,264	4 LA Lakers	6,303,553
5 LA Lakers	2,920,109	5 Galatasary	5,014,189
6 Man Utd	2,417,690	6 Liverpool FC	4,591,090
7 Liverpool FC	2,406,744	7 Arsenal	4,452,250
8 NY Yankees	2,006,441	8 Chelsea FC	4,121,506
9 Besiktas	1,715,125	9 Fenerbahçe	3,439,557
10 Chelsea FC	1,550,475	10 Boston Celtics	3,397,033

It is estimated that interactive television betting will account for almost half of the income generated. Sports betting channels are a potential source of high revenue for sports rights holders but a danger exists if any sport becomes too dependent on this sole source of revenue. A deal between Go Racing and the British Horse Racing Board in 2001 means that the future of UK horse racing in this area now hangs in the balance because of the inability to resell the intellectual property rights associated with the sport. At the same time, there is little to prevent bookmakers who are unwilling to pay the licence fee for those rights from creating their own organic betting properties. Given the existing marketing, advertising and different legal restrictions governing world online international gambling services, it seems inevitable that an affiliation with the broadcaster or sports rights holder will prove key to future customer acquisition. This will become a compelling reason for bookmakers to seek mergers with established media brands, whether these are established sports clubs who own their own sports rights or TV broadcasters.

News Corporation-owned BSkyB has already demonstrated the possibilities of such a merger strategy by paying £250 million in 2000 to forge an alliance with Sports Internet Group. Wap Integrators, a technology company with a UK betting licence, recently signed a revenue share deal with Leeds United Football Club to enable Leeds fans to access unique mobile content from the official Leeds site on a Leeds-branded phone, with the means to place a bet on their team. The I-Race is a horse racing product launched at the end of 2003 that allows betting to take place on virtual horses running in virtual races. The line between the betting industry and the entertainment industry in this case provides for a chain of live virtual races every 10 minutes. The consumer is offered three options: one, to watch the race passively; two, to press the interactive red button, log on and play for fun with a fictional pot of money; and three, the full version that provides the option to register, deposit real money and place real wagers on the races (Britcher, 2004a).

Major League Baseball (MLB) views the advent of the Internet as the key to providing compelling global baseball content to fans as a result of web-based technology. It provides an increased opportunity for fans outside of the US and Japan to tune into live games. The MLB.com figures for 2004 suggest that more than 65 million people visited the site during the 26 days of the Division Series, League Championship Series and the World Series – more than double the 29 million who visited in 2002. An estimated 750 million visitors logged on to MLB.com during 2005, with the link between Internet and mobile phone technology viewed as a future growth area that will provide a quicker return on the investment in improved technology. The logic of capitalism is self-evident in the words of the Chief Executive of MLB, who points out that:

> we will try to take anyone who does not have an economic relationship with us and turn it into one. We estimate about 95 percent of our traffic does not spend money and our goal is not to shift the percentage but shift the numbers so that so instead of 750 million this year we want to do 1.5 billion in two years. Undeniably, across all sectors, the acceptance and the comfort the consumer now has with spending online has helped enormously with paying for better sports content.
>
> (Britcher, 2004b: 27)

For many of the major US sports, the holy grail of global expansion continues to be the attraction of the new media sports platforms, but few have been able to achieve it. The Far East is becoming a hub of interest for both NBA and MLB web offerings. Despite the surge in uptake of broadband Internet usage for sport in 2004, the development across cities and nations remains uneven. The mix between private and public supported infrastructures, plus the new media mix available to sports audiences is diverse. More than 12 million people used the BBC interactive button service during the 2004 Athens Olympic Games, but the level of infrastructure support for new media public service broadcasting in Britain at the time remained lower than, for example, Stockholm in Sweden. Different cities cater for the development of a new media infrastructure in different ways. The Stockholm model reflects the more general Swedish belief in the public provision of fundamental infrastructure. There is a very clear vision in Stockholm that the building of a knowledge economy, the attraction of inward investment and the provision of better public services will all be facilitated by a fibre-based communication infrastructure that wishes to turn Stockholm and Sweden into a wireless hot spot. In Milan, the driver was not the knowledge economy or the desire to put e-learning into schools or do health consultations in people's living rooms, but the demand for video telephony and entertainment provided mainly through private provision by e-Bisom. In places such as Warsaw in Poland, the provision of electronic cabling and connections was based upon a private/public partnership mix.

Sport in the new information age is keen to provide further sporting experiences for the sports fan and connect cities around the world through new media–sports opportunities. Ellen MacArthur's 2005 race around the world by boat may be cited as an example of the way the high-speed Internet connection has revolutionised offshore racing in at least two ways. The sea in parts of the world might be viewed as one of the most remote places on Earth, but modern technology facilitated scenes of this offshore round-the-world boat race to be beamed into people's homes all over the world. From the audience's point of view through TV quality footage and webcams, email and photos, the world was able to communicate with the sailor, and experience the swells of the world's oceans from the comfort of home. For the sailor, tactical and security points of view were informed by up-to-date, high quality weather images and thus routes could be planned more accurately and safely. In short, the performance of media projects, sailing speed and sailor safety took a big step forward due to high-speed connections.

SPORT IN THE INFORMATION AGE

In one of the most sustained attempts to map out and evaluate the impact of the information age, Castells (1998) argues that the emergence of such an age is marked by the rise of networks and the network economy, a new economy that depends on the connections made possible by a global communications network. Telecommunications and computers form the new basis of production. The effects of this production impinge upon personal identity and everyday life to such an extent that Castells (1998: 354) asserts that we no longer control the world we have created. As Castells puts it:

> humankind's nightmare of seeing machines take control of the world seems on the edge of becoming a reality – not in the form of robots that eliminate jobs or government computers that police our lives but as a world-wide electronically based system of financial transactions.

> (Castells, 1998: 56)

235

Yet, the argument goes on, the same power of information technology can serve as a means of local empowerment and community renewal. He thinks it is possible and important to regain more effective control of the global marketplace and that the route to this salvation is through international organisations and countries that have a common interest in regulating and redistributing global capital. The collective efforts of international organisations must, it is asserted (Castells, 1998: 379), have a common interest in regulating international capitalism.

The information age is certainly characterised by the international use of technology but it is also part of a society in which networking appears to be an important organising form of social life in certain parts of the world. It may be more appropriate to say that we live in a networked society rather than an information or knowledge society. Networks theoretically know no boundaries, they exist on an international if not global scale. Networked organisations, including sports organisations, out-compete all other forms of organisations, particularly the rigid, vertical command and control sports bureaucracies. Sports organisations are part of the world of mergers and conglomerates but the successful ones are those based upon flexible networked partnerships that can react and change quickly in response to given information. Since a whole range of social practices, both global and local, communicate through the media space, this space is an important public space of our time, through which sports organisations, activists, fans, chief executives and volunteers can plan, organise and share experiences and information about the sporting landscape that exists or could exist in the twenty-first century. The flexibility, elasticity and interactivity of the media sports text provides the sports media space with an infinite capacity to exchange information, to integrate, to exclude but also influence the boundaries of sport in society and how we think about sport and how we, the audience, are represented and represent sport through the media–sports complex. The networked sports–media complex continues to be a fundamental structuring force in the world of sport today. Networks therefore matter because they are an increasingly underlying structure of not just society and culture, but sport, culture and society.

If television and sport was often seen as a match made in heaven, the same might not be said about social networking and sport. One is often left with the question as to whether or not social networking blights sport or is fulfilling an important role. The medium has a number of inherent benefits that have changed or could change sport further. Lance Armstrong saw it as a powerful tool that, during his return to the Tour de France, he used Twitter for PR purposes to comment each day on his performances. But when the efficient operation of the sports labour markets are at stake, or when good sports fans' relationships are in jeopardy, or when sports management decisions are undermined, then social networking could be argued to have caused more problems.

Sports information and the Fourth World

Castells did not comment on the role of sport, culture and society in the new information age, nor the role of sport as a vehicle for global financial transactions, although he did suggest that the power of technology and information might provide the promise of and opportunity to experience spirituality through leisure. Yet, the idea of the creation of an information-age Fourth World in an unequal world order applies as much to sport, culture and society as it does to other spheres of life. The promise of new technology is intended to provide great benefits in the information age. The promise of unprecedented productivity, taking care of needs and the promise of affluence for all is reminiscent of the sorts of debate that heralded the promise of a post-industrial leisure society of the 1970s. The history of such promises tells us that social polarisation may also have increased substantially throughout the world during the last two decades — a theme we shall return to in the last chapter of this book. There are various dimensions of inequality, such as inequality between countries, inequality between peoples, and inequality between different social groups, but, no matter how social inequality is defined, a substantial gap between rich and poor is maintained. Societies change, explanations change, governments and policies change but somehow the needs and conditions of those at the bottom of society are systematically denied. Consequently, it is vital not to forget that extremism and polarisation are as much a part of sport in the new information age as they were in the era of the old media–sport relationship. In truth, in the transformation from the twentieth century to the twenty-first century, we have also witnessed an extraordinary intensification of social exclusion both between countries and within countries, between and within regions, and between and within metropolitan areas. This may include a Fourth World made up of much of Africa, rural Asia and rural Latin America, but also territories and segments that can be found in many parts of the planet.

There are clear exceptions to such broad generalisations. Appadurai (1995) refers to the decolonisation of sport in India as a process of indigenisation, changing the way sport is managed, patronised and publicised away from its colonial past as a tool of socialisation that spread Victorian upper-middle-class values. He claims the media have played a crucial role in the indigenisation of cricket in India, with radio and television broadcasting in the vernacular languages, and the arrival of television deepening national passion for the game along with the star status of players. Sports fans in the information age may be more distant geographically in the future. The impact of the information age may mean that clusters of virtual fans will be built around hubs of virtual sports activity. Writers such as Smith and Westerbeek (2004: 199) claim that sports organisations must be a virtual place of social experience, a hub of activity and tribal identity. They go on to suggest that communities are about tribal values and that the virtual online providers of new community sport must provide the opportunities for these values to be exposed and encouraged.

Yet, despite such an aspiration, access to the Internet, for example, is highly uneven. In 2002, 88 per cent of the world's Internet users lived in the developed world. North America accounted for more than 50 per cent of all users, although it only contained, at the time, 5 per cent of the total world population. The US is the country with the highest levels of computer ownership and online access. More than 100 million Americans use the Internet, while Germany and Britain both boast more than 10 million users each. In Japan, a country where the Internet craze arrived late, more than 14 per cent of the population, some 18 million people, used the Internet in 2009. Variations in technology and affluence around the world preclude a truly global market for sports technology and sports access through the new and old media forms.

237

The Fourth World does not often relate to the First World, except under extreme circumstances. Castells (1998) argues that, in the emergence of an information age and a networked society, access to education, information, science and technology becomes critical for countries, firms and peoples in the network society. It might be suggested that access to these resources, but also sport in the new media, whether it be access to online sporting gambling opportunities or sport on TV stations, also becomes increasingly unevenly distributed despite the fact that new technology in the First World is often viewed as the saviour of isolated places and spaces. True, there is more and more sports technology in the world but, at the same time, there is also a growing unevenness in people's capacity to properly access and use technology. So there are growing links between globalisation, information, networking, rising inequality and social exclusion, if not isolation. The links are asymmetrical and power-laden; the globalised, informationalised First World countries exploit the devalued, disconnected Fourth World countries. The new media may provide new forms of sports experience but it is questionable whether this is new informationalism or just old-style capitalism. The new information age may provide new possibilities for the sports fan or consumer but it is also an age that is profoundly unjust.

While the power, the promise and the reach of new media sport is undeniable, there are forces within countries that resist and question the onslaught of new media forms primarily produced from and for Western audiences. The rise of international electronic information empires that operate across state borders is often perceived as a threat to cultural and national identity in, for example, many Islamic countries. Reactions have ranged from muted criticism to outright banning of Western satellites. Programmes that offend traditionalism are sometimes prone to being censored. The BBC, and consequently BBC sports coverage, is no longer supported in Saudi Arabia. At least three Islamic states have banned satellite access to Western television – seeing it as a form of cultural pollution supportive of the promotion of Western consumer values. On the other hand, Indian pay television is booming as a healthy mix of sports rights help the growing expansion of digital TV technology, making Neo Sports available to 90 per cent of cable and satellite homes in India, reaching over 77 million households.

As for the future, it is a possibility that technologies will make it far easier for rights owners to broadcast and market television offerings directly to the consumer, cutting out the broadcaster. If Google and Apple TV combine and take off, then the sports business model of advert-funded television network provision may come under pressure, as well as the TV operators. Other themes we are likely to see might include leagues following the US model and retaining a proportion of their live games to launch and distribute their own multi-platform channels, widespread Twitter bans and the creation of super-short variants of all sports because they can be packaged more easily. Certain sports will produce new formats, with the proliferation of apps providing a different trend in terms of both format and revenue streams. This being compared with today, where Internet coverage is mainly considered free of charge. Sports media platforms may have to be more interactive and more personal, with more emphasis being placed upon sharing content and experiences with and by the sports fan. Live sports will probably remain the best unscripted drama on the market, but the way it is delivered, paid for and packaged could all change.

238

SUMMARY

From the sports daily to television, film and the Internet, we live in a world in which the media and networks have a profound influence upon sport and the way it is shaped, represented, presented, consumed and challenged. Sporting heroes and heroines are created and destroyed by the influence of the sports media. The way in which particular sporting events are covered influences what people think about particular sporting action or events. The logic of the media as a form of capitalism continues to permeate sport economically, socially and culturally to such an extent that it remains one of the most powerful influences upon sport and social life in different parts of the world. The First World and the Fourth World are provided for and experience mediated sports opportunities differently. The media promises sport much but the sports–media relationship is one that is both facilitating and problematic. This chapter has set out to explain the impact of both the old and new media upon sport and the way in which the relationship between sport, media and television, in particular, influences the way we think about sport, culture and society.

This chapter has linked developments of the sports–media complex to that of the possibilities and limits brought about by the advent of an information age and increasingly networked sports world. Understanding and mapping out the changing nature of power in a networked society is one of the immediate tasks facing any student, teacher or researcher interested in explaining and influencing the relationship between sport and the media. Power no longer simply resides in individual sports institutions, but through what Castells refers to as the switchers through which networks regulate terms of entry and privilege or exclude interests or positions. As such, it is vital not to lose sight of the fact that, just as sport in the new information age affords new opportunities for the control, ownership and structuring of sport, so too does it afford new opportunities for networked campaigning, providing an increased voice from different parts of the world. The role of the sporting celebrity in promoting and facilitating messages and resources of hope for and by different parts of the world may have a part to play in a new reconstructed civil society. The Internet certainly provides the promise of not just increased gambling opportunities, but also the development of numerous social forums and discussion groups about sporting issues and problems. The media itself faces significant challenges but some of the immediate challenges for sport and the media include those of transparency, knowledge, innovation, regulation, accountability, ownership, citizenship, access and the use of power.

GUIDE TO FURTHER READING

Baym. N. (2010). *Personal Connections in the Digital Age*. Cambridge: Polity.

Crosson, S. and Dine, P. (2011). 'Sport and Media in Ireland'. *Media History*, 17 (2): 109–116.

Hutchins, B. and Rowe, D. (2011). *Sport Beyond Television. The Internet, Digital Media and the Rise of Networked Media Sport*. London: Routledge.

Kennedy, E. and Hills, L. (2009). *Sport, Media and Society*. Oxford: Berg.

Marx, G. (2011). 'Challenges to Mainstream Journalism in Baseball and Politics'. *Forum*, 9 (1): 1–7.

Scherer, J. and Whitson, D (2009). 'Public Broadcasting, Sport and Cultural Citizenship: The Future of Sport on the Canadian Broadcasting Citizenship?'. *International Review for the Sociology of Sport*, 44 (2): 213–231.

Shor, E. and Yonay, Y. (2011). 'Play and Shut Up: The Silencing of Palestinian Athletes in Israeli Media'. *Ethnic and Racial Studies*, 34 (2): 229–247.

Sport et Citoyenneté (2010). *Sport and the Media*. 11 (June/July).

Watson, C. (2010). 'Test Match Special and the Discourse of Cricket: The Sporting Radio Broadcast as Narrative'. *International Review for the Sociology of Sport*, 45 (2): 225–239.

Yu, Chia-chen. (2009). 'A Content Analysis of News Coverage of Asian Female Olympic athletes'. *International Review for the Sociology of Sport*, 44 (2): 283–305.

QUESTIONS

1 Explain the relationship between sport and the press in both the pre- and post-1900s.

2 Describe and critically comment upon the ways in which the media filters sport to produce media sport. You may want to consider how visual and auditory techniques are used to frame a sports story.

3 Does the advent of new media enhance or reduce the possibility of open debate about sport?

4 What are the advantages and disadvantages of the Internet, and how has it developed sports content?

5 Describe what the information age is and its implications for sport. You may want to consider how sport has become part of a networked society and what the implication of this is for different people in different parts of the world.

6 What key trends might be listed to testify to the arrival of a globalised sports media?

7 Use Sport in Focus 9.4 to answer the question: who are the most popular football teams using Facebook?

8 How did sport figure in the newspapers between 1890 and 1950?

9 What are the most popular sports, according to the analysis of sports coverage presented in Sport in Focus 9.3?

10 Consider how the sports media might be change in the future.

PRACTICAL PROJECTS

1   Using newspaper reports of one of the major international tennis championships, compare and contrast the ways in which women players were portrayed in each of the following years: 1970, 1990 and 2010.

2   Access a recording of the opening ceremony of a major international sports spectacle such as the Olympic Games, the rugby or football World Cup, or the Asian or African Games. Using a method of content analysis, describe and explain the themes that have been selected to create a spectacle.

3   Arrange for two similar groups to watch a recording of a major sports event at the same time in two separate rooms. Group A watches the programme with the sound as normal and Group B watches the programme with the sound turned off. Ask the two groups to write up an independent report of the action and what they saw. Compare and contrast the two reports and use the evidence to write 2,000 words on how the commentary influences the views of the audience.

4   In a sport of your choice, use the Internet as a source of information to produce a diagram that traces the network of media interests, marketing, advertising and sponsorship interests in your chosen sport. What does the diagram tell you about media interests and influences upon your chosen sport?

5   Choose 10 separate days, perhaps Mondays, as a basis for carrying out a content analysis of the sports that are covered in your daily newspapers. In what ways are certain sports prioritised and others marginalised? Use the empirical evidence gathered to write 2,000 words on the uneven coverage of sport in a nation of your choice.

KEY CONCEPTS

Audience ■ Colonisation ■ Democracy ■ First World ■ Fourth World ■ Imperialism ■ Information age ■ Internet ■ Knowledge economy ■ Monopoly ■ Narrative ■ New media ■ Network society ■ Online gambling ■ Social media

WEBSITES

The Washington Post Sports
www.washingtonpost.com/sports
A day-by-day coverage of sport through the eyes of the *Washington Post*.

Sport and Citizenship
www.sportetcitoyennete.org/version3/page_anglais.php
A European think tank based at promoting citizenship through sport. See the special edition on sport and the media, as above.

UK Sports Netork – Social Media and Sport
www.theuksportsnetwork.com/
A social media and sports network.

Sports Journalists Network
www.sportsjournalists.co.uk/
The UK Sports Journalists Network and Association.

CBC Sports
www.cbc.ca/sports/
Sports headlines as they appear in Canada.

Chapter 10

Sport, social capital and education

The social value of sport is often underestimated – does sport help to build levels of education and trust between and within communities?

PREVIEW

Key words defined ■ Introduction ■ Barcelona's Youth Academy ■ What is social capital? ■ The importance of social capital ■ Sport and voluntary associations ■ The dark side of social capital ■ Sport and social capital ■ Bowling alone ■ The decline of the public sphere ■ Sport as entertainment or social right? ■ Local sports worlds ■ Sport in a safe and secure world ■ Education through sport ■ Education for all ■ Narrowing the gap and better futures ■ Better future levy ■ Summary

OBJECTIVES

This chapter will:

■ examine the impact of projects that combine sport and education;

■ consider the place of education and sport in reaching marginalised groups;

■ define and discuss the relationship between education, sport and social capital;

■ provide examples of projects where sport has been part of educational interventions; and

■ evaluate whether sport and education are important forms of social capital.

KEY TERMS DEFINED

Community: A social network or group of interacting individuals usually, but not always, concentrated in a defined territory; a human association in which members share a common symbol and wish to cooperate to realise common objectives.

Human capital: Consists of the resources possessed by the individual who can dispose of them with great freedom and without concerns for compensation.

Social capital: Often associated with a theory of social networks and the norms of reciprocity and trust that they facilitate; for some, it is the outcome from the ability to work together with communication, cooperation and political action being some of the key factors.

INTRODUCTION

The contribution that sport makes through education is rarely covered in most of the major texts that comment upon the impact or role of sport in society. Yet, nearly all governments endorse the principle of equal opportunity in education and recognise that restricting access to education not only violates human rights, but reinforces social inequality and holds back economic development. All education systems have to address problems of marginalisation and nearly all the education systems in the world have been experiencing the impact of the economic downturn. The idea that education returns tangible benefits to individuals and societies is rarely questioned, and yet the way in which sport both contributes to education and is a means to education is often forgotten. Education through sport is not about two different sectors working in isolation but it is in part recognition that access to sport through education is but one possible avenue through which a humanitarian and more international understanding of the value of education through sport can in part be realised. The progressive capacity of education and sport to impact upon life chances remains incredibly strong.

Education in sport could be about the enormous, almost unique contribution that education in sport, in particular higher education, has made in relation to developing people, raising aspirations and being a real resource of hope, nationally, internationally and locally. The relationship between social capital and education in calls for an increasing awareness of not only the need for alternative conceptualisations of social capital but an awareness of the diverse number of ways in which this relationship is examined, defined and operationalised (Dika and Singh, 2002). The conceptual umbrella of social capital is often stretched to include a variety of social factors that do not always coherently hang together. Problems with the conceptualisation and measurement of social capital have resulted in a body of research that does not always acknowledge the differential access to social networks and social resources. Thus, much remains to be done if the *social* in social capital is to be fully realised, and acknowledging the potential power of education through sport may make a small contribution. Sport and education have historically been aligned with both notions of social mobility, social capital and, to some extent, social transformation. The common denominator in all of these terms is the word *social*. The term is generally invoked to suggest a commitment to the broader welfare of society rather than the narrow interest of particular elites.

Some may be ambivalent about freedom, but the story of what an education system has given to many people is the priceless ability to recognise the bigger questions, situate your own position in a wider context and think things out for yourself and about what to do about it. Is it worth holding on to the idea that education through sport can contribute to a sense of what Paterson (2003) refers to as ordered freedom? It may be suggested that, in many ways, the partnership of education through sport can really make a difference to the quality of life in many places. It might be useful to evaluate whether the partnership of education through sport continues to provide pathways of hope for many people in different parts of the sports dream, receive basic education or recognise that social, economic and human capital can be enhanced as a result of university-level education. It is important to help to create the conditions to let the relationship of education through sport thrive – that would truly be a partnership in action worth trusting and striving for because education through sport has much to offer.

The notion of citizenship, like the word 'community', is very slippery indeed. Both of these terms carry with them notions of trust and mutual obligation involving others. The notion of citizenship is straightforward in that it implies that individuals owe a duty to one another and the broader society. The collective power of all should be used for the individual good of each. Some have continually argued that, in recognition of our inter-dependence upon one another, people must accept their responsibilities as individuals (Brown, 2002). Community action should never be allowed to be a substitute for personal responsibility to others. There is material to suggest that education through sport can help with some of this. Programmes such as First Tee Golf in America, which had Tiger Woods playing golf with hundreds of inner-city kids in New York, is based upon nine core values, including trusting others, but also making golf more accessible.

Alternatively, consider the approach to education through sport taken by some international sports teams. Sport in Focus 10.1 is illustrative of an attempt by one club to integrate a holistic approach to education and sport.

245

SPORT IN FOCUS 10.1: FC BARCELONA'S YOUTH ACADEMY

La Masia is the celebrated youth academy of FC Barcelona. Lying in the shadow of the famous Camp Nou stadium, it is where the future stars of the club call home through their teenager years as they develop their football skills. The academy has produced a host of big stars in its past, including all three 2010 FIFA Ballon d'Or finalists: Lionel Messi, Andres Iniesta and Xavi Hernandez.

The academy is the creation of the Barcelona legend Johan Cruyff, who modelled La Masia on a similar set-up at Dutch club Ajax. By living, studying, training and eating together, Cruyff believed that the young players were more likely to realise their potential. The daily schedule is balanced between sport and schoolwork so the boys are brought up as well-rounded individuals, rather than just sportsmen. This balance is vital for those who do not make it as professional players. Below is the schedule for the boys on a typical day.

07:00	Get up.
07:30	Communal breakfast.
08:00	Bus to school.
14:00	Return from school, communal lunch.
14:30	Free time for siesta or homework.
16:00	Intense training sessions for two hours.
18:30	Gym or physio session depending on fitness.
21:00	Communal dinner.
22:00	TV, homework, Internet or reading time before lights out.

The intensity of the academy also reinforces the philosophy of the club. Barcelona are known for their 'tiki-taka' style of football; a positive, attacking style that relies on excellent passing and control skills. At La Masia, the young players are drilled in these techniques from an early age so they have the right set of skills to make the transition to the first team when the time comes.

The players at La Masia are all given scholarships by Barcelona that pay for all their needs. This includes food, accommodation, teachers and study materials. The club also pay them a minimum wage to give them a degree of independence. The success of the academy is demonstrated by the number of graduates in the current squad. Barcelona's 5–0 victory over rivals Real Madrid in November 2010 was won with 8 La Masia alumni in the starting 11. The winning team contrasted with the Real Madrid team of 'Galacticos', which featured only one product from their own youth development system.

La Masia is an example of how to create a successful system of education and youth development in sport.

Read more: www.totalbarca.com/2010/news/la-masia-the-footballing-factory-par-excellence/#ixzz1GDKtRsYp

WHAT IS SOCIAL CAPITAL?

While it was the sociologists James Coleman and Pierre Bourdieu who developed the term, it was the political scientist Robert Putnam who packaged and developed a theory of social capital as a basis for analysing American society. Social capital, according to Putnam, meant those features of social life – networks, norms and trusts – that enabled participants to act together more effectively to achieve shared objectives. It has been viewed as the elixir that thickens civil society with the potential to create strong reciprocal relationships and energetic communities. For Putnam, the best indicators and generators of social capital included involvement in voluntary associations: a choir, a political party, a football or a bowling league. James Coleman's (1988) concept of social capital has also become popular within contemporary policy-orientated discourses about sport and leisure (Coalter, 2000; Harris, 1998). Coleman introduced his now well-known concept in a discussion of a society's capacity for educational achievement, but implicit within the notion of social capital was a potential meaning that extended well beyond education in that social capital can be involved in any sphere that involved trust. Since the late 1980s, developing social capital has been viewed as a way of renewing democracy. It refers to the network of social groups and relationships that fosters cooperative working and community well-being. It involves communities and other social groups exercising a certain degree of trust through taking on mutual obligations.

There are at least two reasons why social capital has attracted so much attention. On the one hand, civil society and communities depend upon it. Social capital has been seen as a way of contributing to social inclusion. Social groups and individuals learn more when they can draw upon the cultural resources of people around them. They learn from each other directly but they also learn to trust that the social arrangements are in place to ensure that learning, through a multitude of mediums including sport, will benefit them both culturally and for employment opportunities. They also trust that their own family or friends will grow up in a community that is intellectually stimulating. Social capital can have these effects most readily where it is embodied in the social structure – most notably, formal educational institutions and cultural organisations that have a commitment to other outcomes such as learning.

On the other hand, democracy depends upon social capital. This is true in one very obvious sense: that democracy depends upon everyone trusting that everyone else will operate the system constructively. When that trust breaks down – for example, as a reaction to certain screening practices aimed at the control of drugs in athletes or the failure to deliver sustainable sporting and economic benefits for deprived inner-city urban ghettos, or the adequate funding arrangements for sport in universities or local authorities – the result is cynicism about democracy in general. But the potential role of social capital is more profound than this because citizenship requires knowledge and that people know how to work with others towards common goals.

The political scientist Robert Putnam (1995) documented the decline of social capital in America, which he defined as those features of social life – networks, runs and trusts – that enable participants to work together more effectively to pursue shared objectives. Putnam used this notion to analyse the phenomenon of what he called 'civic disengagement'. By this, he referred to the decline in participation not just in formal political activity, but also in all

247

kinds of social activities, including sport and physical activity. The decline of social capital allegedly included the decreasing membership in voluntary organisations, decreased participation in organised activities and the decrease in time spent in informal socialising and visiting. Americans were viewed as becoming less trusting of one another, with a close correlation existing between social trust and membership of civic associations. Television emerged as the prime suspect in the decline of social capital, with viewing per television in 1995 accounting for more than a 50 per cent increase in viewing time in comparison to the 1950s. Television privatised time for sport and other activities and, in doing so, destroyed the networks and values that supported social capital and the pursuit of shared objectives.

The concept of social capital carries with it a heavy burden of claims that only recently have been subjected to critical review (Johnston and Percy-Smith, 2003). At its heaviest, as typified by writers such as Putnam, the presence or absence of social capital is used as an explanatory factor for economic and political performance. More modest claims are also made for social capital in that it allegedly contributes to the formation of strong formal and informal networks, shared norms and trusting social relationships. In relation to communities, it is asserted that high-trust communities typically experience less crime, antisocial behaviour and social fragmentation. For individuals, social capital, it is suggested, contributes to better health, higher levels of educational attainment and access to employment. Social capital, it is maintained, is a factor that contributes to higher levels of civic and voluntary activity and, in turn, such activity enhances democracy by offering citizens greater choices and opportunities.

The dark side of social capital

On the other hand, Portes (1998) identified four negative consequences associated with social capital. First, the exclusion of outsiders as a result of strong ties that exist within a particular group or community. Second, group or community closure that inhibits the economic success of its members as a result of free-riding on the part of some group members. Third, conformity within the group or community, resulting in restrictions of personal freedom and autonomy. Finally, social capital is partly responsible for a downward levelling as a result of group solidarity that arises out of opposition to mainstream society and inter-generational experiences of exclusion and discrimination. In all of these ways, social capital is viewed as excluding outside influences and enforcing damaging group norms if you do not belong to a community or group. The notion of social capital has a dark side as well as a positive side, and discussion of sport and social capital must be sensitive to both the positive and negative aspects of social capital in action.

SPORT AND SOCIAL CAPITAL

While credit for the notion of social capital remains with sociologists such as James Coleman and Pierre Bourdieu, it was Robert Putnam who packaged and developed the theory subsequently presented in *Bowling Alone: The Collapse and Revival of American Community* (2000) and earlier works. Putnam's firm belief that investment in bowling leagues and other voluntary associations could save democracy and community in the West has been encouraged by both American and British political administrations. Rarely has a work revolving around aspects of sport, culture and society had such a political impact. *Bowling Alone* articulated the unease many, initially Americans, felt about the state of their communities, and Putnam provided the numerical evidence that fuelled those initial fears. Putnam saw deep parallels between the turn of the twentieth century and the turn of the twenty-first century in which major technological, economic and social change was destroying the nation's stock of social capital and yet no action was taken to fix the problem. Between 1890 and 1910, all the major American civic institutions of the twentieth century – from the Urban League to the Knights of Columba – were invented.

At Harvard, Putnam engaged in a range of seminars to encourage a new wave of voluntary associations aimed at rebuilding bonds of civic trust among Americans. Much of what was happening in America also related to the British experience at the turn of the twenty-first century and perhaps expressed most forcibly in the work of David Marquand (2004) in *The Decline of the Public*, in which the writer charts the decline of citizenship, equity and service that had been crucial to both individual fulfilment and social well-being. From the Women's Institutes and the Women's League of Health and Beauty to the working men's club and local sports clubs, Britain has always had a strong record of voluntary association and social capital in sport and other areas of public life. With specific reference to sports clubs in Scotland, a 1999 survey identified the following concerns: 50 per cent identified a general shortage of volunteers, 33 per cent identified a shortage of volunteer staff with technical skills and 29 per cent identified a shortage of volunteer staff with management skills (Jarvie, 2004).

On the other hand, Hunt (2001) points out that we still manage to maintain levels of sociability and community investment commensurate with the 1950s. Yet, at the same time, we are trusting people less, our faith in politics is declining and the kinds of associations we are joining tend to have more to do with private needs than civic engagement. The results of the shift away from ways that were concerned about the public domain and social capital to individualism and market fundamentalism are there for everyone to see, according to Marquand (2004); resource-starved public services, the marketisation of the public sector, the soul-destroying targets and audits that go with it and the erosion of public trust. One further observation upon this general malaise is made, and that is the observation that citizenship rights are by definition equal. Market rewards are, by definition, unequal. If the public domain of sport is annexed to, or invaded by, the market domain of buying and selling, the primordial democratic promise of equal citizenship and sporting equity will be negated.

The promise in the notion of social capital is that sport and other associational activity can make a contribution to building up levels of trust in sport, culture and society, and consequently contributing to democracy, community spirit and a weakening public domain. Yet, the explanatory power of the relationship between sport and the promise of renewed forms of social capital needs to carry with it a cautionary note. The work on sport and social capital has been predominantly based upon evidence drawn from British and American sport and recreational activity, and if broader international comparisons with other places were brought into play the picture may be different. There is little evidence of the decline in associational activity in certain parts of Europe and in Scandinavia, and in other parts of the world such as South America it may still be constant, if not increasing (Da Costa *et al.*, 2002). Stolle's (1998) work in Germany and Sweden suggests that sport and the arts facilitate few

249

bridging links with ethnic groups. Whereas sport and the arts may encourage bonding at the expense of bridging, little contribution is made to linking disadvantaged groups to other levels of the decision-making hierarchy. Insofar as many people are excluded from sport, how can the notion that sport is said to increase social capital be accepted as a general or universal truth? Are there not differences between regions, within nations and, more importantly, between rich and poor parts of the world?

While not wanting to imply that an uncritical devotion to certain observations and facts does not mean that sport cannot make a contribution to social capital or healthy democratic communities, it is important to heed Putnam's (2000: 77) own words in *Bowling Alone* where he challenges readers to understand the complexities involved in creating civic engagement and just precisely what types of organisations and networks most effectively embody or generate social capital in the sense of mutual reciprocity, social obligations and community action. Many on the left have viewed the politics of social capital and civic renewal as a diversion from the politics of social democracy and, as such, students, teachers and researchers may want to consider or emphasise that, in sport, culture and society, social capital is a complement and not an alternative to the more egalitarian fundamentals of social democracy, and a more just and equal world beyond Britain and America.

Current debates about social capital and social cohesion may, at one level, raise questions concerning the direction of sport within urban policies. Sports have been at the heart of city life in many parts of the world for some time and yet urban policy needs to address the issue of whether the role of sport remains that of entertainment or whether sport is a social right, or both. If sport were to facilitate social capital, then cities, rather than using sport as a basis for attracting the national and international destination of major events or sports festivals, might wish to resurrect the notion of sport as a social right rather than a spectacle or form of entertainment. Cities in all parts of the world are first and foremost places to live for millions of people and yet access to sport remains problematic for many vulnerable groups of people. The citizens who seem the most ignored are those with the fewest resources (Harvey, 2003). The Canadian Council on Social Development points out that more than 60 per cent of children in the poorest households almost never participate in organised sports, whereas the figure is 27 per cent for children from affluent homes. The Council also confirmed the theory that cities that give young people a voice in policy development are more inclusive than others. Thus, it might be argued that, if sport does help to facilitate notions of social capital and/or community, then a prerequisite of any such approach necessitates viewing sport as a social right rather than a form of entertainment. Harvey (2003) is insightful when he suggests that the sociability networks that may develop in and around community sport and recreation initiatives may help to strengthen social bonds, and consequently a potential source of social capital. If this is the case, then sport as a social right for children and all vulnerable groups cannot be left to chance.

EDUCATION THROUGH SPORT

There may be some who believe that we should not have to justify the educational worth of sports activities in order to lend credibility or status to physical activity. The argument of sport for sport's sake is popular and it is believed by some that an over-emphasis on extrinsic

---

SPORT IN FOCUS 10.2: OBJECTIVES OF 2004, THE EUROPEAN YEAR OF EDUCATION THROUGH SPORT

- To raise the awareness of educational and sports organisations of the need for cooperation to develop education through sport and its European dimension.

- To take advantage of the values conveyed by sport to increase knowledge and skills, enabling young people to develop their physical capabilities and inclination to personal effort, as well as social capabilities such as teamwork, solidarity, tolerance and fair play in a multicultural context.

- To raise awareness of the positive contribution made by voluntary work to informal education, particularly for young people.

- To promote the educational value of mobility and pupil exchanges, particularly in a multicultural environment, through the organisation of sports and cultural meetings as part of school activities.

- To encourage the exchange of good practice concerning the potential role of sport in education systems in order to promote the social inclusion of disadvantaged groups.

- To establish a better balanced school life by encouraging sport in school activities.

- To examine the problems linked to the education of young people engaged in competitive sport.

(educational) outcomes distorts the very nature of sport. However, this argument refuses to recognise many things, and not just that educational values are inherent within sport .The pleasure and enjoyment of participating is not lost by placing an emphasis on its educational value. An ideal scenario may be to create healthy, poverty-free and active nations that understand and have the opportunity to access the benefits of physical activity, enjoy participating in sport but also develop human capabilities and further freedoms. Education through sport is also about enhancing individual freedoms and harnessing the social commitment to bring this about.

Sport in Focus 10.2 outlines the key objectives from the European Year of Education through Sport. Education through sport projects have long since been viewed as agents of social change. The following are some of the many popular answers that are given when asked, 'what does education through sport provide us with?'.

- It can increase knowledge and skills and, in a broader sense, contribute to the knowledge economy.

251

- It can help to provide opportunities for life-long learning and sustain not just education, but an involvement in sport and physical activity.
- The voluntary contribution to informal education through sport can make a positive contribution to helping young people.
- Education through sport can help foster and develop critical debate about key public issues.
- Programmes in different parts of the world that involve sport as part of an approach to tackling HIV education clearly view education through sport as an important aspect of international and humanitarian aid efforts.
- Education through sport helps to foster social capital through fostering relationships, networking and making connections.

The effectiveness of this latter point is at the heart of the debate about social capital in the sense that associational activity through both education *and* sport can help people connect through a series of networks, and these networks in themselves then constitute a form of social capital, particularly where networks tend to share common values. These networks through education and sport, therefore, have the potential to act as a form of resource that can be seen, according to Field (2003: 1), as forming a kind of capital.

The challenge of social change is enormous and the promise of education through sport should not detract from the fact that increasing competition within some of the poorest areas of the world often depletes social capital and leaves its potential fragmented. The informal sector sometimes dissolves self-help networks and solidarities essential to the survival of the very poor, and it is often women and children who are the most vulnerable. An NGO worker in Haiti describes the ultimate logic of neo-liberal individualism in a context of absolute immiseration (Davis, 2006: 184):

> Now everything is for sale. The women used to receive you with hospitality, give you coffee, share all that she has in her home. I could go get a plate of food at a neighbour's house; a child could get a coconut at her godmother's, two mangoes at another aunt's. But these acts of solidarity are disappearing with the growth of poverty. Now when you arrive somewhere, either the women offers to sell you a cup of coffee or she has no coffee at all. The tradition of mutual giving that allowed us to help each other and survive – this is all being lost.

Narrowing the gap and better futures

Narrowing the gap through education in sport is about the almost unique contribution that education in sport has made in relation to developing people, raising aspirations and being a real resource of hope, nationally, internationally and locally. Yet, the relationship between social capital and education, as indicated earlier, calls for an increasing awareness of not only the need for alternative conceptualisations of social capital, but an awareness of the diverse number of ways in which this relationship is examined, defined and operationalised (Dika and Singh, 2002). The conceptual umbrella of social capital is often stretched to include a variety of social factors that do not always coherently hang together. Problems with the conceptualisation and measurement of social capital have resulted in a body of research that does not always acknowledge the differential access to social networks and social resources.

The promise of education through sport to narrow the gap or forge new forms of social capital should not be overestimated. An issue might be the right of all people to have access to education and/or sport, and the small contribution that education through sport can make to this goal. With the international campaigns against world debt struggling to find a solution, new ideas and progressive ideas are needed to cure the problems, in part, caused by international finance institutions attempting to solve the debt problem of the global South and other places. Football is popular in places such as Brazil, where it is estimated that some 250,000 children work and a further 250,000 who are not working are not in school. The need to raise money for the family unit through the informal economy means that children often do not have access to education and the failure to study only serves to maintain poverty (Landman, 2004). Yet, some projects highlight the promise, possibilities and limits of education through sport to make a difference, be a ray of hope. Sport cannot do this on its own but swapping international debt for education, including education through sport, may be one of the possible strategies open to a progressive, humanitarian international approach to education through sport that could challenge the very values at the heart of global sport. It may assist in creating the conditions that may allow education through sport to thrive. In short, swapping debt for education, including education through sport, may assist millions of children and others to gain substantive education, transferable skills and enable some, ultimately, to become more active participants in a national economy, secure better life chances and escape the cycle of poverty.

Founded in 1987, the Mathare Youth Sports Association (MYSA) in Kenya lies in one of the country's poorest slum areas. It is an area with a population of nearly one million people and with an average household income, for a family of eight, of about 63 pence a day. Here, sport is placed at the centre of a humanitarian aid programme precisely because it is a point of contact with young kids that can entice young people to learn. It is a vehicle for facilitating mutual self-help and education on a massive scale. Sports leagues far in excess of 14,000 children run on a 'pay it back' approach in which, in return for help with facilities and organisation, players help keep the neighbourhood clean, plant trees, and attend AIDS, pregnancy and drug awareness classes. Scholarships exist for photography, music and drama classes. Teams got points for their work as well as their sport.

Reflecting back on the impact of MYSA, one former goalkeeper said:

> Older kids who have been involved since its beginning have become leaders and role models in the community and football has been the catalyst for *their social, physical and intellectual development.*

The ethos here was pretty straightforward: ask kids what they want, use sport and physical activity as a basis for developing economic and social capital, local solutions to local problems, education and a track record of success, all of which has been recognised internationally through a number of awards. There is the reality of Maria Urrutia, the woman from Colombia who lifted 245 kg to win Colombia's first ever Olympic gold medal at the 2000 Sydney

Olympic Games. The country usually hits the headlines for other reasons, but speaking to her nation following her success, she was clear about how sport had helped her and how it could help other people who may have been disadvantaged or poor. More specifically she said – 'I hope others see that you can make a living, see the world and *get an education*, through sports, or even in music and other arts'.

Alternatively, Sport in Focus 10.3 illustrates how the redistribution of wealth created from football tournaments in different parts of the world could assist in providing basic education in many marginalised communities.

SPORT IN FOCUS 10.3: THE BETTER FUTURE LEVY

Before the 2010 FIFA World Cup in South Africa, the Education For All (EFA) Monitoring Report 2010 proposed that a 'Better Future' levy could be placed on the world's top football leagues and the World Cup to improve basic education in low-income countries.

By placing a 0.4 per cent levy on the media and marketing revenue generated by these leagues and the World Cup, the EFA report calculated that around US$48 million could be raised. A figure such as this could provide basic education for nearly 500,000 out-of-school children around the world until 2015. The table below displays the figures central to the model.

While the model could be seen as an extremely forward-thinking step, similar models already exist. FC Barcelona already spends 0.7 per cent of the club's income on global poverty reduction through its foundation.

Major football leagues	Annual commercial revenue (US$ million)	Revenue from 0.4% school levy (US$ million)	Estimated number of primary school places provided
England	3,511	14	140,430
Germany	2,068	8	82,727
Spain	2,068	8	82,727
Italy	2,044	8	81,749
France	1,422	6	56,897
World Cup	850	3	34,000
Total	11,963	48	478,530

Note: Based on a recurrent unit cost of US$100 per child in primary school. No account is taken of the capital costs (e.g. classrooms) required to provide primary schooling. The commercial revenue for the World Cup is averaged over four years to provide an annual revenue figure.

Sources: Constructed from evidence drawn from: Sportcal (2009); Deloitte LLP (2009); EFA Global Monitoring Report (2010).

The above has been recognised by *2010 Education For All Global Monitoring Report* but so too has a warning. More than a decade has passed since the international community adopted Education for All goals in Dakar in 2000. Many of the world's poorest countries are not on track to meet 2015 targets. Failure to reach the marginalised has denied many people the right to education. While the residual effects of the global economic crisis may continue, it is important to realise that education in many communities is on the front line, and education through sport can play a crucial role in promoting tolerance, peace and understanding between peoples, and yet, at the same time, education through sport is also at risk.

SUMMARY

Community is often missing in the worlds we inhabit, and yet it is potentially a crucial quality to a happier life. The worlds of sport and beyond would be safer, more secure and less vulnerable if community was more of a reality (Bauman, 2001). Given the insecurity and concerns about safety in a rapidly globalising interdependent world, we need to gain control over the conditions under which we struggle with the challenges of life and, for most people, such control can only be gained by working collectively. If there is to be any notion of active community in a world of many individuals, it needs to be a community woven together from sharing and mutual care. If sport can help to provide moments of safety, security and hope for vulnerable groups of people, then it has a part to play in creating a community of concern and responsibility for the equal right to be human and the equal ability to act on that right. Education through sport is a potentially powerful means to an end. This may take at least two different forms: sport being the potential key to *accessing* formal education, and an education through the *process* of being involved in sport. At present, those excluded from sport in many parts of the world do not have access to that right.

This chapter has looked at some of the arguments and some evidence that would support the fact that sport and education or education through sport provides a potential resource of hope that can make a difference to people's lives. Historically, sport and education have keen key avenues of social mobility and an escape from poverty for some. It has been suggested that, rather than capital, the emphasis in social capital should be on 'social' and aligned so that it is necessary to think of ways in which the 'social' in social science, social change and social empowerment may contribute to alternative practices and ways of thinking about sport and education. Thinking systematically about emancipatory alternatives and the part played by sport and education is only one way or element in the process by which the limits of the possible can expand and the promise and possibilities of the power of education through sport can become more of a reality for more people. Many new proposals are continually being tested.

When the former First Minister for Scotland, Jack McConnell, in his St Andrews day speech, talked of talking Scotland up, about starting with Scotland's young people, about renewing democracy, about the importance of cultural activities, including sport, he could have almost been paraphrasing Tom Johnston, the former Secretary of State for Scotland who, in November 1942, charged the then Advisory Council of Education in Scotland with being a parliament of education and seeking how schools could ensure that young people were properly equipped to discharge the duties and exercise the rights of citizenship. It is this promise or possibility that education through sport is about citizenship, social cohesion, social capital and social responsibility that makes it so attractive to different places and forms of social policy.

Education through sport is not simply about the development of human capital, but also the development of human capability. If education helps with a person being more efficient in commodity production, this may enhance the level of human capital. But looking beyond the concept of human capital, it is also helpful to think about how education through sport may also help with closing the gap between different parts of the world in terms of human capability. If a person can become more productive in making commodities through better education and better health it is, as Sen (2009) points out, not unnatural to expect that he or she can achieve more, have the freedom to achieve more and the choice to achieve more. There is more to inequality than disparities of income distribution, but this does not mean that people's ability to choose for themselves, the lives they wish to lead are not drastically curtailed by circumstances they find themselves in. To take care of inequalities of capability, you need more resources of hope from many fronts and the belief that education and lifelong learning can be a resource of hope, to add capability for people in need and many others. Perhaps this is what education through sport can help with, and it is a matter to which we will return in Part 4 of this book.

GUIDE TO FURTHER READING

Altinay, H. (2010). *The Case for Global Civics*. Washington, DC: Brookings Institution.

Benn, T., Dagkas, S. and Jawad, H. (2011). 'Embodied Faith: Islam, Religious Freedom and Educational Practices in Physical Education'. *Sport, Education and Society*, 16 (1): 17–34.

Coalter, F. (2007). *A Wider Social Role for Sport?* London: Routledge.

Dika, S. and Singh, K. (2002). 'Applications of Social Capital in Educational Literature: A Critical Synthesis' in *Review of Educational Research*, Spring, 72 (1): 31–60.

Evans, J. and Davies, B. (2011). 'New Directions, New Questions? Social Theory, Education and Embodiement'. *Sport, Education and Society*, 16 (3): 263–278.

Fabian Society (2006). *Narrowing the Gap: The Fabian Commission on Life Chances and Child Poverty*. London: Fabian Society.

Field, J. (2003). *Social Capital*. London: Routledge.

Houlihan, B. (2008). *Sport and Society*. London: Sage, 254–283.

Nicholson, M. and Hoye, R. (2008). *Sport an Social Capital*. Oxford: Elsevier.

Robbins, C. (2006). *The Giroux Reader*. Boulder, CO: Paradigm Publishers.

Sen, A. (2009). *Identity and Violence: The Illusion of Destiny*. London: Allen Lane.

Sherry, E., King, A. and O'May, F. (2011). 'Social Capital and Sport Events: Spectator Attitudinal Change and the Homeless World Cup'. *Sport in Society*, 14 (1): 111–125.

UNESCO (2010). *Education For All Global Monitoring Report*. Paris: UNESCO Publishing.

QUESTIONS

1 Provide a summary of Putnam's thesis in relation to sport and social capital, and describe ways in which sport might contribute or not contribute to the notions of social bridging and social bonding.

2 What is social capital and does sport help to develop it? Illustrate your answer with at least five examples from sporting contexts.

3 The notion of social capital should not be simply accepted. Explain what is meant by social capital having a dark side.

4 Use the notion of ordered freedom to explain the value of education and education through sport.

5 What were the objectives behind the European Year of Education through Sport?

6 Education and sport have often been viewed as agents of social change. Explain some of the common ways in which education through sport projects have attempted to bring about social change.

7 How can education through sport help with the development of human capabilities, and why might this be important?

8 What does the term 'narrowing the gap' refer to, and how can sport contribute to this?

9 Describe the ethos of the Mathare Youth Sports Association in Kenya.

10 Describe the idea behind the case study provided in Sport in Focus 10.3.

PRACTICAL PROJECTS

1 Examine the policies of five different professional sport academies in any sport, and critically review the way in which these sports approach, sustain and develop the formal education of the athletes.

2 Many universities run scholarship schemes that are designed to help talented athletes combine sport and education. Examine five scholarship schemes, and compare and contrast the way in which sport and education is combined in university sport scholarship schemes.

3 Access the UNESCO website and move to UNESCO education. Read the monitoring reports on conflict (2011) and marginalisation (2010). Provide ten policy statements that would help UNESCO recognise and maximise the combined effect of sport and education to intervene.

4 Talk to ten board members of different types of organisation and ask the members who sport helps to develop and sustain social networks. Ask how the social network

operates and if anybody can access the network. Write a short report drawing on your findings that explains how sport helps or hinders the development of social capital.

5   Interview ten volunteers and explore with them the way in which they see their role in sport as involving the creation of active citizenship, trust, and mutual obligations and responsibility.

KEY CONCEPTS

Education ■ Citizenship ■ Community ■ Democracy ■ Human capital ■ Marginalisation ■ Mutuality ■ Obligations ■ Public realm ■ Social capital ■ Trust ■ Volunteers

WEBSITES

Friends of Edusport
www.friendsedusport.com
A charity that looks to empower communities through sport.

International Sport and Culture Association
www.isca-web.org
Use this international social forum to gain up-to-date information of education through sport. Access the website and use the search engine to access education projects around the world. Use the key word 'education' in the search box.

United Nations Education, Scientific and Cultural Organization
www.unesco.org
Access the UNESCO website and look for key reports on education for all, and search for the different ways in which sport is used.

Council of Europe on Education, Youth and Sport
www.coe.int/lportal/web/coe-portal/what-we-do/education-and-sports/sport-for-al
An explanation of why the Council of Europe sees sport and education as making an important contribution to the lives of young Europeans.

A factbook of information on different countries
https://www.cia.gov/library/publications/the-world-factbook/
Use this resource to examine education systems and educational spend in different countries.

Scotland's University for Sporting Excellence
www.sportingexcellence.stir.ac.uk/
A university dedicated to sport and education – see the research across the university.

Part 3

Sport and contemporary social issues

INTRODUCTION

The six chapters that form the third part of this book critically examine some contemporary social issues and the part that sport has to play in these issues. To what extent has sport a part to play in solving some of the major social problems of our time? Part 3 revolves around six chapters and addresses head on some of the key problems facing the world today such as the environment, health, violence, religion, regeneration, development and the quest for a better lifestyle. Given the importance of the Olympic Games in 2012, the Commonwealth Games in 2014 and the FIFA World Cup in 2022, this chapter looks at the rationale and impact for hosting major sporting events. This section builds upon some of the issues raised in Part 1. Part 3 is divided into six chapters, and the following summaries introduce the areas covered.

Sport and the environment

The environment, environmental movements and environmental policies have impacted upon our knowledge and thinking about sport, culture and society. The historical and systematic relationship between sport and the weather has recently been the subject of enquiry, while the determining impact of the environment has been commented upon regularly in relation to sport. The emergence of Kenyan and Ethiopian dominance in athletics is often misleadingly attributed to single-factor explanations such as high altitude, and this is stressed or prioritised over other environmental–social factors such as lifestyle. The weather and its shifting patterns make the scheduling of events more of a challenge. Changing international weather patterns meant that the absence of adequate quantities of snow brought about by unusually warm winter weather conditions had to be resolved quickly by the 2010 Vancouver Winter Olympics organising committee. The Global Anti-Golf Movement rooted in Asia has been critical of the financial, environmental and societal impact of golf tourism. In some parts of the world, golf tourism is viewed as problematic since its expansion has created problems for many indigenous populations who seem removed from the profits associated with the promotion of golf as a green and environmentally friendly sport. Does sport contribute to a sustainable environment? What would a radical environmental approach to sport entail? What does the term 'environmentalism' mean and how recent is the debate about sport, the environment and society? Chapter 11 introduces and critically examines the ways in which sport, the environment and society have been thought about.

Sport, the body and world health

The body has been the focus of a substantive amount of research in sport, culture and society. Concerns about health and ageing have placed the body and how we look after it at the heart of world health problems. Four main reasons for this are: (i) the importance of the body as a personal project and cultural object; (ii) the impact of feminism and other forms of intervention upon the engendered nature of the body in sport; (iii) the development of the ageing process on sporting bodies; and (iv) the way in which the body in sport is thought of differently within and between different cultures and societies. In the twenty-first century, should sporting bodies be thought of as constrained, symbolic, liberated and/or naturalistic? Body culture has been central to the framing of policies involving sport in many of the Scandinavian countries. Does sport continue to be a vehicle for controlling, regulating, disciplining and punishing the human body? Does high-performance sport have an impact upon the way athletes in later life think about the body? Chapter 12 provides the basis for students and researchers acquiring a sound grasp of some of the fundamental ways in which sports bodies and societies are inextricably linked to issues of identity and world health.

Sport, violence and crime

How do we know that our neighbour is not a serial football hooligan or staunch supporter of blood sports? These are only two sports historically associated with different forms of violence. The duality of sport is such that sport is seen as both a source of violence and crime, but also a partial cure to a perceived problem of violence and youth crime. Within liberal accounts of sports policy sport is often linked to forms of intervention aimed at ameliorating or changing crime rates in different countries or localities. The terrain of sport, violence and deviance is fluid. Player violence, spectator violence, and bodily violence including drug abuse, blood sports and other forms of violence are some of the rich substantive areas that can open up an investigation or critical enquiry. There are a number of liberal and non-liberal explanations of the relationship between sport and violence. The economic argument against sports violence centres on the risk of injury and loss of livelihood as a result of foul play. The issue of violence in women's sport has also been a focus, with debates about the emergence of women's boxing and bullfighting. Chapter 13 draws upon some of these areas while exploring sport, violence and crime in relation to identity and a quest for recognition and excitement. How should we think about the changing relationship between sport, violence and crime?

Sport, religion and spirituality

A British newspaper headline read 'Lewis hands surfers never on a Sunday warning'. The article referred to a clash of cultures between those who viewed Sunday as sacred and those who wanted to develop a remote Outer Hebridean island of the west coast of Scotland as one of the major professional world surfing centres. Athletes in different sports continue to refuse to play on Sundays because of their adherence to religious observances. The evolution of Jewish Maccabi Olympic Games serves as a reminder that faith provides a basis for not only separatist forms of provision in education, religion and welfare, but also in sport. Does religion help sport cope with the uncertainty of competition (i) by providing a platform for the display of religious symbols and rituals; (ii) by providing a psychological edge in the quest for success or coping with failure; and (iii) by establishing team solidarity; or (iv) does sport competition reflect religious divisions and conflict in the world today? Chapter 14 looks at the different ways in which sport and religion have come together while, at the same time, providing a critical overview of the relationship between sport, religion and spirituality. The spiritual experience of sport goes well beyond questions of religion but the very idea of 'religio athletae' has a long history. How and why do various faiths influence sport? Religious faiths carry a premium in the contemporary world and, while some suggest that faith can provide an ethical underpinning for involvement in sport, others suggest that being in possession of a divinely prescribed rulebook does not provide the basis for any moral high ground in sport. At the same time, sport and spirituality is central to many people's motivation for taking part and being driven through pain and suffering to success.

Sport, the Olympics and major sporting events

In 2012, the Olympic Games will return to London for the first time since 1948. It has been argued that they are the key to urban regeneration in the East End of London. The rationale of urban regeneration is also central to the hosting of the Commonwealth Games in Glasgow in 2014. It is estimated that the 2012 Games will involve 15,000 athletes, 203 countries, 70,000 volunteers and 9 million tickets, which will make London 2012 arguably the largest peacetime mobilisation of people and resources in the world. One reason London was successful in its bid to host the Games was that it gave a commitment to provide a lasting, positive economic legacy, and the benefits and opportunities would be distributed across the UK. The economic benefit of hosting major events often rests upon two foundations. First, the building of facilities and the related infrastructure and, second, the influx of tourists and visitors to the local economies. Chapter 15 examines the reasons why cities in different parts of the world both want to and don't want to hold major sporting events. Not all cities can be Olympic cities. Indeed, the Olympics have yet to be held in Africa. African cities have lodged bids for Commonwealth Games and the FIFA 2010 World Cup was hosted in South Africa. China has financed significant sports infrastructure in support of major sports events in Africa – why? The chapter examines the evolution and development of Olympic cities, the major winners and losers, and the consequences for local inhabitants when the Olympics are in town. Major sporting events are very rarely examined from the point of view that they provide insights into the future of societies and the consequences for ordinary people.

Sport, lifestyles and alternative cultures

Sport, lifestyles and alternative cultures have often been associated with the language of opposition, resistance, alienation and exclusion from mainstream sport. Studies have examined windsurfing, snowboarding, skateboarding, surfing and a rapid growth in extreme sports. Alternative sports are invariably defined as offering ideological and practical alternatives to mainstream sport and sport values, yet the process by which alternative lifestyles become mainstream activities is not uncommon. Alternative choices to mainstream sport may also involve choices over sexuality, risk and uncertainty, freedom, expression, universalism, and life politics. Life politics is not the politics of life chances but lifestyle, identity and, in this chapter, the consumption of alternative sports. In a more fragmented, uncertain world of sport, are the future alternative choices primarily associated with Western sporting cultures or are the alternatives to mainstream sports arriving from other worlds and communities? Chapter 16 interrogates the social issues that have emerged from research into sport, lifestyles and alternative cultures, and questions whether the promise and possibilities of freedom carried with these sports are indeed alternative or extreme, or primarily Western fads and fashions.

Chapter 11

Sport and the environment

How should society balance the environmental impact of sport against the economic impact?

PREVIEW

Key terms defined ■ Introduction ■ 2010 Winter Olympic Games ■ Environmental sporting problems and issues ■ Sport and the weather ■ Beijing Olympic Games and the environment ■ The worlds first green cricket match ■ Environmental determinism ■ Radical and reformist approaches to sport and the environment ■ Surfers Against Sewage ■ The green sport agenda and sustainability ■ Nike's green World Cup kits ■ The Olympic Movement and Agenda 21 ■ Environmentalism and the anti-golf movement ■ Summary

OBJECTIVES

This chapter will:

- introduce key themes in the discussion of sport and the environment;
- critically discuss the relationship between sport and the weather;
- consider radical, reformist, light and dark green approaches to sport and the environment;
- answer the question 'what is environmental determinism?'; and
- evaluate ways in which sport and the environment are viewed as anti-global.

KEY TERMS DEFINED

Eco-centrism: A point of view that recognises the ecosphere, rather than the biosphere, as central in importance, and attempts to redress the imbalance created by human influence.

Environmental determinism: The belief that human activities are controlled by the environment. A more general synonym is 'environmentalism'.

Sustainability (or sustainable development): The development that meets the need of the present without compromising the ability of future generations to meet their own needs.

INTRODUCTION

Make a list of environmental problems and issues that are affecting us – the increase of greenhouse gases and consequential global warming, the acidification of the oceans and the collapse of fish stocks, the loss of the rainforest, the spread of deserts, the shortage of arable land, the increase in violent weather, the growth of mega-cities, famine, migration patterns, and population growth. It may be tempting to conclude that sport is not a major driver to environmental change. Yet, sport is both directly and indirectly involved in global environmental politics at a local, national and international level.

The vision for the 2010 Vancouver Winter Olympic Games was to make it not just about Vancouver, but Canada as a whole. 99.1 per cent of Canadians watched some of the Winter Olympic Games. Different days were labelled as British Columbia day or Ontario day. The top 10 US TV markets had between 26 and 36 per cent primetime share of coverage on NBC. Vancouver 2010 reached a record potential audience of 3.8 billion people worldwide and approximately 1.8 billion viewers (Peach, 2010: 17). However, changing international weather patterns meant that challenges such as a lack of snow brought about by unusually warm winter weather conditions had to be resolved quickly. Environmental issues are high

SPORT IN FOCUS 11.1: VANCOUVER 2010 WINTER OLYMPIC GAMES

The 2010 Vancouver Winter Olympic Games required considerable amounts of artificial snow to be transported so that the skiing events took place as scheduled. That being said, the Vancouver Games placed a large emphasis on environmental stability when planning the event, as shown below:

- All venues were built in accordance with Canada's green-building standards.

- Venues used innovative sustainability methods such as capturing rain to irrigate landscaping and capturing the heat from the used bath water.

- Almost 70 per cent of the heating for the Olympic Village was provided by waste heat recovery systems, including heat from sewage.

- The Olympic Village will anchor a sustainable urban neighbourhood that will serve as a model development for other cities.

- The Richmond Oval, the venue for the speed skating events, won numerous awards for environmental design.

- The Vancouver Olympic Committee (VANOC) received the Excellence for Green Building award from the Globe Foundation and the World Green Building Council for building the greenest Olympic district in North America.

- Transportation improvements reduced emissions that encouraged the use of mass transit, bicycling and other forms of transport as an alternative to using cars.

- The most ambitious carbon management programme at any Games included the first official supplier of carbon offsets.

- All construction occurred with community input, and integrated legacy planning from conception.

- VANOC, the IOC and the International Academy developed a sustainable Sports Event Toolkit for major sport events for Sport Science and Technology.

- VANOC assisted the Canadian Standard Association's development of the new Z2010 Sustainable Event Management Standard in Canada.

- A Vancouver City Olympic legacy fund helped to create 40 new garden plots, with 8 accessible to seniors and people with disabilities. Four beds were also used to supply food to agencies that feed the poor.

- The same programme also saw a 3- to 4-acre community garden established so that seniors and people with disabilities could participate in the community gardening.

on the international agenda for a whole generation of political leaders, activists and, to a lesser extent, sports leaders. Understanding the causes and impacts of environmental change may be more of an urgent task in the twenty-first century than it was in the nineteenth, but so too is our knowledge of the impact of the environment upon sport. According to Edward Wilson, the Earth is entering a new evolutionary era – an era of solitude. In effect, it is suggested that humans may destroy the planet and bring about the extinction of themselves and other living beings. It is doubtful if sport will tip the balance of the world's ecosystem and many would no doubt argue that, as important as sport is, nature is more important to human survival. However, current environmental debates about the nature of the world we live in should not ignore the relationship between sport, the environment and communities.

ENVIRONMENTAL SPORTING PROBLEMS AND ISSUES

The United Nations Environment Programme (UNEP) created a sports and environment unit in 1994 that has evaluated and consistently reported upon the environmental impact of hosting international Olympic Sporting Events. UNEP teamed with the International Olympic Committee (IOC) in 1994 with a view to:

- promoting the integration of environmental considerations in sports;
- using the popularity of sports to promote environmental awareness and respect for the environment among the public, especially young people; and
- promoting the development of environmentally friendly sports facilities and the manufacture of environmentally friendly sporting goods.

The IOC requires cities bidding to host the Olympic Games to undertake an environmental impact analysis and, while many of the host cities have looked to minimise the environmental impact, it has only been achieved at a significant financial cost. The growing popularity of sport as a mechanism for delivering powerful messages has not been lost on various social groups and movements such as Greenpeace. The London 2012 Olympic Games environmental action plan revolves around a small number of environmental values such as low-carbon production, zero waste, conserving biodiversity and promoting environmental awareness and partnerships.

Environmental sporting problems are not new. The wettest cricket summers occurred in 1903 and 1924, with recorded rainfalls of 450 mm in 4 months, during which time 44 bowlers averaged fewer than 20 runs and only 2 batsmen achieved an average of more than 50 runs (Kay and Vamplew, 2002: 27). The day Jack Dempsey beat Jess Willard for the heavyweight boxing championship in July 1919, 150,000 sweltered in the heat with hundreds of spectators fainting. In the 1924 Paris Olympic Games 10,000 metres, only 15 of the 39 runners completed the field in temperatures of over 40 degrees Celsius. In June 1952, when Sugar Ray Robinson fought Joey Maxim for the world light-heavyweight championship, he was beaten as much by the heat as his opponent (Kay and Vamplew, 2002: 185). 1947 was one of the coldest post-war British winters, with more than 200 football matches being postponed by mid-March. 1976 was one of the driest, and fast grass, worn courts and dehydrated players struggled in the above average heat accompanying the Wimbledon tennis fortnight. Lightning fatalities occurred at the US Open golf championships of 1988 and 1991. The environment, then, has long had an impact upon sport, although different regions of the world have experienced different conditions unevenly and, as a result, climate in part has determined sporting choice. To take this to an extreme, hot countries are not renowned for their performance in Nordic sports.

A number of sports have a potentially detrimental impact upon the environment. In Austria, the impact of ski tourism meant that, by 1991, there were 2,709 draglifts and 785 cable cars compared with 74 draglifts and 44 cable cars in 1952 (Weiss et al., 1998: 369). The construction of new ski lifts to meet market demand for ski holidays in Austria meant the significant clearing of trees, soil and rocks above 1,500 metres, bringing with it the increased risk of flooding to the habitats below 1,500 metres. The sport itself is not immune from the effects of shifts in climate change. The 2010 Vancouver Winter Olympic Games required considerable amounts of artificial snow to be transported in at the last minute so that the skiing events could take place as scheduled. The advent of snow making itself is not without a potential negative environmental impact given that, in some case, snow making involves diverting natural waters, altering the normal flow of rivers and habitats with the result being dry stream beds, effects on irrigation and the consequences for species that depend upon stream flows.

The hosting of major sporting events creates numerous challenges and has forced major sporting organisations to think about the potential environmental impact and management of hosting such events. By the late twentieth century, the IOC had raised the environment and environmental policy to being the *third dimension* of the Olympic Movement. In 1991, it amended its charter to promote the notion that future Olympic Games were to be held under conditions that were cognisant of the fragile nature of the environment. International environmental sporting issues have not yet emerged as a focus of international politics, but they are part of any current Olympic bid and the focus of a pre-Olympic audit. The UNEP pre-Olympic audit of the 2008 Beijing Olympics arose out of two concerns. The first was to assess Beijing's performance against its commitments and the second was to disseminate lessons learned from the environmental challenges and achievements arising from the Games.

The 2007 Pre-Audit Report noted that the Beijing Olympic Committee (BOCOG) had taken steps to build sustainable venues, paying particular attention to energy efficiency, use of eco-friendly materials, water conservation, and environmental management and control of building sites. An interesting innovation was the widespread use in the venues of ground, water or air source heat pump systems to provide buildings with heat in winter and air conditioning in summer.

Two areas of concern were highlighted. While BOCOG had established guidelines to encourage sustainability in most aspects of the Games, many of its requirements were mandatory or enforceable. Final decisions on the environmental aspects of, for instance, transport, construction, accommodation and catering, were being taken on a voluntary basis. UNEP felt that this reliance on goodwill and trust, while admirable, left too much leeway for taking shortcuts at the expense of environmental sustainability. A further aspect of concern was the absence from commitments and specific undertakings to offset the added carbon dioxide emissions created by staging the Games. This is increasingly a feature of high-profile events, and is being adopted by a growing number of sports organisations and

267

SPORT IN FOCUS 11.2: THE WORLD'S FIRST GREEN CRICKET MATCH

The Punjab Cricket Association (PCA) hosted the world's first green cricket match on 9 April 2010. The carbon neutral event was co-organised by the United Nations Environmental Programme (UNEP) and the Indian Premier League (IPL) as part of the 'Batting for the Environment' initiative, launched in March 2010. The game took place in the Mohali Stadium in Punjab between Mumbai Indians and Kings XI Punjab and was the opening match of third IPL season.

The PCA made certain the carbon footprint of the event was as small as possible by offsetting 580 tonnes of match-related CO_2 emissions. Factors such as travel, accommodations and food consumption of all players, officials and fans travelling to the stadium were all taken into account. To cover unavoidable gas emissions, approximately US$10,150 was spent towards supporting a Rajasthan based residual biomass project. Furthermore, solar panels were installed at the venue to provide 100 kW of energy for the event.

The Batting for the Environment initiative had a wider impact than just one game. Over the 45-day tournament, the programme attempted to increase environmental awareness among millions of cricket fans and the wider public. This was achieved in many ways, including 'green tips' being displayed on the screens at live matches and read out by commentators. These tips advised people on how to limit their greenhouse gas emissions and how to care for the environment around them. There were a further four matches in the season that were carbon neutral.

private sector companies. Excellent examples include the HECTOR project devised by the organising committee of the 20th Olympic Winter Games in Torino (2006), and the Green Goal programme of the 2006 FIFA World Cup. Sport in Focus 11.2 provides some detail surrounding the first cricket match in Pakistan that pioneered an environmentally green approach to cricket.

UNEP, the United Nations' voice on the environment, also helped assist and advise the IPL on a range of ways to improve their green credentials. This included looking at ways to save water and energy, and lessen waste. Moreover, new cricket stadiums in India will be built to sustainable standards, team captains have pledged to reduce their teams' environmental impact and all players, sponsors and partners promised to be more mindful of their carbon footprint.

Over much of human history, the environmental impact on sport has tended to be local, yet the contemporary environmental risks associated with global warming, large scale pollution, over-population, levels of security, changing seasons and nature mean that environmental sporting issues are no longer just local issues, but potentially international and anti-global (Attenborough, 2011: 29). A lack of ground or green spaces for sport and physical activity may be experienced in a particular locality or nation but may also be considered to be more than a local or national problem. Many environmental issues are intrinsically transnational and many explanations for sporting performance draw upon the common environmental features such as high altitude or poverty. Indeed, the nature-versus-nurture dualism to explain aspects of sport is itself not new.

The phrase 'environmental sporting issue' encompasses a wide range of types of problems, issues and challenges and, although they share some common characteristics, each environmental sporting issue needs to be analysed in its own right. Committed sporting eco-warriors or sporting conservationists link sport and the environment to broader political and socio-economic changes that are impacting upon the environment. The sporting eco-warrior may view golf course development as a social pollutant while sporting conservationists might defend the threatened village cricket green in rural England on environmental green grounds but also as a threat to tradition and heritage. Thus, students of sport, culture and society should recognise that many environmental sporting problems and concerns are linked to the generation and distribution of wealth, knowledge, power, patterns of energy consumption, population growth, affluence and poverty. There is an inter-dependence and practical necessity to relate sport and the environment to other spheres of life.

SPORT, THE WEATHER AND ENVIRONMENTAL DETERMINISM

The changing nature of weather and climatic conditions not only poses an environmental threat to many winter sports, but also an economic threat to certain communities that rely upon income from snow reliability and the resulting tourism. Mountain areas are sensitive to climatic change, with less snow leading to receding glaciers, landslides and the concentration of winter sports activities upon high mountain environments. In other words, the ski industry will climb the mountain in order to obtain reliable snow at high altitude. While some regions may be able to maintain their winter tourism with suitable but expensive strategies, studies in Canada, the US, Australia, Switzerland, New Zealand, France and the UK have all shown that the environmental threats to the winter sports industry brought about by climatic change are also real economic threats (Burki et al., 2003). The potential annual cost of climatic change in Switzerland was estimated to be $2.1 billion by the year 2050, which equated to about 0.8 per cent of the Swiss gross national product for 1995, when the study was completed. In Canada, it has been projected that, based upon the current patterns of climatic change, without snowmaking technology the ski industry would decline substantially by between 37 and 57 per cent by 2050.

Kay and Vamplew (2002: 157) remind us that everyone concerned with sport – players, administrators, promoters, spectators and many others – all pay attention to the weather forecaster who referees many a decision concerning whether sport is on, off, likely to be interrupted or likely to be safe from the elements. Information about the weather is a vital determinant that influences the decisions made by event organisers, ground staff, spectators and others. Some sports venues, they point out, such as Wimbledon and Old Trafford, have their own weather centres, while other sports rely on the local meteorological office. The All England Cricket Club has two radar systems while the Professional Golfers Association in the US has two full-time meteorologists on site. Outdoor activities rely upon specialist weather services. Football grounds and race courses require accurate assessments of the weather in advance of match or race day. The weather affects the preparation for Formula 1 races in terms of the tyres that the drivers will put on the car. Thus, it might be argued that the weather is a vital environmental determinant influencing sports events and seasons.

The physical environment, to which Bale (2002a: 152) alludes, has been a factor determining the athletic success of national groups and has been noted in studies of sport since at least 1910. In an article entitled the 'Geography of Games' published in 1919, it was claimed that the climate determines the games we play. In the 1920s and 1930s, environmentally deterministic explanations of Finnish running success were not uncommon. In 1930, there were 12 Finns in the top twenty 5,000-metre runners in the world. In the 1990s and early twenty-first century, high altitude and other environmental factors have been highlighted as being almost a causal explanation in accounting for the phenomenal success of Kenyan and Ethiopian middle-distance runners. The illustrations listed above are examples of ways in which environmental determinism have been used as a kind of legitimating theory to explain sporting performance of different groups of people, but they can also be interpreted as racist.

RADICAL AND REFORMIST APPROACHES TO ENVIRONMENTALISM AND SPORT

It is one of Scotland's most popular surfing bays but campaigners say pollution renders it unsafe. Pease Bay is a haven for surfers. It is close to the community of Cove on the east coast of Scotland (Baynes, 2011: 7). The community of around 600 people is served by Cove sewage station, which is about 1 mile from Pease Bay. The sewage pollution at Pease Bay that has affected the winter surfing community has drawn the attention of Surfers Against Sewage (SAS – www.sas.org.uk), who are tackling the Scottish Water Authorities about the release of effluent into the sea near Pease Bay (Baynes, 2011: 8). Surfers Against Sewage was started after a public meeting on 10 May 1990, by a group of surfers who were *literally sick* of surfing in the sewage-polluted waters of three local beaches (St Agnes, Chapel Porth and Porthtowan), and equally exasperated by the National Rivers Authorities (now the Environment Agency) and the newly privatised water company's apathy and disinterest towards the problem. By the end of the year, just seven months after its inception, SAS had achieved a membership of 2,000 and had gained extensive press, radio, terrestrial and satellite coverage.

In 2007, SAS was awarded a BBC *Coast Magazine* award for the ground-breaking Return To Offender campaign, which addresses the worsening issue of litter on our beaches (www. sas.org.uk). This campaign has subsequently positively influenced industry giants including Coca-Cola. In 2009, SAS launched the Protect Our Waves (POW) campaign to increase protection for UK surf spots from environmental damage, negative impacts on wave quality and to safeguard water users right of access to ensure sports such as windsurfing, surfing, kayaking and others can benefit from the very best sporting wave resources the UK offers. The POW campaign secured a major victory in the Scottish Marine Bill in 2010, securing a place for surfers and other wave riders on Regional Planning Partnerships to help protect the world-class waves Scotland has to offer. In 2010, SAS was again awarded the BBC *Coast Magazine* award for Best Marine Green Project, for its work combating marine litter through its Mermaid's Tears campaign. The 2011 Pease Bay campaign involved petitioning the Scottish Government and asking for a probe into recreational water use at Pease Bay. SAS called for Scottish Ministers to recommend to the Scottish Environmental Protection Agency (SEPA) that Scottish Waters keep their sewage treatment works at Cove at a tertiary level, while a robust survey of recreational water usage at Pease outside the bathing season is undertaken (Baynes, 2011: 9).

SAS's Campaign Manager noted: 'SAS are urging Scottish Ministers to ensure SEPA deliver the same levels of protection English and Welsh wave riders enjoy and ensure that Scottish Water's discharge doesn't impact on popular beaches'.

SAS's Edinburgh Rep noted: 'Pease Bay has a huge community of surfers and receives great surf, especially outside the bathing season. This is when we need full sewage treatment to protect wave riders from potentially harmful bacteria and viruses'.

If it can be established that bathing takes place all year round, then Scottish water may be compelled to carry out a more refined process of water treatment and the SAS campaign will have paid off. The aforementioned is provided as a substantive illustrative example of a protest involving sport and environmental concerns. It is necessary at this point to consider two very different approaches to sport and environmentalism.

Environmentalism broadly refers to a belief in and concern for the importance and influence of the environment within and between societies. The term 'environment' is derived from the French verb *environner*, meaning to surround and therefore, in one sense, the term 'environment' literally means our surroundings (McLean, 1996). The concept of the environment was evident by at least the mid-nineteenth century in that it was empowered through a range of ideas that suggested that human beings are, to a degree, formed by their surroundings. These included Darwin's discovery that the survival of the species was at least partly dependent upon their adaptation and suitability to their surroundings. German geographers, through the notion of *Unwelt*, emphasised the importance of the environment in determining economic and cultural differences between peoples. The history of the term 'environmentalist' has meant primarily a person who believes in the importance of the environment as a determinant of human life. Bale (2002a: 147) observed that, during the nineteenth and twentieth centuries, environmental determinism was a powerful social lens through which the world and its peoples and their sporting potential were read. In essence, often colonialist and racist explanations of physical ability implied that physical activity and many of the qualities associated with sporting performance, vigour, health, energy, were *determined* by environmental factors.

Environmental determinism is but one of many environmental approaches from the standpoint of environmentalism. The concerns of environmentalism and sport can range from issues about architecture and stadium construction, to loss of green space, to explanations of human sporting performance and ability, to raising awareness of environmentalism, to political protest through movements such as the anti-golf movement, to questions about sustainability and a more green approach to world sport. Environmentalists can base arguments upon virtually any known philosophical assumption, including those that are anthropocentric (concerned only with benefits to human beings) and those that are studiously opposed to anthropocentrism.

271

SPORT IN FOCUS 11.3: RADICAL AND REFORMIST APPROACHES TO ENVIRONMENTALISM

Radical sport and the environment (mainly anti-capitalism, tends to be proactive)		Reformist sport and the environment (pro-capitalism, tends to be reactive)	
Deep ecology	Based on ecocentrism, intrinsic value in nature. Sport is not above nature.	Conservatism	Preservationism, NIMBYism, stewardship of nature. Sport as part of natural nurture management programmes would support the notion of sporting estates.
Social ecology	Looks to both humanism and ecocentrism, based on anarchist and feminist principles.	Free-market liberalism	Market mechanisms and privatisation of the commons. The relationship between sport and environment determined by the market.
Eco-socialism	Humanistic and socialist politics (libertarian, decentralist, utopian socialism). Sport as humanitarian values.	Social reformism	Market intervention, e.g. environmental taxes, tradeable pollution rights plus voluntary agreements plus regulation.

Sport in Focus 11.3 differentiates between *radical* and *reformist* approaches to environmentalism, many of which have grown out of Western or mainstream concerns over sport, capitalism and the environment/nature. While the discussion below broadly defines radical and reformist approaches to sport and the environment, some have argued that the differences between the two collective camps of thought may be too profound to place them on the same continuum and that, perhaps, it might be more useful to think of paradigm shifts between each approach rather than a spectrum of thought that can be neatly compartmentalised as a continuum from reformist to radical environmental sporting politics.

Reformist approaches to sport and environmentalism at the end of the twentieth century would have embraced liberal and democratic socialist approaches to sport and the environment. As such, the reformation of the relationship between sport and capitalism would be viewed as the key to reform and yet, in practice, would merely react to environmental problems in sport. The arguments would revolve around a greater or lesser degree of intervention within the sporting market or economy. Free-market liberals would look to increased privatisation to secure further environmental freedoms for sport, while social reformists would increase environmental taxes and incentives while regulating firms and individuals. Elements of conservative thinking would also permeate reformist approaches to mainstream concerns about sport and the environment in that preservation, conservation, and a precautionary incipient approach to change would, in the North, be supported perhaps at the expense of those countries in the South.

Radical environmentalism, on the other hand, is inclined to be proactive, seeking to eliminate environmental sporting problems at their root rather than simply reacting to the normal impulses of international or global capitalism operating through sport. The debate about sport and the environment has shifted out of the cultural/economic mainstream sport debate to become counter-cultural, and often drawing upon counter-cultural traditions of romanticism, anarchism and utopian socialism. At least three different strands of thinking might be mentioned in the first instance: social ecology, eco-socialism and deep ecology. Social ecology looks to both humanism and eco-centrism for inspiration and was often associated with anarchism and feminism. Eco-socialism looked to humanistic ideologies but drew heavily upon socialist politics. Deep ecology was based upon a strong eco-centrism that championed the intrinsic value of nature.

The reformist approach to sport and the environment has, at times, been referred to as the light green or technocratic approach to sport and the environment (Lenskyj, 2008: 156–157). The latter embraces mainstream culture's ideologies of liberalism and democratic socialism and it would aim to reform capitalist sport, to a greater or lesser degree, by adopting a perspective that is technocratic. Techno-centrist approaches to sport and the environment place faith in science, technology and the rational management of nature to solve environmental sporting problems. The arguments mainly relate to how much to intervene in solutions and choices provided through the market economy. The Atlanta 1996 Olympic Games were coined by environmentalists as the disposable Olympic Games because so many of the sporting structures, including the velodrome, the water polo pool, the rowing venue, the archery facilities and much of the seating, fencing and tent space, was dismantled and disposed of afterwards. Such practices clearly fail to qualify as ecologically sustainable development but for reformists they offered a profitable, technical solution that was sensitive to some environmental issues, but not others. The Atlanta 1996 Olympic Games adopted a light green approach to sport and the environment. It might be suggested that the light green approach to sport and the environment involves putting a price on the environment in order to protect it unless degrading it is more profitable.

The discussion of reformist and radical approaches to the environment was often labelled as emphasising anthropo-centric versus eco-centric points of view on ecology (Grundmann, 1991). The anthropo-centric approach had the main advantage of providing a reference point from which to evaluate ecological phenomena. This can be defined in different ways (reference points might be currently living humans, society, future generations or gender) but, no matter how we define it, it establishes clear criteria for how to judge existing environmental or ecological problems. Any eco-centric point of view is bound to be inconsistent unless it adopts a mystical standpoint. Eco-centrism is inconsistent because it tends to define ecological problems purely from the point of view of nature. It starts with the assumptions about nature and natural laws to which humans should adapt. The deep eco-centric approach tends to marginalise the social and, therefore, there would be a place for considering sport's relationship with the environment in social or human terms, and yet it seems the very definition of nature's nature and ecological or environmental balance implies a human element. Sport and the environment may be thought of in terms of social needs, pleasures and desires and, therefore, it seems problematic to accept eco-centrism and see it

273

as necessary to view sport and environmental problems as a result of the consequence of society's dealings with nature.

The radical approach to sport and the environment has, by way of an alternative, been referred to as the dark green or eco-centric approach to sport and the environment. Deep ecology's approach is eco- or bio-centric and is focused upon non-human nature. Eco-socialism is not so radical in that it sees humans as an ultimate source of value and is prepared to elevate human worth above that of plants and animals. Social ecology is said to transcend both anthropo-centrism and bio-centrism. Eco-centric or dark green approaches to sport and the environment would include the support of strategies aimed at energy conservation and use of renewable energy sources, water conservation, waste avoidance and minimisation, protecting human health with appropriate standards of air, water and soil quality and the protection of natural environments from the sports industry. The 2000 Sydney Olympic Games is perhaps the nearest example of a dark green approach to sport and the environment. The work of groups such as Greenpeace to the planning of Olympic Games or the philosophy of the global anti-golf movement may be considered as being eco-friendly, if not totally eco-centric, in outlook. It can be suggested that the dark green approach to sport and the environment views the natural environment as having an intrinsic worth and that existing political and economic systems are to be challenged when they pose a threat to the environment.

In answer to the question of what environmentalism is, it is important for students and researchers to start from the position that there are different environmentalisms. Environmentalism and sport is a wide-ranging, eclectic and diverse area of research that is influenced by, and needs to move beyond, orthodox social reformists and radical political traditions. To return to the weather, not surprisingly instances of cold, wet and snowy weather affect European sport more than issues of blistering heat, but even this is changing as a result of environmental shift. Thus, theoretically, spatially and temporally, it is important to talk of *environmentalisms* and sport. It remains to be seen how global warming will impact upon sport in different parts of the world.

GREEN SPORT, AGENDA 21 AND SUSTAINABILITY?

Many sports and sporting events have strived to become greener. Sport in Focus 11.4 provides but one example of the impact of Nike's association with the 2010 FIFA World Cup and its attempt to market a green image.

In 1972, the UN Conference on the Human Environment was organised in response to the dramatic increase in international environmental concerns. Held in Stockholm, the conference established a number of principles, institutions and programmes that helped to provide a framework for promoting the further development of international responses to transnational environmental problems. Non-governmental groups such as Greenpeace, the World Wildlife Fund and Friends of the Earth became as influential as many diplomats in shaping international environmental agreements. However, the development agendas included in the Action Plan and Declaration of Principles agreed at Stockholm were never seriously followed up. Moreover, UNEP lacked the institutional weight to coordinate other UN agencies and, consequently, largely failed to integrate the environmental agenda

SPORT IN FOCUS 11.4: NIKE'S GREEN WORLD CUP SHIRTS

'All Nike Football Kits are Green'

That was the message Nike sent out to their clients for the 2010 FIFA World Cup in South Africa. While Brazil still wore their famous yellow shirts and the Dutch turned out in orange as always, there was something distinctly green about their attire. This was down to the fact the shirts were made from recycled plastic bottles.

The teams from Australia, Brazil, the Netherlands, New Zealand, Portugal, Serbia, Slovenia, South Korea and the US all wore the environmentally friendly uniforms produced by Nike during the tournament.

Nike claimed each shirt was made from up to eight plastic bottles taken from landfill sites in either Japan or Taiwan. The process reduced energy consumption and carbon emissions by 30 per cent compared with producing the shirts from virgin polyester, while it also limited the need for fresh raw materials. As a result, around 13 million plastic bottles, totalling nearly 254,000 kg of polyester waste, were stopped from going to landfill. Leading green campaigners backed the multinational sportswear firm's claims and have supported their new production methods.

Since the World Cup, Nike has continued to use this greener form of production for the 2010/2011 season kits as well. High-profile clubs such as Manchester United, Arsenal, Inter Milan, Barcelona and Celtic are all wearing the kits.

While this is a relatively small step in terms of the world of sport becoming friendlier to the environment, it is certainly a step in the right direction. Furthermore, it demonstrates that high-quality sportswear can be produced in a way that is not damaging to the environment.

within the UN system. This caused an increasing international concern among many non-First World countries, who suffered exploitation at the behest of transnational, often Western-based, multinational companies. NGOs became increasingly active in international environmental politics.

In 1987, the UN established a World Commission on the Environment and Development chaired by the then Prime Minister of Norway, Gro Harlem Brundtland. The Commission promoted the notion of sustainable development. The Brundtland Commission's shorthand characterisation of development is development that meets the needs of the present without compromising the ability of future generations to meet their own needs. The prominence given to needs reflected a concern to eradicate poverty and meet basic human needs, broadly understood. The exact meaning of the concept of sustainable development remained unclear but it was important because it attracted support from a number of international constituencies. The UN General Assembly in 1989 decided to convene an Earth Summit in Rio de Janeiro in 1992, at which 27 general principles for guiding action on the environment and development were outlined.

Three new conventions were agreed at the Rio conference aimed at limiting climate change, preserving biodiversity and combating desertification. The institutions established in 1992 agreed to promote Agenda 21, aimed at providing a programme of action for sustainable development. The Global Environment Facility provided alongside Agenda 21 is aimed at helping developing countries meet the costs of implementing aspects of Agenda 21. The institutions established to promote the implementation of Agenda 21, including the Olympic Movement, have stimulated the development of national plans for sustainable development and provided forums where plans can be reviewed and where networks of non-governmental groups, government representatives and international secretariats can develop and influence agendas, and yet the influence on overall patterns of sustainable development has been small.

Global environmental issues exist in many different forms and, although they share common characteristics, each area needs specific examination in its own right. There has been a growth of green consciousness, policy and practice in the context of international sport (Maguire *et al.*, 2002: 89). The environmental dimension was critical to Sydney's bid to host the 2000 Olympic Games. The Sydney Olympic Games are viewed as being one of the most successful green Games to date, with the environmental guidelines governing the Olympic Games focusing upon environmental protection and the *sustainable* development of Olympic sites. The Olympic approach to the environment was, in part, brought about by the resolution of the International Olympic Committee to adopt Agenda 21 in 1999 (see Sport in Focus 11.5). The Sydney Olympic Games Committee followed the United Nations Agenda 21 resolution to implement a comprehensive plan of action to safeguard the environment from the impact of human interaction, including the hosting of major sports events, which committed the 2000 Olympics to demonstrating more sustainable site management practices, more sustainable event management measures and raising public awareness about environmental issues related to sport. The Executive Director of UNEP argued, in 2004, that the environment, like sports, knows no barriers or territorial borders and it transcends ideological cleavages. It does not recognise distinctions between North, South, East and West. Athletes, as the main actors in the sports movement are role models and, while only a few of us can aspire to join the Olympics, we should all strive to achieve higher goals in order to help ourselves, our communities and our countries, and most important of all, the environment that we all dependent upon.

The 1999 agreement was re-emphasised in 2001 through the Nagano Declaration on Sport, Environment and Sustainable Development in which the participants of the IVth World Congress on Sport and the Environment resolved to uphold the principles of sustainability in their sports activities and to promote such principles on a global scale so as to ensure that the Earth is given a sporting chance. It is tempting to suggest that by 2004, sports organisations such as the IOC were greener than they were prior to 1992, and it might be suggested that the IOC has uncharacteristically moved on its green policies in a progressive manner. On issues such as resource management and species conservation, several other landmarks were achieved during the 2000 Olympic preparations. The Olympic Village utilised solar power, construction work widely used recycled and plantation timber and an ecologically sustainable approach to design and building methods was pioneered. Major tree-planting projects were planned throughout Australia so that the financial benefits of the Games could be experienced by the whole nation (Maguire *et al.*, 2002: 89).

SPORT IN FOCUS 11.5: THE OLYMPIC MOVEMENT AND AGENDA 21

In 1999, the International Olympic Committee (IOC) adopted Agenda 21, which proposed ways for individuals and groups in sports to develop sustainable societies.

Improving socio-economic conditions

Sustainable development implies satisfying the essential cultural and material needs of every individual to enable him or her to live with dignity and play a positive role in society. As a result, Agenda 21 pays particular attention to the lives of the most disadvantaged and to minorities. This includes helping to combat social exclusion, promoting a new approach to consumption, playing a more active role in health protection, promoting sports facilities that better meet social needs, and better integrating development and environmental concepts into sports policies.

Promoting the socio-economic dimension of Agenda 21 matches the goal of Olympism, as set out in the Fundamental Principles of the Olympic Charter, which is 'everywhere to place sport at the service of the harmonious development of man, with a view to encouraging the establishment of a peaceful society concerned with the preservation of human dignity'.

Conservation and management of resources for sustainable development

The Olympic Movement's environmental protection policy should come within the wider framework of sustainable development. Thus, the environmental work of the Olympic Movement is now focused on the conservation and management of resources and the natural environment necessary to improve socio-economic conditions. These should encourage education about the environment and specific action to help preserve it. This is the most visible aspect of the IOC's environmental work, especially at the Olympic Games.

Strengthening the role of the main groups

To ensure the success of sustainable development, it is helpful if all of the groups that make up society are active and respected players in the process set in motion. To this end, the Olympic Movement can make a meaningful contribution to strengthening the roles of two groups in particular, women and young people.

There is no doubt that Sydney 2000 set an important new threshold for integrating environmental aspects into sports event planning and management. The concept of a green Games with an integrated programme, which paid attention to transport methods, waste, energy, water, materials, pollution and biodiversity issues arguably set a benchmark for future international sporting events. The Sydney 2000 Environment Programme managed to extract pledges from multinational corporations that have added credibility to notions of sustainable environmental development through sport. Corporations such as Coca-Cola pledged to introduce Green Freeze technology through its global operations by the time of the Athens 2004 Olympic Games. The relationship between trade and environmental issues has also served as a reminder that virtually all environmental issues are intimately linked to the dynamics of international, if not global, political and economic, processes. Such concerns have given rise to movements such as the anti-golf movement.

THE ENVIRONMENT AND THE ANTI-GOLF MOVEMENT

The spread of golf courses internationally has not only spawned the global anti-golf movement but has also been a catalyst for a movement that calls for a moratorium on the development of golf courses. Huge amounts of water (2.4 million litres a day worldwide) are needed to keep golf courses bright green and much of this activity takes place in countries where water is scarce. The global anti-golf movement was launched on World Golf Day in April 1993. The three initial sponsoring organisations were the Global Network for Anti-Golf Course Action (GNAGA) based in Japan, the Asian Tourism Network (ANTENNA) based in Thailand and the Asia-Pacific People and Environmental Network (AEN) based in Malaysia. The anti-golf movement is active in Europe, Australia, Asia, Latin America and the US. Various environmental groups are opposed to the construction of golf courses. The anti-golf manifesto revolves around observations that include:

- Golf courses and golf tourism are part of a global package that is capitalist-orientated, with most of the money arising from the activity being exported out of the locality.
- The speculative nature of the industry makes it a high-risk investment for small countries and localities, with many golf courses, resorts and companies becoming bankrupt.
- The environmental impact of golf course development is negative in that it facilitates water depletion and toxic contamination to such an extent that the golf green is fraught with ecological problems.
- It promotes an elitist and exclusive leisure class, with the globalisation of this lifestyle encouraging wealthy urban elites to absorb a particular way of life regardless of the environment and other members of society.
- In the face of growing criticism, the golf industry is falsely promoting the notion of pesticide-free, environmentally friendly golf courses in the knowledge that such a golf course does not exist.

A survey by the UK Sports Turf Research Institute found massive overdosing of British greens with phosphate fertilisers.

278

Between August 1995 and April 1996, the town of Tepoztlan in Mexico was involved in a conflict with a real estate development corporation, the Kladt-Sobri Group (KS), over the construction of a golf course and country club. The project represented a $500 million investment in the town and promised to augment the tourism industry but local activists became concerned about the negative environmental impact of the development. The arguments against the development included excessive water usage, toxic run-off, and the negative social and cultural impacts caused by creating an enclave community of extremely wealthy individuals within a relatively poor community. The opposition group, which called itself the Committee for Tepozteco Unity (CUT), managed to convince the majority of the population that the golf course was a bad idea and they pressurised the town council into promising not to issue the zoning waivers that would facilitate planning permission. The council subsequently issued permits, resulting in their physical expulsion from the town. The state government organised a fraudulent assembly (they bussed people in from other municipalities) to ratify the decision; CUT threw the state government out of town, erected barricades and, a month later, held their own elections to name legitimate authorities. The confrontation between the state, the townspeople and KS continued until April, when an elderly activist was killed in a police ambush. The scandal forced the KS to drop out of the project and the state to suspend its aggressive polices towards the town. Yet, with specific reference to golf, what is required is an increased awareness of the environmental threats posed by the ideas and practices of people involved in the development of golf at local and international levels. Should golf as a sport become a resource-intensive and environmentally harmful activity, then it may be defined as an unsustainable sport. The paradox of sustainable development often means that environmental issues are sidelined in favour of economic development when the latter is more convenient, more commercially attractive and supported by more powerful interest groups (Maguire et al., 2002: 96). However, as the case in Tepoztlan serves to illustrate, organised, committed and locally driven anti-golf protests can succeed in bringing about social and political change at the local level.

The activities of the anti-golf course movement have been highlighted as illustrative of the fact that sport has linked with broader environmental impacts, which in many cases have reflected the way in which different parts of the world connect on an economic, social and political level. The core concerns of the anti-golf movement have been economical and environmental (in the sense that it is a protest against a reliance on toxic chemicals and, in some cases, water wastage) but also social in the sense that the protests have been against the closed-door policies of many golf clubs that leave locals out in the cold in terms of club membership. The profits also bypass local communities in some places. The average cost of developing a golf course in Thailand has been estimated as being as much as $47 million, not including the cost of hiring consultants. In Indonesia, the construction of a golf course in Cimacan, West Java, displaced 287 peasants. The Badung Asri Mulia Construction Company paid villagers who lost their land 1.5 cents per square metre. It is not surprising that sport has become more of a focus for anti-environmental groups but, as Chapters 15 and 19 point out, the framework for Agenda 21 has not yet maximised the potential to bring about social change and social responsibility.

279

SUMMARY

Environmental issues emerged as late as the last quarter of the twentieth century as a major international concern and activity. Sport is not immune from this. Many environmental problems are intrinsically international and stimulate international political activities in response to the degradation of the planet. Sport and the environment problems have connected with international movement. International environmental issues in the field of sports pose significant challenges for students and researchers of sport. They raise questions about the role of states and transnational corporations in the field of environmental politics, the relationship between power and knowledge, and about the distinction between international and domestic spheres of activity. The issues of sport and climatic change, sport and international sporting agendas, sport and environmental thinking, and the notions of dark green and light green sport have figured in this chapter. Sport and the environment has figured in broader social and political protests concerning the control of communities over their own local environment, as is illustrated in the anti-golf movement.

The issue of sport and the environment or the question of how sport can be greener may not be one of the prime directives of the sports industry in the Western world but the environment and survival of human life itself is one of the foremost twenty-first-century concerns. According to Edward O. Wilson, the Earth is entering a new evolutionary era in that we are on the brink of extinction the likes of which have not been seen since the end of the Mesozoic era, 65 million years ago. Species are vanishing and, as Wilson puts it, our children will be practically alone in the world (Gray, 2002a: 27).

Given the magnitude of such concerns, you would expect the environment to be at the centre of public debate, as would be discussion of the alleged causes of concerns about mass destruction. According to most mainstream political parties and environmental organisations, the destruction of the environment is mainly the result of flaws in human institutions. The predominant view of the Northern countries has tended to be that, potentially, we are entering a desolate world with the reason being that humans have over-populated and injustice prevents proper use of the Earth's resources. Such a view is not accepted in many of the world's countries, such as China, Egypt, India and Iran. Ideas about population control tend to be concentrated in or emanate from within rich parts of the world. Such an issue is raised here to illustrate the complexity of implementing a course of action, even if it were to be accepted that Wilson's era of solitude is about to fall upon the world. Sport may not be able to halt major environmental catastrophes but its undoubted popularity in many parts of the world means that it provides a popular target for organisations such as Greenpeace, the anti-golf movement and the IOC to deliver on environmental messages. Perhaps the real question for environmentalists is: can we have sport at all without nature?

GUIDE TO FURTHER READING

Attenborough, D. (2011). 'The Heaving Planet'. *New Statesman*, 25 April: 29–32.

Bale, J. (2002a). 'Lassitude and Latitude: Observations on Sport and Environmental Determinism'. *International Review for the Sociology of Sport*, 37 (2):147–159.

Baynes, R. (2011). 'Making Waves: The Surfers Fighting to Clean Up Our Seas'. *The Herald*, 27 February: 4–11.

Boykoff, J. (2011). 'The Anti- Olympics'. *New Left Review*, 67 (January/February): 41–50.

Environment/Focus (2006). 'Putting the Earth in Play: Environmental Awareness and Sports'. *Environmental Health Perspectives*, 114 (5): May.

Elvin, M. (2010). 'Concepts of Nature'. *New Left Review*, 64 (July/August): 65–84.

Feffer. J. (2010). 'Earthquake Olympics'. *Foreign Policy in Focus*, 5 (13; 30 March): 1–6.

Hayes, G. and Karamichas, J. (eds) (2011). *Olympic Games, Mega-Events and Civil Societies: Globalisation, Environment and Resistance*. Basingstoke: Palgrave.

Mansfield, L. (2009). 'Fitness Cultures and Environmental Injustices'. *International Review for the Sociology of Sport*, 44 (4): 345–362.

Peach, S. (2010). 'What the World Can Learn from Vancouver'. *The Sporting Brief*, 6 June: 16–20.

QUESTIONS

1 Discuss four different approaches to sport and the environment, taking care to differentiate between light green and dark green strategies.

2 Comment upon the potential impact of Agenda 21 on sport in relation to sustainable development in different parts of the world.

3 What are some the environmental arguments for and against the development of golf courses, and are the arguments essentially eco-centric?

4 What considerations would you have to take into account when designing an environmentally friendly sports event?

5 Describe some of the environmental concerns associated with one Summer Olympic Games and one Winter Olympic Games.

6 Outline some of the content of Olympic Agenda 21 in relation to the environment.

7 Explain the objectives and possible outcomes of the Surfers against Sewage campaign.

8 Define the following terms: 'environmental determinism', 'eco-centrism' and 'sustainable development'.

9 Describe and explain the impact of the world's first green cricket match in India.

10 Evaluate the development and philosophy behind the anti-golf movement, and consider whether such policies might be viewed as dark green or light green.

PRACTICAL PROJECTS

1   Carry out a Google search on 'sport + environment'. Look for studies by Rolf Burki, Hans Elsasser and Bru Abegg, and write a synopsis of 500 words explaining how environmental and economic threats to winter sports are brought about by climatic change.

2   Explore the guidelines for the greening of sports events outlined by the Committed to Green Foundation and compare this with the values of the anti-golf movement. Write 1,000 words describing and comparing this specific foundation and movement.

3   Assess the impact of environmental pollution caused by a local sports event. Interview five local residents and five visitors to the event with a view to exploring issues relating to sport and the environment.

4   Keep a diary of the weather in your country or region over the period of (i) a month and (ii) a year, and write a report on how the weather has affected sport.

5   Design two different policy statements in relation to sport and the environment, one that is radical in orientation and one that is reformist in orientation. Each strategy should contain ten items or directives.

KEY CONCEPTS

Agenda 21 ■ Conservation ■ Dark green sport ■ Deep ecology ■ Eco-centrism ■ Eco-socialism ■ Environmental determinism ■ Friends of the Earth ■ Global anti-golf movement ■ Greenpeace ■ Light green sport ■ Olympic Movement ■ Radical environmentalism ■ Reformist environmentalism ■ Social ecology ■ Sustainability ■ Weather

WEBSITES

Anti-Golf Movement
www.antigolf.org/english.html
A insight into the anti-environmental policies associated with one movement in one sport.

Greenpeace
www.greenpeace.org/international/en/
Access the site and use the search facilities for (i) sport and (ii) Olympic updates.

United Nations Environment Programme
www.unep.org/
The United Nations Environment Programme.

Sport and the environment

www.unep.org/sport.env/

The United Nations sport and the environment website.

The IOC Study Centre

www.olympic.org/olympic-studies-centre

Access the official Olympic Games study centre, and search for documents and reports relating to the environment.

Chapter 12

Sport, body and health

How can our understanding of sport today help to redefine what is meant by the body, health, pain, injury and hunger, in not only different social worlds but also different worlds of health?

PREVIEW

Key terms defined ■ Introduction ■ Health-worlds and life chances ■ Sport, body and society ■ The body and social theory ■ Deviant bodies ■ Civilised bodies ■ Natural bodies ■ Sport, the body and religion ■ Sport and the body in social thought ■ Civilised bodies and the quest for excitement ■ Body, class and physical capital ■ Women, body habitus and lifestyles ■ Sexuality and the gendered body ■ The body, power and knowledge ■ The body, identities and differences ■ Other sporting bodies ■ Sport and body culture as cultural policy ■ Summary

OBJECTIVES

This chapter will:

■ introduce students, teachers and researchers to a vast body of research that takes as its focus, in either a minor or major way, sport, body and health;

■ examine some of the key ways in which the sporting/healthy body is thought about today;

■ consider the argument that sport is a vehicle for disciplining, punishing, controlling and constraining the body;

■ critically discuss sport and the body from the perspective of the 'other';

■ explain and illustrate the way in which the body has become a marker for identity, recognition and difference in sport and related areas; and

■ note that the relational nature of human well-being and grounding it in terms of the body means that the analysis provided is not particular to any one world or social context.

KEY TERMS DEFINED

Health: The general condition of the body or mind with reference to soundness and vigour.

Life chances: The life chances approach to understanding health recognises that a gap exists between different communities and places, and the challenge for governments is to narrow the gap in health differences between groups of people. Central to this framework is the question of how to narrow the gap in life chances between the most disadvantaged and the rest.

Well-being: The satisfactory state someone or something should be in, which expands beyond health to factors such as happiness, safety and prosperity.

Sexuality: Including normalised heterosexuality, and other often stigmatised sexualities; homosexuality, minority masculinities, shifting or multiple sexualities.

INTRODUCTION

The assumptions that are made about the relationship between different forms of enhancements in sport and the effect that they have on the body and health are complex and vary between different parts of the world. Various histories of the use of drugs in sport have charted incidents of death and self-induced harm to the body (Dimeo, 2007; Lopez, 2011). Public opinion is far from uniform on this issue but, as Sport in Focus 12.1 illustrates, this is not new. As Eichberg (2011) argues, it is as difficult in the twenty-first century as it was in the nineteenth century to ascertain just exactly what is the normalised body and what is the normalised or accepted truth about drugs in sport, and who defines this truth. The relationship between sport, the body, health and well-being is both complex and culturally and socially varied.

Many have tended to view the body as a fixed, unchanging fact of nature, viewed in biological terms rather than as being social, cultural or historical, or invoking political economy. Naturalistic and social constructionist views have left their mark upon how people have thought about human embodiment in relation to sport, health, fitness and physical activity. Many new ways of thinking about the body have opened up sport, body and society as a vibrant area of research. It is no longer possible to think of the body solely in universal, fundamental or natural terms, but rather in differentiated and plural terms. A striking development has been the extent to which encounters between social and ethical thinkers, as well as Western and non-Western schools of thought have wrestled with explanations of body, health, pain, injury, hunger and contributed not simply to a more comprehensive and complex understanding of different social worlds or sporting worlds, but also health worlds (Germond and Cochrane, 2010).

Earlier interventions such as Shilling's *The Body and Social Theory* (1993), Scott and Morgan's *Body Matters* (1993) and Turner's influential *Body and Society* (1996) all recognised sociology's neglect of the body and argued for divergent approaches to recognising the need to analyse humans as embodied persons. Much of this work has explored the varied cultural meanings attached to bodies and the way they are controlled, regulated and reproduced. Coakley (2003: 140) testified to changes in the ways that bodies have been socially defined and contributed to different exchanges concerning how people think about the body in society. Most notably, in terms of sexuality, ideals of beauty, body image and identity, health, social differences, violence and power, the medical profession and high performance sport.

If you add to this recent research relating to pain, injury, hunger, performance and the management of these (Loland *et al.*, 2006; Waddington, 2001; Eichberg, 2011), then the study of sport, body and health has proliferated into a corpus of knowledge that has:

- challenged traditional Western ideas about the separation of mind and body;
- questioned the moral, cultural and sociological implications relating to how bodies are protected, probed, monitored, tested, trained, manipulated, rehabilitated and disciplined all in the name of sport;
- questioned the simplistic way in which bodies are differentiated and represented as marks of gender, race, disability, age and other social divisions without really thinking about the recognition of difference or the dangers of thinking in differentiated terms;
- questioned the way in which body culture figures as an alternative to conventional notions of sports policy; and
- encouraged health-seeking strategies that draw upon multicultural environments and places, and challenge the notion of normality.

It would be wrong not to relate this introduction to sport, body and health to other chapters in Part 3. The body has figured prominently in accounts of *sports, violence and*

SPORT IN FOCUS 12.1: A HISTORY OF DRUGS IN SPORT

1904   American Thomas Hicks takes strychnine and brandy during the race as he takes the gold in the marathon at the St Louis Olympics.

1935   Scientists synthesise testosterone.

1967   British cyclist Tom Simpson collapses and dies during the Tour de France. The post-mortem examination concludes he had taken amphetamines, which resulted in heart failure. This leads to the introduction of doping tests in the Tour de France.

1968   The IOC introduces the first drug tests at the Winter Olympic Games.

1976   The IOC adds anabolic steroids to its banned list. Athletes at the Montreal Olympics are the first to be tested.

1988   Canadian sprinter Ben Johnson is stripped of his 100 m gold medal and world record at the Seoul Olympics after testing positive for an anabolic steroid.

1990   The NFL introduce a year-round, random steroid-testing programme.

1992   NFL defensive end Lyle Alzado dies from cancer at age 43. Although unproven, Alzado said his cancer was caused by taking muscle-enhancing drugs.

1993   The Association of Tennis Professionals, the Women's Tennis Association and the International Tennis Federation establish an anti-doping programme.

1998   Australian customs agents detain Chinese swimmer Yuan Yuan after they find 13 vials of human growth hormone in her possession as she arrives for the world championships.

2000   The World Anti-Doping Agency (WADA) begins operations.

2000   China cuts 27 athletes and 13 coaches from its team for the Sydney Olympics, stating some athletes had suspicious test results.

2004   A record 24 athletes are thrown out of the Athens Olympics for doping violations.

2005   The National Hockey League establishes a drug-testing policy for performance-enhancing substances. Players are tested twice a year. The first positive test results in a 20-game suspension, the second brings 60 games and the third a permanent ban.

2006   Italian police find 30 packs of drugs, equipment for blood transfusions and blood testing, and more than 100 syringes in raids on residences of Austrian skiers at the Torino Winter Olympics.

2011   Manchester City defender Kolo Touré tests positive for a banned substance and faces a ban of up to two years. Touré says he unwittingly ingested the banned substance when he took some of his wife's slimming pills.

deviance. Cole's (2002) review of sport and the body describes the role of science and technology in the production of a modern sporting body, which she describes in both normal and abnormal terms. Deviant/transgressive bodies are viewed as those that challenge or shock societies' orthodox attitudes to the sporting body. The language of deviance and violence is used to explain the appearance of non-normative bodies that do not conform to the conventional wisdom in a domain that often invests dedication to bodily perfection. Such views are often expressed in relation to female and male bodybuilders, male boxers and female bullfighters. Shilling (1993) refers to the notion of civilised bodies. Elias's analysis of civilised bodies was both sociogenetic and psychogenetic in that it encompasses long-term processes underlying society's development and the personality structures of individuals. Changing rates of bodily violence, body manners and violence in sport have been drawn upon to substantiate and add weight to the theory of the civilising process. To simplify, the relatively civilised bodily characteristics and/or different rates of violence in sport of those involved in sport today are compared with their medieval counterparts as a basis for explaining an ongoing process of change.

So, too, has the body figured in debates about *sport, nature and the environment*. Are our bodies to be thought of purely in biological terms, or does nature or the environment in which bodies are located in time and space affect the relationship between body, self-identity and society? The naturalistic view holds that the capabilities and constraints of human bodies define individuals and generate subsequent social, political and economic relations. Women have challenged and buried the way in which natural bodies have historically been viewed as being a generic male form. Alternatively, socio-biological or natural views of the female sporting body point out that feminists have reproduced a distortion of the natural female body that, because of social pressures, requires women to pursue the tyranny of slenderness or a particular type of body. The notion of feminine embodiment often requires regimes of diet and exercise that are far from healthy. The tyranny of slenderness has been central to studies of feminism, aerobics and the politics of the body. What determines the tyranny of slenderness – the body or the environment? And to what extent can we change, manipulate one or the other, or both? The relationship between natural bodies competing in natural activities in a natural landscape was, suggests Magdalinski (2004), a primary method of understanding the 2000 Sydney Olympic Games. When London was awarded the 2012 Olympic Games, its success was, in part, due to its commitment to producing environmentally friendly places.

Some of the thinking presented in sport, religion and spirituality could equally be pertinent to thinking about the body and healthy worlds. Turner's seminal contributions to both the sociology of religion and the sociology of body provide possibilities for thinking about *sport and religion*. The human body is typically central to shifting debates about whether sport is more or less secular. Hashemi (2000) has reminded us of the constraints that impinge upon the athletic body of Muslim women wishing to train for karate competitions in Afghanistan. In 1998, the second Islamic Women's Games took place – involving athletes from 24 Islamic countries. The relationships between sport and divine bodies, secular bodies and Islamic bodies are potentially rich areas for any student, teacher or researcher wishing to explore sources of human mythology and religious dogma. Add to this the challenge that the regulated body and the metaphors associated with right-handedness or left-footedness as being regarded

288

as symbols and even sources of evil, then the role of religious authority is not just about sport, but all forms of body culture on display at festivals, gatherings and other collective rituals that may provide a rich vein of exploration in the past and the present.

HEALTH WORLDS AND LIFE CHANCES

High-performance sport can be dangerous and life threatening. The physical body experiences a multitude of contexts, many of which involve pain, injury and other threats to the health of the individual. *The Scotsman*, reporting on one injury during an international rugby match between England and Scotland in 2010, ran the headline 'Evans was millimetre from death or paralysis, reveals team doctor' (Mcginty, 2010: 3). The specific injury sustained during the match had caused the sixth cervical vertebrae to move forward by a factor of 50 per cent. This pulled the spinal cord, thus causing a risk of it either rupturing or snapping and leading to paraplegia.

People think about health, illness, pain and injury in different ways. The social and ethical account of pain and injury in sport presented by Loland *et al.* (2006) considers pain as culture, pain as nature and pain as individual subjective experience. The physical body experiencing the pain of, for example, running may be central to the health of the athlete, whether they are injured or not, but the physical body is also a social body and has a relational connection to both exterior and interior aspects of health. Such concerns raise critical questions about how athletes or people understand their health or the management of pain or injury and the choices they make. The physical body is intrinsically social as it is the product of social processes. Society, in part, governs the representation of the exterior body to different worlds or regions. The physical modification of the body, dietary regulation, tattoos, questions of gender and disability are often pivotal to how the body is presented. The interior body, constituted of mind, emotion and spirit is accessed, nurtured and disciplined by engagement of the exterior body. The health of the body is, therefore, inextricably linked through interior, exterior and social factors. These are not distinct aspects, but are in fact bound together.

The idea that sport and the healthy body can help with improving life chances is dependent upon not just structural social and economic differences, but also the idea that it can enable the development of trust, care, belonging, anticipatory hope and other notions that can help reframe our understanding of health, pain, injury and other life concerns (Germond and Cochrane, 2010). The notions of different worlds of health and different life chances are two important sensitising social concepts that help us to think about sport, body and health. The official landscapes of healing, medicine and injury are becoming increasingly more healthy as researchers realise that Western science and medicine is not a bounded or unique system of thought or practice. Different hybrid ways of understanding health and pain are found the world over as societies pursue the endless quest for not just fitness, exercise, and health, but also governance of the body. The notion of health worlds relates to people's conceptions and conditions of health. Individuals' worlds of health are also shared by place, region and community in which they are embedded. Thus, the notion of embodiment can relate to both individual and region, but also time.

One important normative idea that needs to be mentioned is that rival notions of health worlds also contain divergent and often cultural conceptions of not just health and well-being, but freedom and justice. Justice often rests upon the necessity of reciprocity and mutuality in relation to both self, others and regions. Freedom, whether negative or positive, often rests upon the tension between actual and potential realisation of winning or losing further freedoms. As has been argued throughout this book, issues of inequality need to refer to not just inequalities in an economic sense, but also inequalities in capability between people and/or places. The challenge is to narrow the gap in both inequalities of income and capability in an attempt to making both sporting and health worlds more just, transparent and free.

SPORT AND THE BODY IN SOCIAL THOUGHT

The range of social thought about the study of sport, body and society is varied and while much progress has been made it would be misleading to suggest that while the importance of the body to fields such as sports studies is developing apace it remains less developed when compared to the centrality of the body to relatively contemporary concerns of social theory and thought. Nonetheless, various traditions of social thought have informed our understanding of sport and the body and, in this section, I should like to draw attention to some of the key contributions to sport and the body in social thought.

Civilised bodies and the quest for excitement

Although the human body is not the central focus of the work of Norbert Elias, the analysis of bodily functions, bodily manners and bodily acts were substantive areas of concern that contributed to the theory of the civilising process. A key component of the civilising process was a concerted effort to understand how external restraints on behaviour could be replaced by internal, moral regulation. The civilised body, argued Elias (1978: 140), has the ability to rationalise and exert a high degree of control over its emotions, to monitor its actions, and those of others, and to internalise a demarcated set of rules about what is and is not appropriate behaviour. Such a process provided the basis for making a contrast between the civilised and uncivilised body over a period of time (Shilling, 1993).

The notion of the civilising process has informed and sustained a vein of social thought that has been captured in collections of essays such as Dunning and Rojek's (1992) *Sport and Leisure in the Civilising Process* and Dunning *et al.*'s (2004) *Sports Histories*. One of the principal functions of sport and leisure activities talked about within this body of work was that those activities that took place within the spare-time spectrum were partly devoted to bodily maintenance, the control of emotional thresholds, and the enhancement of body appearance through utilising the outer body as a means of display. Thus, the body contributed not only to the performing self, but also to the promoting self. Both the quest for excitement and for identity were involved in physical and emotional bodily activities, such as the controlled decontrolling of emotions and eliciting different rates of excitement, as well as pleasurable acts such as smiling or less pleasurable acts such as wincing with pain, which are both intentionally deployed symbols that can convey a range of messages as a result of involvement in sport and leisure activities. Sport and the civilising process provide a useful way of thinking about and exploring embodied emotions.

Both in society and the fields of sport, the controlled and calculated management of the body becomes increasingly necessary and important for success. Such control is also a prerequisite, according to Shilling (1993: 163), for the development of civilised bodies. The development of the civilising process and civilised bodies has involved a progressive socialisation, rationalisation and individualisation of the body. The rationalisation of bodies has been integral to the emergence of sport as form of physical contest of a relatively non-violent type. Despite decivilising spurts of behaviour, such as in acts of football hooliganism in England in the later decades of the twentieth century, by comparison with past eras in general sport as a form of physical contest of a relatively non-violent type was associated with the reduction of violence in society at large. Sport and physical activity provided an emotional release. The violence into which uninhibited drives were channelled in past eras, it is argued, has now been replaced by individuals witnessing mock contests in which behaviour is governed by rules. Sport provides the civilised body with release, with a re-charging, which helps it to return to highly controlled behavioural norms that help in the governing of society (Shilling, 1993: 166).

Body, class and physical capital

The work of the French sociologist Pierre Bourdieu has also been central to an understanding of social reproduction. Key ideas such as the body as a symbol of distinction, body habitus, physical capital and social field are evoked by Bourdieu to provide a particular theory of social reproduction. Bourdieu described his own work as constructivist structuralism. The production of different bodily forms is central to this theory of social reproduction as the symbolic values accorded to particular bodies vary. People's sporting tastes act as signifiers in the constant struggle for distinction. The instrumental body of the working class is differentiated from the bodies of the dominant class. The interrelationship between social location, habitus and taste helps to produce distinct bodily forms and orientations. Social, cultural and economic processes affect the body.

Habitus as a specific notion refers to the acquired patterns of thought, behaviour and taste that are said to constitute the link between social structures and social practices. It locates the middle ground between structures and actions. Bourdieu (1990a) likens habitus to the feel for the game but the game is the social game embodied and turned into a second nature of doing things without thinking. Being a competent social actor involves having a mastery over social practices that involves a feel for the game. Having a deeply embodied habitus develops this game. The knowledge of what it means to be a boxer involves the development of a particular body habitus. Conceived in this way the absorption of certain actions and specific feelings enables boxers to be at ease within a certain habitus, a boxing habitus. Yet, it is not just membership of particular communities that such practices involve but also membership of humanity as a whole. Thus, the boxer may be part of a particular boxing habitus that, in turn, is part of a broader habitus that is society. Habitus, then, is an embodied, internalised schema that structures but does not determine actions, thoughts and feelings (Jarvie and Maguire, 1994: 191).

291

From Bourdieu's work, it is clear that bodies are involved in the creation and reproduction of social difference. More specifically, bodies bear the imprint of social class because of three main factors: an individual's social location (material circumstances of daily life), the formation of their habitus and the development of their tastes. As a result of these factors, people tend to develop bodies that are valued differently and serve to naturalise social differences through such features as accent, poise and movement. According to Bourdieu (1978), the working classes adopted an instrumental approach to the body in which the body is a means to end. The body tends to be characterised as a machine in relation to health, illness, exercise and lifestyle in that it is always important to put the body right. Working-class attitudes to bodies are marked by the demands of getting by in life and the temporary release from the demands of everyday living. By contrast, the dominant classes are characterised as viewing the body as a project and have available resources to choose whether to place an emphasis on the intrinsic or external functioning of the body. In comparison to working-class groups, middle-class groups are deemed to have more control over their health, which can be exercised by choosing an appropriate lifestyle.

The relationship between physical activities, body habitus and lifestyles has been explored in a number of studies. Laberge and Sankoff (1988: 285) concluded that the structure of relations between different physical practices, different types of attention to the body and various leisure activities provided information about the social meaning of participation in physical activities and the social logics that govern these activities. The variation or pattern of participation by women in physical activities according to social class depended not only upon the different capacities of women with regard to time and money but also the variations in perception and appreciation of the profits and/or immediate or long-term benefits that participation in various physical activities could bring them. The relationship between physical activities, body habitus and lifestyle is determined in part by class habitus.

Social class, according to Bourdieu, was not simply a function of belonging to a particular social category, but also how one perceived one's self in relation to that category. The relationship between the body, class and exercise could not be understood purely in terms of what a group or person did, but how they also perceived what they were doing in relation to class activity. The value of Bourdieu's contribution to this discussion is important because it places the body and sport as bearers of symbolic value. The general importance of the body's orientation through sport and leisure activities may be as an expression of elite status but there might also be a mismatch between a person's orientation to their body and a related taste for sport. Thus, participation in certain sports might be seen as requiring social, cultural and economic capital before actual preferences or tastes are actualised in terms of participation. Such concerns raise critical questions about how people understand their body and physical activity, and how the choices that are made influence life chances.

Sexuality and the gendered body

The headline of a leading newspaper reads 'Row as beauty queen made a role model' (Allardyce, 2010: 7). Such headlines are not uncommon in the UK press. The article was about whether or not a glamour girl and beauty queen was the right person to choose as a role model to promote a campaign aimed at tackling childhood obesity and, in particular, childhood obesity among girls. Her appointment was condemned because the government was using a slim, tall model who loves wearing skimpy clothes to get across a message about body shape and image; the message from the government being that you have to aim at being exceptionally thin and glamorous to have a healthy body.

The physical body has been the focus of much research concerning the construction of gender. Gender is experienced through the body and, therefore, experiences, feelings, representations and the body politic are fundamentally related not only to masculinity and femininity, but heterosexuality, homosexuality and other cultures. Bodybuilding for men and women is not only sport but also a body project that involves a practical recognition and changing understanding of the significance of the body, both as a personal resource and a social symbol of self and a broader identity. The pervasive influence of new forms of health consciousness re-confirms the way the body has become a project, the control of which is central, fundamental to gender politics. Plastic surgery has provided alternatives for radical bodily reconstruction in line with contemporary notions of femininity and masculinity of the time. These notions change over time, space and place, are not neutral, and involve complex social processes and pressures that vary.

It is impossible to provide an exhaustive list of ground that has been covered by researchers in terms of gendered bodies, sport and physicality. It is crucial to realise that some of the orthodox questions, while still not being fully answered, in addition to a new wave of questions, remain important issues. In an overview of this area, Sport in Focus 12.2 draws upon and extends Scraton and Flintoff's (2002) different levels of analysis.

The body, power and knowledge

One of the most provocative lines of analysis that has touched upon all of the above has been the use of the work of Foucault in relation to the body, power and difference. This has not been limited to one particular form of social difference in that Foucault's ideas on control, discipline, punishment and the body have developed as a means of resistance to such control with possibilities for feminism, masculinity, sport and the emotions, and the body. Many have looked to the work of Foucault for insightful use of concepts such as power and resistance, bodily discipline, surveillance and self-surveillance to position the body in a social context. Foucault was particularly interested in the micro-politics of the regulation of the body and the effects of power on it. Self-surveillance was the means through which the individual or athlete, or women monitored their own bodily behaviour to make sure it conformed to a prescribed norm. At the same time, the body could be used to resist such control, and this includes the implications for the use of the body in exercise, sport and leisure.

Foucault's model of power and knowledge explained very clearly that knowledge is used by agencies wielding the power that they have at their disposal but also through the established language structures through which all forms of imposition on society are made. What is truth is decided by a powerful minority, it regiments and systematically regulates the subject to suit its own goals by operating through a discourse. Foucault believed that a group of people could have the power to influence or create a worldview if they had the knowledge. The exercise of power itself involved the creation and cause to form new objects of knowledge

293

SPORT IN FOCUS 12.2: KEY ARGUMENTS ABOUT GENDER, BODY CULTURE AND HEALTH

■ Theorising gender and acknowledging that shifts in thinking and theory are ongoing.

■ The fact that the historical body has also changed, as illustrated when one compares the Victorian cult of the family and the early years of female sport with the contemporary progress made by women's football.

■ The representations of gendered bodies in sport through the media and, for example, how the body is used in displays of sexuality but also that such media representations contribute to the denial of women or the marginalisation of lesbian or homosexual sports coverage.

■ The body diaspora and the ways in which notions of ethnicity, race and diaspora provide alternatives for reassessing the accepted gender hierarchy about sport and the body, for example, the role of the body in offering anti-national, anti-essentialist and non-European sophisticated accounts of the body and sport.

■ Accounts of different masculinities and men's talk in relation to women's sport, female body culture, competition and homophobia.

■ Sexuality and how this manifests itself in sport, gym cultures, exercise clubs, sporting tastes and body movement.

■ The body, physicality and power and how different permutations of these notions manifest themselves in terms of violence, sexual abuse, gender orders in sport, sports organisations and struggles/resistance to produce change.

■ The normative ideas of justice and freedoms are not uniform and the gendered body, like the healthy body or sporting body or athletic body carries with it many constraints and possibilities.

and accumulate new bodies of information. This notion has been applied to discussions about the body and health, the body and sexuality, the body and exercise, the political economy of the body, education and schooling, the body and masculinity to name but a few areas. These areas have been influenced by the idea that power constructs and dominates. The use of power and knowledge has helped to generate discourses about sport, the body, exercise and health that are viewed as natural and normal but are in fact legitimated through the use of power relation and knowledge. Simply put there could be no power relations without the correlative constitution of a field of knowledge, nor any knowledge that did not presuppose and constitute at the same time power relations.

Foucault argued that power was an inevitable part of the production of society, that its presence was dispersed through intellectual and bodily disciplines and that social relations were not to be understood as being dependent upon any single foundation. Gruneau (1999: 121) points out that Foucault's influence forced an older generation of social critics writing about sport to broaden an understanding of the relationship between sport, power and the body not to mention radical politics. Various post-modern critics of sport, culture and society became more sensitive to a new line of critical analysis that focused attention on the problematic nature of any account or discussion of constraint or control that gave priority to any one axis of power, social division or one political subjectivity over another. This happened at the same time as new explanations of body, power and difference called into question the possibility of achieving any kind of universal freedoms in or through sport. The work of Nancy Fraser (2000) points to the fact that such a broad Foucauldian approach to body/sport placing an emphasis on self-defined identity fails to connect with other struggles for recognition. Without any normative standards for evaluating if and when more forms of power are more anxious or self-indulgent, the danger is always that yet another form of identity politics becomes reduced to just another form of lifestyle politics.

For some time, Foucault lorded over the fields of history, literary theory, queer theory, medicine, philosophy, sociology and sport, body and society. Some of his most powerful contributions were that the concept of truth is relative, that madness is a cultural creation and that history is little more than storytelling. The pervading theme in Foucault's philosophy was that human relations are defined by a struggle for power. Right and wrong, truth and falsehood are but illusions and there can be no such thing as values and therefore no such thing as judgement. Many suggested that Foucault was not just wrong, but he erased any possibility of proving himself to be right since he asserted such things as that the author did not exist, since he or she was conditioned to write by the customs of literature, and the mores of the day. Therefore, the body of work that is body, sport and society is nothing more than illusory. By his own philosophy, the logical conclusion leads to the question – how can we believe an author who tells us the author does not exist or the historian who tells us we can't write history or the sociologist of the body who tells us that body and society are illusory? Foucault's contribution to sport, body and society is self-invalidating, and perhaps it is time to assert that it is time to forget Foucault.

THE BODY, IDENTITIES AND DIFFERENCES

The study of the body offers endless possibilities and points of entry and exit from historical, geographical and contemporary examinations of sporting identities and differences. Even the most cursory glance at the critical academic literature on sport and related activities such as exercise, physical culture and health provides the reader with an array of bodies – the athletic body; the sporting body; the fascist body; the racialised body; the black body; the oriental body; the engendered body; the civilised body; the bodybuilder; the female body; the male body; the gay and lesbian bodies; the body habitus; and the African body. The rise of identity politics and the place of the body and sport within what Balakrishnan (2002) refers to as the age of identity has increased our understanding of embodiment in some societies, but such an approach also contains risks.

The discussions that follow are necessarily succinct. The first of these is the notion of identities in relation to the body and sport. Although the term 'identity' has a long history,

295

deriving from the Latin root *idem*, implying sameness and continuity, it was not until the twentieth century that the term came into popular usage. The usage of the term in relation to body, sport and society has taken many forms, all of which have attempted to reinforce and challenge *essentialist* understandings of sport, body and society. Essentialism refers to that which is a core identity or identities after everything else has been peeled away and the extent to which sport and body cultures reproduce and reinforce essential identities. The historical contribution has highlighted the invented or constructed character of identity associated with many sporting traditions and body styles. The historical approach, as with other approaches, views identity as essentialist but also *contingent* in that the identities are associated with body change over time and are, therefore, contingent upon particular histories. The psychodynamic approach to identity, body and sport has attempted to answer the question: who am I, and to what extent are the sporting and bodily practices I am involved in a reflection of self in a psychodynamic sense? The sociological approach to identity also has links to a theory of self in that a sociological tradition of identity theory has been linked to the symbolic interactionism associated with George Herbert Mead, Erving Goffman and Peter Berger. In this sense, body identities have been explained through the process of socialisation, communication and body language, all of which have attempted to reconcile the inner subjective creative bodily 'I' with the more outer, partly determined and objective 'me'. With particular reference to sport, discussions of national identity have drawn upon the notion of sport, helping to construct an imagined community while developmental or process sociologists have asserted that sport and the body are but vehicles for an overall quest for identity.

The notion of *identity crisis* has been evoked to imply that identity only really becomes an issue when a particular, culture, social group, or nation is facing a crisis of identity. The notion of the body or sport reflecting an identity crisis is problematic in that it reduces discussions of body identity to being simply reactionary rather than body or sporting identities being enabling. The framing of debates about the body and/or sport in this way is not sensitive to particular identity crises unique to sport or body culture at a particular point in time. Did the impact of football hooliganism in the 1990s and beyond pose a particular crisis of identity for English football or was English football simply reacting to broader social and cultural forces? If sport is viewed as a key component for the expression of national identity, then the fragmentation of different parts of the world may pose a particular crisis of identity for particular body cultures at local, national and international levels. Identity politics on its own is relatively meaningless and the notion of identity in crisis can contribute to an understanding of sport and body cultures in different parts of the world experiencing large-scale political upheaval or in places where new social forces attempt to dilute, replace or marginalise national identities. To what extent have body cultures helped to reassert a new European identity that threatens national identities? To what extent has sport reflected or enabled forms of reconciliation or a hardened militancy among various ethnic identities? Thus, identities that are forged through sport, body and society may matter more if there is a real or perceived crisis of identity, globally, locally, personally and politically.

A crucial concept is the notion of *difference* in relation to the body and sport. The marking of difference is crucial to the construction of identities in sport, body and society. Identities tend to be formed in relation to other identities and differences are used to signify or represent them. This unsatisfactory trend tends to take the form of binary forms of classification such as us and them; insider and outsider; women and men; black and white; Arab and Jew; Protestant and Catholic; Serb and Croat. All depend upon differences marking particular forms of identity that, in turn, symbolise or represent forms of social and political difference. The notion of difference is integral to the understanding, construction and in some cases invention of identities, all of which tend to be used to legitimate a particular social order or ways of being. More positively the recognition/acceptance of change and differences involving the body and sport may be seen as positively progressive in that it signifies an acceptance of a rich, diverse set of body cultures such as gay and lesbian sporting culture; a sporting Olympiad rather than the able and disabled Olympics; and a secure place for Muslim Pakistani women in sociological accounts of sport and body cultures rather than a predominance of white/other feminist accounts of sport and the body. Differences in and between sport and body cultures and identities may be viewed as a celebration of bodily diversity, heterogeneity and hybridity. The notion of identity is not the same as difference in that one helps in the construction and legitimation of the other.

Representation refers to the ways in which images and texts such as articles, books, radio or television programmes reconstruct an account of sport, body and society. A painting, a photograph, a written text about sport and the body are never just an actual account of real sport or physical activity but how the painting, the photograph or the written text has represented sport and the body. Writers about gender and the body argue that representation is continually creating, challenging, recreating and endorsing stereotypical images, stories, and ideas about identity, sport and the body. The areas of historiography and representation are crucial to developing post-colonial accounts of the sporting body. The work of Bale (2000, 2004) and Dimeo (2004) offered, at the time, alternative epistemological systems or ways of thinking about the sporting body that dislocate Euro-centric or colonial sporting histories and geographies.

Representing accounts of sport identities and the body can never be a neutral activity. Critical representations of sport and the body attempt to wrestle with and provide answers to who am I? What could I be? Who am I like and who do I want to be? Many writers could do a lot worse than take their lead from Edward Saïd, who argued, in *Culture and Imperialism* (1993), that studying the relationship between the West and its dominated cultural other is not just a way of understanding an unequal relationship between unequal stories, but also a point of entry into studying the formation and meaning of Western cultural practices themselves. Thus, Saïd implied that the discrepancy of power between Western and non-Western sport necessitates that any account of global, international or local sport must take such a disparity into account if we are to accurately understand sport, body and society in its totality and not simply as an illusion of totality. It is worthwhile exploring the issue of other sporting bodies in more detail if for no other reason than that they have made a profound contribution to the story of sport, body and society. The politics of representation are such that all accounts of sport and the body that are promoted as authentic, valid and true need to be closely questioned in order to ascertain just exactly where the authority and coherence for such claims may be located.

Many of the issues above are applicable to contemporary issues and debates about the body abd sport. Sport in Focus 12.3 covers the background to the key arguments surrounding the introduction of women's boxing to the 2012 Olympic Games in London, a first in the

297

SPORT IN FOCUS 12.3: OPPOSING CORNERS – THE BOXING DEBATE

Women's boxing will appear in the London 2012 Olympic Games for the first time. The arguments for and against have been summarised below.

For:

- It is a good thing we are trying to bring equality into sport.
- It is much more accessible than other women's sports.
- Having it on TV during the Olympics will raise the profile.
- Women wear the headguards and are medically checked every time they box.
- The risk is no more or less than other women's contact sports such as rugby.

Against:

- The British medical authorities (BMA) are disappointed with the decision to televise women's boxing.
- Since the early 1980s, the BMA has called for boxing to be banned.
- The opposition is based upon medical evidence that the risk to acute injury and brain damage is too great.
- Irrespective of gender, boxers can suffer damage to eyes, ears, nose and brain.
- The cumulative effect of a lifetime in the ring can be irreversible damage.

contest's modern history. Should the debate about women's boxing be framed in terms of medical grounds (the same logic applies to men's boxing) or equality grounds?

Other sporting bodies

In drawing attention to the fact that indigenous Australians grow up in historical contexts of racism both inside and outside of sport, Gardiner (2003: 43) concludes that indigenous players have to confront a sports culture in which traditionally white codes attempt to dictate, order and define black bodies. The texts that have emerged from indigenous people's lives in Australia have begun to produce an 'other' history of Australian football codes. In reality, there is also a rich substantive terrain of women's sport in Africa, Asia and the Middle East but, as Hargreaves (2004: 197) points out, there is a dearth of sport feminist literature from outside the West. She draws our attention to the need to develop multiple complex accounts of women in sport but also to the *vital* point that, to many, homogenous accounts of sporting identity for women tend to conceal many hidden forms of injustice, discrimination and activism in other worlds. This holds true for work on the body and identity as much as it does for sport. Anne Leseth (2003: 243), talking of dance, sport and the body in Dar-es-Salaam contrasts the notion of a Western body image with 'other' points of view and, in doing so, draws upon the words of Betty, a 25-year-old woman living in a squatter area of Dar-es-Salaam, who explains 'it is not important whether you have a body shape like a bodybuilder, a beauty queen or a traditional figure, the crux of the matter is how this person moves when it comes to speed and style' (Leseth, 2003: 242). This powerful piece of ethnography illustrates how the use of sport and dance in Tanzania can produce fundamentally different ways of thinking about bodily practice that take us beyond the traditional way of thinking about colonial sport and the body. It vividly illustrates the power of sport and dance as a means of developing, changing and re-shaping lives in a post-colonial Tanzania.

As has been explored in Part 2 of this book, it is necessary that both research and teaching about sport, body and society listen to the view from the 'other'; that is, from the perspective of women and men who have been marginalised in some way as a result of colonial or other forms of Western sport.

Sport and body culture as cultural policy

Body culture is an important facet of Danish cultural policy in that it provides an alternative or third way of thinking about sport as part of national cultural policy (Danish Ministry of Culture, 1996). Danish cultural policy is informed by a number of underpinning principles. Cultural decentralisation entails that the state must ensure that all population groups and geographic areas have access to cultural products and cultural activities be they art, literature, film, sport, festivals, theatres or libraries. Thus, culture is viewed not simply as art, but as a dynamic social institution that acknowledges all cultural movements, including bodily movements found in play, festivals, dance and sport. The focus of Danish cultural policy since the 1960s has been on the dissemination of culture. The dissemination and production of culture in Denmark involves a division of labour between the state, country and the municipalities. The Ministry of Culture has recognised the need for a pluralistic approach to culture rather than evoking the national mono-cultural approach that endorses one country, one culture. The Ministry of Culture recognises the differences with regard to cultural provision in the capital and the provinces, the city and the country and between various social groups and the population as a whole.

The notion of body culture is much broader than the simple notion of sport, sports cultures or sports policy. The added dimension of body culture moves the notion of sports and sports policy beyond the simple dualism of elite sport versus recreation or high-performance sport versus mass sport or simply thinking of sport as sport without appreciating the nuances of sport, dance, games and sports festivals. The Danish way of sports implies a break from the unitary notion of sport. Sport *as body culture* includes not only competitive sport, with its problematic dualism of elite and mass sport, fitness and health-promoting initiatives, popular games, forms of play and festivals, but all of these and more. Sport and body culture as cultural policy evokes a dialectic interplay between different forms of movement culture, performance and result-orientated sport; the lifestyle-promoting movement of exercise and fitness and popular activities of body culture such as play.

The connection between the body, people and movement presented in Sport in Focus 12.4 is adapted from Eichberg (2004, 2011).

299

SPORT IN FOCUS 12.4: THE BODY, PEOPLE AND MOVEMENT

Bodily movement	Emotional movement	Social movement
Basic experience:		
"We play" motion emotion, motive, motivation	"I am moved" people in motion	"We are the people"
Physical practice	Feelings of togetherness and difference	Self-organisation and conflict
How to discover:		
Sports studies	Psychology/sociology	Sociology/politics
What we discover:		
People in sport, dance, festivals and games	People as social identities	People as civil society/ other cultures
Differentiations and contradictions:		
People in competition	Identity of achievement	People's will
People in discipline	Identity of integration	Popular culture
People in festivity	Identity of encounter	People's solidarity

SUMMARY

New ways of thinking about the body in social and cultural terms have led to an interest in the study of the sport, body and health. The bodily practice of peoples in different parts of the world is a basis for their social life. The body remains central to struggles for recognition. A plethora of studies have been organised around the uses and abuses of the body in and beyond sport that have redressed the cultural and social blindness of biological paradigms that historically limited the body gaze to complex biological concerns. In reality, the body in a physiological, medical, biological, religious and social sense is a key component to the practice of power, democracy, lifestyle and identities. The fact that bodies of knowledge will interconnect and talk to one another is a refreshing breakthrough. This has helped to address some or all of the following concerns:

- the process by which ideas about the body in sport and beyond are viewed as natural, deviant, different and/or biological;
- the ethical, social and legal implications of how bodies are protected, probed, monitored, rehabilitated, disciplined and/or evaluated;

- the extent to which the struggle by different professions for market control over different segments of the body continues to provide the rationale for developing accounts of the body that are driven by political economic concerns;
- the ways in which both old and new media represent bodies in sport;
- the illusory untouchable bodies associated with the marketing of celebrity sports bodies; and
- anthropological studies that have made a real difference to the ways in which the sports academy of knowledge has opened up to other parts of the world.

Future thinking and action in relation to sport, body and health must attend to the dynamics and impact of new markets, social patterning, and state policies in different parts of the world in order to understand the new parameters of any current body politic. On the question of social differences and identities, the relation between the recognition of cultural differences and social equality and justice in different or all parts of the world remains a key tension and a fruitful study ground for teachers, students, activists and researchers interested in broadening or moving interventions or policies beyond just sport. Studies of the body in sport provide for exciting opportunities to consider what is natural, what is ethical and what is social and for these reasons alone they must remain a valuable component of any future evaluation of the potential progressive contribution of sport to society.

GUIDE TO FURTHER READING

Allardyce, J. (2010). 'Row as Beauty Queen Made a Role Model'. *The Sunday Times,* 7 March: 7.

Eichberg, H. (2011). 'The Normal Body: Anthropology of Bodily Otherness'. *International Journal of Physical Culture, Sports Studies and Research,* L (1): 1–16.

Germond, P. and Cochrane, J. (2010). 'Healthworlds: Conceptualizing Landscapes of Health and Healing'. *Sociology,* 44 (2): 307–324.

Hargreaves, J. and Vertinsky, P. (2007). *Physical Culture, Power and the Body.* London: Routledge.

Loland, S., Sklirslad, B. and Waddington, I. (2006). *Pain and Injury in Sport: Social and Ethical Analyses.* London: Routledge.

Lopez, B. (2011). 'The Invention of a Drug of Mass Destruction:Deconstructing the EPO Myth'. *Sport in History,* 31 (1): 84–109.

Luttrell, W. (2011). 'Where Inequality Lives in the Body: Teenage Pregnancy, Public Pedagogies and Individual Lives'. *Sport, Education Society,* 16 (3): 295–308.

Maguire, J. S. (2008). *Fit for Consumption: Sociology and the Business of Fitness.* London: Routledge.

Oswald, A. (2011). 'The Well-Being of Nations'. *Times Higher Education,* 19–25 May: 35–40.

Tang, C. C. (2010). 'Yungdong: One Term for Two Different Body Cultures'. *East Asian Sport Thoughts: The International Journal for the Sociology of Sport,* 1 (1): 73–104.

Waddington, I. (2001). *Sport, Health and Drugs.* London: Routledge.

QUESTIONS

1 Use examples from the literature on sport, body and health to explain the following terms: 'identity', 'difference' and 'representation'.

2 Choose two from the following list of body formations and compare and contrast the social theories behind them: the natural body, the civilised body, the engendered body, the body habitus, the socially constructed body, the fascist body, the African body, the oriental body.

3 Explain the difference between essential and contingent approaches to understanding sport, body and society.

4 Evaluate the contribution that post-colonial thinking has made to our understanding of the body in other cultures.

5 What are the advantages of the broader notion of body culture over sport in terms of policy formulation?

6 Explain the terms 'health worlds' and 'life chances', and consider how they help us think about sport, pain, health and/or illness.

7 What does the term 'other' sporting bodies mean?

8 Provide a short evaluative history of the use of drugs in sport.

9 What is Fraser's critique of Foucault's work on the body and identity?

10 Describe the key points inherent within Eichberg's account of body movement presented in Sport in Focus 12.4.

PRACTICAL PROJECTS

1 Select two popular health magazines and, over a three-month period, carry out a content analysis of the two magazines as a basis for writing a critical report on body representation and health.

2 Go to a local gym or exercise club in your area and carry out a series of interviews with three different populations in order to ascertain what their views are on the perfect body.

3 Identify five different articles in the journal *Body and Society* that have researched aspects of sport, exercise or physical activity, and use these to compile a short case study on *representation* and sport, exercise and/or physical activity.

4 Identify three different local populations in terms of social class participation in exercise. Carry out a series of interviews with each population, enquiring about why exercise is important to the body and what sort of body people would like. Write a

report of about 2,000 words on the body, exercise and social class, drawing on the findings from the three different populations.

5   List ten policy directives that would be derived from developing a policy based upon the broader notion of body culture as opposed to sport. Access the Danish website www.netpublikationer.dk/um/8911/html/chapter01.htm and compare your policy with that of Denmark.

KEY CONCEPTS

Body cultures ■ Difference ■ Disciplined body ■ Distinction ■ Freedom ■ Habitus ■ Health worlds ■ Life chances ■ Other ■ Quest for excitement ■ Naturalism ■ Physicality ■ Power ■ Representation ■ Secular ■ Sexuality

WEBSITES

ESRC Research
www.esrc.ac.uk/impacts-and-findings/research-topics/health-wellbeing-research/
Main findings from ESRC-funded research into health and well-being.

The Scottish Annual Health Report
www.scotland.gov.uk/Resource/Doc/296797/0092270.pdf
A resource that explains the health of one nation in one given year and the trends. The important part of this report is the explicit link between physiological and social well-being.

Body and Society Journal
http://bod.sagepub.com/
A dedicated journal to social and political issues about the body in society.

Rethinking masculinity: Men and their bodies
http://fathom.lse.ac.uk/Seminars/21701720/21701720_session1.html
A seminar on men, masculinity and the body.

A Healthy Australia
www.healthyactive.gov.au/
This website provides a range of information and initiatives on healthy eating, regular physical activity and obesity to assist all Australians to lead healthy and active lives.

Chapter 13

Sport, violence and crime

Is sport more or less violent today than it was in the nineteenth or twentieth century?

PREVIEW

Key terms defined ■ Introduction ■ Violence, sport and the law ■ The Old Firm ■ Shame ■ Violence in North American Ice Hockey ■ Violence in sport and society ■ Deviance, crime and sport ■ Crime prevention through sport and physical activity ■ The Twic Olympics ■ Risk and sexual violence in sport and society ■ London 2012 Olympics crackdown, risk and sex workers ■ States of denial in world sport ■ Summary

OBJECTIVES

This chapter will:

- introduce the reader to previous work linking sport to violence in society;
- evaluate ways in which sport is used to tackle deviance and crime prevention;
- comment upon sport as a facet of risk in society and of a risk society;
- provide illustrative examples of sport, violence and crime; and
- explain the significance of and main ways in which the notion of denial might be considered as a useful analytical tool in the area of sport, violence and crime.

KEY TERMS DEFINED

Crime: An act or ommission prohibited and punished by law, often culturally specific but also framed by international laws.

Normative: The systematic analyses of the ethical, moral and political principles that either govern the norm of behaviour or crime or violence; the belief that theories should be concerned with what ought to be rather than what is.

The Old Firm: The term given to the rivalry between Glasgow Celtic Football Club and Glasgow Rangers Football Club, one of the oldest football club games in the world.

Risk: A probability of threat of damage, injury, liability, loss or other negative occurrence that is caused by external or internal vulnerabilities, and that may be neutralised through pre-emptive action.

Violence: The intentional use of physical force or power, threatened or actual, against another person or against oneself or a group of people, that results in or has a high likelihood or resulting in injury, death, psychological harm, mal-development or deprivation.

INTRODUCTION

'The Old Firm must tackle violence or face penalties' was the headline of an article in the *Sunday Times* the morning after a Scottish Cup tie between Glasgow Rangers and Glasgow Celtic (*Sunday Times*, 3 April 2011: 20). A decade earlier, a survey by the trade union Unison revealed that, after Old Firm football matches, hospital admissions rose and sectarian assaults increased almost tenfold. Domestic violence incidents doubled. Arrests for murder in the hours after the match are usual. After this specific Scottish Cup match between the two teams, there were 300 arrests. One 18-year-old girl was left with serious head injuries.

During the game, three Rangers players were sent off, 13 yellow cards were issued and the managers of the two teams were involved in an incident as the two teams left the field. The following weeks saw the escalation of violence and forms of violence change, with a letter bomb campaign against Neil Lennon (the Celtic manager), Trish Godman (a retired politician and Celtic supporter) and Paul McBride QC. The latter went on to describe Scotland as a a Third World country and said that it was time to tackle the violence and sectarianism that had become intertwined with this football rivalry (*The Herald*, 22 April 2011: 1).

As Sport in Focus 13.1 illustrates, there has been a history of ill-discipline at Old Firm matches between players, coaches and supporters. The 'beautiful game' of football can, at times, look ugly but, as Sport in Focus 13.1 evidences, it is not as if the incidents described above are one-offs. Only a fortnight earlier at another Old Firm match, there had been 250 arrests. An emergency government summit was called for and put in place. The issue at stake is whether Scottish society is highly tolerant of football violence and a blind eye is sometimes turned to the social and physical violence that is mobilised around these football matches. On the one hand, the call is for politicians and police to deal with the problem of football violence by passing the cost of dealing with the violence on to the clubs. Others suggest the European football authorities themselves need to deal with this problem by banning the clubs from playing in Europe. Other calls claim that the clubs cannot deal with this problem and that its root problems lie in schools, families and the social fabric of Scottish society and, in particular, the West of Scotland.

Violence is one of many social issues that is complex, and occurs in different forms and in different places. It is tempting to suggest that incidents need to be looked at on a case-by-case basis but clearly the relationship between sport and violence can take many different forms and is not solely a Scottish problem. On 2 February 2000 in Vancouver, during a National Hockey League (NHL) match, a player took a swing, from behind, at another player's head with his hockey stick. The NHL disciplinary body instigated an enquiry while the federal law courts decided to bring formal charges for assault with a weapon against Marty McSorley. The NHL fought the court action on the grounds that the concussion was sustained during an organised game. The court decided that the actions of the player exceeded the limits of the NHL rulebook. The player was suspended from the NHL for a year. But, as Sport in Focus 13.2 substantiates, violence in North American ice hockey is not new.

Nor is violence in sport a phenomenon that is limited to the West. Regular press briefings from the United Arab Emirates have reported child abuse and human rights violations (Beaumont, 2001: 27). Child jockeys as young as four years old are regularly sought after for camel races in the Gulf because of their light weight and skill in manoeuvring the animals. The Karachi-based Ansar Burney Welfare Trust claimed, in 2001, that as many as 2,000 boys had been smuggled to camps since 1999 despite laws introduced in the UAE in 1998 forbidding the use of young boys in this dangerous sport. The rules of the Emirates Camel Racing Federation forbid the use of riders under the age of 14, or weighing less than 45 kg. The trade in boys for camel racing has been the subject of campaigns by both the United Nations (UN) and Anti-Slavery International. Children are sold for up to $3,000 (£2,100) each (Beaumont, 2001: 27). Anti-slavery campaigners have had some success in returning camel slaves. In 1999, the authorities repatriated an eight-year-old Pakistani boy who had

306

SPORT IN FOCUS 13.1: THE OLD FIRM SHAME GAME

1909: Celtic 1 – 1 Rangers

The replay of the Scottish Cup final ended in another draw, which meant the game would be played again under SFA regulations. The fans became enraged after realising extra time would not occur and went on the rampage. The crowd stormed the changing rooms, fought the police, set the ground on fire, cut up the pitch and slashed the hoses of the firemen trying to extinguish the blaze. More than 50 policemen were injured and both clubs were fined £150 as punishment.

1980: Celtic 1 – 0 Rangers

George McCluskey scored the winner for Celtic in a cup tie at Hampden Park. However, things turned sour after the final whistle. Fans from both sides invaded the pitch and clashed. Unbelievably, there were only 12 police officers inside the stadium to deal with the trouble. After the game, alcohol was banned from games in Scotland – a ban that still stands today.

1988: Rangers 2 – 2 Celtic

Violent scenes erupted on the pitch after a Scottish Premier League match between the rivals. Celtic's Frank McAvennie and Rangers' goalkeeper Chris Woods squared up to each other, before Rangers' skipper Terry Butcher waded in and grabbed McAvennie by the throat. The three players were shown red cards for their behaviour. After the game, they were charged, along with Rangers' Graham Roberts, with breach of the peace. In court, Woods and Butcher were convicted and fined £500 and £250 respectively. The case against Roberts was found not proven and McAvennie was found not guilty.

1997: Celtic 0 – 1 Rangers

During an important league win for Rangers, Malky MacKay and Mark Hateley were shown red cards. However, the worst offenders were Paulo Di Canio and Ian Ferguson. The two clashed on the park, with the Celtic forward Di Canio gesturing that he would snap Ferguson. A brawl erupted in the tunnel between the players at full time.

1999: Celtic 0 – 3 Rangers

Rangers won to secure the league in the home stadium of their arch rivals. There was an uneasy atmosphere in the stadium throughout the game, but the tipping point came after Celtic's Stephane Mahe was sent off. A Celtic fan tried to get on to the pitch to confront referee Hugh Dallas, but was caught by security guards. But, during the chaos, a coin was thrown that hit Dallas on the forehead and he needed to receive medical treatment. There were further pitch invasions, serious violence in Glasgow throughout the night, and Dallas' house windows were smashed.

SPORT IN FOCUS 13.1—*continued*

2011: Celtic 1 – 0 Rangers

There was disarray throughout the stadium during a Scottish Cup replay. Three Rangers players were shown red cards, but the most serious offences took place off the pitch. Celtic claim El-Hadji Diouf barged their physiotherapist, a bust-up between players and staff occured at half time in the tunnel, and after the final whistle the Celtic manager, Neil Lennon, and Rangers coach, Ally McCoist, had to be pulled apart after a spat. In the stands, the police had to make 34 arrests for various sectarian, racial and breach of the peace offences.

been kidnapped to work as a camel jockey. In August 1999, a four-year-old jockey from Bangladesh was found abandoned and close to death in the desert. In 2000, Anti-Slavery International reported the case of another four-year-old jockey from Bangladesh whose employer had burnt him on his legs for under-performing. The boy was left crippled. Although some of the children are taken as indentured labourers with the parents' consent, in other cases children are drugged and abducted. In November 2001, UAE police rescued two Pakistani brothers, aged six and four, who had been kidnapped to work as jockeys (Beaumont, 2001: 27).

In the second half of 2001, the Committee on the Rights of the Child monitored the situation of child rights in Oman, Qatar and the UAE. It expressed serious concern that sometimes very young children are involved, are trafficked, particularly from Africa and South Asia, are denied education and healthcare, and that such an involvement in sport produces serious injuries and fatalities. When questioned about the camel races, members of the delegation from Oman explained that 'camel riding was considered a sport, not a job and that participation of children in it was a source of pride for both children and their parents' (David, 2005: 178). The delegates from Qatar stated that addressing the issue of the involvement of children in camel racing was a priority for the government.

This chapter develops at least three themes by means of providing a critical evaluation of the broad field of sport, violence and crime. At the heart of this is the concerted attempt to emphasise the changing nature of sport, violence and crime and to draw attention to the fact that teachers and researchers in the field of sport, culture and society have moved the study of sport, violence and crime some way beyond the areas of football hooliganism, sport and deviant youth subcultures, violence in sport and changing rates of violence in sport and society through the ages. The aim is simply to prompt thinking about the nature of sport, violence and crime by broadening the horizons of understanding in the hope that a questioning attitude to understanding others might enable us to better understand ourselves with others.

SPORT IN FOCUS 13.2: VIOLENCE IN NORTH AMERICAN ICE HOCKEY

1905   Allan Loney was charged with murder after he clubbed Alcide Laurin to death during a game. The charges were later reduced to manslaughter, and, after claiming self-defence, he was found not guilty.

1907   During a brawl in a match with the Ottawa Victorias, Cornwall player Owen McCourt died after receiving multiple blows to the head with sticks. Ottawa's Charles Masson was charged with manslaughter, but was found not guilty as they were unable to determine which blow had killed McCourt.

1927   Billy Coutu was banned from the NHL for life after he punched a referee during a Stanley Cup game.

1969   Boston Bruins player Ted Green missed the 1969/1970 NHL season after sustaining a fractured skull and brain damage in a violent fight, using sticks, with Wayne Maki of the St Louis Blues. Maki and Green were suspended for 30 days and 13 days respectively, but were both acquitted in court.

1975   Dan Maloney was charged with assault causing bodily harm for an attack on Brian Glennie of the Toronto Maple Leafs. Maloney did not contest the charge, and was given a community service sentence. He was also banned from playing in Toronto for two years.

1988   Dino Ciccareli struck Luke Richardson with his stick. He was charged and convicted of assault, which resulted in one day in prison and a fine of $1,000.

2000   Marty McSorley was convicted and sentenced to 18 months in jail for hitting Donald Brashear in the head with his stick near the end of a game between the Bruins and the Vancouver Canucks. It was seen as a revenge attack after he had lost a brawl with Brashear earlier in the game. McSorley's sentence was later suspended.

2004   Todd Bertuzzi of the Vancouver Canucks knocked Steve Moore of the Colorado Avalanche unconscious with a punch. Bertuzzi then fell on him, his weight smashing Moore's face into the ice. Moore ended up with three broken vertebrae in his neck, concussion and cuts to his face. Bertuzzi pleaded guilty to assault and received a suspended sentence and 80 hours of community service. Bertuzzi lost around $500,000 in pay but returned to the NHL in 2005. Moore has not played hockey since and has failed in several attempts at civil litigation.

2011   Riot police fired tear gas as a mob burned cars and looted shops in Vancouver after the Canucks lost the Stanley Cup final to the Boston Bruins.

VIOLENCE IN SPORT AND SOCIETY

There is a robust body of knowledge about violence in sport. Different forms of violence, rates of violence and varying solutions involving sport in relation to violence have generated a vast amount of research. The above examples are illustrative of a broader critical contribution made by sociologists, historians, psychologists and anthropologists in the study of sports violence in different cultures and societies. Young's (2002) overview of the field of sport and violence directs attention to:

- different explanations and manifestations of *crowd violence* associated with sports events;
- social and legal contributions resulting from the analysis of *player violence* (these include brutal body contact; borderline violence viewed as part of the culture of the game but prohibited by the official rules of the game; quasi-criminal violence that violates the rules of the game or the law of the given land; and the norm accepted by players and criminal violence involving players in which the incidents are so serious that they are deemed to fall outside the boundaries of acceptability and are, therefore, handed over to the criminal courts);
- *other forms of violence related to sport* such as sexual assault and harassment, employment violations of young athletes and the stabbing and stalking of sports heroes and heroines; and
- *sports violence and the mass media*, in particular the role of the mass media in producing, legitimating and reinforcing violent forms of behaviour associated with sport.

Violence is complex and difficult to define (Ray, 2011). In the technical sense of the word, the World Health Organization (2002: 5) defines 'violence' as:

> The intentional use of physical force or power, threatened or actual, against another person or against oneself or a group of people, that results in or has a high likelihood or resulting in injury, death, psychological harm, mal-development or deprivation.

Minimalist accounts often regard violence as being narrowly defined in terms of physical force, bodily response and/or harm. Wrestling and boxing may be seen as violent by some but others point out that people entered the ring on a voluntary basis. Broader generic definitions of violence sometimes define it as actions which inflict, threaten or cause harm. Violence might be both casual and perpetrated by individuals or highly structured and perpetrated by the state. Where states have legitimated violence, it has given rise to destructive and extensive instances of state organised and state sanctioned violence. In such instances, sport has occassionally figured as a tool of diplomacy or a soft form of intervention. To call something violent may suggest that it is morally wrong, but who or what defines what is morally right or wrong? Violence is intimately connected with the body, pain, vulnerability and issues of security, embodiment and power. For peace talks to take place, individuals and communities sometimes need to feel safe and secure as a prerequisite for dialogue.

DEVIANCE, CRIME AND SPORT

Giddens (2001: 237) suggests it would be a mistake to regard crime and deviance wholly in a negative light. Any society that recognises that human beings have diverse values and concerns must find a space for individuals who do not always conform to the norm followed by the majority. Academics who develop new ideas in politics, science, sports studies, art or other fields are often viewed with hostility by those who hold on to orthodox ideas. The introduction of the wearing of seat belts in cars was met with hostility and scepticism when it was first introduced in the UK. The emergence of rule changes in different sports has often been initially met with hostility. People fiercely resisted ideas such as freedom of the individual and equality of opportunity at the time they were introduced and yet they are viewed today as being accepted ideals in parts of the world. To deviate from the dominant norms of any society or sport takes courage and is often a key part of the process of change. Deviance may be viewed as behaviour that transgresses commonly held norms in any culture or society, but it need not be.

The relationship between criminal violence and societies that experience greater individual liberties is interesting. Are crimes of violence inevitable in societies where rigid definitions of conformity are applied? In some societies, such as Holland or the Scandinavian countries, where a wide range of individual freedoms and progressive toleration of activities are deemed to exist, rates of violent crime are relatively low. Conversely, in countries where individual freedoms are restricted, are the levels of violence higher? Giddens (2001) asserts that a society that is tolerant towards deviant behaviour need not necessarily suffer social disruption. Perhaps it is utopian to suggest that a good outcome might be to work towards the norm where individual liberties are joined to social justice in a social order in which inequalities are not so glaringly large and in which everyone has a chance to lead a fulfilling and satisfying life. If freedom is not balanced with equality, and if a lack of self-fulfilment is the norm, then it is likely that deviant behaviour would be channelled towards socially destructive ends. Sport has historically been viewed as a means of social control, a means of curbing or deflecting deviant behaviour, and yet, as Bauman (2001) and others have pointed out, no other form of social control is more efficient than the spectre of insecurity that hangs over the heads of the controlled. The pragmatic key to any strategy that involves sport as a mechanism for either increasing rates of violence or controlling rates of deviant behaviour lies with knowing what is appropriate and what is not, and when and where certain interventions should be taken forward.

According to Coakley and Pike (2009: 197), the study of deviance in sport presents four challenges. First, the forms and causes of deviance in sports are so diverse that no single theory can explain all of them. Second, actions, ideas and characteristics accepted in sports may be defined as deviant in the rest of society. Third, deviance in sports often involves an uncritical acceptance of norms, rather than a rejection of them. Finally, training in sports has become medicalised to the point that athletes use medical technology in ways that push normative limits. It is possible to provide more of a sense of what deviance means in sport. Thinking about deviance in sport has moved beyond the notion of deviance as being attributed to forms of behaviour, or that deviance in sport should be measured against patterns of norm violation in sport, or that deviance is a social construct, a stigma or label bestowed upon participants in sport who breach the changing norms of behaviour in sport at any given time. One of the central tensions inherent in evaluations of deviance in sport or whether sport may be used as an instrument of social control is whether or not it is associated with personal behaviour or whether it is a feature of certain social structures. It is a sympathy for the latter that has, in part, characterised one of the most fluid contributions to the study of sport, namely that deviance through sport may be contingent upon a particular type of society in which it is important for individuals to have a heightened sense of awareness of who they are, an identity that has evolved out of self-awareness (Bauman, 2000b).

In one of the most refreshing contributions to our understanding of violence in sport, Blackshaw and Crabbe (2004) suggest that we need to recast the sociology of deviance as the sociology of 'deviance' – the emphasis here being on the last word. It is suggested that we need a better interpretation in order to understand the complexity of the social world of sport while at the same time recognising that notions of deviance will always be contested and influenced by the events of the time (Blackshaw and Crabbe 2004: 14). In many ways, they play the popular sociology of sport game by claiming that particular aspects of sport in society should be thought of in different ways. They do this by systematically critiquing with approaches to the sociology of deviance that have hitherto got in the way of what they want to say.

The strategy involves:

- arguing that attempts to explain deviance in sport to date have been useful but lacking in some aspects, and are very problematic for understanding deviance in sport today;
- substantiating the case that the everyday make-up of sport is increasingly characterised by the experiences of deviance, and that we need new ways of re-imagining deviance using the notion of performativity; and
- arguing that an examination of the uses of the categorisation of 'deviance' may help to explain how power and social control continue to be exercised in today's world of sport and society.

It is, in many ways, a critical synthesis of the sociology of deviance as applied to sport and has the hallmarks of the strategy adopted by those who used classical sociology in previous decades to stake a claim and direction for certain aspects of sport. Instead of the driving force being a Marx, a Weber, an Elias or Durkheim, the guru behind the mask is the work of Zygmunt Bauman. In a critical statement, Blackshaw and Crabbe (2004: 15) reveal, drawing on Bauman, that if sociology in its twentieth-century format was too preoccupied with the circumstances of conformity, obedience and consensus making, the challenge facing sociology today is the matter of choice between taking responsibility as its focus or by asserting that responsibility for one's actions need not be taken. In their own words, 'their approach then is to create a disorderly inquietude out of what has already been written about the sociology of deviance and provide a new beginning' (Blackshaw and Crabbe, 2004: 15) – rather than an end in itself.

Just as approaches about sport and deviance need rigorous critical scrutiny, so too do questions about sport and physical activity as strategies in crime prevention. Crime prevention is not the primary objective of sport and associated activities but it is often, sometimes mistakenly, argued that such activities may be a positive strategy in crime prevention. The conclusions from one such approach are presented in Sport in Focus 13.3. Many of the arguments about the positive role that sport can play in the area of crime prevention tend to draw upon some or all of the arguments presented in this box.

The role of organised sports and cultural activities for young people in many countries is often linked to the expectation that investment in deprived areas in this way will help to reduce street crime and rates of robbery. In January 2002, Tessa Jowell, then the UK Culture Secretary, hailed the success of 'Splash Extra Schemes', where publicly funded investment in sport and the arts was claimed to have brought about a 5.2 per cent fall in local crime (Jowell, 2002). The five main crimes commonly associated with youth offending are motor crime, domestic burglary, robbery, criminal damage and drug offences. This cross-government street crime initiative in England during the summer of 2001 received £8.8 million of public funds attached to deprived neighbourhoods and city centres, and involved some 91,000 young people between the ages of 13 and 17. The male/female split was approximately 62 per cent to 38 per cent, marking a slight increase in the number of females participating when compared with the previous year. Around 2.5 million hours of activity were delivered at the cost of around £2.60 per hour. The results suggested that street crime and robbery fell by 31 per cent in those parts of the country in which the schemes ran, compared to an increase of 56 per cent in areas where the schemes did not run (Jowell, 2002). Similarly, in other parts of the UK, twilight basketball schemes have been partially aimed at diverting young people from crime and antisocial behaviour while combating drug, alcohol and other physical abuse by young people (www.scottishrocks.co.uk). In an evaluation of the role of sport in preventing crime in areas of deprivation, the then Scottish Executive (2000: 2), drawing on the work of Coalter, Allison and Taylor, suggest that sport is most effective when combined with programmes addressing wider issues of personal and social development, and that short-term funding often means that such interventionist projects rarely last long enough to achieve meaningful, sustainable impacts.

The Twic Olympic Games

Sudan has now divided into North and South Sudan but, as yet, the respective sporting structures remain unclear. For years, sport was part of a deliberate policy of diplomacy and normalisation that attempted to help people suffering as a result of conflict and civil war. Sport is a powerful seductive force in drawing people beyond their immediate circumstances rather than submitting to them. By 2002, Sudan had been at war for the most part of 50 years and its peoples have endured bombing, slave traders and pillaging troops. The staging of the Twic Olympics meant that sport provided a moment of tolerance and compassion – the importance being that the contest had taken place at all (Harris, 2002). The Twic Olympics was the beginning of an aspiration for a Games for southern Sudan. Currently, only the people of the Twic County, one of the border regions that lies adjacent to the Arab land of the north, compete. Twic is divided into six districts, or payams, and each January a team of athletes from each district gather to compete at football, volleyball, dance sport athletics and tug of war. The competitors are people such as James, who was drafted into the army at the age of 11, who 'does not smile and in playing sport points out that nothing

SPORT IN FOCUS 13.3: CRIME PREVENTION THROUGH SPORT AND PHYSICAL ACTIVITY

The following are some of the commonly referred to arguments surrounding sports-based interventions aimed at ameliorating or helping crime reduction:

- It appears that sport and physical activity can reduce crime by providing accessible, appropriate activities in a supportive social context. In other words, sport and physical activity must be connected positively within the social fabric of groups and communities.
- Sport and physical activity-based interventions must be conducted in collaboration with a range of other strategies and sectors.
- Elite sporting bodies can be involved in programmes directly aimed at particular crimes or communities.
- It is essential to consider how the design, location and funding of sporting and recreational infrastructure contributes to social cohesion, and avoids taking sport and physical activity out of its social context.
- The cases do not suggest 'one size fits all' strategies; instead, they represent the value of community development approaches to tailor programmes to particular needs. Nevertheless, this should not prevent us from suggesting common strategies and processes, and collecting examples of good practice.
- Recreation and sport programmes established for the explicit purpose of crime prevention should be subject to rigorous evaluation.
- Programmes should be based on evidence that a problem exists, and that the solution works.
- Programmes should be sustainable.
- Evaluations should aim to identify the factors that influence crime reduction and change in the young person.

is normal for us' (Harris, 2002: 28). James fought the Nuer as a child soldier but as an almost teenage athlete at the Twic Olympics he races with them and against them while commenting that there is now peace between the Dinka and the Nuer (Harris, 2002: 31).

Oil is the reason why tribes such as the Nuer have become displaced in Sudan. It is perhaps the last thing that South Sudan needed because oil in the south means that the north will not let go of the south while there are riches to be wrestled from the ground. Implicit in the conflict are the multinational energy companies such as Canada's Tailsman Energy, Malaysia's Petronas and Sweden's Lundin Oil, and there is little that local people, even rebels, can do to get in the way of the oil companies. The oil violence that is at the heart of the troubles takes place despite the fact that before any oil can be exploited there has to be peace, but in Sudan there are worse atrocities than the oil wars and the thousands of child soldiers. Each dry season, columns of horsemen made up of the nomadic Arab tribes burn villages, kill the men and take women and children back north as slaves. Mowien Akway, a slave whose 15 years of life include 4 spent captive in the north, was branded with a hot iron across his legs with his crime being to complain of long days spent herding his master's cattle. He played volleyball in the Twic Olympics alongside Aguek Athie, who was taken from her home by mounted raiders and would not speak of the suffering she had received at the hands of her Arab master (Harris, 2002: 31). At the end of these Twic Olympic Games, the district with the most medals will be declared the winner, with the prize being a mechanised flour grinding mill. In a country with few roads or even brick buildings, or little of that which is deemed the norm by other standards and values, this is worth competing for.

For nations used to the extravagance of the modern Olympic Games or even the £8.8 million investment in sporting initiatives to help reduce crime in the UK, the Twic Olympics offer a surreal parallel. At the opening ceremony, each district had a flag bearer at its head, carrying a home-made banner with stars, or leopards or bulls crayoned on. Behind them marched the athletes and an effort was made to keep colours uniform within each district. Few in Sudan can afford to choose their clothes with care, none of the athletes wore shoes, and yet the significance was not the dress of the athletes but that it was taking place at all. It is also a reminder that living in an international or even globalised world means being aware of the pain, misery and suffering of countless people whom we will never meet through sport or otherwise. It raises a relative perspective upon questions of both crime and violence. In a world of global dependencies with no corresponding global polity and few tools of global justice, the rich are free to pursue their own interests while paying little attention to the rest – is this not a crime or violence of another order?

It is rare to encounter anyone in the former South Sudan who has not experienced war. The Sudanese civil conflict lasted 22 years and formally ended in 2005. In July 2010, the Republic of South Sudan become a reality with the split from the rest of Sudan and, therefore, the questions, possibilities and options for peace, development and freedom, rather than civil war, violence and conflict, provide for a different future for both North Sudan and South Sudan. Tensions will still exist over resources but the place of sport in nation building, development and peace may provide for a more optimistic future than the role of sport in between periods of conflict. The recognition given to new countries through sport will be explored further in Part 4.

RISK AND SEXUAL VIOLENCE IN SPORT AND SOCIETY

The question still remains as to whether or not a society at risk or a risk society is really as bad as many commentators might suggest. While the spectre of risk increasingly hangs over us in terms of environmental disasters, Blackshaw and Crabbe (2004: 54) remind us that it is the secure, monotonous, repetitive character of the contemporary condition that contributes to individuals engaging with risk. They draw upon Midol and Broyer (1995) to note that it is partly a vision of risk society that influences the take-up of a variety of extreme or whiz sports; Pilz (1996) to suggest that it is the sense of unself-conscious adventure that can help make sense of forms of German football hooliganism; and Rojek (1995) to illuminate that experiences at the edge of leisure are related to testing our limits in order to experience intense moments of pleasure and excitement. Most emphatically, Blackshaw and Crabbe (2004: 55) endorse an adapted working of Rojek's idea of abnormal leisure to suggest that such activities are always likely to occur in societies that set moral limits on what is and is not acceptable normal behaviour.

Debates about the emergence of a risk society also highlight a set of concerns pertinent to the individual at the beginning of the twenty-first century. Just as thinking socially about societies is a reflexive activity, the relationship between risk and identity also involves personal, individual reflexivity. These modern dynamics of identity have helped Cole (2002: 445) make sense of what she refers to as embodied deviance and sport. The body plays a normative/non-normative role in forging identity through developing normal/abnormal bodies that conjure up images of controversial sporting bodies – corrupt, criminal, cyborg, grotesque, hybrid, monstrous, subversive and violent body images, all of which represent forms of identity through sport and a perceived level of risk for the individual. In the contemporary world, argues Giddens (2001), individuals tread a tightrope between risk and opportunity. Individuals are obliged to choose between a vast array of lifestyle choices to the extent that everyday life amounts to an amalgamation of calculated risks. Risk opens up the individual to uncertainty while simultaneously serving the needs of increasingly individualistic cultures and identities. It forces him or her to live an uncertain life because there are so many choices.

While individualisation may appear to be liberating on the surface, it potentially undermines the ontological well-being of the individual. The individual is less and less certain about whether his or her actions are appropriate. He or she is more likely to feel that the world is quite literally spiralling out of control. The march towards global sports consumption may have liberated individuals from the constraints of sport and the local community but, at the same time, traditional forms of protection and support have also been lost as the shift towards global sport has created new political priorities. The violent litigation culture of contemporary professional sport may have contributed to the sense of risk in sport in society also being a paranoid society in which the perception of risk is either real or has grown out of all proportion. In December 2004, the Manchester United and England forward Wayne Rooney was served a three-match suspension after admitting a charge of violent conduct in a match against Bolton Wanderers. Commenting on the incident and changes in the game of professional football, the then Manchester United captain Roy Keane added that:

> a lot of players seem to be getting players booked or sent off . . . There are a lot of cases where players are reacting and trying to get fellow professionals into trouble. It's disgraceful – it needs to stop. Lots of stuff goes on in a game and if you went down every time a player touched you, every player would be down. They are trying to con the referee, con their fellow players and con the crowd.
>
> (*The Herald*, 31 December 2004: 36)

What Keane was actually alluding to was that the objective level of the risk of being sent off and being punished for violent conduct has changed and that the individual antics of players have meant that the perception of the risks associated with violent conduct has grown out of all proportion.

316

Sociologists have portrayed children and/or young people as being at the forefront of both new and old forms of risk and violence. Young people are facing a greater diversity of risks and opportunities than ever before. Traditional family, work, school and sporting environments are more unpredictable and less secure and the journeys into adulthood are for some becoming increasingly precarious. Moreover, because there is a much greater range of pathways to choose from, children may develop the impression that their own route is unique and that the risks they face have to be overcome as individuals rather than members of a collectivity. In concrete terms, Hari (2002: 24) reminds us that poverty is plainly a factor in the formation of what have become labelled 'feral children', the right-wing term referring to some of the most disadvantaged kids in Britain who have been raised without family support in urban inner-city housing estates. Hari (2002: 25) reports, 'It's not like these kids want much, they only ever have one pair of trainers, not five but it is not unreasonable for them to want one pair'. For poor kids in Britain's inner cities, many areas are desolate, shrinking amounts of public space, no leisure centres and children who might once have played in parks, fields or even streets now have nowhere to go.

Ironically, some of the most appealing avenues of escape in certain circumstances are risky forms of behaviour such as drug taking, alcohol consumption, exercise addiction and sports consumption, which simply serve to accentuate the risky and unpredictable nature of youth lifestyles in a changing world. We should not to forget that children are also threatened by the uncertainties of a risk society. Are children today more at risk of sexual abuse and violence in a sports context than in other settings, such as home or school? The author of one of the most comprehensive studies of sexual abuse in sport believes that we know too little to draw any conclusions (Brackenridge, 2001). So far, only one study, in Norway, has compared the prevalence of sexual harassment in and outside the context of sport. The initial results reveal that twice as many athletes as non-athletes have experienced sexual harassment from authority figures (Council of Europe, 2000: 6). Many experts believe that sexual harassment, abuse and violence in sports are widely under-reported. They do not trust the system or society to respect their right to confidentiality and appear to become resigned to frequent acts of verbal and physical harassment in the strongly male-dominated world of sport. In 1998, studies in both Canada and Norway revealed that athletes experience a negative and uncomfortable environment ranging from mild sexual harassment to abuse (David, 2005: 94).

Issues of sex discrimination, sexual harassment and sexual abuse in sport bring into question both the nature of sport within a risk society, but also the very definition of violence that operates within sport, culture and society. Brackenridge (2002: 257) questions any narrow definition of violence in sport from the point of view that one of the most important aspects of power in sport is the power to name or resist definitions made by those in power. With reference to sexual exploitation of children and women, both within and beyond sport, Brackenridge (2002: 257) notes that the power of men to define what does and does not count as violence often leads to narrow definitions that benefit men. Defining sexual violence purely in physical terms ignores the institutional forms of violence in sport against women, such as the violence of discrimination that is involved in pay, resources, career provision,

317

safety, neglect, deprivation, insensitivity and oppression that, asserts Brackenridge (2002: 257), face many women on a day-to-day, week-by-week basis. The solution is simply to define violence as that which violates and consequently allows the issue of violence in sport to be viewed in systemic terms rather than inter-personal terms. Brackenridge is right to question the notion of violence that has tended to operate in sport, and her critique is a progressive and valuable step forward. Any evaluation of this and other research has also to note that paying exclusive attention to coaches and abused sportsmen and sportswomen tends to overlook other groups, including 'experts' who are charged with identifying and protecting young people and/or children and others at risk in sport and society.

London 2012 Olympic crackdown, risk and sex workers

At the same time, the hosting of major sporting events is often associated with clean-up campaigns in local areas. The hosting of the 2012 Olympics in London is no different in this respect. As part of a coordinated clean up campaign ahead of the London 2012 Olympics, Scotland Yard has been targeting brothels in the London boroughs that are expected to play host to the majority of visitors who come to the city to watch the Olympic Games. Figures released to parliament by the Home Office show that 80 brothel raids were carried out between January and August 2010 in the main Olympic boroughs, compared with 29 raids in other parts of London. Similair vice crackdowns and clean-up campaigns have taken place in other countries hosting major sporting events. The London initiative comes among claims that an increased number of sex workers will try to work in the capital during the Olympics. According to the English Collective of Prostitutes, no increase in trafficking of women during major sporting events takes place (*Observer*, 10 April 2011: 19). This point is supported by the London Metropolitan Police, who argue that they have not seen, as yet, any increase in trafficking of sex workers in the five Olympic boroughs. Critics argue that attempts to remove sex workers from the Olympic boroughs will drive trade underground and that prohibition increases risk to women but also distorts the laws of supply and demand. Policy intiatives, it is suggested, should address real problems such as housing, health and safety, and not be based on flawed ideology that distorts the market and endangers the women (*Observer*, 10 April 2011: 19).

The social theory or notion of a risk society may not provide all the answers in helping students, teachers and researchers thinking about risk, violence and sport but what it does do is provide a useful framework or intervention within which you can come to your own conclusion about the nature of the problems and the solutions in the area of sport, violence and crime. If we were to try to prevent all undesirable consequences, the danger might be inactivity due to the nature of the task, however in a society of risks the issues derive not so much from what each person does in isolation but from the very fact that because they often perceive a state of isolation the actions are often uncoordinated and dispersed. If global sport is framed as a risk and if global sporting processes are taken to be a set of processes that nobody controls, then this should not be viewed as a reason for inaction simply because such forces are deemed to be overwhelming. The answer to the magnitude of the challenge of social change is not one of denial.

STATES OF DENIAL IN WORLD SPORT

Imagine for a moment a nice thirty-something couple, interested in sport or fitness or exercise, having just finished a work-out or run and sitting with their coffee and newspaper in New York, London, Paris, Milan, Toronto, or some other epicentre of Western sport. They pick up the sports section of the newspaper and read about: child jockeys being sold into slavery as camel racers; the hundreds of refugees who participated in the Twic Olympic Games in southern Sudan; the street cleansing and removal of people from public spaces that accompanies certain visits of the International Olympic Committee to cities aspiring to host the Olympic Games; the World Cup qualifying game of football that was interrupted because of claims of witchcraft; the illegal trafficking of young football, baseball and ice hockey players across the frontiers of world sport; the sexual violence in sport mentioned in the previous section of this chapter; and/or the opportunities for any sporting life or involvement denied the official number of 15 million AIDS orphans worldwide or the 500 million children who have no access to sanitation facilities or those children who have accounted for 50 per cent of those killed in war between 1990 and 2003 (*The Herald*, 10 December 2004).

To pick but one specific example – the case of Kailu, the Indian boy sold into labour at the age of 14. At his age, other boys might dream of playing cricket or hockey for their country or of playing sport with friends at school and at home but these are areas of life, even dreams, that Kailu does not have access too. Kailu was among 200 boys from one village sold on to landlords to work in sugar, cane and rice fields. The transfer fee for Kailu was 1,200 rupees. He gets up at 7, carries out a 12-hour shift in the field, followed by housework before going to bed at midnight, and then doing the same the next day (*Herald Magazine*, 11 December 2004: 5). What does this news do to our thirty-something sportsmen and sportswomen in New York, London, Paris, Milan or Toronto? What goes through their minds, and does this register as part of the experience or lack of access to world sport today or the response to the uncomfortable personal and political realities of world sport one of denial and evasion by individuals and states? Are these and other states of denial in world sport not also part of the reality of sport, violence and crime in the twenty-first century?

At least one common thread runs through these and many other stories of denial in world sport. People, sports organisations, governments and even societies are often presented with information that is too disturbing, threatening or anomalous to be fully absorbed or acknowledged. The information is, therefore, somehow repressed, disavowed, pushed aside or reinterpreted. Blocking out, turning a blind eye, shutting off, not wanting to know, seeing what we want to see – these are all expressions of denial. At times, denial may appear to be wholly an individual matter, but many forms of denial are public, collective and highly organised. The denial of certain matters of sport in society is often officially subtle – putting a gloss on the truth, setting the public sports agenda, spin-doctoring, leaks to the sports press and media, selecting victims for verbal abuse. Many classic sporting examples exist, none more typical than those fearful words that 'the board is behind the manager' or 'the player is not for sale' or 'no deal has been done behind closed doors'.

Cultural and social denials such as those in sport are neither wholly private nor officially organised by the state, since whole societies may slip into modes of denial independent of the authorities that are the official world of sport, the organisations, the clubs, the ministries and individuals. People, at times, tend to believe information that they know is false or fake in order to express their allegiance to sports slogans and ceremonies and rituals in the name of loyalty, identity, and other structures such as class, nation and religion. When sport denies something is it a conscious or unconscious defence mechanism to protect it from some unwelcome truths? Despite evidence to the contrary, many clubs for decades continued to deny that racism in sport was a problem in Britain – despite the physical and verbal abuse of players, and the lack of a non-white presence in positions of authority in British sport. Can there be cultures of denial in sport and how do organisations such as the United Nations, the Council of Europe, the World Health Organization or the International Olympic Committee try to overcome public indifference in certain countries towards violence in sport, to violations of children's rights and to criminality in the field of sport? The continued need for transparency and accountability in world sport, the greater scrutiny of public figures and the regular exposure of their private lives could no doubt lead to a corrosive cynicism about prospects for change in countries where athletes are bought and sold and where agents and middle men stop monies going to where they are needed. At the very least, it could create a reflex suspicion of official denials with regards to sports, violence and crime.

SUMMARY

The problem of violence in sport and how to lessen or prevent it is perhaps one of the most difficult questions to answer within the area of sport, culture and society. Clashes of viewpoints are often about how we should relate to basic dilemmas and problems. In this sense, the study of sport, violence and crime is no different from many other areas covered within this book. The chapter has kept the notion of violence as wide open as possible in order to emphasise that the study of sport, violence and crime is not just limited to the phenomenon of crowd violence and player violence. It would be a mistake to regard this area of investigation in such narrow terms and as such this chapter has drawn upon the themes of deviance, crime and sport, risk and sexual violence in sport and states of denial in world sport. All of these themes raise issues pertinent to sport and life. Sport is no different to other areas of society in that statements of denial emerge rapidly when the personal and political ways in which many of the uncomfortable realities of sport are evaded by both individuals and states.

The literature on sport, violence and crime is often written as if it is irrelevant to the fact that the free market of sport under capitalism accentuates violence and denial, in the sense that vast swathes of the world's populations are excluded from sport and are viewed as being marginal and superfluous to the real entertainment for the more affluent sectors, countries and regions. The exclusion and segregation of enclaves of losers and redundant sports populations separated from enclaves of winners, health enthusiasts and spectators in their guarded gyms, gated sports stadiums and modern sports villages is in itself a form of violence. The success stories are viewed as the real Olympics and not the Twic Olympics, and yet these two very different outlets for sport are both part of the world of sport.

Furthermore, cultural denials are neither wholly private nor officially organised by global sporting organisations, states or powerful individuals. The social and cultural denials that accompany the façade of drugs in sport, sexual violence, racism and child labour are all areas of investigation that should not be excluded from the coverage of sport, violence and crime in the contemporary world. There is a very real danger of failing to recognise that that which violates is not simply limited to violence for private gain (crime), or violence between states and non-state actors (war, repression, terrorism), cultural and/or personal violence, but all forms of violence. All of this can be acknowledged by the student of sport, culture and society without turning a blind eye to the very positive part played by sport in areas of the world suffering from atrocities of human violence, material greed and forms of conflict.

GUIDE TO FURTHER READING

Blackshaw, T. and Crabbe, T. (2004). *New Perspectives on Sport and Deviance: Consumption, Performativity and Social Control*. London: Routledge.

Bodin, D., Robene, D. and Heas, S. (2005). *Sport and Violence in Europe*. Strasbourg: Council of Europe.

Campsie, A. (2011). 'Terrorists, Thugs and Cowards'. *The Herald,* 22 April: 1.

Coalter, F. (2007). *Sport a Wider Social Role: Who is Keeping the Score*. London: Routledge.

David, P. (2005). *Human Rights in Youth Sport: A Critical Review of Children's Rights in Youth Sport*. London: Routledge.

Doward, J. (2011). 'Sex Workers Put at Risk by Olympics Crackdown'. *Observer,* 10 April: 19.

James, M. and McArdle, D. (2004). 'Player Violence or Violent Players? Vicarious Liability for Sports Participants'. *Tort Law Review*, 131 (12): 131–146.

Ray, L. (2011). *Violence and Society*. London: Sage.

Van Ingen, C. (2011). 'Spatialities of Anger: Emotional Geographies in a Boxing Program for Survivors of Violence'. *Sociology of Sport Journal*, 28 (2): 171–188.

Watt, C. (2010). 'Women Boxers Land a Knockout Blow to Sport's Chauvinists' *The Herald,* 22 October: 3.

QUESTIONS

1 Describe and critique the definition of violence provided by the World Health Organization as it might apply in the area of sport, culture and society.

2 Comment upon the role of sport in the area of crime prevention.

3 Explain what is meant by the notion of a risk society and the place of sport within it.

4 Outline and critically comment upon the correlates of gender violence and abuse based on cross-cultural studies, applied to sport as outlined in Brackenridge (2001: 146).

5 How might the notion of denial be used to investigate aspects of world sport today?

6 While individualisation may appear to be liberating on the surface, it potentially undermines the ontological well-being of the individual. Explain this statement.

7   Provide six of the commonly referred to arguments surrounding sports-based interventions aimed at ameliorating or helping crime reduction.

8   Capitalism itself brings its own forms of violence through sport. What is meant by this statement?

9   What have some of the studies into sport and sexual harrassment uncovered?

10 Read Coalter's (2007) account of the relationship between sport and crime, and discuss the importance of evidence.

PRACTICAL PROJECTS

1   Outline five different policies in which sport is clearly used as an instrument of social control.

2   Compile a report of about 2,500 words on sport and violence in a country of your choice based upon investigating a national newspaper over a five-year period.

3   Use the Internet to find out information about the Twic Olympics and other sports competitions in different parts of the world that are aimed at helping countries affected by violence or even war.

4   Visit the websites of the World Health Organization, the United Nations and the Council of Europe, and write a report on the official positions taken by these organisations on both violence in sport and children's rights as far as they apply to sport, exercise and physical activity.

5   Visit www.harassmentinsport.com, which is sponsored by Sport Canada and provides information and links to other sites on sexual harassment in sport. Develop a 10-point non-tolerance policy statement aimed at curbing sexual harassment in a sport of your choice.

KEY CONCEPTS

Abuse ■ Anti-slavery campaigns ■ Compassion ■ Crowd violence ■ Denial ■ Deprivation ■ Identity ■ Media sports violence ■ Normative values ■ Power ■ Racial violence ■ Risk ■ Risk society ■ Sexual harassment ■ Sexual violence ■ Tolerance

WEBSITES

Rocks Twilight Basketball
www.scottishrocks.co.uk
Looks at the impact of the Shell Twilight Basketball programme.

Sports, culture and the Scottish Executive

www.scotland.gov.uk/crukd01/blue/rsrdua-00.htm

The Scottish government website, which looks at sport, culture and the arts and their role in various social policies.

Twic Olympics play for the prize of peace

www.dadalos.org/frieden_int/grundkurs_5/twic_olympics.htm

The impact and background to a sports initiative aimed at supporting children affected in a war zone in 2009.

ESRC Research on 2012 Olympics – Early Impact

www.esrc.ac.uk/impacts-and-findings/features-casestudies/features/15278/Early_impacts_for_London_2012_Games_.aspx

The early impact of the 2012 Olympics on a range of social and economic indicators.

Chapter 14

Sport, religion and spirituality

The Maccabi Games remain one of the few Jewish international sports festivals. They are associated with the Maccabi Movement and date back to 1895.

What is the relationship between sport, religion and spirituality today?

PREVIEW

Key terms defined ■ Introduction ■ Sport and faith ■ Religion, sport and culture ■ Faith invaders, religion and liberal humanism ■ The Maccabi Games ■ Fundamentalism ■ The promise keepers ■ Muslim fundamentalism, the war against feminism and physical activity ■ Sport and fasting ■ Sport as a civil religion, worship and capitalism ■ Sport as the quest for spirituality ■ Better faith, better ethics, better sport? ■ Summary

OBJECTIVES

This chapter will:

■ highlight the relationship between sport, religion and spirituality;
■ provide examples of single faith orientated sports organisations;
■ critically evaluate the dangers of fundamentalist approaches to religion and sport;
■ examine the relationship between Islam, gender and physical activity; and
■ question the notion of better faith, better ethics and better sport.

KEY TERMS DEFINED

Faith: Confident belief in the truth, value or trustworthiness of a person, idea or thing.

Fundamentalism: Strict adherence to a specific set of theological doctrines, typically in reaction against the theology of modernism.

Religion: The Latin *religonem* refers to respect or care for what is sacred; often refers to systems of belief or rituals focused upon ethics, a divine order and afterlife.

Secular: Not related to religion or spirituality.

Sectarianism: A system of attitudes, actions, beliefs and structures, at personal, communal and institutional levels, which always involves religion, and typically involves a negative mixing of religion and politics.

Spirituality: The practice and outworking of the spirit and the different ways in which this may be developed. Spirituality is relation- and action-centred, and about making connections with different aspects of life.

INTRODUCTION

An article in a 2010 edition of *Scotland on Sunday* carried the heading 'Baptised Lemoncello has faith in himself to deliver' (Woods, 2010: 25). The story went on to explain how an athlete in preparation for the London Marathon had around the same time been baptised as Catholic after a period of study and reflection. The athlete went on to explain that, while there were other reasons for him becoming a Catholic, the new faith had acted as a performance enhancer. He noted:

> It's strengthened me – there are a lot of times when I am out on the road and I can go for a while just drifting away because I am saying a prayer or something. There is a strength that I had never used before.
>
> (Woods, 2010: 25)

325

This is but one example of how an athlete has used a faith to enhance performance. The late Pope John Paul II, in addressing Olympic Committees, championed the role of sport as a vehicle that *contributed* to the harmonious and completed development of body and soul. Watson and White (2007: 62) point out the Vatican established an office for church and sport in the belief that sport could be an instrument of peace among people.

Scholars of religion are often sceptical of efforts to define religion. It is often referred to in terms of rituals, beliefs and ways of life orientated towards an existence or experience different from the realms of ordinary life. Religions often carry metaphysical ideas about the meaning of life, the secular versus the sacred and/or the familiar versus the unfamiliar. Ideals of freedom and equality often contain categories of religion. For many Europeans, a belief in God may have given way to beliefs about democracy, law and human rights. Freedom of religion is rightly considered to be a basic liberty but there is nothing special about religion at the level of fundamental political principle. Understanding the scale and theory of religions is certainly complex. In the 50 countries and territories with an Islamic majority, there are roughly 1.3 billion Muslims – a fifth of the world's population – and yet only recently has this impacted upon studies about sport, culture and society. There is a need for comparative studies of sport, religion and spirituality.

Religion has had a significant historical presence in sport. Sport in Focus 14.1 looks at some of the key arguments about religion that have appeared in research studies about sport, culture and society. It is not an exhaustive list, but the literature suggests that religion and sport have rarely been indifferent to one another. Certain fundamental beliefs have come to form part of the juridical religious dogma that sustains several institutional structures in the West. Sport is not immune from the effects of these. The problem here is not particularly new but is posed today with particular urgency. Sport is far from secular but the issue is, in part, whether doctrinal systems are impenetrable and therefore reduced to either condemning each other or, in the case of fundamentalism, potentially doing battle with one another. The catalogue of atrocities committed in the name of religion shows how dangerous all forms of dogma may be. The relationship between sport and religion is far from innocent.

The clashes between sport and sabbatarianism are not merely early twentieth- or nineteenth-century phenomena. The orthodox history of the relationship between sport and religion has been reproduced in numerous accounts of the connection between amateurism, class, colonialism and religion through the advent of the muscular Christian (Searle, 1987; Parry *et al.*, 2007). Perhaps too much has been made of the moral power of this ideology, exercised through the connections and power of a networked society and closely associated with the British public school system. Too many have uncritically accepted the orthodox story of the development of muscular Christianity emanating from the athletic missionaries of the British, not simply English, public schools. What is often overlooked in these accounts of muscular Christianity is not only its *contemporaneous* meaning for some athletes, such as Jonathan Edwards, the 2000 Olympic triple jump champion, but also that, like all forms of religion, amateurism itself was/is a social system (Allison, 2001). A social system that reproduced power relations, colonialism and sexism. Like all -isms, amateurism as a social practice consisted of sets beliefs and rituals that were supported by social institutions. For the muscular Christian who adhered to amateurism, the attitude towards money and

SPORT IN FOCUS 14.1: KEY ARGUMENTS ABOUT RELIGION IN SPORT, CULTURE AND SOCIETY

- Rates of change in various historical periods with a view to commenting upon whether sport has become more or less secular or religious.

- The relationship between early puritanism and folk games.

- The religious symbolism of sporting festivals and events, most notably the Olympic Games.

- The specific religious identity and stereotypes associated with particular sports teams.

- Muscular Christianity, amateur sport and social class.

- The relationship between body, spirit and mind in the practice of sumo.

- The relationship between a particular sport, particular country and particular faith, such as rugby in Afrikaner South Africa and the Dutch Reformed Church or gymnastics, Catholicism and France.

- The relationship between sport, religion and capitalism.

- The relationship between gender, physical activity and Islam.

- The relationship between religion, health and well-being.

economic reward was viewed as being secondary to other more important aspects of human life (Allison, 2001). The poor across a range of colonised countries were invariably left to live on forms of metaphysical income rather than materially sustainable livelihoods.

FAITH INVADERS, RELIGION AND LIBERAL HUMANISM

In August 2004, on the beaches around the north-western tip of a small Scottish island, could be found Nicola Breciani and Francesco Palatella, professional surfers from Italy, who have dedicated their lives to finding the perfect wave; a quest that had taken them from California, to Costa Rica, Australia, Bali, South Africa, Burma and Scotland. This is one of 'the top places in Europe', raves Palatella, but he is unaware of the controversy that surrounded them about surfing on a Sunday (Martin, 2004: 13). 'Lewis hands surfers never on Sunday warning' was how Martin (2004: 13) introduced her feature story in a leading national newspaper, the *Observer*. The article explained the tension between the quest to increase tourism and income generation and the longstanding tradition of Sunday being a day of worship, rest and reflection. The Rev Iver Martin of the Stornoway Free Church of Scotland, commenting upon the issue of surfing on Sunday pointed out 'that the Sabbath is very special here and we have to fight to keep it sacred' (Martin, 2004: 13). The Rev Martin was referring to plans by a local businessman to host an international surfing competition and festival on the Island of Lewis. The local Western Isles Council had earlier voted unanimously against opening a multi-million pound sports hall on the Sabbath, while a paintball company twice had its application for a Sunday licence refused. Some seven years later, the same Rev Martin, in 2011, attacked the way in which human rights law was being used to undermine the Sabbath (Wade, 2011). He contends that the legislation was designed to stop discrimination against minority faiths and yet, on the Island of Lewis, where the religious community has long held sway, the human rights law could rob an indigenous population of its distinctiveness (Wade, 2011: 4). Logic and the law suggest that, in time, the question may be resolved in favour of seven-day golf or surfing, but the sabbatarian answer as it currently stands is that golf clubs and leisure centres are not unique to island life and that Sunday on the Island of Lewis remains special.

The notion of the sacred Sabbath, as illustrated above, has impacted upon sport in other ways, most notably when sportsmen or sportswomen have been asked to put sport before the Sabbath and have refused to do so. In February 2010, the devoutly Christian Scottish forward, Euan Murray, returned to play for Scotland in a rugby international against Wales. It was the strength of his faith rather than his body that had ruled him out of the opening international match against France because it was due to be played on a Sunday. The issue of sport on Sunday in Scotland has had a long history. By July 1982, David Putnam's film classic *Chariots of Fire* had amassed £49.4 million, making it, at the time, the biggest money-making foreign film in US box office history. The narrative in the film was built around Eric Liddell, the Scottish athlete, later to become a missionary in China, who was picked to run in the 100 yards at the 1924 Paris Olympic Games but refused to run because the final was scheduled for a Sunday. Liddell is introduced in the film as an establishment Scottish rugby international who turns to running as a form of secular preaching. The conflicts in the film between amateurism, idealism, realism, god and nation, sport and social class are crucial to the narrative. Liddell's metaphysical, evangelical running qualities are a core theme through-out the film. Liddell's faith was deep-rooted within a Scottish evangelical fundamentalist tradition. The core of this faith was a burning conviction in personal salvation through the merits of Jesus. To bring men and women to this spiritual climax was one of the ultimate aims of the Scottish evangelicals. The evangelical fundamentalists shared many similarities with the Scottish covenanters; both were fervent, both were puritanical and both in their heyday were anxious to see their ideals adopted by the rest of society. The story presented in *Chariots of Fire* transforms Liddell's evangelical ideology into a metaphorical statement about the ultimate possibilities that could be achieved through sport. The framing of this story about the athlete tended to depoliticise the role of the evangelicals within Scottish society but also framed the notion of freedom within a religious frame of reference.

Puritanical yet wealthy, convinced of their God-given mission to the rest of the world, Saudi Arabia and the US are surprisingly similar in terms of religion, politics and interference in other countries' affairs. Saudi Arabia, in part, is wedded to Wahhabi Islam, while a large section of Middle America is devoted to evangelical Christianity. Historically, they are at odds with one another; both see themselves as exponents of the purest version of their faith, are suspicious of modernity and see no distinction between politics and religion. Both of these spiritual empires have been invading Britain since the late twentieth century. Increasingly, foreign-financed and foreign-inspired religious conservatives have been recruiting volunteers, establishing schools, and setting up publishing houses, think tanks, places of worship and cultural outlets.

A single-faith, Saudi-funded Wahhabi-influenced curriculum has been at the heart of the King Fahd Academy set up in London for 600 primary and secondary school children. Christian evangelical training is at the heart of new theologies such as the Alpha Course, a 10-point plan to salvation that has been heavily supported by middle-class fundamentalist groups. It is perhaps time that the secular establishment accepted that religion now identifies many people in the way that other forms of social division have done in the past. Single-faith organisations have used sport in a number of ways, notably to: (i) promote spiritual growth, (ii) recruit new members and (iii) promote religious beliefs and organisations. Yet, at the heart of these doctrines are certain problematic concerns. Often a strict adherence to absolute interpretations of sacred texts promotes certain forms of behaviour; for example, no drugs, no sex outside of marriage, male superiority over women and a profound conviction that the wider society is living in sin.

The Maccabi Games remains the only exclusively Jewish international sports festival. The games are the largest Jewish teen event in the world, with 6,000 Jewish teenagers between the ages of 13 and 16 participating each summer. The games are sponsored by the Jewish Community Centre Association of North America, the Maccabi World Union, Maccabi Canada and Maccabi USA. The Maccabi Movement began in 1895, with the first games proposed in 1929 and held in 1932. Sport has been one of the many institutions that have sought to conserve religious traditions and ethnic culture, as well as communicate important lessons about Judaism and society. The first American Maccabi Games were held in 1982. Sporting activities held a considerable place within the lives of numerous Jewish women and girls at local, national and international levels. Borish (2002: 90), in particular, points out that Jewish women's participation in American sport was contoured by their gender and ethnic roles in American society and, therefore, sport helped in the construction of what it meant to be a Jewish American woman.

The increasingly common use of sport being caught up with forms of religious identity fails to fully understand the social complexity of the relationship between, faith, religion and liberal humanism. The simplistic affiliation between a sports team, identity of a sports fan and religion often fails to distinguish whether it is a person's main affiliation or loyalty, or just one point of an identity among a group of various reference points. If being a follower of Christianity, Islam, Judaism, Shintu or Hinduism is the only form of primary or personal faith a person has then such religious identification would carry a burden of having to resolve the many choices a person faces in other parts of their lives. Individuals can take up different positions on matters involving social, political, moral or other judgments without ceasing to be a Christian or Muslim. The US, Turkey and India all have secular constitutions but these have the common aim of protecting religion. By not permitting the establishment of any particular faith, secularism seeks to ensure that the state cannot be used as an instrument to persecute minority religions and that no religion can be imposed by law on an unwilling populace. At the same time, too fundamental a view of the relationship between sport and

329

religion fails to recognise that varying attitudes to religious tolerance have been socially important in the history of the world. The basic recognition of a multiplicity of identities would militate against seeing certain sports teams or fans in exclusively religious or sectarian terms.

Fundamentalism

The Promise Keepers, according to Randels and Beal (2002), are a Protestant Christian evangelical group that act as a social movement through religion. In this sense, they are similar to a range of other groups such as the Freemasons, the Knights of St Columba, the Young Women's Hebrew Association and the Young Men's Christian Association. In other senses, they are different. The Promise Keepers do not simply invoke sport in the name of Christianity but as a partial solution to what Randels and Beal (2002) refer to as the crisis of masculinity. By this, it is implied that success in sport might help to define certain aspects of masculinity and religion. They acknowledge that patriarchy is reproduced not just through athletics, but through other fields including politics, business and religion. The Promise Keepers as a movement seeks recognition through a blend of sport, masculinity and religiosity. The Promise Keepers, it is argued, endeavour to enable men to become more Christ-like and masculine (Randels and Beal, 2002: 163). The Promise Keepers reject secularism, use sporting symbols to reach a broader audience and promote an overt relationship between religion and sport. The boundary maintenance offered in promoting such forms of religious and gender exclusivity through sport requires forms of surveillance and soft policing.

The extent to which the Promise Keepers also promote conservative fundamentalist beliefs through sport may be brought into question when tested against a number of political beliefs held by other fundamentalist groups such as pro-life, pro-family and pro-American expansion. Many fundamentalist Christian groups have embraced sport as a mechanism for reducing their separation and exclusion from society while increasing their legitimacy and power within it. Fundamentalists in all religions tend to emphasise a need to return to basic, moral religious roots and develop a personal relationship with God, Allah, Christ, Mohammad, or the Other, whoever that may be. The fundamentalist view is the absolute view that allegedly offers clear-cut answers to personal and social problems. The key point, however, is to recognise that, in the quest for seeking legitimacy and exclusivity, all forms of fundamentalism promote forms of reification and separatism. By shielding internal tensions, a fundamentalist approach to sport would repress forms of communitarianism, and promote conformism, intolerance and patriarchy.

A qualifying comment needs to be made in relation to the liberal humanist claim that religion can be eradicated from human life. This remains an article of faith for many secular humanist groups, and yet it should not be forgotten that (i) at best, liberal humanism itself may have been rooted in nineteenth-century Christian denominations such as the Quakers or the Unitarians and (ii) at worst, in its extreme form liberal humanism itself is often viewed as religion-like in terms of its adherence to particular views about humanity, politics and religion. According to Gray (2002b: 69), liberal humanism is an absolute form of religious doctrine. Gray argues that the secular view that we live in a post-religious era is a Christian, if not Western, invention. Liberal humanism, in other words, is framed as a form of religious humanity forged in a period before the work of John Stuart Mill (1806–1873) and whose intervention, lest we forget, upheld the abolition of slavery. Today's liberal humanism could be viewed as a contemporary version of an eccentric nineteenth-century cult that is clearly modelled on Christianity, despite the secular claims that are made. Yet, the Christian principle of individual liberty contrasts with and is often at conflict with other faiths.

MUSLIM FUNDAMENTALISM, THE WAR AGAINST FEMINISM AND PHYSICAL ACTIVITY

Many of the traditional early sociological thinkers believed that a process of secularisation was bound to occur as societies modernised and became more reliant upon technology and science. In this sense, secularisation was utilised as a comparative concept that described the processes whereby religion lost its influence over various aspects of the social world. By contrast, the notion of fundamentalism is used to describe a strict adherence to a set of principles or beliefs and, within this context, religious fundamentalism describes the approach taken by different religious groups who adhere to a strict interpretation of various religious doctrines, texts, and/or scriptures. The strength of religious fundamentalism is often viewed as an indication that secularisation has not triumphed in the modern world. Religious fundamentalists believe that only one view of the world is possible, and that their view of the world is the correct one.

A number of feminist thinkers have attempted to explain the appeal of fundamentalism in the predominantly Muslim societies of the Middle East, North Africa and Southeast Asia (Afary, 1997; Benn et al., 2011; Fry, 2011). Such studies have generally been divided into at least three groups: those that have (i) stressed the economic and political issues that have given rise to the emergence of fundamentalist movements; (ii) explored the disruptive impact of modernisation on the family; and (iii) argued that militant Islamist movements and organisations have actually empowered students and professional women in certain ways by restricting their lives. Gender relations are not a marginal aspect of such movements because an important facet of the work of many Islamic fundamentalist groups has been the creation of the illusion that a return to traditional patriarchal relations is the answer to the social and economic problems of both Western and non-Western societies (Afary, 1997: 1). The notions of fundamentalism, secularism, traditionalism and modernism are all contested ideas in terms of their continued and precise value to explaining late twentieth- and early twenty-first-century capitalism.

It is clear from the above that the emergence of Muslim beliefs and fundamentalism is a complicated phenomenon. It is only recently that feminist researchers have begun to fuel, question and intensify the stance taken by forms of Muslim fundamentalism in relation to women's physical activity. Walseth and Fasting's (2003) study of Islam's view of physical activity and sport is based upon the interpretations offered by Egyptian women over a four-month period. Studies that have looked at the relationship between Islam and participation in physical activity and sport, they argue, have generally been divided into at least two groups: (i) those that draw upon Islam's positive attitudes towards sport and (ii) those that have focused on women's sports participation in Muslim countries (Walseth and Fasting,

331

2003: 48). What is interesting about the conclusions drawn from this fieldwork is the common opinion that, contained within Islam, was a positive attitude towards participation in sport and physical activity that could be interpreted as a way of pleasing God – a finding that challenges the secular interpretation of the nature of sports participation in certain parts of the world and warns against too much of a Western interpretation being placed on the relationship between sport and religion. The second conclusion from this study was less positive in that it noted that some of the barriers to women's participation in certain physical activities resulted from a different interpretation of Islam in relation to the body, dress, religion, sexuality and the locus of power in society (Walseth and Fasting, 2003: 57).

It has been suggested that certain religious beliefs have curtailed the freedom of expression that women in parts of the world have in comparison to, for example, women in many non-Islamic countries. It has also been recorded that feminist politics is viewed by some religious fundamentalists as a form of fundamentalism which is in part why some traditionalist Islamic fundamentalist groups have waged war on feminism. Afary (1997: 15) contends that for feminist politics to be more effective in this area it must work in conjunction with other grassroots movements in order to mainstream an emancipatory rather than a reactionary feminist agenda as a basis for undermining traditional Islamic fundamentalism. Certainly, progressive alliances might help to produce a more reality-congruent view of the relationship between sport and religion in the twenty-first century. Research into Islam and physical activity needs to become more mainstream to the debate about sport and religion today. The stories of the struggle for Muslim woman attempting to find God through sport and physical activity are much more religious than the moderate view that sport is a form of civil religion or worship contoured by the developments of contemporary capitalism. Yet, other challenges exist within some forms of Islamic belief in relation to the redistribution of wealth within areas of the world that might not be Muslim, that is, in relation to humanity as a whole.

While a facet of some religions has been to fast on certain days, the issue of fasting has, at times, been used against both male and female athletes who observe the practice of fasting. Sport in Focus 14.2 considers the relationship between training for competition and religious fasting.

SPORT AS CIVIL RELIGION, WORSHIP AND CAPITALISM

Many Major League Baseball clubs and more than 100 minor league teams arrange non-denominational religious services each Sunday morning before the Sunday afternoon game. Approximately 50 per cent of all MLB players attend these sessions of prayer and bible reading. The Fellowship of Christian Athletes and other evangelical sports groups are thriving in certain parts of America. Ministers have become part of the army of support services attached to major sport franchises. The Fellowship of Christian Athletes was founded in 1954; it has doubled in size, according to Nixon and Frey (1996: 69); has a multi-million dollar budget; a staff of more than 100 and a membership in excess of 100,000. Signs with biblical references, note Levinson and Christensen (1996: 317), sprout like mushrooms with fans, coaches and athletes during the post-game prayer sessions. Sport is often uncritically described as a form of civil religion, worship and capitalism without necessarily forging the links between these three social forces.

SPORT IN FOCUS 14.2: FASTING AND SPORT

Can athletes cope with the strain of top-level sporting competition, while at the same time observing religious fasts?

Many high-profile athletes, including English Premier League footballers Nicholas Anelka and Kolo Touré, are known to fast during the Islamic fasting month of Ramadan. During this time, Muslim athletes have to perform without taking fluids or food between sunrise and sunset. The issue of fasting in sport is certain to be a talking point during the 2012 London Olympics, as the event will coincide with the holy fasting month.

Many assume that fasting puts the athletes at a disadvantage compared with competitors of other faiths; the then manager of Inter Milan, Jose Mourinho, made comments to the press to suggest that his midfielder Sulley Muntari was lacking in fitness and energy because he was observing Ramadan.

However, experts are unconvinced that fasting does have a negative impact on an athlete's performance. The small number of well-controlled experiments undertaken in this field suggests that there is a negligible decrease in the physical condition of athletes. These observations echo the experiences of Manchester City defender Kolo Touré: 'It doesn't affect me physically. It makes me stronger. You can do it when you believe so strongly in something. A normal human can be without water for much longer than one day'.

Experts concluded that much more research is required into this subject to further understand the effects of intermittent fasting on sporting performance. Perhaps the 2012 London Olympics will prove to be an interesting study of the issue.

The relationship between religion and sport has been explored in *With God on Their Side: Sport in the Service of Religion* (Magdalinski and Chandler, 2002). The assumptions informing this collection are that sport and religion are both cultural institutions with a global reach, a claim that may be more realistic in relation to Catholicism than sport. The authors go on to suggest that each of these institutions is characterised by the ecstatic devotion of followers and ritualistic performances. The premise upon which the historical and geographical case studies of sport and religion, presented in this book, are based upon is one of international pluralism. Thus, Magdalinski and Chandler (2002: 1–2) assert we have conceived of this volume to investigate the role of sport and religion in the social formation of collective groups and we are specifically concerned with the way in which sport might operate in the service of a religious community and assist in the promulgation of its theology.

Magdalinski and Chandler (2002) avoid the common assertion that sport has taken on the character of modern religion. In many cases, such assertions are critically advanced as a statement about the alleged increasing secularism associated with modern life. Consequently, sport is viewed as a form of civil religion, controlled through hierarchical structures of authority, a celebration that seeks to reproduce certain sets of power relations, a sacred form of activity that lifts the human spirit and, like religion, is dependent upon rituals before, during and after major sports events. The extent to which sport is viewed as a modern substitute for religion, a new popular opiate, is often questionable but the idea that sport acts as a form of religion is often a question of emphasis. The most extreme position is to suggest that sport is like a new form of religion, while others stop short of this position by suggesting that sport is *religious-like*, thus sharing certain characteristics with religion but not being a religion or a religious movement.

At its most extreme, the relationship between sport, religion and capitalism is ever present in Smith and Westerbeek's (2004) account of the new sporting cathedrals of the Western world. The writers point out that sport is a kind of religion that satisfies religious needs for participants and spectators and that at the heart of the optimal sporting and religious experience is spiritual enlightenment (Smith and Westerbeek, 2004: 90). The sports business, they warn, could destroy everything that makes sport suitable as a religious substitute (Smith and Westerbeek, 2004: 91). In other words, they believe the specialness of sport can be destroyed by business if it fails to comprehend the spiritual components of the product by diminishing the power of the rituals, the stories, the gods and the temples that can be promoted through sport as religion. The authors uncritically buy into the idea that sport, like religion, mobilises communities, forges identity, provides meaning, infuses passion and enlivens the soul. Many of the problems that limit this sort of analysis are closely tied to a frame of reference that is presented as universal but, in reality, rarely unpacks or delineates within or between matters of faith. Perhaps more importantly, development is based upon spiritual rather than social possibilities. The political implications of this lack of social thinking can often be disturbing. By framing development purely in spiritual and capitalistic terms, Smith and Westerbeek (2004), while acknowledging the potential of the cultural sports business, tend to reproduce certain social arrangements that are idealist and far from liberating for some people.

The tyranny of materialism was a value not simply present within the practice of amateur muscular Christianity but other forms of religion, notably Islam. It was allegedly the clash between profit and faith that led to the rift between Muhammad Ali, the former world heavyweight boxing champion, and Elijah Muhammad, leader of Nation of Islam movement. After Muhammed Ali indicated, in the late 1960s, that he wished to return to the boxing ring because he needed to make money, Elijah Muhammad suspended him from the Nation of Islam. He removed his holy name on the grounds that he had rejected the spiritual platform and replaced it with the search for money. Elijah Muhammad went on to assert that Ali had become too dependent upon white America and his return to the world of sport had revealed a lack of faith in Allah (Smith, 2002: 188). Just as the boxer's sporting popularity had been used to the full advantage of the Nation of Islam movement in the beginning, so too at the end of this association was Muhammad Ali's return to sport used by the Nation of Islam to promote key values. Ironically, one of the movement's most popular messengers was removed from office for returning to the very activity that had provided a popular platform for the Nation of Islam movement. The relationship between sport and religion in this instance was not only contradictory, but paradoxically financially rewarding, providing the movement with an international audience through the fame and athleticism of a boxer. Muhammad Ali continued to follow the Muslim faith after the death of Elijah Muhammad in 1975.

334

SPORT AND THE QUEST FOR SPIRITUALITY

Spiritual gifts, write Walters and Byl (2008: 314), are special abilities or capacities given by God for the edification of other people. Yet, the issue that the writers seek to address is a quest for a Christian and/or spiritual approach to health and well-being. While this contribution to an understanding of physical well-being is as much about the women who seek spirituality through mountain biking as it is about the religious experience of the man who loves to run, it is essentially a Christian guide to healthy body, mind and spirit. It presents a biblical view of the human body, it approaches the notion of well-being through the notions of creationism, evolution, redemption, God's care for your body, the opposite of sinning causing healing, fulfilment. It presents a view of spirituality as directly expressed through a Western Christian narrative and it might be viewed as part a new age movement, or other religious social movements that strive to, in this case, place spirituality at the heart of well-being, health and personal development.

Robinson's (2007) series of essays provide one of most comprehensive overviews of the *promise and possibilities* brought about by the need to explain the relationship between sport and spirituality. It is complex because there is no single definition of what spirituality is or might be and rather than provide a single definition Robinson adopts to provide a model of spirituality that draws upon practice, experience and belief. Spirituality in relation to sport is multi-disciplined, drawing upon history, sociology, psychology, physiology and much more. The notions of hope, faith, acceptance and sense of purpose are practicalities for Robinson and yet, as is illustrated, the spiritual journey can be both individual and corporate. At both of these levels, the quest for spiritual meaning demands a process of, according to Robinson (2007: 41), articulation, reflection, meaning development and a response.

The characteristics of the spiritual journey are outlined and presented below in Sport in Focus 14.3.

SPORT IN FOCUS 14.3: CHARACTERISTICS OF THE SPIRITUAL JOURNEY

■ It is dynamic and responsive.

■ It is a learning experience.

■ It is a relational experience.

■ It stresses the responsibility of the person or group to develop significant life meaning.

■ It values tradition and community as the base of belief systems.

■ It needs a supporting community or environment within which to grow or develop.

■ It leads to creative response, which embodies the vision and purpose of the person or group and shares responsibility.

Source: Parry *et al.* (2007).

The decisive words in the passages above are promises and possibilities, and, although Robinson strives hard to avoid the abstract, the metaphysical and the symbolic, there is little discussion of whether, having travelled along the journey of spirituality, the athlete finds spiritual freedom or something else equally vague. More often than not, the vague suugestions of possibility or promises of something better fail to take account of political and/or economic conditions or whether spiritual freedom is, in fact, something different from human freedom. There can be substantive debates about well-being, freedom and capability and whether the spirituality and the end of the spiritual journey adds real capability that helps the individual or the group achieve, for instance, a better lifestyle or better range of choices, or does the quest for spirituality help constrain the search for human freedoms either through sport or otherwise? If the spiritual journey through sport helps improve social choices and freedoms, then it may be seen as a valuable tool that may or may not increase or decrease the capability gap between nations or groups or individuals.

BETTER FAITH, BETTER ETHICS, BETTER SPORT?

In the contemporary world, is it necessary to have a strong relationship between sport, religion and faith or does an adherence to religious faith make things worse in terms of tolerance, recognition and reconciliation? Faith carries a premium in the contemporary world and yet from faith schools, faith-based welfare through to religious justifications for debt relief and even warfare it is hard to escape from it. Faith-based sports movements continue to exist despite the increasing secularisation of certain societies. Those who support the notion of better faith, better ethics and better sport tend to view forms of faith as an ethical underpinning for debates about religion, spirituality, politics and sport. Those who do not support the notion of better faith, better ethics and better sport tend to argue from a humanist perspective that being in the possession of a divinely prescribed rulebook does not put you on the moral high ground in which there is a hierarchy of moral ideologies. It is worthwhile briefly considering the arguments for and against such propositions.

The arguments for better faith, better ethics and better sport tend to rely on a number of assumptions. The assumed demise of old political ideologies has left all areas of public life, including sport, with a sense of uncertainty about what is right and wrong. Developments in genetic science continue to present ethical dilemmas for sport, not least the possible cloning of athletes. Broader bio-ethical issues such as abortion and euthanasia are rarely out of the headlines. For those who support faith-based answers to difficult problems, it is argued that faith can make an important contribution in the prioritising of policies. Faith groups are frequently sought out by government and related agencies because they contain highly motivated and committed volunteers. A major English study into sport volunteering confirmed the need for more informal patterns of sports volunteering given the chaotic lifestyles of young people in general (Sport England, 2003). Faith-informed volunteers often run local schemes and, while the faith element may be strong, it often remains in the background. The problematic assumption is that better faith, better ethics, better volunteering in sport is part of an answer to the broader crisis of volunteering. Faith-based welfare provision has become so popular in the US and, to a lesser extent, Britain that governments want to remain neutral on matters of faith but all parties, whether it be in politics, religion or sport, seem to want dedicated adherents.

The arguments against better faith, better ethics and better sport also tend to rely upon a number of assumptions primarily associated with humanists or atheists. Humanists tend to deny the possibility of moral rulebooks but believe that certain actions are right and wrong in areas such as freedom, tolerance, equality and justice. Emotive arguments about sport need to be informed by relevant comparative evidence as the possible antidote to making uninformed choices. Humanists view too strong an adherence to religion and sport as divisive and serving self-interests. Humanists would seek to provide forms of intervention that promoted tolerance in areas such as ethnicity and racism in sport and be naturally suspicious of sporting organisations that promoted single-faith sport as a model for better faith, better ethics and better sport. Humanist sport would promote pluralist sport based upon the assumption that cultural and religious-based sporting groups will only come to tolerate each other if they are educated together through sport and other areas. To humanists, seeking to promote or privilege forms of sporting experience at the expense of others is immoral but also dangerous because it promotes a sort of tribalism that capitalism, globalisation and the contemporary world needs to outgrow. Yet, the problem, for anyone seeking faith-based forms of sporting involvement as the antidote to the contradictions of the modern sporting world, or even a faith-based model of global sport, of realism and hierarchies remains with sport as in other facets of life – namely, which faiths and why?

SUMMARY

The sense of allegiance that many hardcore sports fans have for a particular team is almost religious-like, in the sense that fans share a common history and share in a particular relationship and identity with other sports fans and groups. Hardcore sports fans and strong believers of faiths share a common distinguishing aspect of ascriptive identity. Those who belong to such groups identify deeply with them and typically experience membership of such groups as morally significant. The sectarian hate that attaches itself to Scotland's Celtic versus Rangers football matches is often characterised as groups of hardcore football fans partaking in a common history and standing in a particular relationship to another group of fans. It has promoted governemt intervention aimed at eradicating sectarian bigotry in football in Scotland by introducing specific legislation, aspects of which came into effect in late 2011. In other senses, it might also be asked whether to be a Muslim or a Jew or a Christian is also to suggest that one's identity is intimately bound up with membership of a group, or at least the value that such a belief has is fundamentally important to the believer in a similar but also different way that a hardcore Old Firm sports fan values the allegiance to a team.

This chapter has recognised that religions exist in all known societies; religious beliefs and practices vary from culture to culture and to the extent that sport involves a set of symbols and rituals, some of which may be religious, it is not difficult to see why some are quick to point out that sport continues to invoke religion in social life. Today, we find both religious organisations using sport and sports participants turning to religion in different ways. Despite the onward march of secularism in some Western communities, it is far from clear whether sport inhibits or promotes religious beliefs, and whether, in certain instances, such beliefs help to develop social cohesion, networking, or even psychological advantage in sport today.

History has taught us that proclaiming the principle of tolerance and justice in a multi-faith society is not sufficient to make a reality of it. There is some truth in the observation that the cultural wars between the religious and the secular is an important social division locally, nationally and internationally, and yet it is not openly acknowledged in the way that other social divisions such as race, gender and forms of social inequality are. The influence of religion on sport may have declined but it has not disappeared and we have seen in this chapter that the potential influence of different faiths does not necessarily mean better sport or a more acceptable world. While other areas of conflict in the world today have observed the power of fundamental religious groups, conflict in and through sport has not yet been characterised by a class of fundamental religious beliefs or dogma and, in this sense, sport might thankfully be viewed as being more secular than, for example, some other aspects of certain countries' politics, culture and society. Just as the identity model of sport may be viewed as being problematic, so too is the ascriptive identity model of religion in its most fundamentalist forms – a point we shall return to.

GUIDE TO FURTHER READING

Ahmad, A. (2011). ' British Football: Where are the Muslim Female Footballers? Exploring the Connections Between Gender Ethnicity and Islam'. *Soccer and Society*, 12 (3): 443–456.

Benn, T., Dagkas, S. and Jawad, H. (2011). 'Embodied Faith: Islam, Religious Freedom and Educational Practices in Physical Education'. *Sport, Education and Society*, 16 (1): 17–34.

Brown, C. and Bathgare, S. (2011). 'Lennon: We Can't Cure Sectarianism'. *The Scotsman*, 16 April: 1–3.

Deucha, R. and Holligan, C. (2010). 'Gangs, Sectarianism and Social Capital: A Qualitative Study of Young People in Scotland'. *Sociology*, 44 (1): 13–31.

Jiwani, N. and Rail, G. (2010). 'Islam, Hijab and Young Shia Muslim Canadian Women's Discursive Constructions of Physical Activity'. *Sociology of Sport Journal*, 27 (3): 251–267.

New Statesman (2010). 'Faith Speaks Volumes: A Guide to the World's Leading Faiths'. *New Statesman*, 5–8 April: 26–28.

Parry, J., Robinson, S., Watson, N. and Nesti, M. (2007). *Sport and Spirituality*. London: Routledge.

Pattullo, A. (2011). 'Saturday Interview: Ibrox Driving Force'. *The Scotsman*, 23 April: 10–12.

Sen, A. (2006). *Identity and Violence: The Illusion of Destiny*. London: Allen Lane.

Supiot, A. (2003). 'Dogmas and Rights'. *New Left Review*, 21 (May/June): 118–137.

Wade, M. (2011). 'Putting the Fear of Golf in Them' *The Times*, 7 March: 4–6.

Walters, P. and Byl, J. (2008). *Christian Paths to Health and Wellness*. Champaign, IL: Human Kinetics.

QUESTIONS

1 Explain the usage of the following terms to illuminate the relationship between sport and religion today: 'fundamentalism', 'secularism', 'traditionalism' and 'faith'.

2 Evaluate the key themes that have dominated the research literature on sport, religion and society.

3 Explain the assertion that Islam has been both a barrier and a source of empowerment for Muslim women's involvement in sport and physical activity.

4 Argue for and against the idea that the relationship between religion and sport is based upon profit rather than faith. Illustrate your answer using three examples from sport.

5 How would humanists view the adherence to religion from sporting outlets and vice versa?

6 Define the following terms: 'spirituality', 'humanism' and 'religion'.

7 How might religion or faith help with an individual's health and well-being?

8 What are the arguments for better faith, ethics and sport?

9 What are the arguments against better faith, ethics and sport?

10 Consider the case for and against involvement in sport on a Sunday.

PRACTICAL PROJECTS

1 Identify a single-faith organisation of your choice and explain the way in which faith informs the organisation's understanding of its sporting practices.

2 Develop a ten-point strategy aimed at increasing participation in sport and physical activity among Muslim women (www.islam.org.au/articles/19/women.htm).

3 Develop a series of four short historical case studies of any sports clubs that have religious affiliations and use the material you have collected to write a report arguing for or against the notion that sport has become more or less secular over time.

4 Carry out a content analysis of the newspaper coverage of Celtic versus Rangers football matches, or any other two teams associated with forms of religious identity, between 2009 and 2011. List and evaluate references to religious themes associated with this match. Write a research report of about 3,000 words, analysing your findings and providing a set of recommendations aimed at changing fan culture at these matches.

5 Make a list of five actions/behaviours from observing sports that have religious connotations. Explain the action, the meaning of the action and the religion the action is associated with, and give a critical comment.

339

KEY CONCEPTS

Capitalism ■ Catholicism ■ Christianity ■ Civil religion ■ Ethics ■ Faith ■ Fundamentalism ■ Identity ■ Islam ■ Jewishness ■ Liberal humanism ■ Muslim ■ Religion ■ Sabbatarianism ■ Sectarianism ■ Secular ■ Spirituality

WEBSITES

Centre for Sport, Spirituality and Religion

www.glos.ac.uk/research/dse/cssr

A centre based at the University of Gloucestershire that focuses on research and outreach work.

Fellowship of Christian Athletes

www.fca.org/

A non-profit interdenominational ministry that aims to reach out to athletes of the world.

The Maccabi Games

www.jccmaccabi.org/index_home.php

The official website of Maccabi Games, dedicated to bringing Jewish youth of the world together through sport.

Verite Sport

www.veritesport.org/?page=home

Verite Sport exists to promote a Christian presence in sport.

Chapter 15

Sport, the Olympics and major sporting events

What are the real benefits of hosting the Olympic Games or a sporting mega-event?

Some cities or countries cannot host major sporting events and yet Qatar, with a population smaller than many cities, is going to host the 2022 FIFA World Cup – is the justification simply economic or one of justice and recognition for certain places?

PREVIEW

Key terms defined ■ Introduction ■ Economic and well-being reasons for hosting sporting mega-events ■ The London 2012 Olympic and Paralympic Games ■ Thinking socially about Olympic mega-events ■ Anti-Olympism ■ Political economy of global sporting organisations ■ The power of Olympism ■ The economic impact, lessons and the legacy ■ Lessons from hosting major sporting events ■ Turkish delight and tennis ■ Brazil and 2014 ■ Qatar and 2022 ■ 2010 FIFA Legacy Trust Fund ■ Hard and soft legacies ■ Summary

OBJECTIVES

This chapter will:

- introduce some concepts relevant to thinking socially about sporting mega-events;
- explain the reasons why the hosting of sporting events is attractive to some cities;
- provide short case studies of contemporary sporting mega-events;
- introduce the idea that countries may use the hosting of major sporting events to influence broader national and international policy goals;
- explain the background to legacies and the different aspects associated with hard and soft legacies; and
- provide a brief case study of one legacy trust fund associated with one event in one country.

KEY TERMS DEFINED

Authority: Often related to matters of power, to be authoritarian or a system of leadership based upon obedience; forms of authority may be traditional, charismatic and devolved, or centralised.

Governance: The resolution of conflicts of interest. It can occur at every level in society; it is inherent in social relationships and organisations, and is more than government. It may be viewed by some as the art of governement.

Olympism: Olympism, as defined by the Olympic charter, is a philosophy of life, an ideology containing core values, tolerance, generosity, solidarity, friendship, non-discrimination and respect for others — refer to Principle 2 of the Olympic charter.

Sporting mega-events: Cultural and sporting festivals that achieve sufficient size and scope to affect whole economies and receive sustained international media attention — see Roche's work in this area.

Power: In the most general sense, the ability of a political actor to achieve its goals.

INTRODUCTION

The Olympics are the foremost of the genre commonly described as sporting mega-events. Cities vigorously compete to host sporting mega-events for many reasons, not least of which is the belief that, in doing so, images will be enhanced and economies will be stimulated. The hosting of international sporting events requires considerable expenditure on infrastructure, and their organisation and security critically depend upon public subsidies.

The growing size and expense of hosting major sporting events continues unabated. The initial cost overruns and unrealised budget forecasts present the Olympics with a challenge. The reasons for investment in major sporting events include ideals of international diplomacy and development. Four of the football stadiums that were built for the 2010 African Nations Cup in Angola were financed by the Chinese government and yet the planned legacy remains questionable given that the four stadiums in Luanda, Cabana, Benguela and Lunabgo are under-utilised. The rental for a match is US$25,000. No club in the 16-club Angolan league can afford the rent on a regular basis. The Bird's Nest stadium in Beijing, built as a centrepiece attraction for the otherwise successful 2008 Beijing Olympic Games, has rarely been used for sport since. *Winning* cities use the awarding of major sporting events to accelerate, divert and expand infrastructural investment, with the hosting of mega-events being given as a rationale for rejuvenation or regeneration of, usually, urban areas. Schemes that might have encountered resistance from politicians, the public and local communities may be attached to Olympic projects on the basis of added value. Even when bids fail, *losing* cities often gain regeneration impetus that might otherwise not have occurred.

By hosting an estimated 15,000 athletes, 203 countries, 70,000 volunteers, 20,000 media and an Olympic family of around 5,000, the London 2012 Olympic and Paralympic Games is forecast to be the largest peacetime mobilisation of people and resources in the world. Supporters of sporting mega-events such as the Olympics, World Cups and Commonwealth Games claim that such events attract wealth and visitors, increase tourism, and lead to lasting economic benefits for the host cities and/or regions. Such claims are often challenged by those who suggest that Olympic legacies are very rarely met. In May 2011, more than a year before the London 2012 Olympic Games, the Centre for Social Justice argued that the Games will fail to deliver the promise of helping Britain's neediest young people. It is suggetsted that the legacy pledge is no more than an effective sales pitch and that the scale of the challenge is too high for the relatively limited amounts of funding that have been promised for the legacy programmes (*Sunday Herald*, 22 May 2011: 11).

The desire to host sports events is not just limited to those events alluded to above, or even simply economic reasons. Economic impact studies of major sporting events sometimes fail to take account of the associated feel-good factor or psychic income that often stimulates a sense of community and common purpose around a project for a defined period of time – the challenge being to sustain the initial impact. It is worth reflecting upon Oswald's (2011) observation that economists have probably been wrong to assert that economic growth makes rich societies happier and that other factors have to be taken into the equation when attempting to measure the well-being of nations. The extent to which sporting success or failure impacts upon the well-being of nations is rarely considered within the context of hosting major sporting events other than to suggest that it helps with recognition and perhaps a slight home advantage, but also pressure.

THINKING SOCIALLY ABOUT OLYMPIC MEGA EVENTS

The Olympic Games remain the most visible dimension of the Olympic Movement. The Games also contribute to a broader cultural and social phenomenon. This is evident in the cultural Olympiad or festivals that accompany the winning of an Olympic bid. They are also present in the international development work associated with the International Olympic Movement and the protests that form part of the Anti-Olympic Movement. The IOC's official charter forbids the expression of anti-Olympic dissent but, when the Olympics arrive in a host city, protests soon follow. To activists, the Games are seen as the avatar of an unaccountable world order of power, wealth and spectacle that invariably causes permanent social damage to the urban environment (Boykoff, 2011: 45). The cultural dimension extends to specific events such as the opening and closing ceremonies, the symbolic significance of torch relays, and the production and reproduction of local and international symbols. Research that has analysed the cultural significance of the Olympic Games has tended to revolve around: (i) the symbolic or invented ritual of the Olympic Games and Movement; (ii) the lived festival dimension of the Games and the degree of local ownership of events; (iii) the global brand dimension of Games portrayed through the international media and various social networks; and (iv) the extent to which events contribute to the cultural well-being of a place or country. According to Garcia (2010), the Olympics cannot afford to limit the cultural dimension since the real Olympic cultural value lies in the opportunities for intercultural exchange, dialogue, dissent or mutual understanding that is forged between participants, spectators, local residents and international communities. The potential cultural dimension became evident in the guidelines given to the 2016 and 2020 Olympic candidate cities.

The social and cultural significance of sporting mega-events can be considered in different ways. A crucial question is: 'who are these events?', as opposed to 'what are these events?'. According to Roche (2000), events may be considered in terms of their modern/non-modern, national/non-national, and local/non-local features. Different levels of analysis may also consider strategies for the wider dissemination of such events and why they end up in certain cities or countries and not others. The notion of events as particular forms of international public culture allows three further dimensions to be introduced. First, there are the public images of nationalities, ethnicities and 'other' groups that exist within any given host nation. Second, there are images of international societies and agreements that consider universal principles and practices such as human rights or drug reduction in sport held by many national public organisations and, third, there are roles played by international corporations and transnational sports organisations and their approach to culture and communications. Given all of these considerations, sporting mega-events help to create and influence national and international public cultures but also various calendars of events that not only influence tourism, but regular points of intervention for the creation of nationalisms, supra-nationalism and/or forms of internationalism. A connecting theme in this discussion is that of citizenship and whether the Olympic Movement contributes to the development of any global or international forms of citizenship.

The political economy of global sporting organisations is influenced by the complex interaction of states, markets and social patterns and beliefs of members and/or other powerful groups of people at any given point in time. The outcomes of these interactions invariably influence where sporting events can or cannot take place. The re-election of Sepp Blatter as FIFA President in June 2011 was, in part, an election result that was supported by the developing world and a reminder to the former colonial worlds that the historical relations that had supported the power of FIFA in the past had changed. Despite allegations of corruption, the president was re-elected on the basis of the policy to continue to place major football events in previously less favoured continents and countries, and open up the decision-making process that determined where future World Cup events would be staged. There is perhaps less of an ideology of Euro-centrism permeating FIFA. Yet, allied to this is the need for more openness, fairness, and assessments of the effectiveness of governance arrangements impacting upon sport. The problem is exacerbated further by the uncovering of different waves of cheating, corruption and deceptive behaviour in different sports organisations. Global sporting organisations need to continually reconcile socio-economic pressures with changing geopolitical pressures that understand the complex interaction between markets, states and social patterns and opportunities.

The types of authority, status, resources, information and skills that are relevant to the success of sporting events and their different social, as well as economic, outcomes will vary from case to case. A simple approach to the notion of power will not explain outcomes. The decisions to re-elect the President of FIFA, to host the 2012 Olympic Games in London and to award the 2012 European Football Championships jointly to Ukraine and Poland all result from the exercise of power. A one-dimensional view of power may limit the study of power and outcomes to that of a behavioural study of the people involved and, in particular, the decisions made. A two-dimensional view of power is more subtle. It focuses upon both the decisions made and the decisions not made, thus allowing for recognition of the subtle use of silence or non-decision making. This, in itself, entails an exercise of some degree of power brokering. That is to say, it recognises that what a person does not say is not a powerless act. Finally, a more complex but not complete view of power might invoke a three-dimensional approach that recognises intended and unintended, decision making and control of the political agenda, as well as conscious and false conscious intentions. Power, in the most general sense, remains the ability of a political actor to achieve outcomes or goals but the process of power needs to be much more pluralistic in its forms of analysis. The common denominator of all of the above ideas about power is their evaluative character. Power and how it works is central to understanding the practice of sporting mega-events. It can be exercised on at least three levels , the ability to make or influence decisions, the ability to set agendas and prevent decisions being made, and the ability to manipulate what people think and want.

The idea of Olympism, suggests Parry (2007: 213), invokes a political goal of peaceful internationalism and the Olympic Movement per se has sought a closer relationship with the United Nations, since both organisations seek to operate at a global universal level while recognising that differences between them exist. Olympism itself seeks to be universal in its values of respect, tolerance and solidarity while acknowledging that there are very real challenges of the different interpretations associated with such values in different cultures or parts of the world. Parry goes on to suggest that the search for universal representation at the interpersonal and political level of common humanity seems to be the essence of hope and optimism, not just for Olympism, but also internationalism and other forms of humanism. Yet, the interactions between states, markets and social patterns at any given point in time needs always to recognise that the market mechanism for hosting and delivering Olympic sporting events involves considerable use of public resources for purposes in which the social benefits are sometimes far from clear. The far-reaching powers of the market mechanism

345

have to be supplemented by creating social opportunities for social equity and justice. In the context of where Olympic sporting events are held, the challenge remains to allow the market to function with a greater degree of fairness in terms of outcomes, and that the overall achievements of the market are often dependent upon political and social arrangements in terms of states, power and social patterns.

LONDON 2012, OLYMPIC CITIES AND MAJOR SPORTING EVENTS

Sport in Focus 15.1 illustrates the continental spread of some major sporting events. The list is not intended to be exhaustive. The most comprehensive study of Olympic cities and the agendas and planning that goes into these games remains that of Gold and Gold (2011). The most comprehensive study of resistance to the Olympic industry remains Lenskyj (2008). A number of general themes have dominated the London 2012 Olympic Games story to date. It is not necessary to provide an exhaustive list, but some of the issues have been:

- the final cost of the Olympics set against the £2.4m bid price;
- the regeneration of the East End of London in particular;
- access to the Games from the Asian and other ethnic minority groups and the displacement of people as a result of the 2012 Games;
- the actual legacy and, in particular, the international inspiration project;
- the controversy over the ownership and building contracts of the actual Olympic stadium itself;
- the high level of security costs asssociated with 2012 and the difficulty of policing potential international terrorism focused upon the UK as a result of hosting a high-profile sporting mega-event; and
- the impact of the riots in London and other English cities during the month of August 2011.

One of the promises made by the then mayor of London Ken Livingstone when the IOC awarded the 2012 Olympic Games to London was the opportunity to transform the chances of the children living in the East End of London and to break the cycle of poverty. The relocation of 600 residents and over 2,000 businesses prior to Olympic Park construction began in 2006. Council tenants received compensation but not those living in caravans or mobile homes. By 2007, an estimated 1,000 people were facing displacement because of London's Olympic construction plans. This was in a city that already had more than 11,000 homeless people. According to Lenskyj (2008: 49), London was following a clear pattern of development similar to at least five other recent Olympic cities. Local politicians, developers and corporate leaders all joined forces with Olympic supporters to use the Olympic recognition to initiate major urban redevelopment and infrastructure projects, largely at the taxpayer's expense. Lenskyj (2008: 49) goes on to suggest that the poorest neighbourhoods are seen as the prime targets for such enterprises and that the subsequent displacement of low-income residents and the destruction of longstanding working-class communities is rarely acknowledged by those with privilege and power.

🔍

SPORT IN FOCUS 15.1: SOME CONFIRMED GLOBAL GAMES, 2010–2016

2010	FIFA World Cup – South Africa
2010	Asian Games – China
2010	Olympic Youth Games – Singapore
2010	Commonwealth Games – Delhi
2011	Cricket World Cup – India, Pakistan, Sri Lanka and Bangladesh
2011	World Student Games – Shenzen, China
2011	Rugby World Cup – New Zealand
2012	UEFA European Championships – Poland and Ukraine
2012	Olympic Games – London
2013	World Student Games – Kazan, Russia
2014	Winter Olympic Games – Sochi, Russia
2014	Commonwealth Games – Glasgow, Scotland
2014	Ryder Cup – Scotland
2014	African Nations Cup – Libya
2014	FIFA World Cup – Brazil
2014	Asian Games – Incheon, South Korea
2015	Rugby World Cup – England
2015	Pan American Games – Toronto
2016	Olympic Games – Rio de Janeiro

By 2009, the spending on the London 2012 Olympic Games had risen to £12 billion, some £2.7 billion above an agreed public spending contribution of £9.325 billion. The extra £2.7 billion included £1.15 billion spent by new Mayor Boris Johnson's London Development Agency (LDA) to buy and clean up the Olympic site; at least a further £359 million not publicly announced by the LDA (comprising £269 million in interest payments and £90 million in Olympic grants); £389 million for 'Games-specific' transport improvements by Transport for London and Network Rail; about £60 million costs for Whitehall departments working on Games preparations and legacy planning; £240 million spent, or bid for, by local councils; a contribution of £110 million by the Homes and Communities Agency quango to the Olympic Village; £280 million on Olympic-related grassroots and elite sport projects; and almost £100 million in directly Games-related spending by a range of other public bodies, from the Lea Valley Regional Park Authority to the Arts Council and the NHS. None of these amounts were included in the publicly announced figure of £9.3 billion budget to construct Olympic venues, security, most of the Olympic Village and transport improvements. The figure in the original London 2012 bid document of November 2004 was £2.05 billion. The state argued that it would recoup some of the further required investment from land and property sales.

Visitors to London during the 30th Modern Olympic Games are estimated to inject around £2 billion into the British economy. Many local residents in and around London hoped to capitalise upon the opportunity to rent properties during the Olympic period, thus providing a direct boost to the local economy as a result of the Olympics. Powley (2011: 11) suggests that rental rates for a double room (per night) during the Olympics could increase to £200–£275 in St John's Wood, Hampstead, Knightsbridge, Kensington and Chelsea; £200– £250 in Stratford; £150–£200 in Victoria Park Village; £200 in Greenwich and Blackheath; £150– £175 in East Dulwich; and £175 in St Katherine's Dock. Many of the businesses to benefit from the 2010 Olympic boom are expected to be UK listed companies. Three categories in particular are worth mentioning: (i) retailers, (ii) hotels and (iii) media. The cycling specialists Halfords will be looking for the next Chris Hoy (Olympic gold medalist in Beijing) to boost bicycle sales and accessories. Those who failed to get tickets in the ballot are likely to watch the action on television, thus boosting certain broadcasters' share prices.

On the one hand, the London Olympics were drawn into stories about corruption over the awarding of contracts to build facilities. West Ham United Football Club allegedly paid £20,000 to a director of the authority that chose West Ham as the club to benefit from taking over the running of the new stadium after the Olympics were finished. Furthermore, it was suggested that two of the directors one from West Ham United and one from the Olympic Park Legacy Company were in a relationship together and, therefore, a conflict of interest emerged. Tottenham Hotspur Football Club were seeking a judicial review of the decision to award the £550 million Olympic Stadium to West Ham United (Insight, *Sunday Times*, 3 July 2011: 1). In November 2011 the deal to award West Ham the Olympic Stadium after the London 2012 Games collapsed. Stakeholders have all subsequently commented that their individual aims remain the same to get the best outcome for their clubs and the UK Athletics legacy.

On the other hand, London and Britain were honouring projects around the world that were supported through International Inspiration, which ran projects in five continents from the Pacific Island of Palau to Turkey. The programme set out to raise £44 million by the end of 2014, with £39 million having been invested in 16 countries by July 2011. In India, £4 million was invested over three years to improve sport in primary schools. Acknowledging the success of the programme, the Indian government rolled the programme out to 100,000 schools and committed a further £400 million. In 2010, some of the key achievements of International Inspiration included: 6 million children in 15 countries reached through sport, 328 schools linked in the UK with partner countries, 2.3 million children in India involved in sporting events, 27,000 children in Bangladesh learning swimming survival skills, and 700,000 children and young people in Brazil provided with a further chance to play sport. In Mozambique 700 schools and 1,200 pupils were being directly or indirectly resourced (i.e. matched funding as a result of the internal inspiration project). Unique had been working with International Inspiration since 2009 to promote child-friendly schools in Mozambique, with the main challenge being the low number of children, especially girls, enrolling for school and an even lower number going on to complete basic education (UNESCO, 2010).

The London City riots of 2011 also raised concerns about how the rest of the world would view coming to London. The aftermath of the fires, looting and damage to property in parts of London and other cities during August prompted a leading paper to comment on the fact that the riots had forced London to get real for the first time about the Olympic Games. An ambassador for the Games was caught looting, one of the faces of the Games until her parents turned her in to the police. Hayward (2011: 9) argues that, just as Beijing was meant to usher in the Chinese century, so the London Games have told a story about diversity and inclusiveness. The article goes on to suggest that these claims are now dead, as London is exposed to the world as a city in which a greedy and corrupt political and economic elite consign an underclass to urban dumping grounds and dismantle the welfare state that built out of the ruins of World War II around the time that the Olympics last came to London in 1948. London's problem, it is argued, is that it raised the bar of expectation to justify an enormous cost and that, even if London cools down before the 2012 Olympics begin, it will feel different to those sold the 'Cool Britannia' myth. In December 2011 the UK government announced that the total number of people involved in the Olympic Games security operation had been increased to 41,700, forcing a rapid escalation in the total security budget to beyond £1 billion.

THE ECONOMIC IMPACT, LESSONS AND THE LEGACY

The economic case for hosting major events or teams often rests upon two foundations. First, the building of facilities and the related infrastructure and, second, that there will be a large influx of tourists and visitors that benefits local economies. The first of these is often premised upon a boost to the construction industry coupled with knock on effects that will benefit the wider economy. Studies of the economic impact of hosting major sporting events have attempted to measure (i) the direct and indirect effects of sport and major sporting events on economic variables such as employment, output or gross domestic product (GDP), and (ii) the impact of sport on urban and regional regeneration. The opportunities to regenerate the East End of London and the East End of Glasgow were key drivers for the London 2012 Olympic Games and Glasgows 2014 Commonwealth Games bids. The broader rationale for hosting major sporting events also includes national profile and prestige, health improvements, the promise of further economic development and other lasting legacies. The hosting of major sporting events is something that an increasing number of countries want to do. 715 million people viewed the 2010 FIFA World Cup Final between Spain and Holland – the highest viewing figure of any single event to date – and provided a major pro-filing opportunity not only for the two nations in the final, but Africa in general.

Kasimati (2003) has reviewed 13 *ex-ante* studies of the summer Olympics using a variety of methods including input–output models and computable general equilibrium models. The studies showed positive impacts on a number of economic variables including GDP, employ-ment and expenditure. Blake (2005) also provides a review of studies carried out for candidate countries for the 2012 Olympics and provides his own assessment of London 2012. All of these studies find evidence of a positive impact on income and employment. Blake's assessment of the London 2012 Games finds that the Games will increase GDP by £1,936 million and create an additional 8,164 full-time jobs. In the pre-Olympics phase, 2005–11, the biggest

349

boost to the economy was in the construction sector where gross value added was estimated to increase by £506 million and the net gain in full-time equivalent jobs is estimated at 14,354. Blake (2005) also includes detailed analysis on the impact on London and its sub-regions, as well as UK-wide effects. Blake finds a positive legacy effect that derives mainly from improved infrastructure but also from additional tourism beyond 2012.

Many studies have been commissioned by the bodies bidding or organising the Olympic Games, and they have been criticised on the grounds that they over-estimated the impact in order to provide a justification for public subsidies and a rationale for hosting major events. The positive results from *ex-ante* studies of the Atlanta and Los Angeles Olympics carried out by Humphreys and Plummer (1995) and Economics Research Associates (1984) have been challenged by *ex-post* assessments. Baade and Matheson (2002) have used time series data on changes in employment for a period before and after the Los Angeles and Atlanta Olympics as a dependent variable and used a dummy variable to cover the Olympic period and a number of other explanatory variables known to influence employment to control for all other effects. They found that the coefficient on the Olympics dummy variable is insignificant, indicating no effect on employment. There are methodological difficulties with this approach. First, it is difficult to control for all other factors, and second, a number of their explanatory/control variables, such as wages and per capita income are likely to be correlated with each other and with the Olympics effect. This study also ignores the possible positive externalities associated with hosting a major sporting event.

Studies carried out for candidate countries for the 2012 Olympics also found evidence of a positive impact on income and employment. Few economic studies attempt to measure the 'feel-good' factor or 'psychic income' associated with major sporting events. 'Psychic income' takes many forms. It includes a sense of community and common purpose. One US study of the impact of a major sports team in Pittsburgh considered the opportunity costs, in terms of taxation, expenditure and employment effects, and concluded that Pittsburgh was better off with the sports team than without it. Few economic impact studies take account of the possible positive effect on inward investment that may follow a successful sporting event if a host city is able to use the event to rebrand itself and improve its international rating as a 'premier league' city.

The branding of Singapore through the hosting of the first ever Youth Olympic Games in 2010 and other sporting events was part of a medium-term strategy to position Singapore as a sports hub. The success of the Formula 1 Singapore Grand Prix, the Youth Olympic Games, the Asian Games and the Beijing 2008 Olympic Games have all helped to gain recognition for Singapore. There is much to be learned from the hosting of major sporting events, and many of the assumptions need to be continually tested almost on a case-by-case basis. In 2003, there were 14 million visitors to Greece but in 2004, when it hosted the Athens Olympic Games, visitor numbers fell by 1 million to 13 million.

There have been notable successes but also lessons to be learned, and Sport in Focus 15.2 looks at some examples. The cases are drawn from specific Olympic and Commonwealth Games, but a broader range of sporting events might also be mentioned. The following are illustrative but underline the point that sport, countries and events have to be considered on a case-by-case basis.

350

SPORT IN FOCUS 15.2: LESSONS FROM SOME MAJOR SPORTING EVENTS, 1970–2010

Edinburgh 1970 and 1986

Edinburgh has hosted two Commonwealth Games, in 1970 and 1986, but has failed to capitalise on the investment. Sporting facilities in the city suffer from under-investment and, in many cases, disrepair, which, in turn, has affected the city's ability to attract major sporting events to these Commonwealth Games facilities. There is no Sports Act as in Finland, which enshrines a minimum level of provision and quality in local facilities.

Barcelona 1992

The 1992 Olympic Games aimed to convert slums and regenerate decaying brownfield sites and shanty areas. The harbour area of the city was completely transformed on the back of sport. The Games helped promote the city as a leisure tourism venue – viewed as a success.

Atlanta 1996

The major winners at the 1996 Centennial Olympic Games in Atlanta were Coca-Cola – the largest sponsor of the 1996 Olympic Games. The Games made a profit of US$10 million but little in the way of any legacy – no improvement in terms of transport or IT infrastructure and a reduction in the availability of low-income housing units.

Sydney 2000

Sydney followed the example set by Barcelona and regenerated derelict land. Hailed at the time as the best Olympics ever, however, the opportunity to further integrate the Aborigine population was missed, and insufficient attention was paid to having foundation-level coaches in place to cope with the influx of children inspired by what they had seen, hampering legacy development – viewed as a success.

Vancouver 2010 Winter Olympic Games

As previously mentioned, the vision for the 2010 Winter Olympic Games was to make it not about Vancouver, but about Canada. 99.1 per cent of Canadians watched some of the Winter Olympic Games. Different days were labelled as British Columbia day, Ontario day. The top 10 US TV markets had between 26 and 36 per cent primetime share of coverage on NBC. Challenges such as no snow and warm weather patterns at the beginning of a Winter Olympic Games were resolved quickly.

Turkish delight and tennis

The hosting of sporting events may also be used to explode sporting myths or challenge national stereotypes. Tennis has been used to challenge notions of countries such as Turkey being viewed as a developing Muslim nation. Istanbul is the fifth largest city in the world, the second largest metropolis in Europe and a city that has recently used an aggressive sporting events strategy to help further position Turkey on the world stage. The country, despite increasing its international stature in relation to its European candidacy, views sport as a key plank in a strategy that aims to lose its image as a developing Muslim country that is not modern enough for the EU but will ultimately host an Olympics, despite its bid for 2012 being its fourth failed attempt. Sport is highly political in Turkey and has been used to open often strained diplomatic relations with Armenia. It has also been used, writes Erdem, to 'parachute ourselves into Europe through sport' (*The Times*, 31 March 2011: 79).

Istanbul has been named 2012's European Capital of Sport. The Turkish government has recognised the power of sport to showcase Turkey while, at the same time, recognising that it has a problem with grassroots support and therefore a fan base for certain world sports such as tennis. The Turkish Tennis Association transferred about $34.7 million to the WTA. In 2011, Istanbul will host the Turkish Grand Prix, the WTA Championships and the Eurasia Marathon. In 2012, the World Indoor Athletics Championships and the World Swimming Championships will also be hosted in Istanbul. It has already hosted Champions League and UEFA Cup football finals.

Private promise and the public reality: the 2014 FIFA World Cup

Judging by the costs to host the 2014 Brazil World Cup, it would seem that the power of private enterprise to fund such events is diminishing. A study by the TCU (Court of Audit) shows that 98.56 per cent of the $23 billion budgeted for the 2014 event will come out of public funds. This comes less than two years after the President of the COL (Local Organizing Committee), Ricardo Teixeira, declared that most of the funding would be provided by the private sector. Most of the money will come from government banks (CEF and BNDES) and the Infraero state institution that administers the country's airports. Together, three public companies will reportedly invest about $16.5 billion up to the opening of the tournament. Financing the construction of urban infrastructure in the 12 host cities will cost state and local governments about US$6.6 billion. BNDES has already invested US$4.8 billion – $1.2 billion in the development of urban infrastructure and $3.6 billion in the construction of the arenas. According to the TCU's study, Infraero will spend about $5.1 billion on the refurbishing and expansion of airports. The federal agency did not calculate the billions that governments will have to spend to organise the security system of the World Cup. The study shows that the private sector appears to be investing only about $336 million, or 1.44 per cent of the £23 billion cost of the tournament.

This $336 million will not be invested by any individual company but will come from the clubs that will rebuild or build stadiums. International and Atletico-PR have already confirmed that they will invest in their stadiums for the World Cup. It is said the Parana will spend $113 million on the arena, while the Gauchos will earmark $133 million to refurbish the Beira-Rio. In São Paulo, Corinthians are still trying to acquire funding for a new stadium in Itaquera. According to the TCU report, Corinthians will invest $90 million. The club's aim is to host the opening ceremony of the FIFA World Cup in the new stadium. The private money invested in the World Cup is less than 10 per cent of the amount that BNDES will use to finance the construction and refurbishing of the stadiums. In 2007, when the country won the right to host the World Cup for the second time, the CBF, the Brazilian candidate in charge of FIFA, estimated that the country would spend just under $2 billion on stadiums. This amount has already surpassed $5 billion. The projected investment exceeds the amount spent by South Africa in the 2010 World Cup. South Africa paid $3.9 billion to build ten stadiums, two less than in Brazil.

The final case study provided here is that of the Qatar 2022 FIFA World Cup, and it forms the basis of Sport in Focus 15.3.

Girginov and Hills (2008) argue that legacies are constructed and not given. The term 'legacy' itself is difficult to define but the IOC themselves concluded that the effects of legacy have many aspects and dimensions ranging from recognised aspects such as architecture, urban planning, city marketing, sports infrastructure, economic and tourist development to less tangible aspects such as the production of ideas and cultural values, education, archives, voluntarism new sport participants, notoriety on a global scale and knowledge exchange (IOC, 2003). Wilfred Lemke, special adviser to the United Nations secretary general for development and peace, argued that, 'sport has the unique power to attract mobilise and inspire and is by far the most popular activity in which youth engage'. The first significant use of the term 'legacy' occurred in the city of Melbourne's bid to host the 1956 Olympic Games. The 1976 Montreal Olympic Games were intended to provide an inheritance benefit. A survey of official Winter and Summer Olympic reports will indicate that the term 'legacy' became increasingly included in the thinking around the hosting of the Olympics. The 1988 bid to host the Winter Olympics in Calgary mentioned it 42 times, with bids for Atlanta 1996 recording 71 mentions; Sydney 2000, 43 mentions; Salt Lake City 2002, 55 mentions; and Athens 2004, 23 mentions.

The 2010 FIFA World Cup Legacy Trust Fund for South Africa provides a more detailed insight into the construction and funding of one proposed legacy associated with one mega-event in one country. The 2010 FIFA World Cup Trust Fund is one of a line of legacies that FIFA have put in place since 2005, including 20 Football for Hope Centers, the Win in Africa with Africa project, and the 11 for Health campaign and the 2010 FIFA World Cup Ticket Fund, which allocated 120,000 complimentary tickets to South Africans to participate in the various social and developmental activities organised around the 2010 event. The legacy trust fund amounts to US$100 million – $80 million of which is allocated to social community projects and $20 million to the South African Football Association in the build-up to 2010. The trust is administered by Ernst and Young accountants. All of the projects are aimed at public benefit only and divided into football development, education and development, health care, and humanitarian activities.

It is possible to think of sporting legacies in both hard and soft terms. Hard legacies are infrastructure matters such as facilities, amenities, technology and transport, and are relatively simple to both measure and assess the impact. Soft legacies are more often about people, communities or segments of communities and, consequently, the extent to which soft legacies

SPORT IN FOCUS 15.3: CAN QATAR HOST THE 2022 FIFA WORLD CUP?

FIFA shocked the world when it announced that Qatar would host the 2022 World Cup. The small Middle Eastern nation beat sporting superpowers such as Australia and the US for the right to stage football's premier event. Since the announcement, controversy has surrounded the bidding process, and with allegations of bribery and corruption, some have called for a re-vote on the 2022 World Cup host selection.

Setting aside any allegations of foul play in the bidding process, there have been questions about Qatar's ability to host the tournament due to a number of obstacles. The summer temperatures can reach up to 50°C (122°F), potentially making afternoon games dangerous; 9 of the 12 stadiums to be used will be within 30 km of the capital city Doha; and, with a population of around 1.7 million, selling the 2,869,000 match tickets could prove to be a struggle.

However, the organising committee has already outlined how these problems will be overcome. The searing heat will be tackled by solar-powered zero-carbon cooling technology for stadiums; while Qatar has a small population, tickets are expected to be in high demand across the Middle East, as there has never been a World Cup in the area; and the issue of unused stadiums after the tournament will be dealt with by gifting them to less developed nations. Many of the brand new stadiums will be dismantled and shipped to countries in which they would be of more use. The legacy of 2022 World Cup infrastructure existing outside of the host nation is something that is reported to have been particularly appealing to FIFA when selecting Qatar as hosts.

But there have also been political questions raised about Qatar's non-recognition of Israel (what if they were to qualify?) and laws in the country on homosexuality, drinking alcohol and public displays of affection. These issues have been less well dealt with, with only general assurances that these will not be a problem.

The Qatari bid had strong backing from high-profile and powerful figures in the game such as Zinedine Zidane, Barcelona coach Pep Guardiola, and Dutch legends Frank and Ronald de Boer, of whom all except Zidane played club football in Qatar. However, with many vocal doubters as well, it remains to be seen whether Qatar can successfully host the 2022 World Cup.

influence sustainable regeneration are more problematic since they take longer to measure and are less tangible in terms of assessing impact. Did the street children of Delhi benefit from the hosting of the 2010 Commonwealth Games? Do the homeless in the East End of London benefit from the 2012 London Olympics? And did the shanty dwellers in Johannesburg benefit from the hosting of the 2010 FIFA World Cup in South Africa? Lenskyj (2008) asserts that, far from bringing communities together, the Olympic cities of Seoul, Barcelona, Atlanta, Athens, Beijing and London have been responsible for the displacement of some two million people. Part of the hidden cost of the FIFA World Cup in South Africa was the thousands of families already living in relative poverty that were evicted to tin shacks, sometimes many miles away from their homes and far away from the media attention. The whole notion of legacies attached to sporting events has to be considered carefully.

SUMMARY

This chapter has looked at the reasons why cities and countries wish to hold sporting mega-events. It looks forward to Qatar 2022. Bidding and winning major sporting events gets a mixed reception around the world. Critics argue that communities are often displaced, ordinary people are excluded from involvement and expensive facilities sometimes become white elephants. This criticism has to be balanced against the fact that such events provide economic, social and cultural opportunities. Tournaments can draw a spotlight on the increasing social responsibility of sports federations. This chapter points out that the legacy of hosting major sports events needs to be looked at on a case-by-case basis. The benefits of hosting major sporting events do not always justify the costs. Economists will tell you with some confidence that the determinants of Olympic medal-winning nations are basic economic variables such as GDP per capita and population size, but predicting FIFA World Cup outcome is much harder.

Hosting the tournament in the case of the Olympics is an absolute determinant in terms of Olympic medal wins but the uncertainty of the outcome in the football World Cup makes it a lot harder. With specific reference to the 2010 FIFA World Cup in South Africa, President Jacob Zuma concluded that the World Cup had to contribute to long-term economic growth and the creation of decent jobs in South Africa. The politics of sport today are such that the international public and diplomatic social role of sporting mega-events provides the opportunity to carry messages about the much broader role of sport in international development, conflict resolution and the hosting of major world events such as the World Cup and what this investment can do in terms of regeneration.

No single agent, group or movement can carry the hopes of humanity but there are many entry and exit points or engagement with politics that give causes for optimism that things can get better. While sport can certainly provide some hope, it cannot do this on its own. Sport needs to be more just and less charitable; however, it continues to provide a pathway for hope for some in different parts of the world and the hosting of major sporting events is often seen as a key opportunity for some but an impossibility for others. This chapter considers that sport continues to hold both a promise and possibilities for some in different parts of world. It is precisely this focus on sport as a resource of hope that the final part of this book goes on to consider.

GUIDE TO FURTHER READING

Curi, M., Knijnik, J. and Mascarenhas, G. (2011). 'The Pan-American Games in Rio de Janeiro 2007: Consequences of Sport Mega-Event on a BRIC Country'. *International Journal of Sports Policy and Politics*, 46 (2): 140–156.

Garcia, B. (2010). *The Olympic Games and Cultural Policy*. New York: Routledge.

Gold, J. and Gold, M. (2011). *Olympic Cities: City Agenda's, Planning and the World Games, 1896–2016*. London: Routledge.

Kavetsos, G. and Szymanski, S. (2009). 'From the Olympics to the Grassroots: What Will London 2012 Mean for Sport Funding and Participation in Britain?'. *Public Policy Review*, Institute for Public Policy Research, 16 (3): 192–196.

Lenskyj, H. (2008). *Olympic Industry Resistance: Challenging Olympic Power and Propaganda*. Albany, NY: State University of New York Press.

Oswald, A. (2011). 'The Well-Being of Nations'. *Times Higher Education*, 19 May: 35–39.

Parry, J. (2007). 'The Religious Athlete, Olympism and Peace'. In Parry, J., Robinson, S., Watson, N. and Nesti, M. (eds). *Sport and Spirituality: An Introduction*. London: Routledge, 2001–2014.

Powley, T. (2011). 'Olympic Hopes for Rentals' . *Financial Times*, 7 August: 11.

Roche, M. (2008). 'Putting the London Olympics into Perspective: The Challenge of Understanding Mega-Events'. In '21st Century Society', *Journal of the Academy of Social Sciences*, 3 (3): 285–290.

Sport in Society. (2011). Special Issue on Olympic Reform. *Sport in Society*, 44 (3) 289–402.

QUESTIONS

1 Explain the key reasons for cities wanting to host major sporting events.

2 Consider the impact of different sporting legacies following the hosting of various Olympic Games.

3 Discuss the notion of power and the limitations of a one-dimensional approach to power.

4 Outline how Turkey has used major sporting events to influence entry into the European Union.

5 Consider the deficiency of current approaches to thinking about the well-being of nations through sport.

6 Evaluate the public funding of the 2014 football World Cup due to be held in Brazil.

7 Differentiate between universal and particular goals and hopes for Olympism, and reflect upon how the Olympic Movement might share similar goals to that of the United Nations.

8 Explain the four aspects of the legacy trust fund linked to the 2010 FIFA World Cup.

9 What are some of the barriers to hosting sporting events in cities, and is this fair?

10 What are some of the key values (up to five) associated with Olympism?

PRACTICAL PROJECTS

1   Identify one city that has hosted an Olympic or Commonwealth Games in the twenty-first century and write a short report on the key aspects of the bid document.

2   Carry out a case study of the legacy aspect of any one major sporting event and consider if the legacy has been a success or a failure.

3   Identify the key people associated with the decision to award a sporting mega-event to a city or country, and critically evaluate who the key power brokers were and how they voted and influenced the decision.

4   Map out the location of football, rugby and cricket World Cups and the hosting of the Commonwealth and Olympic Games, and consider if the spread of these events has been geopolitically fair, in terms of location of events within countries and continents since 1948. Which country or continent has held the greatest and least number of events? Identify any trends.

5   Identify any one anti-Olympic set of protests associated with any one Olympic Games and write a report on what were key elements of the protest.

KEY CONCEPTS

Authority ■ Capitalism ■ Cultural impact ■ Economic impact ■ Governance ■ Justice ■ Legacy ■ Nationalism ■ National well-being ■ Internationalism ■ Olympism ■ sporting mega-event ■ Power ■ Social impact

WEBSITES

Olympic Games Monitor
www.gamesmonitor.org.uk/node/1171
A network site that provides information and awareness of issues arising out of the development and processes associated with the 2012 London Olympic Games.

Academic Olympic Papers
www.olympic.org/Assets/OSC%20Section/pdf/Ac%20Ac_2E.pdf
The papers provided through this site give a wide-ranging insight into studies of the the Olympic Games, Olympism and the Olympic Movement.

International Inspiration through sport
www.uksport.gov.uk/pages/international-inspiration/
The research provided here in the International Inspiration annual reviews will provide an account of international inspiration through sport's main achievements. For instance, in

2010, 6 million children in 15 countries were reached through sport thanks to International Inspiration.

London 2012 investment figures
www.uksport.gov.uk/pages/london-2012/
The website of the UK National Sports Agency provides access to current levels of investment in not only the London 2012 Olympics, but high-performance sport elsewhere.

Olympism in Action
www.olympic.org/olympism-in-action
An insight into the social impact of the Olympism in different parts of the world.

Glasgow 2014 legacy framework for the Commonwealth Games
www.glasgow2014.com
The official website of the 2014 Commonwealth Games – look at the Games Legacy documents.

Chapter 16

Sport, lifestyles and alternative cultures

Do extreme sports really provide an alternative to mainstream sports? Have they become mainstream or simply a reflection of indulgent societies – often, but not always, Western societies?

PREVIEW

Key terms defined ■ Introduction ■ Alternative, extreme and free sports ■ The growth of alternative sports in the USA ■ Alternative versus mainstream sports trends ■ Alternative sports and the IOC ■ Rationales and arguments about extreme sports ■ Sports, subcultures and lifestyle sports ■ Sport as popular resistance and hegemony ■ Freedom, constraint and alienation – an old sporting paradox ■ Negative freedom ■ Positive freedom ■ Liberation and sport ■ Sport and alienation ■ Alternative or lifestyle sports as social movements ■ Utopian alternatives ■ Sport as a social movement or social forum ■ Summary

OBJECTIVES

This chapter will:

■ examine the emergence of extreme sports and the differences between extreme and alternative sports;

■ introduce concepts for thinking about sport, lifestyles and alternative cultures;

■ discuss the processes by which some alternative sports threaten to evolve into mainstream sports;

■ evaluate the use of the term 'freedom' in relation to alternative sports cultures; and

■ suggest ways in which sports, lifestyles and alternative cultures might be thought of as social movements.

KEY TERMS DEFINED

Alienation: The state of being an outsider or the feeling of being isolated, as from society.

Freedom: The state of being free or at liberty.

Lifestyle: A way of life or style of living that reflects the attitude and values of a person or group.

Social movement: Many definitions exist. Social movements have traditionally been defined as organised efforts to bring about social change. A number of components are common to most definitions: an antagonist group; joint collective action; change-orientated goals; and some social solidarity around common goals. They often involve collective challenges (to elites, authorities, other groups or cultural codes) by people with common purpose and solidarity in sustained interactions with elites, opponents and authorities.

INTRODUCTION

Alternative sports, like alternative cultures, have often been linked ideologically and in practice as an expression of resistance to both mainstream sport and mainstream culture. Alternative sports have also been linked to extreme, action and/or free sports. *One* approach to activities coming under the banner of free sports has been to locate or associate such activities firmly with counter-cultures or 'other' alternatives to mainstream sport. Data from the US illustrates that the demand for alternatives to mainstream sport choices has emerged at such a rate that the large traditional commercial powerbrokers in American sport may struggle to win back a generational cross-section of traditional devotees to sports such as baseball, basketball and American football. The values associated with alternative sports have often been linked with notions of individualism, lifestyle, risk, freedom, alienation, excitement, voluntarism and invoking a high degree of agency when compared with mainstream sport and mainstream lifestyles. The spectre of generation X or Y rebelling or protesting against the way things are is not new, since counter-cultural movements have been active throughout the twentieth century and before. BMX biking and skateboarding have more than a 30-year history, but it is only relatively recently that they have been brought to the attention of mainstream advertising. It is not so long ago that the popular trend of jogging struggled to become a mainstream form of activity for certain groups of people and yet, at the beginning of the twenty-first century, the attraction of organised fun runs, marathons and half-marathons continues to be a pull for people of all ages. The same cannot be said for pursuits such as surfboarding, skateboarding, snowboarding, BMX biking or undertaking the eco-challenge, all of which mean different things to different groups of people and oscillate between conformity and fighting to remain alternative. Some see the difference between alternative sport as a cult or a religion being purely a question of numbers. If this is the case, then when does an alternative lifestyle become a mainstream activity? Or, given the demographic ageing profile in countries such as the UK, are there likely to be as many alternatives in the future as there have been in the past?

Research carried out by the Sporting Goods Manufacturers Association in the US indicates that the growth rates of skateboarding and snowboarding remain around the 50 per cent a year mark and that 5 of the top 10 fastest growing sports in the US can be described as extreme or free sports. The issue is complicated not just by the emergence of a diverse range of sports, but by genre and geographical location. The evolution of non-mainstream sport is not simply youthful rebellion against the sporting choices of parents or elders. Between 1987 and 2000, surfing remained the second most popular sport to soccer in Brazil and yet, in America, skateboarding, windsurfing and snowboarding are all associated with rebellion against the sports participation of one's parents. This included those who were part of the free sports Californian surfing communities of the 1950s. Many traditional sports in America are in decline in terms of participation growth (sports such as baseball, basketball and tennis have all been in declinè; Jarvie, 2006: 270). Mainstream sports lag behind alternative sports in terms of US participation trends but not number of participants. The story can be repeated in different parts of the world, particularly in Australia and Europe, where the lifestyle choices inherent in extreme sports make them an attractive alternative to those that were available to their parents (Gillis, 2001: 15).

In the US, the term 'generation Y', also known as the new millennials, is specifically used to refer to the 75 million children between the ages of 6 and 24 who allegedly show a higher degree of individualism than their predecessors. There is no longer a youth culture, but youth cultures plural, that are turned off the old school of sport. Yet, what you do is still seen to be an important part of the type of person you are. As Gillis (2001: 15) reminds us, there is no contest when you ask a contemporary 18 year old whether they like snowboarding, skateboarding, bands, girls and boys, or rugby, baseball or cricket. Further defining the nature of generation Y is a disdain for authority and the desire for sport is, in part, characterised not by the traditional values of team sport, but by the desire for risk-taking, with the common denominators being the thrill-seeking experience culminating in an adrenaline rush. The choice of sports for future rulers of twenty-first-century America may, in fact, be organised on a continuum not according to health, safety and cooperation, but the likelihood of danger, recklessness, and potential injury. It is estimated that generation Y will grow at twice the rate of the general population and that the future leaders of American society will be those weaned not on baseball, basketball and American football but also extreme sports. For the time being, the link between Obama and basketball remains strong.

The emergence of alternative sports has also had an impact upon an International Olympic Committee eager to develop youth appeal and take a hard line on traditional minority specialist sports. In 2004, alarmed that the Olympics were increasingly viewed as being too staid and out of touch, IOC president Jacques Rogge suggested to senior IOC officials that younger people were into newer more demanding pursuits, such as dirt biking and extreme sports. In 2002, Rogge had tried to axe modern pentathlon, baseball and softball, and pointed out how sports such as equestrianism and tae kwan do often draw very small crowds. In 2004, the IOC wrote to five governing bodies of sport concerning potential inclusion in the programme for the 2012 Olympic Games – squash, karate, golf, roller sport and rugby. At the Beijing 2008 Olympic Games, it was agreed to substitute two track cycling events with two BMX cycling events. Keen to make the games a more truly global or international event, it has been argued that people in every country in the world play golf but that only a few do modern pentathlon (Campbell, 2004). The inclusion of Rugby Sevens would open up opportunities for many 'other' countries to participate, and not simply the traditional rugby nations such as Britain and Australia. Yet, if extreme or alternative sports were to become part of a mainstream attraction such as the Olympic Games, does this mean that they would lose something of the essence of being extreme or alternative in the first place? Would the

SPORT IN FOCUS 16.1: EXTREME SPORTS SURFING TO SUCCESS

Some facts

✔ US surf industry retail sales: $7.22 billion (£5 billion).

✔ US participation rates in top 5 most popular extreme sports: 46 million.

✔ Top 5 most popular extreme sports: mountain biking (10.0 million); skateboarding (9.90 million); in-line roller skating (9.5 million); paintball (6.80 million); and alpine skiing (6.70 million).

✔ About 8 per cent of UK population express an interest in extreme sports but only about 1 per cent take part.

✔ The government of China set up a Chinese Extreme Sports Association in 2009 and invested $22 million in an extreme sports park in Beijing.

Compiled from various sources, including Global Industry Analysts Annual Reports, Surf Industry Manufacturers Association Reports, Leisure Trends Group Research and Mintel.

SPORT IN FOCUS 16.2: KEY THEMES IN THE DEBATE BETWEEN ALTERNATIVE AND MAINSTREAM SPORT

- Sports labelled 'alternative', 'extreme', 'gravity', 'lifestyle' and 'adventure' have proliferated transnationally.

- Contributions from cultural studies, anthropology, sociology, history, literary criticism and other areas of knowledge have impacted upon the study and interpretation of extreme sports.

- While the individual, as opposed to team, approach and the fundamental nature of present-day alternative sports remains, the march of corporate capital and the promise of lucrative sponsorship has encroached upon many of these activities.

- The image of class-related freedom that is often attached to certain activities when they are presented as cultural commodities in film and photography is frequently an illusion, if not a misleading image.

- While grassroots communities of surfers, snowboarders, skateboarders and windsurfers remain, the participants are conscious of their insider/outsider status brought about by the different reasons and values attached to the consumption of alternative sports.

- The history of many extreme sports illustrates the potential to explode and threaten the monopoly of mainstream sport and yet, at the same time, struggle to avoid being absorbed into the mainstream and consequently lose the essence of the attraction to the sport in the first place.

- Speed, time, risk, uncertainty, temporal issues and adrenaline rushes are all central to the ontology of being in alternative sports.

- Notions of identity, consumption and difference remain prominent analytical angles for grasping the phenomenon that is alternative sport today.

threat of being absorbed into the arena of international capitalist sport mean that extreme or alternative sports would lose their appeal through becoming associated with other values and pressures?

Sport in Focus 16.1 provides some facts concerning extreme sports as of May 2010, while Sport in Focus 16.2 provides a summary of some of the themes that have shaped the debate about alternative and/or extreme sports.

Let us consider some of these central issues in more detail.

SPORTS, SUBCULTURES AND LIFESTYLE SPORTS

Throughout at least the last quarter of the twentieth century, the notion of subcultural theory was formative in discussions of sport, culture and society. The formation of subcultures as a collective solution or resolution to problems of blocked aspirations of certain sections of society was widely used in discussion of youth sport, violence and sport, and the much wider usage of the way in which hegemony operated through sport. In this sense, sport was framed as a site of popular resistance and cultural struggle. While the politics of state involvement in sport continued to dominate much of the politics of sport literature, at the time the question of sport's capacity to provide resistance to what was then a debate about sport and capitalism rested very much upon the role of sport in civil society and its capacity to define itself as a credible social alternative.

A significant impact was made by those researchers who set out to illustrate the oppositional promise of sport, the meaning of style, the significance of sporting rituals and alienation from mainstream sport in the sense that many dropped out of sport. As mainstream society becomes increasingly subject to potential processes of globalisation, there are those who, through their actions, seek to dissociate themselves from what is perceived to be the homogenising nature of global culture. Many feel that they do not wish to consume the products of a global culture and seek to find alternative sources of pleasure, while others simply reject the process of globalisation. Yet, the uneven development of alternative sports and lifestyles among the peoples of the world increasingly points to the uneven distribution of those sports mentioned in the introduction to this chapter. Is alternative sport a metaphor for Western or affluent sporting cultures and places? Consider this question in relation to Sport in Focus 16.3.

One of the significant dangers in this sort of work was that many critical studies of sport that set out to analyse the wide variety of apparent popular forms of resistance to hegemony were drawn into theoretical and practical positions that lost sight of the importance of political economy and what was then discussed as capitalism's powerful forces of containment. One of the greatest weaknesses of contemporary discussions about sport today is the continued failure to realise that the new parameters of political ideas and action in sport result not so much from the demands of global markets and states and various social patternings in sport. but the tension between all three of these planes (see Chapter 3). It is within this triangle of states, markets and social patternings that political ideas about sport gain ascendancy and political action occurs. More than quarter of a century ago, the Canadian writer Richard Gruneau (1988: 126) wrote that the moment of resistance always needs to be understood both in the way it opposes hegemony and is often contained by it. It is a common mistake to associate all alternative sports with extreme sports. Many extreme sports fall under the umbrella of alternative sport but not all alternative sports are extreme. Any sport that may threaten a particularly powerful ideology may be deemed to be an alternative sport, and yet not all alternative sports are associated with lifestyle and opposition or have the potential to be a social movement. Many sports that have positioned themselves as being alternative to mainstream sports tastes and choices may share some of the same characteristics as the mainstream – perhaps male dominated, suburban and exclusive to certain groups. Traditionally, alternative sports have been enjoyed by smaller groups of

SPORT IN FOCUS 16.3: PARKOUR

Parkour is a difficult thing to describe. Part sport, part philosophy, it is the creation of Frenchman David Belle and his childhood friend Sebastian Foucan. Parkour is the art of forward movement.

Parkour is the minimalistic idea of getting from point A to point B in a straight line as fast as possible. This could require jumping between tall buildings, climbing walls, swinging from branches or vaulting obstacles in the way. Practitioners need to immerse themselves totally in their environment to be able to deal with any obstruction.

Often confused with free-running, there is a blurred crossover between the two. Some argue that free-running is simply the English name for parkour. However, there are others who disagree. Traceurs, the practitioners of parkour, often separate themselves totally from free-runners, stating the philosophy of the two terms is very different. Free-running often incorporates flips, spins and other unnecessary tricks to display athleticism and skill.

Obviously, there is a health benefit gained from being involved in such a physical activity, but traceurs also highlight the mental benefits of parkour. They believe that overcoming physical obstacles while running, such as climbing a high wall, improves their determination to succeed in other areas of their life. Similarly, making a dangerous jump helps them to take risks and battle their fear.

David Belle perhaps described Parkour's philosophy best when he said, 'Obstacles are found everywhere, and in overcoming them we nourish ourselves'.

people, and cherish a lack of competition, organisation and commercial intervention. Yet, sports such as surfing have their own Grand Prix world circuit, with surfing in 1999 being Coca-Cola's third largest sporting sponsorship deal behind international football and the Olympic Games. Beal's (1995) exploration of forms of social resistance presented through the subculture of skateboarding tried to tease out a contemporary statement about the differences between skateboarding as an alternative to mainstream sport. Three factors highlighted as important were:

1 participant control of the sport;
2 a desire to individualise the sport as standing apart from corporate sponsorship and thus being a symbol of self-determination and definition; and
3 the devaluing of competition in that, what tended to define high status was not competitiveness, which was viewed as negative, but skilfulness and a willing cooperation in sharing experiences and expertise with group members.

FREEDOM, CONSTRAINT AND ALIENATION: AN OLD SPORTING PARADOX

The notion of freedom has often been associated with alternative sports and subcultures, and yet the popularity of the term 'freedom' is often matched by confusion about what it actually means. Does freedom mean being left alone to act as one chooses or does it imply some kind of fulfilment, self-realisation, personal and social development, or simply escape? One of the most popular ideologies associated with the consumption of lifestyle or alternative sports is the close association with fun, hedonism, involvement, self-actualisation and expression. If we are to avoid simplistic views that alternative or lifestyle sports are simply expressions of freedom, voluntarism or even spontaneity, then we have to be more sensitive to the complexity of meanings and possibilities attached to the term freedom.

'Freedom' is a difficult term to discuss because it is employed by sociologists, philosophers and others as commonly as political theorists. In each case, the concern with the notion of freedom is rather different. In philosophy, freedom is usually examined as a property of the will. Do individuals possess free will? Do individuals possess free will to enjoy sport or are their actions entirely determined? Clearly, the answer to this question depends upon one's conception of human nature, opportunity and, perhaps more importantly, the human mind. In economics and sociology, freedom is invariably thought of as a human social relationship. To what extent are individuals or groups free agents in sport, able to exercise choice and enjoy privileges in relation to others or other places? By contrast, political theorists often treat freedom as an ethical ideal or normative principle, perhaps as one of the most vital principles. Moreover, throughout the twentieth century, the language of freedom became closely associated with other notions such as liberation. This took many forms, such as national liberation, women's liberation, sexual liberation, racial liberation and, consequently, the question must be asked: to what extent has sport contributed to the notion of liberation? The idea of liberation seems to promise a more complete inner fulfilment than that implied by emancipation or liberty. This notion is addressed in some depth in Part 4 of this book.

Perhaps sport continues to be haunted by the same fundamental paradox alluded to by Gruneau (1999) more than a decade ago, namely that forms of sport can, at times, give the impression of being at once an independent and spontaneous aspect of human activity and action, while at the same time being a dependent and regulated aspect of it. Certain sports, at times, allow us to be totally frivolous and escapist from the stresses, strains and realities of hardship in everyday life, and yet the very same sports remain inherently rule-bound, structured through not just rules and rituals, but space and time, and therefore the paradox is simply this: how can something that is essentially structured, rule-bound, ritualised and culturally specific be free? Forms of sport might be seen to entail a high degree of freedom, choice and voluntarism but, at the same time, be constrained by the rules, tensions and pressures that are themselves constitutive of the same social reality. How free are we in sport? To what extent are the runners at the beginning of a race standing on the same starting line all equal? Are some more equal than others, more free than others? Has sport contributed to the politics of liberation or has sport won freedoms for different groups of people in different parts of the world?

At its worst, sport goes beyond the notion of constraint in that, for many, it is deemed to be alienating. The notion of alienation has historically been central to discussions about young women and sport and, more generally, youth and sport. The notion of a certain type of freedom was clearly reflected in Marx's concept of alienation. By virtue of not being able to control the product of their labour, Marx asserted that workers would suffer from alienation in that they would become de-personalised by market forces and separated from their own genuine or essential natures. Such ideas have been used to provide insights into the world of contemporary sport, particularly where athletes drop out of sport or where they have little control over their own labour as athletes. Thus, dropping out from sport may be explained by suggesting that such athletes or that sports labour have experienced the process of being alienated from labour itself, alienated from their fellow athletes and finally alienated from their true selves. This use of the term 'alienation' from sport is presented in such a way that freedom is linked to personal fulfilment that only unalienated labour could bring about. At the same time, the popularity of sport was also linked to alienation in the sense that sport was viewed as historically helping people cope with alienation at work.

Thus, the fairly simple question – are people free to participate in sport or do alternative sports provide a sense of freedom that is no longer encapsulated in mainstream sport? – turns out to be not that simple at all. In its simplest sense, freedom means the absence of constraints or restrictions. There is a distinction drawn between the liberty to do anything or participate in anything, and a licence to do anything and participate in anything. It is often unclear whether liberty becomes licence when rights are abused, when harm is done to others or when freedom is unequally shared out. Thus, the most common qualified answer to the question of whether people are free to participate in sport is often 'yes, but only within certain limits and possibilities'. Although a formal neutral definition of freedom is possible, negative and positive conceptions of freedom have commonly been advanced. Negative freedom means non-interference, the absence of external constraints, while positive freedom is conceived variously as autonomy, self-mastery, personal self-development and/or some form of moral or inner freedom.

ALTERNATIVE SPORTS, LIFESTYLE OR SOCIAL MOVEMENTS?

As Sport in Focus 16.4 illustrates, many of the world's most extreme races require an inner strength of body and mind. As the individuals are seeking the adrenaline rush of seeking new challenges, they provide an alternative to mainstream forms of activity not always in the same sense that social movements are sometimes linked to the notion of alternative. One of the most commonly cited reasons for people focusing upon extreme sport is not only a search for the self, a quest to push back barriers, but also an urge to escape the increasingly materialistic and sometimes utilitarian Western forms of lifestyle. Many involve long periods of isolation but, in the sense that they work within the system and not against the system, they are not alternative in the same way that many social movements may be seen as alternative.

Social movements play a significant role in radical politics not so much because of what they try to achieve, but because they dramatise alternatives that might otherwise go unnoticed. It is clear that social movements favour different politics and, while the aspirations

SPORT IN FOCUS 16.4: THE SPARTATHLON

The Spartathlon is one of the world's most demanding foot races. The ultramarathon is a punishing 246 km (152.85 mile) run that takes place in Greece every September. The race is based on the legend of the Athenian messenger Pheidippides, who travelled to Sparta to persuade the city to aid Athens in the war against the Persians. He supposedly arrived the day after he set off on the journey.

The modern race began when four British Royal Air Force servicemen undertook the journey in 1982 to test whether it was possible for a person to cover the distance in such a time. Three of the four servicemen finished the race in less than 40 hours. However, in the years since, this time has been drastically lowered. The most successful participant is Yiannis Kouros, who holds the four fastest times, with the quickest finish in 20 hours and 25 minutes.

The extreme physical exertion needed to finish the race means the organisers have to impose strict entry requirements. Runners must fulfill one of the following requirements within three years of the race:

1. The athlete has finished a race of at least 100 km in less than 10.5 hours.
2. The athlete has competed in the Spartathlon race and has reached checkpoint Nestani (172 km) in less than 24.5 hours.
3. The athlete has reached the finishing point when competing in the Sparathlon.
4. The athlete has competed in an event of more than 200 km and has finished the race, regardless of the time.

of some social movements may be close to forms of socialism or a progressive way of life, their objectives are disparate and sometimes actively opposed to one another. Social movements are not totalising, nor do they all promise social reform or a clear strategy of social development aimed at social change or moving beyond the existing order. Grassroots organising remains crucial for building up relationships of mutual support and coalitions of resistance. Yet, organising from below while remaining the life-blood of many social movements remains a fragile process.

Writers such as Kusz (2004) have attempted to make sense of the emergence of extreme sports in America during the 1990s and beyond by praising the identities, values and desires that the American press have articulated and associated with the growth of extreme sports. The story that is told is that extreme sports are a symbol of a revival of 'traditional American values' such as individualism, self-reliance, risk-taking and progress. What Kusz means by this is that extreme sports have enabled and celebrated the return of white masculinity, white privilege, and a close articulation between American images and whiteness brought by the mainstream space colonised by white, male participation in extreme sports. To quote directly from Kusz (2004: 209), 'extreme sports are celebrated . . . because they enable the apparent return of the strong, confident white male no longer paralysed by feelings of anxiety, uncertainty, resentment and paranoia'. Thus, the rise of extreme sports in America is caught up in the cultural logics of white male backlash politics of the 1990s.

The story told by Wheaton (2004: 149) and Beal (1996), while acknowledging that gender relations and competing notions of masculinity remain core entry points for thinking about and participating in windsurfing cultures, is slightly different from that presented by Kusz (2004). The accounts presented here are not of any single monolithic sporting masculinity, but of perceived strains in the sport/masculinity relationship in windsurfing and other lifestyle sports. Add to this the rejection of formal competitiveness and the overt emphasis on winning, then the ethos, action and representation of sports such as windsurfing and skateboarding culture in the US and the UK is slightly different from that referred to by Kusz (2004). The examples serve to illustrate that alternative or extreme sports are capable of mobilising meanings, networks, resources and ideologies. They may contribute to social conflict or at least have the potential to realign aspects of alternative or lifestyle sports with aspects of larger social movements, such as the women's movement, the ecological or green movement or other socially driven movements that have been seeking social change.

Worldwide, 60 per cent of learner surfers are women. Women and girls, while not forming themselves as a social movement, have made and won space for themselves in the world of surfing. The first Australian surfer was a woman, Isabel Letham, who started surfing in 1914 and is now in the Australian Surfing Hall of Fame. In California, women started surfing in the 1920s. During the 1960s, the skill and number of female surfers increased. Margo Godfrey, in particular, represented a new breed of female surfer – athletic and aggressive – and later became the first female professional. Layne Beachley is the most successful female surfer of all time to date and her success has helped to attract more girls to take up the sport. She acknowledges the importance of powerful women such as Pam Burridge, Freida Zamba and Lisa Anderson, who broke down barriers, adding:

> Now there is an industry that supports women's surfing with all-girls magazines, movies and professional circuits all of which have contributed to social change within the sport of surfing. At one National Surf Centre in Britain in 2003, 40 per cent of new surfers coming through are women.
>
> (Pearson, 2003: 14)

The extent to which it can be claimed that alternative or extreme sports may be considered as a social movement or making a contribution to a new social movement remains open to question. The term 'new social movements' is often applied to a set of social movements that have arisen primarily in Western cultures since the 1960s in direct response to the changing risks facing human societies. While the ways in which sports contribute to risk, uncertainty, agency, values and certain notions of freedom can be illustrated, the extent to which alternative and/or extreme sports consciously form new social movements remains uncertain. Wheaton (2004) notes that any understanding of such sports necessitates challenging the characteristic hegemonic masculinity associated with traditional and/or mainstream sport; not all alternative subcultures or lifestyles have to be linked to the promise, utopian or otherwise, of an alternative future. Utopian alternatives to mainstream sport would remain inoperative without the visions of alternative futures and utopian

369

transformations presented in certain alternative lifestyle sports, and in that sense they remain both an important component of, and a threat to, any social movement in sport. It is clear, however, in the research by Wheaton (2004: 4) and others that part of the particular experience of, for example, windsurfing was the lifestyle that participants sought – a lifestyle that was distinctive, often alternative and closely associated with social identity, although not necessarily in the progressive sense of the word. Whether it be in the promise of the surfing subcultures of the 1960s or twenty-first century; or adventure racing and epic expeditions as 'another kind of life' (Bell, 2003: 219); or the uncertainty or risk experienced in what Watters (2003: 257), in his accounts of kayaking, refers to as 'the wrong side of the thin edge'; or style, prestige and tension encountered in Booth's (2003: 315) research into surfing in Hawaii, California and Australia, something has to be said about the pleasures and compulsions of the potential utopias presented through these and other lifestyle or alternative sports.

Wheaton (2004) insightfully suggests that, like other alternative lifestyle groupings that have emerged out of counter-culture movements, sporting cultures may, at times, invoke certain identity politics and lifestyle practices. While the emergence of lifestyle politics and lifestyle sports in the late twentieth and early twenty-first centuries may have deflected from the ideal of social class as a driver of social change, it remains clear that the politics of sport, lifestyles and alternative cultures remains one of the key terrains of any post-twentieth-century politics of sport. Yet, without firmly associating at least some of the terrain of sports, lifestyles and alternative cultures with notions of social movement or social forums, the promise of these alternative sporting lifestyles and alternative cultures may remain utopian.

Social movements are among the most powerful forms of collective action. Social movements come in all shapes and sizes, and often arise with the aim of bringing about change on a public issue. Many claim that the term 'new social movements' seeks to differentiate contemporary social movements from that which preceded them in earlier decades and is, in part, a reflection of changing risks facing human societies. The cumulative effect of new challenges and risks is often expressed in a sense that people are losing control of their own lives in the midst of rapid change. The notion of sport as an old or new social movement in itself or contributing to broader social movements may help to acknowledge the collective efforts to promote or resist political and/or cultural change in and through these sports. A change that acknowledges that alternative, extreme or free sports may be viewed as a collective or individual attempt to conquer risk, take control of part of one's sporting life separate from global sport or that the sort of grassroots organising remains a crucial aspect, perhaps a primary or core reason why people participate in old or new alternative/extreme sports. These characteristics are not unlike some of the key reasons that give rise to the development of social movements. The notion of sport as a social movement remains a fruitful area of exploration for students, teachers or researchers interested in sport, culture and society.

The idea of skateboarding as a social movement aligning itself with feminist, environmental, anti-global or civil or human rights movements is a key silence within the contemporary story of lifestyle sports. While Wheaton (2004) acknowledges the potential power of skateboarding and the transforming nature of twenty-first-century sport in the US, the analysis stops short of asking: what is the transformative or even liberating capacity of these sports to link themselves to progressive or even social forms of change? If the notion of social movements can add anything to the story of sport, lifestyles and alternative cultures, it is simply that the very essence of social movements through and in sports involves a collective attempt to further common interests by collaborative action outside the sphere of mainstream sport and/or society. This would appear to echo many of the stated values, spirit and forgotten promises within contemporary discussions of sports, lifestyles and alternative cultures.

In Chapter 3, we have already indicated the ways in which political space has changed under the impact of new social patterns. It should be noted that newly emerging forms of sporting politics exist, as well as traditional ones, rather than replacing them. New politics of sport have come on to the agenda, such as lifestyle politics, human rights in sport and environmental politics, as well as old ones such as inequality, violence, nationalism and internationalism. The characteristics often associated with lifestyle sports cultures such as those of choice, self-expression or freedom of expression, differentiation, individuality, creativity, health, fitness and the body may be seen not simply as some of the variables that attract different groups of people to lifestyle sports, but also as a set of values that have the possibility to unite a sea of people looking for something different from that provided by global or mainstream sporting forms. Alternative sports and lifestyle sport have been referred to as being an expression of people's cultural beliefs and values, but potentially they are much more since the various sports may be viewed not simply as a widely differentiated set of sports, but also as containing a mutual link to an expanding network of anti-global pleasures, pastimes and protest.

SUMMARY

This chapter recognises that sports, lifestyles and alternative cultures have attracted a considerable degree of attention, not least because they have offered a popular alternative to mainstream sport. So popular have alternative sports become that multinational corporations have seized upon the opportunity to capitalise upon the commercialisation of them. The media endorsement of athletes such as Tony Hawk meant that, at age 14, the skateboarder could command a market value estimated at $250 million. The arrival of new alternative sports, in the broadest sense of the word, continues to pose new questions, new issues and demand new notions of explanation. They also necessitate an ongoing evaluation of the real social choices that are offered by such new developments and if they are, for example, characterised by colonial powers, world markets and transnational companies. The thirst for risk, uncertainty, adrenaline rushes, chance and the quest for excitement are not new, but the limits and possibilities presented by sport, lifestyles and alternative cultures in the twenty-first century are also matched by unpredictability, uncertainty, and a new set of parameters from those that were faced in the mid-twentieth century. This chapter asks and answers the question: 'why are people and/or groups looking for new social forms of sport today?'.

It would be unfortunate if the spirit of lifestyle or alternative sports were left solely to either theories of collective behaviour or the politics of utopia. At least two practical issues are at play in the struggle over alternative and/or extreme sports. On the one hand, the notion of grassroots involvement and an antithesis to the essence of sports such as surfing, skateboarding and others being defined primarily by the need for alternative forms of competition would seem to indicate that the notion of alternative sports is more closely aligned to social-democratic reform than mainstream sport. On the other hand, the inherent potential within alternative sports to become mainstream due in part to their free-market potential would seem to indicate that the notion of alternative extreme sports is also closely aligned to free-market fundamentalism due to its potential of being absorbed by free-market forces and transformed into being a mainstream popular alternative to traditional sports. A genuine confrontation with such utopias remains possible within a broader social forum or movement involving alternative sport forms and the lifestyle politics of sport. Without visions of alternative futures in and through sport, utopian transformation remains politically and existentially inoperative, mere thought experiments and mental games without visceral commitment.

Thus, it has been suggested in this chapter that the possibilities of real freedoms in and through alternative sporting choices may be achieved if alternative and/or extreme sports actively engage with the spirit and ethos of new social movements and social forums of the time rather than identifying with the ethos of free-market individualism or being lost to identity politics. Alternative and/or extreme sports must become more than just the choices of a Western play-world; the options of real lifestyle sports choices must remain open to all parts of the world and not simply be a North/South divide in lifestyle and/or sport as a facet of lifestyle politics. The cooperation so evident within Wheaton's (2005) early accounts of lifestyle sports must move beyond being a symbol of experience and identity to making room for a more international alternative sports forum that can accommodate innumerable lifestyles and sport for life projects. Such an orientation may be discernable in embryonic form among those, primarily young people, who commit themselves to a new politics of sport today. Or is this utopia in itself?

GUIDE TO KEY READING

Booth, D. (2004). 'Surf Lifesavers and Surfers: Cultural and Spatial Conflict on the Australian Beach'. In Vertinsky, P. and Bale, J. (eds). *Sites of Sport: Space, Place and Experience.* London: Routledge, 115–131.

Campbell, D. (2004). 'Game Over for Minor Olympic Events'. *Observer,* 3 October: 5–6.

Jameson, F. (2004). 'The Politics of Utopia'. *New Left Review,* 25 (January/February): 35–54.

Parry, J., Robinson, S., Watson, N. and Nesti, M. (2007). *Sport and Spirituality.* London: Routledge.

Pearson, B. (2003). 'Say Aloha to Sisters of Surf'. *The Herald,* 12 April: 14.

Rinehart, R. (2002). 'Arriving Sport: Alternatives to Formal Sports'. In Coakley, J. and Dunning, E. (eds). *Handbook of Sports Studies.* London: Sage, 504–519.

Rinehart, R. and Sydnor, S. (eds) (2003). *To the Extreme: Alternative Sports Inside and Out.* Albany, NY: Suny Press.

Wheaton, B. (ed.) (2004). *Understanding Lifestyle Sports: Consumption, Identity and Difference.* London: Routledge.

Wheaton, B. (2005). 'Selling Out? The Commercialisation and Globalisation of Lifestyle Sport'. In Allison, L. (ed). *The Global Politics of Sport: The Role of Global Institutions in Sport.* London: Routledge: 140–161.

Wheaton , B. (2008). 'From the Pavement to the Beach: Politics and Identity in Surfers Against Sewage'. In Atkinson, M. and Young, K. (eds). *Tribal Play : Subcultural Journeys through Sport.* Bingley, UK: Jai, 113–134.

QUESTIONS

1 To what extent do participants experience a sense of freedom in lifestyle sports?

2 List and critically and evaluate six of the main themes that have been used to frame discussions about alternative or extreme sports.

3 What does the term 'alienation' mean, and how might it be used to explain the emergence of alternative sports and cultures?

4 Define both negative and positive freedom, and explain how these notions differ in relation to alternative sporting cultures.

5 In relation to lifestyle politics and sport, in what sense might we consider these activities as forming a social movement or social forum?

6 What are the politics of utopia, and how does sport contribute to this perspective?

7 What does the data presented in Sport in Focus 16.1 tell us? Drawing on this data, outline five trends.

8 What do the terms 'positive freedoms' and 'negative freedoms' mean?

9 Explain why any of the cases presented in Sport in Focus 16.3 or 16.4 might be seen as extreme or alternative, and what do they tell us about the society we live in?

10 Consider the relationship between sport, spirituality and the quest for escape or an alternative.

PRACTICAL PROJECTS

1 Identify five extreme sports websites and write a short report (1,000 words) on how these differ from mainstream sport choices today.

2 Choose any alternative sport, interview five individuals who regularly participate and form a discussion group from this sport. List the reasons they give for participating in the sport.

3 Use either newspaper or television coverage of alternative or extreme sport events to critically examine how these events are reported by the media. How would you make sense of what you have found?

4   What arguments would you use to forge a policy aimed at increasing provision for alternative sports in your area? What objections would you envisage coming from the authorities and how would you address these objections or concerns? Draft a letter to your local authority making the case for the increased provision of alternative sports in your area.

5   Choose two different lifestyle sports and, using ethnographic methods of enquiry, write a comparative report explaining how the different subcultures within these two sports experience the sport.

KEY CONCEPTS

Alienation ■ Alternative sports ■ Constraint ■ Counter-culture ■ Environmental politics ■ Extreme sports ■ Liberation ■ Lifestyle sports ■ Negative freedom ■ Positive freedom ■ Risk ■ Spirituality ■ Social movements ■ Uncertainty ■ Utopia

WEBSITES

American sports data
www.americansportsdata.com/pr_01-15-02.asp
A source of consumer survey research dedicated to American sports.

BBC News – extreme Sports Surfing to success
www.bbc.co.uk/news/10130842
An insight into the top five extreme sports in the US in 2010, with a commentary.

Extreme sports
www.itzalist.com/spo/extreme-sports/
A source of information of extreme sports – also Google 'extreme sports' for further information.

Sufers against Sewage
www.sas.org
An environmental campaign group with a mission to clear the UK coastline of sewage.

Parkour
www.parkour.org
The website of the UK Parkour Association, providing up-to-date news on events, articles and general news.

Sport as a resource of hope

INTRODUCTION

The chapters that form the final part of this book emphasise issues of social change, social intervention and the extent to which sport can act as a resource of hope today. They champion the power of sport to produce change and make a small difference to people's lives. What arguments and evidence do we have that sport can be an inspiration to different parts of the world? Part 4 of this book focuses upon the extent to which sport has figured in various campaigns and policies aimed at producing change in and through sport. The final chapter of this book explains some of the excitement, commitment and challenges facing the student, researcher or teacher who is captivated by and committed to the power of education through sport today. The conclusion draws together key points that have informed *Sport, Culture and Society*.

Sport, social inequality and social movement

Chapter 17 examines different forms of social inequality that have impacted upon contemporary sport. The chapter examines inequalities that are present in the sports participation. It draws upon research from other countries in order to provide an international perspective. It examines new forms of inequality and some of the ways in which sport has helped to support social change. It suggests that future researchers and students might examine the relationship between sport and social inequality in at least three ways: (i) inequality of condition, (ii) inequality of opportunity and (iii) inequality of capability. The chapter supports the argument that sport has a part to play in improving the life chances. It considers the way in which sport has contributed to broader social movements. Many forms of social inequality have contributed to specific social movements Sport, social inequality and social movement provides a preliminary discussion of aspects of sport and social change that are developed further in Chapter 19.

Sport, poverty and international development

Chapter 18 recognises that, despite the aspirations of many groups to bring about social change, the world continues to experience human rights violations and both absolute and relative forms of poverty. The power of sport to influence poverty is negligible but sport itself should not hide from the fact that it has been a vehicle for help in many parts of the world. Talking of the political responsibility of the athlete, the former Olympic 1,500 metre gold medalist Haile Gebreselassie commented that:

> eradicating poverty, this is all that matters in my country. When I am training I think about this a lot; when I am running it is going over in my mind — as a country we cannot move forward until we eradicate poverty and whereas sport can help — the real problems will not be overcome just by helping Ethiopians to run fast.

This chapter examines the ways in which sport has been used to help with international development and poverty in parts of the world today. It questions the way in which humanitarian aid is used and whether sport can contribute to humanitarian aid/peace efforts. It recognises Collier's (2007) observations that a *Bottom Billion* people always seems to exist. Those who are committed to advancing opportunities not just for a more humane sporting world but also a more humane world should not lose sight of the role of sport in helping to produce social change in a world that is left wanting on so many fronts. It seems that governments and policies may change but the need remains the same.

Sport and social change

In the introduction to this book, one of the core questions that was raised was: 'what is the transformative capacity of sport?'. It has been stressed throughout this book that it is important to go beyond simply explaining sport by asking the question: 'what difference can sport make?'. Chapter 19 answers this question by looking at where sport has been part of campaigns and policies aimed at bringing about social change. The chapter draws upon illustrative examples of where sport has contributed to campaigns to bring about change in society at large and internal campaigns where the focus of change has been sport itself. Many of the examples relate to sport and forms of inequality but also anti-global, anti-environmental and anti-Olympic pressures to bring about change. The chapter is conscious of the fact that the underlying factors linked to social inequality are also geographical, and that students interested in thinking about social change in sport must acknowledge that the root causes of many of the social injustices in sport today may also involve geo-political as well as socio-economic differences. The chapter explains that, in practical terms, the formulation of sports policy is but one of the most effective methods of bringing about social change in sport. The link between analysis and action for change can take many forms but, ultimately, the student, teacher, university and/or researcher of sport must move beyond the issues of what is going on in sport and how we make sense of it to decide what is to be done about what is going on. Chapter 19 argues for informed social intervention in and through sport. It alerts readers to the idea that some have referred to the era from 2010 until the present as an age of activism.

Sport, the public intellectual and the university

Part 4 concludes by questioning the role of the public intellectual, students and, indeed, universities and other agencies that have the potential to draw attention to the some of the world's problems, uncover silences and speak the truth to those in power. Chapter 20 asks: What are universities for? What are public intellectuals for? It would be wrong to assert that what is being argued for here is simply more activism from those involved in university sport, whether it be research, teaching or student sport, but if universities do not ask the vital questions of the day then they are, in part, failing to engage with one of their many key roles, which is to challenge and maintain a healthy scepticism about the societies of which they are a part of. Students may well decide that they do not have any social or political responsibilities towards sport. Yet, the public realm of sport is part of the interdependent world that we live in, and universities and university teachers have a vital role to play in preparing students for life in, if not a more just world, then certainly life in an interdependent world. Sport is also very much part of the public realm but only occasionally does sport figure in the consciousness of those politicians who have the power to make at least parts of the world a better place.

Conclusion: theses on sport, culture and society

Each of the chapters that make up *Sport, Culture and Society* has attempted to address key issues and concerns about sport and how they might be approached. The book has consistently asked three core questions:

1 What is going on in the world of sport today?
2 How should this be explained?
3 How should the question of social change be kept alive in the contemporary world of sport today?

The book has asserted that it is the interrelated nature of these questions that is important. What is going on? How do you explain and substantiate it, and what are you going to do about it? Behind the book is a thesis about sport itself. More than thirty years ago, the French sociologist Jean Marie Brohm concluded that sport was a prison of measured time and that certain theses on sport needed to be presented. In the conclusion, the arguments about sport were presented and, while this book does not attempt to emulate Jean Marie Brohm, it concludes in the same way by presenting key theses – which inform this book and the world of sport, culture and society today.

Chapter 17

Sport, social inequality and social movement

Social movements have traditionally been defined as organized efforts to bring about social change but what part does sport have to play in bringing about social change and how?

OBJECTIVES

This chapter will:

- introduce key terms for analysing social inequality and social movements;
- consider some of the social inequalities that are prevalent within contemporary patterns of sports participation;
- critically discuss new categories of social inequality;
- explain and illustrate the way in which sport may act as a social movement; and
- suggest that future researchers examining the relationship between sport and social inequality might think of this in at least three ways: (i) inequality of condition, (ii) inequality of opportunity and (iii) inequality of capability.

KEY TERMS DEFINED

Life chances: The life chances approach to policy recognises the importance of opportunities and risks. It is a framework for examining policy. It prioritises three areas for any policy: what does this do for life chances; what does it do for the life chances of the most disadvantaged; and is it likely to narrow the gap between the most disadvantaged and the rest?

Social capability: An approach to inequality that is broader than just material aspects of inequality but recognises that a gap may exist between groups or countries in terms of capability. Inequalities of capability need to be recognised as much as economic inequalities. The approach is closely associated with the work of Amartya Sen.

Social divisions: A social division is a principle of social organisation resulting in a distinction between two or more logically interrelated categotries of people which are socially sanctioned as substantially different from one another in material, cultural, social and other ways. The coherence of analysing social divisions is that it considers hierarchies of social inequality and social injustice that permeate life.

Social inequality: Unequal rewards or opportunities for different individuals within a group or groups within or between societies. Inequality is often limited to two notions of inequality namely inequality of condition and inequality of opportunity. The notion of power is important in relation to patterns of social inequality as is the notion of uneven development between areas of the world.

Social movement: Many definitions exist. Social movements have traditionally been defined as organised efforts to bring about social change. A number of components are common to most definitions: an antagonist group; joint collective action; change orientated goals; some social solidarity around common goals. They often involve collective challenges (to elites, authorities, other groups or cultural codes) by people with common purpose and solidarity in sustained interactions with elites, opponents and authorities.

INTRODUCTION

This chapter examines different forms of social division and social inequality that impact upon contemporary sport. It draws upon contemporary sports participation data in one country but also research from countries in order to provide a international perspective. It examines new forms of inequality and some of the ways in which sport has helped to support social change. It suggests that future work examining the relationship between sport and social inequality might think of this in at least three ways: (i) inequality of condition, (ii) inequality of opportunity and (iii) inequality of capability. The chapter supports the argument that sport has a part to play in improving the life chances.

It is impossible to think about sport, culture and society without immediately recognising the social differences that exist. It is useful to think of sport in terms of limits and possibilities in the sense that people are free to participate in sport but only within certain limits. Such limits are not necessarily of people's own choosing, with some of the most regularly commented upon limits being social divisions such as class, gender and ethnicity, but also age, health and location. Different people have different degrees of freedom and the fact that they differ in their freedom of choice and the range of actions they decide to take is, according to Bauman (2001: 113), the essence of social inequality. The difference in the degree of freedom is often considered as a difference in power in the sense that power is an enabling capacity and the more power that people have at their disposal the wider is the range of sports choices available to them. Nobody is powerless but being less powerful often, sometimes wrongly, equates to moderating one's choices and dreams of what is or could be possible.

Whenever one is pondering the dynamics of social divisions or forms of inequality in sport, it is always useful to consider: who is sport and how have social structures provided both continuity and change in sport? Smith (2010) reminds us that uneven development is as much about the social inequalities of space and place as it is about traditional social patterns of inequality. Undoubtedly, a global gap continues to define today's world, with more than 1.2 billion people living on less than $1 a day. 46 per cent of the world's population lives on less than $2 a day. The gap in social inequality is both between countries as well as within countries. To put this in some comparative context, for the season 2003/2004, the wage and transfer bill of the four English football divisions stood at £1,049 billion, a figure that eclipses the gross domestic product of some small African nations such as Lesotho and Mauritania, and could wipe out most of the debt of many countries, both within and outside of Africa. The transfer of sporting capital, both in terms of human and physical forms, helps to sustain social divisions and inequalities between different parts of the world, as well as promote the illusion or myth of social inclusion – a much over-used term. While recognising that traditional forms of inequality exist, this chapter considers the way in which sport reinforces old and new forms of social inequality while providing a resource of hope for some people.

The notion of social movements may encompass political parties and campaigning organisations but also individuals who are not part of any formal organisational structure. They are organised around ideas and can provide a means of introducing new ways of thinking to political and social agendas. From at least the 1960s onwards, social movements unaligned with political parties have become a component of Western and some non-Western democracies. Social movements have *at least* four characteristics, they may be conceived as informal interaction networks, having shared beliefs and solidarity, a focus on specific conflicts through collective action and finally they make frequent use of different forms of protest. In some senses, struggles over gender, class and race through sport have reflected broader social movements. The advent of improved mechanisms for social networking has meant that communication between and within social movements is much quicker and accessible. The discussion of sport and social movements introduced in this chapter should not be seen in isolation from Chapter 19 on sport and social change.

This chapter is structured around five themes:

1   social divisions and the new tribes that introduce new forms of inequality in the UK based upon people's attitudes to equality and fairness;
2   sport and social class that eschews traditional class barriers in sport while acknowledging campaigns for change – some of which are outside of the UK;
3   the role of gender and sporting heroines in challenging traditional forms of authority;
4   the impact of the Obama phenomenon in the US and, in particular, the part played by sport in providing a contribution to what Obama refers to as the audacity of hope; and
5   an introduction to sport as a form of social movement.

These themes are not exhaustive of all the different forms of social division that permeate sport today, but they do, nonetheless, reflect upon the ways in which sport – despite exaggerated claims of social inclusion or exclusion in some countries – continues to provide many possibilities within certain limits. They also inform and provide an introduction or link to further chapters that look at forms of sport and social change.

SOCIAL DIVISIONS AND NEW TRIBES

Socio-economic systems differ in the degree to which they constrain the rights and powers of different groups of people in different countries. The class structure in the UK is not the same as the class structure in the US or Asia. Patterns of interaction between different social divisions, at times, disproportionately marginalise segments of the population. In the US, while the class structure at the beginning of the twenty-first century includes an extremely rich capitalist class and corporate managerial class, living at extraordinarily high consumption standards, with fluctuating constraints on their exercise of economic power following the emergence of a recession in 2008, it also reflects a pattern of interaction between race and class in which the working poor and marginalised populations are often disproportionately made up of racial minorities.

The potential coherence of social divisions lies in the notions of hierarchy, social inequality and social injustice that permeate sport. Complex social divisions are not just about the reality of everyday sport, but rather they reinforce the fact that, whatever categories are used, unequal access to sport tends to continually impinge upon the same categories of people. The gap between rich and poor remains a significant gap. Any discussion of sport and social inequality that relates solely to class, ethnicity, gender, or any singular category fails to raise issues of poverty, capability, injustice, and the precise nature of the limits and possibilities that are open to people. No single story can address every form of oppression, identity or political aspiration but sport in the world today has to be much more sensitive to the shear diversity of the multiple axes of power and inequality.

New social divisions are emerging all the time but in the Britain of the twenty-first century new attitudes towards inequality and fairness might suggest that the orthodox traditional forms of inequality are themselves not as important as they were in the twentieth century. Researchers in the UK have begun to ask new questions about social inequality (Hampson and Olchawski, 2009). Four fairly equal clusters of opinions and groups seem to be emerging out of this recent research. The traditional egalitarians (22 per cent) support measures to tackle inequality at both the top and the bottom. They tend to be older and more heavily weighted towards Labour, with 55 per cent in socio-economic group C2DE. The traditional free marketers (20 per cent) oppose measures to tackle inequality at both the top and the bottom. They are overwhelmingly in socio-economic group ABC1 (70 per cent) and are much more heavily weighted towards the Conservative party than the country as a whole. The angry middle (26 per cent) support measures to tackle inequality at the top, while opposing measures to tackle inequality at the bottom. They are slightly more weighted towards the Conservatives than the country as a whole and 53 per cent are ABC1. Finally, a fourth grouping, the post-ideological liberals (52 per cent) support certain measures to tackle inequality at the top (although they have more positive attitudes towards those at the top than traditional egalitarians) without having negative attitudes towards those in poverty or being opposed to tackling inequality at the bottom (unlike the traditional free marketers and the angry middle). Most of the new tribes are strongly attracted to a social vision framed around improving the quality of life for all and not just some.

SPORT AND SOCIAL CLASS

Sport has long been viewed as a graphic symbol of meritocracy despite the fact that sociologists and others have been questioning the substantive basis for such a claim. The popular image of sport as an unquestioned democracy of ability and practice is somewhat over-exaggerated. Generally speaking, the term 'democratisation' tends to imply a widening degree of opportunity or a diminishing degree of separatism in varying forms of sports involvement. The term has been used to describe the process whereby employees or clients have more control over sporting decisions and sporting bodies. The expansion of opportunities in sport has been used at one level to argue that sport, at least in the West, has become more open, and yet the reality in Britain is that the extremes of privilege and poverty remain sharply drawn. An emphasis on social class cannot explain all aspects of the development of British sport but there is good reason for believing that sport and social class have been mutually reinforcing categories in British society for a long time.

It is important to ask who plays sport. The figures presented below relate to sports participation and social class in one country towards the end of the twentieth century (Jarvie, 2006; Sportscotland, 2010). Key points are that:

1   The most popular participatory sports among class category AB were curling, cricket skiing, sailing and tennis.

2   The most popular sports among DE category included snooker/billiards/pool, ice skating/ice hockey, fishing/angling, dancing and walking.

3   Sports participation in all sports is most popular among social class C1 (30%); followed by DE (26%), AB (23%) and C2 (21%).

4   With reference to particular sports, golf participation by social class is made up of AB (33%), C1 (32%), C2 (20%) and DE (15%); football participation by social class is made up of AB (19%), C1 (32%), C2 (25%) and DE (24%); bowls participation by social class is made up of AB (22%), C1 (32%), C2 (21%) and DE (25%); and athletics participation by social class is made up of AB (24%), C1 (30%), C2 (24%) and DE (16%).

5   Sports such as squash would appear to be extremely elitist in terms of participation – AB (39%) and DE (5%).

6   Some sports are fairly democratic in terms of participation, such as walking: AB (24%), C1 (30%), C2 (20%) and DE (26%); swimming: AB (26%), C1 (31%), C2 (21%) and DE (22%); and cycling: AB (27%), C1 (32%), C2 (20%) and DE (21%).

Such evidence is never complete but it addresses the question 'who is sport' rather than 'what is sport?'. Arguments about sport and social class have tended to suggest:

- that it is possible to identify a leisure class that is involved in the conspicuous consumption of sport;
- that sport helps to sustain and reproduce status, prestige and power;
- that the struggle for sport has been influenced by social class;
- that the practice of sport is socially stratified and differentiated by social class;
- that sport within and between social classes acts as a hallmark of distinction;
- that sport is intimately associated with classes that exist on the basis of the differential distribution of wealth , power and other characteristics;
- that sport contributes to a distinct way of life associated with certain class categories;
- that social class has contributed to the discourse of colonial sport within and between certain former colonies and nations; and
- that class networks continue to afford capacity and opportunity for some.

Sport and social class is not dead but perhaps the monolithic social imagery of class as a driver of change is not as forceful in the twenty-first century as it was in the twentieth century.

There are times in human history when liberalisation in the direction of harmless fun can be absorbed in an upward movement of an optimistic and expansive society. For many in Britain in much of the second half of the twentieth century, the answer lay in labour with a small and large L, in work itself, in the organisation of people who did the work so that their rewards began to match the value of their efforts and in the progress of a political party that historically represented the working class, the un-represented and those in poverty. This traditional synergy as declined. For many, the relationship between sport, class and the lottery in the twenty-first century is just another symptom of decline, a change of focus, a feeling of uncertainty and insecurity in a world in which collectivism and solidarity, in many instances, has been replaced by irreverence and individualism. A nation of subjects who historically felt that they had some control over their fate through elections, security of pensions, representation and the communities where they lived has been replaced by a loose collection of individuals living in a global world of uncertainty where even the winnings from the sports lottery are distributed elsewhere. A nation of ricocheting pinballs in some vast global bagatelle machine in which the anonymous financial bankers of the universe pulled the levers, which gave rise to the beginning of an economic recession in 2008.

The National Lottery has become an icon of uncertainty, individualism, false hope, which even in sporting terms has failed to supply the financial security and provision that was promised. The number of good causes funded through lottery provision has meant reduced funding for sport in many if not all parts of Britain – a Britain in which some people are doing rather well for themselves while other remain marginalised, disadvantaged within sport and in terms of the opportunities for physical activity. A 30/30/40 society, in which the privileged 40 per cent remain comfortable, can access private sporting clubs and have sustained their power in the market place; a further 30 per cent that, due to their changing relationship to the marketplace, insecurity of pension provision and an ageing society, have become marginalised but also increasingly politically active as a result of the changes; and a further 30 per cent who remain disadvantaged. In 2005, 25 per cent of children living in Scotland under the age of 16 continued to live in poverty (*The Herald*, 31 March 2005: 2). Thirteen million people live in poverty in the UK, including one in three children (Hampson and Olchawski, 2009). It has been suggested in the Britain of the twenty-first century that, while the lottery draws more working-class support in terms of distribution, the distribution of prize money is disproportionately biased towards middle- and upper-class sporting tastes. The poor have always had to live with insecurity and uncertainty and, while sport used to be a traditional avenue of social mobility, this has been increasingly left to chance.

The relationship between sport, social class and campaigns for social change remains a relevant challenge to equitable, neo-liberal notions of global sport. It would be misleading to suggest that, as a major driver of social change, social class is no longer relevant to bringing about transformation in sport. It is evident, even in sport, that social class cannot be viewed as a static entity. It has a life form that changes as a result of social and historical processes and consequently finds different forms of expression in political movements that endorse forms of social change in and through sport. Many forms of class conflict have been deflected into anti-immigrant and anti-Muslim campaigns. Many forms of traditional urban and rural forms of social class activism have re-emerged and confronted each other over the fight to ban fox hunting in Scotland and England. The International Labour Organization, in conjunction with FIFA and UNICEF, launched the Red Card to Child Labour campaign in conjunction with the 2002 African Nations Cup, while Fabians, in the twenty-first century, have campaigned not only against corruption in world sport, but also the need to develop a more progressive politics of sport that promotes cooperation, mutuality and a fostering of trust between different groups who share such concerns (Katwala, 2004). The traditional working-class game of football struggles through partially state-sponsored movements such as supporter's trusts to gain or cease an increased say in the running of clubs. The very cost of viewing elite football is in itself a barrier to many people. The average price of a season ticket for Manchester United Football Club in the 2009/2010 season was £730.

In other countries where football is deemed to be important, such as Brazil, governments have taken alternative steps to bring about social change through football. In 2002, Luiz Inacio Lula de Silva was elected president of Brazil. The content of the administration's policies were also influenced by football in that the first two laws that the president signed in May 2002 concerned football. Football in Brazil was one of the key grounds upon which the battle to make the country a fairer place was being fought. The sport had been run by a network of unaccountable, largely corrupt figures known as carrolas or 'top hats' who had become obscenely wealthy while the domestic football scene remained broken and demoralised (Bellos, 2003: 32). The public plundering of football was viewed by the president as a continual reminder of the previous administration's failure to stamp out corruption in areas of public life. Lula, in an attempt to force the football authorities to become transparent, ratified a 'Law of Moralisation' in sport that enforced transparency in club administration (Bellos, 2003: 32). On the same day, he sanctioned a more ambitious and wide-ranging law, the 'Fans Statute', a bill of rights for the football fan.

Social class continues to impact upon campaigns for social change in sport, and yet this particular expression of social class activism has combined diverse social and political protests with different forms of ideological awareness. While one of the elements of the erosion of deference has been the creation of new forms of rebellious collectivism, the motor of sport and social class as an engine of social change is not dead; it may have shifted geographically. Many of the progressive successes and challenges in and for world sport continue to be linked to traditional areas of concern such as poverty and labour. Classical irreverent collectivism linked to sport and working-class movements may have passed its historical high point and may be progressively weakening, and yet it would be foolish and unscientific not to acknowledge the continuing significance of social class politics in bringing about social change in sport. There may be less class but there is certainly more irreverence, which may also express itself in repulsive forms in xenophobia, violence or crime. It may also still reassert itself in struggles over the ownership and direction of football clubs in the UK.

The very poor, of course, are not in the main seats and, as John Underwood, writing in the *New York Times*, has explained:

> The great damage done by this new elitism is that even the cheapest seats in almost every big-league facility are now priced out of reach of a large segment of the population. Those who are most critically in need of affordable entertainment, the underclass (and even the lower middle class), have been effectively shut out. And this is especially hateful because spectator sport by its very nature has been the great escape for men and women who have worked all day for little pay and traditionally have provided the biggest number of a sports core support. As it now stands, they are as good as disenfranchised- a vast number of the taxpaying public who will never set foot inside these stadiums and arena.
>
> (Cited in Eitzen 2003: 18)

More recently, a reporter commented (Reid, 2011) that the hot news from Washington was that Barack Obama and John Boehner, the Republican speaker of the House of

Representatives, had arranged a round of golf together but went on to assert that the place of the challenge would certainly not be at the Congressional Country Club before the 2011 US Open. This was deemed a pity since the opulent and exclusive home of the 2011 US Open, founded almost 90 years ago, has remained an exclusive Congressional Country Club. The membership list reads like a 'who's who' of America's well-heeled elite, including a political elite numbering some seven former presidents.

SPORTING HEROINES, FEMINISM AND THE POST-NEO-LIBERAL ERA

There are layers of power within sport that are influenced by gender relations (Travers, 2011). Sport in Focus 17.1 outlines some of the ways in which gendered power relations are embedded within sport.

It is often suggested that the most widely helped view of second-wave feminism is the sharp contrast between the relative success in transforming cultures and the relative failure in transforming institutions. This assessment is double edged given that feminist ideals of gender inequality now sit squarely in the social mainstream but have yet to be fully realised in practice. Thus, feminist critiques of sexual harassment, sexual trafficking and unequal pay are widely espoused today but the level of sea-change in such attitudes has no means eliminated such practices. Thus issues of gender justice in the present period just like other forms of social division need to be concerned with issues of redistribution, recognition as well as representation. Global capitalism is itself at a crossroads given that the global financial crisis and the election of Barack Obama may signal a further challenge to the neo-liberal project but it remains to be seen as to whether the optimism of a further period of transformation is to be realised. There is a need to continue to link hopes for change for women in and through sport with a vision of hope for a better society or worlds of sport in a post-neo-liberal era.

SPORT IN FOCUS 17.1: GENDERED POWER RELATIONS

- The language, ideas, beliefs, norms and values in sport that, for instance, promote the belief that women's sport is not as valuable as men's sport or that men are better.
- The space for sport is structured by other factors such as women's freedom to go running in open spaces or at night for fear of attack.
- Hierarchical and institutionalised practices in sport.
- Embodied sporting practices that result in physical activity and sport being performed in certain ways also reproduce power relationsips.
- Historically, specific forms and notions of sport that change over time.

The very same question about who is sport is just as important in the context of a discussion of sporting heroines. The figures presented below relate to sports participation by women in one country towards the end of the twentieth century (Jarvie, 2006; Sportscotland 2010). They indicate that:

- The most popular participatory sports among women are aerobics (75%), dancing (74%), swimming (60%), yoga (87%) and horse-riding (75%) while the least popular sports in terms of participation are football (7%), fishing/angling (8%), rugby (8%), golf (12%) and squash (15%).
- The most popular participatory sports among men are football (93%), rugby (92%), golf (88%), fishing/angling (92%) and squash (84%), while the least popular sports in terms of participation are yoga (13%), aerobics (25%), dancing (26%), horse riding (25%) and gymnastics (29%).
- Women's participation in sport in this country is dominated by four activities, while men participate in a much wider range of sports, with twelve sports having participation rates of above 5% compared with six such sports for women.
- Sports that have the smallest gender gap in terms of participation include curling (51% male and 48% female), badminton (52% male and 48% female), bowling (53% male and 47% female), hockey (53% male and 47% female).
- In terms of total sports participation, a gender gap of 4% exists between men (52%) and women (48%).

Arguments about sport and women have suggested that:

- Different structures of masculinity and femininity have historically influenced the development of sport.
- It is necessary to ask the question where are the women in sport in order to highlight issues of oppression, marginality and empowerment of women in sport.
- Gender is a fundamental category through which all aspects of life are organised and experienced including sport.
- Experiences of gender in sport need to be sensitive and aware of 'other' experiences of sporting struggle outwith mainstream and/or colonial gender relations.
- Body culture and physicality are important facets of gender relations that also need to be explored and explained in terms of social division and social differences.
- Sport and gender relations have contributed to both reformist, emancipatory and evolutionary aspects of social change and continuity.
- Sport and gender remains an important and insightful element of social division in its own right.

Key areas of social change fought for by women in and through sport continue to include the struggle for:

- a more representative coverage for women within the Women's International Sports Movement;

387

■ concerns over the existence and strategies aimed at the amelioration of sexual harassment in sport;

■ raising awareness of women in sport across the world;

■ improved conditions for women in sport;

■ increased representation for women in sport both through the existing structures and new structures;

■ women's health and well-being in all parts of the world;

■ ensuring that the women executives in positions of power listen to and do not distance themselves from ordinary women who are the majority; and

■ acknowledge that the culture of movement is different for ordinary women in different parts of the world.

The Women's International Sports Movement has been an effective advocate for change in sport but also a successful conduit between sport and other organisations such as the United Nations. The reality of speaking as one voice may be utopian, but cooperative work between women in sport has meant that there is a greater potential or hope for the international voice of women in sport being heard within the mainstream of other international movements supporting and advocating for women in different parts of the world. The Women's International Sports Movement struggled with the question of representation but the future of a global sports feminism and the Women's International Sports Movement lies in the potential to unite women across social divisions and differences and, as such, the future remains international in focus, and dependent upon effective coalitions both within sport and between sport and other forms of difference including generations of feminisms.

In 1792, more than 200 years ago, commenting upon the vindication of the rights of women, Mary Wollstonecraft noted that it was justice and not charity that was wanting in the world at that time. Women and feminist movements have continually questioned male radical leadership of movements for liberation and equality in which traditional gender roles have remained unchanged. Overall, feminism has been a movement of the left, in the broadest sense, although more so in Western Europe and, in its own way, in the Third World – questioning the masculinist rule of capital as well as patriarchy – than in the US. Whether or not the contemporary women's movement or other forms of activism involving women's issues provides the prototypical alternative social movement is open to question, but certainly struggles for women's sport have benefited from international support, collectivism and forms of solidarity. Struggles for women's sport and other forms of justice for women have been sensitive to other traditions of emancipatory internationalism and, in this sense, a similarity exists between labour and women's movements. One of the major reasons for the advances, policies and interventions won by women in sport has not only been the heightened sense of forms of common orientation, but also the linkage of the women's movement to struggles for women in different parts of the world.

Fraser (2009: 114) has pointed out the advantages of contemporary dangerous liaisons between feminism and neo-liberalism based upon a mutual critique of traditional authority that may exist. Such authority as male-dominated forms of sport is a longstanding target of feminist activism. However, traditional authority also appears in some periods as an obstacle to capitalist expansion and, therefore, in this current moment the two critiques of traditional authority, one feminist and the other neo-liberal, seem to converge. If the feminist critique of sport integrated in a more balanced way issues of redistribution, recognition and the idea of justice, then should it not be possible to reconnect such a feminist critique of sport and social inclusion under capitalism? The current ongoing recession and the impending transformation of the public realm provide the opportunity to redirect sport in the direction of justice – and not only with regards to gender.

SPORT AND RACISM AND AN ERA OF AUDACITY

Arguments about the relationship between sport, racism and ethnicity have tended to rely upon some of the following arguments. That sport:

- is inherently conservative and helps to consolidate patriotism, nationalism and racism;
- has some inherent property that makes it a possible instrument of integration and harmonious ethnic and race relations;
- as a form of cultural politics has been central to processes of colonialism, imperialism and post-colonialism in different parts of the world;
- has contributed to unique political struggles that have involved black and ethnic political mobilisation and the struggle for equality of and for black peoples and ethnic minority groups;
- is an important facet of ethnic and racial identities;
- has produced stereotypes, prejudices and myths about ethnic minority groups that have contributed both to discrimination against and an under-representation of ethnic minority peoples within certain sports;
- has race and ethnicity factors that are influencing choices that people make when they chose to join or not join certain sports clubs; and
- needs to develop a more complex set of tools for understanding the limits and possibilities that influence sport, racism and ethnicity and, in particular, the way such categories historically articulate with other categories and social divisions.

In 2000, four broad generalisations were made about sports participation in England (Jarvie, 2006; UK Sport, 2010). These included that:

- black African (60%) and black other (80%) men have higher participation rates than the national average for England (54%);
- Indian (47%), black Caribbean (45%), Bangladeshi (46%) and Pakistani (42%) men are less likely to participate in sport than men in the population as a whole;
- national participation rates for women (39%) are matched or exceeded by women from black other (45%), other (41%) and Chinese (39% ethnic groups; and
- women who classify themselves as black Caribbean (34%), black African (34%), Indian (31%), Pakistani (21%) and Bangladeshi (19%) have participation rates below the national average for all women.

At the same time, sport has also been explicitly involved with campaigns, activism, policies and protests aimed at discrediting explicit racism and the power of colonialism. The struggle for sport has involved drawing attention to the fact that, up until the 1960s, many black and other peoples of colour in the US were still denied human and civil rights. The de-colonisation of Africa, the attempt to defeat institutional racism in the US, the overthrow of apartheid in South Africa and the defeat of US imperialism in Cuba and Vietnam have all implicated sport as an area of activism, if not policy intervention.

Some of the most prominent areas of legislation and injustice in sport have grown out of struggles over racism:

- The period of *apartheid* sport in South Africa from 1948 to 1992 when specific racial legislation that separated the practice of sport by racial groupings gave rise to the international slogan 'You cannot have normal sport in an abnormal society'.
- The practice of *colonialism* in many parts of the world that formed the backcloth to sporting relations between many countries. During the 1960s and 1970s, the cricket rivalry between England and the West Indies reflected racial tensions and racism rooted in years of colonial struggle. Terms such as White Wash and Black Wash were used to refer to English or West Indian victories while, at the same time, sport took on the mantle of symbolic colonial/anti-colonial struggle both between the two teams, but also in the selection of the West Indian team, as is explained in C. L. R. James's (1963) classic period account of West Indian cricket.
- The popularity and worldwide coverage of sport has meant that *sport as vehicle for protest* has been a successful medium for drawing attention to the treatment of black Americans as second-class citizens in the US and in American Sport, as evidenced by the Black Power protests at the 1968 Mexico Olympic Games. The extent to which Aborigines or Inuit peoples have also been marginalised in mainstream Australian or Canadian sport has also been a target for sporting activists. For example, much of the coverage of the 2000 Sydney Olympic Games revolved around the performances of the 400 metre Olympic gold medallist Cathy Freeman and the plight of Aborigines living in contemporary Australia.
- *Legislation* such as the Race Relations Acts of 1976 and 2004 in Britain, which provides the legal machinery of the law to investigate and act against racism in all walks of life in Britain, including sport.

Equally, there are important historical moments that can symbolise a prejudice, a protest, an ideology or a breaking down of barriers. Sport has both been racist but also provided some of the most poignant anti-racist moments. In 1881 Andrew Watson became the first black player to play for Scotland at football/soccer. In August 1936, Jesse Owens won an unprecedented four gold medals at the 1936 Berlin Olympic Games in Nazi-occupied Germany. Two years later, Joe Louis crushed Max Smelling to signal the end of a period of white supremacy in boxing. In 1967, Muhammed Ali, the world heavyweight boxing champion, condemned the war in Vietnam, arguing that he did not have any quarrel with the Vietcong. One year later, in October 1968, American black athletes protested from the Olympic medal rostrum against the treatment of black people in America and elsewhere, notably South Africa. Evonne Cawley (Goolagong) became the first aboriginal Australian to play in a Wimbledon tennis final in 1971, four years before Arthur Ashe became the first black American to win the Wimbledon men's tennis championship in 1973. In 1995, Nelson Mandela, following South Africa's victory in the Rugby World Cup, talked of sport as a force that could mobilise the sentiments of a people in a way that nothing else could. Three years later, when Zinedine Zidane lifted the FIFA World Cup for France, the French President talked of the French football team as being symbolic of the new multi-racial integrated France. In 2001, arguably the world's greatest footballer, Pele, endorsed a worldwide anti-racist campaign in football, with the words that racism is cowardice that comes from fear, a fear of difference. In February 2002, Vonetta Flowers became the first African American to win a gold medal at the Winter Olympic Games. In 2006, England bowler Monty Panesar became the first Sikh to represent any nation except India in test match cricket (Armstrong, 2008).

In 1997, when Tiger Woods won the Masters and donned the green jacket that accompanied the winning of the coveted title, golf became thrilling to watch for an entirely new audience. On the hallowed putting greens of Augusta, where Woods would not have been allowed membership a few years earlier, history had been made. Social change through sport occurred and, at the time, America did not have the language to deal with the change. Not since Lee Elder squared off against Jack Nicklaus in a sudden death playoff at the American Golf Classic in 1968 had a black golfer gained so much televised attention (Bass, 2002). The sports press cast the feat of Woods as breaking a modern colour line, yet no one, including Woods himself, could fully describe exactly what colour line had been broken. The press conveyed his parental heritage as variously African American, Asian and Native American; overwhelmingly others portrayed Woods as a black athlete, a golfer who had brought about change in the same way attributed to the likes of Jesse Owens, Tommie Smith, John Carlos, Muhammad Ali, Tydie Pickett, Louise Stokes, Vonetta Flowers and Alice Cochrane. Woods himself did not consider himself in such terms but embraced a more nuanced racial heritage more representative of the melting pot imagery associated with American history and a determining demographic factor of Generation X (Bass, 2002: xvi). Drawing upon some of the thinking presented in Carrington (2010: 5), it is worth mentioning in relation to some aspects of race, sport and politics that Carrington recognises that, through shifts between what he refers to as human freedom and unfreedom, a history of racial signification of sport can be used to mark both change and stasis, and sport contributes to both.

This book has been written as the impact of the financial crisis of 2008 and beyond continues to unfold and the age of extremes would appear to have been replaced by the age of austerity and tempered the audacity of hope reflected in the aspirations of a new American president – President Obama. As is pointed out in the introduction to this book, on the eve of the election for the new president of the United States of America, both Barack Obama and John McCain were interviewed on the half-time show of *Monday Night Football*. Asked the same questions, they differed significantly on only one: if you could change one thing about American sports, what would it be? McCain offered something worthy about sorting out the steroid problem while Obama wanted a college football play-off. Obama is not only the first black president of the US, but the first president to identify himself primarily as a basketball fan. The perception of being seen to be a sports fan associated with certain sports is not new – Reagan played football at college, Bushes senior and junior were both baseball men, Clinton did play basketball at Oxford, but Obama's basketball credentials are good. It has been widely reported that he shook off Election Day nerves playing basketball. *In Dreams of My Father,* Obama writes 'that I was trying to raise myself to being a black man in America and, beyond the given of my appearance, no one around me seemed to know what that meant' (Obama, 2008: 9). One thing it means is, in basketball, the dominance of African Americans on the basketball court is so well established and documented that it is hardly commented upon anymore. In 2009, the Washington Wizards, Obama's new local team, had 15 players on the roster, 13 of them African American. Obama's presidency coincided with an aggressive expansion by the National Basketball Association (NBA) and it hopes to establish a club in Europe within this time. One of the problems it faces is the NBA draft laws, which are the American method of dividing up young talent, that might just be too socialist for European employment law (Markovits, 2003: 28).

FREEDOMS, MYTHS AND SOCIAL MOVEMENTS

The notion of inequality can in itself be limiting, in that the focus on different forms of inequality can, at times, detract from a focus on the additional freedoms that can or cannot be won at any given point in time. These freedoms can be at the level of the individual or much broader communities of social networks. In a normative sense, substantive forms of inequality and the winning of further freedoms that help ameliorate from inequality are critical. The success of a society or community or continent can be evaluated, in part, by the substantive freedoms that members of that society enjoy. However, the focus of the argument presented in this book is that perhaps too much emphasis has been placed upon identifying forms of inequality in sport, culture and society rather than identifying the possibility of the expansion of capabilities that can be won through sport, culture and society. Greater freedoms can enhance the ability of groups and individuals to help themselves, narrow the gap, improve life chances, but not simply by identifying forms of social inequality. If the attention is drawn away from concentrating on just indices and measurements of inequality and poverty to focus upon a broader approach that includes impacting upon levels of capability, then a broader and more hopeful picture of success may emerge as opposed to one of simply measuring inequality, deprivation and poverty.

The winning of freedoms through sport, culture and society may operate at two levels. For instance, if we consider the ability of Brazil, Spain or another team to subdue all other football-playing countries, the object of discussion becomes the capability of the Brazilian or Spanish football team and not any individual player such as Messi or Pele. In perhaps the same way, the focus upon governments or organisations to solve the problem of inequality fails to acknowledge that individuals also have the opportunity to influence inequalities. Therefore, it might be asserted that considerations of inequality, justice and poverty might also allow for considerations of not only group capability, but also individual capability to make a difference to the situation. The advent of additional freedoms being won in and through sport may result from the actions of various social movements or organisations fighting to reduce forms of inequality, but they might also be influenced by sporting heroes or heroines, or ordinary people.

The women's movement, the Black Power movement, the gay rights movement, the labour movement, religious movements, and the environmental Greenpeace movement may all be viewed, in one way or another, as forms of social movement. Such movements have, at times, impacted upon sport, culture and society but very rarely is sport viewed as a social movement in its own right and, when it is, perhaps its is correct to marginalise such a thought as utopian thinking. Yet, when one reflects upon studies of social movements, it is not unreasonable to think about sport, freedoms and social movements as really important facets of any social approach to understanding sport, culture and society. More is stated in the next chapter, so it is suffice here to outline some of the key means by which sport may be considered as contributing to social movement thinking and practice. Social movements sometimes operate in the space between governments and civil society. Ad hoc commissions, new government ministries, local government committees, public protests and marches all constitute channels to access to the decision making process frequently used by social movement organisations in attempts to win further freedoms and/or influence public policies.

The study of social movements is diverse but a concern for at least four characteristics might be mentioned:

1   Movements may be conceived as informal interaction networks between a plurality of individuals, groups and/or organisations.
2   To be considered a social movement, an interacting collectivity often requires a set of beliefs and shared belonging, which can generate a sense of solidarity.
3   Social movements are invariably engaged with collective action focusing on conflicts, which may be aimed at promoting or imposing social change at either the systemic or non-systemic level.
4   The way in which social movements frequently use various forms of protest.

It has been suggested above that the impact of the women's movement internationally on sport may lend itself to a good illustrative example of a social movement changing and adapting over time. Considering social movements as potential vehicles for social or political transformation in or through sport often requires a note to be taken of the tangible outcomes gained.

By means of summary and an introduction, it might be suggested that the research into sport and social movements, to date, has tended to rely upon some or all of the following arguments, that:

- a sport-for-development movement exists that has grown out of a broad concern or framework for human rights;
- Olympism/anti-Olympism itself is both conceptually and organisationally a social movement;
- the women's international movement has been an effective social movement;
- sport has contributed to the struggles of the international labour movement;

393

- the hosting of sporting mega-events provides a regular calendar for various social movements to target and focus upon specific forms of protest; and
- sport in various forms is a social movement in the sense that it has traditionally been involved in efforts to bring about social change both within and through sport.

The very notion that sport for development/sport development initiatives may be a movement in itself was raised by Kidd (2008a) as a possibility, although not a reality, as early as 2008. The idea that the Olympic Movement and its wider contributions to society would benefit from monitoring and evaluating in order to provide a more reality congruent body of knowledge was also called for by the same author (Kidd, 2008a). Such concerns about the mythopoeic claims made by sport in a wide variety of fields have been called into question for more than a decade by researchers such as Coalter (2007, 2008, 2010) who have consistently argued that the weak evidence base for the regular systematically positive outcomes associated with sport remains problematic. The mythopoeic thesis is examined further in the chapter on sport, poverty and international development but suffice it is to say at present that, in the broader context of this chapter, the extent to which sport is a social movement remains an open question; although the extent to which the notion of development and freedoms as poorly theorised building blocks for thinking about sporting capabilities has, in part, been refuted in this chapter. Again, more shall be said about this in the remaining chapters.

The International Sport and Culture Association (ISCA) is but one example of a contemporary social movement that operates around promoting social change through sport. In March 2001, ISCA was adopted as a member of the World Social Forum's International Council. The World Social Forum is characterised by its plurality and diversity, non-governmental and non-political party focus. That is to say it is a social movement, a social network and a social forum advocating and acting to promote social change (Mertes, 2004). It is an organisation engaged in concrete action towards building another world at any level form the local to the international. ISCA association through the forum is provided here as an illustrative example of a sports movement contributing to global social change as part of a strong worldwide alliance of NGOs, volunteers, activists, researchers, students and politicians.

SUMMARY

This chapter has examined the complex reality of sport and social inequality. It has noted that social inequalities have traditionally referred to the differences in people's share of and access to resources and opportunities. It has suggested that the term 'social inequality' in relation to sport and other areas needs to be thought of in at least three senses:

1 inequality of condition, which may refer to variations in factors such as income, education, occupation or the amount of time to spend on sport, exercise and recreation;

2 inequality of opportunity, which focuses more on the individual and is concerned with the degree of freedoms that people have in moving within and between the restrictions set by a reward structure; and

3 inequality of capability, which refers to the differences that individuals or groups may have as a result of inequalities in power and capability.

A redistribution of income resources may clearly affect different social divisions and people living in different countries but it is what people do with this resource that is important. For social thinkers such as Sen (2009) the issue of inequality of capabilities – in other words, what people do with resources – literacy, nutrition, access to sport and the power to participate in the social life of the community is also crucial. It has been suggested here that sport can have a part to play in improving or influencing the capability gap and consequently make a contribution to improving life chances for some.

Improving life chances requires a coordinated effort and, as such, any contribution that sport can make must also build upon a wider coalition of sustained support for other social and progressive policies. The life chances approach to narrowing the gap between rich and poor has a key role to play in producing social change. It requires harnessing a strong political narrative and action plan that fits with many people's intuitive understanding that life should not be determined by socio-economic position and that people do have choices. The thesis presented in *Idea of Justice* exposes the idea that, to be genuinely free, you have to have a capability set. What Sen (2009) argued was that the market economy is not a free-standing institution, nor a self-regulating one. You need support from other institutions. You need other resources of hope. You need supervision from the state, you need supplementation by the state and society to take care of poverty, ill health, illiteracy, and educational achievement and opportunity. The question this chapter has posed is whether sport can be part of these other resources of hope.

While explaining economic, social and comparative aspects of what sport can do for society, the more important intellectual and practical questions often emanate from questions relating to social change. Historically, the potential of sport lies not with the values promoted by global sport or particular forms of capitalism for as we have also shown in this chapter these are invariably unjust and uneven. The possibilities that exist within sport are those that can help with radically different views of the world perhaps based upon opportunities to foster trust, obligations, redistribution and respect for sport in a more socially orientated humane world. Yet, the cautionary mythopoeic thesis is a warning that needs to be engaged with further.

The notion that sport can contribute to or be a social movement for change in its own right is explored further in the next chapter but it has been introduced here because so many social forms of inequality have influenced the very social nature of other social movements in and through sport. Organisations such as ISCA are examples of non-governmental organisations aimed at bringing about change through sport. They act as a social movement in some senses.

GUIDE TO FURTHER READING

Bass, A. (2002). *The Triumph but the Struggle: The 1968 Olympics and the Making of the Black Athlete*. Minneapolis, MN: University of Minnesota Press.

Coalter, F. (2010). 'The Politics of Sport for Development: Limited Focus Programmes and Broad Gauge Problems?'. *International Review for the Sociology of Sport*, 45 (3): 295–314.

Kidd, B. (2008). 'A New Social Movement: Sport for Development and Peace'. *Sport and Society*, 11 (4): 370–380.

Mertes, T. (2004). *A Movement of Movements*. New York: Verso.

Sen, A. (2009). *The Idea of Justice*. London: Allen Lane.

Travers, A. (2011). 'Women's Ski Jumping, the 2010 Olympic Games and the Deafening Silence of Sex Segregation, Whiteness and Wealth'. *Journal of Sport and Social Issues*, 25 (2) May: 126–141.

QUESTIONS

1 Outline the five arguments that are made about the relationship between sport, racism and ethnicity.

2 Explain the impact on racism of struggles over sport in South Africa, America and other places. Have these struggles made a difference to the lives of minority groups of people?

3 Fraser's argument might provide direction for thinking about women in sport. What are the points made with regards to feminism, capitalism and inequality, and how might these be applied to analysis or new ways of thinking about sport today?

4 Discuss the role of freedom in sport and the limitations of thinking that freedoms can only be won at the level of structure.

5 Provide four characteristics that often constitute the making of social movements.

6 Outline forms of inequality that have impacted upon sports participation in the UK and substantiate your answer with the evidence provided.

7 What new social divisions are introduced in this chapter? What are the key forms of social inequality in your country today? Comment upon how some of these interact with each other and impact upon sport.

8 Discuss the assertion that power relationships are central to understanding sport and gender relations.

9 Outline three important ways in which inequality is talked about in this chapter. Why are they important in relation to the idea of improved life chances?

10 Provide arguments for and against the charge that the concepts and substantive base for considering sport to be a power for good are mythopoeic.

PRACTICAL PROJECTS

1   Visit the International Olympic Committee's main website (www.olympic.org). Choose 5 projects that illustrate Olympism in action and write 500 words evaluating each of them.

2   Look at the ISCA website (www.isca-web.org). Use examples from the work of ISCA to illustrate how ISCA might be viewed as a social movement for sport.

3   Having researched some of the evidence provided by the Women's Sports Foundation (www.womenssportsfoundation.org) and the Black Women in Sports Foundation (www.blackwomeninsport.org), outline five policy statements that would help promote equality in sport for all women.

4   Consider how an organisation such as unicef (www.unicef.org) use sport to help promote children's rights. Using the search facility, carry out a search for sport and read 10–15 of the documents that result from your search.

5   The United Nations history of promoting sport for development can be found at www.sportanddev.org. Provide a short history of the United Nations involvement in sport and development work from 2000 until the present. List the resolutions adopted by the United Nations General Assembly in relation to sport from 2003.

KEY CONCEPTS

Anti-racism ■ Capability ■ Ethnicity ■ Feminism ■ Freedom ■ Gender ■ Life Chances ■ Olympism ■ Power relations ■ Racism ■ Social change ■ Social class ■ Social inequality ■ Social movement ■ Sport for development

WEBSITES

Black Athlete sports network
www.blackathlete.com
A support network for black athletes that covers issues in sport in society. For instance, a call to support the President of the United States in 'Support our President Please'.

European Women and Sport group
www.ews-online.com/
A nework of European sports organisations supporting women and equality through sport.

International Sport and Culture Association

www.isca-web.org

This website will take you into the work of a sports organisation aimed at building international relations between people, cultures, organisations and sectors. Seeing sport as a culture of movement, it aims to develop opportunities for learning, inspiration and action to induce social change.

The Centre for Sports Policy Studies

www.physical.utoronto.ca/Centre_for_Sport_Policy_Studies.aspx

Access to campaigns, projects and publications involving the University of Toronto centre.

Let's Kick Racism out of Football

www.kickitout.org

A source of information that provides up-to-date knowledge about sport and racism, and the ongoing actions to eradicate racism from sport.

Women's Sports Foundation

www.womenssportsfoundation.org

The work of the Women's Sports Foundation is cited in this chapter as an example of a dedicated foundation contributing to the broader work of the Women's International Sports Movement. It has the potential to unite women across social divisions and differences and, as such, its future remains international in focus and dependent upon effective coalitions, both within sport and between sport and other forms of difference.

Chapter 18

Sport, poverty and international development

Sports are often associated with fighting forms of inequality and poverty. Can sport make a difference?

Is it a utopian project to expect sport to make a difference?

PREVIEW

Key terms defined ■ Introduction ■ Millennium Development Goals ■ Homeless World Cup ■ Sport, poverty and the bottom billion ■ Absolute and relative poverty ■ Tiger Club project ■ Sports labour migration ■ Running to escape poverty and survive ■ Haile Gebreselassie ■ Sport and international development ■ Common assumptions ■ Types of international development projects involving sport ■ Peace and sport ■ Aid, poverty, recognition and freedom ■ Summary

OBJECTIVES

This chapter will:

■ explore the notion of sport as a form of humanitarian aid;
■ answer the question: 'how can sport serve the international development agenda?';
■ evaluate the relationship between sport and poverty;
■ identify a number of sports campaigns that might be viewed as humanitarian; and
■ argue for a solution that prioritises recognition and redistribution through sport, culture and society.

KEY TERMS DEFINED

Freedom: The state of being free or at liberty.

Human development: A capability-orientated approach to development that seeks to expand the range of things that people can do and can be. It recognises that an inequality gap may exist in terms of different capabilities in different parts of the world, which contributes to uneven development.

Humanitarian intervention: The principle that the international community has a right to intervene in states that have suffered large-scale loss of life or genocide, wheter due to deliberate action by its governemnt or because of the collapse of broader governace. The question is whether sport can contribute as a basis for paving the way for various forms of intervention.

Millennium Development Goals: A set of time-limited targets and commitments enshrined within the United Nations Millennium Declaration to improve eight areas: poverty and hunger; primary education; gender equality; child mortality; maternal health; tackling diseases such as HIV/AIDS and malaria; environmental sustainability; and partnership working.

Poverty: In the most orthodox view, a situation suffered by people who do not have money to buy food and satisfy other basic material needs. In an alternative view, a situation suffered by people who are not able to meet their material and non-material needs through their own effort.

INTRODUCTION

In early 2009, international communities were struggling to understand the significance of the New Depression – its causes, its duration, its consequences and its possible solutions. The global crisis that began in the summer of 2007 with the onset of a credit crunch and the unravelling of the world financial systems also marked a potential fundamental shift in the balance of international power. Such a shift may constitute one of the most profound, financial, economic, political and ideological crisis facing the West since the 1930s. A meeting of the G20 leaders in London in 2009 delivered more than symbolism. The very fact that a meeting of the top 20 leaders took place is an indicator of a shift in the global balance of economic power from the rich countries to one involving more of the developing world. The April 2009 summit of world leaders agreed a $1.1 trillion package of funding to secure stability, growth and jobs in the light of an economic recession. The G20 solution to tackling the economic crisis included commitments to financial regulation, sanctions against tax havens, increasing resources made available through the International Monetary Fund, commitments to global trade, and a degree of protectionism for developing countries. If development is about anything, it may be about giving hope to ordinary people that their children will live in a society that has caught up with the rest of the world and, if sport in development is about anything, then it ought to act as a resource of hope in this process.

Earlier in 2000, at a Millennium Summit in New York, 189 world leaders agreed to implement a series of Millennium Development Goals (MDGs) by the year 2015. These goals included:

1   reducing world poverty and hunger by 50 per cent;
2   achieving universal primary education;
3   empowering women and promoting gender equality;
4   reducing child mortality;
5   improving maternal health;
6   combating HIV/Aids and other diseases such as malaria;
7   ensuring environmental sustainability; and
8   developing a global partnership for development.

(Ogi, 2004)

Talking of the role of sport in international development, in 2005, Kofi Annan, then United Nations secretary-general, noted the potential of sport to effectively convey humanitarian messages and help to improve the quality of people's lives while helping to promote peace and reconciliation. In 2010, the United Nations reaffirmed the importance of sport as a vehicle for education, health, development and peace. At the 2010 Summit on the MDG, the 65th United Nations General Assembly adopted a resolution recognising the power of sport in helping to attain such objectives by 2015.

Improving life chances certainly requires a coordinated effort and, as such, any contribution that sport can make must build upon a wider coalition of sustained support for social and progressive policies. The life chances approach to narrowing the gap between rich and poor has a key role to play in producing social change. It requires harnessing a strong political narrative and action plan that fits with many people's intuitive understanding that life should not be determined by socio-economic or even geographical position and that people do have choices, while drawing attention to the fact that some people and places face greater risks and more limited opportunities. Equalising life chances and focusing on areas such as poverty should sit together as part of a vision for a better society and sport has its part to play. In part, the promise and possibilities of sport are encapsulated in the words of the former Olympic and Commonwealth athlete Kip Keino:

> I believe in this world that sport is one of the tools that can unite youth – sport is something different from fighting in war and it can make a difference – we can change this world by using sport as a tool.
>
> I've run a lot for water charities and children's charities. I believe we share in this world with members of our society who are less fortunate. This is important. We came to this world with nothing and we leave this world with nothing. So we can be able to make a better world for those who need assistance.
>
> (interview with the author, 5 February 2007)

Sport is clearly not an answer to the eradication of absolute or relative poverty in that in certain circumstances it can only make a contribution. In certain parts of the world, it may contribute to escaping from certain local contexts but this in itself does not change the context. Certain celebrity role models may draw attention to the plight of many of the world's poor and underprivileged but the number of socially committed sporting role models is more than often outweighed by the overall impact of global sport that in itself is part of the problem. Athletes on the world stage can keep the issue of human rights and poverty in the media headlines for a small period of time. There are humanitarian support initiatives, such as Sport Relief held in the UK in July 2002, which helped to raise £10 million for projects aimed at improving the lives of children and young people suffering from the effects of poverty and deprivation. Numerous initiatives involving education through sport, in which sport is viewed as a means to an end, have been cited in this chapter. It is evident, according to a former chairman of Olympic Aid, J. O. Koss, that participating in sport may provide a number of psychosocial benefits (Roberts, 2002: 24). One thing to remember about poverty and the exploitation of human rights is that they continue to exist whether the spotlight is turned on or off, and while governments, policies and initiatives may change, the need often remains the same.

Many of the poorest countries in the world continue to defy repeated attempts by international communities to provide sustainable help. Sport has historically been used as a key facet of humanitarian aid and a proven avenue of social mobility for many athletes from developing countries. The historical writings on sport and capitalism are rich with proven examples of how sport has intervened in the past (Kidd, 2008a; Kidd and Donnelly, 2000). Observations made by Collier (2007) acknowledge that the real development challenge is one of closing the gap between a rich world and a poor world in which the world's poorest people – the bottom billion – face a tragedy that is growing inexorably worse. Helping the bottom billion remains a key challenge for the world in the twenty-first century. The question is whether sport has a part to play in this process.

SPORT, POVERTY AND THE BOTTOM BILLION

Nelson Mandela described it as the modern slavery; thousands have demonstrated against it; and it has been the object of fundraising campaigns by some of the world's top musicians and sportsmen and women. In July 2004, James Wolfensohn, head of the World Bank, noted that, in terms of expenditure, the priorities in world spending were roughly $900 billion on defence, $350 billion on agriculture and $60 billion on aid, of which about half gets there in cash (Settle, 2004: 16). Oxfam noted that it would cost £3.2 billion to send all the world's children to school. Poverty may be a truly international phenomenon in that, in relative and absolute terms, it exists worldwide and the needs of the world's poor invariably remain the same.

The notion of poverty is not new but it is often suppressed in the academic literature about sport, culture and society as other debates take centre stage. Discussions of poverty have tended to draw upon some or all of the following ways of thinking about poverty:

- poverty is a matter of behaviour;
- poverty does not exist but some people are too unequal;
- poverty must be viewed in both relative and absolute terms;
- a symptom of poverty is social exclusion;
- poverty is about how society distributes its resources through its structures and processes;
- poverty is what economists say it is but also much more in terms of social poverty;
- poverty is about having an income below some statistical percentage of the national income distribution; and
- poverty is not just relational in socio-economic terms, but also geopolitical terms.

(Alcock, 1997; Davis, 2006; Lister, 2004; Pacione, 2001)

Many NGOs have been at the forefront of initiatives involving sport as a facet of humanitarian aid in attacking the social and economic consequences of poverty. The Tiger Club Project in Kampala, Uganda, is one of many initiatives that use sport as a basis for reaching street children and young people in need. The objectives of the Tiger Club include: (i) helping street children and young people in need; (ii) providing children with food, clothing and other physical needs; (iii) helping with education and development; (iv) enabling children to realise their potential so that they can gain employment; (v) providing assistance to the natural families or foster carers of children and young adults; and (vi) providing medical and welfare assistance (Tiger Club Project, 2003). The 2003 annual report reported that, in 2002, 263 children had been offered a permanent alternative to the street; a further 116 street children and young people were in the START programme, which meant full-time schooling; and 161 young people were resettled in their village of origin and provided with means for income generation. Of those resettled children, 76 per cent have remained in their villages (Tiger Club Project, 2003: 2).

403

SPORT IN FOCUS 18.1: THE HOMELESS WORLD CUP IMPACT REPORT, 2007

381 players participated at the Homeless World Cup 2007 in Copenhagen. Six months after the tournament, research conducted showed:

- 93% had a new motivation for life (354 players);
- 83% had improved social relations (316 players);
- 71% had significantly changed their life (271 players);
- 29% found employment (110 players);
- 38% improved their housing situation (145 players);
- 32% went into education (122 players);
- 118 players addressed a drug or alcohol dependency;
- 71% now play football on a regular basis (271 players); and
- 18 women participated (up from 5 in Edinburgh 2005).

Statistics are just one story. Here are some of the personal stories behind the figures:

- Michelle, female player of the tournament, was selected for Brazil's national team (under 20s) for the South American Cup.
- Cheerie from Liberia was awarded a four-year academic scholarship at a college in the US.
- Eugene from Ghana addressed a drug dependency and also found employment that gave him enough money to pay rent and have a home.
- Dave, manager of Scotland, himself a player in the Gothenburg 2004 Homeless World Cup, led Scotland to victory. He has bought his own home, addressed an alcohol issue, and passed an HND in community development.
- Aaron from Wales has acquired the confidence to train and get a job as a forklift truck driver.

Every year, about 200 million people move in search of employment – about 3 per cent of the world's population (Seabrook, 2003: 32). Legal migrants who leave their homes in poor countries to provide labour or entertainment in other parts of the world are generally regarded as privileged. Researchers have helped to pave the way for an extensive body of research into the causes of sports labour migration across different parts of the world, and yet very little has been written about the part played by some athletes in earning money to support whole families, even villages, in their country of origin. When the career of a leading world athlete from a developing country is brought to a premature end, the consequences often extend far beyond the track. The Mozambican Maria Mutola, the Olympic and five-time world indoor 800 metres world record holder, routinely sends track winnings back to her country of origin. Chamanchulo, the suburb of Maputo in which Mutola grew up, is ravaged by HIV, passed on in childbirth or breast milk to 40 per cent of the children (Gillon, 2004: 30). In 2003, when Mutola became the first athlete to collect $1 million for outright victory on the Golden League Athletic Grand Prix Circuit, part of the cash went to the foundation she endowed to help provide scholarships, kit, education and coaching for young athletes (Gillon, 2004: 30).

Running to escape poverty and survive

A survey of more than 250 Kenyan women athletes prioritised the following motivations for women athletes wanting to run:

1 money (48%);
2 role models (22%);
3 to run in the Olympics (12%);
4 scholarships (6%);
5 significant others (6%);
6 fitness (4%); and
7 fun (2%).

(Jarvie and Macintosh, 2006)

The most prominent barrier facing Kenyan women was a lack of money, with a staggering 98.5 per cent finding this prohibitive. Closely related to this was a lack of equipment (97.5 per cent). These barriers were also faced by young boys starting out on an athletic career, but boys were much more likely to receive support from their families, the government and the Kenyan Amateur Athletic Association. The findings from the survey are supported by other sources of information that support the priority of money as the main motivation for women athletes in Kenya (Jarvie and Sykes, 2012).

The 3,000 metre steeplechase at the 2005 World Athletic Championships held in Helsinki was won by Saif Saaeed Shaheen in a time of 8 minutes, 13.31 seconds. The official world championship records will show that the gold medal went to Qatar, a country in which Saif Saaeed Shaheen is viewed as an athletic icon. The athlete's successful defence of this gold medal was his twenty-first successive victory since 2002. His elder brother Chris Kosgei won the gold for Kenya in 1999 but, unlike Shaheen, did not defect to Qatar. Saif Saaeed Shaheen, born Stephen Cherono, won his first world steeplechase title 17 days after defecting to the oil-rich state that had granted him a passport. In that same race, Shaheen's brother ran for Kenya, refused to call him anything other than Stephen and did not congratulate him after the race. Kenyan athletic officials, writes Gillon, were so upset at losing this steeplechase world title for the first time since 1987 that they stopped Shaheen running for Qatar at the 2004 Athens Olympics through enforcing athlete eligibility rules following his migration. Kenya won gold, silver and bronze medals in the men's 3000 metre steeplechase at the 2004 Athens Olympic Games.

Athletes such as Shaheen are single-minded and mono-causal when it comes to explaining both personal and Kenyan athletic success. It is important here not to be confused by simple Western stereotypes about non-Western cultures. The context is such that, as a boy, Shaheen's family 'had 60 cows and 30 goats until a drought . . . left the family with 7 cattle and 3 goats . . . and it cost him his education', since the animals would have been sold to

405

pay for his school fees. As Stephen Cherono, he was raised in Kamelilo a village in Keyo in which there was no water tap and every day after school, which cost $2 for 3 days, he walked 3 km to collect 10 litres of water. The move to Qatar was allegedly based upon an offer of a least $1,000 dollars a month for life. About 50 people now depend upon that athlete's success for their livelihoods. He puts eight children through school, with two at college in America and, when asked to explain Kenyan running success, said that the answer is simple: 'an athlete in Kenya runs to escape poverty' and 'I fight to survive' (Jarvie, 2010).

The Ethiopian athlete and politician, once Olympic champion and world record holder, Haile Gebreselassie left us in no doubt about both the social and political responsibility of the athlete but also the limits and possibilities of sport in relation to poverty in his country. In an interview with the athlete reported in *The Times* of March 2002, in an article entitled 'Gebreselassies's rise provides hope in the long run', the Ethiopian drew attention to the context and circumstances of his life aged 15:

> This was all at a time when my father was cross with me because I was doing athletics and my country was going through famine in which millions died and all I had was running – I just ran and ran all the time and I got better and better.

Talking of the necessity to run:

> I only started running because I had to – we were six miles from school and there was so much to be done on the farm that I ran to school and back again to have enough time to do farming as well as school work.

Finally, talking of the political responsibility of the athlete we were left in no doubt about the priorities:

> Eradicating poverty – this is all that matters in my country. When I am training I think about this a lot; when I am running it is going over in mind – as a country we cannot move forward until we eradicate poverty and whereas sport can help – the real problems will not be overcome just by helping Ethiopians to run fast.

In reality, sport can only make a small contribution but small contributions can sometimes make a difference. How sport can help in the fight against poverty should not be shelved as a historical question until much more has been done to fight both relative and absolute experiences of poverty worldwide.

In the same way that the all-too-easily accepted truths about globalisation have ignored the uneven and differentiated forms of capitalism emerging in the twenty-first century, so too it is crucial not to ignore the injustices and uneven patterns of sports labour migration. It is essential that any contemporary understanding of sport must actively listen and engage with other sporting communities, places and voices. Perhaps it is impossible for humanity or sport to arrive at an understanding of the values that unite it, but if the leading capitalist nations ceased to impose their own ideas on the rest of the sporting world and start to take cognisance of 'other' sporting cultures, then the aspiration of sport may become more just and less charitable. It is not charity that Africa or African runners want, but the tools by which Africans can determine their own well-being and life chances in a more equable sporting world. If large parts of Africa are kept poor as a result of unfair trade arrangements, which facilitate cheap European and American imports that keep parts of Africa poor and dependent, then why should the resources afforded by running not be viewed as a viable route out of poverty for those that can make it?

The issue is put more explicitly in the work of Collier (2007), who asserts that single-factor theories about development fail to recognise that a one-size-fits-all theory of development fails to acknowledge the distinct poverty traps that some developing countries face. For the past 50 years or more, what we have defined as developing countries tend to encompass about 5 billion of the 6 billion people in the world. Those whose development has failed face potentially intractable problems and account for the bottom billion people and about 50 failing states. This bottom billion live on less than a dollar a day and, while the rest of the world moves steadily forward, this forgotten billion is left further behind and the gap between rich and poor fails to diminish in economic terms. Conventional international aid has been unable to impact in areas of the world in which corruption, political instability and resource management lie at the root of many problems. The lack of growth in the countries of the bottom billion needs particular strategies for particular circumstances. The object of international development should not be aid, but growth. The politics of the bottom billion is not a contest between the rich developed world and a number of economically poorer worlds, but it is difficult for parts of Africa, Haiti, Bolivia, Laos, Cambodia, Yemen, Burma and North Korea to compete with the likes of China, India and/or Brazil. The 58 countries that make up Collier's bottom billion people have fewer people than China or India combined. One of the few forums where the heads of the major governments meet is the G20.

SPORT AND INTERNATIONAL DEVELOPMENT

A significant contribution to research into sport, culture and society has been made by those who have started to address and question the role of sport in development (Bolton, 2008; Coalter, 2010; Levermore and Beacom, 2009). Much of this research has talked to a world that existed before the emergence of the credit crunch, the economic recession, the election of a new American president and the emergence of a new world order symbolically represented by the G20. The role that sport has to play in the field of international development has been advanced through the work of Levermore and Beacom (2009). The aim of this work was to initiate debate, in primarily academic international development circles, upon the 'use of sport based initiatives to establish and assist development' (Levermore and Beacom, 2009: 5). The collection of essays remains the most comprehensive coverage of a potential new sports agenda in the field of international development and provides a body of evidence that testifies to the idea that power in world sport has become increasingly dispersed. The dispersal of power in world sport means that the control, management and organisation of sport does not simply occur at local or global levels.

The research associating sport with international development tends to rely on some or all of the following arguments presented in Sport in Focus 18.2.

407

SPORT IN FOCUS 18.2: ASSUMPTIONS RELATING TO SPORT AND INTERNATIONAL DEVELOPMENT

- Sport represents a number of theoretical positions within the field of development.

- Sport can be part of the process for development in a diverse range of different circumstances and contexts.

- The evidence to support the claim that sport can produce social change is, at best, limited. We need to be clear about the limitations of sport as well as the possibilities.

- Sport has only recently figured within the goals of modernisation/neo-liberal development thinking.

- Sport reproduces and helps to sustain the gap in resources between different parts of the world.

- Sport has some capacity to act both as a conduit for traditional development but also as an agent of change in its own right.

- New forms of internationality and cooperation between countries provide a more realistic opportunity for progress rather than those that simply emanate from Westphalia or state-organised capitalism.

Historically (see Chapter 10), sport and education have been key avenues of social mobility and an escape from poverty. Thinking systematically about emancipatory alternatives and the part played by sport is one way or element in the process by which the limits of the possible can expand. Education through sport projects have been viewed as agents of social change, with the rationale being that they can:

- increase knowledge and skills and, in a broader sense, contribute to the knowledge economy;
- help to provide opportunities for life-long learning and sustain not just education, but an involvement in sport and physical activity;
- make a voluntary contribution to informal education through sport that can make a positive contribution to helping young people;
- help foster and develop critical debate about key public issues;
- support programmes in different parts of the world that involve sport as part of an approach to tackling HIV education; and
- help to foster social capital through fostering relationships, networking and making connections.

These networks through education and sport have the potential to act as a form of human resource.

Research suggests that sport can contribute to the development process, particularly where traditional approaches to development have found it difficult to engage with communities. The benefits from using sports as a development tool or for peace building involve not just sport, but education through sport. Such programmes have long since been viewed as agents of social change for individuals, with the rationale being that they can: provide opportunities for life-long learning and sustain not just education, but an involvement in sport and physical activity; increase knowledge and skills and, in a broader sense, contribute to the knowledge economy; foster social capital through building relationships, networking, and making connections; and support development programmes across the world that use sport as a tool or incentive for participation. Levermore and Beacom's (2009: 9) review of sports projects that were aimed at sport and development tended to initially group such projects around certain themes. These were aimed at helping with:

- conflict resolution and international understanding;
- building physical, social, sport and community infrastructure;
- raising awareness, particularly through education;
- empowerment;
- direct impact upon physical and psychological health as well as general welfare; and
- economic development/poverty alleviation.

International recognition for the potential role that sport can play in attempting to achieve the Millennium Development Goals has undoubtedly placed sport higher up the agenda of organisations aiming to facilitate humanitarian aid packages for countries in need. New dimensions to the understanding of the role of sport are being further developed as a result of an increasing emphasis on the part played by sport in international development and/or as a facet of humanitarian aid. Sport, in a number of ways, has been seen to be part of a programme of social intervention and welfare aimed at supporting people who have been traumatised by conflict and by helping in situations of military conflict where sport is used to draw people out of routines of violence. Projects such as Peace and Sport are, in part, specifically targeted at parts of the world, such as Haiti, that have experienced some of the issues alluded to above.

In a recent overview, Coalter (2010), questioning the promise of sport to help with development makes a number of salient points about work in this area. Coalter (2010: 298) suggests that approaches to sport can be classified based upon the degree of emphasis placed upon sport to deliver certain objectives. Such approaches include traditional forms of provision for sport in which sport is assumed to have inherent development properties. Sport plus approaches in which sport is augmented with parallel programmes in order to achieve development objective. Plus, sport approaches in which sport's popularity is used to attract young people to programmes of education and training but very little attention is paid to the systematic strategic development of sport itself. In a tightly worded phrase Coalter (2010: 311) concludes that a development approach involving sport must recognise that some desired outcomes with some sports for some people in certain circumstances must be better

409

SPORT IN FOCUS 18.3: PEACE AND SPORT

Peace and Sport, or L'Organisation pour la Paix par le Sport, is a global initiative that works for sustainable peace throughout the world. Set up in 2007 by current president Joel Bouzou, the former modern pentathlon world champion, the organisation is under the High Patronage of Prince Albert II of Monaco. Peace and Sport aims to achieve its goal of sustainable peace by promoting the practise of structured sport and sporting values to educate young generations and help foster social stability, reconciliation and dialogue between communities. It uses the following actions in its work:

- a networking platform and a resource centre to enhance collaboration between stakeholders;
- locally-based projects, programmes based in the field;
- the Peace and Sport International Forum, a place where all stakeholders can meet and exchange ideas; and
- the Peace and Sport Awards, to reward initiatives and individuals who make a difference in the field.

An example of the organisation's impact is in Timor Leste (East Timor), where Peace and Sport have organised various sporting activities aimed at street gang members in order to contain violence. Over 700 young boys and girls have had the chance to regularly participate in football, volleyball, tae kwon do, table tennis and badminton. Furthermore, they have trained local instructors, renovated local sports areas, provided equipment, and organised sporting event between communities to promote social integration.

The project in Timor Leste has made an impact in the areas in works in by reconnecting with disenfranchised young people, encourage peace among gang leaders, and creating better communication between young communities. Prime Minister Xanana Gusmaso said of the project:

Sport is an important factor for peace. It can impose itself as a driving force to change the state of mind and the behaviour of our youth. Peace will be established by creating an environment of tolerance, and Peace and Sport is in a good position to bring about this change thanks to its field programmes for martial arts gangs.

understood, evaluated and evidenced. He goes on to sympathise with analysts who indicate that honest analysis may lead to programme improvement.

Inequality is a complex issue and varies both within and *between* countries and communities. An important although not causal determinant would be the inequality of opportunity or lack of access to good education, healthcare, clean water, poor economic and social services, markets, information and the lack of democratic right to participate in the key decision making processes. Often, the root cause of poverty, marginalisation and injustice is the un-equal power distribution that impacts upon many regions and areas of the South. There are historical causes linked to colonial impositions, extraction of resources (human and natural) and the reality of globalisation and international affairs only seems to perpetuate certain benefits of power. Within the South, there are cultural, social, political and historical reasons today for poor governance and power in certain groups and places. Most noticeable are the major fault lines between the North and South. This is to say that there exists a very definite tension, sometimes ideologically based and sometimes intuitively based between the demands of those from the wealthy countries and those from the poorer countries.

Writers such as Coalter (2010) continually remind us of the substantive basis for such claims. If there is any doubt about the potential of trade to reduce poverty far more effectively than aid, then it will not be because of the efforts to alleviate poverty within certain parts of Africa. If the main aim of the MDGs, to halve the proportion of people of the world living in poverty by 2015, is likely to be met, then it will not be because of Africa, but because China, Brazil and India have been making progress on the back of increased trade with Western markets. Yet, the major unanswered question remains whether the structures through which we manage trade as a world community give poor countries a real chance to help themselves. While China, India and Brazil continue to develop, the very poorest countries of the world may lack the economic power to negotiate favourable trading terms. OECD research suggests that the emigration of highly skilled workers, including athletes, may in fact prevent the poorest countries in the world from reaching the critical mass of human resources necessary to foster long-term development. What is undeniable is that part of the root of the problem lies in countries in the West failing to manage their own needs and poorer countries paying the price in terms of the emigration of national talent. It is often the poorest countries with the fewest opportunities and smallest salaries who suffer most. China, India and Brazil are reckoned to be losing about 5 per cent of their highly skilled workers while, in countries such as Mozambique, Ghana and Tanzania, the figure is closer to 50 per cent.

The promise and possibilities arising out of any new world order of power should not detract from the fact that increasing competition within some of the poorest areas of the world often depletes social capital and leaves its potential fragmented. The informal sector sometimes dissolves self-help networks and solidarities essential to the survival of the very poor, and it is often women and children who are the most vulnerable. An NGO worker in Haiti describes the ultimate logic of neo-liberal individualism in a context of absolute immiseration:

> Now everything is for sale. The women used to receive you with hospitality, give you coffee, share all that she has in her home. I could go get a plate of food at a neighbour's house; a child could get a coconut at her godmother's, two mangoes at another aunt's. But these acts of solidarity are disappearing with the growth of poverty. Now when you arrive somewhere, either the women offers to sell you a cup of coffee or she has no coffee at all. The tradition of mutual giving that allowed us to help each other and survive – this is all being lost.

> (Davis, 2006: 15)

411

AID, POVERTY, RECOGNITION AND FREEDOM

There are initially two ways of reflecting about sport and capitalism. The first is to think of capitalism in terms of what it represents as a set of contemporary relationships between people and countries. The truth about sport as a universal creed is that it is also an engine of injustice between nations and peoples. The second is to think of the relationship between sport and capitalism in historical terms. Sport potentially provides a resource of hope for many people and places but it also runs the danger of aligning itself with historical calls proclaiming the principles of equality, justice, and the eradication of poverty. Past interventions through sport have not sufficed to make a reality of any of these aforementioned possibilities. The social dimension and possibilities of global sport remain as empty slogans amid constant historical reminders that proclaiming the principles of equality, justice and the eradication of poverty does not suffice to make a reality of it. There is just one thing that many corporate lobbyists and social movements both understand, and that is that the real issue is not trade but power. A fundamental gap continues to exist both within sport and capitalism between the outcome of universal, often Western prescriptions and local realities.

At least four as yet unresolved questions might be raised to close this chapter.

A question of aid

The notion that sport can form or act as humanitarian aid is relatively unexplored and yet its potential has been recognised by the United Nations. International aid has been unable to impact in areas of the world in which corruption, political instability and resource management lie at the root of many problems. The lack of growth in the countries of the bottom billion needs particular strategies for particular circumstances. The object of international development should not be aid, but growth. It is difficult for parts of Africa, Haiti, Bolivia, Laos, Cambodia, Yemen, Burma, North Korea to compete with the likes of China, India and/or Brazil. Fifty-eight countries make up Collier's (2007) bottom billion people.

A question of poverty

A monetary-based conception of poverty has been almost universalised among governments and international organisations. The orthodox view sees poverty as a situation suffered by people who do not have the means to buy or satisfy basic material needs. Alternative views suggest that poverty may be a situation suffered by people who are not able to meet their material or non-material needs through their own efforts. Poverty, as a material reality, constrains and often scars the lives of those who have experienced it. Absolute and relative approaches to poverty acknowledge that differences exist between and within populations. In reality, no one definition of poverty will suffice since poverty itself cannot stand outside of the history and culture that it is a part of.

The Brookings Institution's (2011) analysis of the changing state of global poverty from 2005–15 reminds us that the bulk of the world's poor live in three areas: East Asia, South Asia and Sub-Saharan Africa. Asia's share of global poverty is expected to fall from two-thirds to one-third, while Africa's share more than doubles from 28 per cent to 60 per cent. Poverty will thus increasingly be seen as an African problem, despite clear progress. OECD research suggests that the emigration of highly skilled workers, including athletes, may in fact prevent the poorest countries in the world from reaching the critical mass of human resources necessary to foster long-term development. It is often the poorest countries with the fewest opportunities and smallest salaries who suffer most. China, India and Brazil are reckoned to be losing about 5 per cent of their highly skilled workers compared to places such as Mozambique, Ghana and Tanzania, where the figure is closer to 50 per cent.

Poverty may be one of the few truly global phenomena in that, in relative and absolute terms, it exists worldwide and, while governments and policies change, the needs of the world's poor invariably remain the same. The notion of poverty is not new but it is often suppressed, not just in the literature and research about sport, culture and society, but in some case it is highlighted in this chapter as a fundamental reason and motivation for why some athletes run. Historically, sport used to be a possible route out of poverty in the Western world. Many NGOs have been at the forefront of initiatives involving sport as a facet of humanitarian aid in attacking the social and economic consequences of poverty. In reality, sport can only make a small contribution, but small contributions can sometimes make a difference.

A question of recognition

The work of Nancy Fraser was viewed earlier as providing an insight into the weakness of accounts of sport that were uncoupled from questions of recognition and redistribution. Although she does not write about poverty, Fraser's recognition is helpful here. The mode of thinking that is encouraged through Fraser's work is to view recognition and redistribution as key social, cultural and economic dimensions to understanding social justice and injustice. Fraser contends that the politics of recognition and redistribution are central to thinking about social justice, and the same might be said for thinking about sport and poverty. People in poverty are often denied participatory parity for a multitude of reasons: material deprivation, processes of otherness, the infringement of human and citizen rights, lack of voice, and relative powerlessness. The continuing struggle for social justice in sport at both a socio-economic and geopolitical level necessitates not simply discussion and analysis involving redistribution, recognition and the development of mutual trust (social capital), but also intervention. The debate and problem of global sport is notoriously silent on all of these issues as if the public intellectuals, among others, have no place or voice in this world – a point we shall return to in the last chapter. However, the point that is being made here in relation to sport, poverty and international development is that, if Fraser's thinking is a way forward, then the politics of sport, poverty and international development necessitates an understanding not just of the politics of redistribution, but also a politics of recognition and respect, a parity of recognition. In other words, a redistribution of resources in and through sport is not enough.

A question of freedom

The redistribution of resources and income have not always been central to narrowing the gap between rich and poor through sport but, while resources matter, so too does what people are able to do with those resources – in other words, their capabilities. You can, at times, increase people's income without necessarily increasing people's ability to choose for themselves the kinds of lives they aspire to lead. Sports development projects are sometimes criticised on a number of grounds. They are often time limited and dependent upon short-term funding. They may while raising awareness not necessarily produce an increased capability set to help create more equal and sustainable choices for people through sport. Those involved need to consider the sustainability of such projects and be prepared to commit to long terms capacity and social relationship building. What much of the sport and development literature has failed to capitalise upon is not so much the notion of sport, development *and* freedom, but sport and development *as* freedom. It is for this reason that Sen's (2006) ideas on justice, inequality and capability are all relevant to thinking about sport, culture and society in a more just world.

SUMMARY

This chapter has reflected upon the way in which sport has been linked with the ideas of poverty, international development and as a soft form of humanitarian aid. The relationship between sport and poverty is often characterised in at least three ways: (i) sport can be an escape from poverty for some and, therefore, sport has been closely linked to social mobility; (ii) the popularity for sport has meant that it has been used as a symbol to bring attention to some of the world's areas of need; and (iii) it has been used as a means to an end in the sense that other resources or capabilities have been part of a welfare or humanitarian package that involves sport. The chapter has also drawn attention to the fact that many of the poorest states, the bottom billion, have struggled to escape the poverty trap for a number of reasons.

The chapter has also reflected upon sport's assocation with both international development and development. It has considered Sen's powerful notion that the issue is not development and freedom, but development as freedom, an issue we shall return to in the last two chapters. Some researchers are sceptical about the ability of sport to help, while others recognise that some athletes, as an example, regularly redistribute wealth and consider taking on broader political roles, building up their celebrity status gained through a life in and through sport.

The notion of poverty is not new but it is often suppressed, not just in the literature and research about sport and society. However, it is highlighted here as a fundamental reason and motivation for some athletes. Manny Pacquiao, the Filipino congressman, the only boxer in history to hold world titles in eight weight divisions, prepared to fight the American boxer Shane Mosley in May 2011. The boxer was set to earn £12 million for his night's work. The message Pacquiao delivered on the eve of the fight was not dissimilar from that of other athletes who have tried to indirectly and directly help development in their home countries through sport. The boxer's thoughts were not so much about boxing, but in his own words:

All my life, I have had to fight, as a child I had to fight just to eat but I believe the biggest fight of my life is not in boxing – the biggest fight in my life is how to end poverty in my country.

(Davies, 2011: 1)

The lack of growth in the countries of the bottom billion needs particular strategies for particular circumstances. The object of international development should not be aid, but growth. The politics of the bottom billion is not a contest between the rich, developed world and a number of economically poorer worlds, but about sustained help for those in need.

GUIDE TO FURTHER READING

Collier, P. (2007). *The Bottom Billion*. Oxford: Oxford University Press.

Davis, M. (2006) *Planet of Slums*. London: Verso.

Haughton, J. and Khandker, S. (2009). *Handbook on Poverty and Inequality*. Washington, DC: World Bank.

Huish, R. (2011). 'Punching Above It's Weight: Cuba's Use of Sport for South–South Co-operation'. *Third World Quarterly*, 32 (3) April: 417–433.

Jarvie, G. (2010). 'Sport, Development and Aid: Can Sport Make a Difference?'. *Sport and Society,* 14 (2): 241–252.

Levermore, R. and Beacom, A. (eds). (2009). *Sport and International Development*. Basingstoke: Palgrave Macmillan.

Sen, A. (2000). *Development as Freedom*. London: Allen and Unwin.

QUESTIONS

1 What are the key ways in which sport and development projects figure within United Nations initiatives?

2 Describe orthodox and alternative notions of poverty and why single-factor accounts of poverty are problematic.

3 Explain the role of sport in assisting with the Millennium Development Goals.

4 Why is the work of Fraser and Sen important in explaining poverty and/or development?

5 To what extent is Collier correct when he argues that the bottom billion remain unaltered, and does sport have a role to play in terms of helping capabilities?

6 Provide six ways in which sport may help with development.

7 Describe Coalter's typology of the way in which sport could help with development.

8 What motivations might Kenyan women runners give for running, and which is the most important reason provided?

9 Critically evaluate the failure of international aid to achieve many of its intended outcomes.

10 Explain the differences between socio-economic and geopolitical approaches to sport, poverty and development.

PRACTICAL PROJECTS

1   Carry out two separate Internet searches using the search words 'sport' and 'poverty', and write a 1,000-word report on your findings from each of the searches.

2   Examine the background to the Homeless World Cup and evaluate its impact.

3   Research the different ways in which four sporting celebrities of your choice have used their public profile to bring attention to poverty in the world today.

4   Develop a case study of a sports association or club such as the Mathare Youth Sports Association or Peace and Sport initiative, explaining how sport has helped contribute to humanitarian causes.

5   Research the work of the United Nations and explain how it has used sport to address social and economic development goals.

KEY CONCEPTS

Absolute poverty ■ Citizenship ■ Common resource ■ Development ■ Freedom ■ Human rights ■ Inequality ■ Justice ■ Obligations ■ Recognition ■ Redistribution ■ Relative poverty ■ Social rights ■ Sport as aid ■ Uneven development

WEBSITES

Magic Bus Charity
http://magicbusindia.org/magicbus/
An Indian-based charity aimed at changing lives through sport.

Human Rights Watch
www.hrw.org
An organisation dedicated to protecting the rights of people around the world. Place the word 'sport' into the search facility and read the results of your search.

The Mathare Youth Sports Association – Kenya
www.mysakenya.org/
A grassroots community-based development programme.

The Homeless World Cup
www.homelessworldcup.org/
The Homeless World Cup was established in 2003 although conceived of in 2001. It was established with backing from the International Network of Street Papers. It was and is developed to promote social opportunities, including access to support services for

participants experiencing homelessness and other associated social disadvantage. The website provides an empirical assessment of the impact of the Homeless World Cup.

Football for Hope

www.streetfootballworld.org

Football for Hope is a movement that uses the power of football for positive social change. It is led by FIFA.

The Right to Play

www.righttoplay.com

The Right to Play organisation outlines its history, impact and research. Its mission is to improve the lives of children in some of the most disadvantaged areas of the world by using the power of sport and play for development, health and peace.

United Nations

www.unitednations.org

The main United Nations website, which outlines the work of the organisation. In particular, look at the sport and development work carried out by the United Nations under consecutive secretary-generals of the United Nations General Assembly – also refer to www.sportanddev.org.

Sport against Poverty

www.sportagainstpoverty.com/

A charity that partners together athletics and education to help children in East Africa by providing opportunities for advancement in education and sport. The charity aims to help with the overall process of educational development and recognizes the popularity of sport as tool that can help in the process of development.

Chapter 19

Sport and social change

Some athletes acknowledge that they run to escape poverty but also that winnings from the world of sport can help to support not only their families but their communities. Is sport a form of soft power?

PREVIEW

Key terms defined ■ Capitalism ■ Global sport and capitalism ■ Brazilian sports policy ■ Sport in South Africa ■ Jesse Owens 1936 ■ Tommie Smith 1968 ■ An age of activism ■ Sport and social intervention (1) ■ Anti-global sport ■ Sport et Citoyenneté ■ Sporting events as adversarial sites ■ Anti-Olympic sport ■ Sport and social intervention (2) ■ Sport, power and the South ■ Sport and social intervention (3) ■ Sport, social change and social forums ■ Sport, the United Nations and internationalism ■ Sport and social intervention (4) ■ Summary

---

OBJECTIVES

This chapter will:

- examine ways in which sport has contributed to bringing about social change;
- consider examples of campaigns for social and political change through sport;
- illustrate that sport is not immune from campaigns for change not only between groups, but also within and between countries and regions;
- examine further sport's contribution to the politics of social forums and movements; and
- draw upon empirical material as a basis for a critique of neo-liberal sport.

KEY TERMS DEFINED

Anti-global: The anti-globalisation movement is critical of globalisation. The movement is also commonly referred to as the global justice movement or alter-globalisation movement, or movement against neo-liberal globalisation.

Neo-liberalism: Represents the reassertion of the classical liberal concern to promote the maximum possible liberty and/or economic efficiency. Developed in the 1970s, it advocates measures to promote economic development, and is used to guide the transition from planned to market economies in former communist countries.

Social change: Various social processes whereby the values, attitudes or institutions of society, such as education, sport, family, religion and politics, become modified. It includes both the natural process and action programmes initiated by members of the community. Not to be confused with social development or social movements.

INTRODUCTION

In 1919, Canadian sport was divided between amateur and professional, east and west, male and female, bourgeois and workers' sports organisations; so wrote the Canadian historian of sport, Bruce Kidd. The struggle for Canadian sport is a text that still remains an exemplar for students, teachers and researchers thinking about the capacity of sport to produce social change. Kidd (1996: 270) concluded that capitalist sport had triumphed and that the effort to create alternatives to commercial sports culture continued to be an uphill fight. Any progressive strategy aimed at bringing about social change in sport, suggested Kidd (1996: 270), while fighting for scarce resources and political support must, at some point, confront consumer loyalties, conventional wisdom, economic power and the political force generated by sports corporations. But such alternatives do exist and they have an active history in the world of sport.

Football influenced the content, as well as the form of former Presidents administration. Lula was elected on a leftwing platform of social reforms; his priority, he said, was to end hunger. Yet in May, the first two laws he signed as president both concerned football A point that was expanded upon earlier in chapter 17. Brazil's dispossessed millions were denied the rights of citizens in much of their lives – but the popular President recognized that helping to tackle corruption in football was not only popular but it allowed the fans to have certain rights.

The content of the administration's policies were also influenced by football in that the first two laws that the president signed in May 2002 concerned football. Football in Brazil is one of the key battlegrounds upon which the struggle to make the country a fairer place was being fought. The sport had been run by a network of unaccountable, largely corrupt figures known as *carrolas* or 'top hats' who had become obscenely wealthy while the domestic football scene remained broken and demoralised (Bellos, 2003: 32). The public plundering of football was viewed by the president as a continual reminder of the previous administration's failure to stamp out corruption in areas of public life. Lula, in an attempt to force the football authorities to become transparent, ratified a 'Law of Moralisation' in sport that enforced transparency in club administration (Bellos, 2003: 32). On the same day, he sanctioned a more ambitious and wide-ranging law, the 'Fans Statute', a bill of rights for the football fan.

The international campaign against apartheid sport in South Africa helped to topple a system of legalised racism in South Africa. The notion of 'no normal sport in an abnormal society' was not the causal factor that brought about change, but it was an important facet of the strategy for reform adopted by the African National Congress (ANC) prior to coming to power in 1992 under the leadership of Nelson Mandela. Given the history of struggle for social and political change in South Africa, and the place of sport within that campaign, it is ironic that both South Africa and countries such as Great Britain have been less than progressive in relation to democracy in Zimbabwe under the leadership of Robert Mugabe. Thabo Mbeki, South Africa's premier in 2005, refused to decry the regime of Robert Mugabe, a stance that has hurt the international reputation of the new South Africa. Both the *Mail* and *Guardian* newspapers, valiant supporters of the ANC during the era of apartheid, reported that South Africa had lost the moral high ground and that democracy had been sacrificed by both the South African and Zimbabwean governments (*Sunday Herald*, 27 March 2005: 19).

Just before the 2010 FIFA World Cup in South Africa, there was a violent demonstration in the township of Riverlea. The residents of Riverlea were protesting against the fact that the government was pouring money into the hosting of the World Cup but not housing or jobs. Traffic passing through the township was stoned by demonstrators who fought with police and who, in turn, fired rubber bullets to dampen the unrest (*The Times*, 22 October 2009). On the one hand, the scenes were reminiscent of the way in which sport was at the heart of the struggle for social and political change in South Africa during the apartheid era but, on the other hand, it is also a reminder of how major international sporting events have become targets for various campaigns from groups seeking action, publicity and change

420

around a variety of socio-economic and geo-political struggles. Various researchers (Boykoff, 2011; Lenskyj, 2008) have drawn attention to the fact that new generations of social movements have woken up to the potential of sporting mega-events as a means of protest against the ethics of neo-liberal globalisation.

An important priority in any contemporary discussion of capitalism is to first acknowledge that it exists but, perhaps more importantly, to acknowledge that it exists in new forms. Capital today is much more fluid, it flows much more readily, looking for the optimum conditions with which to reproduce itself and, in turn, accumulate greater capital. Sports businesses look around the world, not just around the locale, the region or the nation, for greater profit. Contemporary capitalism is still marked by the rise to pre-eminence of the transnational corporations that, in terms of their size and power, are able to take advantage of whatever opportunities exist to lower the costs of production, typically by shifting aspects of sports production from wealthier to relatively poorer countries, or through consolidation, mergers or takeovers. Contemporary capitalism also takes place within an alleged regime of international governance that seeks to accommodate the interests of nation states and the needs of transnational capital. While some businesses have taken on the agenda of social responsibility, various recessionary dips in the world economy between 2008 and 2012 were invariably viewed in terms of a stand-off between pecuniary bankers and governments who failed to take account of the very real hardships that people in many countries were experiencing.

There is the almost unquestionable challenge that global sport, in many ways, is part of the hallmark of the triumph of capitalism coupled with the growing ascendancy of economics over politics, of the corporate demands for sport over public policy and of private sporting interest over public sporting interests. Neo-liberal thinking about sport, in many ways, implies the end of politics because of the centrality of the market as the resource allocator and the submission of public life and the commons to commodification. But what if this does not work, and social groups wishing to bring about change recognise that they need to bypass the conventional orthodox channels for bringing about political change? It is tempting to suggest that globalisation represents a further acceleration towards the capitalisation of the sporting world but to accept such an analogy would be to acknowledge *uncritically* the rhetorical promotion of globalisation as capitalism and the submission of public life and the commons to commodification. That is to say that, at one level, the services that remain in the public sector according to neo-liberalism have to be compelled to run themselves as private enterprises, and the role of different sporting worlds is simply to compete for customers. At another level, global neo-liberalism also advocates a clear path towards economic convergence between the richest and poorest parts of the world if the governments of poor countries strictly adhere to liberal policies. While global neo-liberalism is an intellectually complex body of knowledge involving diverse strands of argument, its politics are pristinely simple in that politics ceases to have any meaning beyond terms prescribed by the market.

To accept such logic would be to deny or reduce to a matter of insignificance the many opportunities for social change and reform that are presented by and through contemporary sport. To deny that such opportunities exist would be just as utopian as thinking that older variants of capitalism remain the way of the twenty-first century – this is not the case.

SPORT IN FOCUS 19.1: OLYMPIC ATHLETES FIGHTING FOR CHANGE IN SOCIETY

'We all have dreams' – Jesse Owens, 1936

In 1936, the Olympic Games were held in Berlin and Hitler wanted to use them to prove to the world that the Aryan people were the dominant race. To the German leader's obvious anger, Jesse Owens won four gold medals. He was and still is an inspirational figure to millions.

> We all have dreams. But in order to make dreams come into reality, it takes an awful lot of determination, dedication, self-discipline and effort.

'Black America will understand what we did tonight' – Tommie Smith, 1968

On October 17 1968, at the height of the civil rights struggles in America, two black athletes – Tommie Smith and John Carlos – made a silent protest at the presentation of the 200 metres race by raising their fists in the Black Power salute during the playback of the US national anthem. They were subsequently suspended from the team, banned from the Olympic Village and stripped of their medals. At a later press conference, Tommie Smith gave the following reason:

> If I win I am an American, not a black American. But if I did something bad then they would say 'a Negro'. We are black and we are proud of being black. Black America will understand what we did tonight.

Effective reform, whether it be radical or evolutionary, can only be based upon an understanding of current global or international pressures, sporting tensions or fault lines, and these are continually shifting. While much attention has focused upon the emerging real or mythical notion of a global civil society with the power to engage with and challenge institutions of global governance, the place of sport has not figured greatly within such developments. Where sport has figured has mainly been where it has provided a means to an end rather than focusing upon being a progressive end in itself.

The relationship between sport and social change must encapsulate and acknowledge both forms of activity in that sport and social change may refer to social change within sport itself, but also the way in which sport has been instrumental in contributing to broader campaigns for social and political change.

New parameters of global politics exist just as capitalism continues to forge an increasing inter-dependence with global sport. As outlined in Chapter 4, politics are thought and fought, policies are forged and implemented, political ideas wax and wane within an increasingly global space that, at one level, is geo-political and, at another level, is socio-economic. Opportunities for social change in and through sport exist at both these levels and arise in both intended and unintended ways. Different people at different times have taken a stand and used sporting moments to speak out for a different world or society or change. Sport in Focus 19.1 provides such examples.

AN AGE OF ACTIVISM?

The historian Eric Hobsbawm conveniently divided eras of history as the Age of Empire (1789–1848), the Age of Revolution (1848–75), the Age of Capital (1875–1914) and the Age of Extremes (1914–91). Writing in March 2011, Feffer (2011: 1) noted that the world is convulsed in protest and that, perhaps, it is worth reflecting on whether the world has entered the Age of Activism (1991–present). Certainly, during 2010 and early 2011, people filled the streets in different places in the Middle East, the Balkans, Africa and parts of the US. Their targets were invariably local autocratic leaders, unelected governments and poor performing economies. In most cases, protesters and activists were demonstrating against specific local sets of conditions, but underlying common tensions existed which meant that the protests which contributed to the 'Arab Spring' uprisings shared some concerns with the protesters on the streets in Greece, Italy, Spain and other parts of the world who were affected by downturns in the international markets and economies. In reality, activism in different parts of the world is caused by a number of factors but initially three might be mentioned: the economic recession, the call for transparency and the increased capacity to socially network through technological advances.

The confluence of these three factors is different in different places. Nonetheless, rising food prices caused considerable discontent in Egypt, limited economic opportunities created frustration and anxiety in Tunisia, while austerity measures imposed by the Greek government brought hundreds of thousands of protesters on to the street. With unemployment rates of near to 35 per cent among young people in Greece, many Greeks were looking to exodus the country. Similar high levels of unemployment among young people were causing concerns across Europe and countries outside of the European Union. A second concern has been the lack of transparency into the lavish lifestyles of ruling elites. In Croatia, protesters nearly brought the country to a standstill by drawing attention to the lavish lifestyle of Croatian politicians. In China, apartment owners have complained against the management of their buildings in attempts to bring democracy closer to ground floor. This is the same class of people who occupied Tahrir Square in Egypt and pushed out President Hosni Mubarak – the first generation of people to use the Internet and new generations of people thinking about the possibility of buying a home, however small. A third factor has been the influence of new technologies and the capacity of Twitter and Facebook to easily coordinate movements, communicate and mobilise groups ahead of the state being aware of tensions. The impact of technology has meant that global civil society and grassroots globalism can mobilise much more effectively.

423

SPORT IN FOCUS 19.2: SPORT AND SOCIAL INTERVENTION (1) – INDIVIDUAL SOCIAL MOBILITY

The women from Colombia

The normative potential of sport to produce social change is self-evident in the following example from the Sydney 2000 Olympic Games. Maria Isabel Urrutia was a gold medal winner having lifted 75 kg in the clean and jerk weightlifting category. The Olympic gold medal winner represents a country where young athletes have had to pass through guerrilla and paramilitary roadblocks while travelling between cities to national competitions. Colombia holds the unfortunate distinction of being the world's leading country in terms of kidnapping, with some 3,000 reported cases per year. Commenting on her gold medal victory, Urrutia said that 'she hoped that her victory would reach others like her – poor, black and female' (*Sunday Herald*, 1 October 2000: 18). She went on:

> As a poor person, I hope others see that you can make a living, see the world and get an education through sports or even music and other arts. As a woman, I hope that girls who are now 13, like I was when I started, now realise that they don't have to become teenage mothers and as a black person I hope the country sees that there's another Urrutia besides the white man who signs our pesos.
>
> (*Sunday Herald*, 1 October 2000: 18)

The man from Sudan

Luol Deng left Sudan, age five, just one of many forced into exile by a civil war that, at the time, had claimed 1.9 million lives. The refugee turned basketball player made his fame and fortune playing for the Chicago Bulls and securing a contract worth £52 million. He is reportedly Obama's favourite player but he is also a hero in Sudan, where he returned from exile for a spell in 2010. In one youth centre visited by the player, they had a song, ' The Luol Deng Referendum'. He guested for the then South Sudan Basketball Association in a game where he met a teammate from the same Dinka Tribe – a fellow lost boy – who tried to escape to Ethiopia. While Deng went to London, his friend moved on to Somalia and then Kenya, while Luol moved on to the US. Sudan's lost boy who found fame in Chicago through sport acknowledged that he was lucky and that they so easily could have traded places. Sport was the key to social mobility for Luol Deng, a resource of hope for an athlete who hasn't forgotten his roots or lost the ability to see beyond the abnormal world of the wealthy sports star into reality and try to help.

In the Age of Activism, protesters have not simply been working against authoritarian governments, but they have also been present on the streets, protesting against democratic governments in Croatia, Greece and Wisconsin, and a potential issue is whether the fundamental contemporary concern is over the activities of the state and its very nature today. The current wave of activism challenges the state as a vehicle for the enrichment of elites at the expense of the common good. In the UK, politicians of different political parties have been sent to prison for mishandling their expense claims and the misuse of public funds. The Age of Activism is also not just about progressives but also Tea Party activists in the US, radical Islamists, and European racists. The rotation of elites through election and/or selection is being viewed as problematic and the state itself is being brought into question (Feffer, 2011).

Sport itself is rarely, if at all, seen as contributing to any strategy of change, whether this been systemic of anti-systemic. But there are numerous points of entry that exist for sport to take its place in any politics of social change. At a general level, these might include local, national and international protests but also individual, anti-global, anti-Olympic or anti-environmental entry points. Sport in Focus 19.2 illustrates the normative potential of sport to help with social mobility for some, and the question remains how to bring this about for many.

In 2010, the highest number of refugees came from Afghanistan, Iraq, Somalia, the Democratic Republic of Congo, Burma, Colombia, Sudan, Vietnam, Eritrea and China. The highest number of refugees entered Pakistan, Iran, Syria, Germany, Jordan, Kenya, Chad, China, the US and the UK.

ANTI-GLOBAL SPORT

What do we mean by the term 'anti-global'? The term is often associated with a real or imaginery anti-global movement but also associated with many other names: anti-corporate, anti-capitalist, anti-free-trade, anti-environmental and anti-Olympic, to name but a few. By focusing on the work of corporations, organisers graphically draw attention to issues of social, economic and ecological justice but no one corporation or movement will transform the world economy, redistribute wealth or provide recognition. Many diverse local movements commonly focus on the way neo-liberal politics are challenged on a number of areas – homelessness, wage stagnation, rent escalation, violence, land theft and lack of safe public common ground for things such as sport. Neo-liberal economics is based upon centralisation, consolidation, homogenisation and, at one level, there needs to be many local solutions and a diversity of opposition from many groups. It often finds expression in calls for social as well as economic and enviromental responsibility. The spirit of this is acknowledged in classic practical works such as Naomi Klein's (2004) reworked version of *Reclaiming the Commons*.

We should acknowledge that the values associated with globalisation and global sport have been subject to pressures for change. The movement for global change is most commonly referred to as an anti-globalisation or anti-capitalist movement. Some have argued that this movement emerged in Seattle in the mid-1990s as a result of protests against the World Trade Organization and the International Monetary Fund. Others maintain that it began

425

more than 500 years ago when colonists first told indigenous peoples that they were going to have to do things differently if they were to develop or be eligible for trade. Whatever the point of origin, the privatisation of every aspect of life and, in particular, the transformation of every activity and value into a commodity has resulted in a number of oppositional threads that have taken the form of many different campaigns and movements.

Sport has not been immune from these campaigns for change. Landless Thai peasants have taken over and planted vegetables on over-irrigated golf courses, and the power of Nike has been challenged on several American university campuses. Students facing a corporate takeover of their campuses by Nike linked up with workers producing Nike clothing, parents who were concerned at the commercialisation of youth, and church-goers campaigning against child labour in the production of sports goods. Red Card to Child Labour was a worldwide campaign against the use of child labour in football. The Red Card to Child Labour campaign is symbolised by the red card handed out by referees for serious violations of rules on the soccer field. The then International Labour Organization (ILO) director, General Juan Somavia, said, 'Working hand in hand with the world's most popular sport, we hope to galvanise the global campaign against child labour with this potent symbol – the red card means you're out of the game' (www.un.org/pubs/chronicle/2002/p19). The Portugal and then Real Madrid star Luis Figo, who was voted World Footballer of the Year in 2001, supported the campaign. The ILO, in conjunction with FIFA and UNICEF, launched the campaign to coincide with the 2002 Africa Football Cup of Nations. The initiative was aimed at highlighting the harsh reality of child labour in sport.

There are at least two competing concepts of anti-globalisation, one termed 'radical' and one termed 'moderate'. The radical wing views globalisation as a process largely designed to ensure that wealthy elites become wealthier at the expense of poorer countries. It would argue, for instance, that globalisation undermines the working conditions and pay of sports personnel in wealthy countries, while at the same time exploiting cheap sports labour in other parts of the world. The radical wing sees transnational corporations as the main cause of the problem in that they have so much power that international sporting organisations undermine the power and decision making of national governing bodies of sport. Furthermore, it is suggested that indigenous sporting cultures have been threatened as a result of global sport or capitalist sport that has tended to market uniform sports products across the globe. Whereas 20 years ago children in local communities might have worn the sports gear of local sports teams, children today tend to wear more uniform sports brands such as Nike. The view expressed here is that globalisation as a process is fundamentally flawed and immoral.

Solutions to these problems offered by the radical wing are various, depending upon the situation. In a sporting context, the solutions to combating global intervention in sport might include some or all of the following strategies: (i) re-assertion of the power of national and local sports organisations; (ii) the return of economic, political and cultural power to localities; (iii) quotas on the migration of sports talent into the country; (iv) re-evaluation and redistribution of wealth derived from sport to alleviate poverty; and (v) support for campaigns such as Sport Relief and critical evaluation of the role of companies such as Nike.

The moderate wing, although more difficult to define, tends to share the view that globalisation has the potential to be good or bad. It has the potential to provide for a sharing of cultures paid for out of the economic growth provided by free trade, but because the institutions and rules that govern the world are currently controlled by wealthy elites, then inequality, instability and injustice are inevitable. In a sporting context, a corollary of this might be to argue that traditional cultural rights and sporting traditions need to be at least equally recognised as socially and culturally, if not economically, as important as market-supported forms of commercialised sport. For the moderate wing, the solution to many of the above problems lies with reforming the institutions that govern world sport. The proposed reforms are multiple, but they might include some or all of the following: (i) a tax on international transfers of sports labour, the revenue of which could be used to promote sports development in poorer countries; (ii) a total reformulation of rules and remits of international sporting bodies to allow for greater representation on the boards from poorer and essentially non-Western countries; (iii) a greater role of the international court of sports arbitration in promoting the role that sport can play in the promotion of justice, the environment, human rights, and loss of work through, for example, doping scandals; and (iv) recognition of the emergence of individual or extreme sports as alternative forms of leisure to more global sporting forms such as football. Indeed, it might be argued that the rise of extreme or alternative forms of sports in itself is a form of protest against global or capitalist forms of sport.

'Globalism' is an all-consuming term that, by definition, does not recognise the possible existence of those outside. Although post-modern intellectuals such as Fukuyama, Baudrillard, Lyotard and Foucault encouraged the extinction of words such as 'opposition', 'resistance' and 'critical vocabulary', the role of the student as future public intellectual in the field of sport, culture and society necessitates a re-examining of the world of sport outside the gaze of the transnational corporation or globalism. The global Nike economy is only global in the sense that giant corporations have free access to every space in the world, if they so choose. To the extent that the money and production flow is beneficial to the privileged few and inaccessible to many, resistance is perhaps inevitable. The baggage of national sport and the nation state has never been adequate because the issues of nationalism and ethno-centrism tend to travel with it, and yet the state and internationalism are but some of the areas that will not halt the march to global sport. However, they illustrate that there is another world of sport, or at least a world of sport outside the zone of the transnational corporation.

Progressive think tanks such as Sport et Citoyenneté or the Jimmy Reid Foundation have recognised the need for left-of-centre thinking and solutions to contemporary social issues. Sport et Citoyenneté claims to be the first European think tank focused on sport. They recognise that sport can play a major role in bringinging together citizens from all over the world who share common values, and that sport has a part to play in building European citizenship. Apart from building up and promoting shared international expertise to comment upon social and political aspects of sport, Sport et Citoyenneté aims to develop further public dialogue on sport, and campaign for recognition for the specificity of sport and what it can do socially, educationally and in a civic sense, but also reaffirm the right to access sport and fight against forms of dicrimination in line with Article 21 of the Charter of Fundamental Rights of the European Union (EU).

Numerous scholars have recognised that mega-events including sporting events reflect both the political dynamics of the time and context in which they take place, but also that

427

they capture the imagination and provide opportunities to open up possibilities for change (Hayes and Karamichas, 2011; Horne and Manzenreiter, 2006; Kelly, 2010). In one sense, the hosting of major sporting mega-events confirms a prevailing neo-liberal agenda and is an affirmation of an alleged globalised order but they are also vehicles for campaigning. The ownership and legacy of events, living conditions of some people affected by the hosting of events, the local and international planning process, and whether mythical or alleged material benefits narrow or exacerbate socio-economic and geopolitical inequalities all provide opportunities for politicians, activists and planners for change. Kelly (2010) points out that sporting mega events have always been sites of protest but what is new is that new generations of social movements have woken up to the politics of mega events, including sporting events. They are capable of posing hard questions about the ethics of neo-liberalism and global sport. The anti-Olympic movement makes a contribution to this.

ANTI-OLYMPIC AND SOCIALLY RESPONSIBLE OLYMPIC SPORT

The work of Helen Lenskyj (2000, 2002, 2003, 2004, 2008) in documenting and challenging the Olympic industry is a stellar example of the public intellectual at work. Her call for social responsibility to be the fourth pillar of the Olympic Movement is based upon expanding the framework of Agenda 21 (see Chapter 11) and evidence-based reports such as COHRE (2007), a report that documents housing trends in Olympic host cities – eviction of tenants from low-rent housing, inflated real estate prices, suppression of human rights such as freedom of assembly and decrease in boarding house stock. The proposal to consolidate an international campaign to pressure the IOC to take action over a reformed Agenda 21 is premised upon the observation that the IOC is unlikely to be influenced by non-governmental organisations struggling for social justice *within* the Olympic Movement. Instead, a number of effective routes for challenging the Olympic industry in particular are listed (Lenskyj, 2008: 152) and adapted in Sport in Focus 19.3.

There exists a substantial body of work that highlights sporting mega events as adversarial sites and draws such events into the politics of place and time, but there needs to be at least a common narrative throughout these events if they are going to live up to the promise of the term 'social movement'. They certainly need to provide an alternative to the neo-liberal narrative in order that at least two points of view are presented. Forms of activism around major sporting events invariably fall into a number of categories such as spontaneous uprisings, grass-roots mobilisation and protest and special interest groups. Such events might not be a form of hard power on every occasion but they can act as soft power through arguing for transparency, accountability, local involvement and increased capability in reaching Millenium Development Goals, among others.

SPORT, POWER AND THE SOUTH

The struggles for social change commented have been linked to issues of social inequality and the distribution of resources between different groups. Inequality is a complex issue and varies both within and *between* countries and communities. An important, although not causal,

---

SPORT IN FOCUS 19.3: SPORT AND SOCIAL INTERVENTION (2) – THE OLYMPICS

- Lobby elected politicians and support local governemnt candidates running an Olympic watchdog campaign.

- Demand responsible factual local journalism and support independent media websites to provide an alternative factual view.

- Peaceful protest and non-violent actions.

- Encourage whistle-blowers to inform from within the Olympic industry.

- Demand that public intellectuals are present and produce credible research and leadership.

- Support both Olympic role model approaches to promote sport but also community-based alternatives.

- Act to stop the exploitation of children, homeless, local communities and sport itself as a result of Olympic propaganda.

- Ensure local universities, colleges and authorities support ethical involvement, run international education programmes and host socially responsible countries.

---

determinant would be the inequality of opportunity or lack of access to good education, healthcare, clean water; others would be poor economic and social services, markets, information and the lack of democratic right to participate in the key decision-making processes. Often, the root cause of poverty, marginalisation and injustice is the unequal power distribution that impacts upon many regions and areas of the South. There are historical causes linked to colonial impositions, extraction of resources (human and natural) and the reality of globalisation, and international affairs only seem to perpetuate certain benefits of power. Within the South, there are cultural, social, political and historical reasons today for poor governance and power in certain groups and places. Most noticeable are the fault lines between the North and South. This is to say that there exists a very definite tension, sometimes ideologically based and sometimes intuitively based between the demands of those from the wealthy countries and those from the poorer countries.

This issue has a long history, with the following being but illustrative examples. The Games of the Newly Emerging Forces, or GANEFO Games, were founded in Indonesia in 1962 in response to sanctions imposed upon Indonesia by the International Olympic Committee in 1963 when it suspended Indonesia indefinitely from the IOC. Indonesia responded by going ahead with plans for the GANEFO Games, an idea that had originally been proposed by the Indonesian President Sukarno in a speech in November 1962 in Tokyo. In November 1963, 3,000 athletes from 48 nations participated in the first GANEFO Games. The hope had been to establish a quadrennial competition, with the 1967 games to be held in Cairo or Peking. Shifting political alliances meant that, following a coup in Indonesia, the government established business relationships with Taiwan while relationships with mainland China cooled. In September of 1965, a smaller group called the Asian GANEFO was formed, with the first and last Asian GANEFO Games being held in December of 1966 in Phnom Penh, Cambodia, with 15 nations participating.

The female badminton player Susi Susanti became the first Olympic athlete to wear a gold medal for Indonesia, at the time the world's most populous Muslim nation. In 1992, the Islamic Countries Women's Sports Solidarity Congress gathered to decide on the manner of organising sports competitions for women from Islamic states, primarily from the countries of the South such as those Islamic countries in Asia, Africa and the Arabic region. Faezeh Hashemi opened the First Islamic Countries Women's Sports Solidarity Games in Iran in 1993 (www.salamiran.org/Women/Olympic/history.html). For many Muslim sports-women, Islamic traditions can have a direct influence upon participation in international sports events such as the Olympics. Faezeh Hashemi is the daughter of the former Iranian President Rafsanjani and was director of a women's organisation tied to the Foreign Ministry in Tehran. She brought female athletes together from the Third World in 1993 for the first Islamic Women's Olympic Games. At the time, 33 Islamic countries did not send women to the Olympics in fear of compromising Islamic dress codes. The group, called Atlanta–Sydney–Athens Plus, started to campaign after the 1992 Olympics, when 35 countries – half of them Muslim – sent no female athletes to the Olympic Games. Only nine countries failed to send women to the Sydney 2000 Olympic Games, with most of these male-only delegations coming from Middle Eastern countries. In Athens, in 2004, Robina Muqimar and Friba Rezihi were the first ever women to represent the primarily Muslim country of Afghanistan. In March 2005, Laleh Seddigh became the first female champion, in the otherwise all-male field, to win the national motor speed race championship in Tehran (*Sunday Herald*, 27 March 2005: 21). For Faezeh Hashemi, women's sports are an important step to evoking social change because they promote an awareness of women's physical strength and thus foster a spirit of self-awareness.

The flow and distribution of resources between Europe and Asia resulting from television broadcasting has become increasingly subject to criticism by Asian broadcasters (Roberts, 2005: 27). The way forward, according to Total Sports Asia, is first to recognise the unique characteristics of the Asian broadcasting market and facilitate local operators controlling the international sports opportunities that are arising out of Asia. Put more critically, each territory in Asia is different and independent and international broadcasting companies located in the West, argues the Chief Executive of Total Sports Asia, need to recognise that Asia is not a golden goose designed to service European television demands for sport. European companies, 'if they wish to help develop the local in Asia need to show a commitment and the days are gone when you can sit in Europe and expect it all happen for you' (Roberts, 2005: 27). The Asian sports market is still expanding, and more and more initiatives are coming up with new channels, broadband and video-on-demand services. There has been a massive investment in infrastructure, with the result that Asia is arguably ahead of other parts of the world. Asia is an increasingly sophisticated television sports market and gone are the days, points out Mike Mackay, of Octagon CSI, when Asia 'was a dumping ground for content from the rest of the world' (Roberts, 2005: 27). Asian broadcasting is utilised here to illustrate and emphasise the dynamics of sporting capital and the potential of the local in the South to challenge and produce change within broader international sporting opportunities that have traditionally been controlled outwith the South.

Unlike the actions taken by President Luiz Inacio Lula da Silva of Brazil in passing legislation in relation to the morality of Brazilian football, when faced with the option of intervening to prevent England cricketers touring Zimbabwe, both the chairman of the England and Wales Cricket Board and Jack Straw, the then British Foreign Secretary, accepted by their actions that morality had no part to play in English cricket (Wilson, 2004: 27). In contrast, Stuart MacGill, the Australian cricketer who refused to make himself available for the Australian cricket tour of Zimbabwe on the grounds that he could not maintain a conscience in the light of the human rights violations being perpetrated in Zimbabwe, was commended by both the Australian prime minister and foreign secretary. One year earlier, two members of the Zimbabwean cricket team, Henry Olonga and Andy Flower, made a powerful political statement by wearing black armbands as they took the field in a World Cup match in Harare – a protest, in their words, against the death of democracy in Zimbabwe. A group of church leaders in Bulawayo hailed the gesture as hitting a six for freedom and democracy, and which cost both players their positions in the side. While the International Cricket Council (ICC) did not allow tours to be cancelled on political or moral grounds, they did allow for *force majeure*, and it was this failure by Jack Straw to issue a clear statement by the government cancelling the tour, on these grounds, that was a missed opportunity. Despite the preparation of a framework paper that could have lead to the abandonment of the 2003 tour, in the end the foreign secretary stated that he did not have the power to order sportsmen around, even when they begged to be ordered, and this was from a government that had no problem with finding powers to invade Iraq on the basis of little substantive evidence of weapons of mass destruction.

In passing, it is necessary to draw clear parallels between the position in which the ICC finds itself today and the position of the major sporting bodies under apartheid-ruled South Africa more than a decade ago. The South Africans' experience taught them that they could have no normal sport in an abnormal society. The ICC and other sporting bodies and governments who support the approach taken by the ICC to cricket in Zimbabwe have to learn that lesson all over again. The most enthusiastic sporting authorities in South Africa eventually had to face the truth that there were occasions when overriding social, if not moral, considerations need to transcend the interests of sport. In the end the power of capital and loss of cricketing funds influenced the decision to tour Zimbabwe rather than influence both social change and cricket in Zimbabwe. Both were let down by weak actions from a former foreign secretary, and betrayed by an international cricket community dominated by the financial vested interests of the first-class countries. How wise were the words of C. L. R. James: 'What do they know of cricket who only cricket know?' (James, 1963: ix).

These examples help to illustrate factors that impact upon sporting worlds that are only partially governed and influenced by unbalanced power structures that operate along or between different fault lines between Northern–Southern geopolitical sporting worlds. That is to emphasise the fact that sporting worlds are differentiated not only as a result of social patterning, but also geo-political power structures and markets. How capital is allocated or misallocated is important for the success or failure of sporting development in different parts of the world. Sport can help in the development of different parts of the world by virtue of

431

SPORT IN FOCUS 19.4: SPORT AND SOCIAL INTERVENTION (3) – GLOBAL SPORT

It is not necessary to view sport as irrelevant to the geopolitical concerns that might figure in the reform of sporting structures and power balances that cause fissures within the North–South fault line or divide. Some or all of the following actions might figure in the reform of neo-liberal or global sport:

■ to reform global sporting institutions to permit greater representation of currently under-represented groups and regions of the South and beyond;

■ to develop sporting treaties and legislation to draw attention to secure better working conditions on a universal basis and the end of child labour in sport;

■ to recognise that the primary causes of child labour lie in poverty and, traditionally, sport has been an avenue for escape from poverty in many parts of the world;

■ to support and publicise attempts by women from Islamic countries to participate in international sporting forums and competitions;

■ to draw upon existing charters, declarations, covenants and laws that point the way to a more humane form of international sport not only within, but also between countries and communities;

■ to monitor and evaluate the percentage of profit made from migrant sports labour and sporting exiles and ensure that it returns South and does not simply remain circulating within the North;

■ to legislate to ensure that sport addresses and chases corruption with the same zeal that it chases the ideal of drug-free sport;

■ to recognise the common concerns of activists demonstrating at successive major international sporting events; and

■ to make sporting exchange and trade work for the poor.

its visibility and capacity to publicise the need for social change in different places. The differential relationship of sport and power is evident between, for example, northern and southern hemispheres' influences; the migration of sporting talent; the support for local or indigenous sport; the flows of sporting capital in and out of certain places; rates of child labour violations and human rights violations. The worry is that continuing injustices in sport and the failings of global sport will contribute to the undermining of trust not only in sport, but also between local, regional and international communities.

SPORT, SOCIAL CHANGE AND SOCIAL FORUMS

We should not over-emphasise the capacity of sport to collapse social barriers. At the same time, it is crucial to acknowledge the capacity of sport to facilitate social change within sport. The ways in which sport may contribute to other alternatives should not be over-emphasised either, but neither should they be ignored. The strength of sport's capacity to produce change perhaps lies in its popularity in different parts of the world, its capacity to symbolise graphically and poignantly social and political success and failure. The old and new politics of sport have been commented upon in Chapter 4, while this chapter has illustrated further some of the ways in which sport has attempted to produce and struggle for alternative ways of change, of reform and intervention. Such alternatives both influence and are influenced by different visions of a world that continues to struggle with inequality, turmoil and lack of clarity about the nature of both capitalism and democracy. It is a mistake to think that contemporary researchers, teachers and thinkers about sport in the world today have not been concerned about the type of world we do or could live in.

In a general sense, sport has contributed to at least three different visions of what the world is and should be. These might be referred to as:

1   the global neo-liberal view of sport in society in which the convergence of the opportunity gap between sport in the richest and poorest parts of the world might be possible (dependent upon a strict adherence to liberal policies);
2   the hard third way view of sport in society that requires a more limited adherence to democracy but an enthusiasm for sporting partnerships funded between private/public sources, decentralisation, arm's length sports policy, an acceptance of global sporting values and less of a concern with sporting inequality, while still embracing certain egalitarian goals through provision for targeted or vulnerable sports groups; and
3   a softer but less likely way in which sporting relief is used as part of an overall policy of managing capitalism's social contradictions with the typical role for sport being that of being a means to an end or a bridge-builder of reconciliation in areas of conflict.

Within this model, Third World democracy and sport as a facet of social welfare come first, not last.

Much attention has focused, in recent years, on the possibility of an emerging global civil society with the power to engage with and challenge institutions of governance. The protests of Seattle, Washington, Chiapas, Prague, Barcelona, Genoa, Porto Alegre and elsewhere have all highlighted the presence and work of civil society. Non-governmental organisations (NGOs) and various social movements have found themselves in the limelight, becoming front-page news and the subject of international debate and action. The development of, at a European level, civil society over the past 10 years has been impressive. NGOs from the local to the international level have increasingly realised the importance of organising themselves into coherent alliances in order to gain influence within the European Union. Both European and World Social Forums have been set up in the early part of the twenty-first century as focal points for various activists, students, intellectuals, environmentalists, economists and researchers, among others, to meet and link together in an expanding network of opposition to the neo-liberal cause.

The geography of the current climate of social and political protest and change in many ways signals a new political landscape – one that is arguing for diverse forms of social change and points towards an entirely new ideological, political and geographical design than that which characterised the cold war or other ideologically driven left-versus-right sporting

433

battlegrounds of the twentieth century. The social and geographical diversity of calls for social and political change can be found in places such as Chiapas, an impoverished region of southern Mexico; Seattle, the symbol of the microchip and American post-modernity; and Porto Alegre, a European city in Brazil's deep south, not to mention the many smaller specialist campaigns that have revolved around single issues such as the environment, poverty, hunger, child labour, religion, democracy and war, to name but a few. What has happened is that new groupings, new emblems of protest and new possibilities have given rise to a host of hopes, fears, illusions, questions and actions for change. In a way, that differs somewhat from liberalism; the ideas of civil society, social forums, NGOs and social movements have been used to voice and proclaim opposition to irresponsible states, governments, parliaments and political parties while at the same time searching for effective partnerships with socially responsible and responsive multinational corporations.

Thus, a new form of internationalism is emerging in a way that is entirely different from the old historical internationalism in which solidarity was premised upon the universalised exploitation of labour. In 2005, UN Secretary-General Kofi Annan pointed out that sport was a universal language that could bring people together, no matter what their origin, background, and religious beliefs or economic status (www.un.org/sport2005/index.html). The use of child labour in sport is still very much part of the use of a debate about labour in sport, and it is vital that such areas of concern are not isolated as single areas unconnected to other local and/or international forms of resistance. The use of child labour in sport is related to labour rights and the rights of the child. The movements that emerged so effectively in Seattle in November 1999 resulted from ecological, feminist, ethnic, human rights and other movements combining with anti-world trade groups that created new space. The notion of the social forum as a meeting place for anti-systemic forces to gather at a world level is attractive both in terms of its diversity, but also because it creates a space in which anti-neo-liberal struggles can escape from the narrow limitations of the global sport versus national or local sport binary. The common framework provides not so much an alternative to globalisation and global sport, but a different kind of globalisation and global sport. The advent of social forums represents a milestone and marks the possibility of a shift from sterile debates about global sport or identity sport to that of asserting, yet again, the idea that sport can contribute to social change but also articulate international, political, social and cultural concerns about neo-liberal sport and overcome them.

A number of contemporary think tanks have also woken up to the fact that sport can be both a popular and effective form of protest, demonstration and lobbying. In Chapter 18, we drew attention to the activities of an International Sport and Culture Association (ISCA) that, in March 2011, became a member of the World Social Forum's International Council. The World Social Forum is characterised by both plurality and diversity, non-confessional, non-governmental and non-party. It proposes to facilitate decentralised coordination and networking among organisations engaged in concrete action towards building another world – at any level from the local to the international. In announcing ISCA'S membership, the president embraced the opportunity for sport to contribute to socal change as part of strong worldwide alliance of NGOs, volunteers, activists, researchers and politicians and, by doing so, recognised the place and part to be played by universities and public intellectuals.

434

SPORT IN FOCUS 19.5: SPORT AND SOCIAL INTERVENTION (4) – RUNNING TO ESCAPE

As Saif Saeed Shaheen (formerly Stephen Cherono), the former world record holder in the 3,000 metre steeplechase, has explained, 'I was raised in Kamelilo, a village in Keiyo in which there was no water tap and every day after school, which cost $2 for 3 days, I walked 3 km to collect 10 litres of water'. The athlete later chose to run for Qatar, a move that was allegedly based upon an offer of a least $1,000 dollars a month for life. About 50 people became dependent upon his success for their livelihoods. He put eight children through school, with two at college in America and, when asked to explain Kenyan running success, said that the answer is simple: 'an athlete in Kenya runs to escape poverty' and 'I fight to survive' (Jarvie, 2011).

SUMMARY

In this chapter, we have examined different ways in which sport has contributed to bringing about social change. It is crucial that workers in the field of sport, culture and society do not lose sight of the many forms of intervention that have helped to contribute to what sport in the world is today. Forms of legislation, declarations of policy, political party manifestos and single and multi-lateral issue campaigns about sport have all had an impact and are continually in a state of flux. This chapter has also questioned the comprehensive nature of capitalist triumph in sport by drawing attention to the campaigns that effectively have been against globalisation and consequently global sport. Furthermore, it has built upon the old and new political successes and failures of sport outlined in Chapter 4.

At the beginning of this book, we asserted that one of the key sporting questions of our time needed to be: 'what is the transformative capacity of sport to produce social change?'. There are a number of fault lines running through the different worlds of sport that have sustained progressive agendas for change. Any number of entry and exit points may be chosen as a basis for substantiating the transformative capacity of sport. Forms of action may be classified along the continuum from reformism to radicalism or from ideological to non-ideological, or from issue-orientated to more collective forms of action. Forms of change may also have both intended and unintended outcomes but, whatever the basis for thinking about sport and social change in the early twenty-first century, it is imperative to acknowledge that the parameters of sport and social change are both geopolitical and socio-economic. The analytical distinction and separation of these two elements does not, of course, imply that they are literally distinct. In the different worlds of sport, these two fault lines may become conjoined but, as a method of thinking about sport and social change, they help to highlight not just the particular social patterning of movements for change in sport, but also that the impetus and pressure for change may result from a more geopolitical faultline of North and South or East and West.

GUIDE TO FURTHER READING

Bass, A. (2002). *Not the Triumph but the Struggle: The 1968 Olympics and the Making of the Black Athlete*. Minneapolis, MN: University of Minnesota Press.

Bellos, A. (2003). 'The President Wins the Midfield Battle'. *New Statesman*, 3 November: 32–34.

Boykoff, J. (2011). 'The Anti-Olympics'. *New Left Review*, 67 (January/February): 41–61.

Harvey, J., Horne, J. and Safai, P. (2009). 'Alterglobalization, Global Social Movements, and the Possibility of Political Transformation Through Sport'. *Sociology of Sport Journal*, 26 (3).

Hayes, G. and Karamichas, J. (eds) (2011). *Olympic Games, Mega-Events and Civil Societies: Globalisation, Environemnt and Resistance*. Basingstoke: Palgrave.

Kidd, B. (1996). *The Struggle for Canadian Sport*. Toronto: University of Toronto Press.

Lenskyj, H. (2008). *Olympic Industry Resistance: Challenging Olympic Power and Propaganda*. Albany, NY: State University of New York Press.

QUESTIONS

1 List four different forms of activism that may be utilised to bring about social change in sport.

2 Consider a further four ways in which neo-liberal ideals of global sport might be challenged.

3 Compare the actions open to radical and moderate anti-global movements.

4 Explore the Sport et Citoyenneté website (www.sportcitoyennete.org) and list the aims of the organisation.

5 List eight ways to challenge the global sports movement in general, and the Olympic industry in particular.

6 How did the following people involve sport to challenge or bring attention to the need for change in society: Jesse Owens, Nelson Mandela, Kofi Annan, Billie Jean King, Muhammad Ali and Cathy Freeman?

7 Explore any one campaign that uses sport to tackle racism or child labour or poverty, and list the aims of the campaign and comment upon its work.

8 Explore the UNESCO website (www.unesco.org/new/en/social-and-human-sciences/themes/sport/physical-education-and-sport/) and summarise the work of any one project that uses sport to intervene socially.

9 How has the Centre for Sports Policy Studies taken forward the notion of advocacy through sport (www.physical.utoronto.ca/Centre_for_Sport_Policy_Studies/Advocacy.aspx)?

10 Access the following site or any other international labour movement (www.imfmetal. org/index.cfm?n=616) and use the search facility to look for campaigns or reports involving sport. Place the word 'sport' in the search box.

PRACTICAL PROJECTS

1   Carry out a Google search using the terms 'sport _ social change', 'sport _ social movements' and 'sport _ reform', and write a 1,000-word report explaining how sport contributes to campaigns aimed at bringing about social change in the world today.

2   Collect a series of about 10–20 charters, declarations and/or laws that have been specific to sport and develop a 10-point charter of your own aimed at bringing about social change in some aspect of sport in your locality.

3   Use the Internet and newspaper sources to research the way in which major sports organisations such as FIFA, the IOC or any other major sports organisation of your choice have associated themselves with movements or examples of solidarity in the world today.

4   Imagine you are the leader of an international political party and an important part of your party manifesto is going to address the question of how sport can make the world a better place today. What would your key party pledges be in relation to your sports policy for international sport? List and explain 10 points of intervention aimed at bringing about social change in and through the world of sport.

5   Monitor and evaluate five contemporary and/or historical initiatives that have used sport as a means of addressing poverty. Write a report of 1,000 words, thinking about the relationship between sport and poverty. Finish your report with a list of five recommendations.

KEY CONCEPTS

Anti-environmental ■ Anti-global ■ Anti-Olympic ■ Anti-systemic ■ Capitalism ■ Civil society ■ Neo-liberalism ■ North/South divide ■ Power ■ Reform ■ Social change ■ Social intervention ■ Social movements

WEBSITES

Sport and Development Platform
www.sportanddev.org/
The platform is a website dedicated to sport and development. It is an online resource and communication tool.

United Nations and Sport

www.un.org/wcm/content/site/sport/home

Explore the role of the United Nations in promoting peace and development through the resources on this website.

The Centre for Sports Policy Studies

www.physical.utoronto.ca/Centre_for_Sport_Policy_Studies.aspx

Access to campaigns, projects and publications involving the University of Toronto centre.

Peace and Sport

www.peace-sport.org/

An international forum supported by the UN dedicated to peace, sport and development.

FARE, Football against Racism in Europe

www.farenet.org/

An anti-racist campaign against racism in football in Europe.

International Year of Sport and Physical Education

www.un.org/sport2005

The United Nations website for the 2005 International Year of Sport and Education supported by Kofi Annan.

Chapter 20

Sport, the public intellectual and universities

The legendary Jesse Owens once commented, 'We all have dreams but who has the courage, capacity and opportunity to speak the truth to power today?'

What are universities for and what opportunities are provided by sport to speak the truth to power?

Are those involved in sport in our universities talking to the societies they inhabit in an attempt to make the world a better place? What are you doing?

PREVIEW

Key terms defined ■ Introduction ■ Key questions and activities ■ First principles ■ Sport, social change and the public intellectual ■ Kofi Annan on sport ■ Amaryta Sen and capability ■ Sport organic intellectuals ■ Bruce Kidd and the struggle for Canadian sport ■ Saïd and the intellectual ■ Sport and the vernacular intellectuals ■ Sporting issues ■ Muhammad Ali ■ Sania Mirza ■ Sport and the role of universities ■ Sport and the university as a resource of hope ■ Maria Mutola ■ Summary

OBJECTIVES

This chapter will:

- introduce key terms for thinking about the role of the public intellectual;
- examine some of the key roles of sport and universities today;
- consider the notion that sport may help as a resource of hope;
- examine key myths about the difference between organic and traditional intellectuals in the field of sport;
- suggest that future students, teachers, researchers, sports enthusiasts and critics examining the relationship between sport, culture and society recognise the interrelated nature of their work and the opportunity, promise and possibility that sport affords; and
- consider what universities are for today.

KEY TERMS DEFINED

Public intellectual: Able to work on behalf of the public on public issues for the public and those who speak the truth to power.

Organic intellectual: All people are intellectuals but not all people have the opportunity to function as intellectuals (adapted from Gramsci).

Traditional intellectual: Able to work on behalf of or in opposition to the status quo.

Vernacular intellectual: Intellectuals as individuals who address and confront social injustice from both inside and outside traditional academic or political spheres; the vernacular intellectual, unlike the traditional or organic intellectual, is in no way connected to organised political structures.

INTRODUCTION

At the outset of this book, it was suggested that those working in the field of sport, culture and society need to engage with a number of key questions and activities. These are:

- What empirical evidence can we draw upon to substantiate aspects of sport, culture and society? (What is happening in sport?)
- What theories, ideas and concepts can we draw upon to explain and analyse this substantive evidence? (How can we make sense of what is happening in sport?)
- What capacity does sport have to transform or intervene to produce social change? (What can be done to produce change?)
- What is the contemporary role of the student, intellectual, researcher, sports enthusiast, university in the public arena? (What are you going to do about it?)

440

One of the objectives of the book has been to encourage students, researchers, members of the public, people to reflect upon sport, drawing upon concepts, ideas and themes but also a body of substantive research from different sports, societies and communities. It is the interplay between theory, explanation, evidence and intervention that is one of the hallmarks of the approach adopted. The student of sport, culture and society will continually be faced with three interrelated challenges. Although the production of knowledge and policy rarely comes in such a neat package or process, these can be summarised as: what evidence do you have, how are you going to make sense of it and what actions, interventions and recommendations are you going to make as a result these first two exercises?

Many authors of rival books to sport, culture and society often seem to overlook the fact that they are written by people working in universities and the very nature of the work provides a glorious opportunity to engage with a very popular subject and highly visible public arena. In this final chapter, it is worth thinking about two further questions that are rarely commented upon by other authors: what is the role or idea of the university and what is the role of the engaged public intellectual – in the broadest inclusive, non-elitist sense of the term – working in the area of sport? Those working in universities are but one diverse community of people who have a part to play in the above. It is the contention of this book that more could be done if students, teachers, researchers and others recognised fully the interrelated nature of their work in this area. The university in different parts of the world has found itself to be besieged and under attack on a number of fronts. Yet, most governments repeatedly stress the importance of the university and acknowledge that the success of different places is increasingly driven by a knowledge economy and by human and intellectual capital.

The term 'university' has current challenges and possible futures, whether the term refers to institutions that actually bear the name university or the complex set of ideas that have accrued over centuries in developing thoughts as to what the very idea of a university might be. For the university both as an idea and as an institution embodies or has embodied extraordinary hopes and profound values. However, if a body of work referred to as 'sport, culture and society' is important to both the university as an institution but also the idea or promise of a university, then it needs to contribute to some or all of the following:

- produce internationally aware graduates who are capable of making sound judgements on the basis of a humane and liberal higher education;
- provide a professionally skilled and well-trained workforce;
- contribute to the creation of knowledge as part of an international effort;
- contribute to a country, area or places of international presence and significance;
- provide a research base for business and industry;
- produce ideas, some of which may turn into marketable products and some which are valued simply as ideas;
- provide social mobility; and
- contribute to independent, dispassionate and informed discussion, critique and analysis of the societies of which it is a part of.

It is the totality of this promise that is important as one of the few places where the totality of the world and those in the university may or should be brought together.

There is much in common with the approach to sport, culture and society adopted in this book and what Docherty (2011) has championed as the first principles of the university in the world today. Universities need to be well managed but also understood and valued. In the twenty-first century, it is quite common in certain parts of the world to ask where a university or area of work might provide value for money but it is equally the case that the question might be turned around to ask where a university might find money for values and what should those be. If one accepts the principles explored by Docherty in relation to the future of the university, then they might equally be applied to the promise and possibility of sport, culture and society as championed in this contribution. These terms are not exhaustive but that sport, culture and society is about *research* because the university is, in part, governed by actions of discovery and inventiveness and the possibilities that are opened up through the ongoing adventure of discovery. Individuals working in universities in the area of sport do research are involved in discovery and add value in a number of ways. An openness of possibility requires a spirit of freedom and that the idea of a university exists for the extension of *freedom and/as development*. This, in turn, allows sport, culture and society to attend to questions of judgment and judgment in turn allows those working in universities and others to search for the *idea of justice* or what constitutes justice. If justice is to be shaped or shared by a community, then it will depend upon a certain kind of *democracy*. Whether it is through research, the student experience and/or public engagement, the promise and possibilities of sport, culture and society and the idea of a university are both helped by these first principles.

The concern in this chapter relates to the question of the public intellectual or some better term to encapsulate not a culture of anti-intellectualism, but one that embraces the public realm, public issues and concerns, and reverses what Marquand (2004) and others have referred to as the decline of the public realm and a search for a common purpose. Sport, culture and society affords the opportunity not only to challenge the very nature of the ivory tower university, but also be at the forefront of solving popular issues contributing to social change and helping with capabilities in a post-recessionary world. Whether it is through theoretical, technical or ethical activity (in reality, the integrated nature of this knowledge), the public intellectual working in the field of sport has the opportunity to speak the truth to power on a number of fronts. There is more to this than just a public engagement strategy – important as these are. It is a committed and sustained effort to make a difference in the communities and societies in which sport and universities are involved. Yet, very rarely do sport and related areas figure on the lists of people making a significant impact upon public discussion and action. Some have mistakenly conflated the notions of public intellectual activity and social activism but at least British and American intellectuals commenting on sport are noticeable in terms of a silence while, at the same time, those lists of people who are likely to have an impact on the world in the future only occasionally come from the field of sport, but not necessarily the university world of sport.

SPORT AND PUBLIC INTELLECTUALS

Despite the existence of many social issues and problems involving sport, a silence continues to exist that only adds weight to the contemporary assertion that there is a character missing from the cast of social and public life – the public intellectual (Jarvie, 2007). While the French have usually celebrated their public intellectuals, the British, according to Naughton (2011: 8), generally seem to regard the term 'intellectual' as a term of abuse. Public intellectualism may be considered at three different levels: writing for the public about an area in which one has a particular knowledge, in this case sport, culture and society; speaking about and writing about one's own area and how it connects with the social, political and economic world; and finally by invitation where one is provided a platform to talk to an issue or represent a body of knowledge but also speak on public issues of the day. Other possibilities also exist. Most intellectuals manage to perform the social role assigned to them by Gramsci in either a traditional or organic sense but only a tiny minority, according to Saïd, manage to speak the truth to power, or set themselves apart in order to become dispassionate and effective, ask embarrassing questions, confront orthodoxy and dogma, and resist being co-opted easily by governments, institutions or corporations.

The very notion of the public intellectual has been addressed by a range of researchers such as Saïd (2001), Klein (2001), Sontag (2002), Small (2002), Farred (2003), Gourley (2002), Giroux (2006), Ritzer (2006), Turner (2006), Misztal (2007), Sokmen and Ertur (2008) and Altinay (2010). Furedi (2004: 67) asked where all the intellectuals have gone and suggested that 'there was clearly a sense that the role of the public intellectual is changing – or might have in fact ended?'. Consternation about the place of the public intellectual in public life has been associated with a further set of arguments about the decline of the public realm, public space and public engagement. The alleged decline in public engagement has been associated, most notably, with the work of Marquand (2002, 2004, 2006) and Mair (2006). Civic engagement appears to be less of a potent force, and public values are seemingly rendered invisible, in light of the growing power of multinational corporations not only to shape the content of the media but also increasingly privatise and commercialise public spaces (Walljasper, 2005). The decline of the Murdoch media empire in 2011 brought about by unethical journalistic practices was, in part, caused by public action, concern and intervention. In *The Decline of the Public*, Marquand (2004) charted the decline of citizenship, equity and service that had been deemed crucial to both individual fulfilment and social well-being. Contemporary trends such as trusting people less, a lack of faith in politics and the kinds of associations that groups of people are joining tend, according to Marquand (2004), to have more to do with private needs than concerns about civic engagement and public responsibility. Mair (2006) has raised the spectre of a void in democracy emerging as ruling elites retreat and voters abstain from mass electoral politics with the paradox being the emergence of a governing class bereft of legitimacy as parties become appendages of the state. The above arguments are complex, however, such concerns and the need for active public intellectuals engaging in the political arguments of the day about and through sport are also vital facets of this concern. They are all needed if Mair's democratic void or Marquand's decline of the public realm are to be addressed not to mention the need for alternative or progressive visions for sport in society. If the public domain of sport is annexed to, or invaded by, the market domain of buying and selling then the promise and possibilities of sport forging higher levels of trust and mutuality run the risk of also being sacrificed on the alter of individualism.

443

SPORT IN FOCUS 20.1: KOFI ANNAN ON SPORT AND MUCH MORE

Kofi Annan was appointed the seventh secretary-general of the United Nations in 1996. He was awarded the Nobel Peace Prize in 2001 and endured being shunned by the US and the UK because of his fierce resistance to the Iraq War. His period of office ended on 31 December 2006 but, during this period of office, he recognised that the language of sport could help with conflict resolution.

Kofi Annan launched the International Year of Sport and Physical Activity by recognising that, 'Sport is a universal language that can bring people together, no matter what their origin, background, religious beliefs or economic status'.

It is not being suggested that public intellectuals only work in universities, that would not only be absurd but traditional and elitist. Sport in Focus 20.1 looks at the position on sport taken by one United Nations Secretary General and asks if this is a public intellectual fighting for the potential or sport or paying lip service to the potential of sport.

What is being suggested here is far from utopian. The previous chapters of *Sport, Culture and Society* have helped to evidence that sport can help to (i) change some people's lives; (ii) symbolise change; and (iii) contribute to and facilitate social change. Sport has the potential to work across societies and agencies to attempt make the world a better place. In a general sense, the potential of sport to contribute to different visions of what the world is and/or should be should not be overstated, nor underestimated. It certainly should not be ignored in what Altinay (2010) refers to as a global veil of ignorance that maintains a state of play in which famine exists in one part of the world and food mountains exist in other parts of the world, or that sport can help in a limited sense. There remain a number of fault lines running through the different worlds of sport and any number of entry and exit points that may be chosen as a basis for public intellectuals to be involved with a progressive agenda for change involving sport. Forms of action may be classified along the continuum from reformism to radicalism or from ideological to non-ideological or from issue-orientated to more collective forms of action. Forms of change may also have both intended and unintended outcomes but, whatever the basis for thinking about sport in the twenty-first century, it is imperative to acknowledge that the parameters of sport are both geo-political and socio-economic. The analytical distinction and separation of these two elements does not imply that they are distinct. In the different worlds of sport, these two fault lines may become conjoined but, as a method of thinking about sport and social change, they help to highlight not just the particular social patterning of movements for change in sport, but also that the impetus and pressure for change may often result from a more geo-political fault line of North and South or East and West. Parts of the world would like to hold major sporting events but cannot do this alone. The distribution of wealth from sport is uneven and certainly not based upon the notion of a countries need.

When Reeves (2003: 24) was asking whether 'There is a character missing from the cast of social and political life: the Public Intellectual', he was in fact asking serious questions about the role of the academic in public life and the nature of academic life – a role that he and other commentators have observed is much in decline. Furedi (2004: 67) asks the question where have all he intellectuals gone – people with genuine learning, breadth of vision and a concern for public issues? In the age of the knowledge economy, we have some-how managed to combine the widest ever participation in higher education – in some places – with a reduced participation of the intellectual in public life. The argument ends with a plea for the recreation of public spheres in which intellectuals and the general public can genuinely debate the issues of the day. Is there a space, a person or a character missing in between the slow ivory tower scholars who have little time for public politics and the furiously peddling politician with little time for theory or sport . The Oxford political philosopher Adam Swift (quoted in Reeves 2003) remarks that the politicians think that the philosophers are only interested in talking to each other in arcane journals and the philosophers think that the politicians have no interest in real philosophical concepts – both observations may be true. At the same time, there also exist plenty of commentators in the media studios who have limited knowledge and expertise in the areas they pronounce upon. Debate is governed by the quick and the clever rather than the thoughtful or the learned, the former being characterised by what the French sociologist Bourdieu (1988: 19) observed as 'Le Fast Talker', who was often heard to be ruling the airwaves. Meanwhile, we have the modern academic who has devoted his or her life to a particular subject lying undisturbed and invisible, perhaps preparing for Research Assessment Exercises (RAEs), writing in one of the peculiar languages of scholarship to an audience of peers, with no inclination, incentive or often ability to participate in the rough and tumble of public debate. So we have plenty of intellectuals and plenty of public commentators – what Plato might have called rhetoricians – but a declining overlap between the two. *Sport, Culture and Society* is a plea for this to happen.

It is not as if there is a shortage of ideas, writing and commentary from academics about the decline of the public realm, public sociology or indeed a common purpose. The cult of genuine expertise being replaced or challenged by the cult of punditry in which there is no place for, never mind value for genuine debate about things unless they are aligned to policy, government, the quest for power and/or authority. Some remind us of the warnings in Huxley's *Brave New World*, in where we willingly enslave ourselves by coming to adore the technologies that undo our capacity to think. Donald Wood (1996), in *Post-Intellectualism and the Decline of Democracy*, argued some 15 years ago that we must manifest an even stronger commitment to reason and responsibility but we fail to do so. He suggested, then, that we are opting out of a serious responsibility if we continue along this path and that the very essence of democracy might be put at risk. Public intellectuals are defined in Posner's (2001: 3) *Public Intellectuals: A Study of Decline* as those who write for the general public or at least for a broader than merely academic or specialist audience on public affairs. More specifically 'a public intellectual is not merely someone who does intellectual work in public but she does intellectual work on public issues' (Posner, 2001: 3). Sport in Focus 20.2 considers another case despite the fact that Sen commented minimally on sport and when he did it was usually cricket. However, the ideas represented in the work of Amartya Sen raise important questions and actions pertinent to sport, culture and society.

SPORT IN FOCUS 20.2: AMARTYA SEN AND CAPABILITY

The Nobel Prize-winning economist Amartya Sen declared that social justice means capability and power for everyone. His work is an example of a corpus of work that speaks to both fellow economists and fellow citizens. He challenged many policy makers to think not only about economic inequalities but also inequalities of capability. He has been described at times as an authentic public intellectual but in this specific sport in focus we present a number of ideas that are presented in Sen's thinking that are valuable to more progressive thinkinging about sport, culture and society. These are:

- the idea that inequalities in capability are as important as inequalities in wealth and power;
- the notion that inequalities of capability may occur between individuals but also nations and commuities;
- redistribution of resources and income is important but also what people do with these resources;
- the greatest injustice is when people cannot achieve their goals because someone else with power stops them;
- to be genuinely free, people need to have a capability set and the question of sport is whether and under what circumstances can sport add to this capability set;
- when asking the question of inequality in sport, perhaps the first issue is to consider 'inequality of what?';
- you can increase people's income in a number of ways but literacy, nutrition, and the power to participate in social life of the community are resources that can help, and is sport resourcful enough to help build capabilities or even social mobility?

The questions and themes presented above are illustrative of issues arising out of a capability approach that may help to guide thinking about the effectiveness of sport as aid, welfare and a resource.

Perhaps the function of the public intellectual is to puncture the myth makers to avoid utopian thinking and be sceptical about grand claims, whether it be the victory of the free market, worldwide genetic enhancement, or the myth of global sport. Scepticism towards elected politicians is nothing new. At least 60 years ago, Schumpeter (1947: 288) warned against relying too heavily on those who were emerging from the electoral process, and suggested that others had to be involved in the process of forging popular democracies otherwise the 'administrators' would distance themselves from the matters that were most important to ordinary people. What was being implied was that, unless we had healthy contributions from a variety of groups and people on matters of public concern, then the elected parties and their civil servants or advisors shifted away from having expressive or representative functions that were in tune with the matters that concerned ordinary people, and became much closer to becoming potential appendages of the state.

SPORT AND ORGANIC INTELLECTUALS

In a critique of the very notion of the public intellectual, Bairner (2009) asserts that much of decline in public intellectualism has been down to the changing nature of the environment in which academics now work and that public intellectuals should not be confused with social activism. The article goes on to suggest that it might be difficult for those working in sport in universities and in particular sociologists of sport, to assume the mantle of the public intellectual in the field of sport. Drawing upon Lightman (2004) and then Gramsci, Bairner outlines three levels of public intellectualism before activating Gramsci's theory of intellectuals. Bairner tries to indirectly draw too narrow a distinction between public intellectuals in the widest sense of the term and social activists working in the field of university sport. The lack of public engagement with sport, according to Bairner (2009: 117) might be put down to some or all of the following:

- the constrains of academic life, particularly in UK universities that have an impact upon intellectuals working in higher education;
- that sociologists of sport, among others, may have become too close to sport or government in a way that mitigates against speaking the truth to power; in other words, they have become civil servant-like;
- that, rather than act as organic intellectuals in the Gramscian sense, some 'well intentioned traditional public intellectualism can only achieve so much in the world of sport' (Bairner, 2009: 127); and
- what is required is organic intellectuals helping public sociology convey important messages to multiple publics.

That being said, Bairner offers some helpful pointers in relation to academics being accepted or rejected by the world of sport itself, which, in some senses, aims at avoiding some sort of double jeopardy of being marginalised by sport because of taking critical stances and being rejected by the academy because of being involved in sport. In both cases, the degree of power one has may be affected but this is as much a question of strategy as reality, and need not result in the picture painted by this researcher.

Consider for example, just one example of the effective politician working as athlete, intellectual, researcher and activist all in one.

It is accepted here, as Gramsci did, that intellectuals compose a large and variegated social body, connected to social movements, class in the strict Gramscian sense, traditions and fulfilling all kinds of social roles. Most intellectuals have the opportunity to achieve the social role ascribed to them by Gramsci but writers such as Saïd, drawing on the work of Julien Benda, went further to evoke the notion that one of the ideas prescribed to the category of intellectual was to be 'set apart, someone able to speak the truth to power, a crusty, eloquent, fantastically courageous and angry individual for whom no worldly power is too

447

SPORT IN FOCUS 20.3: BRUCE KIDD AND *THE STRUGGLE FOR CANADIAN SPORT*

The examples of the academic-cum-athlete who operates as public intellectual and high level policy developer are many but the example used from the Canadian context is valuable in a numner of ways. Published in 1996, *The Struggle for Canadian Sport* is perhaps a prisoner of time and context but it was written by Professor Bruce Kidd, formerly head of school at the University of Toronto, international athlete and valued sports administrator. *The Struggle for Canadian Sport* raises a number of questions – more than can be illustrated here. The following five issues and questions could be added as a result of reading and acting as per the example given by the author:

■ The politcal economic analysis of Canadian sport tells the story of the struggle for Canadian sport.

■ It maps out not only socio-economic fault lines in and through sport, but also geopolitical fault lines between countries, notably Canada and the US.

■ It explores the idea that, to enhance athletes' health, education and social capacities, as well as sporting skills, it is vital to strive for a health environment – one that is free from sexual harrassment and dsicrimination.

■ It paints a picture not only of better sport, but a better society and, therefore, the question of sport is inextricably linked to working for a better society, providing and contributing to the model of a better society – the same needs to be done today.

■ Finally, the struggle for Canadian sport not only adds to our understanding of the material and social conditions under which sport operates, but also that it is necessary not to explain conditions but work to change such conditions.

In many ways, a link exists between this and the more recent idea of justice elaborated by Sen and presented in Sport in Focus 20.2.

big and imposing to be criticised and pointedly taken to task' (Sokmen and Ertur, 2008: 54). It may be that the context or the intellectuals to which Saïd applied such thinking no longer exist, but aspects of it do, and there are lessons here for sport, culture and society and those who earn a living from it. Even Saïd might not have been blind to the political possibilities of sport and Palestine. Saïd, as far as the authors are aware, never commented on the potential of sport to recognise Palestine, while other social institutions and governments did not. This was an oversight but Saïd acknowledged that public intellectuals, while taking the side of the downtrodden and those in need, were not completely free from social constraints (constraints of universities, government and other social institutions). The prime threat facing the public intellectual wanting to engage with sporting issues and problems comes from a more insidious pressure, namely the seduction of silence and compromise offered under the disguise of professionalism. The proper role of the public intellectual involved in sport is partly to maintain intellectual and political integrity and to speak the truth to power.

Despite Bairner's (2009) pointers, qualifications and decisions about tactical entry points into the debate about sport, culture and society, there is undoubtedly a considerable cynicism, perhaps premature cynicism about the demise of national mainstream politics, the prospects of a more just and less charitable social order in which important social and political problems are not reduced to matters of efficiency or profit. For those interested in sport, there are a number of fault lines running through the different worlds of sport that have sustained agendas for change and have illustrated that any number of entry and exit points may be chosen as a basis for substantiating and encouraging change in and through sport. Writers such as Sontag (2002), Saïd (2001), Sen (2009) and others remind us of the impressive array of opportunities offered by the lecture platform, the pamphlet, the radio, the interview, the Internet, the research newsletter, the guest lecture, the letter to the newspaper open to a wide variety of public intellectuals. Gilroy (2011) acknowledges the role of the public intellectual in the US while recognising that new technologies impact upon the idea of public intellectuals directly. New technologies provide a very different kind of platform. To ignore the capacity of sport to assist with social change is perhaps not an option for the public intellectual interested and steeped in an understanding of what sport can do.

Durkheim once insisted professional associations should always be an integral part of national political life – and not just function to defend their own narrow professional interests. A public intellectual involved in sport would not simply be an intellectual who does work in public but does intellectual work in public on public sporting issues and concerns. One of the most important roles of the public intellectual in sport is the capacity to see above and beyond existing debates, to get off the tramlines of discussion – perhaps to rock the boat but certainly provide a level of independence that think tanks cannot often provide because of funding constraints. Bairner, I would add, forgets that Saïd (2001: 16) was openly explicit about the role of the intellectual, which was to 'uncover the contest, to challenge and defeat both an imposed silence and the normalised quiet of unseen power' wherever and whenever possible. Saïd laid out a powerful case for regarding intellectuals as those who are never more themselves than when moved by metaphysical passions and disinterested principles of justice and truth, they denounce corruption, defend the weak and defy imperfect or oppressive authority. They are those who speak the truth to power and refuse the constraints of disciplinarity and specialisation that Saïd believed tended to weaken and depoliticise the intellectual strengths of academic writing.

SPORT AND THE VERNACULAR INTELLECTUALS

In a study of four vernacular intellectuals, Farred (2003) develops a category of involved thinker as the vernacular intellectual. It is clear to Farred (2003: 15) that a transition is made from the organic to the vernacular and the key issues are how the organic intellectual becomes a vernacular figure. How does the intellectual's work change in the process? What marks the point of transition from one mode to another and how is it sustained? Finally, what are the limitations and advantages of all of these labels? It is perhaps worth reminding ourselves here that the purpose of this debate is not to confuse or add complexity to a debate about intellectuals, but it is about the individuals working in university settings who have a range of platforms and opportunities to influence and move forward public debate and issues about a wide range of concerns arising out of an interest and commitment to sport, culture and society.

In Chapter 3 of this book, we listed a number of concerns or potential public issues that need commenting upon today:

- sport and poverty;
- human rights and aid in sport;
- sporting irreverence and identity;
- post-colonial sport;
- sport and the environment;
- lifestyle politics;
- sport and corruption; and
- hosting of major sporting events.

These areas and issues will change with the context and time period but they are some of the issues that are in the public arena and would be potential concerns for organic, traditional, vernacular and/or all public intellectuals. Extending Gramsci's notion of the organic intellectual, Farred conceives of vernacular intellectuals as individuals who address and confront social injustice from both inside and outside traditional academic or political spheres. According to Farred (2003: 22) the vernacular intellectual, unlike the traditional or organic intellectual, is in no way connected to organised political structures. These figures emerge

SPORT IN FOCUS 20.4: MUHAMMAD ALI, BOXING, VIETNAM AND AFRICA

- Renounced the name Cassius Clay (born 1942) for Muhammad Ali in 1964 – the boxer aligned himself with not just America, but Africa and Asia in particular.
- Positioned himself as an international, black, postcolonial figure who opposed US imperialism.
- Refused to enlist in the army to fight in Vietnam in 1967 and was stripped of his world title.
- Aligned himself with conservative republican politics of the Regan era.
- Supported decolonisation in Kenya, Zaire and other parts of Africa.
- Lived the journey of social mobility and escape from poverty through sport.
- Took on selective struggles and used the platform provided through fame to publicly take on certain political causes.

SPORT IN FOCUS 20.5: SANIA MIRZA, TENNIS AND THE MUSLIM WORLD

Sania Mirza was once ranked as one of the most powerful future people in the world because of the symbolism attached to her tennis and beliefs. In 2000, in a list of the top 10 people likely to have an impact on the world, she stood at number 10, behind a then unelected Barack Obama, who stood at number 1. In tenth place was this young athlete – a then 18-year-old female tennis player from India ranked number 37 in the world – Sania Mirza. The first female Indian tennis player to be ranked in the top 40 had the potential to be a role model for an entire generation of Muslim girls in a country where women have typically been discouraged from taking part in sport. At Wimbledon, she wore a T-shirt bearing the slogan 'well-behaved women rarely make history'. At the US Open, where she lost in the quarter finals to Maria Sharapova, she wore another T-shirt that read 'You can either agree with me or be wrong'. She has been attacked by Muslim clerics who, all too well, have recognised the impact of sport in changing attitudes and the power of a young, attractive, media-smart teenage Muslim tennis star to shake traditional hierarchies.

out of the vernacular experience, they craft a public space, and they address issues of the day that directly affect the communities in which they operate. Figures such as Muhammad Ali, C. L. R. James, Bob Marley, argues Farred (2003: 23), are grounded in the vernacular, speak for the vernacular but stand slightly removed from the experience in it. In this sense, the description is close to Saïd's notion of the public intellectual. Celebrity status often empowers minority athletes to pronounce on a range of subjects in the civic domain. Ideologically mobile, such celebrities can often, if not talk for, then certainly connect with a body of subjects often excluded from public platforms and formal public debate. For instance, those athletes who spoke out from and around the Olympic platform at the 1968 Mexico Olympic Games and questioned the political responsibility of the black American athlete who experienced life as a second-class citizen outside of the athletic arena and life as first-class citizens as long as they were winning inside the athletic arena. The former world heavyweight boxing champion Muhammad Ali took on such a role on a number of occasions. Throughout his career, the boxer engaged with a number of social and political issues, and some of these are captured in Sport in Focus 20.4.

The difference between vernacular and organic intellectuals is that the former are grounded in often disenfranchised communities and, for Farred (2003: 12), it is this situation or location that is one of the differences. Vernacular intellectuals, in this sense, are grounded in sport, or from sport, and understand the challenges and language of sport because of their immersion in it. Farred recognises that female athletes such as Althea Gibson, the openly gay Martina Navratilova, or the Williams sisters Venus and Serena have not been afraid to challenge the accepted image or world of women's tennis. Billie Jean King and Evonne

Goolagong also challenged issues of equal pay and the all-white world of women's tennis at particular points in time. If public intellectuals are taken as people who move public debates forward or say something that everybody knows to be true but is afraid to express, then the opportunity of many entry and exit points into public issues is open to a wide range of people. The Indian tennis player Sania Mirza, at the beginning of the twenty-first century, found herself on a list, indeed in the top 10, of the potentially most powerful people in the world alongside, at the time, an emerging presidential hopeful, Barack Obama.

SPORT AND THE VITAL ROLE OF UNIVERSITIES

Much of what has been written here in *Sport, Culture and Society* has been written from the privileged position of chair or university employee in different universities in different countries. Sport and its impact within cultures and societies has the potential to impact both within and, perhaps more importantly, outwith the university. It can help to be that missing ingredient that many chancellors and presidents/principals and politicians are looking for but do not fully understand other than its celebrity or community potential. One of the ideal venues and places for debate and action about sport, culture and society is certainly the university campus but, perhaps more importantly, the spaces and places beyond the campus. If universities in the twenty-first century do not provide their students with the forums and tools to at least discuss and discover what their responsibilities are to their fellow human beings, and help develop the requisite normative compass to navigate the treacherous path of increasing or decreasing interdependence, then they could be failing in their mission. Universities should be key sites about asking, if not solving, the problems of our time. *Sport, Culture and Society* has attempted to connect with many of the key questions of our time but it has, in particular, wished to underline not only the social and political importance of the area, but it has also challenged the idea of the university and the necessity of it and its members to revive politics in relation to the question of the university and its place in the world we live in today.

Much more could be done if researchers, students and teachers of sport regarded themselves less as academics and more as a public resource to help or intervene in some or all of the many worlds of sport. The notion of the public intellectual may not be perfect, but it is a useful starter. There is much more to this than public engagement strategies put forward by the university or the faculty. The role of the public intellectual in sport is fundamentally different from the role of the academic. Public intellectuals are not only different from academics, but almost the opposite of them. Academics usually, *but not always*, plough a narrow disciplinary/conservative inter-disciplinary path, whereas public intellectuals roam ambitiously from one area to another. Academics are interested in ideas, research and analysis, whereas public intellectuals are more concerned with the intersection between research, analysis and public debate, ideas and helping ordinary people. The decisions about sport and the part of the social contract that involves matters of sport can only work if we have honest argument, real information and not the spurious confessions of spin-doctors.

The role of sport in many universities is multi-functional, invariably uneven, rarely understood and often unjust in terms of socio-economic divisions or geopolitical divisions but also status within university strategies. The norm is quite often for separate academic and recreation/athletic divisions, the promise and possibility of sport is often justified on a number of orthodox grounds but rarely in terms of how it can help students and/or individuals deepen their understanding of an increasingly interdependent world in which sport has a part to play in the development of social, human and economic capital. Sport also has a vital role to play in answering the question 'what are universities for?'. By this, it is not meant that the utilitarian function of sport in universities to help with recruitment and retention or enhance the quality of life of students, staff and the wider community or provide businees benefits, volunteering benefits, or national and international recognition through sport are not important – they are. It is about all of the aforementioned but also the much more active necessity of harnessing the power of sport and education to address the problems of the day or equip students and staff with the necessary annalytical tools to better exercise command of their lives. The potential of sport to contribute to an analysis and vision for both the idea of a university but also a forum for debate and action should not be underestimated. We need, more than ever, visionary universities that have a strong normative comitment to ensure that all, not just graduates and public intellectuals, have answers to the seminal questions of the day but are also prepared to do something about them. We need public engagement to be recognised as part of the normal criteria for selection in the same way that research expertise and inspirational teaching is valued.

For the student or faculty member interested in the study of sport, culture and society, it is not just enough to be interested in ideas, but rather one must participate in debate to clarify issues, expose the errors of other public intellectuals, draw attention to neglected issues and generally be a catalyst for public discussion and discovery. Edward Saïd saw the public intellectual as the scoffer whose place it was to publicly raise embarrassing questions, to confront orthodoxy and dogma. None of these provide exact or sharp definitions of the role of the public intellectual but the role should not be lost among the global demands and uncertainties that see universities caught between ever-rising social expectations and the

SPORT IN FOCUS 20.6: MARIA MUTOLA, ATHLETIC RESOURCE AND REDISTRIBUTION

Maria Mutola, the Mozambican, former Olympic and five-time world indoor 800 metre champion and world record holder, routinely sends track winnings back to her country of origin. Chamanchulo, the suburb of Maputo in which Mutola grew up, is ravaged by HIV, passed on in childbirth or breast milk to 40 per cent of the children. When Mutola became the first athlete to collect $1 million for outright victory on the Golden League Athletic Grand Prix Circuit, part of the cash went to the foundation she endowed to help provide scholarships, kit, education and coaching for young athletes. Farms and small businesses were sustained by her winnings on the circuit, which helped provide for the purchasing of tractors, fertilisers and the facilities to drill small wells. The redistribution of wealth through athletics earnings served as a resource of hope for some.

demand for improved economic performance. At times, there is a deep insecurity for many academics, staff, students and managers but also, more broadly, for the society and world that we live in. This need not be the case if one reflects on what the university will be and how the worlds in which we live in need the discovery of new knowledge and the solutions to problems. It is not necessary to view a university education as just a public good that contributes to the social, economic and cultural vitality of society or just a private good that primarily enhances the economic and social welfare of the student, but it is both and much more. Those interested in sport, culture and society have the opportunity to make a difference in a number of ways, and the opportunities need to be grasped.

SPORT AND THE UNIVERSITY AS A RESOURCE OF HOPE? [[AQ130]]

Perhaps sport should be thought of as a resource of hope in that sport has some limited capacity to assist with social change, have an impact on life chances and be part of a holistic approach to what a recent report by a international think tank referred to as 'Narrowing the Gap'. As indicated earlier, intervention can come in many forms: legislation, policy writing, investigating, uncovering silences, pressure groups, social forums, campaigns and activism, re-allocation of resources and not accepting injustice in sport. There is no single agent, group or movement that can carry the hopes of humanity, but there are many points of engagement through sport that offer good causes for optimism that things can get better. As the introduction to this book illustrates, there are many points or levels of engagement with sport, culture and society that can lead important areas of research, debate and action.

Perhaps the university might also be considered as a resource of hope. The university is certainly one of the places where we can figure out the future in terms of imagining possibilities. Some question the real value of university education but it is just one invaluable function of the university namely to educate, to innovate and to discover knowledge but also much more. Consider the following analogy. Whether people use the roads or railways, they benefit from the country having a transport system that helps so many places and communities facilitate commerce or transport food and, therefore, may be seen to contribute to life itself. In the same way, if we were to follow Docherty (2011), then the university has a leadership role to play in the communities in which it works to ensure that everyone benefits. This may mean encouraging dissent rather than conformity and, as Docherty (2011: 124) states, this dissent becomes the language that shapes possible futures and keeps them as possibilities. This is not too far removed from what Said referred to as the role of the public intellectual, since Docherty applies this same principle to the idea of being an active university.

It might be suggested that, since the banking crisis that emerged in 2008, a moral vaccuum has opened up in places across Europe and America and elsewhere, and the idea of the university helping to fill this void in leadership should be grasped. This clearly goes beyond the world of sport, culture and society, but sport has a part to play because it connects publicly with so many social, cultural, political, economic communities and issues and therefore helps to provide resources of hope. We need the authority and leadership provided by a properly functioning university to assume a servant-leadership role within the public sphere. That is to say, leadership in the university is perhaps not as important as universities leading through committed public engagement by and through its public intellectuals (in the broadest sense of the term). We need what Docherty (2011: 125) refers to as the authority of the institution as a defence against forms of authoritarianism that threaten not just the idea of the university but also public life.

SUMMARY

The word 'intellectual' itself is not the best of phrases but we have commented upon different uses of the term in relation to the organic, traditional, vernacular and public. None of the definitions offered is sharp enough to be conclusive. However the key point being made in this chapter is simply that the notion of the public intellectual needs to be kept broad and that while many, many people are in their own right public intellectuals not everybody has the opportunity to act as a public intellectual. Those that do need to fully grasp the vast array of openings and platforms that are open to those working in the field of sport in universities and other places. The commitment, courage and solidarity with the downtrodden and dispossessed were for Saïd the indispensable requirements of the oppositional public intellectual.

The passing away of the writer Susan Sontag may have marked the end of an era but the late novelist once said that any novel worth reading is an education of the heart; it enlarges your sense of human possibilities and what human nature can be. She was a fervent believer in the capacity of art to delight, to inform and transform the world in which we live in. Does this make sense in relation to sport does it fulfil its potential to enlarge your sense of human possibilities, to delight, to inform and transform the worlds in which we live? The possibilities that exist within sport are those that can help with radically different views of the world perhaps based upon opportunities to foster trust, obligations, redistribution and respect for sport in a more socially orientated humane world. For those working in universities and related institutions, the platforms for action and impact are endless but not always grasped.

This chapter has also drawn our attention to a revitalised idea of the role of the university in leading and serving public life. Certainly in the UK, where the authors work, we need a much broader debate about the idea of the university and the place of the university and its people in public life. We need a debate and action plan for recognising the the role of the university as an international social institution which can lead and fill the vacuum left by the banking crisis. It is time to revitalise the political will of not just those working in the area of sport, culture and society and related areas, but the university itself and its very public role in terms of engagement, democaracy, justice, and freedom as development.

GUIDE TO FURTHER READING

Bairner, A. (2009). 'Sport, Intellectuals and Public Sociology: Obstacles and Opportunities'. *International Review for the Sociology of Sport,* 44 (2–3): 115–131.

Docherty, T. (2011). *For the University: Democracy and the Future of the Institution.* New York: Bloomsbury.

Farred, A. (2003). *What's My Name: Black Vernacular Intellectuals.* Minneapolis, MN: University of Minnesota Press.

Gourlay, B. (2003). 'In Defence of the Intellectual'. Robbins Lecture: University of Stirling.

Naughton, J. (2011). 'The French Have Always Celebrated Their Intellectuals: Why Are We So Ashamed of Ours?'. *Observer*, 8 May: 8–12.

Saïd, E. (2001). 'The Case for the Intellectual' *The Age,* May: 5–12.

Sen, A. (2009). *The Idea of Justice.* London: Allen Lane.

Sokmen, G. and Ertur, B. (2008). *Waiting for the Barbarians: A Tribute to Edward Saïd.* London: Verso.

QUESTIONS

1 What four key questions and/or activities have informed the thinking behind this book?

2 This chapter outlines at least eight different areas in which the work of universities are vital. List five of these areas.

3 What key principles are explored by Docherty (2011)?

4 Public intellectualism can be thought of in at least three different ways – what are they?

5 How does the work of Kofi Annan and Amartya Sen help us to think about sport, culture and society?

6 What are vernacular intellectuals and how should we harness their power to help with sport and social issues?

7 What was the role of the public intellectual, according to Saïd, and how does this take us beyond that of the work of the organic intellectual working in sport?

8 Outline the role of sport in and through the universities in the broadest possible terms.

9 Explain why athletes and universities might be viewed as resources of hope today.

10 The potential leadership role of universities is commenetd upon by Docherty (2011). Explain how the concerns and ideas raised by Docherty help to position universities as both leaders and public servants, and apply this thinking to the part played by sport in culture and society.

PRACTICAL PROJECTS

1 Access, through the Internet, the university strategy for 10 universities in at least 4 different countries, and consider how these strategies involve sport and how they might be improved through fully understanding what sport has to offer universities, communities, students and academics or public intellectuals.

2   Read five similar books to *Sport, Culture and Society* to identify if they add under-standing to the potential role of the student and/or academic or public intellectual who grasps the potential of sport, culture and society activities around public issues and concerns of the time. Draw up your own list of top five issues and a plan for action for each issue.

3   Gather information on any project or campaign carried out by the United Nations or UNESCO that specifically involves sport (you may wish to consider the objectives, the outcomes and the key facts).

4   Research the involvement of up to four sportspeople or celebrities who have been involved with international humanitarian aid projects. Provide a short report on the projects, the communities involved and the objectives.

5   Develop any five key action points or outcomes that would address any one specific social issue raised in this book. Outcomes usually begin with words or phrases that show you want to change something – for example, 'improve', 'reduce', 'develop', 'expand' and/or 'sustain', or useful ways of approaching such outcomes.

KEY CONCEPTS

Capability ■ Democracy ■ Freedom as development ■ Justice ■ Public engagement ■ Public intellectual ■ Public realm ■ Organic intellectual ■ Sport ■ Traditional intellectual ■ Vernacular intellectual ■ The idea of a university

WEBSITES

The Centre for Sports Policy Studies at the University of Toronto
www.physical.utoronto.ca/Centre_for_Sport_Policy_Studies.
A university-based centre and a resource of research papers, studies and activism in sport.

The Brookings Institution
www.brookings.edu/global
A source of policy information about the global economy and development.

The British Sociological Association
www.britsoc.co.uk
A professional membership organisation representing the intellectual and sociological interests of the members.

Peace and Sport
www.peace-sport.org
A resource centre for peace and sport.

Sport et Citoyenneté

www.sportcitoyennete.org

A European think tank and membership organisation that aims to promote public dialogue around sport and social issues and promote European citizenship. The organisation publishes a number of informative research briefs on key topics.

Conclusion: Theses on sport, culture and society

Can sport change the world, individual lives and/or communities?

Can sport help make the world a better place?

1   While it is true that humanity has always been involved in sport, culture and society, it is false to claim that sport has always existed or that sport is the answer to the social problems and issues of the day. Sport itself can be part of the problem but it can also contribute as a resource of hope. The task ahead involves a fourfold exercise. The practice of sport, culture and society requires a sound grasp of sport but also a commitment to evidence, analysis and, ultimately, an attempt to contribute to social change and intervention.

2   It is the interrelated nature of four initial tasks that provide so much ground for those interested in the limits and possibilities of sport both to excite and disappoint, but also strive to make the world a better place. The first task is to collect the evidence and ask the question 'what is going on out there in the world of sport?'. The second task is to provide an analysis and explanation – how do I make sense of what is going out there

in the world of sport? The third task is to identify what needs to be done and what is the best strategy and/or tools of intervention for bringing about social change in and through sport. The final task is to consider what you yourself can do to act or help in this process. That is to say, what am I going to do in order to make sport and the worlds in which sport is located a better place, a more just place, a more humane place, a more trusting, safe and secure place to be?

3   There exist many entry and exit points for addressing the problems and possibilities that sport brings. The ones presented in this book are not exhaustive. The social problems and issues presented in sections of this book are not exhaustive. It remains to be seen as to whether this intervention provides the most comprehensive authored coverage of sport, culture and society, but whether it does or not is incidental. The broader challenge is to act upon the methodology presented in point 2. It is the interrelated nature of the four tasks that are important and not any one part of the exercise.

4   There is no single agent, movement, group or form of governance that can carry the hopes of humanity but there are many points of entry or engagement about sport that offer good causes for optimism that things can get better. It is crucial that you engage with the current and future politics of sport.

THE BROADER CONTEXT

5   The first four chapters provide an examination of the broader context in which sport operates. At one level, it examines various frameworks that are used to both prioritise some questions but also suppress others. It acknowledges that capitalism exists in many different forms and that the trade in world sport is far from equal. It also acknowledges that, while many researchers have been quick to identify economic and financial inequalities existing between and within sports and between and within different countries and places, the body of research that is sport, culture and society has not necessarily acknowledged that inequalities in capabilities may also exist.

6   Thinking socially about sport, culture and society necessitates and invokes a historical, economic and political understanding of sport in the past and the present. Having acquired such an understanding, there is no guarantee that one can dissolve or change the realities of everyday life for many people and places, but if there were not this understanding, then the chance of further freedoms being won in and through sport would be slimmer still. Sport has been most recently linked with international development and humanitarian aid agendas, but what much of the work to date has failed to capitalise upon is the idea is not so much about development and freedom through sport, but development as freedom through sport.

7   Sport is part of a system, perhaps a global system, that continues to perpetuate a gap between rich and poor. Governments change, policies change, countries change but the need to narrow the gap between rich and poor seems to stay the same, at best. Sport should be seen to be part of a broader movement, striving to narrow the gap and improve life chances for all. Helping the bottom billion remains a key challenge facing the world and the question is 'what part has sport and global politics to play?'.

GLOBAL SPORT AND OTHER COMMUNITIES

8   The idea of global sport needs to be evaluated. The values associated with global sport need to be challenged. Far too often, states, markets, ideas and even social patternings that have been influenced by the West drive the idea of global sport. Yet, the trade in world sport remains uneven, unjust and lacking in accountability and transparency. The basic idea remains that global sport is not value free, but is affected by states, markets and social patterns.

9   Global sport does not offer a single coherent challenge, but many different challenges. It may even be a myth but certainly the debate about global sport within sport, culture and society, while recognising the local and the national needs to further recognise anti-global, and anti-Olympic alternatives. A primary concern for those working in the field of sport, culture and society should be to question and move beyond any neo-liberal consensus that often characterises the debate about global sport. The values associated with sport in Asia, Africa, America and Europe are complex and different in many cases. The challenge to global sport is also a challenge about governance and democracy in and through sport.

10 Sport has contributed to identity building in many nations but so too has sport helped with internationalism and reconciliation between countries. It is not necessarily identity that countries are looking for, but recognition and a redistribution of resource that may contribute to more freedoms through development and a narrowing of the development gap. Sport has a part to play in the development of capability.

11 The idea that education returns tangible benefits to individuals and societies is rarely questioned. The progressive impact of sport and education, and education through sport, remains incredibly strong. Education through sport is not simply about the development of human capital, but also the development of human capability. The UNESCO Education for All monitoring report proposed that a better future levy could be placed on the world's top footballing leagues to help improve basic education in low-income countries.

SOCIAL ISSUES AND PROBLEMS

12 At one level, sport, culture and society has identified some contemporary themes that are central to understanding the world in which we live in to day. There remains a debate over the consequences of globalisation on everyday life. Concerns about identity in the world are not just about individual and collective identity, but also about ideas of justice, recognition and redistribution. New world orders are emerging and yet the flow of athletes between countries often flows in limited directions. The issue of social inequality remains central to sport, culture and society in both a socio-economic and geo-political sense. At the same time, sport is as much about inequalities in capability as income. You can, at times, increase people or countries' incomes without necessarily impacting upon people or countries' abilities to choose for themselves the kinds of lives they aspire to lead, including sporting choices.

461

13 On the environment, debates and actions concerning the nature of the world we live in should not ignore the relationship between sport, the environment and communities.

14 On sport, body and health, issues of well-being, happiness, safety and prosperity are inter-linked. Sport can contribute to different worlds of health and, consequently, contribute to narrowing the gap in life chances. The idea that sport, health and the body can enable further developments in trust, care, belonging, anticipatory hope, and well-being while also helping a better understanding of health, pain and injury in different people and regions is worth fighting for. Boxing for both men and women will appear in the Olympics for the first time in London 2012.

15 On violence and crime, the impact of sport is more robust than some other areas, and yet states of denial in world sport continue to exist. The social and cultural denials that often accompany the façade of drugs in sport, sexual violence, trafficking, child labour, and racism all appear in different forms in different places. Investment in sport in inner-city areas seems to impact favourably upon crime rates but issues of investment are often left to political choices that need to be hard won and fought for.

16 On sport, religion and spirituality, clashes between different practices and belief systems fly in the face of different dogmas. Sport is far from secular. Sport satisfies religious needs, including the relationship between sport, religion and capitalism. Sport is implicated in the quest for spirituality. Faith-based sports movements exist and history has taught us that proclaiming the principle of tolerance and justice in a multi-faith society is not sufficient to make a reality of it. Sport needs better faith, better ethics and, consequently, better sport.

17 On the hosting of major sporting events, the question of hard and soft legacies are often to the fore. The hosting of major sporting events may be used to explore sporting myths or challenge national stereotypes. The geopolitical capability to put on such events is uneven. The promise of urban or rural regeneration is realised by some but the extent to which sporting success or failure impacts upon the well-being of host nations and others is rarely considered. Critics argue that communities are often displaced, ordinary people excluded from involvement. The sponsors always appear to win.

18 On lifestyles and alternative cultures, sport has the capacity to offer alternatives to both mainstream sport and lifestyle. It would be unfortunate if the spirit of alternative and/or lifestyle sports were simply explained on the basis of alternative collective behaviour, escapism or the politics of utopia. It may be suggested that the possibilities of real freedoms in and through alternative sporting choices may be realised not just from social movements or social forums, but also through realising that real lifestyle sporting choices must remain options for all parts of the world and not just some. The geopolitical dimensions of alternative lifestyle or sporting cultures need to be clear on the normative question of an alternative to poverty or urban living or materialism, or something else.

SPORT AS A RESOURCE OF HOPE

19 The relationship between sport and social inequality exists in at least three ways: (i) inequality of condition; (ii) inequality of opportunity; and (iii) inequality of capability. For social thinkers, the issue of inequality of capabilities – in other words, what people do with resources such as literacy, nutrition, access to sport and the power to participate in the social life of the community, is also crucial. It has been suggested here that sport can have a part to play, with improving or influencing the capability gap and consequently make a contribution to improving life chances for some. Many social forms of inequality have influenced the social nature of other social movements in and through sport. Organisations such as ISCA are examples of non-governmental organisations aimed at bringing about change through sport. They act as a social movement in some senses.

20 Many of the poorest countries in the world continue to defy repeated attempts by international communities to provide sustainable help. Sport has historically been used as a key facet of humanitarian aid and a proven avenue of social mobility for many athletes from developing countries. The real development challenge is one of closing the gap between a rich world and a poor world in which the world's poorest people – the bottom billion – face a tragedy that is growing inexorably worse. Helping the bottom billion remains a key challenge for the world. The question is whether sport has a part to play and, if so, what? Questions of aid, poverty, recognition and development as freedom remain unresolved. The lack of growth in the countries of the bottom billion needs particular strategies for particular circumstances. The object of international development should not be aid, but growth. The politics of the bottom billion is not a contest between the rich developed world and a number of economically poorer worlds, but about sustained help for those in need.

21 Opportunities for social change in and through sport exist at different levels and arise in both intended and unintended ways. Different people at different times have taken a stand and used sporting moments to speak out for a different world or society or change. Sport itself is rarely, if at all, seen as a contributing to any strategy of change, whether this be systemic or anti-systemic. But there are numerous points of entry and exit for sport to take its place in any politics of social change. At a general level, these might include local, national and international protests but also individual, anti-global, anti-Olympic and anti-environmental points of entry. Forms of action may be classified along the continuum from reformism to radicalism or from ideological to non-ideological or from issue-orientated to more collective forms of action.

22 It is time to revitalise the political will of not just those working in the area of sport, culture and society and related areas, but the university itself and its very public role in terms of engagement, democracy, justice, and freedom as development. Despite the existence of many social issues and problems involving sport, a silence continues to exist that only adds weight to the contemporary assertion that there is at least one character missing from the cast of social and public life – the public intellectual. The word 'intellectual' itself is not the best of phrases but we have commented upon different uses of the term in relation to the organic, traditional, vernacular and public. None of the definitions offered is sharp enough to be conclusive. However, the key point being made

463

is simply that the notion of the public intellectual needs to be kept broad and that, while many, many people are in their own right public intellectuals, not everybody has the opportunity to act as a public intellectual, and those that do need to fully grasp the vast array of openings and platforms that are open to those working in the field of sport in universities and other places. The commitment, courage and solidarity with the downtrodden and dispossessed were, for some, the indispensable requirements of the oppositional public intellectual.

23 Sport itself can contribute as a resource of hope, but it cannot do this on its own. Other resources are needed if sport is to win further freedoms through development, or sporting choices being increased and alternative visions of the world we live in realised through social change and improved life chance.

If you have suggestions on how to make this book better or to provide future Sport in Focus case studies, please write to: grantjarvie1@gmail.com

Bibliography

The bibliography presented here is the complete list of sources, including books, articles, conference papers, newspaper sources, web-based sources, official reports, unpublished papers and dissertations used to research this study of sport, culture and society.

Adams, M. (2010). 'From Mixed-Sex Sport to Sport for Girls: The Feminization of Figure Skating'. *Sport in History*, 30 (2): 218–242.

Afary, J. (1997). 'The War Against Feminism in the Name of the Almighty: Making Sense of Gender and Muslim Fundamentalism'. *New Left Review*, 24 (July/August): 1–21.

Ahlfeldt, G. and Maening, W. (2010). 'Stadium Architecture and Urban Development from the Perspective of Urban Economics'. *International Journal of Urban and Regional Research*, 34 (3): 629–646.

Ahmad, A. (2011). 'British Football: Where Are the Muslim Female Footballers? Exploring the Connections Between Gender Ethnicity and Islam'. *Soccer and Society*, 12 (3): 443–456.

Ahmed, A. (2000). *Post-modernism and Islam*. London: Routledge.

Alabarces, P. (2000). *Peligro de Gol: Estudios Sobre Deporte Y Sociedad En America, Latina*. Buenos Aires: Clacso.

Alcock, P. (1997). *Understanding Poverty*. Basingstoke: Palgrave.

Alexander, T. (2003). 'Uniting Humanity – Strategies for Global Democracy and Progressive Globalisation'. *Fabian Global Forum*. London: Fabian Society (www.fabianglobalforum. net/forum/article026.html).

Ali, T. (2003). 'Re-Colonizing Iraq'. *New Left Review*, 21 (May): 5–20.

Allardyce, J. (2010). 'Row as Beauty Queen Made a Role Model'. *Sunday Times*, 7 March: 7.

Allison, L. (2005). *The Global Politics of Sport: The Role of Global Institutions in Sport*. London: Routledge.

Allison, L. (2002). 'Sport and Nationalism'. In Coakley, J. and Dunning, E. (eds). *Handbook of Sports Studies*. London: Sage, 344–356.

Allison, L. (2001). *Amateurism in Sport*. London: Frank Cass.

Altinay, H. (2010). *The Case for Global Civics*. Washington, DC: Brookings Institution.

Amir, G. (2011). *Global History: A View from the South*. Oxford: Pambazuka Press.

Anderson, B. (1991). *Imagined Communities: Reflections on the Origin and Spread of Nationalism*. London: Verso.

Anderson, P. (2002). 'Internationalism: A Breviary'. *New Left Review*, 14 (March/April): 5–25.

465

Appadurai, A. (1995). 'Playing with Modernity: The Decolonisation of Indian Cricket'. In Breckenridge, C. (ed.). *Consuming Modernity: Public Culture in a South Asian World.* Minneapolis, MN: University of Minnesota Press, 23–48.

Arbena, J. (1999). *Latin American Sport: An Annotated Bibliography, 1988–1999.* Westport, CT: Greenwood Press.

Archetti, E. (1999). *Masculinities: Football, Polo and the Tango in Argentina.* Oxford: Berg.

Armstrong, G. (2004). 'The Lords of Misrule: Football and the Rights of the Child in Liberia, West Africa'. *Sport in Society,* 7 (3): 473–502.

Armstrong, G. and Giulianotti, R. (eds) (2004). *Football in Africa: Conflict, Conciliation and Community.* Basingstoke: Palgrave.

Armstrong, G. and Giulianotti, R. (1997). *Entering The Field: New Perspectives on World Football.* Oxford: Berg.

Armstrong, S. (2008). 'Is British Sport Still Racist?'. *New Statesman,* 18 November: 32–34.

Arrighi, G. (2002). 'The African Crisis'. *New Left Review,* 15 (May/June): 5–39.

Attenborough, D. (2011). 'The Heaving Planet'. *New Statesman,* 25 April: 29–32.

Australian Government (2004). 'Crime Prevention through Sport and Physical Activity'. Australian Institute of Criminology. Paper 165 (www.aic.gov.au/publications/tandi/tandi165.html).

Baade, R. and Matheson, V. (2002). 'Bidding for Fool's Gold' in Baros, C., Ibrahimo, P. and Szymanski, S. (eds). *Transatlantic Sport: The Comparative Economics of North American and European Sport.* Cheltenham: Edward Edgar, 121–151.

Back, L., Crabbe, T. and Solomos, J. (2001). *The Changing Face of Football: Racism, Identity and Multiculture in the English Game.* Oxford: Berg.

Bairner, A. (2011). 'Soccer and Society in Eva Menasse's Vienna'. *Sport in History,* 31 (1): 32–48.

Bairner, A. (2009). 'Sport, Intellectuals and Public Sociology: Obstacles and Opportunities'. *International Review for the Sociology of Sport,* 44 (2–3): 115–130.

Bairner, A. (2001). *Sport, Nationalism and Globalization.* Albany, NY: State University of New York Press.

Balakrishnan, G. (2002). 'The Age of Identity'. *New Left Review,* 16: 130–142.

Bale, J. (2007). 'Kenyan running before the 1968 Mexico Olympic games'. In Pitsiladis, Y., Bale, J., Sharp, C. and Noakes, T. (eds). *East African Running.* London: Routledge, pp11-24.

Bale, J. (2004). *Running Cultures: Racing in Time and Space.* London: Routledge.

Bale, J. (2003). *Sports Geography.* London: Routledge.

Bale, J. (2002a). 'Lassitude and Latitude: Observations on Sport and Environmental Determinism'. *International Review of the Sociology of Sport,* 37 (2): 147–159.

Bale, J. (2002b). 'Human Geography and the Study of Sport'. In Coakley, J. and Dunning, E. (eds). *Handbook of Sports Studies.* London: Sage, 170–186.

Bale, J. (2000). 'The Rhetoric of Running: The Representation of Kenyan Body Culture in the Early Twentieth Century'. In Hansen, J. and Nielsen, N. (eds). *Sports, Body and Health.* Odense: Odense University Press, 123–133.

Bale, J. (1998). 'Capturing the African Body? Visual Images and Imaginative Sports'. *Journal of Sports History,* 25 (2): 234–252.

Bale, J. (1994). *Landscapes of Modern Sport.* London: Leicester University Press.

Bale, J. and Cronin, M. (2003). *Sport and Post-colonialism.* Oxford: Berg Publishers.

466

Bale, J. and Philo, C. (eds) (1998). *Body Cultures: Essays on Sport, Space and Identity: Henning Eichberg*. London: Routledge.

Bale, J. and Sang, J. (1996). *Kenyan Running: Movement, Culture, Geography and Global Change*. London: Cass.

Barros, C., Ibrahimo, M. and Szymanski, S. (2002). *Transatlantic Sport: The Comparative Economics of North American and European Sports*. Northampton, MA: Edward Elgar.

Bass, A. (2002). *The Triumph But the Struggle: The 1968 Olympics and the Making of the Black Athlete*. Minneapolis, MN: University of Minnesota Press.

Bauman, Z. (2001). *Community: Seeking Safety in an Insecure World*. Cambridge: Polity Press.

Bauman, Z. (2000a). *Liquid Modernity*. Cambridge: Polity Press.

Bauman, Z. (2000b). 'Whatever Happened to Compassion in the Global Era?'. In Bentley, T. and Stedman Jones, D. (eds). *The Moral Universe*. London: Demos, 51–57.

Bauman, Z. (1990). *Thinking Sociologically*. Oxford: Basil Blackwell.

Bauman, Z. and May, T. (2001). *Thinking Sociologically*. Oxford: Blackwell.

Baylis, J., Smith, S. and Owens, P. (2008). *The Globalisation of World Politics*. Oxford: Oxford University Press.

Baym, N. (2010). *Personal Connections in the Digital Age*. Cambridge: Polity.

Baynes, R. (2011). 'Making Waves: The Surfers Fighting to Clean Up Our Seas'. *The Herald*, 27 February: 4–11.

Beacom, A. (2000). 'Sport in International Relations: The Case for Cross-Disciplinary Investigation'. *The Sports Historian*, 20 (2): 1–25.

Beal, B. (1996). 'Alternative Masculinity and its Effects on Gender Relations in the Subculture of Skateboarding'. *Journal of Sport Behaviour*, 19: 204–220.

Beal, B. (1995). 'Disqualifying the Official: An Exploration of Social Resistance through the Sub-culture of Skateboarding'. *Sociology of Sport Journal*, 12 (4): 252–267.

Beaumont, P. (2001). 'Kidnapped Children Sold into Slavery as Camel Racers'. *Observer*, 3 June: 27.

Beer, S. (2002). 'Better Faith, Better Ethics?'. *Fabian Review*, Spring: 8–12.

Begg, Z. (2000). 'What the Olympics Really Celebrate'. (www.greenleft.org.au/back/2000/441717p14.htm).

Bell, M. (2003). 'Another Kind of Life'. In Rinehart, R. and Sydnor, S. (eds). *To the Extreme: Alternative Sports Inside and Out*. Albany, NY: Suny Press, 219–257.

Bellos, A. (2003). 'The President Wins the Midfield Battle'. *New Statesman*, 3 November: 32–34.

Benedict, J. (1997). 'Arrest and Conviction Rates of Athletes Accused of Sexual Assault'. *Sociology of Sport Journal*, 17 (2): 171–197.

Benn, T., Dagkas, S. and Jawad, H. (2011). 'Embodied Faith: Islam, Religious Freedom and Educational Practices in Physical Education'. *Sport, Education and Society*, 16 (1): 17–34.

Bentley, T. and Stedman-Jones, D. (2001). *The Moral Universe*. London: Demos.

Bhabha, H. (1983). 'The Postcolonial Critic'. *Arena*, 96: 47–63.

Billings, A. and Tambosi, F. (2004). 'Portraying the United States vs. Portraying a Champion: US Network Bias in the 2002 World Cup'. *International Review for the Sociology of Sport*, 39 (2): 157–167.

Blackshaw, I. (2002). 'Law and Human Rights'. *Sports Business International*, November: 42–44.

Blackshaw, T. (2002). 'The Sociology of Sport Reassessed in the Light of the Phenomenon of Zygmunt Bauman'. *International Review of the Sociology of Sport,* 37 (2): 199–218.

Blackshaw, T. and Crabbe, T. (2004). *New Perspectives on Sport and Deviance: Consumption, Performativity and Social Control.* London: Routledge.

Blaikie, A., Sartan, S., Hepworth, M., Holmes, M., Howson, A. and Inglis, D. (2003). *The Body: Critical Concepts in Sociology.* London: Routledge.

Blake, A. (2005). 'The Economic Impact of the 2012 Olympic Games'. University of Technology Sydney. Sydney: Research Papers. 1–33.

Blanchard, K. (2002). 'The Anthropology of Sport'. In Coakley, J. and Dunning, E. (eds). *Handbook of Sports Studies.* London: Sage, 144–157.

Bliers, H. (2003). *Communities in Control: Public Services and Local Socialism.* London: Fabian Society.

Blitz, R. (2011). 'FIFA Set to Launch Probe into Bribery Allegations'. *Financial Times,* 11 May: 1–3.

Bloomfield, S. (2010). *Africa United.* Edinburgh: Canongate.

Bodin, D., Robene, D. and Heas, S. (2005). *Sport and Violence in Europe.* Strasbourg: Council of Europe.

Bolton. G. (2008). *Aid and Other Dirty Business.* Reading: Edbury Press.

Bonnett, A. (2009). 'Green Agendas and Grey Dawns'. *New Statesman,* 6 March: 28–31.

Booth, D. (2010). 'Beyond History: Racial Emancipation and Ethics in Apartheid Sport'. *Rethinking History,* 14 (4): 461–481.

Booth, D. (2004). 'Surf Lifesavers and Surfers: Cultural and Spatial Conflict on the Australian Beach'. In Vertinsky, P. and Bale, J. (eds). *Sites of Sport: Space, Place and Experience.* London: Routledge, 115–131.

Booth, D. (2003). 'Expression Sessions: Surfing, Style and Prestige'. In Rinehart, R. and Sydnor, S. (eds). *To the Extreme: Alternative Sports Inside and Out.* Albany, NY: Suny Press, 315–337.

Booth, D. (2001). *Australian Beach Cultures: The History of Sun, Sand and Surf.* London: Frank Cass.

Borish, L. (2002). 'Women, Sport and American Jewish Identity in the Late Nineteenth and Early Twentieth Century'. In Magdalinski, T. and Chandler, T. (eds). *With God on Their Side: Sport in the Service of Religion.* London: Routledge, 71–98.

Bose, M. (2006). *The Magic of Indian Cricket (Sport in the Global Society).* London: Routledge.

Bourdieu, P. (1990a). *In Other Words: Essays Towards a Reflexive Sociology.* Cambridge: Polity Press.

Bourdieu, P. (1990b). *The Logic of Practice.* Cambridge: Polity Press.

Bourdieu, P. (1988). *Homo Academicus.* Stanford: Stanford University Press.

Bourdieu, P. (1978). 'Sport and Social Class'. *Social Science Information,* 17 (6): 819–840.

Boykoff, J. (2011). 'The Anti-Olympics'. *New Left Review,* 67 (Jan/Feb): 41–61.

Boyle, R. and Haynes, R. (2004). *Football in the New Media Age.* London: Routledge.

Boyle, R. and Haynes, R. (2000). *Power Play: Sport, the Media and Popular Culture.* Harlow: Longman.

Brackenridge, C. (2004). 'Women and Children First? Child Abuse and Child Protection in Sport'. *Sport in Society,* 7 (3): 322–337.

Brackenridge, C. (2002). 'Men Loving Men Hating Women: The Crisis of Masculinity and Violence to Women In Sport'. In Scraton, S. and Flintoff, A. (eds). *Gender and Sport: A Reader*. London: Routledge, 255–269.

Brackenridge, C. (2001). 'Gender, Abuse and Violence: Men Loving Men Hating Women – The Crisis of Masculinity in Sport'. In Ruskin, H. and Lammer, M. (eds). *Fair Play: Violence in Sport and Society*. Jerusalem: Magnes Press, 127–158.

Bradley, H. (2000). 'Social Inequalities: Coming to Terms with Complexity'. In Browning, G., Halcli, A. and Webster, F. (eds). *Understanding Contemporary Society: Theories of the Present*. London: Sage, 476–489.

Bradley, J. (ed.) (2004). *Celtic Minded: Essays on Religion, Politics, Society, Identity and Football*. Glendaruel: Argyll Publishing.

Bradley, J. (1999). 'British and Irish Sport: The Garrison Game and the GAA in Scotland'. *The Sports Historian*, 19 (1): 81–96.

Brennan, T. (2003). *Globalization and its Terrors: Daily Life in the West*. London: Routledge.

Brennan, T. (2001). 'Rooted Cosmopolitan v International'. *New Left Review*, 7: 75–85.

Bricknell, P. (2000). *People Before Structures*. London: Demos.

Bridgland, F. (2010). 'Big Men, Big Money: No Holds Barred for the Wrestlers More Famous than Footballers'. *The Sunday Herald*, 18 April: 32.

Britcher, C. (2004a). 'Virtual Horses for Virtual Courses'. *Sport Business International*, 88 (February): 28–30.

Britcher, C. (2004b). 'MLB Upwardly Mobile'. *Sport Business International*, 86 (January): 25–28.

Brookings Institution (2011). 'Poverty in Numbers: The Changing State of Global Poverty from 2005 to 2015'. *Policy Brief 2011–01*. Washington: Brookings Institution.

Brown, C. and Bathgare, S. (2011). 'Lennon: We Can't Cure Sectarianism'. *The Scotsman*, 16 April: 1–3.

Brown, G. (2002). *Maxton*. Edinburgh: Edinburgh University Press.

Brown, K. and Connolly, C. (2010). 'The Role of Law in Promoting Women in Elite Athletics: An Examination of Four Nations'. *International Review for the Sociology of Sport*, 45 (1): 3–21.

Brownell, S. (1999). 'The Body and the Beautiful in Chinese Nationalism: Sportswomen and Fashion Models in the Reform Era'. *China Information*, XIII (2/3): 36–58.

Brownell, S. (1995). *Training the Body for China: Sports in the Moral Order of The People's Republic*. Chicago, IL: Chicago University Press.

Browning, G., Halcli, A. and Webster, F. (2000). *Understanding Contemporary Society: Theories of the Present*. London: Sage.

Burki, R., Elsasser, H. and Abegg, B. (2006). 'Climate Change and Winter Sports: Environmental and Economic Threats' (www.viewsfromtheworld.com/Climate-Change-and-Winter-Sports, 006). Accessed 16 January 2012..

Burnett, J. (2000). *Riot, Revelry and Rout: Sport in Lowland Scotland Before 1860*. East Linton: Tuckwell Press.

Callaghan, T. and Mullin, M. (2000). 'This Sporting Lie'. *Index on Censorship*, April: 37–47.

Cameron, M. and Macdougall, C. (2004) 'Crime Prevention through Sport and Physical Activity'. Australian Government: Australian Institute of Criminology. Paper 165 (www.aic.gov.au/publications/tandi/tandi1165.html).

Cammack, P. (2002). 'Attacking the Global Poor'. *New Left Review*, 13 (January/February): 125–136.

Campbell, D. (2004). 'Game Over for Minor Olympic Events'. *Observer*, 3 October: 5–6.

Campbell, R. (2011). 'Staging Globalization for National Projects: Global Sports Markets and Elite Athletic Transnational Labour in Qatar'. *International Review for the Sociology of Sport*, 46 (1): 45–60.

Campsie, A. (2011). 'Terrorists, Thugs and Cowards'. *The Herald*, 22 April: 1.

Cantelon, H. and Letters, M. (2000). 'The Making of the IOC Environmental Policy as the Third Dimension of the Olympic Movement'. *International Review for the Sociology of Sport*, 35 (3): 249–308.

Cardoza, A. (2010). 'Making Italians? Cycling and National Identity in Italy: 1900–1950'. *Journal of Modern Italian Studies*, 15 (3): 354–377.

Carlin, J. (2003). 'Rwanda's Magic Moment'. *Observer*, 13 July: 14.

Carrington, B. (2010). *Race, Sport and Politics: The Sporting Black Diaspora*. London: Sage.

Cashmore, E. (2010). *Making Sense of Sports*. London: Routledge.

Castells, M. (1998). *The Information Age*: *Economy, Society and Culture*, 111. Oxford: Blackwell Publishers.

Centre on Housing Rights and Evictions. (2007). *Fair Play for Housing Rights*. Geneva: COHRE. www.cohre.org.

Cha, V. (2009). *Beyond the Final Score: The Politics of Sport in Asia*. New York: Columbia University Press.

Chaker, A. N. (2004). *Good Governance in Sport*. Strasbourg: Council of Europe.

Chandy, C. and Gertz, G. (2011). 'Poverty in Numbers the Changing State of Global Poverty'. *Policy Brief 2011* (1). Washington: The Brooking Institute.

Charlton, T. (2010). 'Grow and Sustain: The Role of Community Sports Provision in Promoting a Participation Legacy for the 2012 Olympic Games'. *International Journal of Sports Policy and Politics*, 2 (3): 347–366.

Chatterjee, P. (1993). 'Clubbing South East Asia: The Impacts of Golf Sports Development' (http://multinationalmonitor.org/hyper/issues/1993/11/mm1193_13.html).

Chiba, N., Ebihara, O. and Morino, S. (2001). 'Globalization, Naturalization and Identity: The Case of Borderless Elite Athletes in Japan'. *International Review for the Sociology of Sport*, 36 (2): 203–221.

Chisari, F. (2004). 'Shouting Housewives!: The 1966 World Cup and British Television'. *Sport in History*, 24 (1): 94–109.

Chung, H. (2003). 'Sport Star vs Rock Star in Globalizing Popular Culture: Similarities, Difference and Paradox in Discussion of Celebrities'. *International Review for the Sociology of Sport*, 38 (1): 99–108.

Clapson, M. (1986). *A Bit of a Flutter: Popular Gambling and English Society, c. 1823–1961*. Manchester: Manchester University Press.

Clarke, J. and Critcher, C. (1985). *The Devil Makes Work*: *Leisure in Capitalist Britain*. London: Macmillan.

Coakley, J. (2003). *Sport in Society: Issues and Controversies*, Eighth Edition. Boston, MA: McGraw Hill.

Coakley, J. and Dunning, E. (2000). *Handbook of Sports Studies*. London: Sage.

Coakley, J. and Pike, E. (2009). *Sports in Society: Issues and Controversies*. Boston, MA: McGraw Hill Companies.

Coalter, F. (2010). 'The Politics of Sport for Development: Limited Focus Programmes and Broad Gauge Problems?'. *International Review for the Sociology of Sport*, 45 (3): 295–314.

Coalter, F. (2008). 'Sport-in-Development: Development in and Through Sport?'. In Hoyle, R. and Nicholson, M. (eds). *Sport and Social Capital*. London: Elsevier.

Coalter, F. (2007). *A Wider Social Role for Sport: Who is Keeping the Score?* London: Routledge.

Coalter, F. (2000). *Role of Sport in Re-generating Deprived Urban Communities*. Edinburgh: Scottish Executive Publications (www.scotland.gov.uk/crukd01/blue/rsrdua-00.htm).

Cohen, S. (2001). *States of Denial: Knowing About Atrocities and Suffering*. Cambridge: Polity Press.

Cole, C. (2002). 'Body Studies in the Sociology of Sport'. In: Coakley, J. and Dunning, E. (eds). *Handbook of Sports Studies*. London: Sage, 439–461.

Coleman, J. (1988). 'Social Capital in the Creation of Human Capital'. *American Journal of Sociology*, 94: 95–119.

Collier, P. (2007). *The Bottom Billion*. Oxford: Oxford University Press.

Collins, T. (1996). 'Myth and Reality in the 1895 Rugby Split'. *The Sports Historian*, 16: 33–41.

Council of Europe (2000). 'Background Studies on the Problem of Sexual Harassment in Sport, Especially With Regard to Women and Children'. *9th Council of Europe Conference of Ministers Responsible for Sport*. Bratislava, Slovakia, 30–31 May.

Crompton. J. (2001). 'Public Subsidies to Professional Team Sports Facilities' in Gratton, C. and Henry, I. (eds). *Sport in the City: The Role of Sport in Economic and Social Regeneration*. London: Routledge, 15–35.

Cronin, M. (2005). 'Sam Maguire: Forgotten Hero and National Icon'. In *Sport in History*, 25, (2): 189–205.

Cronin, M. (1999). *Sport and Nationalism in Ireland: Gaelic Games, Soccer and Irish Identity since 1884*. Dublin: Four Courts Press.

Crosset, T. (1995). *Outsiders in the Clubhouse: The World of Women's Professional Golf*. Albany, NY: New York University Press.

Crosson, S. and Dine, P. (2011). 'Sport and Media in Ireland'. *Media History*. 17 (2): 109–116.

Cunningham, J. and Beneforti, M. (2005). 'Investigating Indicators for Measuring the Health and Social Impact of Sport and Recreation Programs in Australian Indigenous Communities'. *International Review for the Sociology of Sport*, 40 (1): 89–98.

Curi, M., Knijnik, J. and Mascarenhas, G. (2011). 'The Pan-American Games in Rio de Janeiro 2007: Consequences of Sport Mega-Event on a BRIC Country'. *International Journal of Sports Policy and Politics*, 46 (2): 140–156.

Da Costa, L., Lamartine, P. and Miragaya, A. (2002). *Worldwide Experience and Trends in Sport for All*. Aachen, Germany: Meyer and Meyer Sports Books.

Danish Ministry of Culture (1996). *Politics of Culture in Denmark*. Arhus: Danish Ministry of Culture.

Darnell, S. and Black, D. (2011). 'Mainstreaming Sport into International Development Studies'. *Third World Quarterly*, 32 (3): 367–378.

David, P. (2005). *Human Rights in Youth Sport: A Critical Review of Children's Rights in Youth Sport*. London: Routledge.

Davies, G. (2011). 'Manny Pacquiao, the Pauper Turned Poverty-Fighter Prepares to Face Shane Mosley in Sun City'. *The Telegraph*, 5 May: 1.

Davies, H. (2005). 'The Fan'. *New Statesman*, 14: 59–60.

Davis, M. (2006). *Planet of Slums*. London: Verso.

Deacon, B. (2003). 'Global Social Governance Reform'. *Fabian Global Forum*. London: The Fabian Society (www.fabianglobalforum.net/forum/article033.html).

Della Porta, D. and Diani, M. (2005). *Social Movements: An Introduction*. Oxford: Blackwell Publishing.

Deloitte LLP. (2009). *Deloitte Annual Football Finance Review*. London: Deloitte.

Department of Sport and Recreation (1997). 'Pulling it Together: Developing a Sport and Recreation Policy that Meets the Needs of the Nation'. South African Department of Sport and Recreation. Cape Town: Unpublished Paper.

Deucha, R. and Holligan, C. (2010). 'Gangs, Sectarianism and Social Capital: A Qualitative Study of Young People in Scotland'. *Sociology*, 44 (1): 13–31.

Dika, S. and Singh, K. (2002). 'Applications of Social Capital in Educational Literature: A Critical Synthesis'. *Review of Educational Research*, Spring, 72 (1): 31–60.

Dimeo, P. (2007). *A History of Drug use in Sport*. New York: Routledge.

Dimeo, P. (2005). 'Cricket and the Misrepresentation of Indian Sports History'. *Historical Studies*, 20: 98–111.

Dimeo, P. (2004). '"A Parcel of Dummies?" Sport and the Body in Indian History'. In Mills, J. and Sen, S. (eds). *Confronting the Body*: *The Politics of Physicality in Colonial and Post-Colonial India*. London: Anthem, 39–57.

Dimeo, P. (2002). 'Colonial Bodies, Colonial Sport: "Martial" Punjabis, "Effeminate" Bengalis and the Development of Indian Football'. *International Journal of the History of Sport*, 19 (1): 72–90.

Docherty, T. (2011). *For the University: Democracy and the Future of the Institution*. New York: Bloomsbury.

Doherty, A. and Misener, K. (2008). ' Community Sport Networks' in Nicholson, M. and Hoyle, R. (eds). *Sport and Social Capital*. New York: Elsevier, 113–143.

Dominic, M. (2011). *The Social Organization of Sports Medicine*. London: Routledge.

Donnelly, P. (2003). 'Sport and Social Theory'. In Houlihan, B. (ed.). *Sport and Society*: *A Student Introduction*. London: Sage, 1–28.

Donnelly, P. (2002). 'Interpretative Approaches to the Sociology of Sport'. In Coakley, J. and Dunning, E. (eds). *Handbook of Sports Studies*. London: Sage, 77–91.

Donnelly, P. (1993). 'Sub-cultures in Sport: Resilience and Transformation'. In Ingham, A. and Loy, J. (eds). *Sport in Social Development*: *Traditions, Transitions and Transformations*. Champaign, IL: Human Kinetics, 119–147.

Donnelly, P. (1988). 'Sport as a Site of Popular Resistance'. In Gruneau, R. (ed.). *Popular Cultures and Political Practices*. Toronto: Garamond Press, 69–82.

Donnelly, P. and Petherick, L. (2004). 'Workers Playtime? Child Labour at the Extremes of the Sporting Spectrum'. *Sport in Society*, 7 (3): 301–321.

Doward, J. (2011). 'Sex Workers Put at Risk by Olympics Crackdown'. *Observer*, 10 April: 19.

Duncan, J. (2000). *In The Red Corner: A Journey into Cuban Boxing*. London: Yellow Jersey Press.

Dunning, E. (1999). *Sport Matters: Sociological Studies of Sport, Violence and Civilization.* London: Routledge.

Dunning, E. and Rojek, C. (1992). *Sport and Leisure in the Civilizing Process: Critique and Counter-Critique.* London: Macmillan.

Dunning, E. and Sheard, K. (1979). *Barbarians, Gentlemen and Players: A Sociological Study of the Development of Rugby Football.* Oxford: Martin Robertson.

Dunning, E., Murphy, P. and Malcolm, D. (2004). *Sports Histories: Figurational Studies in the Development of Modern Sport.* London: Routledge.

Dyck, N. (2000). *Games, Sports and Cultures.* Oxford: Berg.

Dyck, N. and Archetti, E. (2003). *Sport, Dance and Embodied Identities.* Oxford: Berg.

Dyreson, M. (2001). 'Maybe It's Better to Bowl Alone: Sport, Community and Democracy in American Thought'. *Culture, Sport, Society,* 4 (1): 19–30.

Dyson, S. (1994). 'Be Like Mike: Michael Jordan and the Pedagogy of Desire'. In Giroux, H. and McLaren, P. (eds). *Between Borders*: *Pedagogy and the Politics of Cultural Studies.* Routledge: New York, 119–127.

Economic Research Associates. (1984). 'The Economic Impact of the Olympic Games' in *PricewaterhouseCoopers European Economic Outlook,* June (27): 18–27.

EFA Global Monitoring Report. (2010). *Reaching the Marginalised.* Oxford: Oxford University Press.

Eichberg, H. (2011). 'The Normal Body: Anthropology of Bodily Otherness'. *International Journal of Physical Culture, Sports Studies and Research,* L (1): 1–16.

Eichberg, H. (2004). *The People of Democracy: Understanding Self-Determination on the Basis of Body and Movement.* Arhus: Klim.

Eilling, A., De Knop, P. and Knoppers, A. (2003). 'Gay/Lesbian Sport Clubs and Events: Places of Homo-Social Bonding and Cultural Resistance'. *International Review for the Sociology of Sport,* 38 (4): 441–456.

Eitzen, D. (2003). *Fair and Foul*: *Beyond the Myths and Paradoxes of Sport.* New York: Rowman & Littlefield Publishers.

Elias, N. (1983). *The Court Society.* Oxford: Blackwell.

Elias, N. (1978). *What Is Sociology?* London: Hutchinson.

Elias, R. (2010). 'The Foreign Policy of Baseball'. *Foreign Policy in Focus,* April: 1–7.

Elliott, A. (2009). *Contemporary Social Theory: An Introduction.* London: Routledge.

Elvin, M. (2010). 'Concepts of Nature'. *New Left Review,* 64 (July/August): 65–84.

Evans, J. and Davies, B. (2011). 'New Directions, New Questions? Social Theory, Education and Embodiement'. *Sport, Education and Society,* 16 (3): 263–278.

Fabian Review (2003). 'Non-economic Boycotts'. *Fabian Review,* Spring: 8–10.

Fabian Society (2006). *Narrowing the Gap: The Fabian Commission on Life Chances and Child Poverty.* London: Fabian Society.

Fabian Society (2003). 'Human Rights'. *Fabian Global Forum,* London: Fabian Society (www.fabianglobalforum.net/knowledge/article002.html).

Fan Hong (1997). *Footbinding, Feminism and Freedom: The Liberation of Women's Bodies in China.* London: Frank Cass.

Farred, G. (2003). *What is My Name? Black Vernacular Intellectuals.* Minneapolis, MN: University of Minnesota Press.

473

Fasting, K. (1989). 'Women's Leadership in Sport'. In *Women and Sport Taking the Lead*. London: Council of Europe, 6–17.

Featherstone, S. (2011). 'Late Cuts: C. L. R James, Cricket, and Postcolonial England'. *Sport in History*, 31 (1): 49–62.

Feffer, J. (2011). 'The Age of Activism'. *Foreign Policy in Focus*, 6 (11): 1–6.

Feffer, J. (2010a). 'Earthquake Olympics'. *Foreign Policy in Focus*, 5 (13) 30 March: 1–6.

Feffer, J. (2010b). 'Blood Sports' *Foreign Policy in Focus*, 5 (14) April: 1–8.

Field, J. (2003). *Social Capital*. London: Routledge.

Foster, J. and Pope, N. (2004). *Political Economy of Global Sporting Organisations*. London: Routledge.

Foster, K. (2005). 'Alternative Models for the Regulation of Global Sport'. In Allison, L. (eds). *The Global Politics of Sport*. London: Routledge, 63–86.

Foster, K. (2000). 'How Can Sport Be Regulated?'. In Greenfield, S. and Osborn, G. (eds). *Law and Sport in Contemporary Society*. London: Frank Cass, 268–285.

Fraser, N. (2009) 'Feminism Co-Opted'. *New Left Review*, 56 (March/April): 97–118.

Fraser, N. (2003). 'Social Justice in the Age of Identity Politics'. In Fraser, N. and Honneth, A. (eds). *Redistribution or Recognition?* London: Verso, 45–61.

Fraser, N. (2000). 'Re-thinking Recognition?'. *New Left Review*, 3 (May/June): 107–120.

Fraser, N. (1995). 'From Redistribution to Recognition? Dilemmas of Justice in a Post-Socialist Age'. *New Left Review*, 12 (July/August): 1–24.

Fraser, N. and Honneth, A. (2003). *Redistribution or Recognition?* London: Verso.

Frazer, E. (2000). 'Communitarianism'. In Browning, G., Halcli, A. and Webster, F. (eds). *Understanding Contemporary Society*. London: Sage, 46–58.

Fry, J.M. (2011). 'Muslim, Women and Sport'. *Sport, Education and Society* 16 (1): 127–130.

Fukuyama, F. (1992). *The End of History and the Last Man*. Harmondsworth: Penguin Books.

Fukuyama, F. (1989). 'The End of History'. *The National Interest*, 16: 3–18.

Furedi, F. (2004). *Where Have All the Intellectuals Gone? Confronting 21st Century Philistinism*. New York: Continuum.

Garcia, B. (2010). *The Olympic Games and Cultural Policy*. New York: Routledge.

Garcia, B. (2009). 'Challenges and Opportunities for the Olympic Movement: Balancing the Games Lived Festival Experience and its Global Media Projection' (www.olympic.org/Assets/OSC%20Section/pdf/Ac%20Ac_2E.pdf).

Gardiner, G. (2003). 'Black Bodies – White Codes: Indigenous Footballers, Racism and the Australian Football League's Racial and Religious Vilification Code'. In Bale, J. and Cronin, M. (eds). *Sport and Post-colonialism*. Oxford: Berg, 29–45.

Gardiner, S., James, M., O'Leary, J., Welch, R., Blackshaw, I., Boyes, S. and Caiger, A. (eds) (2001). *Sports Law*. London: Cavendish Publishing.

Gems, G. (1995). 'Blocked Shot: The Development of Baseball in the African-American Community of Chicago'. *Journal of Sports History*, 22 (2): 135–148.

Gen Doy, A. (1996). 'Out of Africa: Orientalism, Race and the Female Body'. *Body and Society*, 2 (4): 17–45.

George, J. (2010). 'Ladies First: Establishing a Place for Women Golfers in British Golf Clubs, 1867–1914'. *Sport in History*, 30 (2): 196–217.

Germond, P. and Cochrane, J. (2010). 'Healthworlds: Conceptualizing Landscapes of Health and Healing'. *Sociology*, 44 (2): 307–324.

Giddens, A. (2001). *Sociology*. Cambridge: Polity Press.

Gilchrist, P. and Holden, R. (2011). 'Introduction: the Politics of Sport, Community, Mobility and Identity'. *Sport in Society*, 14 (2): 151–159.

Gillis, R. (2001). 'Ready to Board?'. *SportsBusiness*, August: 14–17.

Gillon, D. (2005). 'View from Man Who Races to Escape Poverty'. *The Herald*, 15 January: 10.

Gillon, D. (2004). 'Candle Who Brings a Ray of Hope'. *The Herald*, 3 May: 24.

Gillon, D. (2003). 'A Winner Who Had to Admit Defeat'. *The Herald*, 19 July: 15.

Girginov, V. and Hills, L. (2008). 'A Sustainable Sports Legacy : Creating a Link Between London Olympics and Sports Participation'. *International Journal of the History of Sport*, 25 (14), 2091–2116.

Giroux, H. (2006). *The Giroux Reader*. London: Paradigm Publishers.

Giroux, H. and McLaren, P. (eds) (1994). *Between Borders*: *Pedagogy and the Politics of Cultural Studies*. Routledge: New York.

Gitlin, T. (1993). 'The Rise of Identity Politics an Examination and Critique'. *Dissent*, Spring: 172–179.

Giulianotti, R. (2011). 'Sport, Transnational Peacemaking and Global Civil Society: Exploring the Reflective Discourses of Sport, Development and Peace Project Officials'. *Journal of Sport and Social Issues*, 35 (1): 50–71.

Giulianotti, R. (2005). *Sport: A Critical Sociology*. Cambridge: Polity Press.

Giulianotti, R. and Armstrong, G. (2011). 'Sport, the Military and Peacekeeping: History and Possiilities'. *Third World Quarterly*, 32 (3): 379–394.

Giulianotti, R. and McArdle, D. (eds) (2005). *Sport, Civil Liberties and Human Rights*. London: Routledge.

Giulianotti, R. and McArdle, A. (2004). *Sport in Society*. Special Issue on Sport, Civil Liberties and Human Rights. 7(3). Autumn.

Glendinning, M. (2009). 'Crimes and Misdemeanours: The Latest Hot-Spots in Sports Law'. *Sportsbusiness International*, 151 (November): 48–52.

Gold, J. and Gold, M. (2011). *Olympic Cities: City Agenda's, Planning and the World Games, 1896–2016*. London: Routledge.

Gold, J. and Gold, M. (2009). 'Future Indefinite? London 2012, the Spectre of Retrenchment and the Challenge of Olympic Sports Legacy'. *London Journal*, 34: 180–197.

Goldman, R. and Papson, S. (1998). *Nike Culture*. London: Sage Publications.

Gorman, J. (2003). *Rights and Reasons: An Introduction to the Philosophy of Rights*. Chesham: Acumen Publishing.

Gourley, B. (2002). 'In Defence of the Intellectual'. Robbins Papers. Stirling: Stirling University.

Gratton, C., Shibili, S. and Coleman, R. (2005). 'Sport and Economic Regeneration in Cities'. *Urban Studies*, 42: 985–999.

Gray, J. (2002a). 'When the Forests Go, Shall We Be Alone?'. *New Statesman*, 22 July: 27–30.

Gray, J. (2002b). 'The Myth of Secularism?'. *New Statesman*, 20 December: 69–70.

Gray, J. (2001). 'The Era of Globalisation is Over'. *New Statesman*, 24 September: 25–27.

Greenberg, E. (2004). 'Coach: Title IX Protects Me From Retaliation' (www.cnn.com/2004/LAW/12/01/jackson/).

Grenfell, C. and Rinehart, R. (2003). 'Skating on Thin Ice: Human Rights in Youth Figure Skating'. *International Review for the Sociology of Sport*, 38 (1): 79–98.

Grundmann, R. (1991). 'The Ecological Challenge to Marxism'. *New Left Review*, 187 (May/June): 1–15.

Gruneau, R. (1999). *Class, Sports and Social Development*. Champaign, IL: Human Kinetics.

Gruneau, R. (1988). 'Notes on Popular Culture and Political Resistance'. In Gruneau, R. (ed). *Popular Cultures and Political Practices*. Toronto: Garamond Press, 1–33.

Gruneau, R. (1976). *Canadian Sport: Sociological Perspectives*. Toronto: Addison-Wesley.

Gruneau, R. and Whitson, D. (1993). *Hockey Night in Canada: Sport, Identities and Cultural Politics*. Toronto: Garamond Press.

Guha, R. (2002). *A Corner of a Foreign Field: The Indian History of a British Sport*. London: Picador.

Gunnell, R. (2004). 'Religion: Why Do We Still Give a Damn?'. *New Statesman*, 3 (May): 18–22.

Gupta, B. (2011) 'Asian Engine Room'. *Sportbusiness International*. 165: 40–43.

Guttmann, A. (1996). 'Sumo'. In Levinson, D. and Christensen, K. (eds). *Encyclopaedia of World Sport*. Oxford: ABC-CLIO, 380–381.

Guttmann, A. (1978). *From Ritual to Record: The Nature of Modern Sport*. New York: Columbia University Press.

Guttmann, A. and Thompson, L. (2001). *Japanese Sports: A History*. Honolulu, HI: University of Hawaii Press.

Gyulai, I. (2003). Transfers of Nationality. *IAAF News,* 64: 2–4.

Habermas, J. (1989). *The Structural Transformation of the Public Sphere: An Enquiry into a Category of Bourgeois Society*. Cambridge: Polity Press.

Hague, E. and Mercer, J. (1998). 'Geographical Memory and Urban Identity in Scotland: Raith Rovers FC and Kirkaldy'. *Geography*, 83 (2): 105–116.

Hampson, T. and Olchawski, J. (2009). *Is Equality Fair*. London: Fabian Society.

Hansen, J. and Nielsen, N. (2000). *Sports, Body and Health*. Odense: Odense University Press.

Harding, G. (2003). 'Bosman in Baghdad'. *Observer*, 23 March: 12.

Harding, L. (2003). 'The Big Match Unites a Country of Two Halves'. *Guardian*, 1 March: 1.

Hargreaves, I. (1999). *New Mutualism: In From the Cold*. London: Trafford Press Ltd.

Hargreaves, J. (2004). 'Querying Sport Feminism: Personal or Political?'. In Giulianotti, R. (ed). *Sport and Modern Social Theorists*. Basingstoke: Palgrave, 187–207.

Hargreaves, J. (2000). *Heroines of Sport: The Politics of Difference and Identity*. London: Routledge.

Hargreaves, J. A. (1994). *Sporting Females: Critical Issues in the History and Sociology of Women's Sports*. London: Routledge.

Hargreaves, J. and Vertinsky, P. (2007). *Physical Culture, Power and the Body*. New York: Routledge.

Hari, J. (2002). 'Yahoo Boo to a Daily Mail Myth'. *New Statesman*, September, 23–25.

Harris, J. (1998). 'Civil Society, Physical Activity and the Involvement of Sport Sociologists in the Preparation of Physical Activity Professionals'. *Sociology of Sport*, 15: 138–153.

Harris, J. and Parker. A. (2009). *Sport and Social Identities*. Basingstoke: Palgrave Macmillan

Harris, N. (2011). 'Cream of the Crop'. *The Herald*, 22 April: 11.

Harris, P. (2002). 'Jumping the Gun'. *Observer: Sports Monthly*, March: 27–34.

Harvey, D. (2010). 'Forward to Uneven Development'. In Smith, M. (ed). *Uneven Development: Nature Capital and the Production of Space*. New York: Verso, 1–8.

Harvey, J. (2003). 'Sports and Recreation: Entertainment or Social Right?' (http://polyresearch. gc.ca/page.asp?pagenm=v5nl_art_07).

Harvey, J. and Cantelon, H. (eds) (1988). *Not Just A Game: Essays in Canadian Sport Sociology*. Ottawa: University of Ottawa Press.

Harvey, J. Horne, J. and Safai, P. (2009). 'Alterglobalization, Global Social Movements, and the Possibility of Political Transformation Through Sport'. *Sociology of Sport Journal*, 26 (3).

Hashemi, F. (2000). 'Flying the Chador'. *Index on Censorship: This Sporting Lie*, 4: 70–73.

Haughton, J. and Khandker, S. (2009). *Handbook on Poverty and Inequality*. Washington, DC: World Bank.

Hawkins, B. (1998). 'Evening Basketball Leagues: The Use of Sport to Reduce African American Youth Criminal Activity'. *International Sports Journal*, 2 (2): 68–77.

Hay, R. (2003). 'The Last Night of the Poms: Australia as a Postcolonial Sporting Society'. In Bale, J. and Cronin, M. (eds). *Sport and Post-colonialism*. Oxford: Berg, 15–28.

Hayes, G. and Karamichas, J. (eds) (2011). *Olympic Games, Mega-Events and Civil Societies: Globalisation, Environment and Resistance*. Basingstoke: Palgrave.

Hayward, P. (2011). 'Riots Force London to Get Real Over Olympics'. *The Observer*, 4 August: 9.

Hedenborg, S. (2009). 'Unknown Soldiers and Very Pretty Ladies: Challenges to the Social Order of Sports in Post-War Sweden'. *Spirit in History*, 29 (4): 601–623.

Henry, I. and Thedoraki, A. (2002). 'Management, Organizations and Theory in the Governance of Sport'. In Coakley, J. and Dunning, E. (eds). *Handbook of Sport Studies*. London: Sage, 490–503.

Henry, I., Amara, M. and Al-Tauqui, M. (2003). 'Sport, Arab Nationalism and the Pan-Arab Games'. *International Review for the Sociology of Sport*, 38 (3): 295–311.

Heywood, L. and Montgomery, M. (2008). 'Ambassadors of the Last Wilderness? Surfers, Environmental Ethics, and Activism in America'. In Atkinson, M. and Young, K. (eds). *Tribal Play: Sub Cultural Journeys Through Sport*. Bingley: Jai, 153–172.

Hill, J. (2006). *Sport and the Literary Imagination: Essays in History, Literature and Sport*. Oxford: Peter Lang.

Hill, J. (2002). *Sport, Leisure and Culture in Twentieth Century Britain*. Basingstoke: Palgrave.

Hill, J. (1996). 'British Sports History: A Post-Modern Future?'. *Journal of Sports History*, 23 (1): 1–19.

Hill, J. and Varsasi, F. (1997). 'Creating Wembley: The Construction of a National Monument'. *The Sports Historian*, 17 (2): 28–44.

Hirst, P. and Thompson, G. (1999). *Globalization in Question*. Oxford: Polity Press.

Hoberman, J. (1997). *Darwin's Athletes: How Sport Has Damaged Black America and Preserved the Myth of Race*. Boston, MA: Houghton.

Hobsbawm, E. (1997). *On History*. London: Weidenfeld & Nicholson.

Hogenstad, H. and Tollisen, A. (2004). 'Playing Against Deprivation: Football and Development in Nairobi, Kenya'. In Armstrong, G. and Giulianotti, R. (eds). *Football in Africa: Conflict, Conciliation and Community*. Basingstoke: Palgrave, 210–229.

Holden, R. (2011). 'Never Forget You're Welsh: The Role of Sport as a Political Device in Post-Devolution Wales'. *Sport in Society*, 14 (2): 272–288.

Holt, R. (2000). 'The Uses of History in Comparative Physical Culture'. In Tollener, J. and Renson, R. (eds). *Old Borders, New Borders, No Borders: Sport and Physical Education in a Period of Change*. Oxford: Meyer and Meyer Sport, 49–57.

Holt, R. and Mason, T. (2000). *Sport in Britain 1945–2000*. Oxford: Blackwell.

hooks, b. (2000). *Talking Back: Thinking Feminist, Thinking Black*. Boston, MA: Southend Press.

Horne, J. and Manzenreiter, W. (eds) (2010). *Sports Mega Events*. Oxford: Blackwell Publishing.

Houlihan, B. (2008). *Sport and Society: A Student Introduction*. London: Sage.

Houlihan, B. (2002). 'Politics and Sport'. In Coakley, J. and Dunning, E. (eds). *Handbook of Sports Studies*. London: Sage, 213–227.

Hoye, R., Nicholson, M. and Houlihan, B. (2010). *Sport and Policy: Issues and Analysis*. Oxford: Butterworth-Heinemann.

Huggins, M. (2008). 'Sport and the Upper Classes'. *Sport in History*, 28 (3): 351–364.

Huish, R. (2011). 'Punching Above Its Weight: Cuba's Use of Sport for South–South Co-operation'. *Third World Quarterly*, 32 (3) April: 417–433.

Humphreys, J.M. and Plummer, M.K. (1995a). ' Upon Further Review: An Examination of Sporting Event Economic Impact Studies'. *The Sports Journal*, 14: 1–15.

Humphreys, J.M. and Plummer, M.K. (1995b). 'The Economic Impact on the State of Georgia of Hosting the 1996 Summer Olympic Games'. *Mimeograph*. Athens, GA: Selig Center for Economic Growth, The University of Georgia.

Hunt, D. (2001). *Communities in Control: Public Services and Local Socialism*. London: Fabian Society.

Hwang, T. (2001). 'Sport, Nationalism and the Early Chinese Republic 1912–1927'. *The Sports Historian*, 21 (2): 1–20.

Hwang, D. and Chiu, W. (2010). 'Sport and National Identity in Taiwan: Some Preliminary Observations'. *East Asian Sport Thoughts: The International Journal of the Sociology of Sport*, 1 (1): 39–71.

Insight (2011). 'Olympics Boss Paid Secret Cash'. *The Sunday Times*, 3 July: 1.

IOC (2003). *The Legacy of the Olympic Games 1984–2000*. Marketing Report, Lausanne: International Olympic Committee.

Jacques, M. (2009). 'No One Rules the World'. *New Statesman*, 30 March: 22–25.

James, C. L. R. (1963). *Beyond a Boundary*. London: Stanley Paul.

James, M. and McArdle, D. (2004). 'Player Violence or Violent Players? Vicarious Liability for Sports Participants'. *Tort Law Review*, 131 (12): 131–146.

Jameson, F. (2004). 'The Politics of Utopia'. *New Left Review*, 25 (January/February): 35–54.

Jarvie, G. (2011). 'Sport Development and Aid: Can Sport Make a Difference?'. *Sport and Society*. 14 (2): 241–253.

Jarvie, G. (2010). 'Sport, Development and Aid: Can Sport Make a Difference'. *Sport and Society*, 14 (2): 241–252.

Jarvie, G. (2008). 'Sport as a Resource of Hope'. *Foreign Policy in Focus*, 18 August: 1–8.

Jarvie, G. (2007). 'Sport, Social Change and the Public Intellectual'. *International Review for the Sociology of Sport*, 42 (4): 411–425.

Jarvie, G. (2006). *Sport, Culture and Society*, first edition. London: Routledge.

Jarvie, G. (2005). 'The North American Émigré and Highland Games in International Communities'. In Ray, C. (ed.). *Transatlantic Scots*. Tuscaloosa, AL: University of Alabama Press, 80–96.

Jarvie, G. (2004). 'Sport in Changing Times and Places'. *British Journal of Sociology*, 55 (4): 579–587.

Jarvie, G. (2003a). 'Internationalism and Sport in the Making of Nations'. *Identities*: *Studies in Global Culture and Power*, 10 (4): 537–551.

Jarvie, G. (2003b). 'Sport, Communitarianism and Social Capital: A Neighbourly Insight Into Scottish Sport'. *International Review for the Sociology of Sport*, 38 (2): 139–153.

Jarvie, G. (1993). 'Sport, Nationalism and Cultural Identity'. In Allison, L. (ed.). *The Changing Politics of Sport*. Manchester: Manchester University Press, 58–83.

Jarvie, G. and Macintosh, T. (2006). 'The Promise and Possibilities of Running in and Out of East Africa'. In Pitsiladis, Y. and Bale, J. (eds) *East African Running*. London: Routledge, 1–15.

Jarvie, G. and Maguire, J. (1994). *Sport and Leisure in Social Thought*. London: Routledge.

Jarvie, G. and Sykes. M. (2012). 'Running as a Resource of Hope: Voices from Eldoret'. *Review of African Political Economy*. Forthcoming.

Jarvie, G., Hwang, D. and Brennan, J. (2008). *Sport, Revolution and the Beijing Olympics*. London: Berg Publishers.

Jiwani, N. and Rail, G. (2010). 'Islam, Hijab and Young Shia Muslim Canadian Women's Dioscusrsive Constructions of Physical Activity'. *Sociology of Sport*, 27 (3): 251–267.

Johnston, G. and Percy-Smith, J. (2003). 'In Search of Social Capital'. *Policy and Politics*, 31 (3): 321–334.

Jones, S. (1988). *Sport, Politics and the Working Class: Organised Labour and Sport in Interwar Britain*. Manchester: Manchester University Press.

Jones, S. (1986). *Workers at Play: A Social and Economic History of Leisure, 1918–1939*. London: Routledge.

Jowell, T. (2002). 'Culture Can Cut Crime'. Available online: www.cjp.org.uk/news/archive/culture-can-cut-crime-says-tessa-jowell-13-01-2003. Accessed 6 November 2011.

Jung, W. and Maguire, J. (2009). 'Global Festivals through a National Prism. The Global National Nexus in South Korean Media Challenge of the 2004 Athens Olympic Games'. *International Review for the Sociology of Sport*. 44 (1): 5–25.

Kasimati, E. (2003). 'Economic Aspects and the Summer Olympics: a Review of Related Research'. *International Journal of Tourism Research*, 5: 433–444

Katwala, S. (2004). 'Political Footballs'. *Fabian Review: The Age of Terror?*, 116 (2): 14–16.

Katwala, S. (2001). 'Can Sport be Reformed?' Available online: http://observer.guardian.co.uk/sport/issues/story/0,,721825,00.html. Accessed 6 November 2011.

Katwala, S. (2000a). *Democratising Global Sport*. London: The Foreign Policy Centre.

Katwala, S. (2000b). 'The Crisis of Confidence in Global Sport' (www.observer.co.uk/Print0, 3858,4421203,00.html).

Kavetsos, G. and Szymanski, S. (2009). 'From the Olympics to the Grassroots: What will London 2012 Mean for Sport Funding and Participation in Britain?'. *Public Policy Review*, Institute for Public Policy Research, 16 (3): 192–196.

Kay, J. (2010). 'A Window of Opportunity? Preliminary Thoughts on Women's Sport in Post-War Britain'. *Sport in History*, 30 (2): 196–217.

Kay, J. and Vamplew, W. (2002). *Weather Beaten: Sport in the British Climate*. Edinburgh: Mainstream Publishing.

Kay, T. (2003). 'Sport and Gender'. In Houlihan, B, (ed.). *Sport and Society: An Introduction*. London: Sage, 89–104.

Keene, J. (1988). *Civil Society and the State*. London: Verso.

Kennedy, E. and Hills, L. (2009). *Sport, Media and Society*. Oxford: Berg.

Kenny, M. (2004). *The Politics of Identity*. Cambridge: Polity Press.

Kidd, B. (2008a). 'A New Social Movement: Sport for Development and Peace'. *Sport and Society*, 11 (4): 370–380.

Kidd, B. (2008b). 'The Olympic Movement and Its Contribution to Society: A Proposal for Monitoring and Evaluating the Realization of Olympism'. Olympic Study Centre, International Olympic Committee (www.olympic.org/Documents/OSC/Relations%20universit%c3%a9/English/Appendix%207%20eng.pdf).

Kidd, B. (1996). *The Struggle for Canadian Sport*. Toronto: University of Toronto Press.

Kidd, B. (1982). *Athletes' Rights in Canada*. Toronto: Ministry of Tourism and Recreation.

Kidd, B. and Donnelly, P. (2000). 'Human Rights in Sport'. *International Review for the Sociology of Sport*, 35 (2): 131–148.

Kietlinski, R. (2011). 'One World One Dream? Twenty-first Century Japanese Perspectives on Hosting the Olympic Games'. *Sport in Society*, 14 (4): 454–465.

King, A. (2002). *The End of the Terraces*. London: Leicester University Press.

Kingsley, P. (2012). 'A Natural High?'. *The Guardian*, 5 January: 10–14.

Kinnock, G. (2003). 'It's All About Justice'. *Fabian Global Forum For Progressive Global Politics* (www.fabianglobalforum.net/forum/article027.html).

Klein, N. (2007). *The Shock Doctrine: The Rise of Disaster Capitalism*. New York: Metropolitan Books.

Klein, N. (2001). 'Reclaiming the Commons'. *New Left Review*, 9: 81–90.

Kluckohn, T. (1951). 'Dominant and Substitute Profiles of Cultural Orientation'. *Social Forces*, 28: 376–393.

Knoppers, A. and Elling, A. (2004). 'We Do Not Engage in Promotional Journalism: Discursive Strategies Used by Sports Journalists to Describe the Selection Process'. *International Review for the Sociology of Sport*, 39 (1): 57–75.

Krieger, J. (2000). *British Politics in the Global Age: Can Social Democracy Survive?* Cambridge: Polity Press.

Kruger, A. and Riordan, J. (1996). *The Story of Worker Sport*. Champaign, IL: Human Kinetics.

Kusz, K. (2004). 'Extreme America: The Cultural Products of Extreme Sports in 1990s America'. In Wheaton, B. (ed.). *Understanding Lifestyle Sports: Consumption, Identity and Difference*. London: Routledge, 197–215.

Laberge, S. and Sankoff, D. (1988). 'Physical Activities, Body Habitus and Lifestyles'. In Harvey, J. and Cantelon, H. (eds). *Not Just A Game: Essays in Canadian Sport Sociology*. Ottawa: University of Ottawa Press, 268–286.

Landman, T. (2004). 'Swapping Debt for Education' (www.fabianglobalforum.net/forum/article012.html).

Leadbeater, C. (2002). 'Globalisation: Want the Good News'. *New Statesman*, 1 July: 29–31.

Leader, P. (2003). 'Why Boycott Zimbabwe But Not China?' *New Statesman*, 6 January: 4–5.

Lenskyj, H. (2008). *Olympic Industry Resistance: Challenging Olympic Power and Propaganda*. Albany, NY: State University of New York Press.

Lenskyj, H. (2004). 'Funding Canadian University Sports Facilities: The University of Toronto Stadium Referendum'. *Journal of Sport and Social Issues*, 28 (4): 379–396.

Lenskyj, H. (2003). *Out on the Field: Gender, Sport and Sexualities*. Toronto: Women's Press.

Lenskyj, H. (2002). *The Best Olympics Ever? The Social Impacts of Sydney 2000*. Albany: University of New York Press.

Lenskyj, H. (2000). *Inside the Olympic Industry*: *Power, Politics and Activism*. New York: New York University Press.

Lenskyj, H. (1990). *Sex Equality in the Olympics: A Report to the Toronto Olympic Task Force*. April.

Leseth, A. (2003). 'Dance, Sport and Politics in Dar-es-Salaam, Tanzania'. In Dyck, N. and Archetti, E. (eds). *Sport, Dance and Embodied Identities*. Oxford: Berg, 231–249.

Levermore, R and Beacom, A. (2009). *Sport and International Development*, New York: Palgrave Macmillan.

Levermore, R. and Budd, A. (2004). *Sport and International Relations*. London: Routledge.

Levinson, D. and Christensen, K. (2005). *Berkshire Encyclopedia of World Sport*, Vols 1–4. Great Barrington: Berkshire Publishing Group.

Levinson, D. and Christensen, K. (1996). *Encyclopaedia of World Sport*. Oxford: ABC-CLIO.

Lightman, A. (2004). 'The Role of the Public Intellectual'. *MIT Communications Forum*. Available online: http://web.mit.edu/comm-forum/papers/lightman.html. Accessed 6 November 2011.

Lister, R. (2004). *Poverty*: *Key Concepts*. Cambridge: Polity Press.

Lloyd, M. (1996). 'Feminism, Aerobics and the Politics of the Body'. *Body and Society*, 2 (2): 79–98.

Loland, S., Sklirslad, B. and Waddington, I. (2006). *Pain and Injury in Sport: Social and Ethical Analyses*. London: Routledge.

Lopez, B. (2011). 'The Invention of a Drug of Mass Destruction: Deconstructing the EPO Myth'. *Sport in History*, 31 (1): 84–109.

Luttrell, W. (2011). 'Where Inequality Lives in the Body: Teenage Pregnancy, Public Pedagogies and Individual Lives'. *Sport, Education Society*, 16 (3): 295–308.

Macintyre, S. (2010). ' Nazi Cricket Rules'. *The Scotsman*, 3 March: 11.

Magdalinski, T. (2004). 'Homebush: Site of the Clean/sed and Natural Australian Athlete'. In Vertinsky, P. and Bale, J. (eds). *Sites of Sport*: *Space, Place and Experience*. London: Routledge, 101–114.

Magdalinski, T. and Chandler, T. (eds) (2002). *With God on Their Side*: *Sport in the Service of Religion*. London: Routledge.

Maguire, J. (2005). *Power and Global Sport: Zones of Prestige, Emulation and Resistance*. London: Routledge.

Maguire, J. (1999). *Global Sport*: *Identities, Societies, Civilizations*. Cambridge: Polity Press.

Maguire, J., Jarvie, G., Mansfield, L. and Bradley, J. (2002). *Sport Worlds*: *A Sociological Perspective*. Champaign, IL: Human Kinetics.

Maguire, J. S. (2008). *Fit for Consumption: Sociology and the Business of Fitness*. London: Routledge.

Mair, D. (2006). 'Ruling the Void? The Hollowing of Western Democracy'. *New Left Review*, 42: 25–51.

Mansfield, L. (2009). 'Fitness Cultures and Environmental Injustices'. *International Review for the Sociology of Sport*, 44 (4): 345–362.

Markovits, B. (2003). 'The Colours of Sport'. *New Left Review*, 22 (July/August): 151–160.

Marquand, D. (2006). 'New Statesman Essay'. *New Statesman*, 16 January.

Marquand, D. (2004). *Decline of the Public Realm*. Cambridge: Polity Press.

Marquand, D. (2002). 'The Fall of Civic Culture'. *New Statesman*, November: 34–38.

Marquand, D. (2000). 'The Fall of Civic Culture'. *New Statesman*, November: 27–30.

481

Marquand, D. (1988). *The Unprincipled Society*. London: Jonathan Cape.

Marqusee, M. (2000). 'Sydney and the Olympics: Corruption and Corporatism Versus a Positive Social Role for the Olympics'. In *Workers Liberty Australia Newsletter*, October (archive. workersliberty.org/Australia/Newsletter/Oct00/olympics.html).

Martin, L. (2004). 'Lewis Hands Surfers Never on Sunday Warning'. *Observer*, 8 August: 13.

Marx, G. (2011). 'Challenges to Mainstream Journalism in Baseball and Politics'. *Forum*, 9 (1): 1–7.

Mason, T. (1993). 'All the Winners and the Half Times'. *The Sports Historian*, 13 (May): 3–11.

McAlpine, J. (2005). 'Africa Has Spoken, But Did Any of Us Bother to Listen?'. *The Herald*, 7 July: 20.

McCarthy, H., Miller, P. and Skidmore, P. (2004) *Network Logic*. London: Demos.

McCrone, D. (2000). *A Sociology of Nationalism*. London: Routledge.

Mcginty, S. (2010). 'Evans Was Millimetre from Death or Paralysis, Reveals Team Doctor'. *The Scotsman*, 27 February: 3.

McGovern, P. (2000). 'Globalization or Internationalization? Foreign Footballers in the English League, 1946–95'. *Sociology*, 36 (1): 23–42.

McKibben, R. (1994). *Ideologies of Class: Social Relations in Britain 1880–1950*. Oxford: Clarendon Press.

McLean, I. (1996). *Oxford Concise Dictionary of Politics*. Oxford: Oxford University Press.

Mertes, T. (2004). *A Movement of Movements*. New York: Verso.

Mertes, T. (2002). 'Grass-Roots Globalism'. *New Left Review*, 17 (October): 101–112.

Metcalfe, A. (2006). *Leisure and Recreation in a Victorian Mining Community*. London: Routledge.

Metcalfe, A. (1991). *Canada Learns to Play: The Emergence of Organised Sport, 1807–1904*. Toronto: McClelland and Stewart.

Mewett, P. G. (2003). 'Conspiring to Run: Women, Their Bodies and Athletics Training'. *International Review for the Sociology of Sport*, 38 (3): 331–349.

Meyer, T. (2002). 'Towards a New Political Regime'. *Fabian Review*, Winter: 16–19.

Mia, A. (2004). *Genetically Modified Athletes*. London: Routledge.

Middleton, K. (2000). 'European Community Law Sport'. In Stewart, W. (ed.). *Sport and the Law: The Scots Perspective*. Edinburgh: T&T Clark, 79–100.

Midol, N. and Broyer, G. (1995). 'Toward an Anthropological Study of New Sports Cultures: The Case of Whiz Sports in France'. *Sociology of Sport Journal*, 12: 204–212.

Mills, C. W. (1970). *The Sociological Imagination*. Harmondsworth: Penguin Books.

Mills, J. and Dimeo, P. (2003). 'When Gold is Fired it Shines: Sport, the Imagination and the Body in Colonial and Postcolonial India'. In Bale, J. and Cronin, M. (eds). *Sport and Post-colonialism*. Oxford: Berg, 107–122.

Misztal, B. (2007). *The Public Intellectuals and Public Good*. London: Routledge.

Miyoshi, M. (1997). 'Sites of Resistance in the Global Economy'. In Pearson, K., Parry, B. and Squires, J. (eds). *Cultural Readings of Imperialism*. London: Lawrence and Wishart, 49–66.

Moffat, G. (2000). 'The Secret Golf Club'. *New Statesman*, 20 September: 33.

Moller, J. and Andersen, J. (1998). *Society's Watchdog – Or Showbiz' Pet? Inspiration for a Better Sports Journalism*. Vingsted, Denmark: Danish Gymnastics and Sports Association.

Morris, P. and Spink, K. (2000). 'The Court of Arbitration for Sport'. In Stewart, W. (ed). *Sport and the Law: The Scots Perspective*. Edinburgh: T&T Clark, 61–76.

Morrow, S. (2003). *The People's Game? Football, Finance and Society.* Basingstoke: Palgrave Macmillan.

Morrow, S. (2000a). 'Mutual Sport and Trust: The Case Study of Celtic *PLC'. Irish Journal of Accounting,* 15: 14–27.

Morrow, S. (2000b). 'If You Know The History: A Study of Celtic'. In *Singer and Friedlander Review 1999–2000.* London: Singer and Friedlander.

Morrow, S. (1999). *The New Business of Football.* London: Macmillan.

Nair, M. (2010). 'Time for Asian Capitalist Values to Shine'. *Financial Times.* 8 May: 9.

Nash, K. (2001). 'The Cultural Turn in Social Theory: Towards a Theory of Cultural Politics'. *Sociology,* 35 (1): 77–92.

Naughton, J. (2011). 'The French Have Always Celebrated Their Public Intellectuals: Why Are We so Ashamed of Ours?' *Observer,* 8 May: 8–13.

Nauright, J. (1997). *Sport, Cultures and Identities in South Africa.* London: Leicester University Press.

New Statesman (2010). 'Faith Speaks Volumes: A Guide to the World's Leading Faiths'. *New Statesman,* 5–8 (April): 26–28.

New Statesman (2009). 'Alex Ferguson on Football Politics and Much Else'. *New Statesman,* 22 March: 20–24.

New Statesman (2004). 'After Switch Over: What Next for Public Service Television?'. 15 November: i–xv.

Nicholson, M. and Hoye, R. (2008). *Sport and Social Capital.* New York: Elsevier.

Niethammer, L. (2003). 'The Infancy of Tarzan'. *New Left Review,* 19 (January/February): 79–91.

Nixon, H. and Frey, J., (1996). *A Sociology of Sport.* Albany, NY: Wadsworth.

Novick, J. (2004). 'World of Sport'. *The Herald,* 15 October: 24.

Obama, B. (2008). *The Audacity of Hope.* New York: Three Rivers Press.

Ogi, L. (2004). 'Sport Serving Development and Peace'. Unpublished Address to the ISCA World Congress on Sport For All, 21 May, Copenhagen: Denmark.

O'Hear, M. (2001). 'Blue-collar Crimes/White-collar Criminals: Sentencing Elite Athletes who Commit Violent Crimes'. *Marquette Sports Law Review,* 12 (1): 427–447.

Okayasu, I., Kawahara, Y. and Nogowa, H. (2010). 'The Relationship Between Community Sports Clubs and Social Capital in Japan: A Comparative Study Between the Comprehensive Community Sports Clubs and Traditional Community Sports Clubs'. *International Review for the Sociology of Sport,* 45 (2): 163–186.

Olsen, K. (2008). *Adding Insult to Injury: Nancy Fraser Debates Her Critics.* London: Verso.

Opp, K. (2009). *Theories of Political Protest and Social Movemnents.* London: Routledge.

Osborne, C. and Skillen, F. (2010). 'Introduction. The State of Play: Women in British Sports History'. *Sport in History,* 30 (2): 189–196.

Oswald, A. (2011). 'The Well-being of Nations'. *Times Higher Education,* 19–25 May: 35–40.

Ouellet, J. G. and Donnelly, P. (2003). 'Sport Policy, Citizenship and Social Inclusion' (http://policyresearch.gc.ca/page.asp?pagenm=horsunset_06_01).

Ozawa-De Silva, C. (2002). 'Beyond the Body/Mind? Japanese Contemporary Thinkers on Alternative Sociologies of the Body'. *Body and Society,* 8 (2): 21–38.

Pacione, M. (2001). *Urban Geography: A Global Perspective.* London: Routledge.

Palm, J. (2003). *Global Perspectives on Sport, Community and Inclusion: Sport for All in Policy and Practice*. London: Routledge.

Paraschak, V. (2007). 'Doing Race, Doing Gender: First Nations, "Sport", and Gender Relations'. In Young, K. and White, P. (eds). *Sport and Gender in Canada*, Second Edition. Don Mills, ON: Oxford University Press, 137–154.

Paraschak, V. (1995). 'The Native Sport and Recreation Programme, 1972–1981: Patterns of Resistance, Patterns of Reproduction'. *Canadian Journal of the History of Sport*, 26 (1): 1–18.

Paraschak, V. (1990). 'Organised Sport for Native Females on the Six Nations Reserve, Ontario, 1968–1980'. *Canadian Journal of the History of Sport*, 21 (1): 70–80.

Park, R. (2011). 'Physicians, Scientists, Exercise and Athletics in Britain and America from the 1867 Boat Race to the Four-Minute Mile'. *Sport in History*, 31 (1): 1–31.

Parker, A. and Harris, J. (2009). *Sport and Social Identities*. Basingstoke: Palgrave Macmillan.

Parratt, C. (1998). 'About Turns: Reflecting on Sport History in the 1990s'. *Sport, History Review*, 29 (1): 4–17.

Parratt, C. (1989). 'Athletic Womanhood: Explaining Sources for Female Sport in Victorian and Edwardian England'. *Journal of the History of Sport*, 16 (2): 140–157.

Parrish, R. (2003). *Sports Law and Policy in the European Union*. Manchester: Manchester University Press.

Parry, J. (2007). 'The Religious Athlete, Olympism and Peace'. In Parry, J., Robinson, S., Watson, N. and Nesti, M. (eds). *Sport and Spirituality: An Introduction*. London: Routledge, 2001–2014.

Parry, J., Robinson, S., Watson, N. and Nesti, M. (2007). *Sport and Spirituality*. London: Routledge.

Paterson, L. (2003), *Scottish Education in the Twentieth Century*. Edinburgh: Edinburgh University Press.

Paton, A. (2003). 'Surf's Up'. *Sunday Herald*, 5 October: 20.

Pattullo, A. (2011). 'Saturday Interview: Ibrox Driving Force'. *The Scotsman*, 23 April: 10–12.

Payne, G. (2000). *Social Divisions*. Basingstoke: Palgrave.

Peach, S. (2010). 'What the World Can Learn from Vancouver'. *The Sporting Brief*, 6 June: 16–20.

Pearson, B. (2003). 'Say Aloha to Sisters of Surf'. *The Herald*, 12 April: 14.

Persson, T. (2008). 'Social Capital and Social Responsibility in Denmark'. *International Review for the Sociology of Sport*, 43 (1): 35–51.

Pfister, G. (1990). 'The Medical Discourse on Female Physical Culture in Germany in the 19th and Early 20th Centuries'. *Journal of Sport History*, (17) 2: 183–189.

Piggin, J., Jackson, S. and Lewis, M. (2009). 'Knowledge, Power and Politics: Contesting Evidence Based National Sports Policy'. *International Review for the Sociology of Sport*, 44 (1): 87–102.

Pilz, G. (1996). 'Social Factors Influencing Sport and Violence: On the Problem of Football Violence in Germany'. *International Review for the Sociology of Sport*, 31: 49–65.

Pine, N. (2010). 'The Role of Athletics in the Academy: An Alternative Approach to Financial Investment'. *Journal of Sport and Social Issues*, 34 (3): 475–480.

Pink, S. (2003). 'She Wasn't Tall Enough and Breasts Get in the Way: Why Would a Woman

Bullfighter Retire?'. *Identities: Studies in Global Culture and Power*, 10 (4): 427–450.

Pink, S. (1996). 'Breasts in the Bullring: Female Psychology, Female Bullfighters and Competing Femininities'. *Body and Society*, 2 (1): 34–51.

Pitsiladis, Y., Bale, J., Sharp, C. and Noakes, T. (2007). *East African Running: Toward a Cross-Disciplinary Perspective*. London: Routledge.

Poli, R. (2010). 'Understanding Globalization through Football: The New International Division of Labour, Migratory Channels and Transnational Trade Circuits'. *International Review for the Sociology of Sport*, 45 (4): 491–506.

Polley, M. (2008). 'History and Sport' 1st Edn. In Houlihan, B. (ed.). *Sport and Society*. London: Sage, 56–75.

Polley, M. (2003). 'History and Sport' 2nd Edn. In Houlihan, B. (ed.). *Sport and Society*. London: Sage, 49–64.

Polley, M. (1998). *Moving the Goalposts: A History of Sport and Society since 1945*. London: Routledge.

Pope, D. and Schweitzer, M. (2011). 'Is Tiger Woods Loss Averse? Persistent Bias in the Face of Experience, Competition and High Stakes'. *American Economic Review*, 101 (1): 129–157.

Pope, S. (1998). 'Sport History: Into the 21st Century'. *Journal of Sports History*, 25 (2): i–x.

Pope, S. W. and Nauright, J. (eds) (2010). *The Routledge Companion to Sports History*. London: Routledge.

Portes, A. (1998). 'Social Capital: Its Origins and Applications in Modern Sociology'. *Annual Review of Sociology*, 24: 1–24.

Posner, R. (2001). *Public Intellectuals: A Study of Decline*. Cambridge, MA: Harvard University.

Powley, T. (2011). 'Olympic Hopes for Rentals'. *Financial Times*, 7 August: 11.

Putnam, R. (2000). *Bowling Alone: The Collapse and Revival of American Community*. New York: Simon & Schuster.

Putnam, R. (1995) 'Bowling Alone: America's Declining Social Capital'. *Journal of Democracy*, 6: 65–78.

Ramsamy, S. (2002). 'Olympic Values in Shaping Social Bonds and Nation Building at Schools' (www.gov.za/Conf_Wshops_Events/Values/Sam_Ramsamy.htm).

Randels, G. and Beal, B. (2002) 'What Makes a Man? Religion, Sport and Negotiating Masculine Identity in the Promise Keepers'. In Magdalinski, T. and Chandler, T. (eds). *With God on Their Side: Sport in the Service of Religion*. London: Routledge, 160–177.

Ray, C. (2005). *Transatlantic Scots*. Tuscaloosa, AL: University of Alabama Press.

Ray, C. (2001). *Highland Heritage: Scottish Americans in the American South*. London: The University of North Carolina Press.

Ray, L. (2011). *Violence and Society*. London: Sage.

Rees, J. (2008). 'The Global Soul' *New Statesman*, 15 December: 24–28.

Reeves, R. (2003). 'Public Life and the Public Intellectual'. *New Statesman*, 7 July: 23–28.

Reid, A. (2011). 'Politicians Meet Their Match'. *Sunday Herald*, 12 June: 15.

Rinehart, R. (2002). 'Arriving Sport: Alternatives to Formal Sports'. In Coakley, J. and Dunning, E. (eds). *Handbook of Sports Studies*. London: Sage, 504–519.

Rinehart, R. and Grenfell, C. (2002). 'BMX Spaces: Children's Grass Roots, Courses and Corporate Sponsored Tracks'. *Sociology of Sport Journal*, 19 (3): 302–314.

Rinehart, R. and Sydnor, S. (eds) (2003). *To the Extreme*: *Alternative Sports Inside and Out*. Albany, NY: Suny Press.

Riordan, J. and Kruger, A. (eds) (1999). *The International Politics of Sport in the 20th Century*. London: E & F N Spon.

Ritzer, G. 'Who's a Public Intellectual'. *British Journal of Sociology*, 56 (2): 209–214.

Robbins, C. (2006). *The Giroux Reader*. Boulder, CO: Paradigm Publishers.

Roberts, K. (2005). 'Taking the Local Approach to International Sporting Opportunities'. *SportsBusiness*, 101 (April): 25–27.

Roberts, K. (2002). 'Sport's Helping Hand'. *SportsBusiness International*, November: 24–27.

Robinson, S. (2007) 'Sport and Spirituality'. In Parry, J., Robinson, S., Watson, N. and Nesti, M. (eds). *Sport and Spirituality: An Introduction*. London: Routledge, pp1-38.

Roche, M. (2008). 'Putting the London Olympics into Perspective: The Challenge of Understanding Mega-events'. *Journal of the Academy of Social Sciences*, 3 (3): 285–290.

Roche, M. (2000). *Mega-Events Modernity: Olympics and Expos in the Growth of Global Culture*. London: Routledge.

Rogers, H. (2010). *Green Gone Wrong*. New York: Verso.

Rojek, C. (1995). *Decentring Leisure: Rethinking Leisure Theory*. London: Sage.

Rottenberg. S. (1956). 'The Baseball Player's Labour Market'. *Journal of Political Economy*, 64 (3): 242–258.

Rowe, D. (2003). 'Sport and the Repudiation of the Global'. *International Review for the Sociology of Sport*, 38 (3): 281–295.

Rowe, N. and Champion, R. (2000). *Sports Participation and Ethnicity in England*: *National Survey 1999/2000*. London: Sport England (www.english.sports.gov.uk).

Runciman, D. (2006). 'They Can Play but They Can Never Win'. *New Statesman*, 29 May: 14–18.

Rushen, S. (1999). 'Economic Input of the Pirates on the Pittsburgh Region'. *Public Administration Quarterly*, 23 (3): 19–2.

Russell, D. (1997). *Football and the English: A Social History of Association Football in England, 1863–1995*. Preston: Carnegie Publishing.

Russo, G. (2004). 'Brutal History of a Beautiful Game'. *The Herald*, 11 December: 5.

Ruthven, M. (2000). *Islam: A Very Short Introduction*. Oxford: Oxford University Press.

Sader, E. (2002). 'Beyond Civil Society'. *New Left Review*, 17 (September/October): 87–101.

Saïd, E. (2001). 'The Case for the Intellectual'. *The Age*, May: 5–12.

Saïd, E. (1993). *Culture and Imperialism*. London: Chatto and Windus.

Sandy, R., Sloane, P. and Rosentraub, M. (2004). *The Economics of Sport: An International Perspective*. Basingstoke: Palgrave Macmillan.

Scheerder, J., Vanreusel, B. and Renson, J. (2002). 'Social Sports Stratification in Flanders 1969–1999'. *International Review for the Sociology of Sport*, 37 (2): 219–245.

Scherer, J. and Whitson, D. (2009). 'Public Broadcasting, Sport and Cultural Citizenship: The Future of Sport on the Canadian Broadcasting Citizenship?'. *International Review for the Sociology of Sport*, 44 (2): 213–231.

Schmidt, C.W. (2006). 'Putting the Earth in Play: Environmental Awareness and Sports'. *Environmental Health Perspectives*, 114: A286–A295.

Schontz, L. (2002). 'Fast Forward: The Rise of Kenya's Women Runners'. *Pittsburgh Post Gazette*, 22 October: 1214.

Schultz, J. (2011). 'Contesting the Master Narrative: The Arthur Ashe Statue and Monument Avenue in Richmond, Virginia'. *International Journal of the History of Sport,* 28 (8/9) May: 1235–1251.

Schumpeter, J. (1947). 'The Creative Response in Economic History'. *Journal of Economic History,* 2 (2): 149–159.

Scott, S. and Morgan, D. (1993). *Body Matters.* London: Falmer Press.

Scottish Executive (2005) *Record of the Summit on Sectarianism.* Edinburgh: Scottish Executive Publications.

Scottish Executive (2000). *Role of Sport in Re-generating Deprived Urban Communities.* Edinburgh: Scottish Executive Publications (www.scotland.gov.uk/crukd01/blue/rsrdua-00. htm).

Scottish Journal of Political Economy (2007). Special Edition on the Economics of Sport.

Scraton, S. and Flintoff, A. (eds) (2002). *Gender and Sports: A Reader.* London: Routledge.

Seabrook, J. (2003). 'Don't Punish the Poor for Being Poor'. *New Statesman,* 23 September: 6–7.

Searle, J. (1987). *On the Right Track: Contemporary Christians in Sport.* Basingstoke: Marshall-Princeton.

Sen, A. (2009). *The Idea of Justice.* London: Allen Lane.

Sen, A. (2006). *Identity and Violence: The Illusion of Destiny.* London: Allen Lane.

Sen, A. (2000). *Development as Freedom.* London: Allen Lane.

Settle, D. (2004). *Fighting Poverty: The Facts.* Swindon: ESRC.

Sherry, E., King, A. and O'May, F. (2011). 'Social Capital and Sport Events: Spectator Attitudinal Change and the Homeless World Cup'. *Sport in Society,* 14 (1): 111–125.

Shilling, C. (1993). *The Body and Social Theory.* London: Sage Publications.

Shor, E. and Yonay, Y. (2011). 'Play Up and Shut Up: The Silencing of Palestinian Athletes in Israeli Media'. *Ethnic and Racial Studies,* 34 (2): 229–247.

Simms, A. and Rendell, M. (2004). 'The Global Trade in Muscle'. *New Statesman.* 7 September: 24–26.

Sloane, P. (2004). *The Economics of Sport,* Basingstoke: Palgrave Macmillan.

Sloane, P. (2002). 'The Regulation of Professional Team Sports'. In Barros, C., Ibrahimo, M. and Szymanski, S. (eds). *Transatlantic Sport: The Comparative Economics of North American and European Sports.* Northampton, MA: Edward Elgar, 50–69.

Slowikowski, S. (1993). 'Cultural Performance and Sport Mascots'. *Journal of Sport and Social Issues,* 17 (1): 23–33.

Small, H. (2002). *The Public Intellectual.* Oxford: Blackwell.

Smith, A. and Porter, D. (2004). *Sport and National Identity In the Post-War World.* London: Routledge.

Smith, A. and Westerbeek, H. (2004). *The SportsBusiness Future.* Basingstoke: Palgrave Macmillan, 90–117.

Smith, M. (2002). 'Muhammad Speaks and Muhammad Ali: Intersections of the Nation of Islam and Sport in the 1960s'. In Magdalinski, T. and Chandler, T. (eds). *With God on Their Side: Sport in the Service of Religion.* London: Routledge, 177–196.

Smith, N. (2010). *Uneven Development: Nature, Capital and the Production of Space.* London: Routledge.

Sobel, A. (2009). *Challenges of Globalization: Immigration, Social Welfare and Global Governance*. London: Routledge.

Sokmen, G. and Ertur, B. (2008). *Waiting for the Barbarians: A Tribute to Edward Said*. London: Verso.

Sontag, S. (2002). *Where the Stress Falls*. London: Jonathan Cape.

Sorek, T. (2007). *Arab Soccer in a Jewish State*. Cambridge: Cambridge University Press.

Southgate, B. (1996). *History: What and Why? Ancient, Modern and Postmodern Perspectives*. London: Routledge.

Spivey, P. (1985). *Sport in America: New Historical Perspectives*. Westport, CT: Greenwood Press.

Sport England (1998). *The Social Value of Sport*. London: Sport England.

Sport England (2003). *Sports Volunteering in England 2002*. London: Sport England.

Sport et Citoyenneté (2010) Special Edition on The Governance of Sport in Europe. No 10, December.

Sport et Citoyenneté (2010). *Sport and the Media*. 11: June/July.

Sportcal (2009). *The Sports Marketing Insight: 2010 FIFA World Cup in South Africa*. London: Sportscal Global Communications.

Sportscotland (2010) *A Ten Year Analysis of Sports Participation Data* Edinburgh: Sportscotland.

Sportscotland (2001). 'Sports Participation in Scotland 2000'. *Research Digest 84*. Edinburgh: Sportscotland.

Sports Policy Research Initiative Canada (www.pch.gc.ca/pgm/sc/pol/pcs-csp/index-eng.cfm).

Stead, P. and Williams, G. (2008). *Wales and Its Boxers: The Fighting Tradition*. Cardiff: University of Wales Press

Stephen, D. (2000). 'What's in a Game? Class and History'. *New Statesman and Society*, June: 20–22.

Stevenson, D. (1997). 'Olympic Arts: Sydney 2000 and the Cultural Olympiad'. *International Review of the Sociology of Sport*, 32 (3): 227–238.

Stewart, W. (ed) (2000). *Sport and the Law: The Scots Perspective*. Edinburgh: T&T Clark.

Stoddart, B. (1998). 'Other Cultures'. In Stoddart, B. and Sandiford, K. (eds). *The Imperial Game*. Manchester: Manchester University Press, 135–149.

Stoddart, B. and Sandiford, K. (1998). *The Imperial Game*. Manchester: Manchester University Press.

Stolle, D. (1998). 'Bowling Together, Bowling Alone: The Development of Generalized Trust in Voluntary Associations'. *Political Psychology*, 19 (3): 497–525.

Stone, E. (2001). 'Disability, Sport and the Body in China'. *Sociology of Sport Journal*, 18 (1): 51–68.

Stranger, M. (1999). 'The Aesthetics of Risk: A Study of Surfing'. *International Review for the Sociology of Sport*, 34 (3): 265–276.

Struna, N. (2002). 'Social History and Sport'. In Coakley, J. and Dunning, E. (eds). *Handbook of Sports Studies*. London: Sage, 187–203.

Sugden, J. (1996). *Boxing and Society: An International Analysis*. Manchester: Manchester University Press.

Sugden, J. and Bairner, A. (1993). *Sport, Sectarianism and Society in a Divided Ireland*. London: Leicester University Press.

Sugden, J. and Tomlinson, A. (eds) (2002). *Power Games: A Critical Sociology of Sport*. London: Routledge.

Sugden, J. and Tomlinson, A. (1999). 'Digging the Dirt and Staying Clean: Retrieving the Investigative Tradition for a Critical Sociology of Sport'. *International Review of the Sociology of Sport*, 34 (4): 385–397.

Sunday Times (2011). 'The Sunday Times: Sport Rich List'. *Sunday Times*, 15 May: 1–15.

Supiot, A. (2003). 'Dogmas and Rights'. *New Left Review*, 21 (May/June): 118–137.

Szymanski, S. (2002). 'The Economic Impact of the World Cup'. *World Economics*, 3 (1) January: 169–177.

Szymanski, S. and Zimbalist. A. (2006). *Handbook on the Economics of Sport*. London: Routledge.

Szymanski, S. and Zimbalist. A. (2005). *National Pastime: How Americans Play Baseball and the Rest of the World Plays Soccer*. Washington, DC: Brookings Institution Press.

Tait, R. (2005). 'The Little Schumacher Who is Driving Iran Round the Feminist Bend'. *The Herald*, 27 March: 21.

Tang, C. C. (2010). 'Yungdong: One Term for Two Different Body Cultures'. *East Asian Sport Thoughts: The International Journal for the Sociology of Sport*, 1 (1): 73–104.

Tatchell, P. (2003). 'Ambassadors of Tyranny: Zimbabwe Cricket Tour'. *New Statesman*, 19 May: 16.

Taylor, I. (1987). 'Putting the Boot into a Working Class Sport: British Soccer after Bradford and Brussels'. *Sociology of Sport Journal*, 4 (3): 171–191.

Theberge, N. (2009). 'We Have All the Bases Covered: Constructions of Professional Boundaries in Sport Medicine'. *International Review for the Sociology of Sport*, 44 (92–93): 265–283.

Therborn, G. (2007). 'Mapping Social Theory'. *New Left Review*, 43 (Jan/Feb): 63–116.

Therborn, G. (2001). 'Into the 21st Century'. *New Left Review*, 10 (May): 87–111.

Tiessen, R. (2011).'Global Subjects or Objects of Globalisation? The Promotion of Global Citizenship in Organisations Offering Sport for Development and/or Peace Programmes'. *Third World Quarterly*, 32 (3): 571–587.

Tiger Club Project (2003) *Annual Report 2003*. Kampala, Uganda: Tiger Club Project.

Tormey, S. (2004). *Anti-Capitalism*. Oxford: Oneworld Publications.

Tranter, N. (1998). *Sport, Economy and Society in Britain*. Cambridge: Cambridge University Press.

Travers, A. (2011). 'Women's Ski Jumping, the 2010 Olympic Games and the Deafening Silence of Sex Segregation, Whiteness and Wealth'. *Journal of Sport and Social Issues*, 25 (2) May: 126–14.

Turner, B. (2006). 'Public Intellectuals, Globalization and the Sociological Calling: A Reply to Critics'. *British Journal of Sociology*, 57 (3): 345–351.

Turner, B. (1996). *Body and Society*. Oxford: Blackwell.

Tutu, D. (2010). Quoted in 'Reflections on Coupe Du Monde De La FIFA 2010'. *Sport et Citoyennete: Special Issue on Coupe Du Monde La FIFA 2010: L'Heure de L'Afrique?*, Paris: Sport et Citoyennete, 5.

UK Sport (2010). *Is UK Sport Equal?*. London: UK Sport.

UNESCO (2010). *Education For All Global Monitoring Report*. Paris: UNESCO Publishing.

Underwood, J. (2009). 'Sport No Longer for the Poor'. *New York Times*, 12 April: 7.

Vamplew, W. (1998). 'Facts and Artefacts: Sports Historians and Sports Museums'. *Journal of Sports History*, 25 (2): 268–283.

Vamplew, W. (1988). *Professional Sport in Britain, 1875–1914: Pay Up and Play the Game*. Cambridge: Cambridge University Press.

Vamplew, W. and Stoddart, B. (1994). *Sport in Australia*: *A Social History*. Cambridge: Cambridge University Press.

Van Ingen, C. (2011). 'Spatialities of Anger: Emotional Geographies in a Boxing Program for Survivors of Violence'. *Sociology of Sport Journal*, 28 (2): 171–188.

Van Ingen, C. (2003). 'Geographies of Gender, Sexuality and Race: Reframing the Focus on Space in Sport Sociology'. *International Review for the Sociology of Sport*, 38 (2): 201–216.

Vaugrand, H. (2001). 'Pierre Bourdieu and Jean-Marie Brohm: The Schemes of Intelligibility and Issues towards a Theory of Knowledge in the Sociology of Sport'. *International Review of the Sociology of Sport*, 36 (2): 183–220.

Vertinsky, P. (1994). 'The Social Construction of the Gendered Body'. *The International Journal of the History of Sport*, 11 (2): 147–171.

Vertinsky, P. and Bale, J. (eds) (2004). *Sites of Sport*: *Space, Place and Experience*. London: Routledge.

Vidacs, B. (2003). 'The Postcolonial and the Level Playing Field in the 1998 World Cup'. In Bale, J. and Cronin, M. (eds). *Sport and Post-colonialism*. Oxford: Berg, 147–158.

Waddington, I. (2001). *Sport, Health and Drugs*. London: Routledge.

Wade, M. (2011). 'Putting the Fear of Golf in Them'. *The Times*, 7 March: 4–6.

Walia, S. (2001). *Edward Saïd*: *Writings and Interpretations*. London: Icon Books.

Walljasper, J. (2005). 'New Statesman Essay', *New Statesman*, 16 January: 22–24.

Wallerstein, I. (2002). 'New Revolts Against the System'. *New Left Review*, 18 (November/December): 29–41.

Walseth, K. and Fasting, K. (2003). 'Islam's View on Physical Activity and Sport: Egyptian Women Interpreting Islam'. *International Review for the Sociology of Sport*, 38 (1): 45–61.

Walters, P. and Byl, J. (2008). *Christian Paths to Health and Wellness*. Champaign, IL: Human Kinetics.

Ward, N. (1996). 'Surfers, Sewage and the New Politics of Pollution'. *Area*, 28: 331–338.

Watson, C. (2010). 'Test Match Special and the Discourse of Cricket: The Sporting Radio Broadcast as Narrative'. *International Review for the Sociology of Sport*, 45 (2): 225–239.

Watson, N. and White, J. (2007). ' Winning at all Costs in Modern Sport: Reflections on Pride and Humility in the Writings of C.S. Lewis'. In Parry, J., Robinson, S., Watson, N. and Nesti, M. (eds) *Sport and Spirituality: An Introduction*. London: Routledge, 61–80.

Watt, C. (2010). 'Women Boxers Land a Knockout Blow to Sport's Chauvinists'. *The Herald*, 22 October: 3.

Watters, R. (2003). 'The Wrong Side of the Thin Edge'. In Rinehart, R. and Sydnor, S. (eds). *To the Extreme*: *Alternative Sports Inside and Out*. Albany, NY: Suny Press, 257–267.

Wearing, B. (1998). *Leisure and Feminist Theory*. London: Sage.

Weiss, O., Norden, G., Hilscher, P. and Vanreusel, B. (1998). 'Ski-Tourism and Environmental Problems: Ecological Awareness Among Different Groups'. *International Review for the Sociology of Sport*, 33 (4): 367–369.

West, P. (2004). 'The Philosopher as Dangerous Liar'. *New Statesman*, 28 June: 24–25.

Whannel, G. (2002). 'Sport and the Media'. In Coakley, J. and Dunning, E. (eds). *Handbook of Sports Studies*. London: Sage, 291–308.

Whannel, G. (1992). *Fields of Vision: Television Sport and Cultural Transformation*. London: Routledge.

Wheaton, B. (2008). 'From the Pavement to the Beach: Politics and Identity in Surfers Against Sewage'. In Atkinson, M. and Young, K. (eds). *Tribal Play: Subcultural Journeys Through Sport*. Bingley: Jai, 113–134.

Wheaton, B. (2007). 'Identity, Politics, and the Beach: Environmental Activism in Surfers Against Sewage'. *Leisure Studies*, 26: 279–302.

Wheaton, B. (2005). 'Selling Out? The Commercialisation and Globalisation of Lifestyle Sport'. In Allison, L. (ed.). *The Global Politics of Sport: The Role of Global Institutions in Sport*. London: Routledge, 140–161.

Wheaton, B. (ed.) (2004). *Understanding Lifestyle Sports: Consumption, Identity and Difference*. London: Routledge.

Wheaton, B. and Beal, B. (2003). 'Keeping it Real: Sub-cultural Media and the Discourses of Authenticity in Alternative Sports'. *International Review for the Sociology of Sport*, 38 (2): 155–176.

White, J. (2004). 'Interview with Haile Gerselassie' (http://sport.guardian.co.uk/athleticsstory/0,10082,680623,00.html).

White, S. (2009). 'Thinking the Future-Ideological Map'. *New Statesman*, 7 September: 19–28.

Wilkinson, J. (2010). 'Personal Communities'. *Sociology*, 44 (3): 453–471.

Williams, G. (1991). 'From Grand Slam to Grand Slump: Economy, Society and Rugby Football in Wales during the Depression'. In Williams. G. *1905 and All That*. Llandysul, UK: Gomer Press, 175–201.

Wilner, D. (2004). 'The Media Value Problem'. *SportsBusiness*, March: 12–14.

Wilson, D. (2004). 'Cricket's Shame: The Inside Story'. *New Statesman*, 6 December: 27–30.

Wood, D. (1996). *Post Intellectualism and the Decline of Democracy*. London: Praeger.

Woods, D. (2010) 'Baptised Lemoncello has Faith in Himself to Deliver'. *Scotland on Sunday,* 12 February: 25.

World Health Organization (WHO) (2002). *World Report on Violence and Health*. Krug, E., Dahlberg, L., Mercy, J., Zuri, A. and Lozano, R. (eds). Geneva: WHO.

Wright, E. O. (2009). 'Class Patternings'. *New Left Review*, 60 (November/December): 101–118.

Wynsberghe, R. and Ritchie, I. (1998). '(Ir)relevant Ring: The Symbolic Consumption of the Olympic Logo in Postmodern Media Culture'. In Rail, G. (ed.). *Sport and Postmodern Times*. New York: State University of New York Press, 367–384.

Young, K. (2002). 'Sport and Violence'. In Coakley, J. and Dunning, E. (eds). *Handbook of Sports Studies*. London: Sage, 382–408.

Yu, Chia-chen. (2009). 'A Content Analysis of News Coverage of Asian Female Olympic Athletes'. *International Review for the Sociology of Sport*, 44 (2): 283–305.

Zuma, J. (2010). Quoted in 'Reflections on Coupe Du Monde De La FIFA 2010'. *Sport et Citoyennete: Special issue on Coupe Du Monde La FIFA 2010: L'Heure de L'Afrique?*, Paris: Sport et Citoyennete, 6.

Index